Special Education in Canada

Third Edition

Special Education in Canada

Alan Edmunds | Gail Edmunds

OXFORD
UNIVERSITY PRESS

OXFORD
UNIVERSITY PRESS

Oxford University Press is a department of the University of Oxford.
It furthers the University's objective of excellence in research, scholarship,
and education by publishing worldwide. Oxford is a registered trade mark of
Oxford University Press in the UK and in certain other countries.

Published in Canada by
Oxford University Press
8 Sampson Mews, Suite 204,
Don Mills, Ontario M3C 0H5 Canada

www.oupcanada.com

Library and Archives Canada Cataloguing in Publication

Edmunds, Alan Louis, 1956–, author
Special education in Canada / Alan Edmunds, Gail Edmunds. — Third edition.

Includes bibliographical references and index.
Issued in print and electronic formats.
ISBN 978-0-19-902665-4 (softcover).—ISBN 978-0-19-902668-5 (PDF)

1. Special education—Canada—Textbooks. 2. Special education—Canada—Case
studies. 3. Textbooks. I. Edmunds, Gail, 1956–, author II. Title.

LC3984.E35 2018   371.90971   C2017-906478-9
                                                          C2017-906479-7

Cover image: Gunther Kleinert / EyeEm/Getty Images
Cover and interior design: Laurie McGregor

Oxford University Press is committed to our environment.
Wherever possible, our books are printed on paper which comes from
responsible sources.

Printed and bound in Canada

1 2 3 4 — 21 20 19 18

This book is dedicated to Gail Annette Edmunds.
A loving mother and wife, gifted scholar, and
exemplary researcher. Hands together, forever.

Brief Contents

Contents   viii

Preface   xiii

From the Publisher   xv

CHAPTER 1   Meaningful Stories: Meaningful Learning   1

CHAPTER 2   Introduction to Special Education   11

CHAPTER 3   The Assessment and IEP Process   38

CHAPTER 4   Creating Exemplary Learning Environments   71

CHAPTER 5   Students with Specific Learning Disorders   101

CHAPTER 6   Students with Behavioural Disorders   143

CHAPTER 7   Students Who Are Gifted and Talented   182

CHAPTER 8   Students with Intellectual Disabilities   219

CHAPTER 9   Students with Autism   256

CHAPTER 10   Students with Sensory Impairments   297

CHAPTER 11   Students with Multiple Disabilities   332

CHAPTER 12   Students Who Are At-Risk   365

CHAPTER 13   Creating Your Own Special Stories   394

Glossary   403

References   407

Index   418

Contents

Preface   xiii

From the Publisher   xv

CHAPTER 1   **Meaningful Stories: Meaningful Learning**   1

A Constructivist Approach   2

The Framework of the Text   3

A Reminder   10

CHAPTER 2   **Introduction to Special Education**   11

What Is Special Education?   12

The Modern History of Special Education   12

Prevalence of Students with Exceptionalities   24

Inclusionary Practices   27

Approaches to Special Education in Canada   31

Summary   35

Learning More about Special Education in Canada and around the World   37

CHAPTER 3   **The Assessment and IEP Process**   38

Special Education: The Implementation of Exemplary Teaching Practices   39

What Is Assessment?   39

Why Is Assessment Important?   40

The Assessment and IEP Process   41

Summary   69

Learning More about the Assessment and IEP Process   70

CHAPTER 4   **Creating Exemplary Learning Environments**   71

Exemplary Learning Environments   72

Classroom Behaviour   73

The Tenets of Classroom Management   77

Phase 1—Understanding the Causes of Problematic Behaviours   77

Phase 2—Establishing a Psychologically Secure Classroom   84

Summary   99

Learning More about Exemplary Learning Environments   100

CHAPTER 5   Students with Specific Learning Disorders   101

Karl's File   102

Why Is Karl Considered to Have a Learning Disability?   110

What Factors Contributed to Karl's Learning Disabilities?   115

How Have Karl's Learning Disabilities Affected His Development?   116

What Is School Like for Karl?   121

What Educational Approach Is Best for Karl?   123

How Is Karl Different from Other Students Who Have Learning Disabilities?   131

Closing Karl's File   136

Updating Karl's Story   137

Summary   139

Learning More about Students with Learning Disabilities   140

Taking It into Your Classroom   142

CHAPTER 6   Students with Behavioural Disorders   143

Lindsey's File   144

Why Is Lindsey Considered to Have a Behavioural Disorder?   152

What Factors Contributed to Lindsey's Behavioural Disorder?   157

How Has Lindsey's Behavioural Disorder Affected Her Development?   158

What Is School Like for Lindsey?   163

What Educational Approach Is Best for Lindsey?   164

How Is Lindsey Different from Other Students Who Have Behavioural Disorders?   172

Closing Lindsey's File   174

Updating Lindsey's Story   176

Summary   178

Learning More about Students with Behavioural Disorders   179

Taking It into Your Classroom   181

CHAPTER 7   Students Who Are Gifted and Talented   182

Geoffrey's File   183

Why Is Geoffrey Considered to Be Gifted?   189

What Factors Contributed to Geoffrey's Giftedness?   193

How Has Geoffrey's Giftedness Affected His Development?   195

What Is School Like for Geoffrey?   200

What Educational Approach Is Best for Geoffrey?   202

How Is Geoffrey Different from Other Students Who Are Gifted?   207

Closing Geoffrey's File   213

Updating Geoffrey's Story   214

Summary   215

Learning More about Students Who Are Gifted and Talented   216

Taking It into Your Classroom   218

CHAPTER 8   Students with Intellectual Disabilities   219

David's File   220

Why Is David Considered to Have an Intellectual Disability?   231

What Factors Contributed to David's Intellectual Disability?   234

How Has David's Intellectual Disability Affected His Development?   235

What Is School Like for David?   239

What Educational Approach Is Best for David?   243

How Is David Different from Other Students Who Have Intellectual
  Disabilities?   248

Closing David's File   251

Updating David's Story   251

Summary   252

Learning More about Students with Intellectual Disabilities   253

Taking It into Your Classroom   255

CHAPTER 9   Students with Autism   256

Zachary's File   257

Why Is Zachary Considered to Be Autistic?   263

What Factors Contributed to Zachary's Autism?   267

How Has Zachary's Autism Affected His Development?   268

What Therapies Did Zachary Experience before
  Entering School?   272

What Was the Transition to School Like for Zachary?   276

What Is School Like for Zachary?   279

What Educational Approach Is Best for Zachary?   281

How Is Zachary Different from Other Students with Autism?   285

Closing Zachary's File   289

Updating Zachary's Story   291

Summary   293

Learning More about Students with Autism   294

Taking It into Your Classroom   296

CHAPTER 10 Students with Sensory Impairments   297

Tyler's File   298

Why Is Tyler Considered to Be Sensory Impaired?   306

What Factors Contributed to Tyler's Sensory Impairment?   311

How Has Tyler's Sensory Impairment Affected His Development?   313

What Is School Like for Tyler?   319

What Educational Approach Is Best for Tyler?   321

How Is Tyler Different from Other Students Who Have Sensory Impairments?   324

Closing Tyler's File   328

Summary   328

Learning More about Students Who Have Sensory Impairments   329

Taking It into Your Classroom   331

CHAPTER 11 Students with Multiple Disabilities   332

Monique's File   333

What Are Monique's Multiple Disabilities?   341

What Factors Contributed to Monique's Disabilities?   345

How Have Monique's Disabilities Affected Her Development?   347

What Is School Like for Monique?   347

What Educational Approach Is Best for Monique?   353

How Is Monique Different from Other Students Who Have Multiple Disabilities?   357

Closing Monique's File   358

Updating Monique's Story   360

Summary   361

Learning More about Students with Multiple Disabilities   362

Taking It into Your Classroom   364

CHAPTER 12 Students Who Are At-Risk   365

Owen's File   366

Why Is Owen Considered to Be At-Risk?   374

How Has Owen's Development Been Affected by the Trauma He Has Experienced?   378

What Has School Been Like for Owen?   381

What Educational Approach Is Best for Owen?   383

How Is Owen Different from Other Students Who Are At-Risk?   388

Closing Owen's File   389

Summary   390

Learning More about Students Who Are At-Risk   391

Taking It into Your Classroom   393

CHAPTER 13   **Creating Your Own Special Stories   394**

Learning More   395

Mentoring 395

Ongoing Professional Development in Special Education   397

Taking It into Your Classroom   399

Your Own Special Stories   401

Closing Our File   402

Glossary   403
References   407
Index   418

Preface

Welcome to the third edition of *Special Education in Canada*. This book tells the stories of nine Canadian students who have experienced specialized forms of education. We feature these real-life case studies because they contextualize the educational realities that are faced by students, their teachers, and their families. We have also included other professionals' perspectives on these stories to provide a uniquely insightful dimension not found in many other texts.

You will find our detailed pedagogical rationale for the book in Chapter 1. As this text will be used by teachers of teachers and by aspiring teachers, we felt strongly that its pedagogy could not be separated from its content. Please consult the From the Publisher section for a preview of the unique pedagogical support found within *Special Education in Canada*.

The Structure of the Text

Chapters 2–4 provide an introduction to the domain of special education and lay out the guiding principles that govern our discussion of (a) its historical and current perspectives; (b) its identification, assessment, and IEP process; and (c) the creation and maintenance of exemplary teaching and learning environments.

Each of the next eight chapters (5–12) contains a story about a student who was identified under a category of exceptionality. These categories include learning disability, behavioural disorder, gifted and talented, autism, intellectual disability, and multiple disabilities. Two new chapters were added to this second edition of the text: Chapter 10 presents the stories of two students who have sensory impairments (hearing and vision) while Chapter 12 introduces the story of an at-risk student.

The last chapter (13) in the text builds on the previous 12 by encouraging beginning educators to continue learning about special education as they are exposed to special stories in their own classrooms.

Acknowledgements

Obviously, we could not have written this text without the amazing contributions of the students and their families. We came to realize that telling and retelling such an intimate family story is not as easy as it seems. While they remain anonymous, they know who they are and we are deeply grateful.

We would also like to thank the reviewers, who offered helpful feedback on the manuscript in various stages of development:

Elina Birmingham, Simon Fraser University
Deanna Friesen, Bishop's University

Joseph Goulet, University of Winnipeg
Randy Hill, Brock University
Elizabeth Jordan, University of British Columbia
Amy Thomas, University of Alberta
Gaby van der Giessen, Laurentian University

Last, but certainly not least, a sincere thanks to the Oxford Press family who helped us throughout this exciting process. In particular, thank you to Stephen Kotowych who got us started and to Amy Gordon and Leanne Rancourt who provided much support from start to finish.

From the Publisher

New to This Edition

The third edition of *Special Education in Canada* builds on the strengths of the second edition to enhance the learning experience for students and instructors.

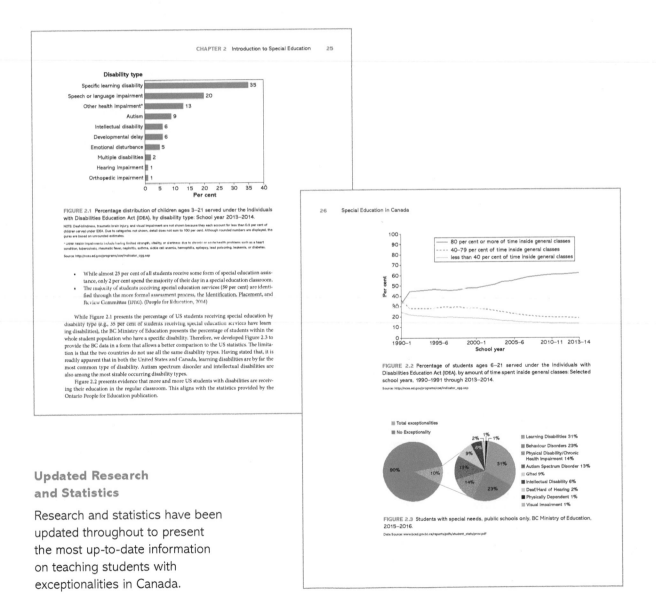

FIGURE 2.1 Percentage distribution of children ages 3–21 served under the Individuals with Disabilities Education Act (IDEA), by disability type: School year 2013–2014.

NOTE: Deaf-blindness, traumatic brain injury, and visual impairment are not shown because they each account for less than 0.5 per cent of children served under IDEA. Due to categories not shown, detail does not sum to 100 per cent. Although rounded numbers are displayed, the gures are based on unrounded estimates.

* Other health impairments include having limited strength, vitality, or alertness due to chronic or acute health problems such as a heart condition, tuberculosis, rheumatic fever, nephritis, asthma, sickle cell anemia, hemophilia, epilepsy, lead poisoning, leukemia, or diabetes.

Source: http://nces.ed.gov/programs/coe/indicator_cgg.asp

- While almost 25 per cent of all students receive some form of special education assistance, only 2 per cent spend the majority of their day in a special education classroom.
- The majority of students receiving special education services (59 per cent) are identified through the more formal assessment process, the Identification, Placement, and Review Committee (IPRC). (People for Education, 2014)

While Figure 2.1 presents the percentage of US students receiving special education by disability type (e.g., 35 per cent of students receiving special education services have learning disabilities), the BC Ministry of Education presents the percentage of students within the whole student population who have a specific disability. Therefore, we developed Figure 2.3 to provide the BC data in a form that allows a better comparison to the US statistics. The limitation is that the two countries do not use all the same disability types. Having stated that, it is readily apparent that in both the United States and Canada, learning disabilities are by far the most common type of disability. Autism spectrum disorder and intellectual disabilities are also among the most sizable occurring disability types.

Figure 2.2 presents evidence that more and more US students with disabilities are receiving their education in the regular classroom. This aligns with the statistics provided by the Ontario People for Education publication.

FIGURE 2.2 Percentage of students ages 6–21 served under the Individuals with Disabilities Education Act (IDEA), by amount of time spent inside general classes: Selected school years, 1990–1991 through 2013–2014.

Source: http://nces.ed.gov/programs/coe/indicator_cgg.asp

FIGURE 2.3 Students with special needs, public schools only, BC Ministry of Education, 2015–2016.

Data Source: www.bced.gov.bc.ca/reports/pdfs/student_stats/prov.pdf

Updated Research and Statistics

Research and statistics have been updated throughout to present the most up-to-date information on teaching students with exceptionalities in Canada.

New End-of-Book Glossary

A compiled list of key terms and definitions at the end of the book provides additional study support for students. Key terms are also still defined in the margins throughout.

Revised and Expanded "What We Know" Boxes

"What We Know" boxes have been revised, replaced, and updated throughout, incorporating contemporary understanding of exceptionalities and teaching methods, as well as the most current assistive technological options available.

Dynamic Pedagogical Program

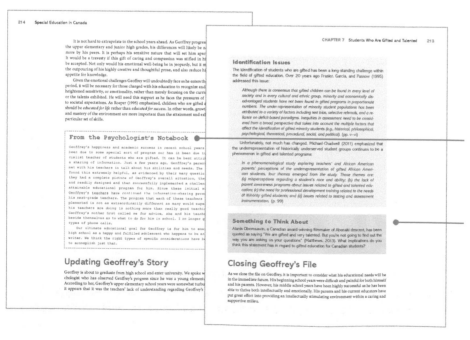

The "From the Psychologist's Notebook" feature highlights professional observations and facilitates a deeper understanding of the student case study and the topic under consideration.

"Something to Think About" boxes encourage critical thinking by posing thought-provoking questions.

"What We Know" boxes provide additional information from professional literature and research.

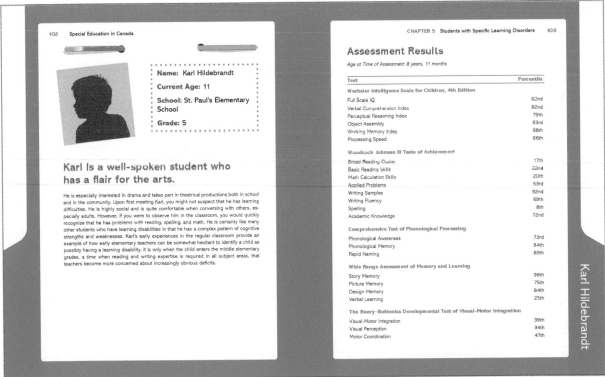

Chapter-opening student files in Chapters 5–12 include actual source documents pertaining to the student case study. Documents such as test results, excerpts from IEPS, samples of student writing and artwork, teacher and parent observations, and school reports encourage genuine engagement with each student case study.

Learning objectives set quantifiable goals for each chapter.

CHAPTER 9
Students with Autism

LEARNING OBJECTIVES

After learning the material in this chapter, you should be able to:

- Describe how autism spectrum disorder is diagnosed.
- Outline the levels of severity associated with autism spectrum disorder.
- Discuss the possible causes of autism.
- Describe the effects that autism can have on a child's development.
- Discuss how dysfunctional sensory systems can affect individuals with autism.
- Outline strategies for teaching students with autism.
- Differentiate between the three identified levels of autism.
- Discuss strategies that educators can use to reduce stress in educational settings.

44   Special Education in Canada

be acquiring reading skills like all the other Grade 3 students in the class, or a student appears overly aggressive toward her peers when on the playground. A high school guidance counsellor may observe that a student seems particularly anxious during school social activities. These intuitive and educated hunches that something is amiss usually mark the beginning of the assessment process.

Most students who are eventually identified as having exceptional learning and behavioural needs are initially identified through screening assessments. *Screening assessments* are most often classroom activities carried out by teachers or other school personnel to determine which students may be at risk for learning or behavioural difficulties. These assessments may include the use of teacher-made investigative tools used on an individual basis to investigate the educated hunches that parents and teachers have about a student's performance. Teachers frequently rely on observation strategies (e.g., time sampling, frequency sampling, and anecdotes) to gain a better understanding of student behaviour. Assessments may also involve the implementation of commercially available tests that are administered to large groups of students, such as entire classes, entire grades, or sometimes groups of grades.

Regardless of the type of assessment tool used, screening assessments are most often implemented at critical junctures in the school curricula, usually at points where students are expected to engage in more complex and sophisticated thinking and learning or at grades where the curricula or teaching methods change dramatically. The most common critical junctures are (a) upon entry to school to determine school readiness; (b) in Grades 2, 3, and 4, where students make the transition from learning to read to the more complex school activity of reading to learn; (c) at the transition from elementary to junior high (or middle school), where students are taught by several different teachers, where the curricula become more demanding, and where students are expected to be autonomous learners; and (d) at the transition from junior high to senior high school, where curricular demands and student products are expected to be more sophisticated and adult-like.

An example of a screening assessment at a critical education juncture is the completion of a variety of spelling and reading exercises at the beginning of the Grade 3 year to see which children may need special attention when tackling the more demanding language elements of the Grade 3 curricula. When properly implemented and carefully evaluated, the results of these screening activities can be used to identify and eliminate minor problems that can be rectified by proper instruction. There is a vast difference between a student who simply cannot read and a student who cannot read because he or she did not receive adequate instruction. Both of these poor readers may score the same on the screening measure, but their requirements for reading instruction will be quite different. In the first instance, special reading interventions will be required and the teacher may have to enlist the services of the school resource teacher. In the second instance, the teacher will simply do what he or she normally does when teaching reading—keep a watchful eye on the student's progress while being cognizant of the fact that the student has a lot of catching up to do.

Whether activated by a hunch or by a formal screening activity or test, the early identification of learning or behavioural differences is the important first step in a comprehensive assessment process that is typically used to determine whether a student may need special education services. Since Bloom's (1964) seminal work on the positive relationship between stimulating environments and intellectual growth and learning, there has been an abundance of research evidence that has consistently and clearly indicated that the sooner a student's difficulties are identified and the sooner proper educational interventions are

time sampling
Observations of student behaviour that are recorded at fixed, regular intervals.

frequency sampling
Counting how many times a particular behaviour occurs during a designated period of time.

anecdote
A brief narrative account of a student's behaviour that is of interest to the observer.

autonomous learners
Students who can learn, solve problems, and develop new ideas with minimal external guidance.

A marginal glossary defines key terms in the margins.

CHAPTER 7   Students Who Are Gifted and Talented   215

needs rather than the actual school placement that had this effect. Subsequently, Geoffrey was home-schooled for his Grade 7 year. Conversely, high school was an extremely positive experience. Geoffrey attended a public high school where he was enrolled in a literary arts program. This meant he took advanced courses in literature and writing while attending regular classes for all other subjects. The psychologist described this mix of programming as "very suitable for Geoffrey's social, emotional, and academic needs." Apparently, Geoffrey excelled in all subject areas, especially writing, and received several awards for his efforts. His closest friends were his literary arts peers among whom he was well-accepted; together they attended regular school functions and socialized with those outside of their particular program. Asked to sum up Geoffrey's latter school years, the psychologist noted that when we wrote the first edition of this text her hope was that Geoffrey would emerge from high school as a happy and fulfilled adolescent who happens to be an amazing writer. "That has been accomplished . . . he had some terrific teachers along the way . . . in high school, he was challenged to further develop his literary expertise and he was acknowledged when he did just that, he experienced teenage life along with his peers in a regular high school, and he continued to have a very supportive home life. He is ready to move on to university, where I am sure he will thrive in a more intense academic setting."

Summary

Giftedness, or the capability of high performance because of outstanding abilities, is considered a genetic endowment that can be influenced by environmental factors. It is typically identified in Canadian schools through observation and the completion of a standardized intelligence test. While students who are gifted may exhibit common characteristics (e.g., how they learn and what motivates them), their superior abilities are displayed through a wide range of behaviours (e.g., academic proficiency, artistic abilities, and athletic prowess). These students are not always as easily identified as one may think, especially when they are not equally capable across all school-related tasks. For example, students may be learning or physically disabled as well as gifted. It is also apparent that some students who are gifted are not identified due to the fact that they are underachievers, sometimes purposefully. As evidenced from Geoffrey's story, it is critical that educators carefully consider the academic and social or emotional needs of students who are gifted.

Chapter summaries succinctly review key concepts.

140   Special Education in Canada

Learning More about Students with Learning Disabilities

Academic Journals

Exceptional Children
Journal of Learning Disabilities
Journal of Special Education
Learning Disabilities: A Multidisciplinary Journal
Learning Disabilities Research & Practice
Learning Disability Quarterly

Books

Bender, W. N. (2012). *Differentiating instruction for students with learning disabilities: New best practices for general and special educators* (3rd ed.). Thousand Oaks, CA: Sage Publications Inc.

Dawson, P., & Guare, R. (2012). *Coaching students with executive skills deficit.* New York, NY: The Guilford Press.

Lerner, J. W., & Johns, B. (2014). *Learning disabilities and related disabilities* (13th ed.). Stamford, CT: Cengage Learning.

Wong, B., Graham, L., Hoskyn, M., & Berman, J. (Eds.). (2008). *The ABCs of learning disabilities* (2nd ed.). Burlington, MA: Elsevier Academic Press.

Web Links

LD Online

www.ldonline.org
This site features hundreds of articles on learning disabilities and ADHD as well as monthly columns by noted experts, a comprehensive resource guide, and active forums. Educators will find information on attention-deficit disorder (ADD/ADHD), dyslexia, dysgraphia, dyscalculia, dysnomia, reading difficulties, and speech and related disorders.

LD@School

www.ldatschool.ca
LD@school is the first resource of its kind in Ontario dedicated to serving the needs of educators. It provides educators with information, resources, and research related to teaching students with learning disabilities.

Learning Disabilities Association of Ontario

www.ldao.ca
Besides providing information about types of learning disabilities and common signs of learning disabilities, this site includes a section devoted to how to help students with learning disabilities in different environments, such as at school and at home.

The "Learning More About" sections offer annotated suggestions for further reading.

The "Taking It into Your Classroom" sections provide a bulleted synopsis of key topics from the chapter with space for personal notes.

142   Special Education in Canada

Taking It into Your Classroom . . .

Including Students Who Have Specific Learning Disorders

When a student who has a learning disability is first placed in my classroom, I will

- review what I know about learning disabilities and locate resource materials,
- read the student's file,
- consult with the student's previous teachers,
- consult with the student's parents, and
- meet with the school-based team to discuss the student's current school year.
- Other: _____

When I suspect a student in my classroom has a learning disability, I will

- review what I know about learning disabilities and locate resource materials,
- collect information about the student through classroom interventions,
- consult with other school personnel who are familiar with the student,
- consult with the student's parents, and
- meet with the school-based team to present the information I have collected.
- Other: _____

Key points to remember in my daily interactions with a student who has a learning disability:

- The student may have low self-esteem and low self-concept.
- The student may exhibit a discrepancy between ability and performance.
- The student may be impulsive and speak without thinking.
- The student may not be able to interpret body language and tone of voice.
- The student may have difficulty understanding spoken language.
- The student may not react well to change.
- Other: _____

Key points regarding curriculum differentiation for a student who has a learning disability:

- Change, modify, or adapt the curriculum according to the student's IEP.
- Use visual aids to supplement oral and written information.
- Include hands-on activities rather than just having the student listen and observe.
- Use learning aids such as assistive technology to motivate the student.
- Implement any additional supports recommended in the student's IEP.
- Other: _____

Key points regarding evaluation of the progress made by a student who has a learning disability:

- Follow the evaluation plan outlined in the student's IEP.
- Consider the student's current learning expectations to determine his or her progress.
- Observe how the student's behaviour affects his or her learning.
- Recognize the student's strengths.
- Modify existing learning expectations or develop new ones as needed.
- Implement new learning supports as needed.
- Other: _____

Instructor Resources

Special Education in Canada is supported by outstanding ancillary material for the instructor.

Instructor's Manual

- This fully revised resource includes a chapter overview, lecture outline, learning objectives, key terms list, discussion questions, class assignments/activities, suggested further readings, recommended websites, and recommended videos for each chapter.

PowerPoint Slides

- PowerPoint slides for each chapter are ideal for use in lecture presentations.

Test Bank

- The test bank contains fully revised multiple-choice, true/false, short-answer, and essay questions, as well as an answer key.
- Details on instructor's supplements are available from your Oxford University Press sales representative or at our website:

 www.oupcanada.com/EdmundsSE3e

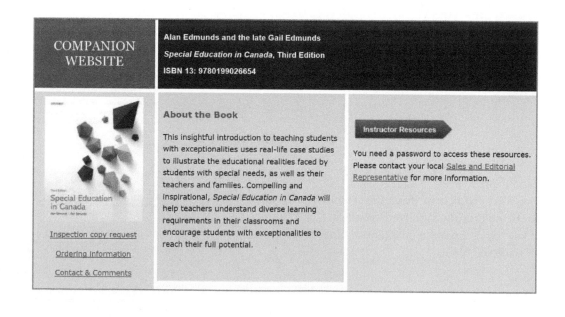

COMPANION WEBSITE

Alan Edmunds and the late Gail Edmunds
Special Education in Canada, Third Edition
ISBN 13: 9780199026654

Special Education in Canada

Inspection copy request

Ordering information

Contact & Comments

About the Book

This insightful introduction to teaching students with exceptionalities uses real-life case studies to illustrate the educational realities faced by students with special needs, as well as their teachers and families. Compelling and inspirational, *Special Education in Canada* will help teachers understand diverse learning requirements in their classrooms and encourage students with exceptionalities to reach their full potential.

Instructor Resources

You need a password to access these resources. Please contact your local Sales and Editorial Representative for more information.

CHAPTER 1
Meaningful Stories: Meaningful Learning

From the Psychologist's Notebook

We would like to welcome you to the third edition of *Special Education in Canada*. We hope you find it as interesting and educational as we envision it to be. The first edition of our book came about for three reasons: (a) We felt a different kind of special education textbook was needed; (b) the publisher had the foresight and conviction to break away from the traditional textbook mould; and (c) both parties wanted a textbook that made special education come to life. In the second edition of the text, we added two new chapters (students with sensory impairments and at-risk students) in an effort to broaden our coverage of students with exceptionalities. This third edition provides updated information in all chapters, including changes based on feedback from users, to ensure that our book addresses the latest and most important special education issues. Please note that the students' stories remain factual and authentic.

For more than 30 years we have been working with students with exceptionalities, helping their teachers and parents, and conducting research in the areas of educational psychology and special education. As well, we have been involved in the design and development of curricula, instructors' manuals, and assessment tools. Along the way, we have read, examined, and utilized several very good special education textbooks, but we cannot say that any of these books stands out as being different or novel in terms of the presentation of information. Most books of this genre are presented in a similar, if not identical, fashion, and despite excellent and comprehensive information about exceptionalities and teaching methodologies, there still seems to be something missing.

The more we thought about it, the more we realized that what these texts lack is the authentic context of the "stories" that education students love to hear when studying special education. From our experience, when we talk about children with exceptionalities and provide examples of their school-related endeavours, students ask lots of questions and seek out additional

Continued

readings or websites. This regularly happens from course to course and from year to year. Unfortunately, the same level and amount of interest does not occur when students are simply assigned textbook readings to discuss in class. This approach often results in the memorization of facts and a failure to recall the information not long afterward. For example, many in education are aware of the Emily Eaton decision in 1997 in which the Supreme Court of Canada ruled that the Brant County Board of Education had the right to judiciously place Emily in a specialized classroom, despite the legal protest of her parents (*Eaton v. Brant*, 1997). However, because Emily's story was mostly presented from a legal (factual) perspective and little emphasis was placed on Emily's life situation, few people remember that this 11-year-old girl had cerebral palsy and experienced considerable difficulty when trying to communicate with others. Further, many in education may not even be aware that up until the time the legal issues began, Emily was a member of a regular classroom where she had the full-time support of an educational assistant. We contend that providing more information regarding Emily and her school experiences would have made the details surrounding her situation more memorable and, therefore, more accurately recalled and discussed at a later date.

This keen level of curiosity regarding the lives of students with special needs is not limited to those who are involved in the field of education. We have noticed that when we informally share children's stories with people who are not even remotely connected to our field, their interest is piqued. We have a friend who, even after many years, always asks about Geoffrey (Chapter 7) because he finds "Geoffrey's story" fascinating. We became convinced that if this approach could have such a positive learning effect on a non-educator, it would be invaluable for aspiring and experienced teachers. We know there is something special about compelling stories, so it made sense to write a book about students with exceptionalities that was first and foremost a collection of stories that people would want to read.

But, as educators, we also know that gripping stories do more than merely spark curiosity: They also set the stage for excellent learning by association. The reason stories are so riveting is because individuals immediately identify with the characters and their particular circumstances. This does not readily happen if information is presented without a captivating context. It is likely that every person who reads this book will know of children with exceptionalities, and many will have witnessed or will have heard about the lives of these children. This instant association will enable readers to easily expand upon what they already know about special education.

A Constructivist Approach

While the beginning chapters of this book serve as an introduction to special education issues, the latter chapters present the stories of students with exceptionalities. Each of the student's stories is presented as an in-depth and comprehensive case study. The case study is an effective teaching and learning method that has been around ever since people started sharing educational information, and it has certainly become the instructional method of choice in law, business, engineering, and medicine. Recently, there has been considerable research evidence that effective teacher preparation programs are using well-developed case studies more often.

Cases addressing educational issues can be developed from portrayals of typical or atypical students or they can be centred on common and recurrent themes or problems that students and teachers encounter in schools every day. The intrinsic learning value of cases is that they allow the reader to vicariously participate in the experiences of the story being told. Jay's (2004) research clearly demonstrated that an instructor's use of different types of cases provides students with a deeper understanding of complex issues. According to Kuntz and Hessler (1998), the most important feature of the case study is that it provides educators with opportunities to have their students (a) employ higher-order thinking skills, (b) generalize learning to actual classrooms, (c) question assumptions about the theories presented, (d) engage in self-analysis, and (e) become aware of and understand the complex nature of teaching.

As you can see, the effects that cases can have on student thinking are consistent with the fundamental tenet of constructivism, which advocates that instead of students passively receiving knowledge from their instructors they should actively and meaningfully construct their own knowledge and understandings (Kantar, 2013; Nath, 2005). Therefore, the cases in this book are not presented simply as information to read and comprehend. They are meant to encourage analysis, discussion, and debate by both instructors and students as they engage in interactive dialogue. Interactive dialogue is an effective social constructivist approach to teaching and learning because it emphasizes the value of the context within which learning strategies and knowledge are mutually constructed. With this emphasis, all students gain a better personal understanding of the topics at hand because their representations are distilled from and compared to what their peers and instructors think and say. Rather than assuming that learning takes place in the minds of individuals, it is better to assume that learning is more efficient and knowledge is better constructed when it is the result of interactions between people.

It is also important to note that the cases in this book are real-life accounts of Canadian children who are operating under real-world circumstances. Learning about the facts of these cases, and then comparing and contrasting them to their own lived experiences, will enable students to experience situated cognition—thinking and learning that becomes located and enhanced by the specific context of each case (King, 2000). Furthermore, the cases in this book will extend students' engagement beyond typical applications of situated cognition because they will be expected to extrapolate and transfer their knowledge and their thinking to the real world—their classrooms. The ultimate goal of this text is to present thought-provoking cases that will stimulate discussion. We want all learners to contribute to their own understanding of students with exceptionalities as they interpret and make meaning of their learning through the cases presented here. We are convinced that these special stories, in the form of comprehensive case studies, will result in enhanced learning.

The Framework of the Text

What Does the Text Include?

In Chapters 1–4, we introduce special education and discuss the identification of students with exceptionalities and their need for exemplary learning environments. Then, in each of Chapters 5–11, we examine a particular exceptionality by focusing on the story of a real child with that exceptionality. These chapters open with extracts from the student's actual school file followed by details of the student's school life. In Chapter 12 we present the concept of being "at-risk," again using the story of a child who falls into this category. We conclude the book with Chapter 13, where we offer advice to future educators on how they can best ensure they are prepared to assist the students who will become the stories in their classroom.

How Were the Special Stories Chosen?

You may be wondering why we chose to tell the stories of the particular students included in this text; undoubtedly, there are endless fascinating stories to be told. Originally, in the first edition of *Special Education in Canada*, we wanted to focus on the high-incidence categories of exceptionality because these categories represent the vast majority of students with exceptionalities. They include the students most frequently encountered by regular classroom teachers. High-incidence exceptionalities typically include learning disabilities, behavioural disorders, giftedness, and intellectual disabilities. The first edition of this text also provided an introduction to low-incidence exceptionalities—Zachary (Chapter 9) and Monique (Chapter 11). Low-incidence exceptionalities usually refer to the more moderate and more severe disabilities that occur less frequently in the general population, such as autism, hearing and visual impairments, serious health impairments, and multiple disabilities. In the second edition of the text, we added two stories in Chapter 10—the stories of Tyler and Veena—that address hearing and visual impairments. We also added the story of Owen (Chapter 12) as students like him are present in many classrooms. He is best described as an at-risk student who has received special education services throughout his school life.

Other reasons for choosing the particular stories presented in this text included the need to cover a wide range of grade levels (i.e., students who are currently enrolled in the lower elementary grades, middle grades, and secondary grades) and the need to reflect the fact that in the general population there are more boys with exceptionalities than girls. As well, we had to choose the stories of students whose parents were willing to share the details of their children's lives. It is interesting to note that all parents we approached were more than willing to have their children's stories included in this text. They were excited that teachers would have the opportunity to learn from the experiences of real children. As one parent stated, "the problems we faced within the school system have a better chance of being fixed if teachers are able to objectively examine what happened to our child . . . we can all learn by looking back at what worked and what didn't work."

Having obtained permission to write about these children and their families, we respected the need to preserve the confidentiality of all individuals involved. Therefore, names have been changed and, in some instances, slight alterations were made to the children's stories. Nonetheless, in an effort to retain contextual authenticity, we have remained true to each individual's special story as much as professionally possible. We chose to do this because even though these real-life educational stories are less-than-perfect depictions of what "should happen," we, like the parents, are convinced that much can be learned from educational situations, decisions, and actions that are sometimes less than exemplary.

What Do These Special Stories Have to Offer Students and Instructors?

We sincerely believe that our unique and innovative approach will make the topic of students with exceptionalities come alive for both students and instructors. If you are a student, we want you to be fully engaged in each story while you learn about this exciting domain, and we want you to take away valuable information that will positively affect your teaching for years to come. If you are an instructor, we offer you each story as a starting point for the specific topics you want to teach. We presume you will use modified and adapted perspectives of each story to suit the emphases of your course. Our overall intention is that the themes of the stories will evoke probing questions from students and instructors alike, such as:

- Why did the Supreme Court decide in favour of the school board in the *Eaton* case? (Chapter 1)
- Why did the Cognitive Credit Card learning strategy work for Karl when other strategies did not? (Chapter 5)
- What are the different ways that students can be identified as being gifted and talented? (Chapter 7)
- How can a student with autism cope with all the sensory input that occurs in a regular classroom? (Chapter 9)
- What is it like for a student to have a cochlear implant and suddenly hear many new sounds? (Chapter 10)

Does the Text Only Address the Learning Experiences of Nine Students?

We recognize that not all aspects of an exceptionality apply to any one child regardless of his or her exceptional condition or the life situations he or she experiences. The obvious question for us was, "How will the text portray all of the different aspects of a particular exceptionality if the focus is on one child's story?" We accomplish this in each chapter with *What We Know* boxes. The information contained in these boxes presents aspects of the exceptionality that do not necessarily apply to the story being told. This special feature brings additional professional literature into every chapter, and it expands the coverage of each category of exceptionality. Once readers are aware of the complete picture, they can then have more reasoned and informed discussions about the exceptionality at hand. For example, now that you know that Emily Eaton was a student with a physical disability and struggled considerably with communication, you can readily compare and contrast her traits, characteristics, and school experiences with those of other students with similar conditions. This will undoubtedly help you to understand the broader spectrum of all students with intellectual and developmental disabilities. Even though Emily's case is not one of the cases in this book, we present more details of her story below in a *What We Know* box to demonstrate its form and purpose. The details in the box are from Bedgell and Molloy (1995) and the Learning Disabilities Association of Canada (2005).

Emily Eaton, age 22.

Used with permission from Carol and Clay Eaton.

What We Know . . .

Emily Eaton's Story

Emily lives in Burford, Ontario. She has cerebral palsy and she is unable to communicate through speech, sign language, or other communication systems. She also has a visual impairment and is mobility impaired, and therefore requires the use of a wheelchair. Although she was identified as an "exceptional student" upon her entry into school, Emily, at her parents' request, was placed in an age-appropriate kindergarten in her neighbourhood school in the public system on a trial basis. As dictated by her high needs, Emily was assigned a full-time educational assistant.

In Emily's Grade 3 year, school personnel concluded that this placement was not in her best interest because of her lack of academic progress and a social environment she had great difficulty managing. Emily's parents refused to allow their daughter to be moved to a segregated class because they strongly believed that her needs could be met in the regular class; that she would be psychologically harmed in a segregated classroom; and that in order to truly be part of her community, Emily needed to go to her neighbourhood school with her peers. Emily's parents were essentially arguing for the concepts that are at the heart of the philosophy of inclusion.

When the Identification Placement and Review Committee (IPRC) determined that Emily should be placed in a special education class, her parents appealed that decision to a Special Education Appeal Board, which confirmed the IPRC decision. The parents appealed again to the Ontario Special Education Tribunal, which also confirmed the decision. The parents then lost in Ontario's Divisional Court, but the Ontario Court of Appeal found in favour of the parents, stating that segregation violated Emily's equality rights under Section 15(1) of the Canadian Charter of Rights and Freedoms. The court held that making distinctions on the basis of disability was discriminatory and that the Ontario Education Act itself violated the Charter in giving school boards the discretion to place children with disabilities in segregated classes against their parents' wishes.

The Brant County School Board appealed this judgment to the Supreme Court of Canada, which set aside the decision of the court of appeal. The Supreme Court ruled that the educators and the tribunal had not violated the equality rights of Emily Eaton; rather they had balanced her educational interests appropriately, taking into account her special needs. The Supreme Court observed that a disability, as a prohibited ground of discrimination, differs from other grounds such as race and gender because of the vastly different circumstances of each individual and that, related to education, inclusion can be either a benefit or a burden depending on whether the child can profit from the advantages that inclusion provides. This meant that educational decisions affecting placement must be based on the child's best educational interests, not on what adults want for their children.

Source: Excerpted from Bedgell & Molloy (1995) and the Learning Disabilities Association of Canada (2005).

As you can see, the information presented in the *What We Know* box enhances Emily's story and provides further insight into her case. You are now in a position to discuss and debate the placement of students like Emily in specialized settings versus their placement in the regular classroom. The discussion can be expanded to include an examination of the varying implications each placement scenario has for teachers and how each would affect their curricular choices and instructional methods. As you can see, the opportunities for learning are numerous and there is no doubt they all emanate from the basic story of one child. For your information, most students with exceptionalities are not educated in specialized settings, but that is not the point. The point is that Emily's story, even though only briefly presented here, has grabbed your attention. Imagine what a full-blown story covering several years of schooling will do!

What Other Special Features Does This Text Include?

The *What We Know* boxes are just one component of a consistent framework that systematically supports each of the student's stories. Another special component is *From the Psychologist's Notebook*. These boxes provide a professional's insightful observations about the child and his or her situation. These types of observations are not often found in special education textbooks, yet they have much to offer in terms of facilitating a deeper understanding of the student who has special needs. An example of this type of box is presented below. It refers again to Emily Eaton's story.

```
From the Psychologist's Notebook

I interviewed Emily Eaton's parents 10 years after the Supreme Court of
Canada handed down its landmark decision to find out more about Emily's spe-
cial story. I met Clayton, Carol, and Emily at their family home in Burford.
Emily was to turn 23 in a few weeks. She remains verbally uncommunicative
and has limited use of her limbs. However, she uses gestures to indicate her
likes and dislikes, and according to her parents she does this quite often
and quite clearly.

    Both of Emily's parents described having had experience working in the
education system. Clayton was once a teacher but, at the time of the in-
terview, he was working for the Ontario Ministry of Education as a resource
consultant for students with visual impairments. Carol had previously worked
as a school counsellor at W. Ross MacDonald School.

    Emily graduated from high school when she was 21. Once out of school,
Carol and Clayton designed a program for her that mostly involves partici-
pating in social activities and doing everyday things like going to the den-
tist, getting groceries, and so on. Emily still needs constant supervision
and assistance to do most things. She has the services of a personal care
worker whose salary is paid by the Ontario government. Her current worker
is a young woman who is Emily's age. On the day I visited, the two of them
were off to see a movie with other friends.
                                                              Continued
```

At the beginning of the administrative wrangling over Emily's educational placement, the Eatons were confused by the school board's decision to place her in a segregated classroom. For two years previous, Emily was provided a full-time educational assistant (EA) and she was fully included in all regular class activities. By Clayton and Carol's account, all went well for those two years and they were very pleased with Emily's overall schooling experiences. In her Grade 3 year, the school board stipulated that Emily would only have EA support for half a day but provided no reason for this decision other than budgetary restraints. When the Eatons argued that this was contrary to the board's previous decisions, and that Emily's educational needs had not changed enough to warrant such an action, the board stated that if the Eatons wanted full-time support for Emily, she would have to be in a segregated class. This contentious position never changed throughout the legal process.

Immediately after the Special Education Tribunal's ruling in favour of a segregated placement, Clayton and Carol moved Emily to another local elementary school, one that fell under the Catholic Board. She continued her elementary education there and completed her secondary education at one of the Catholic high schools in nearby Brantford. For all of those years, until she was 21 years old, Emily had a full-time EA and was educated in regular classrooms with her peers. She left the classroom only for specialized interventions in speech, physical therapy, and occupational therapy. Clayton and Carol were extremely pleased with how it all turned out and could not say enough about the kindness and compassion of nearly all of Emily's teachers and classmates in both schools.

When asked why this seemingly obvious solution was not possible in the public system, Clayton and Carol explained how they had often suggested this very solution but were rebuked at every turn. They felt that once the battle lines had been drawn, the board did not want to back off from its original position.

I asked if anyone or any of the ruling bodies involved in the entire case had ever suggested the above educational solution for Emily. They informed me that the Supreme Court ruling was not really about Emily, per se; rather, the decision had more to do with ruling on the legitimacy of the school board policy. Therefore, nobody wanted to get into the details of Emily's specific case and no such suggestions were proposed, except by the Eatons themselves. In a twist of fate, and after all they had been through, their local Catholic school said they would welcome Emily into the regular classroom. It was as simple as going down the road to another school. It could have been as simple as providing her with a full-time EA at her original school.

Carol and Clayton were emphatic that parents of students with exceptionalities need to be vigilant about their child's schooling and not be afraid to advocate on their child's behalf whenever necessary. Despite their long ordeal, they found that constant diplomatic pressure coupled with precise and copious documentation made a significant difference in getting their point across. They also made it clear that, regardless of training or special expertise, teachers who are open-minded about a child's condition, and kind and compassionate in their teaching of that child, make more of a difference than any specialized programs. While they admitted that not all of Emily's teachers were exemplary, the majority were appreciated because of the reasons stated above.

It is difficult to comment on Emily's case because it focused more on policies and responsibilities than on Emily's education in particular. It is heartwarming that all went well for Emily eventually, but I think her parents paid an emotional price along the way. Currently, they are skeptical of what educational policy documents "say" about students with exceptionalities and place much more value on what educators "actually do" to support what is stated. In support of inclusive practices, the Eatons continue to share their experiences in an effort to help other families as well as educators (York University's Daily News, 2013).

Unfortunately, Emily and her parents were victims of their own time. I am convinced that if Emily's situation were to arise today, her case would never be argued beyond the jurisdiction of the governing school board, and it certainly would not make it to the Supreme Court. Educational decision makers, aware of the prevailing research on the best educational practices and policies for students with exceptionalities, would make the appropriate accommodations. There is no question that the overarching objective for the education of all students with exceptionalities should be to actualize their potential by providing exemplary educational opportunities. It is only under the auspices of valid, reliable, and proven special educational practices and policies that this is possible.

Also included in this text are the *Something to Think About* boxes that pose specific questions designed to encourage critical thinking about educational issues that extend beyond each child's respective case. Each of the student's stories concludes with a section entitled *Taking It into Your Classroom*, which presents a synopsis of the important points from the chapter. This box also allows readers to add their own points, or reminders, that they feel will be important to remember when teaching students with exceptionalities.

At the end of each chapter, we have also included some resources you can access. If you are mostly interested in research findings, you should explore the academic journals that are listed. General information, including teaching strategies, can usually be found in the books we have suggested. Both theoretical and practical information can be located through searches on the Internet.

Something to Think About

As you begin to learn about special education, it is important to reflect on your current feelings about the field and the experiences you have had that have led to the formation of these feelings. For example, you may have some negative thoughts about teaching students with exceptionalities that you can trace back to your own school years when you were in classrooms where disruptive students took all of the teacher's time. Perhaps it would be helpful to express your feelings on paper and revisit your writing after you have completed your coursework. It may be the case that more knowledge about the field will alter your feelings about special education. In any event, it is important to recognize the views you bring to your study of this topic.

A Reminder

As you learn about special education through the meaningful stories presented in this text, keep in mind that it was never our intent to provide comprehensive information that would qualify you as an expert once you had read and discussed the material. In the field of special education, there are entire textbooks that cover many of the topics presented in the chapters of this text. It is our intention, therefore, to introduce you to these topics and pique your interest so that you continue to pursue knowledge in this area throughout your teaching career. We hope you come to realize that teaching students with exceptionalities is not as daunting as it is sometimes portrayed. While there are new teaching skills to learn, they are not that different from the skills you use to teach all students.

CHAPTER 2
Introduction to Special Education

LEARNING OBJECTIVES

After learning the material in this chapter, you should be able to:

- Define the terms *students with exceptionalities* and *special education*.

- Describe the modern history of special education, including legislation that has affected the direction it has taken.

- Explain how the use of non-stigmatizing professional terminology relates to the field of special education.

- Differentiate between special education in Canada and special education in the United States, including the role that the Charter of Rights and Freedoms has played in special education in Canada.

- Define and differentiate between the terms *inclusion*, *integration*, and *mainstreaming*, and discuss why inclusion is considered the better option.

- Differentiate between the *categorical model* and the *non-categorical model* of special education, and discuss the strengths and weaknesses of each approach.

What Is Special Education?

In every classroom, in every school, on any given day, teachers know they will face groups of students who have different abilities and behaviours. They fully expect that not all students will learn at the same rate, or act and react to their environment in the same manner. Teachers are known to frequently teach lessons while purposefully wandering around their classrooms providing instructional prompts, extra help, or guidance so that each child can better understand the topic. Teachers also seem to intuitively know when a particular look or verbal reminder is necessary to nip potentially problematic behaviour in the bud. As a result of their education and classroom experiences, teachers develop a wide range of teaching and classroom management strategies to accommodate the typical range of student diversity.

However, in these very same classrooms, there will also be students whose learning and behaviours differ considerably from the norm. Without specialized knowledge, teachers will likely lack the educational tools needed to teach and manage these students properly. We refer to this group of children as *students with exceptionalities*—students who exhibit differences in learning and behaviour that significantly affect their educational potential and whose exceptional needs cannot be met by typical approaches to schooling. This group of students is just as varied and diverse as the rest of the school population. For example, their needs may include physical accommodations, behavioural interventions, specialized computers, particular learning strategies, modified curricula, or advanced placement university exams. According to the Council for Exceptional Children (2013), "special education refers to educational services provided to children and youth with exceptionalities; it includes specially designed instruction, supplementary aids and services, related services and early intervention." *Special education*, then, is a particular type of schooling that is constructed and delivered to suit the specific strengths and needs of students with exceptionalities. It is founded on the premise that if their education is properly differentiated, more of these children will reach their full potential.

The Modern History of Special Education

There is ample historical evidence that special types of educational services were provided for individuals with exceptionalities as far back as the eighteenth century. Often, these services were designed as convenient measures to thwart perceived threats to the education of normal students (Taylor & Harrington, 2001). As unpalatable as it may be, we have to remember that the early forms and types of special education were not always designed with the best interests of children with exceptionalities in mind.

It is not commonly known that some Canadian provinces were enacting legislation to ensure the education of students with exceptionalities as far back as 1969 (Goguen, 1993) and earlier. For example, "By 1955, the [British Columbia] provincial government introduced funding for programs for 'handicapped' children as part of the basic grant to school districts" (Siegel, 2000, p. 8). Another example occurred in Alberta where "in 1950, there were 256 identified exceptional students, in 16 classrooms across the province, and there were three categories of student exceptionality that were recognized" (Lupart, 2000, p. 5).

What We Know . . .

Dr. Helen MacMurchy— Inspector of the Feeble-Minded in Ontario

Ellis (2014) wrote about a medical doctor who was appointed "Inspector of the Feeble-Minded" in Ontario in 1906. The following excerpt describes the role Helen MacMurchy played in the history of special education in Canada:

> In 1910 in Toronto, a pioneering medical doctor, women and children's health expert, and social reformer named Helen MacMurchy played a vital role in getting special education classes for children then called "mentally defective." (While terms such as "mentally defective," "feeble-minded," or "sub-normal" to our ears sound harsh and offensive, they were the only terms that people a century ago had to talk about intellectual disabilities.) MacMurchy believed that people with intellectual disabilities in particular, whom she called feeble-minded or mentally defective, were a menace to other Canadians. Her fears were founded on her firmly held beliefs that the feeble-minded caused social problems, such as pauperism, prostitution, and unemployment, that feeble-mindedness was a hereditary disease, and that feeble-minded people were having more children than the rest of the population. MacMurchy thought that special education classes could help in a bigger effort to control the feeble-minded.
>
> MacMurchy wrote that "auxiliary classes" (special education classes) could be used as "clearing houses" for the training schools she wanted the government to build for feeble-minded people. The classes could be used to identify and train feeble-minded children while they waited to be transferred to training schools for the feeble-minded. In the training schools that eugenicists planned, feeble-minded people would be separated from the general population. The managers of the institutions could also monitor the feeble-minded so that they did not have children. (Later, eugenicists would advocate for sterilization to accomplish this aim.) MacMurchy also believed that the training schools, called "farm colonies," would be safe places for people with disabilities, where they would be happy and other people would not take advantage of them. MacMurchy's farm colonies were never built. But between approximately 1910 and 1945, multiple special education classes were opened in the schools of Vancouver, Victoria, Edmonton, Calgary, Regina, Saskatoon, Winnipeg, Brandon, Toronto, Ottawa, Montreal, Saint John, Halifax, and elsewhere in Canada and the United States as well.

Source: Ellis (2014). *Special education.* Retrieved from: http://eugenicsarchive.ca/discover/encyclopedia/535eee5c7095aa000000025d

However, the modern era of special education really began in the 1960s with the emergence of human rights issues. For example, in Ontario in 1968 the Hall–Dennis Report, *Living and Learning: The Report of the Provincial Committee on Aims and Objectives of Education in the Schools of Ontario*, emphasized "the right of every individual to have equal access to the learning experience best suited to his needs, and the responsibility of every school authority to provide a child centred learning continuum that invites learning by individual discovery and inquiry" (SEAC Learning, 2007). According to SEAC Learning, this report served as a catalyst for dramatic changes in classrooms and in teaching throughout the province.

During the 1960s nearly everyone associated with education rejected the existing practice of housing and educating students who were different in institutional settings. There was a strong movement across North America advocating that all individuals had the right to live, learn, and work with all other individuals. This represented a monumental change in our social consciousness. More and more educators of the day questioned the validity and effectiveness of the non-egalitarian approach that prevailed, and as a result special education came into its own.

Legislation Affecting Special Education

In Canada, education is the jurisdictional responsibility of the 13 individual provinces and territories. This means that each province and territory has its own respective education regulations, policies, and guidelines that govern the education of students with exceptionalities; however, these provisions are not laws per se. The situation is different in the United States, where the Department of Education governs special education by ensuring the implementation of federally mandated laws. It is important to consider these US laws, because they continue to have an effect on special education practices in Canada and around the world.

The passage of the US laws started in the late 1960s, flourished in the 1970s, and carry on today as educational perceptions about best practices continually evolve. It is generally perceived that the ground-breaking legislation for special education across North America occurred in 1975 with the signing of US Public Law 94–142, the Education for All Handicapped Children Act. The most influential feature of this law was its emphasis on individualized instruction that emerged from a child's individualized education program or IEP (see Chapter 3 for full details). Along with individualized programs, PL 94–142 also required that all students with special needs be educated in the *least restrictive environment*—the most appropriate classroom setting for each child's instructional needs. In addition, this landmark law contained provisions for the mandatory identification of students with exceptional needs, the use of non-discriminatory assessment criteria, and child and parental access to due process for dispute settlement. As well, it outlined and defined the 10 specific *categories* under which students could be identified. These mandated features of PL 94–142 had to be implemented for a state to receive supplementary funding for the education of students with special needs. In 1978, PL 95–561, and later the Jacob Javits Gifted and Talented Students Education Act of 1988, were enacted to address the educational needs of students who are gifted and talented, thus bringing the number of identifiable categories to 11. However, because PL 94–142 only mandated special education for children aged 6 to 18 years, another law, PL 99–457, was passed in 1986 to provide services for infants (0–3 years) and for preschoolers (3–6 years). This legislation set the stage for early intervention services for young children with special needs. The next major revision of PL 94–142 occurred in 1990 with the introduction of the Individuals with Disabilities Education Act (IDEA). This legislation added traumatic brain injury and autism to the collection of identifiable categories, thus resulting in the 13 categories that are widely used today. As well, IDEA was the first law to implement a people-first approach, using terms like "children with disabilities" instead of "disabled children." IDEA was further refined in 1997 as PL 105–17 when it made teachers accountable for

individualized education program

A document that describes a student's specialized learning expectations and the educational services that will be implemented to help the student meet these expectations.

student progress relative to the regular curriculum and required that the regular curriculum be the preferred starting point for all student outcome measures. This change put the onus on classroom teachers to directly involve students with exceptionalities in the regular courses of study.

Something to Think About

As well as implementing good teaching methods in a particular way and for particular purposes, special education, like all other professional disciplines, also requires the use of precise and professional terminology. You will note that throughout this book we use non-stigmatizing professional terms that emphasize a "people-first" approach, just as was implemented in the IDEA legislation. We speak of the child first and of his or her disabling condition second. We encourage you to immediately begin using terms like *students with learning disabilities* and *students who are gifted and talented*, rather than *LD students* and *gifted students*. Do you think it makes a difference to use this professionally accepted language? How might it affect both the student and those who work with the student?

The No Child Left Behind Act (NCLB)

The US legislation that has had perhaps the most significant impact on special education over the last 20 years is the No Child Left Behind Act of 2001 (NCLB, PL 107–110), which existed until 2015. This act was signed into law in January 2002 and established a sweeping set of reforms for the discipline. It was designed to improve the academic success of all students but especially the academic success of those who have exceptional learning and behavioural needs. According to the US Department of Education (2002), the act addressed four basic education reform principles: (a) stronger accountability for results, (b) increased flexibility and local control, (c) expanded options for parents, and (d) an emphasis on proven teaching methods. The NCLB also mandated that teachers be fully qualified, that non–English speaking children receive intensive instruction in English, and that schools be safe and drug free. The most noteworthy implication of NCLB was that schools may be subject to remedial action if students with exceptionalities failed to progress (we interpret this to mean the withholding of special education funding).

There was much debate over the NCLB legislation. One of the major criticisms of the original law voiced frequently and strongly by teachers and researchers in special education was that the NCLB assessment requirements did not exempt students with exceptionalities from district-wide or state-wide yearly achievement tests. Measuring the progress of these students against the general curricula went against everything that speaks to the individualized nature of special education and had the potential of undermining their access to programming based on their IEPs. The US Department of Education responded to these concerns by introducing a flexibility option:

The newly released proposed regulations for the 2 Per cent Flexibility Option give states and districts more leeway in assessing students with disabilities. States can develop modified assessments for 2 per cent of their students with disabilities who do not meet grade-level standards despite high quality instruction, including special education services. Though the modified assessments must be aligned with grade-level content standards, they may differ in breadth or depth from the achievement standards for non-disabled students. The proposed regulations make it clear that high expectations will be held for students with disabilities who take modified assessments. The students must have access to grade-level instruction, and the modified standards cannot preclude the students from receiving a regular diploma. Further, the students must be appropriately assessed on modified achievement standards. The IEP team will play a critical role in determining not only which students will take modified assessments, but also the type of modified assessment individual students will take. (Council for Exceptional Children, 2006)

Other criticisms of NCLB included the lack of funding available under the law and the pressure for educators to focus their teaching solely on the content of the student achievement tests. According to Mertler (2011), educators believed this approach was having a negative impact on instructional and curricular practices, not to mention the stress that came with demands for improved student performance. Educators also worried about the apparent narrowing of the scope of the overall curricula (and accompanying assessments). There was a sense that the increased focus on math and reading was at the expense of other curricular topics (McKenzie, 2003).

Every Student Succeeds Act

The Every Student Succeeds Act (ESSA), which replaced the NCLB act, was signed by President Obama on 10 December 2015. The president explained that "The goals of No Child Left Behind . . . were the right ones: High standards. Accountability. Closing the achievement gap. But in practice, it often fell short. It didn't always consider the specific needs of each community. It led to too much testing during classroom time. It often forced schools and school districts into cookie-cutter reforms that didn't always produce the kinds of results that we wanted to see" (Korte, 2015).

According to the Council for Exceptional Children (2016), the following are some of the provisions of ESSA that are relevant to children and youth with disabilities and gifts and talents:

General

- Transfers authority for accountability, educator evaluations, and school improvement from the federal government to the states and local districts

Assessments and Accountability

- Maintains annual, state-wide assessments in reading and math in Grades 3 through 8 and once in high school, as well as science tests given three times between Grades 3 and 12
- Repeals adequate yearly progress and replaces it with a state-wide accountability system
- Includes the use of multiple measures in school performance
- Maintains annual reporting of data disaggregated by subgroups of children, including students with disabilities

Associated Press

Pictured here at the signing, President Barack Obama signed the Every Student Succeeds Act into law in December 2015.

- Maintains with some modifications provisions for a cap of 1 per cent of students with the most significant cognitive disabilities who can take the alternate assessment aligned to the alternate academic achievements standards
- Helps states to improve low performing schools (bottom 5 per cent of schools)
- Actions to be determined locally, not federally
- Authorizes the use of federal funds for states and local school districts to conduct audits of state and local assessment systems to eliminate assessments that do not contribute to student learning

Gifted and Talented

- Authorizes the Jacob Javits Gifted and Talented Students Education Act supporting high-ability learners and learning
- Includes strong provisions for the disaggregation of student achievement data by subgroup at each achievement level on state and local report cards
- Provides options to include the identification of and service to students with gifts and talents in local education agency plans
- Provides options to include professional development plans for gifted and talented educators in Title II

Children with Disabilities

- Ensures access to the general education curriculum
- Ensures access to accommodations on assessments
- Ensures concepts of Universal Design for Learning

- Includes provisions that require local education agencies to provide evidence-based interventions in schools with consistently underperforming subgroups
- Requires states in Title I plans to address how they will improve conditions for learning, including reducing incidents of bullying and harassment in schools, overuse of discipline practices, and use of aversive behavioural interventions

As Canadian teachers, researchers, and policy makers continue to share ideas with their US colleagues, it will be interesting to see which, if any, elements of ESSA find their way into Canadian policies and classrooms.

How Is Special Education in Canada and the United States Similar?

The practice of educating students with exceptionalities in Canada is so similar to the practices implemented in the United States that not many individuals, even educators, would be able to tell the difference between the jurisdictions if they walked into comparable schools or classrooms. This is because the basic practices of special education follow the same conceptual models reported in literature worldwide; these are models that know no political boundaries.

Canadian Charter of Rights and Freedoms

As stated earlier, there is one major difference between special education in Canada and in the United States—the way in which it is governed. The closest that Canada comes to having a federal law regarding special education is the Canadian Charter of Rights and Freedoms. Section 15 of the Charter states that "Every individual is equal before and under the law and has the right to the equal protection and equal benefit of the law without discrimination and, in particular, without discrimination based on race, national or ethnic origin, colour, religion, sex, age or mental or physical disability" [s. 15 (1)]. To date, the Supreme Court of Canada has consistently interpreted Section 15 of the Charter to mean that the best interests of the individual child must be considered when determining a child's educational placement and intervention program. As you will see in the following *What We Know* box, the court has been consistent in that decisions regarding the provision of special education made thus far have been determined on a child-by-child basis. While the *Elwood* case below was not decided at the Supreme Court level (the parties reached an out-of-court settlement), it was the first challenge to segregated educational placements under Section 15 of the Charter. The parents of the child used Charter Sections 15 (equality), 2 (freedom of expression), and 7 (right to life, liberty, and security) to negotiate for their child's placement in the regular classroom. The *Moore* case decision was made more recently at the Supreme Court level some years after the student had completed his education.

Thus, while the Supreme Court of Canada did not render a decision in the *Elwood* case, the Charter shaped educational policy in favour of the best interests of the child (regular classroom), as it did soon after in its decision regarding Emily Eaton (segregated classroom; see Emily's story in Chapter 1). This is a highly significant development for special education because it means that the interpretations of the Charter were not precedent setting, as is usually the case with legal decisions of such magnitude. It is perhaps even more significant because the highest court in our land is adhering to the most fundamental tenet of special education—educational decisions are to be made in the best interests of each and every individual child who is exceptional. On one hand, this means that not all students with exceptionalities will be included in regular classrooms, but on the other hand, it also means that children will not be excluded from the regular classroom unless their situation warrants it. In terms of the *Moore* case, the Supreme Court determined that the student suffered discrimination in terms of the provision of a general education.

What We Know . . .

Elwood v. The Halifax County-Bedford District School Board

Luke Elwood of Halifax, Nova Scotia, was 9 years old and in a special education class for the "trainable mentally handicapped" until 1986 when his parents enrolled him in a regular class in nearby Lawrencetown for the coming year. The Halifax County-Bedford District School Board asked his parents, Maureen and Rick Elwood, to place him back in his special education class in Halifax. When they refused, the board held a formal meeting where they decided that Luke would continue in his special education placement.

After many legal manoeuvres wherein the parents attempted to keep their child in a regular class and the board attempted to prevent it, an injunction was granted to allow Luke to stay in a regular classroom until the dispute was resolved. The board's basic argument was that if the parents had the right to choose their child's educational placement, the board would be obliged to develop a new and different education program. They had no way of providing an appropriate education for Luke other than in his segregated and specialized classroom. Immediately prior to the deciding court date in June 1997, the board and the parents came to an out-of-court settlement.

The important point here is that the parents used Charter Sections 15 (equality), 2 (freedom of expression), and 7 (right to life, liberty, and security) to (a) secure the injunction while awaiting the court date, and (b) successfully negotiate with the board for their child's placement in the regular classroom. The board was unsuccessful in arguing that education was a provincial matter as defined by statutes and regulations and as directed by educational administrators.

Source: MacKay (1987).

Moore v. British Columbia (Education) (2012 SCC 61)

In November 2012, the Supreme Court of Canada ruled in a unanimous decision that the British Columbia Ministry of Education (Board of Education of School District No. 44, North Vancouver) failed to provide the special education supports that Jeffrey Moore needed to get meaningful access to general education. The court determined that according to the Human Rights Code (R.S.B.C. 1996, c. 210, s. 8) and what constitutes meaningful access to education for students with learning disabilities in British Columbia (School Act, S.B.C. 1989, c. 61), the board discriminated against Jeffrey by failing to provide necessary remediation. The court found that Jeffrey's access to the education he

Continued

was entitled to was denied based on four facts: (a) there was no dispute that Jeffrey's dyslexia was a disability, (b) there was equally no question that the adverse educational impact he suffered was related to his disability, (c) Jeffrey undeniably required intensive remediation to have meaningful access to education, and (d) the board did not provide sufficiently intensive remediation for Jeffrey's learning disability. The court determined that Jeffrey's access to general education should have been the same as that available to *all* students and that he should have received an education that provided him the opportunity to develop to his full educational potential.

Source: http://scc.lexum.org/decisia-scc-csc/scc-csc/scc-csc/en/12680/1/document.do

Globe and Mail/The Canadian Press

Now a successful plumber, Jeffrey Moore and his family won a major human rights victory in the Supreme Court of Canada on 9 November 2012.

From the Psychologist's Notebook

Jeffrey Moore suffers from severe dyslexia. In his Grade 2 year, a board psychologist recommended that since he could not get the intensive remedial help he needed at his school, he should attend the local Diagnostic Centre to receive the necessary remediation. Despite the fact that the board had classified severe learning disabilities as a high-incidence, low-cost disability, the Diagnostic Centre was closed by the board due to fiscal restraint. Jeffrey entered a private school in his Grade 4 year to get the level and type of instruction he needed. The remedial instruction he received there was successful, and his reading abilities improved significantly.

Jeffrey's father filed a complaint under Section 8 of the BC Human Rights Code with the BC Human Rights Tribunal against the board and the province on the grounds that Jeffrey had been denied a "service customarily available to the public." The tribunal (and later the Supreme Court of Canada) defined this service as "general education." The tribunal concluded there was discrimination against Jeffrey by the board and the province and ordered remedies against both, including a reimbursement to the family for tuition costs charged by the private school and an award of $10,000 for pain and suffering. The tribunal's decision was first overturned by the reviewing judge of the Supreme Court of British Columbia (2010 BCCA 478), who argued that Jeffrey's situation should be compared to that of other students with exceptionalities, not to the general population of students. Subsequently, a majority in the British Columbia Court of Appeal agreed that Jeffrey ought to be compared to other students with exceptionalities and dismissed the family's appeal. Believing fully in their case, the Moore family appealed to the Supreme Court of Canada.

The Supreme Court determined that the purpose of the School Act in British Columbia is to ensure that "all learners . . . develop their individual potential and . . . acquire the knowledge, skills and attitudes needed to contribute to a healthy, democratic and pluralistic society and a prosperous and sustainable economy." According to the court, adequate special education is therefore not a dispensable luxury; for students with severe learning disabilities, special education is the ramp that provides them access to the statutory commitment to the education of all students made by the province. Therefore, the "service" to which Jeffrey was entitled under Section 8 of the BC Human Rights Code was not special education as argued by the board; rather, it was general education. The court declared that to define special education as the service risked descending into the "separate but equal" approach that had been previously quashed in US litigation. If Jeffrey was only compared to other students with exceptionalities, full consideration could not be given as to whether he had meaningful access to the education to which all students in British Columbia were entitled. This risked perpetuating the very disadvantage and exclusion the Human Rights Code is intended to remedy.

Several statements in the court's decision have major implications for educators across Canada. The court accepted the general agreement among the testifying experts that significant negative long-term consequences are experienced by students when learning disabilities are not remediated. The court also stated that educators have an obligation to provide individualized educational programs for students based on appropriate assessment. The court found that the board failed to assess Jeffrey's learning disability early enough. The court also found that intensive supports were needed to remedy Jeffrey's learning disability and that the remediation he received was far from adequate. The court rejected the board's expert who stated that Jeffrey had received the services he needed at his public school and that the interventions had been of appropriate intensity.

The court noted that the BC School Act (1991) set out minimum spending levels for high-incidence, low-cost and low-incidence, high-cost students.

Continued

This means that once a child is identified as having a severe learning disability, necessary services including early intervention are mandatory, thus establishing the right of all students with learning disabilities to adequate, individualized special education programs and services, including intensive evidence-based interventions for those who need them. The court rejected the board's argument that it was justified in providing no meaningful access to education for Jeffrey because it had no economic choice.

Because the Diagnostic Centre was being closed, Jeffrey's necessary instruction was available only at Kenneth Gordon Maplewood School, a private school specializing in teaching children who have learning disabilities. The court found that the board had not considered any reasonable alternatives for meeting the needs of students with severe learning disabilities before cutting available services such as the Diagnostic Centre. The board admitted in cross-examination that "the sole reason for the closure was financial." The court stated that there was no reason to think that the board's funding cuts necessarily had to affect the support of students with severe learning disabilities.

While the board stated that it contemplated a cascade model of service delivery, whereby a range of placements were available including highly specialized education environments for small numbers of students (British Columbia Ministry of Education, 1985, ss. 4.1 and 4.2), the court found that the board's predominant policy of integrating students with exceptionalities into the general classroom whenever possible was the usual practice. The board argued that its educational philosophy of integration, in part, warranted the closure of the Diagnostic Centre. The court rejected this position, stating that it was clear from the evidence provided by all the board's witnesses that they thought the Diagnostic Centre provided a useful service.

The ruling is a clear and unequivocal reconfirmation that a cascade or continuum of specialized educational interventions to meet a range of students' individualized educational needs is not a "luxury"; rather, it is the standard that must be applied. The Supreme Court stated that program decisions must be based on the subjective, child-centred "individual needs" of each student and that equal treatment may be discriminatory if it violates individual rights. The court rejected the board's argument that its integration/inclusion policy and its use of learning assistance to accommodate Jeffrey were valid. The court deemed it discriminatory to expect that Jeffrey could simply be "accommodated" to meaningfully access general education, when what Jeffrey actually needed was to be accommodated to suit the severity of his disability. The court found that the board had no specific plan in place to replace Jeffrey's services. It declared that the board's eventual plan of supporting Jeffrey via learning assistance was, by definition and purpose, ill-suited for the task. The court also made it clear that such mandatory and specific accommodations are not a question of "mere efficiency" and discretionary educational initiatives (e.g., outdoor education, concert band, field trips) cannot be compared with the documented accommodations necessary to make the core curriculum accessible to students with severe learning disabilities.

This ruling counters the view of some individuals that the regular classroom is the universal placement option for all students with exceptionalities. It puts to rest the notion that the one-placement model implied by inclusion is best for all students. The court cited Lieberman (1992), who pointed out that many advocates (primarily parents) for those with learning disabilities have significant concerns about the wholesale move toward inclusion. Their concerns stem from the fact that they have had to fight long and hard for appropriate services and programs for their children. They recognize that students with learning disabilities do not progress academically without individualized attention to their educational needs.

The court's finding that Jeffrey suffered discrimination and was therefore entitled to a consequential personal remedy has clear broad remedial repercussions for how all boards of education in Canada deal with and educate all students with exceptionalities. The court clearly inferred that if school boards want to avoid similar claims, they will have to ensure they provide a range of services for students with exceptionalities in accordance with related educational policies, and that fiscal expediency is not a defence against inadequate special education services. In a reasonable and justified move, the court did not hold the province liable for any of the costs awarded. It determined that the order for reimbursement and damages should apply only against the board because the board alone made the decisions that led to the discrimination.

How Do Special Education Practices in Canada Compare to the Practices Implemented Outside of North America?

While special education practices in North America and in countries such as Australia and New Zealand are currently focused on the inclusion of students with exceptionalities in regular classroom settings, this is not the case around the world. As Kohama (2012) pointed out, while inclusion is recognized as an excellent idea, it takes considerable effort to make it happen. She used the example of India where the government "has attempted to create policies that are inclusive for people with disabilities, [but] their implementation efforts have not resulted in an inclusive system of education, nor have they reached their goal of 'education for all' across the country" (p. 3)

In Europe, legislative progress regarding inclusion has been achieved in many countries where segregated special-needs education systems exist. Enculescu (2015) noted, however, that in many EU member states (e.g., Belgium, Germany, the Netherlands, Hungary, Greece, Lithuania, and Romania) many students with intellectual disabilities are still placed in segregated schools. Meijer (2010) explained that while the trend in Europe is toward more inclusive services, the situation is complicated by the growing pressure for better achievement outcomes and the fact that schools are free to admit students of their choice. Meijer concluded that little progress was made toward inclusion in Europe; in fact, there was a slight increase in segregation.

Impediments to the successful implementation of inclusive education also exist in South Africa. According to the Human Rights Watch (2016):

Hundreds of thousands of children are still out of school, but the government has not yet presented accurate data to show how many children with disabilities are out of school. The government continues to prioritize funding for special schools . . . [and]

has not yet adopted a strong focus on inclusive education . . . In 2015 and 2016, care-givers of children and adolescents with disabilities from Orange Farm, a township in Gauteng province, wrote letters telling their experiences of navigating the complex system, tackling discrimination against their children, and the impact on their children when they are not in school.

In summary, it is quite clear that barriers to inclusive education are not uncommon in many countries outside of North America. While special education services are available on a segregated basis, inclusionary practices, like those evident in Canada, are not as widely implemented.

Prevalence of Students with Exceptionalities

When discussing students with exceptionalities, many aspiring teachers want to know how likely it is they will have these students in their classrooms or how many students fall under the broad definition of "exceptional student." The fact is that the vast majority of classrooms now include students with exceptionalities, and nearly all teachers are required to teach and manage these students on a daily basis.

Exact statistics regarding the inclusion of students with exceptionalities in the regular classroom are difficult to acquire in Canada. Canada does not have a process that parallels the federal function of the US Department of Education which, through its mandated annual report to the US Congress, tracks the number of students with disabilities who receive special education funding and services. Despite the slightly different criteria used in some states, these reports are the most complete and accurate information on how many students in the United States have exceptionalities. It is important to note that students who are identified as gifted and talented are not included in this report as it only deals with students who are considered disabled. The generally accepted percentage of students identified as gifted and talented is 2–5 per cent depending on the jurisdiction and the criteria used. Because of the similarities between Canada and the United States in terms of special education practices, we have extracted some of the pertinent statistics and descriptions from the US National Center for Education Statistics (http://nces.ed.gov) to provide you with a general indication of what teachers might expect in regard to special education (see Figures 2.1 and 2.2).

In the absence of country-wide statistics on Canadian students with exceptionalities, it is useful to consider the statistics of two of the larger jurisdictions (British Columbia and Ontario) to determine how they compare with the US statistics. In 2016, the British Columbia Ministry of Education reported statistics for the 2015–2016 school year in its document *Student Statistics: Public and Independent Schools Combined*. Some of their findings for special education (public schools only) can be seen in Figure 2.3.

In 2014, People for Education produced a report titled *Special Education* detailing the current state of affairs in Ontario. The following statistics were highlighted:

- In publicly funded schools, 17 per cent of elementary students and 22 per cent of secondary school students receive special education assistance—percentages which have increased steadily over the last two decades.

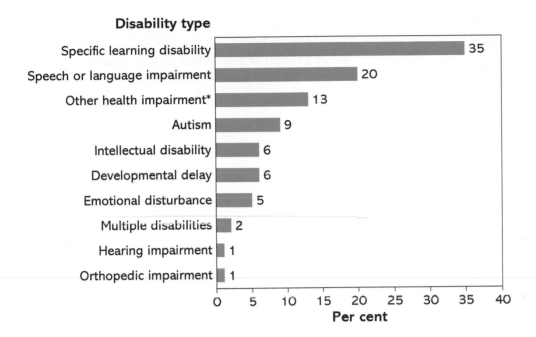

FIGURE 2.1 Percentage distribution of children ages 3–21 served under the Individuals with Disabilities Education Act (IDEA), by disability type: School year 2013–2014.

NOTE: Deaf-blindness, traumatic brain injury, and visual impairment are not shown because they each account for less than 0.5 per cent of children served under IDEA. Due to categories not shown, detail does not sum to 100 per cent. Although rounded numbers are displayed, the gures are based on unrounded estimates.

* Other health impairments include having limited strength, vitality, or alertness due to chronic or acute health problems such as a heart condition, tuberculosis, rheumatic fever, nephritis, asthma, sickle cell anemia, hemophilia, epilepsy, lead poisoning, leukemia, or diabetes.

Source: http://nces.ed.gov/programs/coe/indicator_cgg.asp

- While almost 25 per cent of all students receive some form of special education assistance, only 2 per cent spend the majority of their day in a special education classroom.
- The majority of students receiving special education services (59 per cent) are identified through the more formal assessment process, the Identification, Placement, and Review Committee (IPRC). (People for Education, 2014)

While Figure 2.1 presents the percentage of US students receiving special education by disability type (e.g., 35 per cent of students receiving special education services have learning disabilities), the BC Ministry of Education presents the percentage of students within the whole student population who have a specific disability. Therefore, we developed Figure 2.3 to provide the BC data in a form that allows a better comparison to the US statistics. The limitation is that the two countries do not use all the same disability types. Having stated that, it is readily apparent that in both the United States and Canada, learning disabilities are by far the most common type of disability. Autism spectrum disorder and intellectual disabilities are also among the most sizable occurring disability types.

Figure 2.2 presents evidence that more and more US students with disabilities are receiving their education in the regular classroom. This aligns with the statistics provided by the Ontario People for Education publication.

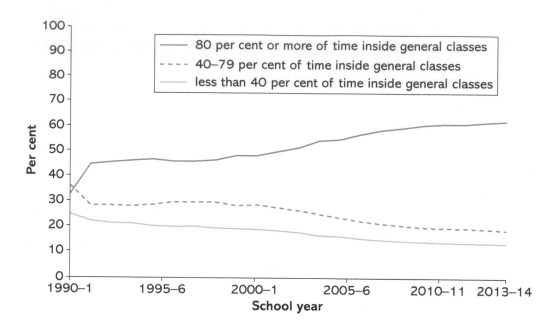

FIGURE 2.2 Percentage of students ages 6–21 served under the Individuals with Disabilities Education Act (IDEA), by amount of time spent inside general classes: Selected school years, 1990–1991 through 2013–2014.

Source: http://nces.ed.gov/programs/coe/indicator_cgg.asp

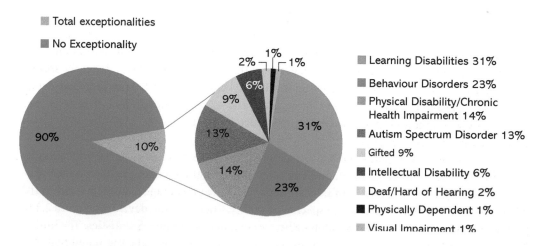

FIGURE 2.3 Students with special needs, public schools only, BC Ministry of Education, 2015–2016.

Data Source: www.bced.gov.bc.ca/reports/pdfs/student_stats/prov.pdf

In general then, the BC and Ontario statistics are not unlike those presented by the US Department of Education. Based on this consistency, we can assume that they are fairly representative of what is happening across Canada.

Inclusionary Practices

Until the early to mid-1980s, most special education services in Canada were traditionally provided through specialized programming that was delivered in classrooms and other settings that were wholly or partially separated from the regular classroom. Today, as mentioned earlier in this chapter, because nearly all Canadian provinces and territories have adopted the philosophy of inclusion, most students with exceptionalities receive their specialized programs in regular classroom settings.

It is important to reiterate that inclusion does not necessarily mean that all students with exceptionalities will be in the regular classroom with their age-appropriate peers all the time. Students must still be provided with appropriate educational programming in the most appropriate educational environment possible. Therefore, while it is preferred that the regular classroom be the first placement option for students with exceptionalities (perhaps with instructional methods and curricula that are considerably modified), it would be inappropriate to say that this arrangement is the only alternative. It is essential that educators clearly recognize that to properly meet the specific needs of some students, these students may need specialized assistance through pull-out programs or resource teacher support, or they may require the help of highly specialized teachers in specialized and separate classrooms. To think that the regular classroom is the only option for students with exceptionalities is an abuse of the fundamental tenet of inclusion, which is to provide an appropriate education for all students.

To date, inclusion is the best philosophical approach we have had to direct the education of students with exceptionalities. It is considered better than integration or mainstreaming because it seeks to change educational systems and classroom environments to suit the needs of the child rather than trying to "fix the child" to suit the system (FSU Center for Prevention & Early Intervention Policy, 2002). Nonetheless, the term *special education* cannot simply be replaced with the term *inclusion*, as has occurred in some Canadian provinces and territories. Inclusion is primarily an overarching philosophy that advocates for the regular classroom as the first placement option for students with exceptionalities, but it does not provide specific definitions as to how that implementation is supposed to take place. Without effective implementation principles, inclusion runs the risk of being perceived as an ivory tower concept that has no credence with educators in everyday classrooms. This has been consistently evidenced in numerous examinations of educators' perceptions of inclusion. These examinations have revealed that educators support the philosophical tenets of inclusion but are concerned about implementation issues (Bennett, 2009; Crawford, 2005; Edmunds, 2003; Edmunds, Halsall, Macmillan, & Edmunds, 2000; King & Edmunds, 2001; Sokal & Sharma, 2014). Therefore, the specifics of implementation still have to come from the effective and proven procedures that have served special education so well for so long.

integration
The process of reintegrating students with exceptionalities back into the regular classroom, if possible.

mainstreaming
The selective placement of students with exceptionalities in regular classrooms on a part-time basis where possible (dependent on ability).

What We Know . . .

The Concept of Inclusion in Canadian Jurisdictions

An examination of the provincial and territorial governments' statements of philosophy for special education reveals the importance that is now placed on inclusionary practices. Excerpts from some of these statements of philosophy follow:

Alberta	. . . a way of thinking and acting that demonstrates universal acceptance and promotes a sense of belonging for all learners. Inclusion is not just about learners with special needs. It is an attitude and approach that embraces diversity and learner differences and promotes equal opportunities for all learners in Alberta . . . Source: https://education.alberta.ca/inclusive-education/?searchMode=3
Manitoba	. . . a way of thinking and acting that allows every individual to feel accepted, valued, and safe. An inclusive community consciously evolves to meet the changing needs of its members. Through recognition and support, an inclusive community provides meaningful involvement and equal access to the benefits of citizenship . . . Source: www.edu.gov.mb.ca/k12/specedu/aep/inclusion.html
New Brunswick	. . . the pairing of philosophy and pedagogical practices that allows each student to feel respected, confident and safe so he or she can participate with peers in the common learning environment and learn and develop to his or her full potential . . . [Inclusion] promotes social cohesion, belonging, active participation in learning, a complete school experience, and positive interactions with peers and others in the school community . . . Source: http://ie.cacl.flywheelsites.com/wp-content/uploads/sites/3/2013/11/6-322a-new-brunswick-2013-inclusive-education-policy-1.pdf, p. 2
Newfoundland and Labrador	. . . the right of all students to attend school with their peers, and to receive appropriate and quality programming . . . [and] a continuum of supports and services in the most appropriate setting (large group, small group, individualized) respecting the dignity of the child . . . Source: www.ed.gov.nl.ca/edu/k12/inclusion.html
Northwest Territories	. . . classrooms need to include a diversity of students, and schools must work to support individual learners and their place in the learning community through early intervention and effective research-based strategies. For teachers, sometimes this is described as "teaching the student, not the grade" . . . Source: www.ece.gov.nt.ca/sites/www.ece.gov.nt.ca/files/024-renewal_framework_en_proof_2.pdf

Nova Scotia	. . . the basic right of all students to receive appropriate and quality educational programming and services in the company of their peers . . . [which] facilitates the membership, participation, and learning of all students in school programs and activities . . .
	Source: http://studentservices.ednet.ns.ca/sites/default/files/inclusion.pdf
Nunavut	. . . an attitude and a belief, a way of life, and a way of living and working together in schools. In Nunavut, inclusion builds on the Inuit belief that each individual is valuable, belongs and contributes to the group. Inclusion infuses all aspects of school life . . .
	Source: http://kugluktukhighschool.ca/4inuglugijaittuq-inclusive.pdf, p. 20

It is important to note that the term *inclusion* is often used to refer to a much broader approach to education, not just the education of students with disabilities. Some regions of Canada, like Alberta, use the term to describe an education system that provides all students (no matter their ability, disability, language, cultural background, gender, or age) with the most appropriate learning environments.

It should be noted that when educators use the term *special education*, some incorrectly emphasize the word "special," resulting in special education being construed as something magical and mystical that only a limited number of teachers know how to deliver. We feel that the emphasis needs to be on the word "education" so that special education is seen as nothing more than very good teaching that happens to be applied differently for very special students. With this understanding and emphasis, special education becomes something that many more teachers can expect to deliver effectively.

What We Know . . .

Canadian Teachers' Views of Inclusion

Research on the Canada-wide implementation of inclusive education is scarce. However, there are several insightful publications, dating back to 2003, that present Canadian teachers' views of inclusion.

In 2003, the journal *Exceptionality Education Canada* produced a special edition that focused on the issues surrounding the preparation of Canadian teachers for inclusion. The following research findings were presented:

- Teacher candidates expressed a need for extended, mandatory studies in special education within pre-service teacher education programs. They also emphasized the importance of having opportunities to work with knowledgeable associate or mentor teachers during their practicums and having this mentoring continue once they become practising teachers (Woloshyn, Bennett, & Berrill, 2003).

Continued

- While regular classroom teachers' attitudes toward inclusion were positive, many reported they felt unprepared to teach students with special needs. They stated that they do not have the skills necessary to effectively adapt curricula to meet the needs of these students. They also reported that inclusion has increased their teaching workload considerably. They expressed a desire to have the opportunity to acquire the skills that will allow them to be good teachers in an inclusive setting (Edmunds, 2003).
- For the most part, teachers indicated their support of the educational soundness of a full-inclusion model. Attitudes were most positive at the elementary level. However, teachers did express concerns regarding the effects that inclusion has on their workload. They also reported significant concerns about the relationship between teachers and support staff (Pudlas, 2003).

In 2005, a summit on inclusive education in Canada revealed the following:

- IEPs are burdensome for many teachers, and teachers typically have only limited background in this area. The practical usefulness of IEPs is highly questionable where they do not inform and guide instructional practices, which in many cases they do not.
- There is confusion among teachers and educational assistants about their respective roles and responsibilities. Teachers often leave the prime responsibility for educating students with significant disabilities to teacher assistants. However, assistants should be playing a supplementary, not a lead, role.
- Pre-service and in-service professional development on issues of inclusion is by no means assured; teachers need more and better professional development, incentives for undertaking the professional development, and recognition for having done so (Crawford, 2005).

Unfortunately, Bennett (2009) revealed that teacher concerns regarding inclusion had not dissipated. She remarked, "while there is a demonstrable willingness on the part of teachers to include students with exceptionalities in their classrooms, real concerns remain over lack of training, classroom management issues, general and special education collaboration, as well as a perceived lack of support and resources" (p. 1). Sokal and Sharma (2014) found that teachers who had some training in special education were less concerned than their colleagues about teaching in inclusive classrooms. However, more recently, the New Brunswick Teachers' Association called for a review of the inclusive education policy in that province over concerns of disruptions and violence in the classroom (*CBC News*, 2016). It is clear, then, that teachers continue to struggle with the implementation of inclusion despite their support of the inclusive education concept.

Something to Think About

Imagine that you are a teacher in an inclusive classroom. Two of your students have an intellectual disability and require a slower pace of instruction. On occasion, they can be somewhat disruptive. Several parents approach you with concerns that their children are not getting the best possible educational experiences because of the time and attention paid to these two "special" students. How would you respond to the concerns of these parents?

Approaches to Special Education in Canada

There are two predominant approaches to special education used in Canada—the categorical approach and the non-categorical approach. A description of each, as well as a comparison of the two, follows.

The Categorical Approach

The intent of special education is to modify educational approaches to suit the educational requirements of children with exceptionalities. In our estimation, to properly and professionally accomplish this goal, students' abilities and needs must first be defined and then identified, classified, and categorized. Therefore, the *categorical* approach to special education is the one adhered to in this text as it is a logical and systematized way of identifying and defining the specialized and diverse needs of children. In fact, it is the most widely used and accepted approach because it provides distinct definitions for each of the categories of exceptionality. These definitions allow educators to separate and classify students according to their unique abilities and needs. This approach clearly establishes the full parameters of each category so that educators do not confuse one with the others, even though children in different categories may exhibit similar skills or needs. By paying close attention to the specific criteria that apply to each particular child, effective educational interventions can be designed to suit the child's unique and special situation. Furthermore, by clearly illustrating how one category can apply to a wide variety of children, all of whom are distinctly different, educators will refrain from overgeneralizing the characteristics of a specific category to any one child. As you will see in the case studies presented in this text, each child meets the identifying criteria of their respective category of exceptionality, but not all other students who fit into the same categories are like the children we have written about here.

As well as facilitating the design and implementation of specific programs for specific children, the categorical approach also provides the basis for specialized training for teachers and for consistency across research studies that investigate the effectiveness of special education interventions. In addition, the categorical approach provides a reliable and consistent way of communicating about exceptionalities. Students often must be described as belonging to specialized categories for educational jurisdictions to be eligible for designated funding and services. Furthermore, this approach has had a significant impact on education in Canada as it is through this approach that more students have been identified as having special needs and, consequently, funding for special education has increased (Lupart & Odishaw, 2003).

The Non-Categorical Approach

In contrast, there are others within the discipline of education who prefer a *non-categorical* approach to special education. This approach evolved as a reaction to the perception that the categorical model emphasized a reliance on labelling to guide testing, assessment, and placement. Advocates of the non-categorical approach feel that the defining labels of the categories are pejorative and therefore frequently stigmatize, isolate, and stereotype individuals with learning, behavioural, or physical differences. They also claim that the categories are arbitrary and that the categorical approach has too much of a diagnostic emphasis and not enough of a functional service purpose.

The non-categorical approach examines student performance relative to expectations, identifies instructional needs, and monitors and evaluates progress in response to intervention, thus resulting in a data-based approach to instructional planning rather than reliance on specific labels (National Association of School Psychologists, 2002; Smith, 2010). Some who support the non-categorical perspective suggest that global efforts toward more effective instructional planning, classroom organization, and the adaptation of teaching and assessment procedures are preferred to individualizing education to suit the specific needs of learners with special needs (Hutchinson, 2010).

Comparing the Categorical and Non-Categorical Approaches

This book was written from an overarching categorical perspective for several fundamental reasons. First, teachers need to know the criteria that are used to identify students with exceptionalities and how the identifying criteria vary across categories. In nearly all instances, these criteria provide beneficial insights as to how curricula, teaching methods, and evaluation can be differentiated to suit the specific needs of each child. In addition, knowing these specific criteria allows teachers to readily notice problems they might otherwise not have noticed. If teachers know what a particular child's needs and abilities are, they can easily make numerous and varied changes to their teaching to help that child.

With non-categorical approaches to special education, teachers do not necessarily know the identifying criteria as well as the differences between the criteria for the various exceptionalities. An observed student difficulty could have one of many causes that each responds best to different interventions. Therefore, without a categorical framework, teachers are not in as strong a position to intervene.

Something to Think About

Despite the delivery of similar special education services across the ten provinces and three territories of Canada, there are differences in the processes used to (a) identify students with exceptionalities, (b) assess their needs, and (c) develop suitable individualized programs for them. There are also differences in the descriptors used to describe exceptionality categories. How do you think this might affect a student with an exceptionality who moves from one jurisdiction to another?

It is important to note that the non-categorical approach is primarily premised on two arguments. The first speaks to the perceived injustices that can arise from the potential misuse of the labels associated with special education. In our view, this is a problematic argument with no foreseeable solution because any word can be used pejoratively; avoiding labels does not prevent mean-spiritedness.

The second argument often presented is that the non-categorical approach is more concerned about functional educational services than the placement outcome emphasis attributed to the categorical model. This argument has been rendered moot by the advent of inclusion, wherein most students with exceptionalities are now educated in the regular classroom.

The current focus of inclusion is on serving students based on their specific educational needs, not based on a special delivery model. There is no doubt that inclusion places more responsibility on all teachers to understand and properly respond to students with exceptionalities. In the final analysis, the categorical approach offers a classification mechanism that can consistently identify a student's educational needs and abilities, thus providing educators with a systematized way of thinking about and evaluating educational interventions.

Let's examine both perspectives in light of the case of a student who has great difficulty reading. Using the categorical approach, this child is referred and assessed and someone— usually a special education specialist or a psychologist—who explains the reasons why the child cannot read as well as he or she needs to in order to complete academic tasks. The assessor then offers suggestions as to how the classroom teacher can adapt or modify teaching methods to suit the child's abilities. For example, the student may have sight word recognition problems, problems decoding, or he or she may struggle so much with reading the words on the page that his or her working memory is unable to process the meaning of the sentences being read (typically called an inability to comprehend). There are several other reasons why individuals do not read well, but the point is that each of them requires a specific type of reading intervention because there is no one general reading intervention that can effectively remediate all of the above problems. This common classroom situation also has significant but different instructional implications if the reading problem is identified when the student is learning to read (up to Grades 3 and 4) as opposed to being identified when the student is expected to read to learn (beyond Grades 3 and 4). More importantly, because the assessment process will have also identified specific learning strengths, the teacher can use these assets to help the student overcome the reading difficulty. In most instances, implementing specific evidence-based reading interventions that suit the diagnosed problem, allowing for some trial and error or slight modifications, will prove beneficial. Note that the categorical approach facilitates the study of specific populations, making the development of evidence-based interventions possible.

In comparison, the non-categorical approach tends to eschew the diagnostic tone of the referral and assessment procedure, preferring to answer the question "How do I adapt my teaching to include these exceptional individuals?" (Hutchinson, 2010). This is an excellent question. Following this approach, however, the teacher knows only that the student cannot read adequately, so he or she is left to try to adapt instruction, sometimes without a clear idea of the nature of the student's specific problem. Without knowing the student's needs and abilities, it will be very difficult for the teacher to effectively facilitate the student's learning in an efficient manner. The teacher runs the risk of frustrating the student by using a trial-and-error approach. It is not uncommon for teachers and special education teachers, who operate under such a mandate, to try something that seems to work one day, yet have it prove extremely ineffective the following day, and not know why.

We believe that the categorical approach advocated here eliminates much of the confusion and frustration that can occur when teaching students with exceptionalities. When educators have expert information regarding students' learning needs, they can efficiently link assessment with intervention. Teachers are quite capable of modifying their curriculum, their teaching, or their classroom environment to facilitate student success.

What We Know . . .

The Use of Categorical and Non-Categorical Approaches in Canada

The following brief quotes excerpted from the government websites of several provinces and territories provide some insight into the approaches taken across Canada in regard to special education:

Province/ Territory	Special Education Approach
Alberta	Every student or ECS child identified with special education needs must have an individualized program plan (IPP) and/or an instructional support plan (ISP) . . . "Individualized Program Plan" means a concise plan of action designed to address students' special education needs, and is based on diagnostic information which provides the basis for intervention strategies . . . Source: https://education.alberta.ca/diverse-learning-needs/special-education-standards/?searchMode=3
British Columbia	The planning process is divided into five phases: 1) identification/assessment; 2) planning; 3) program support/implementation; 4) evaluation; and 5) reporting . . . When extended assessments (e.g., psycho-educational, behavioural, speech and language, orientation and mobility) are requested, the goal is to better understand the student's strengths and needs in order to plan more effectively for that student. Source: www.sd5.bc.ca/programs/StudentServices/Partners%20Hand-book/Documents/4.6%20DEVELOPING%20AN%20IEP%20SPEC.%20ED.%20MANUAL.pdf
Newfoundland and Labrador	The Department of Education and Early Childhood Development uses the term exceptionality to identify patterns of strengths and needs common to groups of students. These strengths and needs may be: cognitive, emotional, behavioural, medical, social, and physical. A student with an exceptionality may access a range of school-based services depending on his or her strengths and needs. Source: www.ed.gov.nl.ca/edu/k12/safeandcaring/handbook_parents_children_exceptionalities.pdf
Nova Scotia	The descriptors cognitive impairments; emotional/behavioural disorders; learning disabilities; physical disabilities and/or health impairments; speech impairments and/or communication disorders; sensory impairments; multiple disabilities; and giftedness should not be used as labels for individual students. Students' strengths and challenges must be the basis for developing appropriate programming and the descriptors should be used only as necessary for administrative purposes related to funding and data collection. Source: https://studentservices.ednet.ns.ca/sites/default/files/speceng.pdf, p. 18

Ontario	Students who have behavioural, communicational, intellectual, physical, or multiple exceptionalities may have educational needs that cannot be met through regular instructional and assessment practices. These needs may be met through accommodations, and/or an educational program that is modified above or below the age-appropriate grade level expectations for a particular subject or course. Such students may be formally identified as exceptional pupils. The Ministry sets out definitions of exceptionalities that must be used by school boards after determining that a student is an "exceptional pupil." Source: www.edu.gov.on.ca/eng/general/elemsec/speced/ontario.html
Prince Edward Island	The Minister's Directive outlines a commitment to provide a continuum of support services based on the philosophy of inclusion. Implicit in this commitment is a non-categorical approach to the determination of special needs. The Directive incorporates a process to ensure students with special educational needs are identified and that appropriate interventions are implemented and reviewed. Source: www.gov.pe.ca/eecd/index.php3?number=1038312&lang=E
Saskatchewan	The identified needs of students are more important in determining programming and essential supports than are the categorical labels of disabilities. However, when needs and diagnostic information are combined, communities can be empowered to ensure supports are in place to meet the needs of all citizens. Source: http://publications.gov.sk.ca/documents/11/82982-intensive-supports-categories.pdf
Yukon	The need for special education may be determined at any time. The process of identifying such need focuses on the impact of the area of special need on the child's or student's functioning in an educational environment. This is accomplished through: a comprehensive, individualized assessment; development of an Individual Education Plan with the involvement of the parent(s) and school personnel; and, a regular review of student needs. Source: www.education.gov.yk.ca/pdf/schools/SSS_Manual_I_Individual_Education_Plans.pdf, p. I-2

Summary

Special education is a particular type of schooling that is constructed and delivered to suit the specific strengths and needs of students with exceptionalities. It is founded on the premise that more children with special needs will reach their full potential if their education is properly differentiated. The history of special education, especially in Canada and the United States, has been defined in terms of the degree of segregation used when educating students with exceptionalities. Currently, the majority of these students receive their education in the regular classroom. This inclusive approach, while widely accepted by educators, is still fraught with implementation difficulties. This is further complicated by the fact that, unlike in the United States, two different approaches to special education are used in Canada—the categorical approach and the non-categorical approach.

Learning More about Special Education in Canada and around the World

Council of Ministers of Education, Canada

www.cmec.ca

The CMEC is an intergovernmental body founded in 1967 by ministers of education to serve as a forum to discuss policy issues; a mechanism through which to undertake activities, projects, and initiatives in areas of mutual interest; and a means by which to consult and co-operate with national education organizations and the federal government.

Departments and Ministries Responsible for Education in Canada

Alberta: *www.education.alberta.ca*
British Columbia: *www.gov.bc.ca/bced*
Manitoba: *www.edu.gov.mb.ca*
New Brunswick: *www2.gnb.ca/content/gnb/en/departments/education.html*
Newfoundland and Labrador: *www.ed.gov.nl.ca/edu*
Northwest Territories: *www.ece.gov.nt.ca*
Nova Scotia: *www.ednet.ns.ca*
Nunavut: *www.gov.nu.ca/education*
Ontario: *www.edu.gov.on.ca*
Prince Edward Island: *www.gov.pe.ca/education*
Quebec: *www.education.gouv.qc.ca*
Saskatchewan: *www.saskatchewan.ca/government/government-structure/ministries/education*
Yukon: *www.education.gov.yk.ca*

Statistics Canada: Education, Training, and Learning

www.statcan.gc.ca/eng/subjects/education_training_and_learning

International Association of Special Education

www.iase.org

The mission of IASE is to promote a professional exchange of information among special educators all over the world. The association encourages international co-operation and collaborative international research.

United States Office of Special Education and Rehabilitative Services

www2.ed.gov/about/offices/list/osers/osep/index.html

The mission of OSERS is to provide the leadership necessary to achieve full integration and participation in society for people with disabilities.

CHAPTER 3
The Assessment and IEP Process

LEARNING OBJECTIVES

After learning the material in this chapter, you should be able to:

- Define the term *psycho-educational assessment* as it applies to special education.

- Describe the fundamental principles of the IEP.

- Outline the major phases involved in the process of evaluating a student's educational situation and determining what changes are needed.

- Discuss how students with learning/behavioural differences are first identified, the importance of early identification, and the role that teachers play in this process.

- Define the term *diagnostic instruction* and discuss why it is important for teachers to document the results of successful teaching adjustments.

- Differentiate between *informal* and *formal* education assessments.

- Discuss the concept of intelligence and provide examples of intelligence measures commonly used in psycho-educational assessments.

- Describe the use of academic achievement tests, tests of perception and perceptual-motor skills, and measures of social and emotional skills.

- Explain the concept of *Universal Design for Learning* and how it relates to the inclusive classroom.

- Define the term *curriculum-based assessment* and discuss why it is the preferred method of determining the academic progress of students with exceptionalities.

Special Education: The Implementation of Exemplary Teaching Practices

As we described in Chapter 2, special education is a particular type of schooling that is constructed and delivered to suit the specific strengths and needs of students with exceptionalities. In this light, special education is a necessary and fundamental part of our educational system because students with exceptionalities, like all other students, have the right to an appropriate education. We also previously described how special education is not something that should be viewed as being highly complex, secretive, or mystical, nor should it be perceived as something that can only be practised by a select few teachers. Rather, special education is best viewed as nothing more than exemplary teaching practices that all teachers can easily implement with some experience, wherein these teaching practices are designed and implemented based on specific types of information. While this perspective may contradict what you have previously heard about special education being so specialized, read on and you will see what we mean when we say that all teachers can effectively engage in special education, given the right conditions.

If special education is simply the implementation of good classroom teaching practices in an effort to provide specialized programming for students with exceptionalities, there are three obvious questions:

1. How do we determine the strengths and needs of students with exceptionalities?
2. What specialized programming is needed to meet the needs of students with exceptionalities, and how does it get constructed?
3. What do teachers have to know and do differently to properly implement specialized programming?

The answers to these interrelated questions all include reference to comprehensive assessments. These assessments reveal how students with exceptionalities differ from their peers, and they also provide the information upon which specialized programming can be constructed, thus providing teachers with descriptions of educational interventions that can be implemented. This brief explanation is provided here to give you an overarching conceptual framework to think about as you read the rest of the chapter. By the time you finish reading, you will see that there clearly is a viable and effective process called special education that can effectively serve students with exceptionalities, their teachers, and their parents. Once you understand what this course of action entails, you will be in an excellent position to modify the process to suit whatever teaching situations you encounter in your career.

What Is Assessment?

Before we go any further, let's carefully examine the term *educational assessment* so we are clear about what it means. If you were to mention this term at a social gathering, many people, regardless of whether they were connected to education or not, would immediately think of "testing someone," perhaps on a variety of topics. Only rarely would someone think of assessment as having a variety of different formats when applied in educational settings. In fact, most individuals would be able to tell you little about what kinds of assessment tools are available or exactly how an assessment is carried out. Instead, their comments would probably be focused on the secrecy and specialness that is often associated with educational assessment (e.g., they had some kind of special test in school but no one ever told them what it was for or what the results were). Another common perception of assessment is that it is a one-time process based on one test, a sort of snapshot in time that sets a student's course for many, if not all, his or her school years. While these perceptions are not totally inaccurate, they are mostly erroneous and they outline the misperceptions that many individuals have about assessment, both within and outside of education.

In general, the term *educational assessment* refers to a comprehensive process of collecting a variety of data for the purpose of making educational decisions about individuals (and sometimes groups). In special education, the term *psycho-educational assessment* is more often used because the data gathered usually includes a variety of indices of social and psychological variables as well as measures of academic achievement. While this process invariably identifies areas of need and deficits in abilities, the predominant emphasis of assessment focuses on a student's current level of functioning so that proper instructional interventions can be designed. Psycho-educational assessment is best viewed as a dynamic process that, as necessitated by the student's abilities or learning environment, involves the gathering of data from multiple sources, across a variety of settings, and using various measures. This is done on multiple occasions so that informed and reliable decision making can occur. It is only from this professional perspective that teachers can begin to alter their teaching or the curricula to suit a student's educational needs.

Why Is Assessment Important?

The assessment process is vital to special education because it provides education professionals with objective, valid, and reliable data upon which suitable and appropriate educational programming can be based. Specialized programming for students with exceptionalities can range from minor modifications to the regular curricula or the typical teaching methods used in the regular classroom, to fully specialized programs that include completely different curricula or teaching methods implemented in a congregated classroom or school. The type and extent of changes that educators make to curricula or teaching methods is entirely dependent upon each individual student's strengths and needs. Therefore, students with exceptionalities are best served by accurate assessments of their abilities and needs, as this type of information makes for the most meaningful educational outcomes (Salvia, Ysseldyke, & Witmer, 2016).

It is worth noting at this juncture that the vast majority of educators, and the psychologists and psychometrists who conduct psycho-educational assessments, are not as concerned today as they were in the past about what causes the majority of differences in student learning (McLoughlin & Lewis, 2005). Most *learning differences* are caused by variables that educators cannot control or remediate (e.g., brain injury). The field has come to realize that, except in very few cases, knowing the root causes of learning differences has limited effects on how educators design and implement effective learning interventions.

On the other hand, educators are quite concerned about the causes of *behavioural differences* because the vast majority of problematic behaviours are caused by learned behaviours or learned reactions, and educators have far greater control over them (Edmunds, Edmunds, & Hogarth, 2012).

psychometrist

A certified specialist who administers educational, psychological, and psychometric tests under the supervision of a psychologist.

The causes of behaviour, commonly referred to as antecedents, are important pieces of information to understand and consider when designing effective behavioural interventions to help children in classrooms. They may not be obvious nor do they appear to be directly linked to the observed behaviour, so assessments of the abilities of students with exceptionalities must be comprehensive.

antecedents
Behaviours that occur immediately before an identified problematic behaviour; often the cause of the behaviour.

The Assessment and IEP Process

Fundamental Principles

The referral, assessment, and educational intervention procedure that we are about to describe depicts the most common procedure currently used throughout Canada and the United States (and in many other countries, such as Great Britain and Australia). It is widely understood that the various provinces, territories, and states of North America have slightly different steps or processes that they follow in their particular assessment procedure, but they all adhere to the following fundamental principles and purposes of educational assessment:

> *The assessment process determines the student's learning and behavioural strengths and needs, the degree to which the student's particular strengths and needs differ from those of his or her peers, and the adjusted educational programming that will be implemented to give the student an excellent opportunity to fulfill his or her educational potential.*

The vast majority of students with exceptionalities receive specialized educational programming outlined in a document called an *individualized education program*, or IEP. Across Canada, there are a variety of names and definitions for this document, none of which are used universally. For example, it is referred to as an IEP or individual education plan in Manitoba and Ontario (Manitoba Education, 2010; Ontario Ministry of Education, 2004), as an IPP or individual program plan in Nova Scotia (Nova Scotia Department of Education, 2009), a PPP or personal program plan in Saskatchewan (Saskatchewan Education, 2009), and an ISSP, or individual services support plan in Newfoundland and Labrador (Newfoundland and Labrador Department of Education, 2007). In Alberta, the IPP may be replaced by the *Inclusive Education Planning Tool*, which is currently being piloted in select schools (Alberta Education, 2013). For the purpose of being consistent throughout this text, we chose the term *individualized education program* because it is the universal term used by the Council for Exceptional Children (CEC, 2013) and it is the official term of the IDEA (Individuals with Disabilities Education Act) legislation (US Department of Education, 2000) as well as the ESSA (Every Student Succeeds Act) legislation.

Given the differences in terminology used across the regions of Canada, it is not surprising to find that the definitions used to describe the IEP are equally different from jurisdiction to jurisdiction. However, most tend to adhere to the following fundamental principles:

> *The IEP is a document that outlines a student's individualized educational goals, the services that a student with exceptionalities will receive, the methods and strategies that will be used to deliver these services to ensure that goals are met, and the placement in which all of these will be provided.*

You will find more details on the content and construction of IEPs later in this chapter.

Something to Think About

What assessment process is followed in your province or territory? How is a student's education plan defined and described? Compare your findings to the fundamental principles presented above.

An Overview of the Process

The assessment and IEP process often gets started when a teacher notices a child struggling with school work. The following is a common scenario:

> *I have observed that James finds it difficult to learn some concepts, and even though he is a conscientious student, he seems to struggle to get his work done on time. He is falling further and further behind in his Grade 7 social studies class. I have talked to another one of James's teachers, and he has noticed similar problems. His parents have expressed similar concerns and told me that James is showing signs of frustration when doing his homework. I'm not sure if he has a disability, but it seems like a definite possibility. What can I do to get someone to investigate my concerns?*

As in James's situation, teachers may be unsure about how procedures in special education are carried out. In the following pages we will walk you through the detailed process that often begins with this very type of teacher observation.

There are usually six major phases involved in the process of evaluating a student's educational situation and determining what changes are needed. These phases include (1) identification, (2) diagnostic instruction, (3) referral, (4) assessment/IEP, (5) educational intervention, and (6) evaluation of student progress. In some cases, the complete process takes very little time and only minor changes to a student's schooling are required. In other instances, the process takes longer and results in major changes to the way things are done. Regardless of how much time it will take, it is time well spent.

The purpose of this six-phase systematized process is to provide educators with a consistent and comprehensive method of coming to reasoned conclusions about a student's future educational path. We have included a schematic figure of the overall process in Figure 3.1. As you will note, there is a cyclical nature to the process that involves an ongoing review and evaluation of the student's situation.

Phase One: Identification

As in the scenario presented above, a student who does not learn readily, does not express his or her learning efficiently, or demonstrates problematic behavioural differences usually catches the attention of parents, caregivers, or teachers. These adults become alerted to the fact that something is not quite right with the student based on their knowledge of children's typical demonstrations of learning or behaviour in particular contexts. For example, in a parent's case, it may be that a child seems to have a limited vocabulary compared to the vocabulary an older sibling had at the same age. In a teacher's case, it may be that a student does not seem to

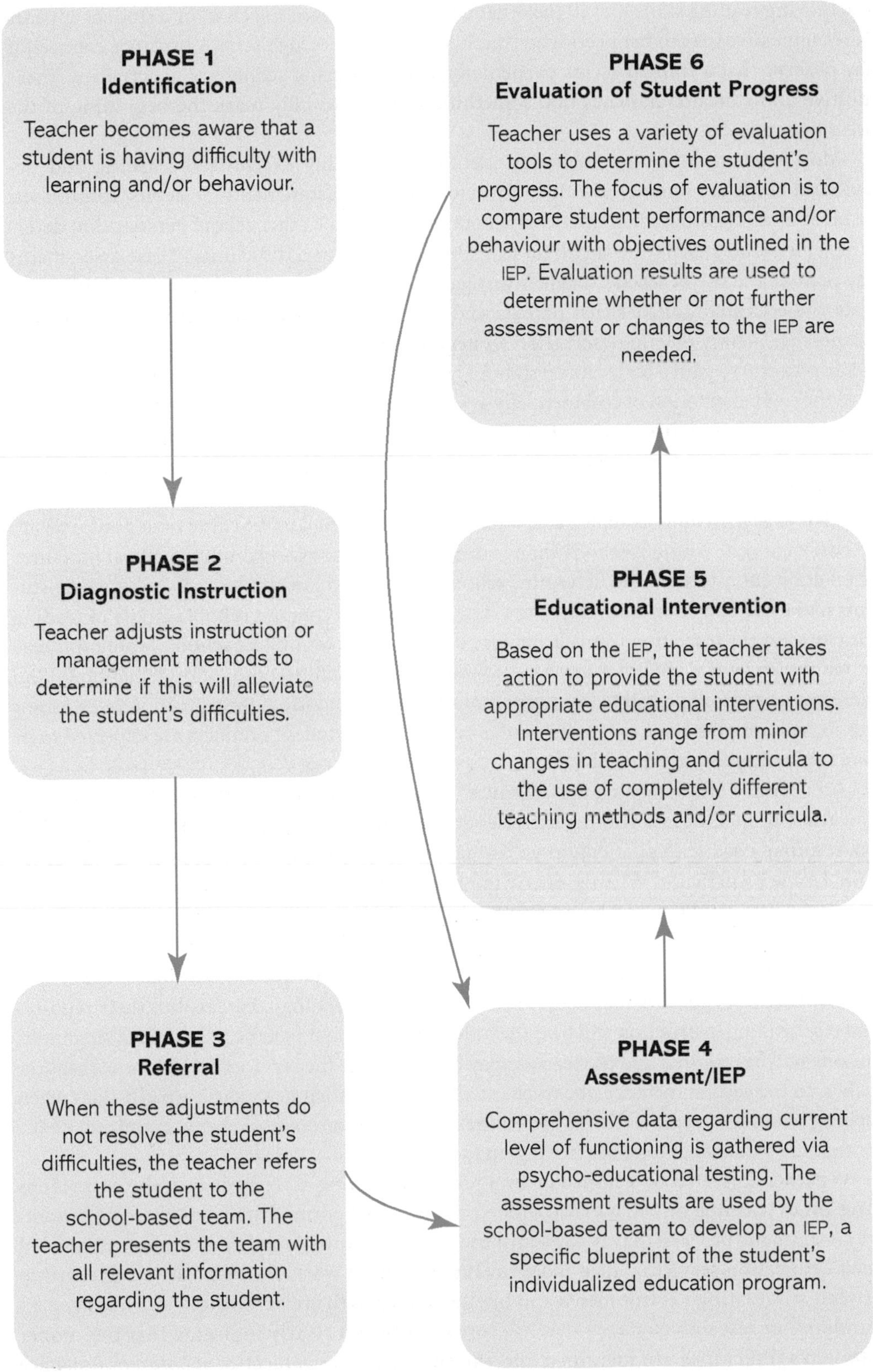

PHASE 1
Identification

Teacher becomes aware that a student is having difficulty with learning and/or behaviour.

PHASE 6
Evaluation of Student Progress

Teacher uses a variety of evaluation tools to determine the student's progress. The focus of evaluation is to compare student performance and/or behaviour with objectives outlined in the IEP. Evaluation results are used to determine whether or not further assessment or changes to the IEP are needed.

PHASE 2
Diagnostic Instruction

Teacher adjusts instruction or management methods to determine if this will alleviate the student's difficulties.

PHASE 5
Educational Intervention

Based on the IEP, the teacher takes action to provide the student with appropriate educational interventions. Interventions range from minor changes in teaching and curricula to the use of completely different teaching methods and/or curricula.

PHASE 3
Referral

When these adjustments do not resolve the student's difficulties, the teacher refers the student to the school-based team. The teacher presents the team with all relevant information regarding the student.

PHASE 4
Assessment/IEP

Comprehensive data regarding current level of functioning is gathered via psycho-educational testing. The assessment results are used by the school-based team to develop an IEP, a specific blueprint of the student's individualized education program.

FIGURE 3.1 The six phases of the assessment and IEP process.

be acquiring reading skills like all the other Grade 3 students in the class, or a student appears overly aggressive toward her peers when on the playground. A high school guidance counsellor may observe that a student seems particularly anxious during school social activities. These intuitive and educated hunches that something is amiss usually mark the beginning of the assessment process.

Most students who are eventually identified as having exceptional learning and behavioural needs are initially identified through screening assessments. *Screening assessments are most often classroom activities carried out by teachers or other school personnel to determine which students may be at risk for learning or behavioural difficulties.* These assessments may include the use of teacher-made investigative tools used on an individual basis to investigate the educated hunches that parents and teachers have about a student's performance. Teachers frequently rely on observation strategies (e.g., time sampling, frequency sampling, and anecdotes) to gain a better understanding of student behaviour. Assessments may also involve the implementation of commercially available tests that are administered to large groups of students, such as entire classes, entire grades, or sometimes groups of grades.

Regardless of the type of assessment tool used, screening assessments are most often implemented at critical junctures in the school curricula, usually at points where students are expected to engage in more complex and sophisticated thinking and learning or at grades where the curricula or teaching methods change dramatically. The most common critical junctures are (a) upon entry to school to determine school readiness; (b) in Grades 2, 3, and 4, where students make the transition from learning to read to the more complex school activity of reading to learn; (c) at the transition from elementary to junior high (or middle school), where students are taught by several different teachers, where the curricula become more demanding, and where students are expected to be autonomous learners; and (d) at the transition from junior high to senior high school, where curricular demands and student products are expected to be more sophisticated and adult-like.

An example of a screening assessment at a critical education juncture is the completion of a variety of spelling and reading exercises at the beginning of the Grade 3 year to see which children may need special attention when tackling the more demanding language elements of the Grade 3 curricula. When properly implemented and carefully evaluated, the results of these screening activities can be used to identify and eliminate minor problems that can be rectified by proper instruction. There is a vast difference between a student who simply cannot read and a student who cannot read because he or she did not receive adequate instruction. Both of these poor readers may score the same on the screening measure, but their requirements for reading instruction will be quite different. In the first instance, special reading interventions will be required and the teacher may have to enlist the services of the school resource teacher. In the second instance, the teacher will simply do what he or she normally does when teaching reading—keep a watchful eye on the student's progress while being cognizant of the fact that the student has a lot of catching up to do.

Whether activated by a hunch or by a formal screening activity or test, the early identification of learning or behavioural differences is the important first step in a comprehensive assessment process that is typically used to determine whether a student may need special education services. Since Bloom's (1964) seminal work on the positive relationship between stimulating environments and intellectual growth and learning, there has been an abundance of research evidence that has consistently and clearly indicated that the sooner a student's difficulties are identified and the sooner proper educational interventions are

time sampling
Observations of student behaviour that are recorded at fixed, regular intervals.

frequency sampling
Counting how many times a particular behaviour occurs during a designated period of time.

anecdote
A brief narrative account of a student's behaviour that is of interest to the observer.

autonomous learners
Students who can learn, solve problems, and develop new ideas with minimal external guidance.

©Monkey Business/Thinkstock.com

Reading exercises at the beginning of Grade 3 help determine if a child may need special attention to meet the curriculum requirements.

provided, the more likely it is that the student will learn more, and learn more efficiently. With regard to behavioural and emotional disorders, there is no doubt that an earlier rather than later identification and intervention process provides educators with a much better chance of both halting the progress of deficits or improving a student's ability to cope with their deficits.

The important point demonstrated above is that teachers play a variety of vital and necessary roles in the early identification process. We contend that the more teachers know about the specific traits of students with special needs and the identification processes that can have positive outcomes for these students, the more diligent teachers will be in reacting to observed student differences. It should be noted that while early identification is best and desirable, late identification is always better than no identification at all.

Phase Two: Diagnostic Instruction

The next step in the assessment process is called *diagnostic instruction*. Teachers are instructional experts, and when it comes to understanding their curricula they usually know many different and effective ways to present the same content. Therefore, diagnostic instruction is simply a purposeful implementation of their best teaching skills.

Any teachers who become aware that a student is having difficulty learning academic content can make adjustments to their instructional approach to determine whether these adjustments alleviate the student's learning difficulties. Often, students themselves (from Grade 2 or 3 onward) can also provide suggestions on how teachers can better help them learn. The following is an actual example of a student's input into the diagnostic instruction process:

> *A Grade 7 teacher noticed that one of his students seemed to excel on some parts of the tests he presented but also did very poorly on other parts of the same tests. This inconsistent performance led the teacher to talk to the student about the situation and check the student's class notes. In this instance, class notes were the primary information base that students studied from for their tests. The teacher discovered that the student had a hard time keeping up with his instruction while note-taking, and she was too embarrassed to ask classmates for their notes for fear she would look incompetent. Upon further discussion, the teacher found out that while the student's notes were accurate and well organized, she simply could not write fast enough to keep up. The teacher and student agreed that the student would continue to take notes in class because the teacher knew the value of having students write their own notes from information they have processed. The teacher promised to be more aware of the speed at which he presented material. Through further discussion and observation, the teacher noted that the student did not necessarily have a writing speed problem as much as she appeared to need more time to process the information that was on the board before she could write it down. The teacher decided that he would provide the student with photocopies of his teaching notes after his classes so that the student could be sure to get all the necessary information. As a result of this diagnostic process, the student performed exceptionally well on subsequent class tests.*

Unfortunately, the problem that this student experienced with note-taking is quite common. Numerous students with learning disabilities indicate that they learn a lot more in class by paying attention to the teacher's spoken comments rather than by writing notes. Another instructional option in this instance is for the teacher to provide photocopies of the notes in cloze format so that the student only has to write down key words or phrases. This allows the student to focus on learning rather than writing. In both of these instructional examples, the teacher is required to make slight adjustments so that the typical teaching method does not exacerbate the student's learning weaknesses. Instead, the adjustments take advantage of the student's strengths.

Here is another example that regularly occurs for students who have simultaneous processing difficulties:

> *A Grade 9 science teacher noticed that one of her students struggled considerably with some of the concepts presented in class. When she asked the student why this was the case, the student replied that she got very confused when the teacher used more than one example to explain a new concept. While this is an excellent teaching strategy employed by many teachers, it was not serving this student very well at all. The student also stated that she usually understood a new concept after the first explanation, but she then had a hard time relating the slightly different information in the extra examples to her newly acquired information. After discussing several options, they agreed that the teacher would indicate to the student when she had fully explained a new concept and this would be the student's signal to not pay attention to the extra examples (if applicable). They also agreed that the teacher would check with the student to make sure the process was working, and the student would approach the teacher if she felt she did not fully grasp a particular concept.*

cloze format

A fill-in-the-blank activity in which students use the context of other written or spoken words to comprehend the concept being conveyed.

simultaneous processing difficulties

A deficit in the ability to efficiently process multiple pieces of information at the same time.

If teaching adjustments are successful like they were in the above-mentioned examples, the teacher should make note of them for three critical reasons: (1) for ongoing personal use and for future use by other teachers of that student, (2) for further modification if necessary, and (3) for consideration at the educational intervention phase of the assessment process (see Phase Five) should the student have other difficulties that need to be addressed. The teacher's effective interventions may provide valuable insight into how other educational interventions should be designed for the student.

Unfortunately, unlike in the scenarios presented above, it is common that a teacher's initial instructional adjustments designed to help a particular student fail to result in positive outcomes. After trying several adjustments, the teacher may decide that the student's needs cannot be met by simply changing the instructional approach. In this situation, the student needs to be referred for a more detailed diagnostic assessment. As previously mentioned, it is imperative that the teacher record what types of adjustments were attempted and the results realized by these efforts. This information is vital to the subsequent phases of the assessment process.

Phase Three: Referral

The primary purpose of a referral is to inform those responsible that a student is experiencing difficulties that affect his or her educational progress and these difficulties do not seem to be alleviated by a variety of instructional adjustments implemented by the student's teacher. The action part of the referral process is usually a simple and straightforward affair. The teacher who identifies that a problem exists fills in a referral form and submits it to the individual in his or her school responsible for such referrals (usually the person in charge of special education issues). This form is accompanied by the following supporting documentation:

- A variety of student products (usually in the form of assignments, work done in class, or tests) that depict the actual problem(s) the student is experiencing
- The student's grades, especially if they indicate a dramatic change in performance across a period of time
- Details of the types of instructional adjustments attempted by the teacher and the outcomes of those attempts
- Any other relevant information that the teacher was able to garner from either the student, the parents, or other individuals that the teacher may have contacted about the problem (such as guidance counsellors or previous teachers)

A comprehensive referral such as this usually ends up being presented to the *school-based team*. While this team is described by different titles throughout North America, its composition and function are basically the same. As the name implies, this team is based within a school and usually comprises the individual responsible for special education, the referring teacher (after all, he or she is most familiar with the situation), other teachers who work with the particular student, a school administrator, and often the guidance counsellor in the case of junior and senior high schools. Depending on the jurisdiction and the nature of the student's difficulty, the parents of the child may be part of the team (although this differs across the country). Parents are almost always included when their child's needs are very high since they usually have a great deal of relevant information to contribute. In instances where the child's specific difficulty is not a high need or has not yet been identified, many school-based teams notify parents if further assessment has been recommended and then invite the parents to participate as team members when the results are to be presented and discussed. Depending on the child's age and his or her ability to contribute information to the team's decision-making process, school-based teams are encouraged to include the affected child as much as possible in their deliberations. In our experience, children with exceptionalities have much to offer, especially when it comes to insights about what helps them learn or what it is that seems to prevent them from learning effectively.

The function of the school-based team is to analyze the referral information and any other applicable information that may be in school files or can be gleaned from other relevant sources (doctors, coaches, etc.). Once the team has analyzed all of the data, team members suggest a course of action that usually falls under one of the following options:

- The use of additional or alternative teaching strategies that have not already been implemented (these are usually implemented for a trial period with a precise date for re-evaluation)
- The completion of further informal assessment measures (usually conducted by the referring teacher or special education personnel)
- The completion of a formal assessment if parental permission is given (usually conducted by a psychologist or a qualified special education teacher, but may also involve other professionals depending on the nature of the child's area of difficulty)

In the case of students with emotional or behavioural problems, the process is exactly the same except the options are slightly different. Keep in mind that the term "behavioural problems" does not only mean behaviours that cause problems between people, it also means behaviours that interfere with learning such as not paying attention, an inability to focus, or an inability to work in groups. Therefore, the team's referral options for behavioural issues are

- the completion of a functional behavioural analysis (FBA) (some straightforward analyses can be performed by teachers, but a full analysis is usually conducted by special education personnel) and the implementation of alternative behavioural interventions as derived from the FBA, or
- the referral of the child to a psychologist or otherwise qualified professional for counselling or the design of a detailed behavioural intervention program.

Most of the students who receive special education services are those who are ultimately referred by the school-based team to psychologists or other assessment experts for a psycho-educational assessment. These assessments are carried out by a variety of experts in consultation with school personnel and usually result in education programs that are developed specifically for each student who is under consideration.

It is not uncommon for students who are referred for a psycho-educational assessment to wait months to receive this service. The question is, "What do teachers do in the meantime?" This is a sensitive issue because it would be inappropriate for a student's schooling to come to a complete halt while waiting for an assessment, but, at the same

informal assessment
A variety of data-gathering processes that allow variation in administration procedures and more subjective interpretations of results.

formal assessment
Testing that has standardized administration procedures, is usually scored on norm-referenced criteria, and uses a formal interpretive procedure to provide reliable and valid assessment data.

functional behavioural analysis (FBA)
A process of determining why a student engages in problematic behaviour and how that behaviour relates to his or her environment.

time, a teacher should not attempt dramatically different approaches until the student's learning needs are determined. Remember, at this point the teacher and the school-based team have already exhausted all the typical educational interventions they could think of, to no avail. Using dramatically different approaches without a valid assessment-based rationale will most likely prove ineffective and will more than likely negatively affect a student's self-efficacy for school work and his or her overall self-esteem. If many changes are repeatedly tried and proven ineffective, the student may feel like he or she is completely incompetent.

As a first course of action, it is highly recommended that the student continue to participate in as much schooling as possible as long as there is a reasonable expectation of successful learning or improved behaviour. Educators do not want to give the student the impression they "don't have to do anything" just because they are waiting for their psycho-educational assessment. In the majority of cases of students who have high-incidence exceptionalities, their difficulties are not so pervasive that all areas of schooling are equally negatively affected. We do not want to give you the impression that during this time teachers are to stop trying to find ways to help the student because they may in fact happen upon something that helps the situation. However, it is more likely that the teacher's solution(s) will need to be augmented by the psychologist's recommendations.

At the same time, we suggest that the school-based team ask the consulting psychologist for an expedited analysis of the student's file and to suggest some assessment tools that can be administered and interpreted by the special education teacher (not all tests used in psycho-educational assessments have to be carried out by a psychologist). After a brief consultation with the psychologist (usually by phone) regarding the findings of such assessments, the special education teacher and the classroom teacher(s) can then map out a new series of educational interventions. Recording the results of these interventions and passing them on to the psychologist provides additional information to be considered when the full-scale assessment is administered.

Despite all of the above, there are instances in which it is obvious to all concerned that the student is in a course or class that is clearly beyond his or her abilities. This mostly happens at the junior high and high school levels. It may be preferable in these cases to assign the student to another comparable, but not-so-demanding, course or class pending the results of the assessment.

Phase Four: Assessment/IEP

The Psycho-Educational Assessment

The psycho-educational assessment is mostly a confirmatory process to determine whether or not problems exist that compromise a student's educational (learning) or social (behaviour) performance. The ultimate goal is to identify a student's abilities and needs so that suitable educational interventions can be designed. The psychologist determines the focus of the assessment by reviewing the comprehensive descriptive information provided in the referral. These details form the starting point for the testing procedure and allow the psychologist to choose a series of tests, most of which are standardized tests and norm-referenced tests, which will best assess the student's strengths and areas of difficulty.

self-efficacy
Beliefs about one's capability to produce certain levels of performance in order to influence events that affect one's life.

self-esteem
Our subconscious beliefs about how worthy, lovable, valuable, and capable we are.

standardized tests
Tests prepared by experts, administered under exactly the same conditions, and used primarily to compare students' performances with other students' performances.

norm-referenced tests
Tests that indicate a student's performance based on how the student's score compares with the scores of other similar students.

From the Psychologist's Notebook

Psychologists are trained to expertly choose, administer, and score the tests used in a psycho-educational assessment. In addition, we have the knowledge that is necessary to interpret the test results so that educators can fully rely on the results when making decisions regarding a student's educational programming. For example, if a referral indicates that a Grade 9 student is having problems with algebra but has no reading problems or related behavioural issues, then I may decide to examine only math and math-related issues using the appropriate tests. The test results may reveal that the student's ability to calculate is fine and the difficulty with algebra is due to an overall deficit in abstract reasoning. Depending on the severity of this deficit, I will recommend one or more educational solutions—ranging from the teacher simply providing more concrete ways to learn algebra, to providing the student with specific assistance in a resource setting, to the more dramatic step of replacing algebra with another math course that is not dominated by abstract reasoning. These solutions are then presented to the school-based team so that the student's educational programming can be finalized.

speech-language pathologist

A certified specialist who evaluates and treats communication disorders.

physical therapist

A certified specialist who evaluates and treats physical ailments using physical therapy programs.

occupational therapist

A certified specialist who evaluates and treats muscle and joint disorders to determine their impact on daily living activities.

social worker

A certified specialist trained in psychotherapy who helps individuals deal with mental health and daily living problems in an effort to improve overall functioning.

Once the psycho-educational assessment has been completed, the results are presented in a comprehensive report. This report typically includes basic information about the student, the reason for the referral, information gathered from other professionals (e.g., speech-language pathologists, physical therapists, occupational therapists, and social workers), a list of all tests used to determine the child's cognitive and behavioural strengths and areas of weakness, a summary of the student's performance on these tests, and recommendations for the student's educational programming (e.g., instructional interventions, curricular adjustments, and behavioural intervention plans). Unfortunately, many educators find these reports somewhat difficult to understand because they are not aware of the cognitive or behavioural abilities assessed by the tests used. It is our contention that when educators gain knowledge about the abilities measured (i.e., the exact cognitive behaviours examined) they are better able to understand the recommendations provided in psycho-educational reports. By knowing both the precise psychological demands that certain test items place on a student and the student's responses to these items, educators can then participate knowledgeably in the construction of effective educational plans that (a) take advantage of the child's cognitive strengths, (b) avoid his or her obvious weaknesses, or (c) address skill areas that need improvement.

Intelligence Tests

Intelligence is an inferred cognitive construct that we deduce from observing and documenting a person's responses to a series of test stimuli. There is consensus within the discipline that intelligence is both a global ability (a measure of general intellectual functioning) and a specific ability (an indication of a discrete skill within a particular cognitive domain). A measure of global intelligence is typically administered during a psycho-educational assessment because it provides an accurate representation of the child's ability to perform the fundamental mental operations that are crucial for efficient learning and problem solving. The link between these mental operations and the learning and problem solving required by schooling is consistent with two of the longest standing and most widely used definitions of intelligence. Wechsler (1974) originally defined intelligence as "the capacity of the individual to act purposefully, to think rationally, and to deal effectively with his or her environment" (p. 3) whereas Sternberg and Salter (1982) referred to intelligence as goal-directed adaptive behaviour. This means that to be intelligent, intellectual abilities are purposefully applied to accomplish something, such as learning or problem solving, and these abilities are adaptable to various learning and problem-solving challenges. The 13 mental operations shown in Table 3.1 are measured by nearly all global intelligence tests.

Table 3.1 Mental Operations Measured in Intelligence Testing

Mental Operation	Description	Example
General Knowledge	An indication of learned factual information.	Can identify that Edmonton is the capital of Alberta.
Discrimination	The ability to determine that some items are different from other similar items.	Can determine that chihuahuas are smaller than Dalmatians, German shepherds, and black Labs.
Generalization	The ability to determine that some items are the same as others.	Can determine that Irish setters are as big as Dalmatians, German shepherds, and black Labs.
Induction	The ability to induce the principle that governs the relationship between objects and ideas.	Can reason that tissue paper is porous because water goes through tissue paper but does not go through wood, glass, or metal.
Vocabulary	An indication of existing vocabulary or the ability to define words.	Can name pictures, point to named objects, define words, and match words to definitions.
Motor Behaviour	The ability to properly execute a required motor skill.	Can touch objects, move a certain way, or copy, trace, or reconstruct objects.
Comprehension	The ability to properly respond to presented situations.	Can answer: What would you do if you saw a train approaching a washed-out bridge?
Sequencing	The ability to arrange items in a progressive series.	Can put blocks in order from smallest to largest.
Analogical Reasoning	The ability to discern a relationship between items based on an identical presented relationship.	Can discern A is to B as C is to ___.
Pattern Completion	The ability to fill in the missing part of a pattern or matrix.	Can identify the missing item in a pattern: 1, 2, ___, 4, 5.
Abstract Reasoning	The ability to analyze and solve problems on a complex, thought-based level.	Can form theories, recognize absurdities, or derive essential meanings from metaphors.
Detail Recognition	The ability to attend to detail when presenting a response to a problem.	Can produce detailed drawings, account for inferred or hidden objects, and identify missing parts.
Memory	The ability to store, retain, and recall information in response to a presented situation.	Can remember a sequence, reproduce a figure, provide a verbatim repetition, or provide the essential meaning of a passage.

Source: Adapted from Salvia, Ysseldyke, & Bolt (2010), pp. 245–249.

Wechsler Intelligence Scale for Children

Individually administered intelligence tests are preferred for psycho-educational assessments because group administered tests are best used for screening purposes or to provide descriptive information about groups of students. One of the most widely used individually administered intelligence tests is the Wechsler Intelligence Scale for Children, more commonly called the WISC (version V was published in 2014). It is designed for children from 6 years and 0 months to 16 years and 11 months and provides measures of global intellectual functioning and measures of four specific cognitive indexes. Brief descriptions of the cognitive demands of the tasks contained in the subtests that comprise the four index scores are provided in Table 3.2.

Based on a variety of literature regarding the WISC, it appears that the global score and the four domain-specific index scores provide good information when determining a child's eligibility for special education services.

Woodcock–Johnson Tests of Cognitive Abilities

Another widely used individually administered intelligence test is the Woodcock–Johnson test, first developed in 1977. The current version, referred to as the WJIV, was published in 2014 and consists of three independent and co-normed batteries (of tests) that can be used independently or in any combination: (a) Tests of Achievement (see Table 3.3); (b) Tests of Cognitive Abilities (see Table 3.4); and (c) Tests of Oral Language (see Table 3.5). The Tests of Achievement can be used to screen, diagnose, and monitor progress in reading, writing, and mathematics achievement areas. The Tests of Cognitive Abilities emphasize measures for identifying individuals' patterns of cognitive strengths and weaknesses through seven different broad abilities.

Table 3.2 Cognitive Indexes of the WISC-V

Index	Cognitive Demand	Description
Verbal Comprehension	Similarities	Asking how two words are alike/similar.
	Vocabulary	Asking to define provided words.
	Information	General knowledge questions.
	Comprehension	Questions about social situations/common concepts.
Visual Spatial	Block Design	Manipulate blocks to reproduce visually presented design.
	Visual Puzzles	View puzzles in a book and choose which three pieces are needed to construct each puzzle.
Fluid Reasoning	Matrix Reasoning	Select missing portion of matrix from five possible responses.
	Figure Weights	Select the shape that keeps the scale balanced.
	Picture Concepts	Select which pictures go together, one from each row.
Working Memory	Digit Span	Recall orally presented digits (forward or backward).
	Picture Span	Select pictures previously viewed, in order if possible.
	Letter-Number	Provide numbers and letters to examiner in a predetermined order.
Processing Speed	Coding	Associate symbols with shapes or numbers and copy onto paper within a time limit.
	Symbol Search	Search, find, and indicate target symbols within a time limit; search group symbols within a time limit.
	Cancellation	Mark target pictures within random or structured arrangements of pictures within a time limit.

Source: Adapted from Salvia, Ysseldyke, & Bolt (2010), pp. 258–259; and Wechsler, D. (2014). *Wechsler Intelligence Scale for Children—Fifth edition.* Bloomington, MN: Pearson.

The Tests of Oral Language were designed to determine and describe an individual's strengths and weaknesses with regard to expressive language.

These batteries provide measures of general intellectual ability, specific cognitive abilities, scholastic aptitude, oral languages, and achievement. The resulting scores appear to be quite useful for determining special education eligibility and for designing specialized educational plans.

Table 3.3 WJIV Tests of Achievement

Standard Battery	Extended Battery
Letter-Word Identification	Reading Recall
Applied Problems	Number Matrices
Spelling	Editing
Passage Comprehension	Word Reading Fluency
Calculation	Spelling of Sounds
Writing Samples	Reading Vocabulary
Word Attack	Science
Oral Reading	Social Studies
Sentence Reading Fluency	Humanities
Math Facts Fluency	
Writing Fluency	

Source: From Woodcock-Johnson IV™ (WJ IV™). Copyright © 2014 Houghton Mifflin Harcourt Publishing Company. All rights reserved. Used by permission of the publisher. Any further duplication is strictly prohibited unless written permission is obtained from Houghton Mifflin Harcourt Publishing Company.

Table 3.4 WJIV Tests of Cognitive Abilities

Standard Battery	Extended Battery
Oral Vocabulary	Numbers Reversed
Number Series	Number Pattern Matching
Verbal Attention	Non-Word Repetition
Letter Pattern Matching	Visual-Auditory Learning
Phonological Processing	Picture Recognition
Story Recall	Analysis–Synthesis
Visualization	Object Number Sequencing
General Information	Pair Cancellation
Concept Formation	Memory for Words

Source: See Table 3.3.

Table 3.5 WJIV Tests of Oral Language

Standard Battery
Picture Vocabulary
Oral Comprehension
Segmentation
Rapid Picture Naming
Sentence Repetition
Understanding Directions
Sound Blending
Retrieval Fluency
Sound Awareness

Source: See Table 3.3.

Stanford–Binet Intelligence Scale

The Stanford–Binet Intelligence Scale, 5th Edition (SB5; Roid, 2003), an individually administered test, is another widely used measure of intellectual ability. Both global ability as well as specific abilities are evaluated. It is considered one of the most robust intelligence tests because it is primarily a power test wherein performance is not dependent upon speed of response. Cognitive skills across the lifespan (ages 2–85) are measured, and a wide range of functioning (very low to very high) can be identified, two features that most other tests cannot claim. Another unique feature of the SB5 is that each of the five measured factors is composed of both a verbal and non-verbal subtest. Brief descriptions of the cognitive demands of the tasks of the 10 subtests that comprise the five broad factor scores are provided in Table 3.6.

The SB5 has good test reliability and test validity across the five domains measured. Factor scores should be used in conjunction with global scores when making important educational decisions, as some of the individual subtests do not have high reliability coefficients.

test reliability

Refers to the consistency of a measure; degree to which test items give the same results.

test validity

Degree to which a test measures what it purports to measure.

Academic Achievement Tests

Academic achievement tests are designed to measure the extent of a child's learning as a result of schooling and life experiences. These multi-skill tests typically provide accurate indications of knowledge and understanding across several curricular areas, such as reading, math, spelling, and writing. Individually administered tests are preferred over group administered tests because the examiner can watch the child working and solving problems. This type of close

Table 3.6 Cognitive Demands of SB5

Broad Factor	Cognitive Demand	Description
Fluid Reasoning	Non-verbal	Can identify geometric objects as well as complete simple and complex patterns and matrices.
	Verbal	Can reason, identify cause and effect and classification, and discern verbal absurdities and analogies.
Knowledge	Non-verbal	Can understand common procedural knowledge and pictorial absurdities.
	Verbal	Can produce vocabulary and language definitions.
Quantitative Reasoning	Non-verbal	Can understand math relationships, counting, algebraic concepts, and patterns, and can use deduced principles to solve novel problems.
	Verbal	Can identify numbers, count, and solve orally presented word problems.
Visual-Spatial Processing	Non-verbal	Can complete geometric patterns and forms.
	Verbal	Can follow spatial directions, provide directions, indicate orientation, and solve visual-spatial story problems.
Working Memory	Non-verbal	Can sort information and repeat simple and complex sequences.
	Verbal	Can remember short and longer sentences as well as simple and complex sentence endings after processing interference.

Source: Adapted from Salvia & Ysseldyke (2007), pp. 314–317. Reproduced by permission of Cengage Learning, Inc. www.cengage.com/permissionslearning.

observation usually provides educators with valuable insights into the child's manner of completing tasks, or lack thereof. These insights are often more informative for educational planning purposes than the child's resulting score.

Screening achievement tests (either group or individually administered) are most frequently used to identify students who may have high or low levels of scholastic attainment. It is important to note that these indicators are merely global estimates of academic ability. Students identified through screening tests, either because of lower-than-average skills or because of exceptionally high skills, need to be assessed further using more precise diagnostic tests that focus on specific scholastic domains. These tests use many more topical test items to measure concepts and skills, thereby allowing for finer analyses of strengths and weaknesses.

Multi-skill achievement tests typically measure abilities that are widely considered to be foundational or basic across and within most curricula in North America. As such, they are suitable indicators of general attainment. If, however, educators want an accurate, reliable, and valid measure of how well or much a child has learned from instruction in school, they must use a test that matches precisely the instruction provided: "Tests that do not match instruction lack content validity, and decisions based on such tests should be restricted" (Salvia & Ysseldyke with Bolt, 2007, p. 382). Therefore, it is quite important for educators to discern whether or not the skills and concepts measured by a particular subtest match the curricular content they are delivering and determine how relevant that information is to their day-to-day teaching. For example, the Spelling subtest of the Canadian Test of Basic Skills does not require students to actually spell words, either orally or by writing or printing the word. It requires students to identify spelling mistakes in words presented in multiple-choice question format; some questions have no spelling mistakes.

The importance of using tests or subtests that have direct relevance to a teacher's curriculum cannot be overstated. These direct connections are such an important factor within educational decision making that some of the more widely used tests are being modified to suit specific curricula. For example, for the latest version of the Canadian Achievement Test (CAT-4; Canadian Test Centre, 2008), the developer/publisher explicitly states that the CAT-4 is modelled to fit various Canadian curricula and it evaluates how well students perform in comparison to other students across the district, region, or in Canada as a whole. Different versions of the test are available depending on the provincial or territorial curricula being taught.

Tests of Perception and Perceptual-Motor Skills

A child's perception and perceptual-motor abilities are assessed because these are important fundamental skills necessary for success in school. These tests measure the ability to acquire, interpret, and organize incoming sensory information and produce respectively appropriate motor behaviours or responses. Some other terms used to describe these types of abilities or behaviours are visual discrimination, spatial problem solving, part-to-whole relationships, and sequential processing. This type of diagnostic data is especially relevant because many scholastic skills require the integrated use of vision, audition, and proprioception (the sense of how your body is oriented in space). Also, there is evidence that early perceptual-motor integration (or lack thereof) can directly affect basic learning processes. This perspective has recently regained favour as more research has focused on processing deficits and learning disabilities.

There are several tests that claim to provide suitable measures of these skills. The most highly regarded test in this category is the Developmental Test of Visual-Motor Integration

(Beery VMI; Beery, Buktenica, & Beery, 2010). It is an individually administered test that assesses the ability to duplicate geometric forms using integrated visual and motor skills. The child produces the images using a pencil and paper. The primary function of this test within a psycho-educational assessment battery is to help identify students who have difficulties coordinating their visual-motor skills. Data from this test should only be used in conjunction with pertinent data from other tests (such as writing and drawing) when making educational decisions.

Tests of Social and Emotional Behaviour

Poor social and emotional behaviours and skills result in problem behaviours that can negatively impact a child's social relationships, development of cognitive learning skills, and overall academic achievement. Problematic behaviour is assessed, therefore, to identify students for special services eligibility and to assist educators in designing proper interventions. These tests measure what are variously referred to as social, emotional, or problematic behaviours. To provide this information, these tests assess specific sets of student actions variously classified or labelled as behavioural, coping, or social skills that are usually indicated in terms of excesses (e.g., excessive verbal outbursts) or deficits (e.g., poor coping skills). Tests of social and emotional behaviour are also important because it is not always obvious whether the child (a) lacks a required or expected behavioural skill; (b) cannot learn the skill; or (c) cannot use it, or chooses not to use it, appropriately. Deciphering why the skill is not being demonstrated is crucial to designing suitable interventions.

The best way to properly determine problem behaviour is to complete a multi-method, multi-dimensional assessment that comprises information gathered from the following sources:

- *Rating scales/tests:* Teachers, parents, peers, or significant others are asked to rate the extent of the target child's demonstration of desirable or undesirable skills.
- *Direct observations of the child:* Over a predetermined period and using a predeveloped recording procedure, an observer notes the presence or absence of defined target behaviours within selected contexts.
- *Situational measure or groups:* Peers are asked to provide indications of the target child's social status within a particular group(s).
- *Interviews:* Usually conducted by experienced and expert professionals, information is gathered from pertinent individuals using structured or unstructured interview processes to gain insights into student patterns of thinking and behaving, social–emotional functioning, educational attitudes, and extracurricular activities.

Behaviour Assessment System for Children

One of the better tests of social and emotional behaviours is the Behaviour Assessment System for Children, Third Edition (BASC-3; Reynolds & Kamphouse, 2015). It is a multi-method, multi-dimensional measure that evaluates adaptive and maladaptive behaviours and self-perceptions in children ages 2–25. Some of the behaviours examined are adaptability, aggression, attention problems, conduct problems, depression, functional communication, hyperactivity, learning problems, social skills, and study skills. Brief descriptions of the areas assessed by the five main measures of behaviour are provided below (adapted from Salvia, Ysseldyke & Bolt, 2010, p. 291):

1. *Teacher Rating Scale:* A teacher rating of adaptive and problem behaviours that children typically exhibit in school and caregiving settings, such as "displays fear in new settings" and "works well with others."
2. *Parent Rating Scale:* A parental rating of adaptive and problem behaviours that children typically exhibit in community and home settings.
3. *Self-Report of Personality:* A student rating providing insight into a child's thoughts and feelings about various topics such as school, interpersonal relations, and self-adequacy.
4. *Structured Developmental History:* A broad-based developmental history that examines the social, psychological, developmental, educational, and medical realms of the child.
5. *Student Observation System:* An observational checklist used to diagnose and monitor specific adaptive and maladaptive behaviours within specific contexts.

The BASC-3 appears to be a comprehensive instrument for conducting clinical diagnoses, providing educational classifications and placements, and conducting behavioural program evaluations. Its strength is that it provides a balanced evaluation of the target child across a variety of contexts.

The Individualized Education Program

Once the psychologist's report is thoroughly reviewed and discussed, a description of how the student's special needs are going to be met is then formally and collaboratively laid out by the school-based team and the parents (and the student when appropriate) in a document we refer to as the IEP or *individualized education program*. The value and importance of this education program cannot be overstated because the essence of special education is individualization. The IEP is designed as a detailed and specific blueprint for one student's personalized instructional program for one school year, and it typically includes the following:

- The student's current level of functioning (learning and behaviour)
- The measurable annual learning and behavioural goals for the student (in the case of students with pervasive or moderate developmental disabilities, post-school goals are also considered)
- The measurable short-term objectives that will be used as benchmarks of the student's progress, broken down by subject or behavioural environment
- The demonstrable special education and related services that the student requires (such as instructional adjustments, curricular modifications, pull-out resource support, or speech therapy)
- When necessary, the environment in which these services will be provided (the regular classroom is usually the first option, but the regular classroom may not always be appropriate)
- The schedule of periodic checks that will be conducted to measure, evaluate, and report on the student's progress

We hope it is now clear why we emphasized the importance of the assessment and data-gathering process in the earlier parts of this chapter. When educators and parents collaborate on the development of a specific blueprint for a student's special type of education, they need the right kind of information to base their decisions on. Without proper assessment there can be no IEPs, without IEPs we do not have an individualization of the learning process, and without individualization we lose the very essence of special education.

While it is necessary that specialized and individualized programs be provided for students with exceptionalities, this does not mean that the regular curriculum will be irrelevant. In fact, this process ensures that all elements of the regular curriculum will have to be *deemed* appropriate for each individual student based on the assessment and decision-making processes described above. For example, the IEP of a student who has a specific learning disability, defined as an expressive oral language disability, would clearly state that the student is required to fulfill all the learning expectations of Grade 10 social studies except for those involving expressive oral language (e.g., public speaking, project presentations, or other oral demonstrations of learning, such as class plays or group discussions). However, the IEP of another student in the same class who also has a learning disability, but not the same learning disability, would clearly state that different learning expectations must be excluded, depending on the exceptional difficulties the student experiences. The purpose behind omitting or altering regular curriculum learning expectations is to allow students with exceptionalities to participate in the regular classroom as much as possible without requiring them to learn or demonstrate their learning by using modes or skills they cannot use very well.

A Condensed Version of the IEP

Despite the vital role that the IEP plays in special education and the benefits it provides for students, there is considerable evidence that the IEP also causes problems. It has been frequently reported that IEPs demand so much time and excessive paperwork that it is one of the major reasons special educators are leaving the profession (Edgar & Pair, 2005; Hale, 2015). We contend that a large part of this problem is due to the often overly complicated IEP forms used in various jurisdictions. Most IEPs are four or five pages long, and some are even as long as eight pages. These documents take onerous amounts of time to develop and complete. When added to the already significant administrative load of teachers, IEPs can be burdensome to revise. In the best interests of students with exceptionalities, it would be ideal if their IEPs were changed whenever substantial changes occurred in their learning ability, their curriculum progress, or their behavioural interactions. If the IEP is to be an accurate representation of a student's current state of functioning and act as the student's educational roadmap for the school year, this amount of change is logical, but probably too time consuming given its length. Most Canadian jurisdictions require an evaluation (and possible revision) of an IEP every 12 months, as a minimum. It should be noted that the principal of the school is the person primarily responsible for the creation, implementation, and management of IEPs.

To solve the various problems that contribute to IEPs being perceived as onerous, we suggest a one-page working document that we feel contains all the relevant and necessary information that should go into an IEP developed for students with *mild disabilities* (see Figure 3.2). The vast majority of Canadian students with exceptionalities have mildly disabling conditions that fall under the high-incidence categories outlined in Chapter 1. In our experience, the majority of IEPs for these students will easily fit into our one-page design. Obviously, students with moderate disabilities and students with severely disabling conditions or those who require multiple services from numerous professionals will require longer IEPs to properly document their unique situations. However, IEPs of this sort will only be required for a very few students.

Our description of what should and should not be part of a student's IEP is a condensed version of the details provided in *The Individualized Education Plan (IEP): A Resource Guide* (Ontario Ministry of Education, 2004):

An IEP is a working written document that outlines, based on appropriate assessment, a specialized educational program for a particular child's learning and/or behavioural strengths and needs. It details the accommodations or modifications required to achieve his or her prescribed learning expectations and outlines how their achievement will be evaluated and reported. An IEP is not a description of everything to be taught, of all teaching strategies to be used, of non-altered learning expectations, nor is it a daily lesson plan.

The reason that most IEPs are so large is that they contain many unnecessary duplications of information contained in reports that were interpreted or consulted to construct the IEP in the first place. This type of information is redundant because these reports are readily available in students' files. It also makes the revision of the IEP an onerous task. Thus, we feel that a one-page document that contains all the necessary information would be received more positively by educators without compromising student learning. This shortened version could be used on a daily basis with updates transferred to the larger file at strategic points in the school year.

As an example, the one-page IEP in Figure 3.2 is a condensed version of the actual six-page IEP designed for Karl, whom we portray in Chapter 5. Our revised version of Karl's IEP provides a demonstration of how a one-page document can contain the critical information necessary to a teacher's understanding of a student's learning needs. This IEP provides answers to the following 12 questions about the student's situation:

1. Who is the student and how old is he or she?
2. What grade is he or she in, what school year is it, and who are the teachers who will implement this plan?
3. Why was the student referred in the first place? (This provides an indication of similar behaviours for which the teachers should be on the alert.)
4. How is the student currently doing in his or her courses and/or subjects? (Barely mastering something is different from struggling with it, which is different from failing it.)
5. What does the student do well, struggle with, or not do at all?
6. What do we want the student to accomplish over the term or school year?
7. What have teachers done before that has proven successful? (This provides information regarding the value of particular interventions and the minor modifications that may make interventions more effective.)
8. Based on the student's strengths and needs, what curricular learning outcomes have to be omitted, added (in the case of students who are gifted), or modified? (These are often called short-term objectives, but we feel that it is better if they are more precisely expressed as learning expectations.)

Student Name: Karl Hildebrandt   Date of Birth: **June 28, 1995**   Age: **11**

Date/Grade/Teacher(s):   **September 1, 2006/Grade 5/Jill McCarthy**

Reason for Referral: Dramatic reduction in academic performance, not reading at grade level

---

Current Levels of Achievement by Relevant Subject: Reading: Level 3 in Grade 4 expectations; Writing: Level 2 in Grade 4 expectations.

Student Strengths and Needs Derived from Assessment: Positive attitude toward learning, above average cognitive abilities, hard worker, verbally expressive, good general knowledge, creative. Difficulty with reading, spelling, and mathematics; can be hyperactive and impulsive; is not well organized.

Short-term Learning Expectations:

Reading: Term 1   Level 4 in Grade 4 expectations

                  Term 2   Level 1 in Grade 5 expectations

                  Term 3   Level 2 in Grade 5 expectations

Writing: Make appropriate progress within each reporting period as Karl moves from Level 2 to Level 3 in Grade 4 expectations.

Long-term Learning Goals: Reading: Level 2 in Grade 5 expectations; Writing: Level 3 in Grade 4 expectations.

Successfully Implemented Teacher Interventions: Reminders for following instructions and turn-taking; reading aloud improved with practice; written work improved with revision and editing; reminders to remember math symbols have improved achievement.

Learning Expectations Omitted/Added/Modified: Karl is expected to fulfill all the Grade 5 learning expectations except for those noted above for reading and writing.

Required Accommodations/Adaptations/Modifications: Cueing from educational assistant or teacher; use of manipulatives in math; teacher provides written notes where appropriate; allow a scribe and extra time for independent tasks and tests; use of quiet work area.

Special Considerations: Candidate for use of assistive technology.

Description of Progress Indicators: Evaluations according to Grade 4 and 5 expectations.

Schedule of Progress Indicators: Reported according to Grade 5 assessment periods.

Principal's Signature: _____ **Date:** _____

Parent/Guardian Signatures: _____ **Date:** _____

Student's Signature: _____ **Date:** _____

Figure 3.2 Karl's IEP (condensed version).

9. What accommodations, adaptations, or modifications are needed to allow the student to successfully attain his or her learning expectations?
10. Are there any unique circumstances that need to be considered, such as whether the student will participate in province-wide testing?
11. How and when will the student's progress be evaluated and reported?
12. Who has agreed that this document constitutes the student's plan for the year?

Something to Think About

Imagine you are a teacher in a regular classroom and you have a student who is going through the assessment/IEP process due to a possible learning disability. What type of assessment data might you provide to the school-based team, and how would you collect it? What would you expect to learn from the qualified professional who conducts the student's formal assessment? What role do you see yourself playing in the development of the IEP?

Phase Five: Educational Intervention

Educational interventions are the actions that teachers and other educators take to provide students with exceptionalities with an appropriate education. Interventions can range from minor changes in teaching and curricula to the use of completely different teaching methods and curricula. The point is that these interventions are carefully and specifically designed and implemented to suit the individual educational requirements of each student based on the information gleaned from assessment data.

From the Psychologist's Notebook

When it comes to designing educational programming for students with exceptionalities, it is important to understand that each child will have both *interpersonal* and *intrapersonal* differences that have to be taken into account. Interpersonal differences are the ways in which a child's abilities are different from his or her peers who are not exceptional, such as inability to read at grade level. Intrapersonal differences are the ways in which each of a child's abilities differ (e.g., a child is proficient at math but is unable to read at grade level). The key concept here is that both types of differences are vital pieces of information when considering program design.

There are a variety of terms used by educators to describe different types of educational interventions, as evidenced by the varied terminology used in different regions of Canada (e.g., accommodations, adaptations, modifications). We will simply present the general categories of educational interventions with examples of each:

- Changes or adjustments can be made to the learning environment to eliminate or reduce minor learning or behavioural differences (e.g., changing seating arrangements to minimize peer interruptions that inhibit learning, installing extra-wide doors for students in wheelchairs, using a Braille printer to produce notes or worksheets for students who are visually impaired). These changes are best thought of as alternate means of arranging the student's surroundings so they are not disadvantaged in any way.

- Changes or adjustments can be made to teaching methods, or teacher or student materials, that allow a student to learn or do something that he or she would not otherwise be able to easily accomplish (e.g., using manipulatives for secondary students who, unlike their peers, cannot master abstract reasoning; consciously and consistently using multi-modal teaching instead of just singular approaches; allowing students options regarding the format they use to present their in-class assignments or homework; providing notes in cloze format for students who have difficulty with note-taking; giving extra time on tests and exams for students who have expressive language processing deficits). These changes are made so that students with exceptionalities can achieve the same academic outcomes as their classmates. In most cases, if these changes were not implemented by teachers, students with exceptionalities would not be successful in school.

- Significant changes can be made to the curricula to accommodate a student's exceptional learning or behavioural strengths and needs (e.g., the Grade 9 math curriculum may be used to teach a mathematically precocious student in Grade 7, a functional reading and writing curriculum may be taught to a Grade 6 student with a mild developmental disability). These major changes are required because the learning expectations of the prescribed curricula are not suitable for the particular student under consideration.

Knowing whether changes such as these are required for any particular student necessitates a clear understanding of what the student is capable of accomplishing and what he or she cannot accomplish without some sort of intervention. It is noteworthy that all of the educational interventions mentioned above, and those detailed in Chapters 5–13, are interventions that teachers either already use or can easily adapt to and master. They are simply examples of good teaching done in a special way for special reasons.

There are many students with exceptionalities who also require various types of therapy to enable them to properly function in their community school setting. These therapies are provided by expert professionals, usually during the school day, but some students may also receive therapy after school hours in clinics or hospitals. Therapeutic interventions can be a student's only special need, as in the case of occupational therapy for perceptual-motor coordination, or they can be additional to a student's instructional needs, such as speech therapy to develop the language skills that support the minor adaptations the teacher makes in her teaching of language arts. Regardless of the form of therapy, these interventions also need to be identified and documented in the student's IEP.

Universal Design for Learning

Given the need for educational interventions that address specific student needs, it is important to consider an overall framework for how this will occur in a classroom. Universal Design for Learning (UDL) is an educational framework based on research in learning, especially the works of Vygotsky (1978). It is a structured process that guides the purposeful development of flexible learning environments to accommodate individual learning differences. In other words, it promotes the design of inclusive curricula for use in inclusive classrooms.

UDL was first defined by the Center for Applied Special Technology (2013). It called for curricula to provide

- *multiple means of representation* to give learners various ways of acquiring information and knowledge;
- *multiple means of expression* to provide learners alternatives for demonstrating what they know; and
- *multiple means of engagement* to tap into learners' interests, challenge them appropriately, and motivate them to learn.

UDL is intended to increase student learning and achievement by reducing or eliminating physical, cognitive, intellectual, and organizational barriers. According to the Council for Exceptional Children (2005), students with exceptionalities need environments where instruction is flexible, equitable, and accessible at all times. UDL does not necessarily remove academic challenges, but it is intended to remove barriers to access using three important principles: representation, engagement, and expression.

What We Know . . .

UDL Principles

Principle of Representation

Learners differ in the ways they perceive and comprehend information presented to them. For example, those with sensory disabilities (e.g., blindness or deafness), learning disabilities (e.g., dyslexia), language or cultural differences, and so forth may all require different ways of approaching content. Others may simply grasp information quicker or more efficiently through visual or auditory means rather than printed text. Also, learning, and the transfer of learning, occurs when multiple representations are used because it allows students to make connections within as well as between concepts. There is no one means of representation that will be optimal for all learners, so providing options for representation is essential:

- *Options for perception*: Learning is impossible if information is imperceptible to the learner, and it is difficult when information is presented in formats that require extraordinary effort or assistance. To reduce barriers to learning, it is important to ensure that key information is equally perceptible to all learners by (a) providing the same information through different modalities (e.g., vision, hearing, or touch) and (b) providing information in formats that allow adjustability by the user (e.g., text that can be enlarged, sounds that can be amplified). Multiple representations not only ensure that information is accessible to learners with particular sensory and perceptual disabilities, but it is also easier to access and comprehend by others.

Continued

- *Options for language, mathematical expressions, and symbols*: Learners vary in their facility with different forms of representation, both linguistic and non-linguistic. Vocabulary that may sharpen and clarify concepts for one learner may be opaque and foreign to another. An equals sign (=) might help some learners understand that the two sides of the equation need to be balanced, but might cause confusion to a student who does not understand what it means. A graph that illustrates the relationship between two variables may be informative to one learner and inaccessible or puzzling to another. A picture or image that carries meaning for some learners may carry very different meanings for learners from differing cultural or familial backgrounds. As a result, inequalities arise when information is presented to all learners through a single form of representation. An important instructional strategy is to ensure that alternative representations are provided not only for accessibility, but for clarity and comprehensibility for all learners.
- *Options for comprehension*: The purpose of education is not to make information accessible, but rather to teach learners how to transform accessible information into useable knowledge. Decades of cognitive science research has demonstrated that the ability to transform accessible information into useable knowledge is an active process. Constructing useable knowledge, knowledge that is accessible for future decision making, depends not upon merely perceiving information, but upon active "information-processing skills" like selective attending, integration of new information with prior knowledge, strategic categorization, and active memorization. Individuals differ greatly in their information-processing skills and in their access to prior knowledge through which they can assimilate new information. The proper design and presentation of information can provide the scaffolds necessary to ensure that all learners have access to knowledge.

Principle of Engagement

Affect is a crucial element of learning, and learners differ markedly in the ways in which they are motivated to learn. Some learners are highly engaged by spontaneity and novelty while other are disengaged or even frightened by those aspects, preferring stricter routine. Some learners like to work alone while others prefer working with peers. In fact, there is not one means of engagement that is optimal for all learners in all contexts, so providing multiple options for engagement is essential:

- *Options to drive interest*: Information that is not attended to or does not engage learner cognition is inaccessible because it goes unnoticed and unprocessed. For this reason, teachers should devote considerable effort toward recruiting learner attention and engagement. But learners differ significantly in what attracts their attention and engages their interest, and these will differ in the same learner over time and across circumstances. This happens because learner interests change as they gain new knowledge and skills, as their brains develop, and as they develop into self-determined adolescents. It is, therefore, important to have alternative ways to generate learner interest, particularly ways that reflect the important inter- and intraindividual differences among learners.
- *Options for sustaining effort and persistence through self-regulation*: Many kinds of learning, especially the learning of new skills and strategies, require sustained

© Liquoricelegs/Dreamstime.com

It is important to have alternative ways to generate learner interest and particularly ways that reflect the important inter- and intraindividual differences among learners.

attention and effort. When motivated to do so, many learners can regulate their attention and affect to sustain the effort and concentration that such learning will require. However, learners differ considerably in their ability to self-regulate in this way. The ability to self-regulate—to strategically modulate one's emotional reactions or states to be more effective at coping and engaging with the environment—is a critical aspect of human development. While many learners develop self-regulatory skills either by trial and error or by observing successful others, many have significant difficulties in developing these skills. Unfortunately, some teachers do not teach these skills explicitly, leaving them as part of the "implicit" curriculum that is often inaccessible or invisible to many. Teachers who address self-regulation explicitly give their students the best opportunity to learn.

Principle of Expression

Learners differ in the ways they can navigate their learning environment and how they can most easily express what they know. For example, individuals with significant movement impairments (e.g., cerebral palsy), those who struggle with strategic and organizational abilities (executive function disorders), those who have language barriers, and so forth approach learning tasks very differently. Some may be able to express themselves well via written text but not via speech, and vice versa. The act of expressing knowledge requires a great deal of strategy, practice, and organization; these skills are other areas by which learners can differ. It is clear that there is not one means of knowledge expression that is optimal for all learners, so providing options for expression is essential:

Continued

- *Options for physical action*: Printed textbooks and workbooks and most interactive software provide only limited means of navigation or interaction. This raises barriers for learners with physical disabilities, blindness, dysgraphia, or those who need executive functioning supports. It is important to provide curricular materials through which individuals with movement impairments can "best" navigate and express what they know, such as those that allow navigation or interaction with a single switch, voice-activated switches, expanded keyboards, and so on.
- *Options for communication and expression*: There is no medium of expression that is equally suited for all learners or for all kinds of communication. Even some media are poorly suited for some kinds of expression or learning. While a learner with dyslexia may excel at storytelling in conversation, he may falter when writing down that same story. It is important to provide alternative modalities for expression so that all learners can best, or easily, express their knowledge, ideas, and concepts.
- *Options for executive functions*: At the highest level of our capacity to act skilfully are our "executive function" skills. These abilities allow us to set long-term goals, plan effective strategies for reaching those goals, monitor the progress of those strategies, and modify them as needed. Unfortunately, for some learners, their executive function skills are limited due to their poor working memory. Executive functioning skills are sharply reduced when (a) most of our executive functioning capacity must be devoted to managing information that is not automatically recalled or fluent, and (b) executive capacity itself is reduced due to an inability to self-design executive strategies. The UDL framework typically involves efforts to expand executive capacity in two ways: (a) by **scaffolding** lower-level skills so that they require less executive processing, and (b) by scaffolding higher-level executive skills and strategies so that they are more numerous, more effective, and better developed.

Source: Adapted from UDL-Universe (2016) (www.udluniverse.com).

scaffolding
A teaching method that enables a student to complete a task through a gradual reduction of teacher support.

Phase Six: Evaluation of Student Progress

Teachers working in inclusive classrooms frequently ask, "How do I evaluate the progress of students who have IEPs?" There are a variety of tools or measures used to determine student academic performance. The most frequently used measures are standardized tests (e.g., provincial curricula tests) and in-class tests developed by teachers, often referred to as *curriculum-based assessment (CBA)*. For students with exceptionalities, CBA is the preferred method of determining academic progress because, as the term implies, it is the teacher's assessment of a student's individual mastery of the curricula that he or she encounters in the classroom on a daily basis (McLoughlin & Lewis, 2005). The foundational assumption of CBA, then, is that one should assess what is taught (Flanagan, Mascola, & Hardy-Braz, 2009).

Standardized tests of curricula are not preferred because they are primarily used to determine the overall performance of groups of students and essentially reveal nothing regarding the educational needs or abilities of students with exceptionalities (Gregory, 2000). If student-to-student performance comparisons are necessary, those derived from CBA results are fairer and more accurate because the student is being compared to his or her immediate classmates and peers. This is opposed to standardized assessment tools that are generically applied to a broad variety of curricular domains, such as board-wide or province-wide tests, and compare children indiscriminately.

CBA directly assesses mastery performance using frequent but brief indicators of both the student's critical skills in core academic domains and the student's ability to execute them (Overton, 1996). For example, a teacher may design an assessment of a student's math skills in problem solving as well as an assessment of his or her organization of the steps to carry out those skills. These CBA indicators are typically derived from the annual and short-term goals outlined in the student's IEP as they relate to the overall expectations of the curricula to be delivered. This makes eminent sense because most students with high-incidence exceptionalities will have IEPs and instructional interventions that are based on the regular curricula. Teachers are encouraged to design and use performance indicators whenever the student progresses from one curricular unit to another, and to systematically record and analyze the data that are collected. In addition to determining the student's curricular performance, these indicators can also be used to monitor the effectiveness of the instructional program in which the student participates. For example, a student may be unsuccessful at completing problem-solving questions, not because he or she cannot perform the calculatory functions of the problem, but rather because the process is misunderstood or he or she has a sequencing problem that causes confusion.

In a comprehensive study examining the effects of CBA on the mastery of IEP objectives and specific instructional objectives, Fuchs and Fuchs (1996) found that CBA was very effective in measuring progress toward the attainment of short-term goals. King-Sears, Burgess, and Lawson (1999) provide an excellent description of the steps for effective CBA:

1. Analyze the curriculum and select the critical skills to be examined based on the match between the student's IEP and the curriculum competencies or expectations.
2. Design assessment tools, sometimes called probes, for each of the skills being examined (e.g., after a brief instructional period in math and an opportunity to practise, the students will answer five questions based on that lesson).
3. Administer the probes on several occasions across an instructional unit.
4. Assess the student's performance on each probe and chart the student's progress on a graph.
5. Analyze the student's progress within the instructional unit.

There are four primary benefits to this approach. First, each probe is specifically designed to meet a particular student's needs. Second, the probes are easy to design because they are extracted directly out of the daily lessons teachers use for instruction. Third, these probes will be specific to the student with an exceptionality, but they will not be dramatically different from the assessment items the teacher will use for the rest of the students in the class. And, fourth, CBA is a formative assessment process that can provide earlier rather than later indications that things are not progressing as they should. Within this approach there is obviously an important interplay between teaching, learning, and assessment (see Figure 3.3).

formative assessment
Determination of a student's level of understanding on an ongoing basis during the instructional period.

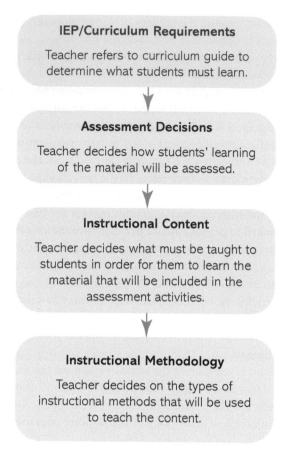

Figure 3.3 CBA and the interplay between teaching, learning, and assessment.

Source: Adapted from Edmunds, A. L., & Edmunds, G. A. (2015). *Educational psychology: Applications in Canadian classrooms* (2nd ed.). Republished with permission of Oxford University Press.

Based on the data gathered from the CBA process, teachers can easily record a student's progress (or lack thereof) at the end of an instructional unit or term and provide clear and precise reports to parents, school administrators, and the school-based team. Depending on the amount and type of progress made, the school-based team then decides with the teacher whether the IEP needs to be changed to reflect the student's next set of short-term curricular goals (or long-term goals if applicable). It is often the case that students with exceptionalities will progress more quickly in one subject than another, so it is probable that only some of the short-term learning expectations of the IEP will be changed while the others remain as they were. In this way, the IEP acts in concert with, and is impacted by, what happens in the classroom. We feel that this purposeful interactivity between the IEP and a student's documented academic progress will do much to bridge the disconnect teachers often claim exists between the IEP and the classroom.

Summary

The identification, referral, assessment, and educational intervention process outlined in this chapter forms the basis of exemplary special education services for students with exceptionalities. This process has proven effective around the world where special education is similarly defined and enacted. Every day, children with exceptionalities demonstrate they cannot cope with the typical expectations of the regular classroom. Without the above process, educators would be unable to determine precisely why these students are different from their peers, and consequently would not be able to effectively intervene on the students' behalf. It should be noted that the assessment process is not designed to label students nor is it designed to unnecessarily place students in special education programs. When properly carried out, the assessment process gathers and interprets multiple forms of data so that educators can make consistent, valid, and reliable education decisions that enhance the teaching and learning that occurs in classrooms.

Learning More about the Assessment and IEP Process

British Columbia: Special Education Manual

www.bced.gov.bc.ca/specialed/special_ed_policy_manual.pdf#page=21
This resource conveys policies, procedures, and guidelines that support the delivery of special education services in British Columbia's public schools.

Canadian Psychological Association: Professional Practice Guidelines for School Psychologists in Canada

www.cpa.ca/cpasite/UserFiles/Documents/publications/CPA%20Practice%20Guide.pdf
This CPA document addresses the roles and responsibilities of school psychologists in Canadian schools.

Council for Exceptional Children—Publications

www.cec.sped.org/Publications?sc_lang=en
The Council for Exceptional Children offers a number of publications that focus on the IEP.

Manitoba Education: A Handbook for Developing and Implementing IEPs

www.edu.gov.mb.ca/k12/specedu/iep/index.html
This handbook is intended to provide professionals with an effective process for deciding which students require IEPs. It is also designed to assist educators in developing, implementing, and evaluating these individual educational plans.

Newfoundland and Labrador Department of Education: Individual Support Services Plan

www.mcscy.nl.ca/issp.html
In their Model for the Coordination of Services to Children and Youth, the Newfoundland and Labrador Department of Education presents details regarding the development and use of the individual support services plan (ISSP).

Ontario Ministry of Education: The Individual Education Plan

www.edu.gov.on.ca/eng/general/elemsec/speced/guide/resource/index.html
This Ontario resource was designed to assist educators in the development, implementation, and monitoring of high-quality IEPs. A five-step process is recommended. Suggestions and examples are provided.

Saskatchewan Ministry of Education: Inclusion and Intervention Plan

www.saskatchewan.ca/residents/education-and-learning/prek-12-education-early-learning-and-schools/supporting-students-with-additional-needs
The Ministry of Education provides a description of the IIP, a document containing a compilation of student outcomes that have the highest priority for a particular student during the current year.

US Department of Education: A Guide to the Individualized Education Program

https://www2.ed.gov/parents/needs/speced/iepguide/index.html
This site provides a comprehensive look at the history and current use of IEPs in the United States.

CHAPTER 4
Creating Exemplary Learning Environments

LEARNING OBJECTIVES

After learning the material in this chapter, you should be able to:

- Discuss why exemplary learning environments are especially important to students with exceptionalities.

- Define the term *classroom management* and discuss how it relates to student socialization and disciplinary interventions.

- Discuss the primary causes of students' problematic behaviours, including psychological factors, learning challenges, and environmental influences.

- Discuss the principles behind *Dynamic Classroom Management* (DCM) as well as the steps involved in implementing this approach.

- Discuss the importance of non-negotiable classroom rules and provide examples.

- Discuss the important considerations teachers should take into account when negotiating rewards and consequences with students.

- Outline the steps to behaviour problem solving in the classroom.

- Discuss how a teacher might plan for a student's return to the classroom after the student has been removed because of problematic behaviour.

- Discuss how teachers can promote students' self-regulation of classroom behaviours.

- Define the terms *functional behaviour assessment* (FBA) and *behaviour intervention plan* (BIP), and discuss how they are used to address students' problematic behaviours.

Exemplary Learning Environments

The academic success of students is dependent on their learning environment and the behaviours present in these environments. Within exemplary learning environments, educators facilitate the pursuit of academic excellence by carefully managing and controlling student behaviours and attitudes. The primary goal of classroom management is to provide all students with optimum opportunities for learning.

In the case of students with exceptionalities, exemplary learning environments are especially important because, by definition, most of these students have difficulty learning what schools present to them. Add to that the fact that many of them have co-occurring attentional, behavioural, and social adjustment problems and it is easy to see why learning environments that are well constructed and well managed are an absolute necessity. Just as Chapter 3 described how teaching students with exceptionalities is nothing more than good teaching, this chapter will outline how creating exemplary learning environments for students with exceptionalities is nothing more than good planning and good classroom management. To accomplish this, the teacher performs the same general management techniques for all students while paying close attention to the management elements that have to be implemented differently for students with special needs. There is no doubt that classroom management is a distinctly different function than other aspects of teaching, such as instruction and assessment. It must, however, operate as part of an overall teaching approach to be most effective.

What We Know . . .

Key Terms and Definitions

Brophy (2006) provided key terms and definitions that are highly relevant to creating exemplary learning environments. It should be noted that the concepts and functions outlined in these definitions need to operate together if a teacher's overall management scheme is to be effective.

- *Classroom management* refers to actions taken to create and maintain a learning environment conducive to successful instruction (arranging the physical environment, establishing rules and procedures, maintaining students' attention to lessons and engagement in activities).
- *Student socialization* refers to actions taken to influence personal or social (including moral and civic) attitudes, beliefs, or behaviours, including the articulation of ideals, the communication of expectations, and the modelling, teaching, and reinforcing of desirable personal attributes and behaviours.
- *Disciplinary interventions* are actions taken to elicit or compel improved behaviour from students who fail to conform to expectations, especially when their misbehaviour is salient or sustained enough to disrupt the classroom management system.

Source: Excerpted from Brophy (2006).

Classroom Behaviour

The Effects of Problematic Behaviour

Every teacher knows that problematic student behaviour can easily undermine well-designed and creative lessons, and even beginning teachers quickly come to understand the emotional costs associated with constantly trying to remedy ongoing disruptions. Preparing lessons that go nowhere, falling behind a tight teaching schedule, and feeling emotionally drained at the end of most days is an overwhelming and daunting combination of factors that detracts significantly from the joy of teaching. Not only do educators feel an inherent professional responsibility to properly manage their classrooms, but they know from media reports that effective classroom management, or a lack thereof, is viewed as a serious educational problem by the general public.

It is not difficult to understand why and how highly disruptive classrooms can negatively affect students' behaviours and their attempts to conduct themselves in appropriate ways (Woolfolk-Hoy & Weinstein, 2006). However, what does not always seem so obvious is the significantly negative effects that disruptive environments have on students' attempts to learn (Levin & Nolan, 2000). This occurs despite the fact that the research literature is replete

©Digital Vision/Thinkstock.com

Effective classroom management is a key component of an environment that is conducive to successful instruction and learning.

meta-analysis
A quantitative and
systematic analysis of
the results of two or
more studies that have
examined the same
issue in the same way.

with evidence that well-managed and exemplary learning environments are conducive to excellent learning (Woolfolk-Hoy & Weinstein, 2006). In fact, Marzano and Marzano's (2003) meta-analysis of all the variables that positively impact on student achievement clearly suggests that classroom management is the single-most-important variable, considerably outperforming instructional and curricular variables.

Unfortunately, classroom management has become such a fundamental educational concern that it consumes as much as 80 per cent of some teachers' instructional days (Sugai & Horner, 1999). Teachers consistently report that managing problematic behaviours is overwhelming (Edmunds, Edmunds, & Hogarth, 2012) and, according to Freidman (2006), classroom management issues are viewed as one of the primary causes of teacher burnout and job dissatisfaction. It is no wonder that classroom management consistently ranks as the most pressing concern of all teachers, whether they are novices or veterans (Jones, 2006).

Current Views

Why has classroom management become such a pressing issue? In our opinion, this serious educational situation has developed because teacher education programs, and the public to a degree, have embraced the postmodernist approach to education. This approach diminishes the importance of positivist concepts such as assessment and testing, direct instruction, and classroom or behaviour management and, as a result, student teachers are not properly trained in these areas.

The fundamental tenet of postmodern philosophy is that all forms of knowledge are exercises in power, and those who construct knowledge have power, while those who do not construct knowledge do not. Or, even worse, those who do not construct knowledge are under the power of those who do. To establish a philosophical foothold and gain power, postmodernists attempt to diminish the power they view as being held by those who use science to construct knowledge. They accomplish this by debasing scientific principles as a way of determining knowledge and by describing science as merely a social construction. The implication is that if science, and therefore knowledge, is socially constructed, then it can be constructed by anyone, not just scientists. Thus, postmodernism renders the findings of science as not objectively or universally true. The final outcome of the postmodernist position is that if the findings of science are not true, then postmodernists do not have to adhere to educational practices that are derived from them.

postmodernist
approach
An approach that
negates the concept
of scientific truth
and supports the
fragmentation of all
academic subjects
into a variety of
perspectives—with no
"answers."

The Effects of Postmodernism on Special Education

In a 2006 series of articles in one of the flagship journals of special education, *Exceptionality*, Kauffman and Sasso (2006a; 2006b) made strong, reasoned, and irrefutable arguments about why and how postmodernism has undermined the guiding principles of special education. We have provided extracts from both articles to briefly, but accurately, outline this perspective:

> . . . the consequences of postmodern philosophy for education in general and for special education in particular are severe and negative. (2006b, p. 118)

> . . . [it] lacks the intellectual resources to answer even the most basic questions regarding how to teach and help children with disabilities. (2006b, p. 117)

The most damaging effect in special education, however, is that postmodern pessimism about finding truth or effective methods of intervention undermines efforts to see that teachers can contribute to a more equitable life for people with disabilities. (Mostert, Kauffman, & Kavale, 2003, as cited in Kauffman & Sasso, 2006a, p. 67)

It is time for the field of special education to expel any vestiges of this form of posturing and move on with the business of helping our students to learn and adapt; to evidence measurably superior outcomes. (2006a, p. 87)

More recently, Farrell (2012) indicated that postmodernism has continued to have negative effects on special education: "Postmodernism incorrectly regards science as a social construction and reduces everything to discourse. It diminishes efforts to apply objective thought to improve the lives of special children" (p. 199).

Relative to classroom and behaviour management, then, postmodernists are not satisfied with how behavioural science systematically explains what it is, nor how it should be designed and implemented. They do not agree with the concept of student differences because of the science that determines those differences, and they loathe the notion that somebody would have the power to make decisions about who was different and to what degree. They argue that student behaviour is socially constructed, that there is no need for differential conceptions of student behaviour, and, thus, that there is no need for different-than-normal ways of managing such behaviour. By extension, there are those within this movement that portray any systematized forms of management, and especially punishment (consequences), as being inflexible and rigid, and therefore unacceptable in teaching.

Somehow, education has totally embraced the notion that a child's behaviour is a direct result of the social context and that the problem with misbehaviour does not lie at all within the child. In adopting this position, education and educators have chosen not to confront and address the fact that a child with behavioural problems is a child who needs help, and a very special type of help. Therefore, the thrust of postmodernism postulates that if students' behaviours are not viewed as different enough to warrant being managed differently, there is no need for specialized courses on this topic in teacher education. The scope of this concern was best expressed by Landrum and Kauffman (2006):

A behavioural view of the management of behaviour in classrooms has been and continues to be a dominant and influential paradigm in both educational research and the preparation of teachers. To say that the behavioural view dominates current classroom practice, however, would be inaccurate . . . despite a rich history and extensive empirical underpinnings, the behavioural perspective on teaching and management is not highly regarded in the education community. (p. 47)

At one time, the non-adherence to the behavioural view was a welcome and necessary philosophical difference among educators as there is evidence that this debate largely contributed to our ecological views of behaviour management (for a detailed explanation see Doyle, 2006). However, when we look at how teachers are trained and what happens daily in classrooms, the following two facts warrant considerable attention: (a) An examination of faculty of education websites across Canada and the United States reveal that many teacher education programs do not have required courses in either behaviour management or classroom management, and (b) teachers consistently report they do not have the training required to properly manage disruptive and challenging behaviour (Greenberg, Putnam & Walsh, 2014; Johnson & Edmunds, 2006).

Educators' Need for Classroom Management Skills

Throughout our years of teaching at the university level, it has been consistently evident that coursework on classroom management, when it is provided, is far and away one of the most popular topics in pre-service education courses and programs. Once aspiring teachers return from practicum placements and realize there is much more to teaching than "knowing-and-saying," they anxiously develop a keen interest in the classroom management aspect of schooling. If, as a student, you have not already experienced this eye-opening phenomenon, you will. In addition, having delivered numerous professional development sessions to experienced teachers across Canada and the United States, it is also evident to us that classroom management is by far the most requested and most appreciated of all the professional development topics available to practising teachers (for a detailed explanation see Jones, 2006). Whether they are novice or experienced educators, teachers have consistently told us that coming to understand the intricacies of establishing and managing an excellent learning environment has dramatically improved their teaching, and particularly their enjoyment of teaching. They report that with this knowledge their classrooms become busy but smooth operations that are home to engaged students who learn co-operatively and independently. These students act and behave responsibly because of their sense of community, rather than to simply avoid getting into trouble with the teacher.

A recent study carried out in Ontario supports what we have heard from teachers. Klopfer (2014) evaluated the effectiveness of a proactive behavioural management course taught at a teacher's college. When comparing those who took the course with those who did not, Klopfer found that the course had a positive effect on pre-service teachers' self-efficacy, teaching style, emotions and reactions toward children, and their use of classroom management strategies. She further stated that enrolment in the behavioural management course "increased pre-service teachers' positive emotions and reactions towards children with learning and behavioural difficulties, decreased their use of psychological pressure as a teaching tactic, increased their overall use of proactive strategies and decreased their use of reactive and ineffective strategies in specific classroom situations" (p. 66).

In summary, we see the disruptive elements of schooling associated with classroom management as more a function of teachers' lack of knowledge and skills, and less a function of students' disruptive behaviours. While there is strong evidence that some of the disruptive behaviours (and outcomes from them) exhibited by students occur because they do not have the skills to cope, the vast majority of behavioural deficits stem from performance deficits (Maag, 2004). Performance deficits, according to Lane, Falk, and Wehby (2006), "refer to those deficits in which students have the expected skill in their behavioural repertoire, yet they choose not to demonstrate a particular skill (e.g., managing conflict with peers or adults) due to a lack of motivation or reinforcement" (p. 439). The implication here is that if teachers can develop the knowledge and skills to properly motivate and reinforce students, the students are more likely to behave in an acceptable manner.

The Tenets of Classroom Management

The fundamental premise guiding our approach to creating exemplary learning environments is that *teachers must have the mindset that the design and management of the learning environment is an integral part of their overall teaching process.* Classroom management cannot be seen as an extra part of the teaching process or as something that is separate from "real teaching." Nor should it be viewed as something that teachers just seem to acquire either by experience or by osmosis. Good learning environments, and the proper management of all behaviours that occur in classrooms, happen by design, not by accident. Teachers who leave the management of their environment to chance have little chance of good management. It is an accident that rarely happens.

The basic ideas that support our premise are excerpted from Johnson and Edmunds's (2006) book *From Chaos to Control: Understanding and Responding to the Behaviours of Students with Exceptionalities.* These basic ideas are as follows:

- Nothing makes a classroom feel more chaotic and less psychologically secure than continually disruptive behaviours that are poorly managed.
- Not all disruptive behaviours occur for the same reason, nor do they cause the same levels of disruption.
- Most problematic behaviours can be anticipated and prepared for, while many others can be prevented altogether.

In keeping with these ideas, teachers need a two-phased approach: (1) They need to understand the causes of problematic behaviours, and (2) they need a comprehensive approach that establishes a psychologically secure environment within which they can effectively manage their classroom and encourage excellent student learning.

Phase 1—Understanding the Causes of Problematic Behaviours

Understanding why children exhibit disruptive behaviours is vital to the attitudes that teachers develop toward particular students. It prevents teachers from merely thinking of some children as "bad students" who choose to make teachers' lives miserable. Understanding the causes of misbehaviours also affects the types of interventions that teachers use to manage children. For example, let's look at two students who engage in the identical disruptive and annoying behaviour of calling out answers when they are supposed to raise their hand or wait their turn. The teacher will obviously react differently to the student who he knows is impulsive and cannot control blurting out her answers than he will to the student who has no such control problems and is merely trying to get attention. The way the teacher perceives and deals with each student will be different, but only because he has an understanding of the causes of the observed behaviour. Without this understanding, most teachers would suspect that both students were simply trying to be annoying and would deal with them in the same manner.

So what are the possible causes of behaviour problems that occur in classrooms, and what do teachers need to know? Quite simply, if we understand why a behaviour occurs, we are in a better position to do something about it. More importantly, we are much less likely to do something to exacerbate the situation. As mentioned in Chapter 3, we are not overly concerned about the causes of *learning* problems because there is little that educators can do about them. There is, however, much to be learned from the causes of *behavioural* problems. In fact, as you will see later in this chapter, in the majority of cases knowing the cause of a particular behaviour is usually the key to an effective behavioural intervention.

There are three main causes of problematic behaviour, and these apply to students with and without exceptionalities: (a) psychological causes, (b) behaviours caused by learning difficulties, and (c) behaviours caused by the learning environment. Let's explore each of these in more depth.

Psychological Causes of Behaviour Problems

Why is it that some children seem to get along well with others and some do not, even when they may be from the same family background? Why is it that some students repeatedly engage in problematic and disruptive behaviours while others only do so occasionally, or not at all? Why is it that some children engage in the same problematic behaviours over and over again despite being constantly reprimanded for these behaviours?

The Need to Be Accepted

The most accepted and widely used explanation for all of the above queries was proposed by Dreikurs and Cassel (1992) in their landmark book *Discipline without Tears*. In it they state that all children have an inherent and powerful need to be liked and accepted by others, but that some are under the illusion they can gain this much-wanted acceptance by engaging in problematic behaviour to (a) gain attention, (b) conceal inadequacy, (c) gain power or control over people or situations, or (d) exact retribution or revenge from real or perceived injuries or slights. Dreikers and Cassel suggested that teachers can improve the behaviours of such children by replacing their mistaken goals with goals that are more positive and appropriate for school settings.

Mistrust of Adults

Another perspective suggests that students are antagonistic toward adults (parents and teachers) because they have developed a strong mistrust of them and do not feel that adults have their best interests at heart (Canter & Canter, 1993). This partly explains why some children, when confronted about their behaviour, will not even comply with the smallest of demands from adults. Obviously, interventions to remedy these behaviours will have to re-establish the children's trust in the adults in their lives.

Neurological Factors

Neurological factors also play a large role in the psychological causes of problematic and disruptive behaviours frequently demonstrated by students, most of which they cannot control without precise and specific interventions. The five most common neurological factors that cause behavioural problems in classrooms are as follows:

1. Oppositional defiance (aggressive and purposefully bothers others, often loses temper, often argues with adults, often refuses to comply, often blames others for mistakes or misbehaviour)
2. Conduct disorder (same as oppositional defiance but the basic rights of others or society rules are constantly violated)
3. Inattentiveness (does not follow directions well, easily distracted, appears not to be listening, shifts from one uncompleted task to another uncompleted task)
4. Hyperactivity (fidgety, talkative, cannot sit still)
5. Impulsivity (acts instantaneously and does so without thinking of the consequences, some of which are dangerous)

The vast majority of students with oppositional defiance disorder and conduct disorder engage in so much disruptive behaviour they usually receive their education in specialized classrooms, working with teachers and para-professionals who have specialized training in behaviour management and cognitive-behavioural interventions. The last three factors are frequently associated with attention-deficit/hyperactivity disorder (ADHD) but often occur in many individuals who are not identified as having ADHD (a detailed description of ADHD can be found in Chapter 6). The problem that teachers experience when they encounter behaviours resulting from inattentiveness, hyperactivity, and impulsiveness is that *everybody* engages in them from time to time. To be classified as having a behavioural problem, however, an individual has to (a) exhibit these behaviours much more frequently, (b) display intense emotions associated with the behaviour, (c) exhibit this emotional intensity for longer-than-normal durations, and (d) mostly engage in these behaviours in completely inappropriate situations. Here is an example of the differences.

Scenario One

A child gets up in the middle of the class to sharpen his pencil and stubs his toe on the leg of a chair. Despite an instinctive attempt to be quiet and suffer in silence, he yells out, gets angry, utters a few choice words under his breath, and maybe takes a swipe at the chair, all the while trying to do so quietly. Shortly, he gets himself under control and hobbles back to his desk, hoping he has not disturbed anyone.

This scenario portrays a fairly common and acceptable way of dealing with an uncomfortable situation, despite the fact that many of the behaviours the student exhibited could be construed as problematic.

Scenario Two

Now, let's look at what typically happens to an individual with a behaviour disorder (or little self-control) who also stubs his toe. He yells out, but with little or no inhibition, and yells and curses loudly and frequently. He gets almost uncontrollably angry, topples the chair, and feels so angry for so long that he cannot get back to attending to his desk work. He intentionally disturbs everyone and has little or no consideration for their need for quiet. The remaining 40 minutes of class time are a disaster, and at the end of the class he is still going to great lengths to tell everyone about his mishap.

This scenario points out the degrees of behaviours and reactions that differentiate students with behavioural problems from those who may engage in the same behaviours, but who are not considered to have behavioural problems.

Temperament

The final contributor to psychological causes of problematic behaviour is *temperament*—a series of traits that account for the differences in the quality and intensity of individuals' emotional reactions (Berk, 1996; Thomas & Chess, 1977). Each of the following key traits operates on a continuum from low to high:

- *Activity level* (the amount of time spent in active movement)
- *Adaptability* (the ease with which one adapts to changes in the environment)
- *Rhythmicity* (the regularity of bodily functions such as eating, sleeping, and eliminating)
- *Distractibility* (how easily environmental stimulation changes one's behaviour)
- *Attention span and persistence* (the length of time one is purposefully engaged in an activity)
- *Approach/withdrawal* (the way in which one responds to new objects or people in their environment)
- *Threshold of responsiveness* (the degree of stimulation required to get a response)
- *Intensity of reaction* (the strength of one's reactions)
- *Quality of mood* (the dominant attitude or feeling one demonstrates)

Unfortunately, temperament is often omitted as a cause or contributor to problematic behaviour when addressing educational remedies, even though it is commonly discussed in the literature on early childhood. It is also conspicuously absent from the factors that account for and describe the interindividual variations that identify and classify students with exceptionalities. It may be that temperament is perceived as being too closely linked to personality and that both are considered out of line with the current thinking that embraces ecological models of special education. It may also be that three of the nine temperamental traits are identical to ADHD behaviours; therefore, the overall concept of temperament gets lost in the discussion. Nonetheless, we think temperament is an important factor to consider when dealing with students who have behavioural problems, because it is a factor that is not explained or accounted for elsewhere. More importantly, we feel that the emotional intensity described by temperament is what makes behaviours less controllable by the individual and more problematic for others to deal with. For example, in the two scenarios above, the first individual will probably be easily consoled by a teacher, parent, or peer. The second individual will likely be inconsolable, and this will make the person offering the comfort feel they have nothing to offer. After several such rejections, the offer of empathy or comfort will stop. When a student consistently displays a number of these unflattering traits at the high end of the continuum, they are typically considered a difficult child (Turecki, 2000). It should be noted that temperament tends to be universally established in childhood and is fairly stable over time but there is evidence that temperament can be changed through the practices of adults (Berk, 1996).

Before we conclude this section, we want to make it clear that the psychological factors that contribute to misbehaviour are not evidence that children are inherently bad. However, it does mean that some children have conditions that need to be clearly understood and acted upon accordingly lest teachers perceive all children's misbehaviour as wilful acts. Much of the difficulty lies in the fact that most of the above behaviours are *expected* to be positively established parts of a child's behavioural repertoire by Grade 3 or 4. If the student exhibits these behaviours beyond the age of expectation, he or she is viewed as engaging in them wilfully. Once teachers and parents think that a student's acts are wilful, they are reluctant to look for reasonable explanations, reluctant to grant lenience, and reluctant to change their own behaviour to help the child.

How Learning Difficulties Cause Behaviour Problems

Efficient learning involves properly perceiving, processing, organizing, using, storing, and retrieving information through our visual, auditory, tactile, kinesthetic, and language modes. Minor or major problems with either the way information is processed or the mode through which it is processed result in a learning difficulty. The vast majority of students with exceptionalities who participate in inclusive classrooms have learning difficulties (see the *What We Know* box), even those students who are primarily classified by behavioural criteria (i.e., emotional/behaviour disorder, ADHD, and autism). These students often become frustrated because of how difficult it is for them to learn. They also develop anxieties about the teaching and learning process because it brings unwelcome attention to their deficits and further heightens their frustrations. Therefore, many students with exceptionalities exhibit problematic behaviours as a result of the emotions associated with their struggles to learn. Johnson & Edmunds (2006, p. 2) suggested that "since many of these students do not have the conceptual, verbal, or language skills required to express their feelings, these feelings are often acted out." It is not difficult to imagine how this continued cycle of failing to learn and getting into trouble for disruptive behaviours can negatively affect a student's self-concept and self-esteem and quickly set school up to be a very unpleasant place. To prevent this from happening, one of the primary functions of the IEP process (see Chapter 3) is to have a professional assess the child's ability to learn, to describe any significant learning problems, and to suggest how teachers can alleviate or circumvent the problems so that the child can learn and perform better. This will not only affect learning but also help with disruptive behaviour.

What We Know . . .

Learning Difficulties

The most prevalent learning deficits and disorders in students with exceptionalities are as follows:

Association reactions	Involuntary body movements as reactions to the movement of other body parts.
Auditory association problems	Difficulty understanding instructions/directions as stated.

Continued

Auditory awareness problems	Difficulty responding properly to unexpected sounds, especially when embedded in background noise.
Auditory discrimination problems	Difficulty discriminating between similar sounds.
Auditory figure-ground problems	Difficulty hearing sounds over background noise.
Auditory processing problems	Difficulty understanding verbal information.
Auditory sequencing problems	Difficulty hearing sounds in the right order.
Catastrophic response	A severe reaction to simultaneous sensory overload.
Cognitive discrimination problems	Difficulty discriminating between similar concepts.
Cognitive sequencing problems	Difficulty thinking in a logical or sequential manner.
Crossing the midline	Difficulty executing tasks where body parts cross the centre of the body.
Depth perception problems	Difficulty determining how far away objects are.
Directional problems	Difficulty distinguishing directions, or directions relative to each other.
Disinhibition	Difficulty regulating one's actions despite knowing the difference.
Dyscalculia	Difficulty with numerical functions and concepts.
Dysgraphia	Difficulty expressing thoughts through writing or printing and/or writing and printing that is distorted/incorrect.
Dyslexia	Difficulty reading words or sentences and/or comprehending what was read.
Dystaxia	Difficulty speaking logically and using extended sequences of words.
Dystonia	Difficulty finding the appropriate words to express thoughts.
Immature tactile abilities	Disliking light touch and preferring heavy pressure touch.
Intersensory problems	Difficulty using multiple senses or processes at the same time.
Perceptual-motor problems	Difficulty using sensory or perceptual skills in conjunction with motor skills.
Sequential processing problems	Difficulty processing multiple pieces of information in the correct sequence.
Short-term memory problems	Difficulty holding information for short periods and retrieving as necessary.

Simultaneous processing problems	Difficulty processing multiple pieces of information at the same time.
Tactile defensiveness	Avoiding touch, usually due to an immature system.
Tactile discrimination problems	Difficulty discriminating between objects that feel similar.
Tactile pressure problems	Difficulty determining how much pressure is appropriate.
Visual discrimination problems	Difficulty seeing differences between similar objects.
Visual figure-ground problems	Difficulty seeing objects against a background.
Visual orientation problems	Difficulty determining objects that are dependent upon their orientation such as "b," "d," "p," and "q."
Visual sequencing problems	Difficulty seeing things in the correct order.

Source: Excerpted from Johnson & Edmunds (2006), pp. 4–17. Reproduced with permission of the University of Western Ontario (The Althouse Press).

Something to Think About

Consider the common learning difficulties experienced by students with exceptionalities presented above and think about how these impediments might affect a student's behaviour. As you go through the list, try to imagine how challenging it is to participate in school activities (e.g., learning how to read, taking a test, or learning a new sport) if you have one or more of these learning difficulties. Keep in mind that these problems do not usually operate as single on-off phenomena; they occur in varying degrees from very minor to severely problematic, and it is not uncommon for many students, especially those with learning disabilities, to have several of these problems concurrently.

Environmental Causes of Behaviour Problems

The psychological characteristics and learning difficulties of students with exceptionalities certainly have the potential on their own to cause persistent behaviour problems. However, an important behavioural concept to understand and embrace as a teacher is that a child's behaviour does not happen in a vacuum. Behaviours mostly occur as the result of interactions between people and in nearly all instances at school, one of those people is a teacher. *Reciprocal determinism* is the key concept in Bandura's (1977; 1986) social cognitive theory that explains this behavioural phenomenon. In short, reciprocal determinism proposes that individuals are constantly engaged in mutual and reciprocal interactions in which their cognitive, personal, and behavioural factors operate as interacting determinants of each other. In the case of teachers, their "behaviour" also includes the physical, social, and attitudinal structures they impose on the classroom environment within which each child interacts. What this really means is that student behaviour is influenced by teacher behaviour, and vice versa, and teachers cannot simply "blame" a student for bad behaviour, even though that student might be quite a handful. Instead, it means that teachers must look at how they may be playing a role in facilitating or causing disruptive behaviours. Now, before we go any further, we want to make it clear that we are definitely not blaming teachers for student misbehaviour; that would be unfair and inaccurate. However, we are saying that the teacher is the one and only person in the room who can positively control nearly all the factors that contribute to problematic behaviour and non-efficient learning environments. By exerting positive control over how a classroom operates, teachers can focus the entire class on increasing good behaviours and attitudes while diminishing bad ones. A student may exhibit behaviours that cause teachers and other students lots of grief but that student's behaviour is not going to suddenly change unless the teacher does something more than simply say, "I don't like that, please don't do it again."

In the pages that follow, we suggest a process for how you can go about creating an exemplary learning environment that is academically productive, well managed, and nearly devoid of common problematic behaviours. If you are a student-teacher, this process should be implemented when you get your first teaching assignment during your first practicum placement. Then, like everything else in teaching, the more you experiment with it and refine it, the better you will be at classroom management when you get your first full-time teaching position.

Phase 2—Establishing a Psychologically Secure Classroom

Establishing a psychologically secure environment starts the moment you say hello and welcome your students to your classroom or course. Once you have finished with attendance issues, class lists, and the obligatory explanations of your course outline (in the case of higher grade levels) or the topics to be learned, your first step is to set a positive, engaging, and determined tone that says in no uncertain terms that it is your intention that each and every student in the class will have a worthwhile and successful learning experience (see Figure 4.1). Notice that the emphasis here is first and foremost on successful learning. The rest of the process is then naturally geared toward designing concepts, attitudes, and management tools that will encourage success to happen.

> Welcome to my class.
>
> I want you to know that in this class we will all work together.
>
> Learning in this class will be fun and challenging. I want every one of you to be very successful.
>
> Let's talk about what we can do to make that happen.
>
> What do we want our classroom to look and feel like?

Figure 4.1 An invitation to students.

Excerpted from Johnson & Edmunds (2006), pp. 58–59. Reproduced with permission of the University of Western Ontario (The Althouse Press).

Dynamic Classroom Management

Teachers can establish this overall positive tone by implementing a proven behaviour management methodology such as *Dynamic Classroom Management (DCM)*, a school-wide approach to building optimal learning environments developed by Alan Edmunds (2010). The DCM approach, which operationalizes positive behavioural interventions and supports (PBIS) theory, was designed in response to Lewis and colleagues' (2006) and Brophy's (2006) calls for additional studies that design and validate classroom management interventions within a school-wide process.

What We Know . . .

PBIS Theory

PBIS is a decision-making framework that is grounded within applied behavioural analysis theory. It addresses a broad range of interrelated systems that examine the contextual factors that contribute to problematic behaviours in schools (Scott, Gagnon, & Nelson, 2008). Using PBIS, educators strive to understand what causes and sustains student misbehaviours. Rather than *de facto* punishment for bad behaviour, students and teachers identify desirable goal behaviours and develop reward structures for successful actions or words. Based on feasibility, desirability, and effectiveness, these reward systems and treatment strategies are specifically designed to have a direct impact on students' abilities to act properly in school. PBIS puts emphasis on intervention elements drawn from historically successful evidence-based practices and systemic, preventative school-wide approaches that enable accurate implementation and sustainability across multiple prevention levels (Sugai et al., 2000). These levels include primary prevention of the development and occurrence of problematic behaviours, secondary prevention through efficient and rapid response mechanisms, and tertiary prevention that reduces the intensity and complexity of escalated behaviours (Lewis et al., 2006). The most important feature of PBIS is its instructional and educational emphasis whereby behavioural expectations are clearly defined and taught to all students. Students' explicit understandings about behaviour requirements virtually eliminate the various interpretations students use to deny or abdicate their behavioural responsibilities.

Source: The Behaviour Management Network (www.edu.uwo.ca/dynamic-classroom-management).

The basis of DCM is that it requires an explicit description of all the elements that operationalize how the environment of the classroom and school will be set up and managed. It emphasizes proactive teacher-student discourses to establish classroom rules, routines, and reminder mechanisms so that explicit rules or routines do not fade. There is an intentional use of the motivational dynamics of self-regulated behaviour: making choices, considering the meaningfulness of choices, executing choices, and reflecting on action outcomes. By proactively engaging students in the design of explicit rules or routines, teachers promote student self-control and a commitment to the rules. This process impedes impulsivity and students' wilful abdication of their behavioural responsibilities. Instead of trying to inferentially change student behaviours (as intended by punishment) the DCM focus is on changing how students think about their actions. With punishment, behaviours will recur as soon as the punishment or threat is removed. However, when students are explicitly taught about and rewarded for desired behaviours, they change their thinking and wilfully change their behaviours.

DCM was developed because one of the major issues in schools is the misunderstandings that occur between educators and students because educators assume that students fully comprehend what was implicitly inferred. It is our experience that educators often fail to be explicit with students about behavioural expectations because they believe these expectations are well ingrained and understood. It is fair to say that in the absence of clearly understood messages, students often interpret messages or infer actions that directly contravene the teacher's intentions. This can happen accidentally and naively, but it can also happen purposefully, particularly if students do not want to be involved in what the teacher wants them to do. Many times students defend their disruptive or negative behaviours with variations on the following phrases: *"Well, I didn't know that's what you meant . . ."* or *"You never said that we couldn't . . ."* or *"How was I supposed to know . . ."* Unfortunately, without the teacher being explicit and clear about the rules of the classroom, these excuses can be viewed as completely valid reasons for misbehaviour, especially when parents become involved in their children's actions at school. However, if educators are explicit about establishing the behavioural parameters of their classrooms and their schools, these phrases become indefensible excuses in light of the mutually agreed-upon rules posted in the classroom and in the non-teaching spaces.

The steps involved in implementing the DCM approach in a school appear in Figure 4.2. First, *all* adults in the school (administrators, teachers, secretaries, custodians, supply teachers, etc.) attend a one-day in-service that focuses on student behaviour and the DCM approach. These adults learn about ways to encourage and support desired student behaviours. Next, there is a DCM implementation period that starts with a school-wide assembly to introduce the DCM concept to students. Upon return to their classrooms, teachers and students engage in discourses as they work together to establish classroom rules, rewards, and consequences. Eventually, all classroom rules are posted, and the administrators are made aware of the rules in each classroom. In addition, during this start-up phase, teachers develop the rules for non-teaching spaces (e.g., hallways, yard, and gym) and parents are invited to the school to learn about DCM. Everyone works together to provide a united approach. Finally, once DCM is implemented across the entire school, the administrators and staff make a concerted effort to evaluate the effectiveness of the approach on a regular basis. This provides an opportunity for modifications as needed.

DCM is conceptually consistent with current notions of classroom management and effective learning because it places the teacher in a proactive mode of purposefully managing education rather than in a disciplinary mode that reacts to educational occurrences (Paintal, 1999). Yes, this process will take some time and effort to implement at the beginning of the school year or semester. However, over the long term it will pay multiple dividends for teachers and students because it allows more class time to be spent on learning activities, it reduces the time spent on non-goal-directed activities, and it prevents the day-to-day operation of the classroom from becoming a competition between the desires of the teacher and the non-complementary actions of students. The DCM approach is an example of how to set the stage for exemplary learning and good classroom management, and it is designed to be easily implemented by all teachers, in all classrooms, and with all students.

TRAINING

↓

One-day in-service on DCM attended by all school staff.

IMPLEMENTATION

↓

School assembly to introduce DCM to all students.

↓

Teachers and students return to classrooms to develop rules as well as rewards and consequences.

↓

Wall of Rules posted in each classroom.

↓

Administrators visit each classroom for presentation of rules by students
(a copy of the rules/rewards/consequences from each classroom kept in office).

↓

Rules/rewards/consequences for non-teaching spaces are determined by staff.

↓

Parents are informed about the DCM approach.

EVALUATION

↓

DCM is discussed at every staff meeting.

↓

Five-week and five-month follow-ups to determine effectiveness of DCM.

Figure 4.2 Dynamic Classroom Management (DCM).

Adapted from Edmunds & Edmunds (2015).

Designing the Class Rules

When using an approach like DCM, we suggest that the classroom rules be first conceptualized through small group discussion and then solidified during an open forum that is facilitated by you, the teacher. Within reason, every aspect of classroom functioning should be open for discussion. This process is known as *participatory decision making* (Lickona, 1987), a collective process among teachers and students that holds students accountable for decisions that influence the quality of classroom life. This means not only being part of the rule making, but also being genuinely involved in the welfare of the classroom and taking responsibility for the actions of all students. At this time, it is worth sharing with students the four principles for establishing classroom rules (Weinstein, 1997):

1. Rules should be reasonable and necessary.
2. Rules should be clear and comprehensible.
3. Rules should be consistent with instructional goals.
4. Classroom rules should be consistent with the school rules.

During the rule-making session, you should also make students acutely aware of the global rules that cannot be changed because they are basic rules designed for school-wide implementation (see "The Big Five" below). This enables students to situate their own rules accordingly and in a complementary fashion. When explaining your global non-negotiable rules to the students, it is best to limit the number of rules that are black or white, or absolute, as these are often perceived as unreasonable or inflexible. However, you may find that some absolutes are necessary. We have provided five global rules, referred to in DCM as "The Big Five," that we suggest you incorporate as a package. In the case of DCM, "The Big Five" are applied school-wide. In other words, they are the starting point in every classroom. Usually, the students in each classroom then add three to four of their own rules to this list.

The Big Five

Rule #1: All our rules will be fair and reasonable and democratically decided upon.
While this is not really a rule *per se*, it serves as a necessary guideline for the entire DCM approach. Being the first rule in "The Big Five," it facilitates a discussion on what is meant by "fair and reasonable." It also prompts a conversation about how the democratic process can work in a classroom.

Rule #2: No disrespect.
An excellent classroom rule is that there will be zero tolerance for disrespectful statements and behaviours, even if they are meant or delivered in a teasing fashion. The two main reasons for this rule are simple: (a) Disrespect in any form is the antithesis of the collective, collaborative, and co-operative intentions of DCM, and (b) there is no positive or constructive rationale for disrespectful behaviour.

Rule #3: Hands off.
One of the most common causes of problematic student behaviour is unwanted touching. Therefore, it is necessary to have a mandatory rule that makes it clear there will be no touching others and no touching things that belong to others. With younger students, it is important to discuss this rule in detail (e.g., what is acceptable and what is not).

Rule #4: Lots of talking.
Another popular and effective global rule is designed to avoid the following common teacher expression, "Aargghh! They never listen to me!" which is usually heard after repeated instances of students talking and not paying attention to the teacher. The discussion about this

rule should go something like this: "There are times when I will ask you to pay attention to me and I would like you to do so. I understand that you like and want to talk to each other, and I think it is a good idea that you do. Therefore, let's agree that you are allowed to talk at a reasonable level unless I am teaching or giving directions or you are writing a test." This approach allows for a reasonable amount of quiet talking when appropriate, yet it restricts student-to-student discussions (disruptions) when the teacher is providing instruction or when students are engaged in work that must be completed individually (e.g., tests). It is a reasonable rule and it conveys the message to students that there is a rationale as to why the teacher will ask for their attention.

Rule #5: The principal will be aware of all classroom rules. The principal will support good behaviour and deal with bad behaviour according to the rules of the classroom and school.

This rule, which like Rule #1 serves to deliver an important guideline of DCM, makes it clear to students that the entire set of class rules will be shared with the principal so that he or she knows how the classroom is supposed to function. The principal is given a copy of these rules, along with the decided upon rewards and consequences, so that when a student is sent to the office because of misbehaviour, there is no question about what rule was broken and what the consequence must be.

The reason for a particular rule should be made clear to students, as in Rule #4 that requires students to refrain from talking when the teacher is providing instruction or when students are engaged in work that must be completed individually.

Something to Think About

As you begin to understand and appreciate the benefits of Dynamic Classroom Management, recall from your own school years the problems that arose in classrooms when teachers did not use an approach such as this. Consider how these problems could have been rectified using DCM. What rules would you have suggested for your classroom, both in elementary school and secondary school?

Designing Consequences and Rewards

It makes little sense for a teacher and a class of students to go through the effort of designing a set of rules for their classroom if they fail to decide upon the rewards for following the rules and the consequences that will occur if the rules are broken. Rewards, whether self-awarded or awarded by others, satisfy our base psychological motivation to experience a positive outcome from both striving toward and accomplishing desirable behavioural goals. Consequences, whether self-imposed or imposed by others, fulfill our understanding that we have to be accountable for our behaviours.

The key here is to allow the students to assume responsibility for the process and its outcomes, as the research has consistently shown that this increases students' commitment to schooling. The most straightforward way of determining both rewards for adherence and the consequences for non-adherence is to do it during the open forum when the rules are selected. The students should complete the following phrases for each rule:

- *A reasonable and fair reward for adhering to this rule is . . .*
- *A reasonable and fair consequence for breaking this rule is . . .*

Both the rewards and consequences have to be meaningful. To determine this, simply ask the students what they want or do not want. By having a serious discussion with them about their preferences, you will quickly determine which rewards and consequences will be effective. If you are in doubt, make suggestions, maybe even outlandish suggestions or modifications to their suggestions. Your students will quickly let you know whether your suggestions are acceptable. Once you have collectively decided what they will be, make it clear that the rewards and consequences are not fixed; they will be reviewed periodically, or at the request of either the students or the teacher.

We strongly recommend that teachers do not in any way assign any form of school work or learning exercise as a consequence for misbehaviour. Practices such as assigning extra written work; handing out more, longer, or more complex assignments or tests; or doling out academic penalties for social misbehaviours are inappropriate. These practices are unfairly punitive and they undermine the productive climate you are trying to create. It also gives your students the message that all their efforts to learn can be for naught if their behaviour is in question. If students have contravened the social contract of the group, they should encounter consequences that are suitable and appropriate.

Enforcing the Class Rules

While it is preferred that the teacher engage students in collectively establishing the rules of the classroom, it always falls to the teacher to enforce the rules. As part of the collective rule-making process, teachers should explicitly state this fact and explain how they will immediately and consistently enforce the rules. When students are clear about what to expect, their psychological security is enhanced and their anxiety about being in a potentially problematic classroom is reduced.

By immediately and consistently enforcing the agreed-upon rules of the classroom, you also send a message to your students that you are concerned for their overall welfare and you are willing to act upon your convictions. Let's take, for example, the zero tolerance rule for disrespectful behaviour mentioned above. If you use this rule, and we highly recommend that you do, you first have to recognize that if students were disrespectful before the rule was agreed upon, they will probably continue to be disrespectful after the rule is initially enacted, although hopefully less so. Take the time to point out and correct infractions as soon as they occur. It may take one or two days of immediate and consistent corrections by a teacher to get things under control and to establish an overall effect, but this approach will heighten students' awareness of disrespectful behaviours and therefore the behaviours are more likely to be extinguished. Because of the class-wide agreement that disrespectful behaviour will not be tolerated, all students will soon be vigilant about contravening behaviours, and there is no better way to eliminate an obnoxious behaviour than through collective peer pressure supported by a teacher who acts immediately. Students quickly become accountable to each other and they realize there is no refuge among their peers if they step out of line and disobey class rules.

We hope that, by now, you have realized that the intent of DCM is to foster within students an ability to self-regulate their classroom behaviour. Nothing is more tiring or annoying for teachers than playing the role of "police officer"; it quickly becomes frustrating to have to constantly be on alert for disruptive behaviour and to constantly battle such behaviour. It is both good educational practice and good self-preservation to divest some of this responsibility to students through a self-regulated behavioural approach like Dynamic Classroom Management. DCM has been proven to promote self-control and commitment and to impede impulsive behaviour.

What We Know . . .

Self-Regulation

According to McCaslin and colleagues (2006), social cognitive theoretical perspective guides much of the research that is done on self-regulated learning and classroom management. They contend that effective behavioural strategies are acquired by methods that are applied to the self by the self. This includes self-monitoring, self-instruction, self-evaluation, self-correction, and self-reinforcement. Ultimately, the goal is to transfer teacher control of student behaviour to student control of their own behaviour. They also point out that what might be an ideal self-regulated learner from a teacher's perspective might not be optimal for students. Therefore, approaches that allow teachers and learners to negotiate the amount of self-regulation are preferred.

This negotiation can include, but is not limited to, the following practices:

1. Providing opportunities for students to make choices, reflect on those choices, and render the personally meaningful experiences and outcomes that accompany them
2. Facilitating student processing of behavioural information that is mediated by mnemonics, cues, or rules
3. Providing a mixture of realistic learning opportunities—not all tasks are interesting and not all classmates are helpful—so that students can learn to persevere, see through, and follow through on commitments
4. Modelling and providing feedback and reinforcement so that students can learn the subprocesses of self-observation, self-judgment, and self-reaction
5. Providing multi-dimensional classrooms so that students can realize their identity and commensurate responsibility within the class
6. Acknowledging that students will not change their behavioural approach without help
7. Initiating a process that explains the reasoning behind the teacher's expectations and goals and teaches students to do the same goes far in promoting the internalization and enactment of desired student behaviour and disposition

Source: McCaslin et al. (2006).

Behaviour Problem Solving

Implementing an approach like DCM does not mean that all behaviour problems in the classroom will be eliminated. There will still be misbehaviours that must be dealt with. We illustrate the six-step problem-solving model in Figure 4.3 because it is consistent with the proactive tenets of DCM and especially because it puts the onus on the student to acknowledge there is a problem and that he or she will be part of the solution. This is a far better system than those systems that put the onus on the teacher to remind the student of the rules that were broken and to be the only one who has a vested interest in the solution. Each step is accompanied by its underlying message.

1. **STOP!! What is the problem we are having?**

   This indicates that there is an inconsistency between what the teacher expects and what the student is doing.

2. **Which of our rules is being broken?**

   This forces the student to acknowledge that there are rules that everyone agreed upon and that he or she broke one of them.

3. **What did we agree would be the consequence(s) for breaking this rule?**

   This forces the student to acknowledge that the consequences were also collectively agreed to, and that the consequences are just and fair.

4. **What can we do about it?**

   This sends the message that the student will have to do something as a result of his or her actions but that the teacher is supportive and will not belittle him or her.

5. **Let's do what we have decided.**

   This sends the message that the consequence has been mutually decided on or agreed to and that there is a plan of action.

6. **Let's check in later and see how we did.**

   This indicates that there will be supportive follow-up.

Figure 4.3 Six steps to behaviour problem solving.

These problem-solving steps are effective at resolving most issues, but there comes a time in every teacher's career when things get so out of hand in the classroom that conventional approaches are not effective and they need support from the principal. Therefore, the final phase of proactively enforcing your rules is having a back-up plan. Like the rest of your overall approach, you should explicitly convey this plan to your students, rather than leaving it unsaid. The following is an example of how you might inform your students of your intentions:

There probably will come a time when I will have tried everything I can to resolve a behavioural problem, or it may be that too much time has been spent on a disciplinary issue, and we need to move along. In those instances, I will ask you to go see the principal. The principal and I have an understanding that when I send you to see him or her, it is because you will not agree to help me resolve the issue and that he/she

will handle it from this point on. As you know, the principal is aware of all our class-
room rules, rewards, and consequences.

This message conveys to your students that you are proactive in your approach to managing your classroom, as opposed to unprepared and reactive.

Often, teachers fail to properly plan for a student's return to the classroom after a visit to the principal's office. In Figure 4.4, we suggest a set of elements to be included in a plan to facilitate this transition.

---

1. **The teacher and the principal will confer about what transpired.**

   This ensures that everyone involved knows what happened and what was done about it.

2. **The teacher indicates to the student that he or she is welcome back into the class.**

   This diminishes the student's feelings of isolation and rejection.

3. **The student has a private conversation with the teacher and they go over the six steps in the behaviour problem-solving model.**

   This refocuses the student's attention on the importance of the issue rather than the punishment (we suggest that teachers facilitate this by stating something similar to, "I really like you but I don't like what you did").

4. **The teacher indicates that he or she is confident that the student will govern himself or herself better from now on.**

   This reconfirms the student's sense that he or she can do it and reconfirms the teacher's expectation that it will be done.

5. **The teacher makes it clear that he or she will be keeping an eye on the student to see how well he or she is doing.**

   This re-establishes normal classroom operations but does not make the student feel picked on.

6. **A very short timeline is set (1–2 days maximum) to review how things are going.**

   This allows the student a chance to behave appropriately and be acknowledged by the teacher; it also provides another opportunity to review the class rules together.

Figure 4.4 Planning for re-entry.

Now that you understand the Dynamic Classroom Management approach, the next step is to consider how your actions will affect your classroom as a whole, and students with exceptionalities in particular.

How DCM Affects the Classroom Environment

It is necessary to carefully examine the effects the DCM approach has on actual classroom environments to fully appreciate its merits. The outcomes described below are consistent with the elements of productive learning environments detailed in one of the most comprehensive books available on the subject, the *Handbook of Classroom Management: Research, Practice and Contemporary Issues* (Evertson & Weinstein, 2006).

Nothing compromises teaching and learning more, and causes additional behaviour problems, than classrooms that are unpredictable, unstructured, or without established routines. A lack of predictability, structure, and routine makes classrooms feel chaotic, seriously undermining the psychological security required for good learning. Worse still, students experiencing chaotic classrooms easily become agitated and frustrated and are likely to engage in problematic behaviours, which, in turn, further contributes to the state of chaos. On the other hand, a teacher who implements an approach like DCM, and explicitly spells out and demonstrates how his or her classroom will operate on a daily or class-by-class basis, will leave no doubt about the logistical efficiency of the environment, especially if students participate in its planning and management. This systematic approach enhances the psychological security of all students. It also reduces the likelihood of problematic behaviours being exhibited by students who can easily become confused or overstimulated by a frantic and chaotic environment. Furthermore, a greater sense of overall predictability allows students to easily adjust to, and cope with, minor changes to a classroom's structure. Psychological security also increases students' confidence about accomplishing learning activities, and it increases their willingness to take on new learning risks. This is an important factor because many acting-out behaviours are due to the anxieties that many students with exceptionalities experience when asked to engage in learning new material. They do not want to risk failing (again!), so they will do anything to avoid the task, even if they might be successful, and even if avoidance gets them into trouble.

What We Know . . .

The Effectiveness of Dynamic Classroom Management

DCM has been implemented and evaluated in many elementary and secondary schools. This has allowed the researchers to adjust and fine-tune the approach under real-world educational conditions. Teacher, administrator, and student data has consistently revealed the following:

- Demonstrable improvements in student behaviours as measured by teacher ratings of existing baseline (pre-intervention) behaviours
- Demonstrable reductions in office referrals as measured by administrator ratings and comparisons with log book data from previous years
- Heightened student awareness of the negative impact of problematic behaviour as measured by teacher and student interviews
- Overall enhancements of the tone of classrooms and schools as measured by administrator ratings

According to Edmunds (2010), the DCM approach was successfully implemented school-wide in an urban elementary school. Eight weeks after an intervention that included a school-wide behavioural analysis and two days of professional development, teachers and administrators reported a sustained reduction of negative behaviours in all classrooms and the necessity for fewer disciplinary actions by teachers and administrators. Administrators reported a 90 per cent reduction in office referrals.

Edmunds, Edmunds, and Hogarth (2012) reported that DCM was successfully implemented in another urban elementary school. This school was chosen because it had a history of significant behaviour problems. After five months of implementation, administrators reported a 41 per cent reduction in suspensions and a 46 per cent reduction in office referrals. Over 70 per cent of teachers indicated that students were more respectful, better at resolving conflicts, better at following rules, and better at helping others.

Source: Edmunds (2010); Edmunds, Edmunds, & Hogarth (2012).

Structure Must Also Be Applied to the Curricula

It is not enough that the organizational structure of the room be predictable, structured, and routine. It is also important that the presentation of the curricula have the same overall sense of structure, moving logically and systematically from general knowledge to more complex ideas, and from concrete examples to more conceptual and abstract portrayals. Just as the organizational function of each day supports good learning, so too does a step-wise progression of the curricula. A curriculum that is presented in a haphazard manner and is not thematic or interconnected in its design will only decrease psychological security and learning efficiency and increase problematic behaviours. This is true for all students, but especially true for students with exceptionalities. However, when both the classroom and the curricula are managed together in a systematized way, teachers are said to have an integrative management approach to their classroom (George, 1991).

How DCM Affects Students with Exceptionalities

In this chapter, we have purposefully not included specific interventions that teachers can use to remedy the particular behavioural problems that students with exceptionalities may display. This is because each child and his or her circumstance is unique, thus making it difficult to explain and prescribe effective interventions for all the possibilities. Nonetheless, in this chapter we do provide several interventions that all teachers can use to manage the majority of student misbehaviours that happen in inclusive classrooms, including the behaviours of students with exceptionalities.

Regarding classroom management and students with exceptionalities, there are three very important issues that need to be addressed. The first concerns the ability or inability of students with exceptionalities to participate in the DCM process. Based on the prevalence of students with exceptionalities in inclusive classrooms, the vast majority will have the cognitive and behavioural abilities to participate in this process. Those whose cognitive or behavioural conditions prohibit full participation can still do so to the best of their abilities or where appropriate. And, of course, they will still benefit from the overall structured and peaceful environment that is created in the classroom.

The second issue concerns the behavioural interventions that will be required for students with exceptionalities whose behaviours are beyond the control of the regular classroom teacher. Most of these students will not be in regular classrooms. For those who *are* in regular classrooms, they will likely have IEPs that clearly delineate their atypical behaviours along with a specifically designed *behavioural intervention plan* (BIP) that suggests remedies for these behaviours (BIPS are described in the next section of this chapter). These students will also likely be accompanied in class by educational assistants who are trained to aid and support them.

The last issue is that, unfortunately, students with exceptionalities will probably engage in more instances of disruptive behaviour than other students, and they will probably be more disturbed by the disruptive behaviours of others. Each of these situations will restrict their learning, negatively affect their sense of well-being, and, in the case of students who have behavioural and emotional problems, exacerbate their inabilities to manage their emotions and inherent misbehaviours. In this sense, these students are considerably *at risk*, a term used to describe students whose circumstances make them susceptible to developing a particular problem or disability. Whelan (1995) has suggested that if the external and internal stresses exerted on a person are great enough, they are at risk for developing extreme behaviours or an emotional disorder. While the primary objective of the DCM approach is to create and sustain a productive learning environment for all students, there is no doubt that students with exceptionalities will benefit most from this approach.

Behaviour Analysis for Effective Intervention of Significant Behaviour Problems

There are times when the DCM approach will not be successful in eliminating behaviour problems. This is most often the case when behaviour problems have more significant underlying causes. Let's consider an example.

A student has been observed hitting a classmate on several occasions despite reminders of the class rules and having to suffer the consequences of breaking those rules. In order to stop this recurring behaviour, the teacher needs to know why the child is hitting his classmate so that she can design a behaviour intervention plan. If she does not carefully examine what consistently happens before, during, and after the student's hitting behaviour, she is forced to guess about its cause. At best, she is likely to be ineffective in her choice of intervention; at worst she will exacerbate the situation.

What We Know . . .

Responding to Problematic Behaviour

When a student constantly and consistently engages in disruptive and problematic behaviours, educators need to respond appropriately. This is such a concern in the United States that they have laws (i.e., IDEA) dictating that school professionals must use precise and systematic procedures to document and analyze behaviour in order to intervene. The two specific processes that are required are a functional behaviour assessment (FBA) and a behaviour intervention plan (BIP):

- A *functional behaviour assessment* is a multi-faceted strategy used to determine the reasons why behaviours occur (their function) and within what situations (their context).

- A *behaviour intervention plan* is a series of strategies that are used to change problematic behaviour.

The FBA/BIP process is slightly differently across jurisdictions, but the basic steps are as follows:

1. Identify and prioritize the problem behaviours and the settings in which they occur.
2. Directly observe and record data about the behaviours (this is often done using the *ABC* technique where *A* stands for the antecedents of the behaviour, *B* stands for the behaviour, and *C* stands for the consequences that result from the behaviour).
3. Collate all other relevant data and analyze the data to determine the function of the behaviour.
4. Design a behaviour intervention plan to deal with the behaviour and change it.
5. Set a trial period after which the intervention will be evaluated.

You may be thinking that this is an awful lot to expect from an already busy teacher, and many teachers have asked how they can conduct a functional behaviour assessment (FBA) if they do not have the luxury of observers in their classes who can perform this task. The simplest method is to make a small and simple one-page chart that you keep close by when teaching the student in question. The chart lists, in point form, (a) the problematic behaviour, (b) any of your own ideas about what might be causing the behaviour, (c) a list of the different environments that the behaviour could possibly happen in, and (d) any of your own ideas as to why the student may be performing the behaviour. Unless you have some experience doing this, we strongly suggest that you focus on only one behaviour at a time, preferably on the one that is most problematic. When the behaviour occurs you simply and quickly place a check mark next to the conditions on your chart that were observable or present. After several instances of the behaviour (and this may only take minutes, or it could take days), you will have some hard data to help you figure out what is going on.

Let's look at how conducting an FBA resulted in a BIP that effectively resolved the scenario of the student who was constantly hitting a classmate for no apparent reason. Prior to implementing the FBA/BIP process, the teacher had tried many disciplinary interventions with the student, all of which were unsuccessful and made the teacher more frustrated. The student was defiant during many of these disciplinary exchanges, and the victim was anxious, constantly felt threatened, and had complained to his parents who urged the principal and the teacher to do something about it.

By systematically documenting what happened before, during, and after the behaviour, the teacher quickly realized that the child only hit his classmate when he moved about the classroom and that he did it mostly for attention, both from the victim and from the teacher. Although the hitter did seem to enjoy having power over his victim (who did not retaliate or tell the teacher), gaining power was eliminated as a cause for the behaviour when the teacher noticed that the child only hit his peer when there was a likelihood that he would be caught, such as when both of the students were in the classroom and when the teacher's attention was only slightly diverted. The teacher also noted that the hitting behaviour did not occur outside the classroom or within the classroom when the teacher was not present (this information was gathered from other students, teachers, and a lunch-room monitor). Once the function of the behaviour was clear, it was simply a matter of using an appropriate intervention to address and change the behaviour. The teacher's BIP had four components that were implemented during a time when the student had not committed the behaviour. This was done to avoid the emotion and attention that an immediate action on the part of the teacher would cause for both parties. The four components of the BIP were as follows:

1. The teacher outlined the problem behaviour and explained the rule it broke and required an acknowledgement of both from the student.
2. The teacher explained that the problematic behaviour was the reason why the child would now be seated immediately opposite the teacher's desk and that the teacher would be keeping an eye on him whenever he moved about the room.
3. The teacher made a point of quietly reminding the student to not engage in the hitting behaviour whenever he got up to move around.
4. The teacher commended the student for his appropriate behaviour.

Not surprisingly, because the student received the attention he wanted, and positive attention at that, it took only one 40-minute class before the behaviour stopped altogether. The student had replaced seeking negative attention from both the victim and the teacher with a positive behaviour, conducting himself appropriately so he could be affirmed by the teacher.

Incorporating the FBA and BIP in the IEP Process

A variety of techniques and strategies are used by educators to identify the reasons for specific student behaviours. In the more serious cases, these data are provided to the school-based team so that appropriate interventions can be selected. This FBA is included in the initial stages of IEP development and functions as an integral component in the reviewing and revising of a student's IEP.

To be most effective, the FBA must look beyond the actual behaviour. The focus should be on identifying any and all factors that may be influencing the specific behaviour that needs correcting, before and after it occurs. This comprehensive analysis of what else is going on in the student's world provides a more complete understanding of what is driving a student's behaviour. With this level of understanding, a BIP can then address "why" a student engages in problematic behaviours, not just provide evidence that problematic behaviours occur. In combination, properly conducted FBAs and well-designed BIPs have been proven effective in addressing a wide range of problematic student behaviours.

The following is a summary of the six steps involved in conducting a formal FBA. A detailed explanation of all of the intricacies of each step can be found at http://csesa.fpg.unc .edu/sites/csesa.fpg.unc.edu/files/ebpbriefs/FBA_Steps_0.pdf. In Steps 1 and 2, the school-based team identifies and defines the problem student behaviour. The more specific this identification and definition process is, the better the resulting assessment/diagnosis will be, and the more likely it will be that the BIP works. In Step 3, the team reviews all available information from all relevant sources, such as school records and information from parents, other students, teachers, administrators, and anyone else who can provide objective observations of the specific student in various settings. Next (Step 4), the team analyzes all the data to determine the probable function/reason for the behaviour and chooses a course of action. If the team has accurately identified the correct behaviour and its purpose and has provided an appropriate intervention, the student's behaviour will improve. In some instances, however, this does not happen and the team must collect and analyze more and different types of data to better discern the cause of the problem behaviour (Step 5). In Step 6, the team develops a BIP and tests and evaluates their approach. It is conceptually beneficial to think of the BIP as a parallel document to the IEP. Both of these are student-specific intervention documents that result from a careful assessment of a child's situation; the FBA and BIP processes deal with the behavioural domain, while the assessment and IEP processes deal with learning issues.

Summary

The purpose of this chapter was to provide you with a functional and practical method of setting up your classroom so it is conducive to exemplary learning. The Dynamic Classroom Management approach involves being explicit about behavioural expectations and systematically planning and managing behavioural variables so that academic excellence can be achieved. We are convinced that teachers who invite students to participate in learning in this manner serve all students well, but we are even more convinced that the creation of psychologically secure environments are most beneficial for students with exceptionalities.

Learning More about Exemplary Learning Environments

American Psychological Association: Classroom Management

www.apa.org/education/k12/classroom-mgmt.aspx
APA offers teacher modules on different aspects of classroom management, including why classroom management works and developmental differences.

Dr. Mac's Amazing Behavior Management Advice Site

www.behavioradvisor.com
This site offers thousands of tips on managing student behaviour and provides step-by-step directions for implementing a great number of standard interventions. It also contains a bulletin board on which you can post your disciplinary concerns and receive intervention suggestions from teachers around the world.

National Association of Special Education Teachers—Classroom Management Series

www.naset.org/783.0.html
NASET provides a series of articles on classroom management that provide teachers with practical guidelines on a variety of topics that help improve learning environments.

PBIS-SCP Canada

https://pbisscpcanada.wordpress.com
This site was designed as a place where individuals at all levels of the positive behaviour interventions and supports process can communicate and collaborate with each other and access relevant research-based resources to support their efforts.

Teacher Vision—Behavior Management Resources

www.teachervision.com/teaching-strategies/behavior-management
This resource website provides numerous articles that will help you manage your classroom. It includes veteran teachers' tips and advice on establishing rules and incorporating effective behaviour techniques.

The Behaviour Management Network

www.edu.uwo.ca/dynamic-classroom-management
This network is devoted to a classroom management approach developed by the authors of this textbook. It includes information about Dynamic Classroom Management as well as the resources needed to implement this approach in both elementary and secondary schools.

The Teacher's Guide—Classroom Management

www.theteachersguide.com/classroommanagement.htm#Classroom_Management_Strategies
The Teacher's Guide provides links to ideas, strategies, and tools for better behaviour management in the classroom.

CHAPTER 5
Students with Specific Learning Disorders

LEARNING OBJECTIVES

After learning the material in this chapter, you should be able to:

- Define the term *learning disability* and explain how it relates to the term *specific learning disorder*.

- Describe how a student is identified as having a specific learning disorder and discuss the use of responsiveness-to-intervention (RTI) in the identification process.

- Discuss the causes of learning disabilities and the effects these disabilities can have on a child's development.

- Define the term *assistive technology* and discuss how technology can assist students who have learning disabilities.

- Outline teaching strategies that can be used to help students who have learning problems with reading, writing, and math.

- Define the term *learning strategy* and provide an example of a learning strategy that may help a student who has a particular learning disability.

- Define the term *attention-deficit/hyperactivity disorder* (ADHD) and discuss how it is related to learning disabilities.

- Define the term *non-verbal learning disorder* and outline common characteristics exhibited by students who have this disability.

- Define the term *dyslexia* and discuss the learning difficulties that may result from this learning disability.

- Discuss the importance of understanding one's learning difficulties, and the success attributes of individuals with learning disabilities.

Name: Karl Hildebrandt

Current Age: 11

School: St. Paul's Elementary School

Grade: 5

Karl is a well-spoken student who has a flair for the arts.

He is especially interested in drama and takes part in theatrical productions both in school and in the community. Upon first meeting Karl, you might not suspect that he has learning difficulties. He is highly social and is quite comfortable when conversing with others, especially adults. However, if you were to observe him in the classroom, you would quickly recognize that he has problems with reading, spelling, and math. He is certainly like many other students who have learning disabilities in that he has a complex pattern of cognitive strengths and weaknesses. Karl's early experiences in the regular classroom provide an example of how early elementary teachers can be somewhat hesitant to identify a child as possibly having a learning disability. It is only when the child enters the middle elementary grades, a time when reading and writing expertise is required in all subject areas, that teachers become more concerned about increasingly obvious deficits.

Assessment Results

Age at Time of Assessment: 8 years, 11 months

Test	Percentile
Wechsler Intelligence Scale for Children, 4th Edition	
Full Scale IQ	82nd
Verbal Comprehension Index	82nd
Perceptual Reasoning Index	79th
Object Assembly	63rd
Working Memory Index	68th
Processing Speed	66th
Woodcock–Johnson III Tests of Achievement	
Broad Reading Cluster	17th
Basic Reading Skills	22nd
Math Calculation Skills	20th
Applied Problems	53rd
Writing Samples	92nd
Writing Fluency	69th
Spelling	8th
Academic Knowledge	72nd
Comprehensive Test of Phonological Processing	
Phonological Awareness	73rd
Phonological Memory	84th
Rapid Naming	89th
Wide Range Assessment of Memory and Learning	
Story Memory	98th
Picture Memory	75th
Design Memory	84th
Verbal Learning	25th
The Beery–Buktenica Developmental Test of Visual-Motor Integration	
Visual-Motor Integration	39th
Visual Perception	34th
Motor Coordination	47th

Karl Hildebrandt

Assessment Summary

Age at Time of Assessment: 8 years, 11 months

The results of Karl's psycho-educational assessment present a complex pattern of cognitive strengths and weaknesses. First and most importantly, Karl is a student with above-average cognitive abilities. In addition to his strong intellect, he is also a hard-working, motivated student who has a positive attitude toward learning. Most of the cognitive skills measured were equally strong, such as phonological processing, learning sound-symbol associations, and many different types of memory (visual, verbal, working or short-term, phonological). Academic strengths were noted in his general academic knowledge and his ability to write detailed, meaningful sentences when errors in punctuation, spelling, and grammar were not penalized. Karl's visual and motor integration skills were in the average range with visual perception and motor coordination also in the average range.

Karl has some difficulties within the areas of academic skills assessed. Reading skills for decoding, fluency, and comprehension were in the low-average range. Spelling was well below average and basic math facts or calculation skills were low-average. When math problems were read aloud to him, Karl was able to solve math problems at an age-appropriate level. Karl does better when he is given a richer context for information to be embedded in. For example, his memory of stories was stronger than his memory for a list of numbers. The context of math problems seemed to help him arrive at correct answers more easily than when he was asked to simply complete rote calculation questions.

Karl seems to have attention-related difficulties as noted in the information collected from his parents and teachers. Given Karl's learning difficulties, it is likely that these attention-related behaviours are secondary to his learning.

There is a significant discrepancy between Karl's full scale IQ and his academic achievement in reading, spelling, and math (1.7 to 2.4 standard deviations). What is not clear is what is causing this discrepancy. At this time, it would appear that perceptual skills, such as his visual and motor integration skills, are affecting his reading and spelling, and to a lesser extent, mathematics. These difficulties are consistent with a diagnosis of a learning disability or learning disorder.

Karl's Strengths and Challenges

Strengths	Challenges
positive attitude toward learning	difficulty with reading
above-average cognitive abilities	difficulty with spelling
hard worker	difficulty with mathematics
verbally expressive	can be hyperactive and impulsive
good general knowledge	not well organized
creative	
artistic	

Teachers' Reports

Ms. Yoon (Kindergarten)

Karl has made excellent progress in learning to read. He knows all the letters of the alphabet in and out of sequence, he is able to read familiar personal words, he can identify words with the same beginning sound, and he attempts to spell words using knowledge of beginning, middle, and final consonants. Karl is also doing well in the area of mathematics. He can count beyond 30, solve addition and subtraction problems greater than five, identify patterns, and complete seatwork with no difficulties. Karl does need some reminders to follow instructions and to stay focused on activities. He also needs to develop his listening skills and learn when it is appropriate to express his opinions.

Mr. King (Grade 3)

Karl's marks have dropped somewhat from the marks he received in Grade 2. He is now receiving mostly Cs in English and mathematics. His written work tends to be short with few complex ideas and details. However, his reading aloud has improved, and he demonstrates good qualities in oral presentations (e.g., eye contact, voice quality). In mathematics, he might perform better if he were to re-read problems to ensure comprehension. He also needs to review his basic facts, concepts, and skills. I am concerned about his inattentiveness and lack of co-operation. He needs to wait his turn to speak.

Mrs. McCarthy (Grade 5)

The implementation of recommendations contained in Karl's IEP has lead to an improvement in his reading and writing skills. He shows a general understanding of the reading material presented and connects ideas that he includes in written responses. He should continue to read every night with an adult to improve fluency and comprehension. I am encouraging Karl to continue to revise and edit his written work carefully using available technology and his spelling wordbook. Karl is also doing well in mathematics. His solutions to problems are usually accurate with minor errors and omissions. He should remember to include appropriate symbols, labels, or units in all calculations. Karl continues to excel in music, visual arts, and drama.

Karl usually works and plays co-operatively with others and usually listens to, acknowledges, and considers differing opinions. He demonstrates a positive attitude toward learning and persists with tasks. Karl worked hard this term and he has shown improvement in homework completion.

Karl Hildebrandt

Excerpt from Karl's IEP

Student: Karl Hildebrandt

Current Grade: 5

Subject Area: English Language

Current Level of Achievement*:

| Reading | Level 3 within the expectations for Grade 4 |
| Writing | Level 2 within the expectations for Grade 4 |

Annual Program Goal*:

| Reading | Level 2 within the expectations for Grade 5 |
| Writing | Level 3 within the expectations for Grade 4 |

TERM 1:

Learning Expectations	Teaching Strategies	Methods for Assessments
Writing		
Spell words correctly	Encourage Karl to use personal word lists of difficult words and book for Everyday Writers.	Note frequency of spelling errors in daily work. Spelling tests.
Reduce letter reversals	Ensure Karl has easy access to an alphabet for referral. Always correct letter reversals.	Informally monitor printing in daily work.
Use the correct conventions for grade level	Cue Karl to slow down when writing. Review basic grammar rules. Provide a proofreading partner (EA, teacher).	Compare Karl's written work over time. Evaluate by provincial standard for grade.
Reading		
Read independently	Review additional decoding strategies, looking at root words, sounding out, etc. Encourage the use of context cues.	Listen to Karl read for fluency and retell for accuracy.

* In the province of Ontario, four levels of achievement are identified for each learning expectation (Level 1: **limited** achievement, Level 2: **some** achievement, Level 3: **considerable** achievement, and Level 4: a **high degree** of achievement).

Samples of Karl's Writing

Age 8: Grade 3

> TO Day is tus June 29 2004
> To Day is my first ful
> DAy of Being ait cool to
> be 9. I got brasis the coler
> are mGold and moreh.
> at person camp I mad a
> mak out of clay it was
> cool for lonch we had pizza.
> Ice-crem and orig jouce it was
> good8 we olsow startid to
> cat out saps for our mobiers
> the saps wer mad out of clay.
> we cam home aho weht
> for a swim the tampa cheor
> was 24° it was can of cowld.
> for biner we had han
> be ger and veges it was yome8
> we went for a hoter swimm
> it had verhd up a bit
> put not to mnch it was 25°
> we bib a skit for the
> parihts it ws caid parints
> parteB

Today Is Tuesday June 29, 2004

Today is my first day of being 9. It cool to be 9. I got braces the colour are medium gold and medium green. At Pearson Camp I made a mask out of clay it was cool for lunch we had pizza, ice cream and orange juice it was good! We also started to cut out shapes for our mobiles the shapes were made out of clay. We came home and went for a swim the temperature was 24C. It was kind of cold. For dinner we had hamburgers and veggies it was yummy! We went for another swim it had warmed up a bit but not too much it was 25C. We did a skit for the parents. It was called parents party!

Age 11: Grade 5

Hurricanes

One summer day there lived a happy orange was walking down the street of New Orleans with his friend apple. They had lived in New Orleans since they were just seeds But one fateful day what they would never forget when Hurricane Brussel Sprout came to town wow what was it oh yes on the day orange said what's that oh it's just a hurricane coming to destroy the town of New Orleans and in two seconds they turned into apple juice/orange juice

Sample of Karl's Artwork

Why Is Karl Considered to Have a Learning Disability?

Definition of Learning Disabilities

According to the Council for Exceptional Children (2013), the largest international professional organization dedicated to improving educational outcomes for individuals with special needs, individuals with learning disabilities, or specific learning disorders, as they are called by the American Psychiatric Association (2013) in the DSM-V, generally have average or above-average intelligence yet they often do not achieve at the same academic levels as their peers. While Karl seemed to progress well in the early elementary grades, his parents became concerned during his Grade 3 year when he began having difficulties with spelling, math, and reading.

Karl's difficulties persisted despite significant support at home. Worrying that Karl may fall further behind in the basic skills required to do well in various subjects and failing to be

What We Know . . .

Definition of Learning Disabilities

The following definition was adopted by the Learning Disabilities Association of Canada (LDAC) in January 2002 and was re-endorsed in March 2015:

"Learning Disabilities" refer to a number of disorders which may affect the acquisition, organization, retention, understanding or use of verbal or non-verbal information. These disorders affect learning in individuals who otherwise demonstrate at least average abilities essential for thinking and/or reasoning. As such, learning disabilities are distinct from global intellectual deficiency.

Learning disabilities result from impairments in one or more processes related to perceiving, thinking, remembering, or learning. These include, but are not limited to: language processing, phonological processing, visual spatial processing, processing speed, memory and attention, and executive functions (e.g., planning and decision-making).

Learning disabilities range in severity and may interfere with the acquisition and use of one or more of the following: oral language (e.g., listening, speaking, and understanding), reading (e.g., decoding, phonetic knowledge, word recognition, comprehension), written language (e.g., spelling and written expression), and mathematics (e.g., computation, problem-solving).

Learning disabilities may also involve difficulties with organizational skills, social perception, social interaction, and perspective taking.

Source: Excerpted from Learning Disabilities Association of Canada (2016). Please note that this box represents only a part of the official definition of learning disabilities adopted by LDAC.

reassured by teachers' statements that Karl was a bright student, his parents took him to an independent psychologist for a complete psycho-educational assessment.

Something to Think About

There is no one definition of learning disabilities (LD) that is universally adhered to by education systems across Canada. Rather, each province and territory has developed its own definition of LD. Even within the provinces and territories, you may find that the conceptual definitions produced by ministries or departments of education are different from the operational definitions used by psychologists. What can you find out about the definitions used in your home province or territory?

Assessing Specific Learning Disorders

Karl was assessed at the end of his Grade 3 year, just before his ninth birthday. The psychologist met with him on three separate days. She reported that Karl was extremely friendly and co-operative. He talked about school and indicated that his teacher was very nice and he really liked working in groups and doing school projects.

During the assessment, Karl worked hard despite being somewhat fidgety. The psychologist noted that it was evident that Karl tired easily while doing many of the tasks, so she allowed several breaks. She also reported that he responded well to praise and encouragement and this type of reinforcement was necessary to facilitate his best performance. He completed most verbal tasks with ease but became discouraged when faced with difficult non-verbal tasks.

From the Psychologist's Notebook

When considering performance on standardized tests, results are interpreted in terms of norm-referenced age equivalency, standard scores, and percentiles. Age equivalencies indicate the age at which typical children obtain the reported score. Standard scores reflect performance in comparison with a standardized sample of same-age peers. On a test with a mean of 100 and a standard deviation of 15, as is the case with most standardized tests, a score between 85 and 115 would be considered to fall within average limits. Percentiles indicate an individual's placement out of all people who have taken the test, with the first percentile representing the low end of performance and the 99th percentile reflecting the highest. Because an individual test-taker is always part of the population that writes the test, the highest percentile score obtainable is the 99th percentile. This score means that the test-taker scored equivalent to or better than all test-takers. A percentile between 16 and 84 would be considered to fall within the range of average limits. Standardized scores provide useful information; however, standardized test results are limited in the scope of skills they measure and limited in the length of time they are considered valid, as an individual's skills and abilities may change with time.

©Digital Vision/Thinkstock.com

Students with specific learning disorders may experience trouble with a variety of reading, writing, and math tasks—for example, learning the alphabet or remembering the sounds that letters make. Guided and independent practice is needed to help students improve these skills.

phonological awareness

The awareness that language is composed of sounds and these sounds (syllables) are related to letters.

phonological memory

The coding of information according to its sounds for temporary storage in working or short-term memory.

visual perception

The ability to see and to interpret what is seen.

However, in general, Karl showed good motivation and effort, leading the psychologist to conclude that her assessment was a fair and accurate estimate of Karl's ability.

The assessment included a battery of standardized tests (see *Assessment Results* on p. 103). The Wechsler Intelligence Scale for Children, Fourth Edition (WISC-IV) contains four indices: Verbal Comprehension, Perceptual Reasoning, Working Memory, and Processing Speed. Karl performed consistently well on this test of cognitive ability, resulting in a Full Scale IQ at the 82nd percentile, which indicates a score equal to or better than 82 per cent of the other scores of all other test-takers (indicating high-average intelligence). The Woodcock–Johnson III Tests of Achievement (WJ-III) provides assessment of reading skills, written language, mathematics skills, oral language, and academic knowledge. This test revealed that Karl has good academic knowledge and a highly developed ability to write meaningful sentences when surface errors are overlooked. However, the WJ-III also revealed that Karl has significant difficulties in the areas of reading, math calculation, and spelling. A further test of reading-related skills was administered to assess Karl's phonological awareness, phonological memory, and his ability to name numbers and letters rapidly. This Comprehensive Test of Phonological Processing (CTOPP) showed that Karl is competent with this type of processing. In an effort to determine why Karl might be having the difficulties evident from the WJ-III, the psychologist administered two other standardized tests. On the Wide Range Assessment of Memory and Learning (WRAML), Karl's weakness was verbal learning, which means he has trouble understanding information that is presented through written and spoken words. The Beery–Buktenica Developmental Test of Visual-Motor Integration (VMI), a test designed to detect deficits in visual perception, fine motor skills, and hand-eye coordination, identified further difficulties experienced by Karl when he attempts to complete tasks that require an integration of his visual and motor abilities. He scored below average on all three subtests. It was these test results that the psychologist used to explain the discrepancy between Karl's cognitive ability and his academic achievement in reading, spelling, and math. She proposed that it is Karl's impaired perceptual skills that are affecting his ability to succeed in school. Because of these findings, she diagnosed Karl as having a learning disorder.

Upon receiving the psychologist's report, Karl's parents approached the Identification, Placement, and Review Committee (IPRC) serving his school to share the information they had learned from this independent assessment. (Note: These committees are legislated by the Ontario Education Act to identify students with exceptionalities, what their needs are, and how these needs will be met.) Early in the fall of Karl's Grade 4 year, the IPRC officially identified him as having an exceptionality and designated this exceptionality as a "learning disability." Their "Statement of Decision" indicated that Karl would be placed in a regular classroom

What We Know . . .

Diagnostic Criteria for Specific Learning Disorder (DSM-V)

A. Difficulties learning and using academic skills, as indicated by the presence of at least one of the following symptoms that have persisted for at least 6 months, despite the provision of interventions that target those difficulties:

1. Inaccurate or slow and effortful word reading.
2. Difficulty understanding the meaning of what is read.
3. Difficulties with spelling.
4. Difficulties with written expression.
5. Difficulties mastering number sense, number facts, or calculation.
6. Difficulties with mathematical reasoning.

B. The affected academic skills are substantially and quantifiably below those expected for the individual's chronological age, and cause significant interference with academic performance.

C. The learning difficulties began during school-age years but may not become fully manifest until the demands for those affected academic skills exceed the individual's limited capacities.

D. The learning difficulties are not better accounted for by intellectual disabilities, uncorrected visual or auditory acuity, other mental or neurological disorders, psychosocial adversity, lack of proficiency in the language of academic instruction, or inadequate educational instruction.

The diagnosed specific learning disorder is classified as mild (can compensate or function with appropriate accommodations or support services), moderate (unlikely to become proficient without some intervals of intensive and specialized teaching), or severe (unlikely to learn without ongoing intensive individualized and specialized teaching for most of school years).

Source: Reprinted with permission from the *Diagnostic and Statistical Manual of Mental Disorders*, Fifth Edition, (Copyright 2013). American Psychiatric Association. All Rights Reserved.

with resource assistance as outlined by his individualized education program (see p. 106 for *Excerpt from Karl's* IEP).

The process that led to Karl's designation as a student who is exceptional is fairly typical of how Canadian students who have learning disabilities are identified within the various education systems. While there is no uniform identification process across the provinces and territories, most students who are identified as having a learning disability have exhibited a discrepancy between their cognitive ability and their academic achievement. This discrepancy is usually noted by parents or teachers in the middle to upper elementary grades when the curricula focus more intensively on reading, writing, and mathematical skills. As in the case of Karl, a psycho-educational assessment confirms a difficulty with one or more of the processes related to perceiving, thinking, remembering, or learning.

From the Psychologist's Notebook

There have been some changes in the US identification process for determining whether or not a student has a learning disability. It is important to consider these changes, since special education in Canada is highly influenced by practices across the border. In 2004, the Individuals with Disabilities Education Improvement Act (IDEA; PL 108-446, 2004) presented changes that permit educators to use responsiveness-to-intervention (RTI) as a substitute for, or as a supplement to, the IQ-achievement discrepancy model of identifying students with learning disabilities (Fuchs, Fuchs, & Compton, 2012). The primary objective of the change was to encourage educators to intervene earlier in identifying students who exhibit learning problems and to decrease the number of children who are identified as having a learning disability when, in fact, their poor achievement is due to poor instruction. According to the National Center on Response to Intervention (2010):

> *Response to intervention integrates assessment and intervention within a multi-level prevention system to maximize student achievement and to reduce behavioural problems. With RTI, schools use data to identify students at risk for poor learning outcomes, monitor students' progress, provide evidence-based interventions and adjust the intensity and nature of those interventions depending on a student's responsiveness, and identify students with learning disabilities or other disabilities. (p. 2)*

According to McIntosh and colleagues (2011), several Canadian provinces have adopted the RTI model: Alberta, British Columbia, New Brunswick, and Saskatchewan. With no federally mandated methodological approach, these provinces are implementing RTI as they see fit. Research studies have reported that a focus on early literacy has improved outcomes for Canadian students.

From my perspective, the RTI process is not much different than the diagnostic instruction phase of the assessment and IEP process described in Chapter 3. The fundamental difference is that RTI interventions are purposefully and gradually intensified and monitored under the guidance of special educators and psychologists. I would endorse this approach if, and only if, these collaborative and research-based supports are omnipresent. RTI should not be used by teachers without these mechanisms in place. Thus far, the main criticisms educators have of RTI are not of its approach or of its intent, but that RTI will be used to replace the more formal and costly assessment and IEP processes as a way of identifying students with learning disabilities. In my estimation, RTI is not a sufficient way to identify a specific learning disability and should therefore only be used in conjunction with the LD discrepancy criteria and other precise indices of specific learning disabilities. Another particular and often-voiced concern is

> *. . . whether RTI is prone to systematic errors in identifying students with LD. For example, the underachievement criterion may exclude some high-ability students with LD from special education. These students, by compensating with their intellectual strengths*

and making good use of support services, often manage to achieve within the normal range and, therefore, are unlikely to receive the early individualized instruction that would enable them to make academic progress consistent with their abilities. (National Joint Committee on Learning Disabilities, 2005, p. 7)

RTI has considerable implications for teachers in regular classrooms who provide instruction to students with exceptionalities. Educators will have to remain vigilant and carefully examine whether studies on the efficacy of RTI empirically demonstrate improved academic achievement for students with learning disabilities.

What Factors Contributed to Karl's Learning Disabilities?

The causes of learning disabilities are diverse and complex and still not clearly understood by researchers today. It is apparent, however, that Karl's brain functioning is atypical in that he does not learn as most children do. The factors that have led to Karl's learning differences can only be considered in terms of the information received from his parents. He has not had any medical tests that have examined the physical aspects of his brain function.

Heredity

Karl's parents both have postsecondary degrees and hold professional jobs in their areas of expertise. Neither parent has experienced any learning difficulties. However, Karl has two uncles who struggle with various aspects of learning. His father's brother has a reading disability that was very apparent during his school years. Despite this difficulty with reading, he excelled in math and went on to become an engineer. Karl's mother also has a brother who struggled in school. He never learned to spell, and his writing skills have always been poor. While he was never diagnosed as having a learning disability, his parents were continually trying to understand why their son failed to attain these basic skills despite being of average intelligence.

According to the Learning Disabilities Association of Canada (2016), learning disabilities do tend to run in families, so some learning disabilities may be inherited. In Karl's case, he has a family history of learning disabilities on both sides—maternal and paternal. If genetics does play a role, he certainly had a significant chance of having learning difficulties. Karl does have a sister who does not have any learning disabilities; however, this does not rule out the possibility that Karl inherited his disorder, because more males than females are diagnosed with learning disabilities. In fact, Karl has no female relatives who have had learning difficulties.

Environment

Teratogens are known as potential prenatal causes of learning disabilities. Karl's mother confirmed that she had a completely normal and healthy pregnancy. She did not drink alcohol nor did she smoke cigarettes or take drugs of any kind. Karl was born full term and there were no

teratogens

Agents classed as radiation, maternal infections, chemicals, or drugs that disturb the development of an embryo or fetus.

difficulties with the birthing process. Karl's development from birth onward has been normal in terms of milestones achieved. He has not experienced any serious injuries nor has he had any medical problems that required medical intervention. He has never been prescribed drugs of any kind. He does not have any vision or hearing problems.

What We Know . . .

The Causes of Learning Disabilities

Researchers do not know exactly what causes learning disabilities, but they appear to be related to differences in brain structure. These differences are present from birth and often are inherited. To improve understanding of learning disabilities, researchers are studying areas of the brain and how they function. Scientists have found that learning disabilities are related to areas of the brain that deal with language and have used imaging studies to show that the brain of a dyslexic person develops and functions differently from a typical brain.

Sometimes factors that affect a developing fetus, such as alcohol or drug use, can lead to a learning disability. Other factors in an infant's environment may play a role as well. These can include poor nutrition and exposure to toxins such as lead in water or paint. In addition, children who do not receive the support necessary to promote their intellectual development early on may show signs of learning disabilities once they start school.

Source: Excerpted from US National Institute of Health (2014). www.nichd.nih.gov/health/topics/learning/conditioninfo/Pages/causes.aspx

Something to Think About

Liam was a high-achieving student until at the age of 10 a car accident left him with an acquired brain injury (see www.traumaticbraininjury.com to learn more about traumatic brain injury). Now Liam has various difficulties with learning and socialization. How might Liam be similar to other students who have been identified as having learning disabilities? How might his situation be different?

How Have Karl's Learning Disabilities Affected His Development?

Cognitive Development

According to Karl's parents, there were no early indicators that he may have learning difficulties. In fact, Karl appeared to be a very bright child right from the start. He spoke single words at 10 months of age and was combining words by 17 months. He loved books and when his parents read to him, he would eagerly chime in with the appropriate rhyming word. His mother

Karl, age 11.

remembers thinking at the time that Karl would obviously have no problems with reading when he entered school. Her prediction seemed to be correct as Karl successfully completed kindergarten and Grade 1. His teachers were very pleased with his progress, both in the areas of reading and math (see *Teachers' Reports* on p. 105).

It was when Karl was in Grade 2 that his mother first thought that "things just weren't quite right." Despite assurances by Karl's Grade 2 teacher that he was an "amazing student," his mother noticed that his reading and spelling skills were not progressing. He was able to read, but he seemed dependent on his excellent memory skills. He also had some difficulties learning how to spell simple words. However, since his teacher was an experienced educator, Karl's mother did not pursue the issue any further. She was just thankful that Karl had such a dedicated teacher who emphasized all of his strengths.

Things really began to unravel in Grade 3 when the first report card came home. For the first time, Karl's marks were no longer all As and Bs. He received Cs in reading, writing, and math. His parents went to the teacher conference with real concerns. They asked his teacher if she thought he may have a learning disability and her reply was, "I don't know much about that." She was a relatively new teacher who had limited experience with children at the Grade 3 level. Unfortunately, this inexperience resulted in no action on her part to determine whether or not Karl did indeed have a learning disability. His parents were left with no answers and decided to wait and see how Karl did during the remainder of the school year. However, before his Grade 3 year ended, Karl's frustrations with learning became more apparent and his mother, convinced there was a significant problem, spoke to a psychologist in the community about Karl's difficulties. The psychologist recommended a complete psycho-educational assessment, and that assessment was completed at the end of Karl's Grade 3 year (see *Assessment Summary* on p. 104).

Despite Karl's learning disabilities, his cognitive development is fairly advanced in the areas of verbal ability and general knowledge. In fact, if you were to have a dialogue with 11-year-old Karl you would be very impressed by his ability to converse in a mature fashion across a number of topics. He is a capable thinker who primarily has problems with reading, writing, and math.

What We Know . . .

Common Characteristics of Young Students with Learning Disabilities

Grades K–4

- Slow to learn the connection between letters and sounds
- Confuses basic words (run, eat, want)
- Makes consistent reading and spelling errors including letter reversals (b/d), inversions (m/w), transpositions (felt/left), and substitutions (house/home)
- Transposes number sequences and confuses arithmetic signs (+, −, ×, /, =)
- Slow to remember facts
- Slow to learn new skills, relies heavily on memorization
- Impulsive, difficulty planning
- Unstable pencil grip
- Trouble learning about time
- Poor coordination, unaware of physical surroundings, prone to accidents

Grades 5–8

- Reverses letter sequences (soiled/solid, left/felt)
- Slow to learn prefixes, suffixes, root words, and other spelling strategies
- Avoids reading aloud
- Trouble with word problems
- Difficulty with handwriting
- Awkward, fist-like, or tight pencil grip
- Avoids writing compositions
- Slow or poor recall of facts
- Difficulty making friends
- Trouble understanding body language and facial expressions

Source: Excerpted from Learning Disabilities Association of Ontario (2015). www.ldao.ca/introduction-to-ldsadhd/what-are-lds/some-common-signs-of-lds/

Social and Emotional Development

Karl is described as a pleasant child by all who know him. He is always enthusiastic and excited about participating in both school and extracurricular activities. However, his mother describes his negative emotions as being just as intense. She said that while he can sometimes get quite despondent over things that do not go well for him, he generally handles negative situations well. When he is having trouble with a task, he sometimes comments to his parents, "Oh well, that's just my learning disability."

Karl has been aware of his learning disabilities since the time of his diagnosis. His parents have been quite open with him right from the start. Prior to the sessions with the psychologist, they talked with him about the assessment process and why it was necessary. They emphasized that the assessment was being done because it would provide information that "would help him learn better." They were careful not to make him feel like he was incapable or unable to do the tasks necessary to be successful in school.

This does not mean that Karl never has moments of frustration when he claims that he just cannot do something. On rare occasions, he attributes his inability to complete school work, especially homework, to being "stupid." However, his parents do not let him use this mechanism to get out of his assigned work. Homework is done at the kitchen table where both parents are available to help him. They will often suggest strategies he can employ to make tasks easier. While Karl is sometimes overwhelmed by the thought of having to do a particular task, he usually responds well once his parents help him break the task down into smaller steps. His negative feelings usually give way to feelings of accomplishment.

Karl's awareness of his learning disability is reflected in his desire to be good at something. He will often ask his parents, "Do you think I am good at this?" Karl is obviously keen to determine what he does well. His parents have been diligent about exposing him to activities that he excels at, especially activities that involve drama since it is one of his passions. However, it is not always possible to completely avoid having his learning difficulties affect his participation in these activities. For example, Karl would have liked to attend a public school for the arts starting in Grade 5. The comprehensive audition for entry into the school required him to complete academic-based tests. He was subsequently not accepted.

When asked about other behaviours that reflect Karl's emotional development, his parents commented that he can be somewhat "fidgety." While they do not believe he is hyperactive, they do feel he has always exhibited some impulsivity. He often "gets wound up," and acts before he thinks. For example, one of his birthday parties was held at a local children's restaurant where an employee organized activities for Karl and his guests. One of the planned activities was to have Karl dip his hands in some paint and then place his hands on a special wall that marked the birthdays of restaurant guests. Karl was already overly excited from the party atmosphere when it was time for him to participate. Upon dipping his hands in the paint, he immediately placed his hands on the employee's shirt. Right away his face showed his emotions; he knew he had done something wrong and he felt very remorseful. He had acted spontaneously without giving the consequences of his actions any thought. It is not uncommon for students with learning disabilities to exhibit behaviours observed in attention-deficit/hyperactivity disorder (ADHD), including inattention, impulsivity, and hyperactivity.

```
┌─────────────────────────────────────────────────────────────────────────────┐
```

From the Psychologist's Notebook

I had Karl's mother and his teacher complete the Behaviour Rating Inventory of Executive Functioning (BRIEF). It is a questionnaire for parents and teachers that professionals use to assess eight aspects of executive functioning: inhibit, shift, emotional control, initiate, working memory, plan/ organize, organization of materials, and monitor. The only significant finding in regard to Karl was that he was rated as slightly elevated on measures of emotional control. Therefore, he may need some extra time and consideration when he gets excited. Both his parents and his teachers should realize that when entering situations where the emotional tone is elevated, Karl may become more excited than others and later need the time and opportunity to calm down. He may also benefit from relaxation techniques and strategies (e.g., visualization, deep breathing).

```
└─────────────────────────────────────────────────────────────────────────────┘
```

Motor Development

Karl walked earlier than most toddlers. He has been an active boy throughout his childhood. His parents describe him as coordinated in terms of large muscle movement. However, they say he is not fast moving and more like "a bull in a china shop" in some situations. In other words, he lacks fluidity and grace. While he has no problems riding his bike or climbing trees, he has had some difficulties learning to skate and learning to swim different strokes. Karl feels that he is not good at sports. While he loves volleyball, he has had negative experiences related to his participation in this sport at school. The other children have called him hurtful names that have referred to his physique and they have also commented on his lack of athletic skills.

Poor motor abilities are a common characteristic of children with learning disabilities. While Karl does exhibit some awkwardness in terms of gross motor abilities, he is certainly not lacking in general coordination. He may not be a star athlete, but he is quite capable physically. Karl is also able to complete fine motor tasks with ease. He enjoys doing craft activities and he has a real flair for drawing, as demonstrated in the samples of his artwork that appear throughout this chapter.

What We Know . . .

Common Characteristics of Children with Learning Disabilities

Characteristic	Description
Disorders of Attention	Does not focus when a lesson is presented. Has short attention span and poor concentration and is easily distracted. May display hyperactivity.
Poor Motor Abilities	Has difficulty with gross motor abilities and fine motor coordination (exhibits general awkwardness and clumsiness).

Psychological Processing Deficits	Has problems in processing auditory or visual information (difficulty interpreting visual and auditory stimuli).
Lack of Phonological Awareness	Is poor at recognizing sounds of language (cannot identify phoneme sounds in spoken language).
Poor Cognitive Strategies	Does not know how to go about the task of learning and studying. Lacks organizational skills. Has a passive learning style (does not direct own learning).
Oral Language Difficulties	Has underlying language disorders (problems in language development, listening, speaking, and vocabulary).
Reading Difficulties	About 80 per cent of students with learning disabilities have disabilities in reading (problems in learning to decode words, basic word-recognition skills, or reading comprehension).
Writing Difficulties	Is poor in tasks requiring written expression, spelling, and handwriting.
Mathematics	Has difficulty with quantitative thinking, arithmetic, time, space, and calculation facts.
Social Skills	Does not know how to act and talk in social situations. Has difficulty establishing satisfying social relationships and friendships.

Source: Republished with permission from Houghton Mifflin Harcourt. *Learning Disabilities and Related Disorders*, by Lerner and Kline, (2006). Permission conveyed through Copyright Clearance Center, Inc.

What Is School Like for Karl?

Karl is quite articulate and able to clearly describe his learning experiences. In the following passage, Karl shares what school is like for him:

I have trouble reading and writing and I don't learn as quick as other people do in these two subjects. With writing, my problem is mostly spelling. I have great ideas, but it is hard for me to get them on paper. I am better at telling people. With reading, I have trouble with the bigger words. I have some trouble with math too. It takes me longer than other people to do the problems and sometimes I need someone to explain the problem to me. But I do some things better than other people in my class, like drawing and playing card games. I am pretty good at playing the piano and I like acting too. Right now I am rehearsing to be the Wolf in "Little Red Riding Hood" in French class. I am good at French. Sometimes I help other people in my class with translation from French to English.

I use a computer at school. It is at the back of the classroom. I am the only kid in the class who uses it right now because the school is just testing it out. Other kids who have problems go to the resource room just like I did last year. But I prefer staying in my classroom because my friend sometimes helps me. If he is walking by and he sees that I am having trouble with something, he will help me with it.

When I am writing, I use WordQ. It will say the word that I wrote and if it is wrong, it will show me a little prediction box and I get to choose the word I meant to write. For reading, I use something called Kurzweil. I scan whatever I am reading into the computer and it will read it back to me. I only use Kurzweil if I have to read a long piece because I still need to practise reading on my own. My teacher usually tells me when I should use the computer. If she doesn't say anything, I know she wants me to try it on my own.

Sometimes school is frustrating. I feel that way when I just want to get something done and I can't get it done as fast as I would like to. But sometimes I like it because I can get extra help. In Grade 1, 2, and 3, before I was told that I had learning disabilities, it was more frustrating because I didn't have any extra help.

My mom got someone to test me for learning disabilities. After we got the whole thing sorted out, I started doing better in school. I don't make a big deal out of having learning disabilities. I am just a bit different from other people. First when I found out though it made me sad. Then I found out that I was going to get some help so it sort of made me happy. In that way, the whole thing made me both happy and sad.

I don't really talk about my learning disabilities to other people. Sometimes I just explain that I have trouble with spelling and reading. My friends don't make a big deal of it. I don't tell some people in my class about my learning disabilities because I think they would call me names. They already tease me about how I do in sports.

The most difficult thing for me to do in school is writing. If I could just use a pencil to write, it would be easier, but then I know I would make a lot of mistakes. So I have to use the computer and that takes more time. I have to find the right keys. I am getting better at keyboarding, so that should help. I just wish I could write with a pencil and not worry about making mistakes. Then I would really enjoy writing.

The easiest subjects for me at school are Religion and Social Studies. I really like historical things. Ever since Grade 1 I have been waiting to do Medieval Times. We finally did it this year and it was so cool. Now we are on to Ancient Civilization. I am going to do my project on Greece. My grandmother has travelled there so she is going to help me. I have a book that shows the outfits and types of helmets they wore during that time. I will write a report and probably draw some pictures to go with it.

I like school. The only thing that really bothers me is how some other kids tease me and my friends. They take things from us and won't give them back. It's the only thing about school that I really don't like.

WordQ

Software designed for those who struggle with writing. It integrates word prediction and text to speech.

Kurzweil

Software designed for those who struggle with reading. It provides a text-to-speech reader.

Karl, age 11.

What We Know . . .

Loneliness and Students with Exceptionalities

According to Nowicki (2006), children with special needs are at a greater risk for social rejection, isolation, and bullying. Some are more vulnerable than others. Those whose disabilities are not readily apparent are less likely to be offered protection by their peer group than those whose disabilities are more visible (Campbell & Missiuna, 2016).

Pavri and Monda-Amaya (2000) noted that school-related loneliness stems from several factors, including boredom, a lack of companionship and friendship, and skill deficits experienced by the child. They emphasized the important role that school personnel play in helping students with exceptionalities feel socially comfortable and accepted at school. Pavri and Monda-Amaya stated that "teachers play an important role, both as leaders of the academic environment and as facilitators of social relationships among students with and without disabilities . . . teachers can create a classroom environment in which they assist students to learn the skills and strategies needed for social problem solving and conflict resolution, for the development of friendships, for learning to work cooperatively with others, and for the enhancement of their self-esteem" (p. 30).

What Educational Approach Is Best for Karl?

When Karl was first designated as "learning disabled" by the school system, an IEP was developed by his classroom teacher, the educational assistant, and the student services support teacher. Based on the psychologist's assessment report, this group of educators decided the learning expectations and type of accommodations that would be most appropriate for Karl. Their goal was to design a program that best facilitated his learning across all subject areas. The resulting IEP reflected the following recommendations made by the psychologist:

- Decrease the amount of written work he has to complete.
- Allow alternatives to written presentations (e.g., oral presentations).
- Allow him to take tests orally or have him write his tests with his peers and later review his answers with him orally.
- Verbally explain instructions that are given in written form.
- Give him extra time to complete written assignments.
- Allow him to use dictionaries, spelling lists, or other aids when doing his work.
- Allow him access to written notes from peers or the teacher.
- Tape a copy of the alphabet to his desk.
- Correct his letter reversals but do not penalize him for them.
- Provide support with study skills, proofreading, editing, and the mechanics of writing.
- Encourage him to use computer-assisted technology (e.g., spell checkers, text-to-voice software, voice-to-text software, reading fluency software).

mnemonics
Simple mental aids such as abbreviations, rhymes, or images that help people remember more complex material.

- Provide small group or individual assistance with reading.
- Encourage him to use mnemonics to help him memorize facts.
- Allow him to use multiplication tables or calculators for math tasks.
- Show him examples of completed work to help him visualize what he has to do.
- Break down tasks into individual steps.

In terms of Karl's *attention-related difficulties*, the psychologist recommended the following:

- Decrease the distractions around him when he is working.
- Have him clear his desk of everything other than what he is working on.
- Decrease or mask the noises around him (e.g., use of headphones or earplugs).
- Chunk his work into shorter bits and change the work frequently so he does not get bored.
- Cue him when giving instructions.
- Tell him ahead of time the question you will ask him in the group discussion so he is less likely to interrupt others.
- Approach him in a low-key manner so he does not get overly excited.

In terms of his *organizational difficulties*, the psychologist recommended the following:

- Help him with strategies such as underlining, outlining a passage, and summarizing.
- Consider the use of coloured folders or binders to help him organize each subject.
- Help him organize his work with checklists and homework books.
- Encourage him to use date books and calendars.
- Check with him to make sure he has all the materials in his backpack that he needs to complete his homework.
- Try to keep things as simple as possible.

Not all of these recommended strategies were incorporated into Karl's IEP, but they are available to his teacher through his school file. They are also available to his parents because they have a copy of the psychologist's report. Karl's father indicated that these recommendations have been very helpful at home, especially in terms of helping Karl with his homework.

What We Know . . .

Teaching Strategies for the Inclusive Classroom

Not all students with learning disabilities have exactly the same problems. However, there are some teaching strategies that have proven effective for most students with learning problems. Lerner and Kline (2006) presented a variety of these strategies for the teaching of math, reading, and writing. They are as follows:

Mathematics

- Determine the students' basic computational skills in addition, subtraction, multiplication, and division.

- Have students use manipulatives to help them understand a concept.
- Teach the students mathematics vocabulary.
- Use visuals and graphics to illustrate concepts to the students.
- Have students make up their own word-story problems.
- Teach students how to use a calculator.
- Teach money concepts by using either real money or play money.
- Teach time by using manipulative clocks.
- Provide many opportunities for practice and review.

Reading

General Modifications

- Increase the amount of repetition and review.
- Allot more time for completing work.
- Provide more examples and activities.
- Introduce the work more slowly.

Phonics

- Play word and rhyming games.
- Analyze the phoneme elements that make up a word.
- Build word families.

Fluency

- Help students recognize sight words.
- Find opportunities for students to re-read passages aloud.
- Use predictable books.
- Use read-along methods.
- Use the language-experience method to let the children read their own language.

Vocabulary

- Teach content vocabulary before reading a chapter in a science or social studies text.
- Find words in the students' areas of interest and use the words for study.
- Use word webs to study vocabulary words.

Reading Comprehension

- Provide students with background knowledge about a story or content-area reading.
- Use the K-W-L strategy (Ogle, 1986) to improve comprehension (see p. 129).
- Have students predict what will happen next in a story.
- Use graphic organizers to visualize the reading passage.
- Show movies or videos about a book to enhance interest.
- Have students act out passages in a story.

Continued

Writing

Written Expression

- Allocate sufficient time for writing (at least four times a week).
- Encourage students in the primary grades to use invented spelling.
- Use brainstorming to create ideas about writing topics.
- Give students a range of writing tasks, both creative and functional.
- Teach students the stages of the writing process.
- Use a graphic organizer, such as Inspiration, to plan a story.
- Use a presentation program, such as PowerPoint, to develop a story.
- Use the Internet to conduct research on a topic.

Spelling

- Limit the number of spelling words to be learned at one time.
- Analyze the phonemes of new words.
- Point out the syllables in multi-syllabic words.
- Teach word families.
- Provide periodic retesting and review.
- Use multi-sensory strategies (e.g., see it, say it, write it in the air, see it in your mind, write it on paper, and compare it to the model).

Handwriting

- Begin with manuscript writing and explain that it consists of lines and circles.
- Say the name of the letter to be written.
- Have the students trace the letter with their finger.
- Use dotted lines for a letter and have the students trace the dots with a pencil.
- Give stroke directions to the students (e.g., first go down).
- Have the students copy a letter (or word) on paper while looking at a model.
- Have the students write the letter from memory while saying the name of the letter.

Source: Republished with permission of South-Western, a part of Cengage Learning, Inc. from *Learning Disabilities and Related Disorders*, (10th ed.), Lerner J.W., & Kline F. (2006). Permission conveyed through Copyright Clearance Center, Inc.

Changes within the Learning Environment

Changes within the classroom that specifically address Karl's learning needs include access to a computer that has software designed to help with reading (Kurzweil) and writing (WordQ), access to concrete materials and number lines for math, an allowance for extra time to complete written assignments, and the provision of extra help when reading math problems. In terms of evaluation, he is sometimes required to complete fewer questions on tests than his peers, and he is asked at times to demonstrate his knowledge orally rather than in written form. These changes to the learning environment have enabled Karl to improve his performance across all subject areas. In fact, in math he now works at grade level.

What We Know . . .

How Assistive Technology Can Help Students with Learning Disabilities

According to Young and MacCormack (2014), **assistive technology** (AT), whether it be low-tech (e.g., pencil grip) or high-tech (e.g., computer programs), can be beneficial to students with learning disabilities. In their review of AT, Young and MacCormack presented the possible benefits and cautions:

assistive technology
Application or device used to maintain or improve physical ability or academic performance.

Computer-Assisted Instruction

- Provides students with dynamic feedback.
- Helps students practise spelling and multiplication drills.
- In order to prevent the technology from being a distraction, students need to be taught how to use technology to support their learning.

Software

- Helps students bypass the task of decoding words. Seeing individual words highlighted as the text is read aloud may help to improve students' sight word vocabulary.
- Bypasses the tasks of handwriting and spelling, allowing the student to concentrate on developing ideas and planning his or her work.
- Bypasses the tasks of handwriting and spelling, allowing the student to concentrate on developing ideas and planning his or her work.

Mid-Tech Devices

- Concept organizers, whether completed electronically or by hand, may contribute to better writing in students with learning disabilities.
- Pentop computers can be used for reading (text to speech), writing (digitizing written words), and math (strategy feedback).
- Calculators can help students with learning disabilities demonstrate their understanding of mathematical computations. Graphing calculators can provide additional support as they verify graph shapes and help solve algebraic equations.

Cautions

- Due to the limited evidence-based research, teachers tend to make decisions about assistive technology based on claims from the software companies.
- To be effective, assistive technology has to be coupled with quality instruction.
- Teachers require training to support their implementation of assistive technology.

Something to Think About

Andrea, who is in Grade 7, has great difficulty with writing and spelling. While her IEP states that she should have access to computer software that will aid her with this learning disability, her parents are hesitant to go along with this recommendation. Their concern is that by allowing Andrea to use AT she will never develop the skills necessary to become a good writer. They consider AT "the easy way out." If you were Andrea's teacher, how would you respond to her parents' concerns?

Learning Strategies

meta-cognitive ability
The ability to understand and monitor one's own cognitive systems and their functioning.

Karl, like many students with learning disabilities, tends to have a limited repertoire of learning strategies, and he does not readily devise new strategies, particularly for novel problems or situations. He also seems to lack the meta-cognitive ability to recognize when the strategy he is using is not producing efficient learning. This presented a perplexing problem for Mrs. McCarthy, his Grade 5 teacher. If she did not teach Karl any learning strategies, he would not learn efficiently. On the other hand, even if she did teach Karl appropriate learning strategies, he still might not use those strategies in the most expeditious manner and he still might not recognize when to stop using an inefficient strategy. Another dilemma for Mrs. McCarthy was that for the teaching of learning strategies to be most effective, she would have to monitor and revise Karl's implementation of strategies on an ongoing basis.

It was a concern that Karl was already becoming somewhat dependent on her for help with his schoolwork.

Efforts to overcome this complex set of problems led Mrs. McCarthy to explore the use of the Cognitive Credit Card (CCC) approach (Edmunds & Blair, 1999). CCCs are credit card–sized laminated sets of cognitive or meta-cognitive cues designed to elicit students' thinking about their thinking as they attempt to learn or problem solve. The design of the CCC allows a student to carry his or her CCCs in a wallet or attached to a binder, thus giving the student some privacy and control over his or her learning.

The process of developing a CCC begins when a teacher recognizes that a student does not use a particular strategy in trying to learn a particular school topic. In Karl's case, he told Mrs. McCarthy that there were "just too many things to keep in my head at the same time" when trying to do subtraction in math class. Together they came up with a set of cues that helped him

©neukind/iStock/Thinkstock.com

A number of tablets and computers can now be customized for students with poor motor abilities. For example, if a student has trouble controlling a mouse, some products allow for keys to be used instead. If a student has difficulty pressing multiple keys at once to perform shortcuts, they can activate a feature (often know as Sticky Keys) that allows them to press the shortcut keys in sequence instead.

Math: Subtraction

- Is the question written in the right form?
- Do I have to borrow?
- Are my numbers in the right places?
- Are my numbers easy to read?
- Are there any symbols I need to include?
- Did I check my answer?
- Does my answer make sense?

Figure 5.1 Karl's CCC for subtraction.

Homework

- What does my notebook say I need to do?
- What materials do I need before I start?
- How do I keep track of what I have completed?
- Did I finish all of my homework?
- Has my mom or dad checked my work?
- Is my work ready to take back to school?

Figure 5.2 Karl's CCC for homework.

think about what he needed to do when subtracting (see Figure 5.1). They revised these cues a number of times until they were exactly what he needed at this period in his skill development. Mrs. McCarthy made sure that the cues were cognitive prompts and that they provided little or no curricular content and little or no content-specific procedural information. The CCC then became a cognitive organizer for Karl. It focused on how he learns rather than on what he is to learn.

Karl and his teacher also developed a CCC to assist with homework (see Figure 5.2).

Both of these CCCs have resulted in positive learning experiences for Karl. He likes the feeling of being able to pull out his "credit cards" when he needs them, and he is proud of the work he accomplishes on his own while using them.

Karl has a similar strategy that he has just begun using to help with reading comprehension (see Figure 5.3). The K-W-L strategy (Ogle, 1986) stands for what I *Know*, what I *Want* to learn, and what I did *Learn*.

My Reading Organizer		
What do I **KNOW** about this already?	What do I **WANT** to know about this?	What did I **LEARN** about this?

Figure 5.3 Karl's reading organizer.

When Karl has a reading assignment, Mrs. McCarthy starts the "know" step by discussing with Karl what he already knows about the topic at hand. She encourages him to brainstorm about where and how he acquired this knowledge, and together they organize the brainstormed ideas into general categories. Then they move on to the "want" step, where Karl is asked to determine what he wants to learn from reading the assigned article. Mrs. McCarthy has him write down the specific questions in which he is most interested. After Karl has read the article, the final "learn" step requires him to write down what he learned from the reading and compare this acquired knowledge with what he identified as "want to learn" in the previous step. According to Karl, he is not keen on having to write all these things down, but he is surprised about how much he does learn from reading.

What We Know . . .

Learning Strategies Instruction

Students with learning disabilities benefit from a combination of direct instruction and strategy instruction. Direct instruction is explicit instruction with clearly specified objectives taught in specific small steps with detailed explanations, demonstrations of steps, and an awareness of connections among concepts. Strategy instruction involves teaching students how to approach tasks and use knowledge to solve a problem. Both direct instruction and strategy instruction involve modelling and demonstration, feedback, guided and independent practice, and transfer.

Teachers can guide students toward independent learning by teaching strategies in a structured way until students can use them in a variety of situations without guidance. The goal is to have students transfer these strategies across subject areas and grades. General tips for teaching strategies to students include the following:

- Teach one strategy at a time.
- Teach a strategy as part of classroom learning, within the context of the curriculum.
- Use direct instruction and be explicit in your language and examples.
- Help students see the benefits of a strategy, using real-world examples.
- Model the step-by-step use of a strategy.
- Reinforce the strategy with visual cues.
- Provide guided practice with easier material.
- Give students opportunities to show what they know.
- Help students make the link between the strategy and different curriculum areas.
- Encourage students to adapt and personalize strategies.

Source: Excerpted from Alberta Education (2010).

Evaluation of Progress

Karl is currently evaluated similarly to the other students in his class, except in the areas of reading and writing. Based on classroom observations and his performance on assigned work, Karl's teacher assigns a grade for each subject area and comments on his strengths and areas of difficulty. While he completes the same class work as his peers in reading and writing, his teacher evaluates his progress based on the appropriate expectations outlined in his IEP.

As mentioned in Chapter 3, the IEP is a key component in the evaluation of a student's progress since it includes the student's short- and long-term learning goals. An evaluation determines whether or not these goals have been met and what goals need to be modified or added to the IEP. As we stated earlier, the IEP is not intended to be a static document; it should be a continually evolving description of the student's education program.

Unfortunately, in Karl's case, the modification of his IEP has been given little attention, especially in terms of noting the teacher interventions that have been implemented successfully and the types of learning supports that have been put in place. Karl's

Karl, age 11.

mother indicated that within Karl's school there is no active school-based team. She feels fortunate that Karl currently has an experienced teacher who understands Karl's needs. As noted in Chapter 2, according to the policies and guidelines that generally govern the implementation of IEPs in Canada (and the United States), there is usually a mandatory requirement that a student's IEP be reviewed and updated (if necessary) at least every 12 months. In Karl's case, his teacher seems to be well in tune with his educational needs, so the educational programming he is receiving is appropriate at this time. However, Karl's parents are justifiably concerned about what will happen when Karl moves on to Grade 6 and a different teacher is responsible for his learning program.

How Is Karl Different from Other Students Who Have Learning Disabilities?

Despite his above-average cognitive abilities, Karl has difficulties with reading, math, and writing. He also has some minor problems with emotional control. Many children with learning disabilities face similar challenges. Like Karl, their poor academic performance is not consistent with their average or above-average performance on tests of general cognitive ability. Like Karl, they have problems in reading; in fact, many students with learning disabilities encounter difficulties that affect their ability to comprehend written language. Like Karl, they also have difficulties with writing; it is understandable that a difficulty with one form of language (e.g., reading) often appears in another form of language (e.g., writing). And like Karl, they have difficulties with math; reading difficulties as well as information-processing deficits can affect an individual's ability to complete math tasks.

However, this is where the similarities with Karl end. Each of these children most likely differs from Karl in the combination of learning challenges each of them has, the severity of each, and the specific instructional changes that are needed to facilitate his or her learning. In other words, children with learning disabilities are a heterogeneous group; each child must be considered as unique and different from other children with learning disabilities. The following examples highlight just some of these differences:

- *ADHD and learning disabilities:* Hoshi is a 16-year-old high school student who has very few close friends. His classmates describe him as "weird" and a "social misfit." They say he just does not know how to act around other people and he embarrasses them constantly by his odd behaviours. To compound his social problems, he is not doing well in school and displays a negative attitude toward learning. Hoshi's parents say that he was a difficult child right from birth. He was an "overactive" preschooler, and once he entered school his short attention span combined with his severe difficulties with reading led to a comprehensive psycho-educational assessment. Hoshi was diagnosed with both ADHD and learning disabilities. For a short period, he was given the stimulant medication Ritalin. While it helped him focus in school, he had trouble sleeping, and the drug was discontinued. Hoshi has failed to learn to read beyond the elementary level. Consequently, he has had many negative school experiences that have led to poor self-esteem and a desire to avoid learning altogether. Now that he is a teenager, his problems with social relations further exacerbate his feelings of failure. He has been thinking of dropping out of school and finding a job.

What We Know . . .

Children with ADHD and Learning Disabilities

It has been known for some time that ADHD (a neurological condition characterized by inattention, impulsivity, and hyperactivity) is a common **co-morbid condition** exhibited by individuals with learning disabilities. In her study, Mayes (2000) found that 70 per cent of children with ADHD were also diagnosed with a learning disability. "Children with LD and ADHD had more severe learning problems than children who had LD but no ADHD, and the former also had more severe attention problems than children who had ADHD but no LD. Further, children with ADHD but no LD had some degree of learning problem, and children with LD but no ADHD had some degree of attention problem. Results suggest that learning and attention problems are on a continuum, are interrelated, and usually coexist" (p. 417). Conte (1998) cautioned that while the co-occurrence of LD and ADHD is quite common, "there is considerable evidence that the two conditions are not causally related. The strongest evidence against a causal relationship stems from neurological evidence that different brain regions seem to be involved in each of the two conditions" (p. 98).

co-morbid condition
A condition evident in an individual at the same time he or she has another distinguishable condition.

- *Non-verbal learning disorders:* Gabrielle is an 8-year-old child who began talking at a very early age. In fact, her parents said that she sounded like a little adult when she was only a preschooler. Her love of books resulted in an ability to read simple stories before she started kindergarten, and she has excelled in oral reading and spelling throughout her first few years of school. Gabrielle has also quickly mastered her math facts and seems to have an excellent memory for recalling factual information. Despite these considerable strengths, Gabrielle has some significant difficulties that affect her in all aspects of her life. She is not well-coordinated and finds it frustrating to participate in physical activities, such as her neighbourhood soccer league and gym classes at school. Her participation in neighbourhood play and school sports are made even more difficult because of her poor social skills and her inability to adjust to new situations. Her mother says that Gabrielle just does not know how to make friends with other children, and when she is placed in a new situation she is simply frozen in fear. These difficulties with social interaction have become more pronounced of late, and they are now affecting Gabrielle's performance in school. Her mother and her teacher have decided that Gabrielle should be assessed by a psychologist.

What We Know . . .

Children with Non-verbal Learning Disorders (NVLD)

NVLDs refer to problems processing visual-spatial information. Students with NVLDs typically possess verbal assets such as strong receptive language and acquire reading skills as expected; but they may have difficulty "reading to learn" and display persistent math problems as well as deficits in motor planning, perceptual reasoning, and verbal prosody. It is important to remember that an individual student may have some, but not all, of the commonly described features.

Some commonly described features of NVLD are as follows:

- Auditory memory is better than visual memory
- Basic reading and spelling skills are better than mathematics skills
- Verbal expression and reasoning are better than written expression
- Difficulties with sense of direction, estimation of size, shape, distance, and time
- Difficulties with spatial orientation (e.g., knowing how things will look when they are rotated)
- Visual figure-ground weakness (e.g., problems finding things on a messy desk)
- Problems interpreting graphs, charts, and maps
- Difficulties with motor skills such as graphomotor skills (related to printing and cursive writing), physical coordination, and balance
- Trouble estimating how long tasks take and managing time
- Trouble seeing the "whole picture" or knowing what details are important
- Trouble organizing, especially non-verbal information
- May become easily lost in an unfamiliar environment

Continued

In addition to these difficulties, some students with NVLDs may have problems with reading non-verbal cues such as body language, facial expressions, and tone of voice. They may not pick up subtle social cues required to monitor their interactions in social settings. However, there are some students with other features of NVLDs who are very successful socially.

Source: From LD@School (2016), www.ldatschool.ca/learn-about-lds/nonverbal-lds/

- *Dyslexia:* Pamela is a 14-year-old high school student who excels in the visual arts and music. Pamela attends a public school for the fine arts where she is able to take many classes in these two subjects. However, school is not a completely positive experience for her. After years of individualized instruction at school and tutoring at home, she still struggles to read at the Grade 4 level. It is an embarrassment to her that she cannot read as fluently as her peers. She knows she is dyslexic but that does not remove the fear she feels when confronted with reading tasks. She would love to be involved in the drama club, but the thought of having to read a script aloud in front of her classmates is just too intimidating. Pamela's parents are supportive of her situation. They have tried to emphasize her strengths by providing her with the opportunity to increase her skill level in art and music. As well, they have brought to her attention people like Jay Leno, Caitlyn Jenner, and Tom Cruise who have excelled despite being dyslexic. While they had hopes early after Pamela's diagnosis that she might be able to overcome her disability, they realize now that dyslexia is something that will affect her throughout her life. They plan to get her some counselling as she faces the difficulties of going through adolescence with a learning disability.

What We Know . . .

Children with Dyslexia

Dyslexia is a specific learning disability that is neurological in origin. It is characterized by difficulties with accurate or fluent word recognition and by poor spelling and decoding abilities. These difficulties typically result from a deficit in the phonological component of language that is often unexpected in relation to other cognitive abilities and the provision of effective classroom instruction. Secondary consequences may include problems in reading comprehension and reduced reading experience that can impede growth of vocabulary and background knowledge.

Source: From International Dyslexia Association (2013), www.interdys.org.

From the Psychologist's Notebook

Karl's set of circumstances are a classic description of a student with a learning disability. However, he is different from a lot of children with LD in that he is in Grade 5 and he still has a fairly positive outlook about school and life in general. Unfortunately, many students with LD do not experience a lot of success in school because of their lack of cognitive strategies, which are the thinking engines that drive effective learning. Their lack of success often leads to a poor perception of themselves and thus leads to low self-esteem and low self-efficacy.

Compare Karl's story to the story of Alan, a high school student I recently met. Alan's school history reveals how cognitive strategy deficits contribute to negative attributions in individuals with LD. It is why we often see high school students with LD who are just no longer interested in school or motivated to even try to do well.

First School Years

Alan was a happy and enthusiastic little guy as he bounded through the doorway of his kindergarten classroom. He knew all his numbers up to 83, all the letters of the alphabet, all the colours in his box of 15 crayons; he could read a few words like "stop," "McDonald's" and "Toronto," and he could write his name and a few other words. His chatty and exuberant behaviour continued through the first few years of school as he really enjoyed the basic academic tasks in those early grades. Like all the other students in his class, his basic cognitive strategies were strong for the tasks presented and learning happened fairly easily. From these encounters, Alan realized that *he had the ability to do what was required and that his effort determined his academic results—good or not-so-good.*

Middle School Years

In November of Alan's Grade 3 year, his teacher sent home a note remarking that Alan seemed to be struggling compared to the rest of the students, particularly in reading and writing. As Grade 3 became Grade 4 and then Grade 5, the complexity and sophistication of most academic tasks, especially reading and writing, pushed Alan's basic strategies to their maximum. Even the newer and better strategies he had learned since coming to school were good for some tasks, but not for all. Alan's perspective changed slightly: "I still have the ability (I successfully accomplish a lot of tasks) but my efforts do not always pay off." His attribution becomes one of, *"I might not have all the cognitive abilities required for what my teacher asks me to do; therefore, I have to try harder to be as successful as my classmates."*

From Grade 5 onward, Alan really struggled with school work because at this point all tasks required complex and sophisticated cognitive strategies. Alan didn't have them and, unfortunately, without specific and individualized help he had no way of developing them. His cognitive strategy deficits were particularly evident because of (a) curricular shifts from "learning to read" to a reliance on "reading to learn" and (b) curricular emphases away from oral communication and manipulatives to a predominance of print formats.

High School Years

Now, in the shadow of senior high, Alan looks around and readily notices that his classmates are doing okay and, because of society's emphasis on doing well in school, "They are okay." Alan's perspective has changed demonstrably: *"I don't have the ability and now my efforts, which were sometimes successful in the past, never pay off. Therefore, trying harder is useless. Another good reason to not try harder is that I will not continually show people that I'm stupid!"*

Closing Karl's File

Karl will not outgrow his disabilities. Undoubtedly, learning will be a continual challenge for him as he progresses through upper elementary school and high school. High school will be particularly demanding as it focuses on mastery of content across all subject areas. These more complex, extensive, and sophisticated curricula will be presented by a number of teachers whose teaching methods will differ and may not be suited to Karl's learning strengths. To make matters worse for Karl, acquiring information through reading will be emphasized, and information will presented at a fast pace. While these characteristics of high school appear daunting in the context of Karl's learning disabilities, he will be better able to handle these challenges as he acquires more effective learning strategies. As well, he will benefit from appropriate supports that are implemented to facilitate his learning. Karl is fortunate to have parents who will continue to advocate for him to ensure that these supports are put in place. His parents' efforts to make him aware of his learning disabilities will also empower him to advocate for himself. As Reiff (2004) pointed out, understanding one's learning disabilities offers a number of benefits: "knowing about one's learning disabilities seems to be related to higher levels of self-esteem . . . such self-awareness provides a greater sense of autonomy . . . such knowledge provides practical advantages, particularly in the areas of self-advocacy and obtaining reasonable accommodations" (p. 187).

When asked about his future, Karl's parents responded with enthusiasm. They expect that with their ongoing support Karl will graduate from high school and enter a postsecondary institution. They do not foresee any major problems in his completion of a degree in whatever field he chooses. His mother said, "He may not get all As, but he will achieve his goals." Right now Karl's goal is to become a computer animator, a police officer, or a priest.

From the Psychologist's Notebook

My advice to Karl's parents is to continue their strong advocacy role. Parents are sometimes better educational advocates than professionals in the field because of their extensive knowledge of the child's complete history, their unparalleled concern and responsibility for the child's well-being, and their ability to speak freely without placing themselves in a conflict of interest with the education system. Unfortunately, many parents do not take on the role of educational advocate for a number of reasons, such as cultural and language difficulties, logistical barriers that restrict participation, a lack of knowledge about special education procedures, negative professional attitudes toward parents, parental burnout, and feelings of alienation from schools (Fiedler, Simpson, & Clark, 2007). Educators should be aware of these barriers and actively encourage parents of children with special needs to participate in the decision-making process that surrounds the education of their child.

In terms of Karl's situation, I also advise both his parents and his future teachers to continue to focus on his strengths. Encourage him to be involved in activities he enjoys and in which he excels. Provide him with opportunities to demonstrate his skills. He has an excellent attitude toward learning and remains motivated to do his best despite the difficulties he encounters on a daily basis. It is important that he continue to receive as much encouragement and positive reinforcement as possible for his efforts and achievements.

What We Know . . .

Success Attributes of Individuals with Learning Disabilities

According to Goldberg, Higgins, Rasking, and Herman (2003), longitudinal research of individuals with learning disabilities has shown that *successful* individuals demonstrated an enhanced self-awareness and the ability to compartmentalize their LD, allowing them to acknowledge strengths as well as weaknesses: "They were engaged in the world financially as well as socially, often rising to leadership roles in the family, at work, and in the community. They were decisive, often consulting others for information or advice, and they took responsibility for outcomes. They showed persistence in their pursuits, yet they could be flexible in altering the path by which they skirted obstacles. Successful individuals set realistic goals for themselves and demonstrated an awareness of the steps that would be required for their attainment. They made use of social support available to them in reaching these goals and sought help when needed. In adulthood, they demonstrated the ability to reciprocate and provide care and support for others. Finally, they developed strong and intimate peer and family relationships that assisted them in many ways to cope with stressful times and maintain emotional stability" (p. 230).

Updating Karl's Story

According to his mother, Karl continued to do very well in his final years of elementary school. She commented that "Karl's adolescence seemed to bring on a whole new positive image for him." He was elected to student council in Grade 8. He started playing hockey, tried out for school teams, continued exploring his artistic side in theatre, and took up the guitar. Unfortunately, however, his transition to high school did not go smoothly. His mother described the move as follows:

> We spent 10 years in the elementary system building him up only to have him squashed like a bug in the first four months of high school. Secondary school is a whole new experience. They expect a lot of self-advocacy in Grade 9. Even though his IEP states that he can use a calculator, he was not allowed to on the first few tests. I had to tell Karl that he needed to advocate for himself. He then started writing in the resource room and calculators were allowed. Academic math seems to be a do-it-yourself course. If you fail a test, the first response by the administration is to drop you to the applied program. Karl's English teacher was unaware of his IEP, and his technology was never encouraged. All the corrections were about his spelling and his grammar or the fact that she could not read his handwriting. Having said all of this, we also need to make sure that Karl is promoting his own needs. I daresay that it is difficult for a 14-year-old boy who tries and is told "no" by a teacher to continue asking for the assistance he requires to be successful in school. He also has realized that secondary school is very different. He did not have to do much outside of school in the elementary grades and he did well. In secondary, he now realizes that he needs to work. I think by the time

he realized this it was almost too late and he had developed a very negative attitude toward school. There were mornings that he was crying because he did not want to go—not something I have ever witnessed in the previous 10 years. Even though he was not an academic star, he found many reasons to go. This term is going better, but we are just at the beginning. I do see more effort in the homework, and perhaps we are on the way out of this downward spiral.

It is interesting to note that a child like Karl who has a good understanding of his learning needs and the support of knowledgeable parents experienced great difficulty transitioning from elementary school to secondary school. Karl's experiences raise several issues about how high school administrators and teachers deal with students who have exceptional needs. The following questions must be considered:

1. What are the best practices in regard to transitioning students with exceptionalities from elementary school to secondary school?
2. What expectations do secondary administrators and teachers have of students with exceptionalities, especially in terms of self-advocacy?
3. What are the responsibilities of secondary teachers in terms of meeting the needs of students with exceptionalities?

What We Know . . .

What Makes a High School a Good High School for Students with Disabilities?

Brigham, Morocco, Clay, and Zigmond (2006) studied positive examples of high schools that successfully included students with disabilities in the general education curriculum and met the research criteria for academic achievement. According to these researchers, these schools consistently implemented five school-wide strategies for educating students with disabilities. They (a) provided a broad array of academic course and program options, (b) provided school-wide support structures that could be combined and customized to the needs and strengths of individual students, (c) worked intentionally to connect students to the school and build their motivation to succeed, (d) created a connected and caring adult community to serve students' academic and social or personal needs, and (e) developed responsive leaders who managed the tensions inherent in the commitment to prepare students with disabilities to be successful in their lives beyond school.

It was obviously disconcerting to learn about Karl's "downward spiral" during his first year of high school. It was especially disturbing to hear about his negative attitude toward school since he had been feeling very positive about himself in the latter elementary grades. The early high school years are a critical period for developing feelings of competence and self-worth. As Wilson, Armstrong, Furrie, and Walcot (2009) reported in their study of the mental health of people aged 15–44, those with learning disabilities were more than twice as likely to report high levels of distress, depression, anxiety disorders, suicidal thoughts, visits to mental health professionals, and poorer overall mental health than individuals without learning disabilities. It is clearly important for secondary school staff to (a) provide students like Karl with positive learning experiences and (b) ensure these students enter adulthood with the belief they can be successful in life and in their chosen career.

Something to Think About

After reading this chapter, how do you feel about having a student like Karl in your classroom? As a new teacher, you will not be expected to be an expert on learning disabilities, but you will be responsible for carrying out students' learning plans. What kind of supports will you need in order to provide students with learning disabilities positive learning experiences?

Summary

Like students with global intellectual deficiency, students with learning disabilities or specific learning disorders often do not achieve at the same academic levels as their peers. However, unlike those with global intellectual deficiency, individuals with learning disabilities generally have average or above-average intelligence. Their difficulties are due to a number of disorders that can affect the acquisition, organization, retention, understanding, or use of verbal or non-verbal information. In the classroom, these students may exhibit difficulties with oral language (e.g., listening, speaking, and understanding), reading (e.g., decoding, phonetic knowledge, word recognition, comprehension), written language (e.g., spelling and written expression), and mathematics (e.g., computation, problem solving). Karl's story highlights the valuable information that can be gained from a psycho-educational assessment. It also details the frustrations experienced by students with learning disabilities in their quest to succeed in school. It is clear that teachers and administrators must be aware of the proven strategies for educating students with disabilities.

Learning More about Students with Learning Disabilities

Academic Journals

Exceptional Children
Journal of Learning Disabilities
Journal of Special Education
Learning Disabilities: A Multidisciplinary Journal
Learning Disabilities Research & Practice
Learning Disability Quarterly

Books

Bender, W. N. (2012). *Differentiating instruction for students with learning disabilities: New best practices for general and special educators* (3rd ed.). Thousand Oaks, CA: Sage Publications Inc.

Dawson, P., & Guare, R. (2012). *Coaching students with executive skills deficit.* New York, NY: The Guilford Press.

Lerner, J. W., & Johns, B. (2014). *Learning disabilities and related disabilities* (13th ed.). Stamford, CT: Cengage Learning.

Wong, B., Graham, L., Hoskyn, M., & Berman, J. (Eds.). (2008). *The ABCs of learning disabilities* (2nd ed.). Burlington, MA: Elsevier Academic Press.

Web Links

LD Online

www.ldonline.org

This site features hundreds of articles on learning disabilities and ADHD as well as monthly columns by noted experts, a comprehensive resource guide, and active forums. Educators will find information on attention-deficit disorder (ADD/ADHD), dyslexia, dysgraphia, dyscalculia, dysnomia, reading difficulties, and speech and related disorders.

LD@School

www.ldatschool.ca

LD@school is the first resource of its kind in Ontario dedicated to serving the needs of educators. It provides educators with information, resources, and research related to teaching students with learning disabilities.

Learning Disabilities Association of Ontario

www.ldao.ca

Besides providing information about types of learning disabilities and common signs of learning disabilities, this site includes a section devoted to how to help students with learning disabilities in different environments, such as at school and at home.

National Center for Learning Disabilities

www.ncld.org

Included on this comprehensive site is basic information about learning disabilities as well as valuable resources for parents and educators.

Youth 2 Youth

www.youth2youth.ca

This site, developed by young Canadians with learning disabilities, provides first-hand information about the transition from high school to secondary school and beyond.

Taking It into Your Classroom . . .

Including Students Who Have Specific Learning Disorders

When a student who has a learning disability is first placed in my classroom, I will

- review what I know about learning disabilities and locate resource materials,
- read the student's file,
- consult with the student's previous teachers,
- consult with the student's parents, and
- meet with the school-based team to discuss the student's current school year.
- Other: _____

When I suspect a student in my classroom has a learning disability, I will

- review what I know about learning disabilities and locate resource materials,
- collect information about the student through classroom interventions,
- consult with other school personnel who are familiar with the student,
- consult with the student's parents, and
- meet with the school-based team to present the information I have collected.
- Other: _____

Key points to remember in my daily interactions with a student who has a learning disability:

- The student may have low self-esteem and low self-concept.
- The student may exhibit a discrepancy between ability and performance.
- The student may be impulsive and speak without thinking.
- The student may not be able to interpret body language and tone of voice.
- The student may have difficulty understanding spoken language.
- The student may not react well to change.
- Other: _____

Key points regarding curriculum differentiation for a student who has a learning disability:

- Change, modify, or adapt the curriculum according to the student's IEP.
- Use visual aids to supplement oral and written information.
- Include hands-on activities rather than just having the student listen and observe.
- Use learning aids such as assistive technology to motivate the student.
- Implement any additional supports recommended in the student's IEP.
- Other: _____

Key points regarding evaluation of the progress made by a student who has a learning disability:

- Follow the evaluation plan outlined in the student's IEP.
- Consider the student's current learning expectations to determine his or her progress.
- Observe how the student's behaviour affects his or her learning.
- Recognize the student's strengths.
- Modify existing learning expectations or develop new ones as needed.
- Implement new learning supports as needed.
- Other: _____

CHAPTER 6

Students with Behavioural Disorders

LEARNING OBJECTIVES

After learning the material in this chapter, you should be able to:

- Define the terms *behavioural disorder* and *emotional disturbance*.

- Discuss the definition of ADHD as it is presented in the DSM-V, and describe the three presentations of ADHD.

- Discuss the use of medication to treat ADHD.

- Discuss the suspected causes of ADHD.

- Describe the effects that behaviour disorders can have on a child's development and discuss the school placement options that may be necessary for these students.

- Outline teaching strategies that may assist the student who has ADHD with learning.

- Define the term *conduct disorder* and discuss some of the possible causes of the disorder.

- Define the term *anxiety disorder* and discuss strategies teachers can use to assist students who have this type of condition.

- Discuss the impact that adolescence can have on students with ADHD and address why students with ADHD may experience difficulties with the demands of high school.

Name: Lindsey Woods

Current Age: 12

School: M.H. Landon School

Grade: 7

Lindsey is a highly creative individual who is considering a career as a visual artist.

Fortunately, her parents support her artistic talents by providing her with private art lessons outside of the school setting. These lessons are a welcome departure from the frustrations Lindsey faces in school. As a child with both attention-deficit/hyperactivity disorder and a learning disability, school is not always pleasant for Lindsey. Like other students with behaviour problems, she has difficulty attending to academic tasks and struggles with the social aspects of school despite her desire to establish friendships with her peers. Lindsey's story allows educators to consider the need for educational placements other than the inclusive classroom for some periods during a particular student's schooling.

Excerpts from Lindsey's Psycho-Educational Assessment

Lindsey's Age at Time of Assessment: 10 years, 9 months

This psycho-educational assessment was requested by Lindsey's parents in an effort to update information on her intellectual and academic functioning. Previous assessments identified Lindsey as having ADHD as well as significant language-based learning difficulties.

Intellectual/Cognitive Functioning

Wide variability in Lindsey's performance on the WISC-IV rendered the reporting of a Full Scale IQ meaningless. Results included:

Skill	Percentile	Range
Auditory-Verbal Skills	8th	Borderline
Verbal Reasoning	16th	Low Average
Perceptual Reasoning	32nd	Average
Working Memory	3rd	Borderline
Processing Speed	84th	Above Average

Executive Functioning

Lindsey's mother completed the *Behaviour Rating Inventory of Executive Functioning* to assess Lindsey's behaviour in the home environment. An elevated score was obtained on the *Working Memory Scale*, which means that Lindsey has difficulty holding in memory the information that is needed to complete a task and, therefore, she also has difficulty sticking to a task. She has a short attention span and is easily distracted. Lindsey also received an elevated score on the *Inhibit Scale*, which means she has difficulty resisting the urge to act on her impulses.

Memory Functioning

On the *Wide Range Assessment of Memory and Learning* (2nd Edition), Lindsey's performance was low average on the *Verbal Memory Index* (19th percentile) and average on the *Visual Memory Index* (34th percentile).

Academic Functioning

The *Woodcock–Johnson Tests of Achievement* were administered to assess Lindsey's current level of functioning in reading, mathematics, and writing. Results indicated the following:

Reading   Lindsey's overall reading skills are in the low average range for her age, and fall around the early Grade 3 level. Reading Fluency was a relative strength while she scored lowest on Reading Vocabulary.

Mathematics   Lindsey's math skills are well below average for her age, falling at the early Grade 2 level. She had significant difficulties with all subtests.

Writing   Lindsey's scores on tests of writing skills are below average for her age, falling at the late Grade 2 level. She scored well below average on all subtests.

Lindsey Woods

Mother's Comments Regarding Lindsey's ADHD

Age at Time of Assessment: 8 years, 11 months

My husband and I adopted Lindsey in Russia when she was just three days old. She has been with us since that time. We are not aware of her family or prenatal history. However, we were told that her birth was uncomplicated and no resuscitation was necessary. Her Apgar scores were nine and ten. When we first saw Lindsey, she was bright and alert. We did meet her birth mother but due to language difficulties we were unable to communicate. She looked to be about 19 or 20 years old and appeared to be healthy and well-nourished. Lindsey was examined by a pediatrician when she was five days old and we were told that she was a healthy baby. She was seen again at one month of age by a specialist and again we were told that she was healthy.

Lindsey was a cuddly, affectionate, and happy baby. She bonded very well to both of us. She bottle fed easily but was colicky during the first few months. We had difficulty switching her to solid foods and there were some concerns about her ability to swallow. Before she was one year of age, we were worried that she was not reaching developmental milestones at the appropriate age. She seemed to be floppy and had low muscle tone. She didn't walk until she was 16 months of age. Her speech was delayed as well. We arranged therapy to address her needs. She also had multiple ear infections during her early years and finally had her tonsils and adenoids removed at age five.

As a toddler, she had extremes in her moods. Most of the time, she was very friendly, affectionate, and happy. Her grandmother once commented that she sometimes seemed "too happy." However, on the other end of the scale, she would have temper tantrums. They were like black storms that would come in very suddenly. Lindsey would scream, cry, and be very upset, and then 20 minutes later, she would be hugging and kissing me and everything would be fine.

She was diagnosed with ADHD early in her Grade 1 year. Lindsey was displaying significant behavioural problems that the school didn't seem to know how to manage. She also had difficulty adapting to change and would easily get wound up. We were referred to a specialist who had both myself and her teacher complete the Conners' Rating Scales. The specialist put her on Ritalin (methylphenidate) at that time. She responded well and has been on medication ever since. She was switched to Concerta when it became available and that is what she currently takes now. A trial of Strattera resulted in a loss of appetite as well as withdrawn, uncommunicative behaviour. The medication was stopped after two weeks. Lindsey also takes Clonidine at bedtime for sleep as she has difficulty falling asleep without it. She used to take Clonidine in the mornings as well because of her physical tics, but it is now being discontinued as the tics seem to have gone away. Her tics may have been a side effect of her medication.

Lindsey has always been a highly sensitive child. Even with medication, she still has problems adapting to new situations and she can get overly excited or overly emotional at times. She is easily distracted, easily frustrated, she does not always listen well, and she often forgets things. But with her medication and the strategies she has learned, her behaviour is definitely better controlled. She's more compliant and co-operative. She is better able to handle peer interactions. We have definitely seen an improvement.

Parent's and Teacher's Assessment of Lindsey's Behaviour

Lindsey's Age at Time of Assessment: 12 years

ADD-H Comprehensive Teacher/Parent Rating Scales (ACTeRS)

Behaviour	Teacher's Rating	Parent's Rating
Attention	major deficit	major deficit
Hyperactivity	major deficit	major deficit
Social Skills	moderate problem	moderate problem
Oppositional	no problem	moderate problem

Conners' Rating Scales

	T-Scores*	
	Parent	School
Oppositional	56	69
Cognitive Problems/Inattention	77	68
Hyperactivity	58	77
Anxious/Shy	58	74
Perfectionism	43	55
Social Problems	50	63
Conners' ADHD Index	79	79
Conners' Global Index: Restless/Impulsive	78	80
Conners' Global Index: Emotional Liability	60	61
Conners' Global Index: Total	74	76
DSM-IV Inattentive	79	70
DSM-IV Hyperactive/Impulsive	74	72
DSM-IV Total	80	74

*A T-score is a standardized score, based on a normal curve. A T-score of 50 is the average score or mean. T-scores that fall between 40 and 60 are within the average range.

Lindsey Woods

Lindsey's Behaviour Plan: Grade 7

Area of Concern: Impulse Control

Lindsey often speaks loudly and over what others are saying. This is particularly evident when she feels she "needs" to say what she is thinking and does not attempt to use cues from others to assist her in stopping. After she has completed what she wants to say, she will then accept cues from others. Lindsey often interjects into conversations or speaks out of turn. She frequently misinterprets conversations and acts and speaks without thinking of the social consequences.

Lindsey is easily distracted when attempting to complete tasks. She will often follow peers to complete tasks. This is not always a beneficial strategy as her peers are often following their own agenda and not necessarily doing what is asked.

Current Goal

Lindsey will listen to communications from others, pause to assess whether she needs to respond, and respond positively if needed.

Intervention

- The school will provide individual counselling to assist Lindsey in understanding the impact of her impulsive comments on others during social interactions.
- School personnel will identify and label social interactions that are both positive and negative at the point of performance to assist Lindsey in recognizing and accepting how her responses affect her relationships with others.
- School personnel will assist Lindsey with her impulsivity during conversations by having her ask questions to clarify what she does not understand. She will be encouraged to respond to information in a positive manner. Lindsey will be given positive feedback upon completion.
- At the end of the day, school personnel will provide positive feedback to Lindsey by recounting situations where she has reacted positively, as well as situations where she has asked for clarification if needed.

Area of Concern: Social Interactions

Lindsey lacks an intuitive understanding of social boundaries. Her attempts to socially interact with peers are often out of context and not received well by others.

Lindsey lacks confidence in social interactions. In order to take part in an interaction, she will often repeat what is said by others in the form of a question; however, her attempts are often out of context and result in an end to the conversation.

Lindsey will often look to peers and follow their lead for direction regarding daily routines and social interactions. She has difficulty initiating both of these areas independently.

Current Goal

At the end of each day, Lindsey will identify to staff one instance when she shared something positive within a conversation.

Intervention

- During weekly social skills sessions, Lindsey's counsellor will focus on the skills needed to enter into a conversation and then participate in a conversation. Personal space will be discussed and demonstrated to assist Lindsey in learning this skill.
- School personnel will provide Lindsey with immediate feedback during social activities and encourage age-appropriate social language. Lindsey will be encouraged to observe peers and their behaviours during positive social interactions.
- The school will include Lindsey in social skills groups where topics such as self-acceptance, feelings, problem solving, and "looking" like a positive learner are discussed.
- The school will provide Lindsey with individual counselling that focuses on having her recognize and accept her own positive and negative social behaviours and their effects on interactions.
- School personnel will encourage Lindsey to take risks during conversations by sharing her own experiences.

Area of Concern: Knowledge of Her Own ADHD and Learning Disabilities

Lindsey has difficulty discussing her strengths and needs and often will avoid conversations about her ADHD and her learning disabilities. She will often comment that she knows all about ADHD.

Lindsey will often make excuses for her behaviours by saying that she has ADHD or learning disabilities. She has difficulty identifying behaviours that need to change.

Lindsey will often respond with a negative tone of voice if she does not understand or misinterprets information. This often leads to a negative response from others and masks the true issue.

Current Goal

During daily interactions, Lindsey will ask questions to clarify information and then respond in a positive tone of voice.

Intervention

- A school staff member will meet with Lindsey on a daily basis to review positive aspects of her day. Lindsey will be encouraged to discuss and identify specific behaviours that are related to her ADHD and her learning disabilities.
- The school will include Lindsey in social skills groups where she has the opportunity to identify what type of learner she is. School personnel will assist Lindsey in using this information so that she takes responsibility for her behaviours and makes changes where necessary.
- The school will provide Lindsey with individual counselling that assists her in identifying when and how her ADHD behaviours interfere with her learning and social interactions. Lindsey's counsellor will emphasize the importance of taking responsibility for changes in her behaviour.
- The school will provide Lindsey with individual counselling that assists her in identifying her feelings when she responds in a negative tone of voice. Lindsey's counsellor will assist her in taking responsibility for her feelings and help her acquire strategies that will lead to more appropriate responses.

Lindsey Woods

Sample of Lindsey's Writing

Age 12, Grade 7

Without you

It's impossible to breath because my heart is broken in two fracause and bleeding there's no beat there without you. I can't sleep at night So I don't have dreams to bring you back to me you are lost forever it seems without loveming you I can't go on I don't know how you are my life I told you that I meant it then, I mean it now My mind has become an echo chamber filled with your memories over and over they repeat there is no release Your shadow is all over me misty eyed tears fall I miss you I do I can't get over you at all I'm a lost soul floating alone in a vast universe and I don't ever in my life remember feeling worses Everything in my life all I ever knew suddenly becomes unreal a lie without you. That how it feels and no one can make it right friends try hard to comfort but they can't help me win this fight For all of your life. wherever you go whever you are I will aways be in your heart your heart Your distant, loving guiding star.

Sample of Lindsey's Artwork

Age 9, Grade 4

Lindsey Woods

Why Is Lindsey Considered to Have a Behavioural Disorder?

Definition of Behavioural Disorders

Although Lindsey's behavioural disorder was not diagnosed until she entered school, her family noticed that she engaged in troubling behaviours at an early age. While Lindsey was an affectionate and contented baby, she began to display significant mood swings during the toddler period. Her mother described them as "black storms" (see *Mother's Comments* on p. 146) that would end as abruptly as they began. They were marked by tantrum-like behaviours that contrasted vividly with the happy, bubbly toddler who loved to give hugs and kisses. Upon entry into kindergarten, more problems arose. Lindsey's teachers noted that she did not pay attention and her behaviour was disrupting classroom activities. She was also having difficulty establishing friendships with the other children. By Grade 1, it was apparent that Lindsey's behaviour needed to be addressed. A medical specialist was consulted, and he confirmed the existence of a behaviour disorder.

What We Know . . .

Definition of Emotional Disturbance

Students with behavioural, mental, and emotional disorders are categorized as having an emotional disturbance. An emotional disturbance is defined as a condition exhibiting one or more of the following characteristics over a long period of time and to a marked degree that adversely affects educational performance:

1. An inability to learn that cannot be explained by intellectual, sensory, or health factors.
2. An inability to build or maintain satisfactory interpersonal relationships with peers and teachers.
3. Inappropriate types of behaviour or feelings under normal circumstances.
4. A general pervasive mood of unhappiness or depression.
5. A tendency to develop physical symptoms or fears associated with personal or school problems.

Source: Excerpted from Individuals with Disabilities Education Act (IDEA) 1997 [Code of Federal Regulations, Title 34, Section 300.7(c)(4)(i)].

Attention-Deficit/Hyperactivity Disorder

Lindsey's behavioural disorder was more specifically diagnosed as attention-deficit/hyperactivity disorder (ADHD), a disorder believed to be caused by a deficiency, imbalance, or inefficiency in brain chemicals that affect certain brain regions (Rief, 2015). It should be noted that ADHD is a psychiatric diagnosis that must be made by a psychiatrist, a clinical psychologist, a physician, or other qualified medical health professional using criteria outlined in the *Diagnostic and Statistical Manual of Mental Disorders,* Fifth Edition (American Psychiatric Association, 2013). There is no simple laboratory test or medical procedure that can lead to a quick and definitive identification of this condition. Rather, the diagnosis is based upon a careful history taken from parents (e.g., age of onset, types of symptoms, duration of symptoms, and degree of impairment), a physical examination, an interview with the child, and input from parents and teachers regarding the child's current behaviour. As is often the case, Lindsey's parents and teachers were asked to complete behaviour rating scales (i.e., Conners' Rating Scales), which use observer ratings to help assess ADHD and evaluate problem behaviour in children and adolescents. For example, in the teacher version of this type of assessment, teachers are presented with common problematic behaviours that students display in school, and they are then asked to rate how often a particular individual has exhibited each behaviour in the past month. In Lindsey's case, her teachers indicated that the following behaviours occurred *"very frequently"* at school:

> **psychiatrist**
> A medical specialist who deals with the diagnosis, treatment, and prevention of mental and emotional disorders.

- Forgets things she has already learned
- Feelings are easily hurt
- Excitable, impulsive
- Emotional
- Inattentive, easily distracted
- Sensitive to criticism
- Short attention span
- Easily distracted by extraneous stimuli

While the above behaviours are problematic in and of themselves, they were even more of an issue because Lindsey also displayed the following co-occurring problematic behaviours, reported by her teachers as occurring *"often"*:

- Has difficulties engaging in tasks that require sustained mental effort
- Has difficulty organizing tasks or activities
- Has difficulty sustaining attention in tasks or play activities
- Has difficulty waiting her turn
- Blurts out answers to questions before the questions have been completed
- Only pays attention to things she is really interested in
- Mood changes quickly and drastically
- Interrupts or intrudes on others

The results obtained from the administration of the parent version of the *Conners' Rating Scale* were similar. In other words, Lindsey's parents reported observing similar frequencies of the same behaviours at home and in other environments outside of school (e.g., extracurricular activities).

Since Lindsey's assessment revealed a significant number of behaviours in all three areas, or presentations, of ADHD (i.e., combined, inattentive, and hyperactive/impulsive) and these had existed for a number of years and across a variety of settings, she was diagnosed as having "ADHD—Combined Presentation." ADHD is actually an umbrella term that describes three presentations of ADHD; the other two presentations are "Predominantly Inattentive," which describes individuals who do not exhibit hyperactivity, and "Predominantly Hyperactive/ Impulsive," which refers to those who have few inattentive symptoms.

What We Know . . .

Diagnosing ADHD

A. A persistent pattern of inattention and/or hyperactivity-impulsivity that interferes with functioning or development, as characterized by (1) and/or (2):

1. *Inattention:* Six (or more) of the following symptoms have persisted for at least six months to a degree that is inconsistent with developmental level and that negatively impacts directly on social and academic/occupational activities:

   a. Often fails to give close attention to details or makes careless mistakes in schoolwork, at work, or during other activities (e.g., overlooks or misses details, work is inaccurate).

   b. Often has difficulty sustaining attention in tasks or play activities (e.g., has difficulty remaining focused during lectures, conversations, or lengthy reading).

   c. Often does not seem to listen when spoken to directly (e.g., mind seems elsewhere, even in the absence of any obvious distraction).

   d. Often does not follow through on instructions and fails to finish schoolwork, chores, or duties in the workplace (e.g., starts tasks but quickly loses focus and is easily sidetracked).

   e. Often has difficulty organizing tasks and activities (e.g., difficulty managing sequential tasks; difficulty keeping materials and belongings in order; messy, disorganized work; has poor time management; fails to meet deadlines).

   f. Often avoids, dislikes, or is reluctant to engage in tasks that require sustained mental effort (e.g., schoolwork or homework; for older adolescents and adults, preparing reports, completing forms, reviewing lengthy papers).

   g. Often loses things necessary for tasks or activities (e.g., school materials, pencils, books, tools, wallets, keys, paperwork, eyeglasses, mobile telephones).

   h. Is often easily distracted by extraneous stimuli (for older adolescents and adults, may include unrelated thoughts).

   i. Is often forgetful in daily activities (e.g., doing chores, running errands; for older adolescents and adults, returning calls, paying bills, keeping appointments).

2.   *Hyperactivity and Impulsivity:* Six (or more) of the following symptoms have persisted for at least six months to a degree that is inconsistent with developmental level and that negatively impacts directly on social and academic/occupational activities:

    a.   Often fidgets with or taps hands or feet or squirms in seat.

    b.   Often leaves seat in situations when remaining seated is expected (e.g., leaves his or her place in the classroom, in the office or other workplace, or in other situations that require remaining in place).

    c.   Often runs about or climbs in situations where it is inappropriate. (In adolescents or adults, may be limited to feeling restless).

    d.   Often unable to play or engage in leisure activities quietly.

    e.   Is often "on the go," acting as if "driven by a motor" (e.g., is unable to be or uncomfortable being still for an extended time, as in restaurants, meetings; may be experienced by others as being restless and difficult to keep up with).

    f.   Often talks excessively.

    g.   Often blurts out an answer before a question has been completed (e.g., completes people's sentences; cannot wait for turn in conversation).

    h.   Often has difficulty waiting his or her turn (e.g., while waiting in line).

    i.   Often interrupts or intrudes on others (e.g., butts into conversations, games, or activities; may start using other people's things without asking or receiving permission; for adolescents or adults, may intrude into or take over what others are doing).

B.   Several inattentive or hyperactive-impulsive symptoms were present prior to age twelve years.

C.   Several inattentive or hyperactive-impulsive symptoms are present in two or more settings (e.g., at home, school, or work; with friends or relatives; in other activities).

D.   There is clear evidence that the symptoms interfere with, or reduce the quality of, social, academic, or occupational functioning.

E.   The symptoms do not occur exclusively during the course of schizophrenia or another psychotic disorder and are not better explained by another mental disorder (e.g., mood disorder, anxiety disorder, dissociative disorder, personality disorder, substance intoxication or withdrawal).

Prevalence of ADHD

According to Bloom, Cohen, and Freeman (2010), 9 per cent of US children between the ages of 3 and 17 have ADHD. Boys are more than twice as likely as girls to have this disorder. When compared with children who have excellent or very good health, children who have a fair or poor health status are also more than twice as likely to have ADHD. While these are

Boys are more than twice as likely as girls to be diagnosed with ADHD.

US statistics, they likely describe the prevalence of ADHD in Canada. Faraone, Sergeant, Gillberg, and Biederman (2003) reported that prevalence worldwide is 8–12 per cent.

ADHD Medication

Upon diagnosis, Lindsey was immediately prescribed the stimulant Ritalin (methylphenidate). Although it may seem odd that a stimulant medication would be prescribed for an already overstimulated child, Ritalin fires up specific neurons in the brain that are not working as they should. These neurons tell us when to pay attention to certain activities and when to ignore other ones. According to the Canadian ADHD Resource Alliance (www.caddra.ca), stimulant medications are an effective treatment for individuals with ADHD. While they are not a cure, they can reduce the symptoms of the disorder. In Lindsey's case, her doctor monitors the effects of her medication and adjusts her dosage accordingly. Lindsey no longer takes Ritalin as it required frequent dosing (i.e., multiple pills a day); she is currently taking Concerta, a once-a-day pill that also contains methylphenidate. Concerta does have possible side effects, one of which is insomnia. Lindsey is prescribed Clonidine to help her sleep.

There is an alternative to stimulant medications. Strattera is a norepinephrine reuptake inhibitor that is used to treat ADHD. It is designed to increase the availability of norepinephrine, which is thought to be essential to the brain's regulation of impulse control, organization, and attention. Lindsey was given a two-week trial of Strattera to see how she would respond. The medication resulted in a loss of appetite as well as withdrawn, uncommunicative behaviour and, therefore, it was stopped and she was placed back on Concerta, which she currently takes today.

When recently asked how her medication affects her, Lindsey described a little "experiment" she conducted:

> *Whenever someone like my doctor asked me how my medication was working, I never really knew what to say because I have taken medication for as long as I can remember. I decided to find out how it affected me by not taking my pill one morning. I slid the pill under my tongue and then spit it out when no one was looking. At school that day, I couldn't stay still in my seat and I was off in la-la land much more than usual. I felt really weird and I just couldn't focus. The teacher even asked me if there was something wrong because I wasn't acting normally. So now I know that my medication does help me. I would never want to try that experiment again!*

Something to Think About

Brain stimulants are among the most commonly prescribed drugs to Canadian children. Many parents and educators of students with ADHD have reported the positive effects these drugs have had on student behaviour. In 2006 and 2011, Health Canada issued public advisories regarding the drugs used to treat ADHD. These advisories warned that certain ADHD drugs carry heart risks, including high blood pressure and increased heart rate. More recently, Health Canada has stated that these drugs may contribute to the risk of suicide. How do you feel about the use of these drugs in the treatment of ADHD?

What Factors Contributed to Lindsey's Behavioural Disorder?

Given the lack of information regarding Lindsey's biological parents and the circumstances of her birth, it is impossible to point to any one factor that may have led to her behavioural disorder. However, given the statistics evident in the literature, it is probable that a genetic factor may have contributed to Lindsey's ADHD. According to the National Institute of Mental Health (2008), attention disorders run in families. In their ADHD genetic research study, the National Human Genome Research Institute (2012) also reported that children who have ADHD usually have at least one close biological relative who has ADHD. Further, they stated that at least one-third of all fathers who had ADHD in their youth have children with ADHD. Many studies of twins have also shown that a strong genetic influence exists in the disorder (Faraone & Biederman, 1998).

What We Know . . .

Combination of ADHD and Poor Emotional Control Runs in Families

According to a study conducted at Massachusetts General Hospital (2011), siblings of individuals with both ADHD and deficient emotional self-regulation had a significantly greater risk of having both conditions than did siblings of those with ADHD alone. Craig Surman, the lead investigator of this study, stated that the "research offers strong evidence that heritable factors influence how we control our emotions . . . Emotion-like capacities such as the ability to pay attention or control physical movement is probably under forms of brain control that we are just beginning to understand. Our findings also indicate that ADHD doesn't just impact things like reading, listening and getting the bills paid on time; it also can impact how people regulate themselves more broadly, including their emotional expression."

There are also suspected environmental causes of ADHD. Banerjee, Middleton, and Faraone (2007) pointed out that some of these biological and environmental factors include food additives/diet, lead contamination, cigarette and alcohol exposure, maternal smoking during pregnancy, and low birth weight. Further, Jensen (2001) pointed out that trauma to the fetus may result in an injury or abnormal brain development that can lead to ADHD. In Lindsey's case, because she was adopted and few details of her mother's pregnancy are available, it is impossible to know whether she was exposed to any of these conditions.

What We Know . . .

Effects of Children's Exposure to Mercury or Lead

According to a study led by Laval University scientist Dr. Gina Muckle, children exposed to higher levels of mercury or lead are three to five times more likely to be identified by teachers as having problems associated with ADHD. The study of Inuit children living in Arctic Canada is the first to find a high rate of attention-deficit symptoms in children highly exposed to mercury in the womb. In addition, the Inuit children more often had hyperactivity symptoms if they were exposed to low levels of lead during childhood. Muckle said the findings, released in 2012, are important because they show for the first time that the effects of mercury in children are not just subtle but are actually noticeable to teachers. One of the most intriguing findings was that mercury was linked to attention deficits while lead was associated with hyperactivity. The difference may be the timing of the exposures: in the womb for mercury and during childhood for lead. The findings "suggest the brain may be sensitive to different environmental chemicals at different times in development," said Harvard epidemiologist Joe Braun.

Source: From Environmental Health News (2012).

There are also a small number of individuals who appear to acquire ADHD after birth through brain injury (LD Online, 2006). According to Lindsey's parents and medical reports, this was not the cause of Lindsey's ADHD. Other than ear infections, Lindsey has had a healthy childhood. She has not experienced any significant illnesses or physical injuries.

How Has Lindsey's Behavioural Disorder Affected Her Development?

Cognitive Development

Lindsey's cognitive abilities were not a concern when she was a young child. She seemed to be a bright, inquisitive child, and her parents were really more focused on her behaviour problems and her delays in speech. It was not until she entered school that there were questions about her ability to learn. Even then, her disruptive behaviours received much more attention from her teachers than did her difficulties with academic tasks. It was not until Grade 3 that a psycho-educational assessment revealed she has significant language-based learning difficulties. Several comprehensive assessments have been conducted since the initial diagnosis (see *Excerpts from Lindsey's Psycho-Educational Assessment* on p. 145) and they have all confirmed that Lindsey has a severe, pervasive language-based learning disability (i.e., receptive, expressive, reasoning, written, social-pragmatic, memory) that has an impact on all aspects of her functioning, especially academic performance. The psychologist who assessed Lindsey over the past several years has been unable to assign a Full Scale IQ score because of the wide variability in Lindsey's performance on the WISC-IV.

What We Know . . .

ADHD and Learning Disabilities

According to the National Institute of Mental Health (2008), there are a number of other disorders that may occur with ADHD. These include learning disabilities, Tourette syndrome, oppositional defiant disorder, conduct disorder, anxiety and depression, and bipolar disorder. Barkley (1998) estimated the prevalence of ADHD among children with LD ranges from 10–25 per cent. In 2006, this estimate was supported by Schnoes, Reid, Wagner, and Marder, who examined data from a nationally representative study of students receiving special education in the United States. More recently, DuPaul, Gormley, and Laracy (2013) suggested the co-morbidity could be as high as 45 per cent. It should be noted, however, that despite the co-occurrence of ADHD and learning disabilities, numerous studies have confirmed that the two are independent conditions (Doyle, Faraone, DuPre, & Biederman, 2001). In other words, just because there are high rates of ADHD in children with learning disabilities and high rates of learning disabilities in children with ADHD, it does not mean they are both symptoms of the same disorder. Each condition requires a separate and distinct clinical diagnosis and treatment. While ADHD is primarily marked by symptoms of inattention, impulsivity, and hyperactivity, learning disabilities are primarily characterized as discrepancies between academic performance and intellectual ability.

Speech and Language Development

Lindsey's parents acted quickly when as a toddler she failed to reach expected language milestones. Speech-language therapy has been a part of Lindsey's life since then. While she does receive some therapy through the school system, Lindsey's mother commented that the 20 minutes a month offered by the school is of little value considering Lindsey's needs. Fortunately, Lindsey's parents are able to provide her with several hours of private therapy every week. Recently, the speech-language pathologist summarized Lindsey's current status and outlined recommended classroom-based adaptations:

> Lindsey, age 12, is a delightful child who continues to demonstrate language impairments. These impairments impact significantly on her learning, literacy development, and academic performance. We are recommending that speech-language treatment

Lindsey, age 12: wood and clay sculpture.

continue with a focus on the following areas: listening comprehension and recall, auditory-verbal learning, oral and written discourse formulation, written spelling and editing, sight word recognition and word attack, conversational and social-pragmatic skills, and articulation of "l" (blends) and "th." Adaptations needed in the classroom include the following:

- *Ensure that you have Lindsey's attention before giving important instructions.*
- *Provide oral directions in small steps, pausing between steps to allow extra processing time.*
- *Pair verbal commands with visuals (e.g., gestures, diagrams, written instructions on the blackboard).*
- *Verify that important instructions and directions are understood (e.g., ask Lindsey to rephrase and review important information).*
- *Provide word retrieval cues (e.g., first sound, word association) instead of saying words for Lindsey when she is struggling.*
- *Teach vocabulary from the curriculum deliberately and explicitly.*
- *Teach memory strategies explicitly and often.*

What We Know . . .

ADHD and Speech-Language Difficulties

It is relatively common for children with ADHD to also experience problems understanding and expressing language (Mueller & Tomblin, 2012). In fact, disorders of grammar, semantics, and pragmatics overlap significantly with childhood psychiatric disorders (Toppelberg & Shapiro, 2000). Furthermore, Cantwell (1999) reported that as many as 50 per cent of individuals with ADHD have communication disorders. While the link between these two disorders is not fully understood, it may be that speech and language difficulties lead to attentional problems in some particular way or that they are both caused by some common underlying factor, such as some type of central nervous system dysfunction.

Social and Emotional Development

Lindsey's social and emotional development has undoubtedly been affected by her difficulties with behaviour, learning, and communication. As her mother commented, Lindsey's tantrum-like behaviour began at the same time that she was having problems with language acquisition. Then her behaviour became even more disruptive when she entered school, where learning and communication were obvious problems. Ongoing difficulties within each of these domains are a source of great frustration for Lindsey. According to her parents, she has always been a child who wants to be socially involved and not being successful in this part of her life is very taxing on her emotionally. While she has an excellent relationship with family members who understand her disabilities, she has not always been a popular girl at school. It is easy to see why inattention (e.g., being easily distracted and not paying attention) and impulsivity (e.g., careless actions, blurting things out, and interrupting others) could lead to social rejection by peers. However, these rejections have not stopped Lindsey from seeking friendships. Her mother reported that she has more friends now that she has entered a provincial demonstration school for learning disabilities where her peer group is made up of students who also have ADHD and/or learning disabilities.

From the Psychologist's Notebook

It is important to realize that ADHD affects all parts of a child's life, not just school. Usually, children make many friendships outside of school, especially when they are taking part in extracurricular activities. This is not always the case for children with exceptionalities. Lindsey has been involved in many extracurricular activities; however, most of these experiences have been cut short because of her behaviour. She has been enrolled in dance classes, a soccer program, skating lessons, and skiing lessons. Her

Continued

instructors have commented on her inability to pay attention and her tendency to be easily distracted. Her father told me about an instance where she basically brought a soccer game to a stop when she was distracted by a butterfly. She also has had difficulty following instructions when they were directed at the group as a whole. Fortunately, Lindsey's parents now understand her needs and they have the financial ability to provide her with one-on-one or small group instruction. She currently takes horseback riding lessons where there are only four other students in the class. The instructor is aware of Lindsey's needs and talks to her before class about the technique they are going to be practising that day. The instructor also knows that Lindsey has difficulty discerning between left and right, so besides using the words during class, she also points to the desired direction and lifts the hand that should be used for a particular manoeuvre. Lindsey also takes private art lessons from an experienced artist and art teacher. Lindsey has never exhibited any behavioural problems in these classes despite the fact that each class is two hours in length. In fact, the instructor has commented on Lindsey's high level of intensity and focus. It is interesting to note that Lindsey has a great passion for art and is quite talented in this area.

Best friend

To describe to me what you mean to me, A friend will just not do, Cause I have never had a friend I've loved as much as you By fate you come into my life to play a special part, And now it seems that you have got a place here in my heart. If I could only find a way to make my wish come true, I'd wish at times when you were sad I could be there with you. Cause I would do my very best to chase away your fears, And hold you cradle in my arms and kiss away your tears And this is just a sample of how much you mean to me, But till they find a better word "Best Friends" we'll have to be.

Lindsey, age 12.

What Is School Like for Lindsey?

According to Lindsey's mother, school has been a source of constant frustration for her child ever since kindergarten. Lindsey was enrolled in a bilingual junior and senior kindergarten. Her JK teacher reported that "Lindsey needs to listen and follow rules better." By the middle of SK, Lindsey's behavioural problems were causing significant disruptions in the classroom and her teacher was unable to manage the situation. Lindsey's parents decided to remove her from the school, and they followed up on the principal's suggestion that a psycho-educational assessment should be conducted. The assessment was completed in June, and Lindsey's parents followed the psychologist's recommendation to move Lindsey to a school where she would not have to attend a bilingual program. Unfortunately, her behaviour problems did not decrease upon enrolment in Grade 1 at the new school. Another assessment at that time led to the diagnosis of ADHD, and Ritalin was prescribed. Lindsey's mother describes how school progressed from there:

> The Grade 1 teacher noted dramatic improvements once the medication was started. However, Lindsey continued to struggle academically. In hindsight, there were a lot of warning signs that these struggles were due to a learning disability.
>
> In Grade 2, the teacher seemed to have a lot of concerns, but she did not recommend an IEP. The only academic support that Lindsey received that year was inclusion in a "Keys to Literacy" group that was composed of about six students. By this time, Lindsey was doing over an hour of homework each night. It was a battle for us, usually with some screaming, weeping, and lots of frustration. Lindsey hated reading and would hide under her bed or throw books, even if I was going to read to her.
>
> Grade 3 was the worst year for all of us. It was the year that Lindsey's stormy behaviour reached its peak. It was also the year that Lindsey talked about wishing to be dead, which was very upsetting for us. Her teacher was really gunning for good results in the Grade 3 testing and it seemed obvious to us that Lindsey represented a big failure. The teacher was not prepared to deal with Lindsey's learning difficulties and interpreted everything that was going on as behaviour problems. A good example of this was when Lindsey was caught stuffing her homework notes in the mesh fence in the schoolyard. Rather than seeing this as Lindsey's way of coping (since she was clearly unable to do the homework), the teacher saw it only as defiant behaviour. It was obvious that there was no empathy for Lindsey. The teacher actually told me that Lindsey did not have any learning problems and was just pulling the wool over everyone's eyes. To me, this was a perfect example of a teacher not understanding learning disabilities. I do admit, however, that it must have been very difficult to have Lindsey in a large class where there was a lot of material to plow through, especially when the majority of the class was capable of keeping up with the fast pace.
>
> It was also during her Grade 3 year that Lindsey began picking at her skin and making it bleed. This was frustrating for us because of all the different problems she was having that year. The school brought in a behavioural specialist to address the picking, and they began to count the number of times she was picking in an hour. In my mind, the picking was clearly anxiety-driven as she would pick at her earlobe and make it bleed or pick at her fingers rather than address what her needs were and why she was so anxious. They told me that the purpose of counting the times she picked

was to determine a baseline for a behaviour modification program. However, that program was never implemented. By the end of the school year, we were offered a spot for her in an LD class at another school.

We were asked to go see this new school and meet the teacher. I remember that day so clearly. We met with the teacher and saw her classroom. She had 10 students, all of whom appeared very happy and friendly. The teacher told us that they all had ADHD and learning disabilities. We spoke for close to an hour and I remember coming out of the school, getting into my car, and crying. I was so happy and overwhelmed that Lindsey would be going into that classroom. I knew right away that it was the right class for her. The program was individualized and while all the kids had ADHD, the room was reasonably quiet, but not suppressed. The teacher was friendly but clearly the boss and in control. The kids obviously loved her and respected her.

Lindsey entered the new school for her Grade 4 year even though the school was a 45 minute bus ride from our house. We quickly decided to move closer to the school when this long bus ride caused us concern. At this time there was no long-acting medication for Lindsey and the extended school day was making it difficult for us to get her medication right without having it wear off too soon or giving her too much. This is just an example of the kind of things parents of children with ADHD have to do to help their children.

In her Grade 4 year, Lindsey finally made some friends. The kids were amazingly accepting of each other and her, even though she was a year younger than the other students. Lindsey stayed with the same teacher in that LD class for Grades 5 and 6. During that time, she never had a suspension, although she did have to go to the principal's office a few times for being rough on the playground. Her teacher also noticed that because of her impulsivity she would follow behind other kids and not use her own good judgment. I really see her making some good gains with this over the past year. We do worry though about high school and her tendency not to think before she acts. In terms of her overall behaviour, she now has fewer stormy periods and seems much more co-operative in general. The worst behaviour we ever saw was during the Grade 3 year, and things got progressively better after that.

Grade 7 has brought Lindsey to another new school as the LD class she attended for Grades 4 to 6 does not extend into Grade 7. We decided to have her assessed for entry into a provincial demonstration school for learning disabilities, and we were successful in having her placed there. We didn't feel she was ready for the regular classroom quite yet as she has just begun to develop some needed self-confidence within the small class setting. This new school offers a one-year program that not only addresses academic difficulties but also deals with ADHD behaviours.

What Educational Approach Is Best for Lindsey?

Placement Options

Demonstration schools were established in Ontario to provide special education programs for students who need intensive help with academics and social skills. The goal is to have these students return to regular programs operated by local school boards within one or two years.

Before entering the demonstration school, Lindsey's school experiences included time in both an inclusive classroom (kindergarten to Grade 3) and a self-contained classroom for students with learning disabilities (Grades 4 to 6). The inclusive classroom was not a good fit for Lindsey at the time because her behaviour and learning difficulties were just being assessed, her teachers were unable to meet her needs, and she had not learned any effective coping strategies. She was very disruptive in the classroom and her frustrations with learning were causing her great anxiety. Her move to the self-contained classroom was definitely a positive one. By this time, her specific needs were established and an experienced teacher of students with ADHD and learning disabilities took responsibility for her education. This teacher was able to provide an environment where Lindsey felt accepted and ready to learn strategies that would assist her with both academics and social skills. According to Lindsey's mother:

> *Lindsey made her most significant gains so far in the LD classroom (Grades 4 to 6). The teacher emphasized organization and routines. She had a very strict requirement that students must constantly refer to a planner where they would record the work that needed to be done and the deadlines that had to be met. The planner had to be signed by her on a regular basis. She also demanded that students keep their notes organized. This teacher just seemed to know how to implement good strategies for teaching students like Lindsey.*
>
> *It was during this time, in Grades 4 to 6, that homework became a less frustrating experience for our family. Lindsey's teacher seemed to have a better understanding of the purpose of homework and how it can be quite a challenge for a student with ADHD. She did things at her end that made it much easier for Lindsey. Homework time at our house became shorter and much more productive. We appreciated this because it made our evenings with Lindsey more enjoyable and not all about her learning difficulties.*

What We Know . . .

Assisting Students with ADHD in the Classroom

Here are some classroom strategies that may assist the student with ADHD:

- Develop a model of behaviour management that is compatible with both the home and classroom environment and which is clear in its expectations. Students with ADHD can be trained to monitor their own behaviours.
- Recognize the issue of compliance versus comprehension and be able to discriminate between these two types of behaviour.
- Set predictable intervals of "no-work" periods that the child may earn as a reward for effort. This helps increase attention span and impulse control through a gradual training process.
- Plan for success. Break tasks into manageable, sequential steps the student can handle with frequent breaks that can be seen as rewards for appropriate behaviour. Provide a sequential checklist for longer assignments and projects.
- Help the student get started with individual tasks.

Continued

- Supplement oral instructions with visual reinforcement, such that the student can frequently check that he or she is following instructions (e.g., write the assignment on the board, photocopy printed instructions, use an overhead, or have matched instructions on tape).
- Encourage the use of a homework journal so that the student has a record of assignments completed and those yet to be done.
- If the student has difficulty taking notes, supply a copy of the notes from another student or from the teacher's notes.
- Frequent breaks can be created by allowing the student with ADHD to compare his or her responses on assignments that require drill and practice with those of a stronger student.
- Modify tests if necessary (e.g., provide extra time or divide the test into two parts to be completed at different times during the day).
- Modify assignments, if necessary (e.g., assign fewer questions in math, use contracts for longer assignments).
- Consider where the student with ADHD is seated. A quiet seat in close proximity to the teacher may assist the student in staying on task.
- Offer a screened corner to your class as an earned privilege rather than a punishment. This avoids segregating the child who may need the screened corner to reduce distractions.
- Try a variety of teaching strategies, including assigning a peer tutor, class-wide peer tutoring, development of class meetings, and life-space interviewing.
- Give responsibilities that can be successfully carried out to help the student feel needed and worthwhile.
- Work with the student to develop social interaction skills (e.g., interpreting non-verbal communication cues). Modelling and role-playing along with reinforcement of appropriate skills tend to be most effective.
- When transitions or unusual events are to occur, try to prepare the child for what is to come by explaining the situation and describing appropriate behaviour in advance.
- Offer the student training in study skills, time management, organizational skills, communication skills, and test taking.

Source: Excerpted from British Columbia Ministry of Education (2006).

From the Psychologist's Notebook

It is clear that Lindsey's parents are not only strong advocates for her in terms of her educational needs, but they also take part in her education, especially in terms of homework. While this can be quite frustrating for parents of a child like Lindsey, it is critical to her progress (both in the learning domain and in the behavioural domain) that she experience consistent messages at home and at school. Lindsey's father spoke to me about how they try very hard to provide Lindsey with a calm home environment. When she was in the early grades, it was necessary for her mother or father to sit with her throughout the entire homework period. They could not even get up from the table where she was working without distracting her. These homework sessions were often quite emotional for both parents and child. Eventually, Lindsey's parents cleared a space in their family room, furnished it with a table and two chairs, and designated it her "work area." Now the television is always off during homework time and an effort is made to provide a quiet atmosphere where Lindsey can focus on the tasks at hand. Her parents make themselves available when needed, whether it is to provide motivation or to actually help with the homework tasks. They have learned to use strategies that are consistent with those used at school. With time, these homework periods have become less emotional and more productive. This is in part due to the willingness of Lindsey's parents to learn how they can best assist their child with the challenges she faces.

What We Know . . .

Homework Tips for Teachers of Students with ADHD

Just as homework was an extremely frustrating activity for Lindsey, it is often a source of stress for many students with ADHD. Rief (2005, pp. 219–222) outlined valuable tips for teachers when considering homework assignments for these students:

- Be responsive to parents who report great frustration surrounding homework. Be willing to make adjustments so that students with ADHD spend a reasonable, but not excessive, amount of time doing their homework.
- Realize that students with ADHD who receive medication during the school day (to help them focus and stay on task) often do not receive medication in the evening. Students with ADHD are in class during their optimal production times, yet they often will not manage to complete their assigned work. It is an unreasonable expectation that parents will be able to get their child to produce at home what you were not able to get them to produce all day at school.
- When assigning homework, realize how critical it is for students with ADHD to participate in extracurricular activities. They need every opportunity to develop areas of strength. Also, remember that these students may work with other professionals or participate in academic training programs outside of school hours.
- Many teachers have a practice of sending home unfinished class work. Avoid doing so with ADHD students. Instead, provide the necessary modifications and supports so that in-school work is in-school work, and homework is homework.
- Remember that homework should be a time for reviewing and practising what students have been taught in class. Don't give assignments involving new information that parents are expected to teach their children.

Continued

- Homework should not be "busy work." Make the homework relevant and purposeful so that time isn't spent on obscure assignments that are not helping to reinforce skills or concepts learned in class.
- Never add on homework as a punishment or consequence for misbehaviour at school.
- Make sure you have explained the homework and clarified any questions.
- Supervise students with ADHD before they walk out the door at the end of the day. Make sure they have materials, books, and recorded assignments in their backpacks.
- Assign a student buddy (or two) to your students with ADHD. They should have one or two classmates, who are willing to answer questions, to call on if necessary in the evenings.
- One of the most important things you can do to help all students (and their parents) keep on top of homework, tests, and long-term projects is to require the use of an assignment calendar. With some students, require that parents initial the assignment calendar daily. This is a good way for you to communicate with parents. You may write a few comments or notes to the parents on the assignment sheet and vice versa.
- Modify the homework for students with special needs. Ask yourself: What is the goal? What do I want the students to learn from the assignment? Can they get the concepts without having to do all the writing? Can they practise the skills in an easier, more motivating format? Can they do fewer practise questions and still accomplish what I want them to?
- Communicate with other teachers who have your students in their classes. Students may be assigned a number of tests, large projects, and reading assignments at the same time from a number of different teachers. Be sensitive to this by staggering due dates.
- Always collect homework and give feedback. It is very frustrating for students to spend a lot of time on assignments that the teacher never bothers to collect.
- Some teachers find it helpful to have their students graph their own homework completion and return rates. Improved performance can result in some kind of reinforcement.
- Provide incentives for turning in homework.

Source: Adapted from Rief (2005).

Lindsey stayed in the special segregated class for three years, the maximum time allowed. As stated earlier, rather than place her back in the regular classroom for Grade 7, her parents, with the support of her teacher and her psychologist, sought a placement in the demonstration school. They all agreed that Lindsey was not ready to re-enter the inclusive classroom. An extensive application process was completed, and Lindsey was accepted to the school.

Lindsey's mother wrote the following letter to the principal of the new school so he would better understand his new student:

Lindsey's strength is her artistic ability. She is confident in her skill as an artist and has begun to formulate a life goal of becoming a visual artist. Not surprisingly, her preferred mode of learning is visual. She finds pictures and visual clues very helpful for following instructions, telling a story, and remembering details. However, even with these types of aids, she must deal every day with the frustration of learning something like addition tables, spelling words, or new vocabulary, only to find the next day that her memory has failed her. She has spent numerous years learning the same material over and over (e.g., the Grade 4 math book has been done three times over three different school years), but each time it seems like it's the first time she has ever experienced the tasks being presented to her. Reading remains a great source of frustration and continues to be the area we have the most struggle with at home. This includes even a dislike of being read to. It is also a source of embarrassment in situations outside of school when she is with a group of her peers and reading is a part of the activity that they are participating in (e.g., camp, church).

We think it is important that Lindsey be able to read at a level sufficient to allow her to move forward in other areas that require reading. We would like her to be able to read, or to use technology to read, material that interests her as well as material that is required to complete her other academic courses. In the past, she has enjoyed novel studies where the teacher has read the chapters out loud and a large part of the course work involved discussing ideas in class. She would completely have missed out on this experience if she had been left to read the novel by herself.

In terms of basic numeracy, she has already made some gains in this area. We have noted that she is making an effort to tell time, and she has begun to understand fractions of the hour. She still does not have the concept of money. She can do some math by rote (e.g., adding with carrying), but we are not sure she fully understands the concepts behind what she is doing.

Lindsey's ADHD affects all parts of life. Her behaviour both at home and at school can affect how others view her and how she views herself. She can be impulsive, blurting

Lindsey, age 10.

out comments before she thinks about what she is saying and interrupting others. She has trouble paying attention and staying focused on tasks. She can become quite anxious at times. Occasionally, she will act silly and out of control and then has trouble calming herself down. She has difficulty with social interactions because of these behaviours.

We have some goals for Lindsey. In the short term, we would like her to become more adventurous and daring in her learning, to not be so anxious about what she does not know or what she thinks she cannot do. We hope she learns not to shy away from a book on art or horses simply because she is afraid she cannot read it. In the long-term, we hope that Lindsey will be able to graduate from high school and perhaps pursue further training in art if that is her choice. We would like her to be able to understand and manage her behaviour so that she can have meaningful, positive interactions with others.

There were some immediate changes to Lindsey's overall education plan when she entered the demonstration school. While she has had an IEP since Grade 4, she now also has a Behaviour Plan (see *Lindsey's Behaviour Plan* on pp. 148–149) that specifically addresses her behavioural needs. This plan describes her current behavioural areas of concern, states the goals that are expected to be met in the short term, and outlines how school staff will intervene to help Lindsey meet these goals. The plan is an ever evolving one. Lindsey's teacher has already provided the following report, one month into Lindsey's first semester at the school:

Lindsey is a positive participant in her new school. She participates in all group activities and is always willing to try her best. Learning the rules and routines of the school has been the focus during the first half of this semester. As noted in her goal areas, Lindsey often follows the lead of her peers to maintain her focus within the program. This has been a successful strategy for her to this point; however, as the program progresses she will be required to maintain more independent programming.

Lindsey has had a difficult time identifying behaviours that have a negative impact on her interactions with others; therefore, internalizing strategies and using these independently are a challenge for her. She has difficulty discussing situations with staff at the point of performance and will often avoid these interactions.

Assisting Lindsey to identify personal strengths and areas to concentrate change will be the focus of the remainder of the semester. Lindsey will continue to be encouraged to take risks to develop new behaviour patterns and to move forward in a positive direction.

Based on this report, Lindsey's current Behaviour Plan identifies three areas of concern (see pp. 148–149). They are impulse control, social interactions, and knowledge of how her ADHD and learning disabilities affect her life. These concerns, the new program goals, and the planned interventions are clearly outlined in the updated plan, and they are familiar to all staff members who work with Lindsey.

From the Psychologist's Notebook

It is clear that, to date, Lindsey has done much better when not in an inclusive classroom. This does not mean that she should never return to such an environment, it simply means that both Lindsey and her teachers will have to be precisely aware of her specific conditions and fully understand the strategies they both will employ to overcome her behavioural and learning difficulties. Lindsey's Grade 3 teacher certainly did not have the knowledge or the skills to help her. Lindsey was probably engaging in exactly the same school work avoidance behaviours displayed by non-ADHD students. And this is often a teacher's dilemma: How do they know if a child is behaving inappropriately on purpose (non-ADHD) or if the child's behaviour is something they do not have full control over (ADHD)? It is in these instances that a teacher's awareness and knowledge can prevent problematic situations from becoming worse. Even if the teacher does not know what to do to correct the child's behaviour, their understanding of the condition can keep them from exacerbating the problem.

Evaluation of Progress

Just as Lindsey's academic progress is measured by the attainment of learning objectives, her behavioural progress is currently measured by the attainment of behavioural goals that are outlined in her Behaviour Plan. Input from her parents, her teachers, and the clinicians who work with her allow decisions to be made regarding future behaviour goals. These individuals use their observational skills to note any increases in desirable behaviours and any decreases in undesirable behaviours. In addition to these observational reports, Lindsey is directly involved in evaluating her behaviour. She is asked for her own assessment on how she is doing and she is actively involved in evaluating past behaviour and formulating new behavioural goals that will help her both inside and outside the classroom. This is a critical component of behaviour management because it will enhance Lindsey's self-regulatory abilities, as we described in Chapter 4. This will, in turn, make the overarching process of classroom management easier for her teachers.

Something to Think About

You find yourself teaching in a regular classroom where two of the students have been diagnosed with ADHD. Both are easily distracted and their hyperactivity is often disruptive to classroom activities. In an attempt to help these students improve their behaviour, you implement behaviour therapy techniques, including **positive reinforcement**, **time-outs**, and **response costs**. One of the students responds particularly well. Her parents notice the difference in her behaviour and begin using the same techniques more consistently at home. The other student shows signs of responding positively to your approach but seems to need "retraining" after weekends and holidays. You talk with his parents regarding your concerns. They indicate that while they would like to help their child, nothing seems to work. Their attempts at discipline all seem to end in yelling and tears. What advice would you give these parents to help them change the situation at home?

positive reinforcement
When desired student behaviour is increased through the use of rewards.

time-out
Removal of a student from a learning activity or learning situation as a consequence of misbehaviour.

response cost
Removal of a student's previously received reward as a consequence of misbehaviour.

How Is Lindsey Different from Other Students Who Have Behavioural Disorders?

Behavioural disorders cover a wide spectrum of behaviours, including attention disorders, conduct disorders, and anxiety disorders. Within each of these groupings, there are obviously many unique combinations of behavioural characteristics. For example, even within ADHD there are three identified presentations (combined, attentive, and hyperactive/impulsive), and within these three presentations two individuals with exactly the same diagnosis can have very different behavioural profiles. As well, someone who has been diagnosed with one type of behavioural disorder may exhibit some of the behaviours common in other disorders. This is true in Lindsey's case as she experiences anxiety in addition to her attention disorder. To complicate matters even further, individuals can be considered exceptional in other areas, thus making their situations even more unique. For example, Lindsey has *both* a learning disability and speech difficulties, and while she has never been identified as gifted, she exhibits remarkable artistic talents.

Despite all of these possible differences, students with behavioural disorders do have one thing in common. Like Lindsey, they all have difficulty meeting societal expectations for acceptable behaviour, especially within the education system. This is apparent in the following two cases, each of which outlines a different behavioural disorder:

dysfunctional environment
Surroundings that contain or perpetuate a persistent series of high-stress incidents that threaten one's sense of psychological security.

- *Conduct disorder:* Ryan is a troubled 13-year-old who comes from a dysfunctional environment. His mother has had an ongoing problem with drug addiction, and Ryan does not even remember his father who left when he was just a toddler. Ryan's chaotic home environment has most likely contributed to his conduct disorder. His school file is full of negative reports regarding his behaviour. He is outspoken, rude, and has no respect for others or their possessions. He has been caught stealing, lying, and using alcohol. Ryan is not well liked by his peers and is considered a bully. Most students in his school are afraid of him. The school principal and Ryan's teachers are finding it more and more difficult to manage him. He is usually very disruptive in the classroom and is beginning to show signs of physical aggressiveness. School suspensions have been ineffective. Ryan seems to enjoy confrontation and, according to him, not having to go to school is a bonus. He is slipping further and further behind in his school work. The school team, along with his social worker, is considering that he be placed temporarily in a special educational facility where he can receive behavioural management and support.

- *Anxiety disorder:* Ellen has always been an anxious, shy child. Even though she is now 13 years old, she still does not like to be away from her parents. She has rarely been away from home overnight, and she worries constantly when one of her parents has to be away for any length of time. Unable to cope with the anxiety of taking the school bus, her mother drives her to school and picks her up each day. If her mother is just a few minutes' late, Ellen panics and fears something horrible has happened to her. Panic attacks are all too familiar to Ellen. She has them frequently, whether it is because she is faced with a new experience (e.g., start of a new school year) or because of social anxiety (e.g., having to give a presentation in front of the class). Unfortunately, there are very few situations that do not cause anxiety for Ellen. The only time she can begin to relax is when she is at home with her parents. Even then she is constantly worrying about what "dangers" she has to face in the coming hours or days: a dentist's appointment, a math test, a neighbourhood picnic. There is nothing in Ellen's life that does not provoke feelings of fear. Ellen's anxiety disorder has become so debilitating that her success in school is being seriously jeopardized. In the early grades, her behaviour was explained away by shyness, but now the behaviour is obviously affecting her more severely. She loves to learn and has an above-average IQ. She completes her homework assignments with ease. However, the demands placed upon her in the classroom are just too overwhelming, and she is failing to complete assigned classroom tasks successfully. A psychologist has recently become involved. Ellen has just begun cognitive-behavioural therapy, and her parents and her teachers are learning how to best support her.

> **cognitive-behavioural therapy**
> An action-oriented form of therapy used to alter distorted attitudes and resulting problem behaviours by identifying and replacing negative or inaccurate thoughts with more positive ones.

What We Know . . .

Conduct Disorder

According to the *Diagnostic and Statistical Manual of Mental Disorders*, Fifth Edition (DSM-5), conduct disorder is the occurrence of a repetitive and persistent pattern of behaviour in which the basic rights of others or major age-appropriate societal norms or rules are violated. This manifests as the presence of at least 3 of the following 15 criteria in the past 12 months from any of the categories below, with at least one criterion present in the past 6 months:

Aggression to people and animals:

- Often bullies, threatens, or intimidates others
- Often initiates physical fights
- Has used a weapon that can cause serious physical harm to others
- Has been physically cruel to people
- Has been physically cruel to animals
- Has stolen while confronting a victim
- Has forced someone into sexual activity

Destruction of property:

- Has deliberately engaged in fire setting with the intention of causing serious damage
- Has deliberately destroyed others' property (other than by fire setting)

Deceitfulness or theft:

- Has broken into someone else's house, building, or car
- Often lies to obtain goods or favours or to avoid obligations
- Has stolen items of nontrivial value without confronting a victim

Serious violations of rules:

- Often stays out at night despite parental prohibitions, beginning before age 13 years
- Has run away from home overnight at least twice while living in the parental or parental surrogate home, or once without returning for a lengthy period
- Is often truant from school, beginning before age 13 years

Continued

Added specifier: The person does not feel bad or guilty when he or she does something wrong (exclude remorse when expressed only when caught or facing punishment). The individual shows a general lack of concern about the negative consequences of his or her actions.

Source: Reprinted with permission from the *Diagnostic and Statistical Manual of Mental Disorders*, Fifth Edition. (Copyright 2013). American Psychiatric Association. All Rights Reserved.

What We Know . . .

Anxiety Disorders

According to Hannell (2006), all anxiety conditions are marked by feelings of fearfulness and apprehension. They may involve physical symptoms, obsessive-compulsive symptoms, or specific phobias. Anxiety disorders often run in families, and a child's tendency to be anxious can be exacerbated by inappropriate treatment by adults. Anxious children are often perfectionists. Treatment for anxiety disorders includes cognitive-behaviour therapy, building up resilience to anxiety triggers, and relaxation training. Teachers can assist students with anxiety disorders by

- providing a predictable, secure, and nurturing environment;
- recognizing situations that the student finds fearful and not forcing participation;
- providing relaxed opportunities for the student to be near his or her anxiety triggers; and,
- providing reassurance and remaining calm during a student's anxiety attack.

Closing Lindsey's File

Lindsey has faced many hurdles in her school life and, to her credit, she still remains motivated and positive about learning. While academic tasks can be frustrating for her, she now finds herself in a supportive school environment where she is becoming more aware of how her behavioural disorder and her learning disability affect her on a daily basis. She is acquiring more strategies that allow her to have both successful social interactions and positive learning experiences. For now, it appears that the provincial demonstration school for learning disabilities is the desired placement for Lindsey. She is making friends and she is motivated to try her best at academic tasks. Lindsey described the changes in her school life as follows:

> When I was first in school, like in Grade 2, I felt completely ignored. The teacher thought I couldn't do anything, so she never called on me in class. I just sat there all day. I only had one friend in that whole school. Then I went to a special class in a different school where all the kids in the class were like me. Our teacher was really nice and seemed to understand us. She could get inside our brain and know why we acted the way we did. Now in my new school I am in an even smaller class with more kids like me. There are only six of us. It feels like a family. We don't have to feel

embarrassed. You can put up your hand and the teacher will listen to what you have to say. I will be sad when I have to leave this school and go back to a regular school. Maybe I will just hide in a box and not go.

Lindsey's mother echoed her daughter's obvious satisfaction with her new school. She and her husband have noticed the following positive changes in Lindsey's behaviour:

Lindsey definitely has more confidence now. While she always had confidence in her artistic abilities, she is now talking about her abilities in other areas like in science and sports. She seems to actually enjoy learning and sharing what she has learned with us. Most surprising is the fact that she is writing poetry and taking an interest in books. Just the other night I found her in her bed using a thesaurus to write a poem. Not that long ago she was doing anything she could to avoid having to read. It is remarkable to see this change in her. She really seems to enjoy school and has made very good friends. In fact, she loves to chat on [online] with her schoolmates when she is at home. Of course, she still has difficulties with learning and behaviour, so we are trying to extend her time at the demonstration school for one more year. She is the youngest student there now and I think one more year will help her mature even more and prepare her for her high school years. We know it will be difficult for her to go back to the regular classroom where her differences will again be more apparent.

From the Psychologist's Notebook

It will be important that Lindsey's parents and her teachers continue to provide her with significant support as she enters her teen years. Recent research by Hinshaw, Owens, Sami, and Fargeon (2006) indicates that adolescent girls with ADHD are at a greater risk than their peers for substance abuse, eating disorders, depression, and anxiety disorders. Given that individuals with ADHD are usually impulsive, it is not hard to see why they may quickly give in to peer pressure and try things like drugs and alcohol. They may also be motivated to partake in inappropriate activities just because they so desperately want to "fit in" and be accepted by their peers. Paradoxically, it is this very problem—lack of social relationships—that can also lead to feelings of depression and anxiety.

Lindsey is certainly at risk as she enters her teen years. She is a sensitive and somewhat anxious child who desires to be an active member of her peer group. Yet she is impulsive and has difficulty interacting with others. The adolescent years will clearly present obstacles for her. Not only will she continue to struggle with academics, but peer relationships and self-esteem issues will become even more of a challenge. Her parents can support her through this period by staying aware of her friendships and her activities; encouraging open communication within the home; and developing mutually agreed-upon rules and consequences for behaviour.

Something to Think About

Suppose you are a secondary teacher who has a student like Lindsey in your class. How might you help support this student as he or she tries to "fit in" with his or her classmates? What actions can you take inside the classroom to influence how your students interact outside the classroom?

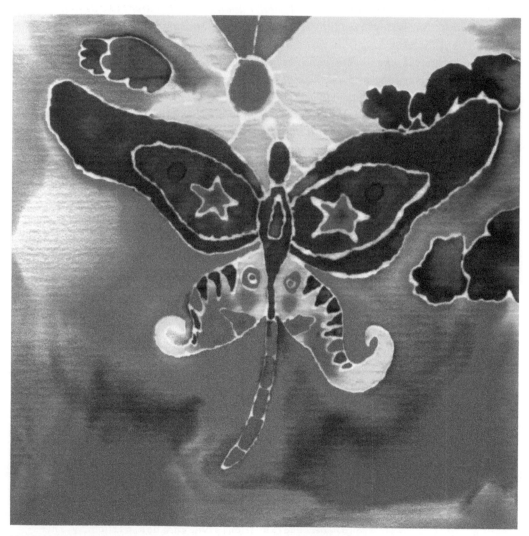

Lindsey, age 10.

Updating Lindsey's Story

Unfortunately, Lindsey continued to have significant difficulties with her schooling after we met her. She stayed in the demonstration school for the maximum time allowed—two years. Her return to the regular classroom was not successful despite the considerable support provided by her parents. This is not surprising given that Lindsey has a significant behaviour disorder as well as learning disabilities. According to Bertin (2011), a student like Lindsey has great difficulty with executive functioning:

> High schools approach academic support for children differently than primary and middle schools do at lower grade levels. Kids, both with and without ADHD, are expected to take responsibility for their education. They are supposed to manage their schedules on their own, handle intense homework loads (and hand everything in on time), and coordinate time around all their after-school activities. The pressure can be intense, but most kids without ADHD sort it out, make a plan, and thrive.
>
> Yet even without ADHD . . . the average teen is still developing their executive function abilities—the mental capacity to regulate emotions and behaviours, organize, plan, manage time, and a host of other related tasks . . . In one way, adolescence is about surviving impulsive decisions and scattered thinking and then to become an older, wiser grown up—as reflected by these changes within the brain . . . Executive function relates to concepts such as "wisdom" and "maturity," and does not plateau in its development until near age thirty. This cognitive progression leads to a decrease in risky behaviours and a better ability to monitor our behaviour and to plan for the future . . .
>
> While most teens struggle with executive function, those with ADHD fall even further behind. Their capacity to organize and plan lags by several years. Because of their neurology they struggle with staying on task, transitioning from activities, keeping track of lists, handing things in, and managing their time. The ability to connect immediate behaviours (I don't feel like going for extra help today) to future consequences may not exist yet.
>
> This attribution to "effort" or "motivation" is the fundamental flaw undermining many academic plans for teens with ADHD. These issues have little, if anything, to do with motivation. Even with lots of effort, if a teen does not possess age-appropriate executive functioning the essentials for school success are not going to be found without the involvement of responsible, caring adults.
>
> Visiting a teacher for after-school support requires the ability to remember the possibility exists, to keep track of time, to put aside the current activity, and to maintain attention from point A to point B. It requires recognizing a need for help, making a plan, and then sticking with the plan over the long haul. As teens fall further behind, the stress increases and at the same time more and more school work accumulates, further taxing their limited executive function skills. For someone with ADHD, it may be too much to ask.
>
> Someone who looks and acts like a teenager may have the executive function and self-monitoring skills of a child years younger. A fifteen year old with frontal lobes going on ten has the capacity of a ten year old to manage his workload and responsibilities. Establishing a school plan for a ninth grader with ADHD is a set up for failure when relying entirely on that teenager for planning and communication. Superficially, it might not seem to make any sense that high school teachers must communicate with parents about school work, but for certain students that intervention is a vital part of short-term planning. Parents stay in the loop, aware within days if work falls behind.

Teens require an opportunity to collaborate, to feel like they are individuals and are being heard, and they may rebel when too much is dictated about their lives. If a particular teen can handle their school work, you can run with it, let him take responsibility and prosper. If he can't stay on top of things because of ADHD and executive function, then he can't.

Some children do lose motivation because they have been struggling for so many years. However, as motivation typically builds from success and a sense of mastery, the initial step to improved motivation is putting the right plan in place. The long term goal of independence doesn't change, but without the support network kids become overwhelmed. (Bertin, 2011)

Summary

Students with behavioural, mental, and emotional disorders are categorized as having an emotional disturbance. Lindsey's emotional disturbance, attention-deficit/hyperactivity disorder, was diagnosed by a psychologist and subsequently treated with a stimulant medication. The cause of Lindsey's ADHD may have been genetic and/or environmental. As can be the case, Lindsey was also identified as having learning disabilities, speech-language difficulties, and anxiety issues. Consequently, school has proven difficult for Lindsey with special placement outside the regular classroom being the most beneficial in terms of her education progress and general well-being. Having effective behavioural, as well as educational, plans in place is most critical for students with ADHD. Even with these plans, students like Lindsey are likely to experience significant challenges in high school.

Learning More about Students with Behavioural Disorders

Academic Journals

Behavioural Disorders
Journal of the American Academy of Child and Adolescent Psychiatry
Journal of Attention Disorders
Journal of Emotional and Behavioral Disorders

Books

Brown, T. E. (2013). *A new understanding of ADHD in children and adults: Executive function impairments.* New York, NY: Routledge.

Rapoport, E. M. (2009). *ADHD and social skills: A step-by-step guide for teachers and parents.* Lanham, MD: Rowman & Littlefield Education.

Reid, R., & Johnson, J. (2012). *Teacher's guide to ADHD.* New York, NY: Guilford Press.

Rief, S. F. (2005). *How to reach and teach children with ADD/ADHD: Practical techniques, strategies, and interventions* (2nd ed.). San Francisco, CA: Jossey-Bass.

Rief, S. F. (2015). *The ADHD book of lists: A practical guide for helping children and teens* (2nd ed.). San Francisco, CA: Jossey-Bass.

Tannock, R. (2007). The educational implications of attention deficit hyperactive disorder. What works? Research into Practice, Research Monograph #3. Toronto, ON: The Literacy and Numeracy Secretariat.

Vaughn, S., & Bos, C. S. (2014). *Strategies for teaching students with learning and behaviour problems* (9th ed.). Upper Saddle River, NJ: Pearson.

Wolraich, M. I ., & DuPaul, G. J. (2010). *ADHD diagnosis and management: A practical guide for the clinic and the classroom.* Baltimore, MD: Paul H. Brookes Pub.

Web Links

A Primer for Teaching Students with ADHD

www.ldatschool.ca/primer-adhd
This primer, compiled for Canadian teachers, provides basic information on ADHD as well as resources and strategies for teaching students with ADHD.

Attention-Deficit/Hyperactivity Disorder (National Institute of Mental Health)

www.nimh.nih.gov/health/publications/adhd-listing.shtml
NIMH presents a detailed booklet on ADHD that describes symptoms, causes, and treatments and provides information on coping.

Behaviour Problems in Children and Adolescents

www.kidsmentalhealth.ca/parents/behaviour.php
Children's Mental Health Ontario presents information for parents and families on behaviour problems exhibited by children and adolescents, including oppositional defiance and conduct disorder.

Canadian Attention Deficit Hyperactivity Disorder Resource Alliance

www.caddra.ca
The CADDRA website presents the voice of doctors who support patients who suffer from ADHD.

Childhood Anxiety Disorders

www.adaa.org/living-with-anxiety/children/childhood-anxiety-disorders
The Anxiety and Depression Society of America presents information on a range of childhood anxiety disorders.

Children and Adults with Attention-Deficit/Hyperactivity Disorder

www.chadd.org
The CHADD organization provides education, advocacy, and support for individuals with ADHD. Its website provides access to the National Resource Center on ADHD (NRC), a clearinghouse for the latest evidence-based information.

Conduct Disorder: Strategies That Make a Difference

www.learnalberta.ca/content/inmdict/html/conduct_disorder.html
Alberta Education presents information for teachers, including implications for planning and awareness, implications for instruction, and implications for social and emotional well-being.

Council for Children with Behavioral Disorders

www.ccbd.net
The CCBD, a division of the Council for Exceptional Children, is committed to promoting and facilitating the education and general welfare of children and youth with emotional or behavioural disorders. Its website includes position papers on relevant issues and a useful "links" section.

Taking It into Your Classroom . . .

Including Students Who Have Behavioural Disorders

When a student who has a behavioural disorder is first placed in my classroom, I will

- review what I know about behavioural disorders and locate resource materials,
- read the student's file,
- consult with the student's previous teachers,
- consult with the student's parents, and
- meet with the school-based team to discuss the student's current school year.
- Other: _____

When I suspect a student in my classroom has a behavioural disorder, I will

- collect information about the student through classroom interventions,
- observe and document behaviours across various times and settings,
- consult with other school personnel who are familiar with the student,
- consult with the student's parents, and
- meet with the school-based team to present the information I have collected.
- Other: _____

Key points to remember in my daily interactions with a student who has a behavioural disorder:

- The student may have difficulty remembering and following directions.
- The student may have difficulty staying focused.
- The student may have trouble staying still.
- The student may talk excessively and interrupt others.
- The student may act before thinking.
- There is a neurobiological reason for the student's behaviour and performance.
- Other: _____

Key points regarding programming for a student who has a behavioural disorder:

- Behavioural expectations should be clearly stated and reinforced.
- The student should be allowed many opportunities to show his or her strengths.
- The student should have options as to where and how he or she works.
- The student may need modified assignments with reduced written work.
- The student may need help with organizational and study skills.
- The student may need more time to complete assigned work.
- Other: _____

Key points regarding evaluation of the progress made by a student who has a behavioural disorder:

- Evaluation should be based on stated behaviour goals.
- Evaluation should include input from those who spend time with the student.
- Evaluation should include observation of the student in different settings.
- Evaluation should identify any increase in desirable behaviours.
- Evaluation should identify any reduction in undesired behaviours.
- Evaluation should include the student's own assessment of his or her behaviour.
- Other: _____

CHAPTER 7
Students Who Are Gifted and Talented

LEARNING OBJECTIVES

After learning the material in this chapter, you should be able to:

- Discuss how the term *giftedness* is defined and differentiate between the terms *gifted*, *prodigy*, *precocious*, *expert*, *creative*, and *genius*.

- Discuss how a student who is gifted is typically identified within the Canadian education system.

- Describe the roles that heredity and the environment play in intelligence.

- Outline the common characteristics found in students who are gifted.

- Discuss the social and emotional development of students who are gifted.

- Define the terms *enriched curriculum* and *grade acceleration*.

- Define the term *differentiated curriculum* and describe the key beliefs and assumptions that guide the development of curricula in gifted education.

- Describe the School-Wide Enrichment Model developed by Renzulli and Reis.

- Describe the student who is a gifted underachiever and discuss how teachers can motivate such a student.

- Outline characteristics of students who are both gifted and learning disabled, as well as those who are both gifted and physically challenged, and outline how teachers can assist these students.

- Discuss why minority students are underrepresented in gifted programs.

Name: Geoffrey MacInnis

Current Age: 9

School: Jackson Elementary Public School for the Gifted

Grade: 4

Geoffrey is a student who excels in language-related tasks.

He is a precocious writer and an avid reader of complex material, particularly books that address scientific and philosophical issues. While he may be described by some as the stereotypical gifted student, his story is real and highlights many of the challenges faced by students with exceptional abilities. Geoffrey's experiences in the regular classroom as well as in a classroom for the gifted provide a consideration of how teachers, not classrooms, make a difference in students' lives. While some may deem the classroom for the gifted the ideal situation, it is important to note that best practices are teacher-driven and can occur in any setting.

Geoffrey MacInnis

Assessment Results

Age at Time of Assessment: 7 years

Informal Assessment

Geoffrey began reading at age three and writing prolifically at age five. He continues to produce numerous literary works, all of which can be considered far more advanced than the writings of his peers. His precocity is not limited to writing; he has advanced skills in science, reading, music, art, and some areas of mathematics.

Strengths

- highly creative
- musical
- inquisitive
- sensitive of social issues
- able to focus intently on tasks of interest
- excellent memory
- keen sense of humour
- wide range of abilities

Challenges

- picking up on social cues
- leaving a task of interest to participate in scheduled classroom activities
- managing stress and anxiety

Formal Assessment

WISC-III (Full-Scale IQ)	139
Raven Standard Progressive Matrices	>99 percentile

Note: An IEP was never developed for Geoffrey. Now that he attends a public school for the gifted, school personnel feel that an IEP is not necessary.

Teachers' Notes

Mr. Campbell (Grade 2)

Geoffrey is a talkative child who finds it difficult to follow instructions. He seems immature and asks endless questions that interrupt most classroom activities. Geoffrey's parents have spoken to me several times about the possibility that Geoffrey is bored. They think he is gifted and they try to prove this by bringing me samples of his writing. The writing is impressive but probably a joint effort by Geoffrey and his parents. He has never produced similar work at school.

I do not think that Geoffrey is bored. However, he does have a problem focusing on what we are doing in class. Yesterday, we were doing a mathematics activity and halfway through Geoffrey stood up and went to look at a book in our library corner. When I asked what he was doing, he said he wanted to finish reading the book on wolves that I had started to read to the class earlier that day. I insisted that he return to his seat immediately and with that he began to cry. I think Geoffrey has been allowed to do whatever he wants at home. He cannot seem to handle being told what to do. I think the best approach is to insist that he focus on his work and refrain from speaking out or leaving his seat during assigned work periods.

Ms. Levesque (Grade 4)

Geoffrey is a caring and compassionate boy who excels in many areas, particularly writing. Last week, I asked the students to work in groups of two on a particular project, and no one would work with Steven because he often exhibits many negative behaviours. Geoffrey spoke in confidence with me, acknowledging Steven's behaviour and the fact that other students would not work with him. Geoffrey told me that he would be willing to have Steven as his part- ner. It was a very kind gesture, and I told him that.

Geoffrey still has some behaviour issues that we are working on. I insist that he "follow the rules" and conform to the behavioural expectations of the classroom. For example, recently Geoffrey left the classroom without asking permission. When I realized that he was missing, I went to find him. He was walking in the hall upon his return from the washroom. I told him in a calm and sincere manner that I was concerned about his absence and the fact that he had not asked for permission to leave the room. Geoffrey asked me why this was important. I carefully explained why it was necessary to notify me of his needs and his whereabouts. I really feel it is necessary to give him an explanation that respects his sensitive nature and his desire to know and understand the reasoning behind a classroom rule.

Geoffrey MacInnis

Mother's Comments Regarding Geoffrey's Emotional Development

When Geoffrey was very young, around age two, I can remember certain parts of stories really upsetting him, as well as loud noises, or Halloween costumes. Even now he is very sensitive to scary videos, television shows, and cartoons. At age five, I remember him having to leave the room when a character fell in the river. It is the same with books, but it became more apparent when he moved out of physics and into fiction at about age seven. He becomes faint and nauseated at any description of graphic violence or injury, even in children's literature.

He is overly sensitive to anger or scolding as well. He has trouble sleeping if he is anxious. He is also very sensitive to the distress of others. He worries or gets upset if George [his brother] is angry at him, or if George is worried or has been scolded. He worries about things that might scare or bother George. I have never heard him tell George that he is stupid and he never presents himself as superior in any way. In fact, when George does a good drawing or writes something, Geoffrey is genuinely enthusiastic and encouraging.

Of course there is a great sensitivity to beauty as well. He likes walks in nature, likes to look at and create paintings, enjoys watching the beauty in sports, and his love of language is remarkable. There is also a strange, sometimes amazing sensitivity around certain holidays. He gets very excited before the event and a great deal of effort is put into writing stories that relate to the holidays, planning activities, and making decorations. For our wedding anniversary, he concocted an elaborate ceremony called the "glorification of the heart," complete with handmade confetti, a confetti dispenser, and a ritual circle dance (he improvised a song and orchestrated what we would do). At Christmas, he planned the Christmas morning festivities himself, sneaking his violin into his room and leading a musical procession with his brother into our bedroom to wake us up. Along with this celebration of the holidays comes a great sadness when the day is actually over.

Tears are probably more frequent than in other kids, not tantrums or manipulative tears but genuine sadness at things that probably do not upset most other children. He frequently says that he just cannot help it.

Aggressive and competitive boy talk seems completely foreign to him. His sensitivity is noticed by other kids—his literary, artistic, musical, non-athletic, and non-aggressive demeanour as well as his physical appearance (small in stature) result in him being called names by many of the boys at school. He also has trouble with any kind of physically rough play. He worries that someone may get hurt.

I think Geoffrey's sensitivity presents more of a challenge at school than at home. There is no doubt that it is more difficult to manage at school, although this year his teachers are doing a great job, mostly by just acknowledging it and giving him time to decompress if he needs to and not making a big deal of it. This is unlike a previous school year that was devastating for Geoffrey. Since he picks up non-verbal signals very well, he knew that his teacher did not like him and thought he was weird. He internalized this and spent the next two years talking about how he was weird. None of this negative self-talk is evident this year. His current teachers seem to strike a good balance between praise and criticism.

Samples of Geoffrey's Writing

(presented exactly as Geoffrey wrote them in terms of spelling and grammar)

Age 5 (written in response to his readings about the universe)

George solved one large irreversibility problem with a theory called Mary Poppins Time. It was a theory of quantum gravity. It istated that whenever tesserarts have their antianti-quarks joined, they merge to form a giant antitesserart (we will discuss antitesserarts in the part The particles of time) called a Megairreversitron, which makes time irreversible. And this is happening everywhere in the universe. Why did he call it Mary Poppins Time? Because he was imaginative. He knew that It was made of sugar, those Megairreversitrons. And he imagined that they were irreversible medicine to cure the universe's reversibility disease. And if you make the sentence "Sugar helping medicine" into a bigger sentence, you end up with "Just a spoon full of sugar helps the medicine go down.

Age 6 (written in response to a newspaper article on Afghanistan)

More terrorists, new government, more attacks, holiday worries, etc. I accept the idea to put a new government in afghanastan, but there is one problem. That means the religious government may become self-supporting terrorists, along with Bin Laden and his gang, which must undergo the same supporting change to keep terrorizing. But if this happens, the war will become longer and more difficult, even with a new government. I wonder if we can send in better peacekeeping forces in Afghanastan and U.S.A? This also may affect holiday season since the terrorists might not even want worldwide Christmas, which is a totally different religion. Who knows? They may even kill Santa. People could maybe use grinch protection.

Age 7 (written in response to his readings about philosophy and religion)

Questionis philosophicus

How can we tell right from wrong? Can religions tell us right from wrong?

If you believe in that certain religion, it can for you. But they do not necessarily vet the basic human moral code. Then what is, or tells us, the basic moral code? I can only tell you the moral code that i believe should be the basic human moral code. I believe humans should not kill, steal, or hate and they should help, care for, and love each other.

What am I?

What's so philosophical about this question? It's really more about the meaning of life, and how you think about yourself, and how other people think about you and how they blend.

Geoffrey MacInnis

So what is the meaning of life?

Now that's a tricky one. It's one of the great philosophica questions of all time. Let's start with animals. Okay. Some people in the old days thought that pigs only lived so that they could be sacrificed. But I think that one isn't true. Wait a minute. I have an idea. Let's skip a bit. What's your idea? Maybe people live so that they can make their unique contribution to the world. What about people who don't? O, Quit simplifying around! Everyone makes contributions to the world.

Age 9 (written in response to a school assignment about the changing seasons)

SPRING

I

Spring opens its eyes
A lonely white crocus
A snowdrop for Blodeuwedd
Across her sea
A young green goddess
Crowned in blue sky
Beats a rhythm on the snowclouds.

He, the crocus
Has known the meltwater
Below the snow.
Where she, spring, is, we know
There soon shall be more green
And soon shall be more snow.
There I sing of spring

II

The pussywillow has flowered
Beneath the willow
Where wanders pussy
In a home of spring
It's something near 10°,
An early, pussywillow-mattressed Spring?
She, young green spring,
Adorns the wood with pussywillow buds,
Detesting the stubborn snow-clouds,
Preferring the young pussy.

(Mated animals
Have their young.)
Showers fall, hope of bright colours
(Blue and then green).
There is an egg, lying in a green
Grass patch, painted.
A single rabbit hops through
The last patch of dirty snow.
The ducks wander from the pond (Gloria!)
A perfect Easter overcast
Ducks in the rain.

He, the crocus, in summer-like bloom,
She, spring, calls for the spring-cleaning broom,
Little pussywillow, their young.

III

Now summer starts,
Or so the old folks say,
For now 'tis May Day.
The forest now is art,
April showers have what they must.
The pussywillow now crowns
The willow in her season,
The flower-crowned, May queen,
Spring goddess of the green.

Why Is Geoffrey Considered to Be Gifted?

Definition of Giftedness

While there is no one universally agreed-upon definition of "giftedness," nor is there consensus about where to set the bar for the gifted and talented range of behaviour (Horowitz, 2009), it is still the case in most education settings that a "gifted" child is one who scores high on an intelligence test or an academic achievement test. While Geoffrey's giftedness was certainly identified by his parents before he even entered school, it was indeed the administration of an intelligence test (a formal assessment tool) by a school psychologist that led to Geoffrey's "gifted" designation within the school system. School personnel also considered Geoffrey's behaviour both at home and in school (part of an informal assessment) to determine his areas of strengths and needs.

What We Know . . .

Definition of Giftedness

The following definition of giftedness, first constructed by former US Commissioner of Education Sidney Marland (1972) in his report to Congress in the early 1970s, continues to be one of the most widely used (with some modifications) both in Canada and the United States:

> Gifted and talented children are those identified by professionally qualified persons who by virtue of outstanding abilities are capable of high performance. These are children who require differentiated educational programs and/or services beyond those normally provided by the regular school program in order to realize their contribution to self and society. Children capable of high performance include those with demonstrated achievement and/or potential ability in any of the following areas, singly or in combination: general intellectual ability; specific academic aptitude; creative or productive thinking; leadership ability; and, visual and performing arts.

Something to Think About

Across the provinces and territories of Canada, educators use a variety of definitions or descriptions of giftedness. Consider the following descriptions that are used in British Columbia, Newfoundland and Labrador, and Nova Scotia:

Continued

British Columbia Ministry of Education

A student is considered gifted when she/he possesses demonstrated or potential abilities that give evidence of exceptionally high capability with respect to intellect, creativity, or the skills associated with specific disciplines. Students who are gifted often demonstrate outstanding abilities in more than one area. They may demonstrate extraordinary intensity of focus in their particular areas of talent or interest. However, they may also have accompanying disabilities and should not be expected to have strengths in all areas of intellectual functioning.

Newfoundland and Labrador Department of Education

Students who are gifted and talented demonstrate, or have the potential to demonstrate, exceptionally high capability with respect to:

- *an exceptional ability to learn, create or perform;*
- *well above average cognitive ability globally or within a specific domain (academic or non-academic)*

If a student is in the very superior range on an overall IQ score, there is little doubt that he or she will exhibit, or has the potential for, gifted behaviours. If a student is gifted in a particular domain, an overall score may not reflect this strength area. The criteria for individual domains will vary according to the domain.

Nova Scotia Department of Education

Although no single criterion can be used to determine giftedness, students who demonstrate above average ability or creativity, or high levels of task commitment may exhibit gifted behaviours at certain times, under certain circumstances, and under certain conditions.

How are these descriptions of giftedness similar? How are they different? How might these descriptions affect the services provided to students who are gifted and talented? If you live in a region of Canada other than the three mentioned here, determine how giftedness is defined in your province or territory.

Sources: British Columbia Ministry of Education (2016), p. 61; Newfoundland and Labrador Department of Education (2013), p. 6; Nova Scotia Department of Education (2010), p. 27.

Other Definitions of Giftedness

There are a variety of terms used to describe extremely capable children such as *gifted, prodigy, precocious, expert, creative,* and *genius.* Many of these terms are used interchangeably because they are accepted common or colloquial descriptors in everyday vernacular. However, when using the categorical model of special education (see Chapter 2), it is always best to be as specific as possible when identifying a child's abilities so that the most effective programs can be implemented. In the case of giftedness, there are precise and discrete definitions of each of the above terms. Gardner (2000) and others (Edmunds & Noel, 2003; Robinson, 2000) have provided an excellent differentiation of their criteria and use; see Table 7.1.

What We Know . . .

Table 7.1 Definitions of Terms Related to Giftedness

Gifted	"At promise" in any domain recognized as involving intelligence
Prodigy	Extreme promise in any domain recognized as involving intelligence; distinguished by performance that is not only promising but also impressive by adult standards
Precocious	Earlier-than-expected, domain-specific development that ranges from mildly advanced to astonishing; distinguished by performance within an age group and not measured against adult standards
Expert	Has achieved a high level of competence in a domain, irrespective of whether the approach is novel or experimental
Creative	Regularly solves problems or fashions products in a domain in a way that is initially seen as novel but that ultimately is recognized as appropriate
Genius	Produces work that is expertly executed and creative and has a profound effect on the domain

Geoffrey is correctly referred to in the educational system as a child who is gifted. However, to be more accurate, Geoffrey is a precocious child in that he is a child writer who has demonstrated a prolific literary output (more than 8,000 pages of writing by age nine) and a complex and sophisticated writing style. This means that Geoffrey's achievements/creations (a) are not measured against adult standards, (b) are precocious when measured against age-relative standards, and (c) focus on the specific tasks of writing.

Assessing Giftedness

Geoffrey was assessed shortly after entering school on the urging of his parents. They were concerned about his unhappiness with school and his apparent boredom with classroom activities. The process began with the collection of information through an informal assessment. Members of the school-based team were interested in Geoffrey's behaviour both at home and in school. Teachers and support staff were asked to comment on how Geoffrey responded to assigned tasks, how he interacted with other children as well as adults, and how he performed in different subject areas. Examples of his in-class work were examined. As well, Geoffrey's parents were interviewed to determine their perspective on his strengths and challenges. They were asked to share examples of the work he completed at home, particularly his writing. The information collected through this informal assessment was compiled and summarized (see *Assessment Results* on p. 184). It served as the impetus for the formal assessment conducted by a school psychologist. In other words, those involved in Geoffrey's education provided enough evidence to warrant further examination of his intellectual abilities.

Geoffrey's formal assessment required him to complete two standardized tests of cognitive ability. The Wechsler Intelligence Scale for Children-III (WISC-III) is a test of general intelligence that is administered individually. It is organized into subtests allowing for an examination of verbal and non-verbal abilities. The test results include three IQ scores: a Verbal IQ, a Performance IQ, and a Full-Scale IQ. In Geoffrey's case, he performed very well across all subtests and was assigned a Full-Scale IQ of 139, putting him in the superior range of general intelligence. The second test that Geoffrey completed during his formal assessment was the Raven's Progressive Matrices (RPM), which is a non-verbal test of figural reasoning. The RPM includes 60 items, each one containing a figure with a missing piece. Below each figure are alternative pieces to complete the figure, only one of which is correct. On this test, Geoffrey scored better than 99 per cent of the same-aged children in the test norming group, confirming Geoffrey's superior ability to understand visual-perceptual relations and to reason by analogy independent of language and formal schooling.

The assessment process that led to Geoffrey's designation of "gifted" was typical of how precocious Canadian students are identified within the education system. Their outstanding academic performance in a particular domain combined with evidence of superior ability on an IQ test allows for a relatively easy decision regarding the necessity of special education programming.

The identification of students who are gifted, but not necessarily precocious, may be somewhat more challenging as these students may not have such visible "gifts." For example, they may simply have above-average abilities across a range of academic subjects, or they may be highly creative and these creative abilities may not be apparent in certain classrooms or situations. While there is no uniform identification process across the provinces and territories to identify children who are gifted and talented, the assessment and identification process should be comprehensive and the "gifted" designation should only rarely be based on one test alone, regardless if it is an IQ test. The preferred process is to use a battery of assessment tools in conjunction with an IQ test. This allows for the full scope of the child's abilities and needs to be examined so that proper educational programming can be provided. Some of the complementary assessment tools that are often used to reach these conclusions are teacher/parent nominations, samples of the student's work, tests of creativity, academic achievement tests, tests of **visual-spatial abilities**, and assessments of social adjustment.

visual-spatial abilities
The ability to efficiently visualize and manipulate objects in space.

It should be noted that, to date, an IEP has never been developed for Geoffrey. While he is recognized as being gifted, it has been left to his teachers to design appropriate curricula for him. As you read about Geoffrey and his school experiences, consider how a well-developed IEP may have made a difference in his school life.

Something to Think About

Across Canada, there is considerable variation in the services provided for students who are gifted. You may find yourself teaching in a school board that offers limited services for these students. Some educators feel that students who are gifted will excel despite the absence of special programming. Do you think it is even necessary to identify students who are gifted as exceptional? Do they really have special needs?

What Factors Contributed to Geoffrey's Giftedness?

Typically, the first question one asks after coming to grips with the reality of Geoffrey's abilities is, "What are the conditions under which he has developed and flourished?"

Heredity

Geoffrey's parents are highly successful individuals. Both his mother and father have graduate degrees that have led them to academic careers in areas that require high degrees of creativity. His mother recalls her frustration with school while growing up. She felt her elementary and secondary schooling failed to provide her with the challenging type of education she needed.

Researchers have long been studying the genetics of intelligence. There is considerable evidence that differences in intelligence are significantly influenced by genetic factors (Plomin, 1997). This does not mean that intelligence is due entirely to genetics, but rather that both genetic and environmental influences play a role in determining general cognitive ability. As Simonton (2005) stated, giftedness has an "elementary connection with biological inheritance" and the environment "plays an important role in the realization of that genetic potential" (p. 278). Given the genetic basis of giftedness, it is not surprising that Geoffrey's parents have two children who are high functioning and exceptionally creative.

Environment

Contrary to the early experiences of many children who are gifted, Geoffrey has thrived without early exposure/practice/repetition and without any urging or pushing from his parents. Even when his verbal precocity and writing talents became obvious, his parents purposefully did not tell him to write. However, they did pay attention to his work and they gently celebrated what he wrote by reading his stories with him and asking questions about characters, pictures, and storylines. This parental approach has continued; Geoffrey's parents just let his prolific writing happen and, within reason, they try to not get in his way. Like any parents, they are enthused by his desire to write and the enjoyment he derives from writing, but they "are not about to let his writing become him." They provide the raw materials such as a multitude of markers and pencils and lots of blank paper. Geoffrey's room is dominated by two pieces of furniture: his adult-sized single bed and an equally large rectangular work table with legs cut down to suit the height of his child's chair.

There is no doubt that Geoffrey's conceptual information comes mostly from what he reads. His parents encourage him to read whatever he is interested in, and while his room and home are filled with numerous books, there are no more books available to him than in other homes where parents value reading and make use of libraries. The major difference is that Geoffrey reads many more books designed for adults. He does this of his own volition with no expectations from his parents. Most importantly, perhaps, his parents do not allow his descriptions or discussions about what he reads to be superficial. They ask him meaningful questions and seek detailed explanations. As his mother explains, "it is like taking the lid off a bottle of pop" because Geoffrey has the wherewithal and verbal precocity to handle their

conceptual information
Mental representations of the knowledge one has about concrete (dog) or abstract (love) objects.

inquiries and they often get more than they bargain for. However, these exchanges are not only of the serious or purposeful variety. There are made-up words and silly repetitive expressions and moments of fun and hilarity for both Geoffrey and his parents. Thus, there do not appear to be any boundaries confining Geoffrey's explorations.

Perhaps the most striking characteristic of Geoffrey's environment is that his time for writing, within the family's schedule, is never questioned. Like clockwork, he goes to his desk and writes, completely unsupervised, and only rarely is he interrupted. This is not to say that the family's life revolves around Geoffrey's writing time; rather, it is to point out that his parents recognize his need for this time and deliberately make the necessary accommodations. Finally, there is no doubt that this highly favourable element of his environment is as much due to Geoffrey's abilities and motivation as it is due to the "space" his parents give him. The point being that one should not conclude that all children would/could thrive as prolific writers under such favourable conditions.

Geoffrey's environment is similar to that of many gifted children; it contains a richness of resources and stimulation. However, except for not allowing Geoffrey to get away with frivolous or illogical descriptions/discussions, his world is without the parental demands for performance frequently presented elsewhere. The conduct of his parents is akin to Fowler's (1981) description of a responsive and incidental parenting style.

From the Psychologist's Notebook

Intelligence, or intellectual ability, is best defined as goal-directed adaptive behaviours (Newman & Just, 2005) that are predominated by problem-solving abilities (Wenke, Frensch, & Funke, 2005). There is considerable agreement among intelligence researchers and theorists that heredity appears to set the limits of one's intellectual ability and that our environment determines how much of that limit is realized (Tucker-Drob, Briley, & Harden, 2013). A good way of thinking about the heredity/environment interactive contribution to the development of intellectual ability is to think of one's intelligence as a bookcase with moveable shelves. Our genetic code (heredity) determines roughly how big the bookcase is in terms of width, height, and depth and the number of shelves it contains. The intellectual stimulation that our environment provides then determines how many different types and sizes of books, magazines, pictures, videos, and so on fill up the various shelves. And, to a limited degree, this overall intellectual influence (called learning) can slightly expand the bookcase or parts of it. Therefore, the more stimulating one's environment, the more complete one's bookcase becomes; the less stimulating one's environment, the less full the bookcase will be. This does not mean, however, that an enriched environment can make a child more intelligent than the capacity provided by his or her genetic code. There is obviously a limit to the number of books an individual's bookcase can hold. It also does not mean that those who may have a larger-than-normal bookcase do not have to do anything to fill it up. Without proper environmental stimulation, those bookcases will be barren. In summary, children's environments (especially school) should be as rich as possible so that they can attain their maximum intellectual potential.

Something to Think About

What are the biological influences on giftedness? In the March 2011 issue of the University of Alberta Alumni News, Jamie Hanlon reported that Dr. Marty Mrazik, a professor in the Faculty of Education at the University of Alberta, and a colleague from Rider University in the United States published a paper in *Roeper Review* linking giftedness (having an IQ score of 130 or higher) to prenatal exposure to higher levels of testosterone (Mrazik & Dombrowsk, 2010). They have hypothesized that, in the same way that physical and cognitive deficiencies can be developed in utero, so, too, can giftedness.

"There seems to be some evidence that excessive prenatal exposure to testosterone facilitates increased connections in the brain, especially in the right prefrontal cortex," said Mrazik. "That's why we see some intellectually gifted people with distinct personality characteristics that you don't see in the normal population."

Mrazik's notion came from observations made during clinical assessments of gifted individuals. He and his fellow researcher observed some specific traits among the subjects. This finding stimulated a conversation on the role of early development in setting the foundation for giftedness: "It gave us some interesting ideas that there could be more to this notion of genius being predetermined from a biological perspective than maybe people gave it credit for," said Mrazik. "It seemed that the bulk of evidence from new technologies (such as functional MRI scans) tell us that there's a little bit more going on than a genetic versus environmental interaction."

Based on their observations, the researchers made the hypothesis that this hormonal "glitch" in the in utero neurobiological development means that gifted children are born with an affinity for certain areas such as the arts, math, or science. Mrazik cautioned that more research is needed to determine what exact processes may cause the development of the gifted brain. He noted that more is known about what derails the brain's normal development, so charting what makes gifted people gifted is very much a new frontier. Mrazik hopes that devices such as the functional MRI scanner will facilitate a deeper understanding of the role of neurobiology in the development of the gifted brain.

How Has Geoffrey's Giftedness Affected His Development?

Cognitive Development

Geoffrey was read to from a very early age, a task that his parents enjoyed and performed quite often. He spoke a few words and phrases at around eight or nine months of age and then, for reasons unknown, he stopped speaking altogether. However, this does not mean that he did not utter a word, it just meant that he did not "speak" in the usual sense. Instead, he transformed the lyrics of songs that he knew into new versions about his family's activities or daily occurrences and sang them joyfully and repeatedly. Similarly, he would recite, verbatim, complete paragraphs from books that his parents had read to him. His parents realized that he was of speaking age and of speaking capacity, so they were considerably frustrated that he did not speak. When he did talk, a late bloomer at two and a half years of age, it was in complete sentences: (to his Mom) "I hear a sound out there but I don't know what it is," and (to his Dad) "I'm not really sure that George understands the difference between a car and a truck." Since that time, the spoken word has literally and figuratively poured out of Geoffrey and, for the most part, his speaking has been purposeful, almost without the meaningless but playful banter in which most children engage.

So, what is it that allows Geoffrey to easily and rapidly absorb and digest what he wants to learn and then re-create it and express it through complex and sophisticated writing? He has extraordinary abilities in a variety of language-related areas, including verbal precocity, reading comprehension, and written expression. Underlying these abilities is a series of cognitive and motivational characteristics that are typically found in gifted children (see *What We Know* on p. 197).

When writing, Geoffrey often demonstrates extraordinary immediate and long-term memory as well as highly developed meta-cognitive abilities for organizing and monitoring his work and for supervising his thinking. These traits are repeatedly evidenced during discussions of his stories, some created years ago, some just underway. Perhaps the best insights into Geoffrey's precocity can be gleaned from his highly developed and sophisticated language abilities, as these have an overarching influence on all that he does. Externally, this is evident in his spoken and written expressiveness while internal manifestations are evident in his logical arguments, book conceptualizations, and the overall planning and execution of writing tasks. His language/thinking has all the adolescent qualities of what Vygotsky (1978) termed "the logicalization of thought," in which words become the principal tool for abstraction and generalization. As Noel and Edmunds (2007) pointed out, Geoffrey uses writing to examine, in a very intentional manner, his own thinking.

Perhaps Geoffrey's most striking characteristic is a dogged persistence to satisfy his need to fully understand what he encounters and to then express what he knows through writing. He possesses a crystal clear determination of purpose, and this is accompanied by his passionate affection for the nuances of language. Therefore, writing not only fulfills his need to express his knowledge, but it also acts as a further consolidation process for what he knows. While his parents provide the milieu, Geoffrey facilitates his own learning trajectory by asking for books on particular topics, making trips to the library for even more books, and engaging whomever he can in spirited conversations about his current topic of interest. His intense involvement and commitment to his domain and his obvious desire to direct this involvement and commitment are the hallmark indicators of precocious children (Goldsmith, 2000). But, Geoffrey's modus operandi is more than motivation, it is what Snow (1994) referred to as an intrinsic "unrest" of the organism, a conscious tendency to act, and a conscious striving by which mental processes or behaviours tend to develop into something else.

Geoffrey also has an extensive attention span and he regularly works for hours without pause. His work sessions are not flurries of activity; they are more the mark of a quiet purposefulness guided only by his penchant for knowing, and then writing and drawing from his knowledge. He shows an intense interest in the details of what he writes and draws, but these are only measured against his own understandings. Toward the end of his first year of writing, he did ask a variety of individuals if they liked his writing/stories, but those questions seemed more a courtesy than attempts to establish a measure of his work.

What We Know . . .

Characteristics of Students Who Are Gifted

Learning Characteristics

- Has unusually advanced vocabulary for age or grade level.
- Possesses a storehouse of information about a variety of topics.
- Has quick mastery and recall of factual information.
- Has rapid insight into cause-and-effect relationships; wants to know what makes things (or people) "tick."
- Has a ready grasp of underlying principles and can quickly make valid generalizations about events, people, or things.
- Is a keen and alert observer; usually "sees more" or "gets more" out of a story, film, and so forth than others.
- Reads a great deal on his or her own; usually prefers adult-level books.
- Tries to understand complicated material by separating it into its respective parts.
- Reasons things out for him or herself; sees logical and common sense answers.

Motivational Characteristics

- Becomes absorbed and truly involved in certain topics or problems; is persistent in seeking task completion.
- Is easily bored with routine tasks.
- Needs little external motivation to follow through in work that initially excites him or her.
- Strives toward perfection; is self-critical.
- Prefers to work independently; requires little direction from the teacher.
- Is interested in many "adult" problems such as religion and politics, more than usual for age level.
- Is often self-assertive or stubborn in his or her beliefs.
- Likes to organize and bring structure to things, people, and situations.
- Is quite concerned with right and wrong.

Creativity Characteristics

- Displays a great deal of curiosity about many things; is constantly asking questions about anything and everything.
- Generates a large number of ideas on problems; often offers unusual, clever responses.
- Is uninhibited in expressions of opinion; is sometimes radical and spirited in disagreement.

Continued

- Is a high risk-taker; is adventurous and speculates.
- Displays a good deal of intellectual playfulness; fantasizes; imagines; is often concerned with adapting, improving, and modifying institutions, objects, and systems.
- Displays a keen sense of humour and sees humour in situations that may not appear to be humorous to others.
- Is unusually aware of his or her impulses and is more open to the irrational in him or herself (freer expression of feminine interest for boys, greater-than-usual amount of independence for girls); shows emotional sensitivity.
- Is sensitive to beauty.
- Is non-conforming.
- Criticizes constructively; is unwilling to accept authoritarian pronouncements without critical examination.

Leadership Characteristics

- Carries responsibility well.
- Is self-confident with children his or her own age, as well as adults.
- Seems to be well liked by his classmates.
- Is co-operative with teachers and classmates.
- Can express him or herself well, has good verbal facility, and is usually well understood.
- Adapts readily to new situations.
- Seems to enjoy being around other people; generally directs the activity in which he or she is involved.
- Participates in most social activities connected with the school.
- Excels in athletic activities; is well coordinated and enjoys all sorts of athletic games.

Source: Coleman & Cross (2001), pp. 35–36, as adapted from Renzulli, Hartman, & Callahan (1971).

Social and Emotional Development

When Geoffrey was six years of age, he was fascinated by the study of the universe, particularly the concept of black holes. It led him to read about Stephen Hawking. He was drawn to this famous scientist and, on his own accord, sent Professor Hawking a Valentine's card. It was with great delight that Geoffrey received a letter from the scientist, thanking him for the first Valentine he had received in many years.

During his Grade 4 year, Valentine's Day proved to be more difficult for Geoffrey. As usual, he looked forward to this special occasion, an opportunity to let those you care about know that they are loved. Geoffrey sent cards to all the girls and boys in his class. Not surprisingly, at this preadolescent stage of development, this was not an act that the other boys appreciated. Unfortunately, this type of behaviour on Geoffrey's part, a genuine caring for others and an outward expression of sensitivity, has already resulted in some school children calling him names.

Students who are gifted can exhibit a number of characteristics. Some examples include keen observations, a preference for working independently, and sensitivity to beauty.

What We Know . . .

The Sensitivity Exhibited by Students Who Are Gifted

The literature on giftedness is abundant with references to sensitivity. While the definition of giftedness is continually debated and modified due to the heterogeneity of the population, the existence of a sensitivity factor among individuals who are gifted appears to be widely accepted. Many compilations of giftedness characteristics, particularly those focusing on the affective domain, include phrases such as *morally sensitive*, *emotionally sensitive*, *personally sensitive*, or *extremely compassionate*. The dictionary defines "sensitive" as being "highly responsive or susceptible" and when referring to a sensitive person, being "delicately aware of the attitudes and feelings of others" and "being easily hurt emotionally" (*Merriam-Webster's Collegiate Dictionary*, 2003). Shavinina (1999) included vulnerability, fragility, empathy, and social responsiveness as manifestations of this sensitivity.

One would think that the sensitivity exhibited by many intellectually gifted children would result in an ability to fit in and get along with others. After all, if an individual is sensitive to others' feelings and perceptions, it would be reasonable to predict that he or she is quite socially competent. Porath (2000) suggested that this may not be the case. She proposed that when a child who is gifted exhibits a depth of understanding in the social domain, this

Continued

may not transfer to actual behaviours. In her research, Porath found that a child who is gifted may experience great sensitivity toward others yet receive low teacher ratings of social acceptance and behavioural conduct. Mendaglio (1995) presented a similar scenario when proposing a definition of sensitivity based on the gifted literature and his counselling experience. His definition, which includes the use of four psychological concepts—self-awareness, perspective taking, emotional experience, and empathy—also emphasizes that "a person's experience of sensitivity is not necessarily expressed directly to others" (p. 171). This lack of expression obviously has implications for the social acceptance of the gifted individual.

Acceptance, however, does not always occur with overt expression of this sensitivity. As Silverman (1993) pointed out, we live in a culture that does not view heightened emotionality in a very positive way. Outward demonstrations of sensitivity are discouraged, especially in boys and men. Perhaps the most critical period for this negative feedback is during pre-adolescence and adolescence. Being gifted already sets children of this age apart from their peers, but adding the sensitivity factor can make life very difficult, or even unbearable. If these children are to benefit from their emotional intensity, which according to Dabrowski (1972) may be the very trait that acts as the catalyst for their intellectual or creative achievements, then researchers, educators, and parents should perhaps focus more attention on their "sensitivities" rather than on their "talents." As Dabrowski and Piechowski (1977) emphasized, there is a strong positive correlation between intellectual level and emotional intensity.

Source: Republished with permission of Taylor and Francis, from "Sensitivity: A double-edged sword for the pre-adolescent and adolescent gifted child," by Edmunds, A.L, & Edmunds, G.A., *Roeper Review*, Volume 27(2), 2005. Permission conveyed through Copyright Clearance Center, Inc.

What Is School Like for Geoffrey?

As Geoffrey's mother remarked, school has not always been a happy place for him. In his first years of school, his experiences were, unfortunately, not unlike the experiences of many other gifted children. There were educators who did not fully understand his gifts and others who did not appreciate his tremendous abilities. There were classrooms that failed to provide an emotionally supportive environment, and others where the curricula were inappropriate for Geoffrey's level of intellectual ability. In an effort to find the most caring and stimulating learning environment for their son, his parents tried several schools, both public and private.

Geoffrey started primary school at the appropriate age but he was very bored. In Grade 2, his teacher ignored his abilities and thought he was a problem child (see *Teachers' Notes* on p. 185). School was particularly difficult for Geoffrey during this time. The curricula were not appropriate and the atmosphere was less than ideal. When asked by Mr. Campbell to write about what he would do if he were in charge of the school, Geoffrey started by saying "I don't know," and then proceeded to repeatedly write the word "don't" for a page and a half. This was his direct response to previously being told by Mr. Campbell to copy lines and letters as punishment. Geoffrey ended the piece by emphasizing again that he did not know what he would do if he were in charge of the school. He advised the reader to "Ask the future or my angel." In a postscript he stated:

I know one thing I would love everyone, be friendly to everyone, not allow punishments bigger than time-outs. I would be nicer to the kids. And I would let them have daily desserts, have a stand for free sweets, only payed for in play money. I would teach them all subjects required.

This was undoubtedly an expression of both his own reaction to his school environment and his understanding of the needs of himself and his peers.

His current school situation is the most successful to date. He attends a public school for children who are gifted. The setting is intellectually stimulating, but perhaps most critical to Geoffrey's well-being, his teachers provide an emotionally supportive environment (see *Teachers' Notes* on p. 185). When he first entered the school, his new teachers took the time to learn about Geoffrey both through observation and meetings with his parents and his psychologist. Their efforts to recognize their new student's strengths and weaknesses have resulted in the implementation of teaching strategies that appropriately address Geoffrey's needs.

Despite the positive classroom environment created by Geoffrey's competent teachers (see the *What We Know* box), he still faces the reality of being a 9-year-old boy who is different from many of his schoolmates, even though they too have been identified as gifted. Geoffrey's precocity includes an intellectual level and an emotional intensity that surpass many of his peers. His preadolescent schoolmates are not always tolerant of his abilities, and they are especially not always tolerant of his sensitivities. It is undoubtedly difficult for them to understand some of Geoffrey's behaviours. This in turn makes school a continuing challenge for Geoffrey, a challenge that must be recognized and addressed if he is to reach his potential.

What We Know . . .

Characteristics of Successful Teachers of Students Who Are Gifted

Personal Characteristics

- Understands, accepts, respects, trusts, and likes self; has outstanding ego strength
- Is sensitive to others, less concerned with self; supports, respects, and trusts others
- Is above-average intellectually; exhibits an intellectual style of conceptualizing, generalizing, creating, initiating, relating, organizing, imagining
- Is flexible, open to new ideas
- Has intellectual interests, literary and cultural
- Desires to learn, increase knowledge; has high achievement needs
- Is enthusiastic
- Is intuitive, perceptive
- Is committed to excellence
- Feels responsible for his or her own behaviour and consequences

Personal-Professional Predispositions

- Guides, rather than coerces or pressures
- Is democratic, rather than autocratic

Continued

- Focuses on process, as well as product
- Is innovative and experimental, rather than conforming
- Uses problem-solving procedures, rather than jumping to unfounded conclusions
- Seeks involvement of others in discovery, rather than giving out answers

Teaching Behaviours

- Develops a flexible, individualized program
- Creates a warm, safe, and permissive atmosphere
- Provides feedback
- Uses varied strategies
- Respects personal self-images and enhances positive ones; respects personal values
- Respects creativity and imagination
- Stimulates higher-order mental processes
- Respects individuality and personal integrity

Source: Lindsey (1980), as cited in Coleman & Cross (2001), p. 321.

Something to Think About

Geoffrey's feelings about school improved when he was transferred to a public school for gifted students. His new teachers took the time to learn about Geoffrey, and they appear to have the knowledge and expertise required to provide him with positive learning experiences. Do you think these positive learning experiences could take place in a regular classroom? How would you feel about having a student like Geoffrey in your classroom? What concerns would you have?

What Educational Approach Is Best for Geoffrey?

The Curricula

Geoffrey did not thrive in the early elementary grades when he was exposed to the regular curricula. He was obviously unhappy with his school experience. This unhappiness spilled over into all parts of his life, including a fixation on the fact that he was different or "weird." As VanTassel-Baska (1997) stated, "an organized curriculum is a key ingredient in the complex blending of circumstances so central to the transformation of a gifted learner's initial capacity for intellectual activity into a mature competence for academic and professional accomplishment" (p. 126).

Geoffrey's parents were given two choices to consider after Geoffrey's assessment by the school psychologist. Should they allow their son to stay with his same-age classmates and experience an enriched curriculum, or should they consider grade acceleration? They decided that an enriched curriculum was the best choice for Geoffrey since they had concerns about putting him at a maturational disadvantage in a classroom of older children. Thinking ahead to the higher grades, they feared that Geoffrey, who is small in stature, highly sensitive, and not athletic, would experience even more intense feelings of being different or "weird."

As a result of his parents' decision, Geoffrey's teachers were required to develop and provide a differentiated curriculum for him. As Renzulli and Reis (1997) described, modifications to the curriculum are designed to: "(1) adjust levels of required learning so that all students are challenged, (2) increase the number of in-depth learning experiences, and (3) introduce various types of enrichment into regular curricular experiences" (p. 145). However, as illustrated by Geoffrey's story, the success of the development and implementation of differentiated curricula depends very much on the skills and attitudes of the teachers involved. Geoffrey's school experiences did not improve significantly until he experienced an appropriate set of curricula delivered by knowledgeable and supportive teachers. In Geoffrey's case, this occurred when he transferred to his current school.

enriched curriculum
A program of study that is expanded beyond its typical depth and scope, usually involving independent study.

grade acceleration
Skipping a grade to participate in appropriate levels of curricula.

differentiated curriculum
A program of study that is altered in content or instructional method to suit the specific needs of a student who has an exceptionality.

What We Know . . .

Differentiated Instruction for the Gifted

Making Content More Abstract

Abstract content focuses less on specific, factual information and more on concepts and generalizations. Building on abstraction means encouraging students to consider ideas in general terms and to move more fluidly between facts and broad understandings. For example, a student who is gifted in math could quickly move beyond manipulatives into identifying patterns and relationships. Artistic representations can challenge students to explore and synthesize concepts in abstract terms. For example, students could identify patterns and relationships through a dance, song, or theatrical presentation. Thinking in more abstract terms can provide greater challenge and complexity for students.

Making Content More Complex

Content can be made more complex by introducing additional variables, other considerations, different sources, and alternate viewpoints to a learning task. The original content remains but is compared, contrasted, or combined with other information or concepts. For example, a basic learning activity of surveying the class to find out how many students come to school by walking, biking, busing, or car could be made more complex by asking students to gather additional information in the survey and use this to compare distance from school with various modes of transport.

Making Content Interrelated

Students who are gifted often spot the potential for applying ideas or methods from one field of study to others. Build on this ability by looking for potential connections from one subject

Continued

© iStock/Highwaystarz-Photography

Artistic representation—in this example, asking students to identify patterns and relationships within a song—promotes the exploration and synthesis of concepts in abstract terms.

to the next and challenging students to use knowledge, processes, and skills in different combinations. For example, students could take science knowledge about weather and climate and use it in a social studies inquiry about how people adapt to their environment. Interrelatedness also can be explored across space or time. For example, students could be challenged to think about how humans adapt to their physical environments across geographic regions or what meaning humans have ascribed to weather conditions throughout history.

Making Content More Constrained

Interestingly enough, making content more constrained can sometimes present as many worthwhile challenges as making it more complex. By lessening the degrees of freedom in an activity, it is possible to concentrate students' focus and encourage them to go more deeply into a particular aspect of a learning outcome. For example, a basic assignment to write a poem about traffic during rush hour could be channelled into a more constrained assignment of writing the poem only about the traffic sounds during rush hour.

Source: Alberta Education (2010), p. 173.

Despite the fact that Geoffrey is now in a classroom where all the students have been identified as gifted, he still requires a differentiated curriculum because of his significantly superior skills in language and writing. For example, in the fall of his Grade 4 year, his teacher taught a unit on the medieval period. She then asked students to write a report on a topic of interest that related to this period in history. Students were directed to either choose a topic from a suggested list or self-select a topic that interested them. The only requirements were that the students must write a paper on their topic, produce artwork that visually displayed their topic, and present the content of their paper to the class. In a private conversation with Geoffrey, the teacher suggested that he self-select a topic of interest based upon his readings of a number of adult-level books on the medieval period. Once he focused in on the question, "Who was King Arthur?" his teacher then encouraged him to compare the ideas of various authors and come to some conclusions of his own. Geoffrey happily immersed himself in this project, reading 10 books before he produced his report on "King Arthur." This paper was divided into two parts: "Arthur of History: Romans, Celts, and Saxons" and "Arthur of Literature: Bards, Historians, and Romancers." For his visual display, Geoffrey presented a sketch of a medieval castle. He had noted from his readings that some of the architecture depicted in this "typical" representation was not consistent with the architecture of the period. Therefore, he built a model of what he calculated an actual medieval castle to look like. He then arranged his visual display so that you could view the "actual" model superimposed on his sketch of the "typical" castle, thus making the differences more obvious. Geoffrey concluded the project by presenting his ideas most succinctly to the teacher and his classmates.

As is evident from the "King Arthur" project, a number of teaching and learning strategies are employed to enhance Geoffrey's education. First, his differentiated curriculum is based on the regular curriculum, yet he is required to explore topics in more depth using higher-level thinking skills such as analyzing, synthesizing, and evaluating. He has some control over the direction of his learning in that he self-selects topics that interest him and he is given the opportunity to work independently. As well, his teacher encourages interdisciplinary learning by allowing him to explore different subject areas within a topic of study. For example, while completing the "King Arthur" project, Geoffrey considered information he gathered from the areas of literature, the visual arts, and architecture. It is apparent, then, that through the completion of this one project, Geoffrey's teacher was able to incorporate many excellent learning experiences. These learning experiences are consistent with those highly recommended by researchers within gifted education (Renzulli & Reis, 2014; Sternberg & Grigorenko, 2003; VanTassel-Baska, 2003; VanTassel-Baska & Brown, 2001).

Other recommended teaching and learning strategies have also been a part of Geoffrey's recent education. He has been encouraged by his parents and his teachers to be creative through brainstorming, problem solving, and role-playing. He has been directed to develop his research skills through exposure to researchers from various fields as well as opportunities to conduct and present his own research. He has been paired with adult mentors, individuals who share the same interests as Geoffrey (i.e., a physics professor and an English professor). He has been given socialization and leadership opportunities through small and large group work within the classroom, as well as through participation in extracurricular activities outside of school (e.g., violin and swimming lessons). All of these learning opportunities have facilitated Geoffrey's development and led to the change in his feelings about school.

What We Know . . .

Curricula for Students Who Are Gifted Learners

The following are some key beliefs and assumptions that guide the development of curricula in gifted education:

- All learners should be provided curriculum opportunities that allow them to attain optimum levels of learning.

Continued

- Gifted learners have different learning needs compared with typical learners. Therefore, curricula must be adapted or designed to accommodate these needs.
- The needs of gifted learners cut across cognitive, affective, social, and aesthetic areas of curricula experiences.
- Gifted learners are best served by a confluent approach that allows for both accelerated and enriched learning.
- Curriculum experiences for gifted learners need to be carefully planned, written down, implemented, and evaluated to maximize potential effect.

Source: VanTassel-Baska (1997), p. 126.

Something to Think About

Geoffrey's parents decided against grade acceleration for their son. How do you feel about moving a child to a higher learning level? What might be the advantages and disadvantages of this approach to educating children who are gifted? Can you suggest some criteria that may be useful when trying to determine whether or not a student is a good candidate for grade acceleration?

What We Know . . .

The School-Wide Enrichment Model

Enrichment of the school curricula can obviously benefit students who are gifted and talented. However, Renzulli and Reis (2014) have demonstrated through their School-Wide Enrichment Model (SEM) that enrichment can enhance the learning experiences of all children. Based on the notion that instruction must take into account the varying abilities, background interests, experiences, and learning styles of each student, the SEM promotes the formation of a talent pool within the school. The membership of the talent pool is not constant and includes students who, at a given point in time, are excited about a topic and demonstrate the ability and commitment to acquire further knowledge in the topic area. These students then complete the regular curriculum at a faster pace and engage in enrichment activities with clusters of similarly interested students from across several grade levels. Usually, these enrichment clusters are led by a resource teacher who has experience in gifted education. After the students have participated in these small group sessions, which focus on higher-order thinking skills and the creative and productive application of skills to real-world situations, they may take their learning experiences one step further by completing an independent study project.

Evaluation of Progress

Just as the curricula must be modified for the student who is gifted, so must the process of evaluation (see the *What We Know* box). For example, Geoffrey's teacher evaluated his knowledge of the medieval period by considering what she expected him to learn from her in-class presentations as well as what she expected him to learn by completing the assigned project. Earlier, when developing these activities and the accompanying learning expectations, she took into account both the provincial learning expectations for that unit and Geoffrey's individualized learning objectives. Her subsequent evaluation of Geoffrey's work was then based on her well-thought-out expectations. The evaluation did not merely assess whether Geoffrey's work was better or worse than that of his classmates. In fact, Geoffrey's project was far more sophisticated than those of most of his peers. This alone does not indicate that learning expectations have been met. Evaluation is only effective when it addresses a student's current strengths and needs and when it provides direction for ongoing instruction within the assigned curriculum. It should be noted that there must be a clear understanding that students who are gifted are not equally advanced in all areas. Otherwise, educators run the risk of failing to make the child's schooling appropriately challenging across all subjects.

What We Know . . .

Assessing the Work of Students Who Are Gifted and Talented

According to Stephens and Karnes (2001), students who are gifted should be involved in establishing the criteria for evaluation of their work. Ideally, a rubric is constructed so that both the teacher and the student are aware of the components of the assigned work as well as the possible exemplary characteristics of each component and their mark value.

Stephens and Karnes also stated that the "evaluation of student products should be multidimensional so students can receive helpful and extensive feedback from a wide array of sources" (p. 198). They suggested that while the teacher and the student can assess the student's work according to preselected criteria, the audience (e.g., classmates, school personnel, family members, topic experts) can also be asked to provide feedback. Once all of the evaluative data have been considered, the student should then be encouraged to reflect on the entire process and learn from both successes and failures.

How Is Geoffrey Different from Other Students Who Are Gifted?

Geoffrey's set of abilities, or gifts, are unique, as are the gifts of all children. There may be children who score exactly as Geoffrey did on the WISC and RPM, but they would likely be very different from him in many ways. In fact, while Geoffrey and these children may display common behaviours in their motivation to learn and how they learn, their superior cognitive abilities may be differentially displayed through a wide range of behaviours, such as academic proficiency, musicality, leadership, artistic ability, athletics, or, like Geoffrey, the ability to write. Geoffrey may be gifted, but unlike many other children who are gifted, he is not athletic nor does he take leadership roles at school. It is critical, then, to consider each child as being distinct and to refrain from stereotyping those who are highly capable in terms of intellect.

In Geoffrey's case, his gifts are most obvious to those who know him and to those who read his written productions. However, not all children who are gifted are quite so visible. The following are examples of children who are gifted yet often overlooked:

- *The gifted underachiever:* Jean-Paul is a 15-year-old high school student who exhibits little interest in learning the Grade 10 curricula. His primary interest outside of school is music as he has the ability to pick up any instrument and play it with little instruction. He scored very high on an IQ test in elementary school, but this has never translated into high academic achievement. Despite little effort on his part, his grades have been consistently average. However, his grades are slipping below average in high school because he has developed very few study skills over the years. He displays no enthusiasm for any subject areas and claims that school is "too boring." He is in constant arguments with his parents regarding "not living up to his potential." On the other hand, he finds great comfort in the fact that he is just like all his friends. This is little solace to his parents, who fear that he will lose interest in school and drop out.

- *The gifted and learning disabled:* Bharati, an energetic, talkative 9-year-old, has great difficulty with reading and writing. However, when these difficulties led to testing by the school psychologist, it was determined that while Bharati has learning disabilities in these two areas, she is of superior intelligence and is remarkably advanced in her verbal abilities. Her parents were relieved when they learned of the assessment results because now they have an explanation for her poor performance at school. Her teachers were also relieved as they too received an explanation for why she performed so poorly on assigned tasks yet constantly demonstrated an ability to be highly creative and to think critically. Knowing Bharati's precise situation enables school personnel and her parents to make constructive decisions regarding her academic programming.

- *The gifted and physically disabled:* Madison is a 10-year-old child who has cerebral palsy, a condition that affects her muscle control. She has great difficulty walking and performing fine motor tasks, such as writing. Her speech is sometimes hard to understand. However, she has a very rich vocabulary and she is a voracious reader, reading books far beyond her grade level. Madison is continually frustrated by the constant focus on her disabilities at school, rather than on her capabilities. Some teachers seem to have low expectations in terms of what she can achieve, even on grade-level tasks. Madison has difficulty demonstrating she is capable of much more in school because it takes her significantly longer than other students to complete written work. She has never been considered for the gifted program.

- *The gifted minority.* Johnny, who is of Southern Tutchone heritage, lives in a major Canadian city. He is a Grade 4 student who is exceptionally thoughtful and introspective. He has produced remarkable artwork and tells captivating and detailed

Like Jean-Paul, many students who are gifted are uncomfortable with the differences be-tween themselves and other students. They prefer to be just like their friends and choose to conform to the expected behaviour of their age group.

stories based on what he gleans from his Elders. His Grade 3 teacher asked that he be assessed as she considered him to be gifted. Johnny did not score above average on the IQ test or the achievement tests that were administered and therefore was not deemed eligible for gifted programming. His current teacher does not encourage Johnny in the areas in which he is gifted. In fact, she discourages him from sketching during class time and she becomes impatient when he does not have immediate answers to her questions. As a result, Johnny is beginning to show a disinterest in school.

What We Know . . .

Underachieving Children Who Are Gifted

Underachievement is seen as a discrepancy between assessed potential and actual performance. The discrepancy may be between two standardized measures (e.g., IQ and achievement tests), or between a standardized measure and classroom performance (e.g., teacher expectation and performance on daily assignments).

Continued

Highly intelligent students who are required to work at the same level and pace as their age-mates, when often they can grasp concepts years ahead, are at great risk of losing interest in school and falling short of their potential. In particular, one problematic area of underachievement is that of gifted children who feel acutely uncomfortable with the differences between themselves and the other children, and quickly adjust to conform to the social and behavioural norms of their age group.

Sources: Colangelo & Assouline (2000), p. 603; Bender (2006), p. 12.

How Teachers Can Motivate Students Who Are Gifted Underachievers

- Explain the purpose of assignments and lessons.
- Help students set short- and long-term academic goals that are meaningful to them.
- Help students see beyond the present activity to the long-term benefits it produces.
- Integrate students' interests into instruction.
- Offer students authentic choices about the ways in which they can learn and show mastery of the material in class.
- Utilize classroom activities that students can master, but not without effort and the use of appropriate strategies.
- Strive to build opportunities for immediate feedback into classroom activities.
- Treat students as if they already are enthusiastic learners.
- Encourage students to think seriously about how their performance in class can affect their future goals, as well as to explicitly articulate their reasons for choosing or failing to put forth effort.
- Discuss with students the obstacles they believe are keeping them from doing well and what options exist for them.
- Avoid letting students use their environment as an excuse.
- Help students set realistic expectations.

Source: From Siegle & McCoach (2005), pp. 23–26.

What We Know . . .

Children Who Are Gifted and Learning Disabled

Characteristics of giftedness include spontaneity, inquisitiveness, imagination, boundless enthusiasm, and emotionality; and these same traits are often observed in children with learning disabilities. Teachers can meet the unique needs of students whose strengths and talents lie outside the narrow view of knowledge by helping students bypass their deficits as they access areas of strengths, modifying assignments and curricula for these students so that their true abilities can be demonstrated, and creating an environment that nurtures personal creativity and intellectual characteristics.

Source: Lerner & Kline (2006), p. 14.

Characteristics of Twice-Exceptional Learners

Areas of Giftedness

- Specific talent or interest area often unrelated to school area
- Superior vocabulary
- Interested in the "big picture" rather than the small details
- High level of problem solving and reasoning
- Penetrating insights into complex issues and topics
- Advanced ideas and opinions that they are uninhibited in expressing
- Highly creative in their approach to tasks, sometimes used as a technique to compensate for their disability
- Unrelenting sense of curiosity
- Unusual imagination
- Advanced sense of humour that, at times, may appear bizarre
- Capable of setting up situations to their own advantage as a means of compensating for their disability

Areas of Challenge

- Inordinately frustrated by school
- Deficient or extremely uneven academic skills resulting in lack of academic initiative and school-task avoidance
- Low self-esteem often masked by inappropriate behaviours such as teasing, clowning, anger, withdrawal, apathy, denial of problems
- Processing deficits may cause them to respond slowly, work slowly, and appear to think slowly
- Difficulty with long-term and short-term memory
- Frequently stubborn and inflexible
- Gross or fine motor difficulties exhibited by clumsiness, poor handwriting, or problems completing paper-and-pencil tasks
- Lack of organizational and study skills
- Difficulty thinking linearly, resulting in an inability to understand cause and effect or to follow directions
- Extremely impulsive
- Highly distractible
- Poor social skills sometimes demonstrated by antisocial behaviours

Source: Republished with permission of Sage publishing, from Nielsen (2002), as cited in Nielsen & Higgins (2005), p. 9. From Nielsen, M.E., & Higgins, L.D. (2005). "The eye of the storm: Services and programs for twice-exceptional learners." *Teaching Exceptional Children*, 38(1). Permission conveyed through Copyright Clearance Center, Inc.

What We Know . . .

Children Who Are Gifted and Physically Disabled

Attention to the gifts of individuals with disabilities has been sorely neglected. Identification procedures must consist of multiple measures, including informal observation. Teachers must expand their knowledge of how children's abilities and disabilities affect learning. They must become proficient in disability-related instruction and technology, adaptive curricular strategies, communication, and collaborative teaming. Service provision must also include counselling to assist the student with disabilities in the development of a positive and realistic self-concept. The low self-esteem that often develops around the disability is combined with the often low and unrealistic expectations by others. Successful approaches are ones that accentuate a student's strengths and individual interests, as opposed to those that focus on remediating deficits.

Source: Johnson, Karnes, & Carr (1997), pp. 521–522.

How Teachers Can Assist the Child Who Is Gifted and Physically Disabled

- Encourage the use of technology to allow the child to be placed in the most "natural" and advantageous setting where academic self-esteem can be maintained.
- Teach to the child's strengths. Allow the child to use what they do well to compensate for, and to remediate, weaknesses (e.g., replace map-making skills with map-reading skills).
- Facilitate the development of independent learning and study skills to combat dependency habits and to assist the child in areas of weakness (e.g., time management).
- Explain the child's disability to fellow students to foster acceptance by classmates.
- Encourage the child to interact with others through co-operative learning opportunities.
- Expose the child to mentors and take the child on field trips in an effort to overcome possible experiential deprivation.

Source: Baldwin & Vialle (1999), pp. 192–194.

What We Know . . .

Minority Students Who Are Gifted

Minority students are underrepresented in gifted programs. They are less likely to be nominated by teachers as potential candidates for gifted programs and, if nominated, they are less likely to be selected for the program, particularly when such traditional measures as IQ and achievement tests are used for identification.

Source: Olszewski-Kubilius, Lee, Ngoi, & Ngoi (2004), p. 129.

Identification Issues

The identification of students who are gifted has been a long-standing challenge within the field of gifted education. Over 20 years ago Frasier, García, and Passow (1995) addressed this issue:

> Although there is consensus that gifted children can be found in every level of society and in every cultural and ethnic group, minority and economically disadvantaged students have not been found in gifted programs in proportionate numbers. The under-representation of minority student populations has been attributed to a variety of factors including test bias, selective referrals, and a reliance on deficit-based paradigms. Inequities in assessment need to be considered from a broad perspective that takes into account the multiple factors that affect the identification of gifted minority students (e.g., historical, philosophical, psychological, theoretical, procedural, social, and political). (pp. v–vi)

Unfortunately, not much has changed. Michael-Chadwell (2011) emphasized that the underrepresentation of historically underserved student groups continues to be a phenomenon in gifted and talented programs:

> In a phenomenological study exploring teachers' and African American parents' perceptions of the underrepresentation of gifted African American students, four themes emerged from the study. Those themes are: (a) misperceptions regarding a student's race and ability; (b) the lack of parent awareness programs about issues related to gifted and talented education; (c) the need for professional development training related to the needs of minority gifted students; and (d) issues related to testing and assessment instrumentation. (p. 99)

Something to Think About

Alanis Obomsawin, a Canadian award-winning filmmaker of Abenaki descent, has been quoted as saying "We are gifted and very talented. But you're not going to find out the way you are asking us your questions" (Matthews, 2013). What implications do you think this statement has in regard to gifted education for Canadian students?

Closing Geoffrey's File

As we close the file on Geoffrey, it is important to consider what his educational needs will be in the immediate future. His beginning school years were difficult and painful for both himself and his parents. However, his middle school years have been highly successful as he has been able to thrive both intellectually and emotionally. His parents and his current educators have put great effort into providing an intellectually stimulating environment within a caring and supportive milieu.

It is not hard to extrapolate to the school years ahead. As Geoffrey progresses through the upper elementary and junior high grades, his differences will likely be noticed even more by his peers. It is perhaps his sensitive nature that will set him apart the most. It would be a travesty if this gift of caring and compassion was stifled in his efforts to be accepted. Not only would his emotional well-being be in jeopardy, but it may dampen the outpouring of his highly creative and thoughtful prose, and also reduce his insatiable appetite for knowledge.

Given the emotional challenges Geoffrey will undoubtedly face as he enters the adolescent period, it will be necessary for those charged with his education to recognize and support his heightened sensitivity, or emotionality, rather than merely focusing on the curricula learned or the talents exhibited. He will need this support as he faces the pressures of conforming to societal expectations. As Roeper (1995) emphasized, children who are gifted and talented should be *educated for life* rather than *educated for success*. In other words, growth of the self and mastery of the environment are more important than the attainment and exhibition of a particular set of skills.

From the Psychologist's Notebook

Geoffrey's happiness and academic success in recent school years has not been due to some special sort of program nor has it been due to a specialist teacher of students who are gifted. It can be best attributed to a sharing of information. Just a few years ago, Geoffrey's parents and I met with his teachers to talk about his abilities and needs. The teachers found this extremely helpful, as evidenced by their many questions. Once they had a complete picture of Geoffrey's overall situation, they easily and readily designed and then successfully implemented a challenging but attainable educational program for him. Since these initial meetings, Geoffrey's teachers have continued the information-sharing process with his next-grade teachers. The program that each of these teachers have implemented is not as extraordinarily different as many would expect. What his teachers are doing is nothing more than really good teaching. When Geoffrey's mother first called me for advice, she and his teachers were beside themselves as to what to do for him in school. I no longer get these types of phone calls.

Our ultimate educational goal for Geoffrey is for him to emerge from high school as a happy and fulfilled adolescent who happens to be an amazing writer. We think the right types of specific considerations have been made to accomplish just that.

Updating Geoffrey's Story

Geoffrey is about to graduate from high school and enter university. We spoke with the psychologist who has observed Geoffrey's progress since he was a young elementary student. According to her, Geoffrey's upper elementary school years were somewhat turbulent. Again, it appears that it was the teachers' lack of understanding regarding Geoffrey's educational needs rather than the actual school placement that had this effect. Subsequently, Geoffrey was home-schooled for his Grade 7 year. Conversely, high school was an extremely positive experience. Geoffrey attended a public high school where he was enrolled in a literary arts program. This meant he took advanced courses in literature and writing while attending regular classes for all other subjects. The psychologist described this mix of programming as "very suitable for Geoffrey's social, emotional, and academic needs." Apparently, Geoffrey excelled in all subject areas, especially writing, and received several awards for his efforts. His closest friends were his literary arts peers among whom he was well-accepted; together they attended regular school functions and socialized with those outside of their particular program. Asked to sum up Geoffrey's latter school years, the psychologist noted that when we wrote the first edition of this text her hope was that Geoffrey would emerge from high school as a happy and fulfilled adolescent who happens to be an amazing writer. "That has been accomplished . . . he had some terrific teachers along the way . . . in high school, he was challenged to further develop his literary expertise and he was acknowledged when he did just that, he experienced teenage life along with his peers in a regular high school, and he continued to have a very supportive home life. He is ready to move on to university, where I am sure he will thrive in a more intense academic setting."

Summary

Giftedness, or the capability of high performance because of outstanding abilities, is considered a genetic endowment that can be influenced by environmental factors. It is typically identified in Canadian schools through observation and the completion of a standardized intelligence test. While students who are gifted may exhibit common characteristics (e.g., how they learn and what motivates them), their superior abilities are displayed through a wide range of behaviours (e.g., academic proficiency, artistic abilities, and athletic prowess). These students are not always as easily identified as one may think, especially when they are not equally capable across all school-related tasks. For example, students may be learning or physically disabled as well as gifted. It is also apparent that some students who are gifted are not identified due to the fact that they are underachievers, sometimes purposefully. As evidenced from Geoffrey's story, it is critical that educators carefully consider the academic and social or emotional needs of students who are gifted.

Learning More about Students Who Are Gifted and Talented

Academic Journals

Gifted and Talented International
Gifted Child Quarterly
Journal for the Education of the Gifted
Journal of the Gifted and Talented Education Council of the Alberta Teachers' Association (AGATE)
Journal of Secondary Gifted Education
Roeper Review

Books

Callahan, C. M. (2012). *Fundamentals of gifted education: Considering multiple perspectives.* New York, NY: Routledge.

Coleman, L. J. & Cross, T. L. (2005). *Being gifted in school: An introduction to development, guidance, and teaching* (2nd ed.). Waco, TX: Prufrock Press Inc.

Heller, K. A., Monks F. J., Sternberg, R. J., & Subotnik, R. F. (Eds.) (2000). *International handbook of giftedness and talent* (2nd ed.). Oxford, UK: Elsevier Science Ltd.

Karnes, F. A. & Bean, S. M. (Eds.) (2015). *Methods and materials for teaching the gifted* (4th ed.). Waco, TX: Prufrock Press Inc.

Kaufman, J. C. (2009). *Creativity 101.* New York, NY: Springer Publishing Company.

Robinson, A., Shore, B. M., & Enersen, D. L. (2007). *Best practices in gifted education.* Waco, TX: Prufrock Press Inc./National Association for Gifted Children.

Stephens, K. R. & Karnes, F. A. (2016). *Introduction to curriculum design in gifted education.* Waco, TX: Prufrock Press Inc.

Sternberg, R. J., Jarvin, L., & Grigorenko, E. L. (2011). *Explorations in giftedness.* New York, NY: Cambridge University Press.

Tomlinson, C. A. (2001). *How to differentiate instruction in mixed-ability classrooms* (2nd ed.). Upper Saddle River, NJ: Merrill Prentice Hall.

Vantassel-Baska, J. L., Cross, T. L., & Olenchak, F. R. (Eds.) (2009). *Social-emotional curriculum with gifted and talented students.* Waco, TX: Prufrock Press, Inc./National Association for Gifted Children.

Web Links

Accelerating Gifted Students in Canada

http://journals.sfu.ca/cje/index.php/cje-rce/article/view/1201/1596
This research report, published in the *Canadian Journal of Education*, addresses Canadian policies related to gifted education in general and acceleration in particular.

Council for Exceptional Children: Gifted Education

www.cec.sped.org/Special-Ed-Topics/Specialty-Areas/Gifted

The CEC provides resources to help you learn more about gifted education, connect you with other gifted education professionals, and better understand the issue of underrepresentation of minority and low-income students.

GATE—Gifted and Talented Education Parent Association

www.gatecalgary.ca
The GATE Program, which is in several Calgary schools, is a special education program for learners who are gifted. The parent association is committed to supporting a congregated setting for students who are gifted.

Gifted Education: A Resource Guide for Teachers (BC Ministry of Education)

www.bced.gov.bc.ca/specialed/gifted
The Ministry of Education in British Columbia designed this guide for teachers who may be seeking information on gifted education, including strategies for meeting the needs of the gifted learner in the regular classroom.

National Association for Gifted Children

www.nagc.org
The NAGC website reflects the primary goals of the association: They strive to train teachers, encourage parents, and educate administrators and policy-makers in regard to the needs of children who are gifted.

Renzulli Center for Creativity, Gifted Education, and Talent Development

http://gifted.uconn.edu/schoolwide-enrichment-model/sem3rd
This website provides links to many downloadable tools that teachers can use when implementing the School-Wide Enrichment Model.

The Association for Bright Children of Ontario

www.abcontario.ca
This site provides information on giftedness, including an FAQ section and a resource titled "Developing Individual Education Plans for Gifted Students."

World Council for Gifted and Talented Children

www.world-gifted.org
The WCGTC is a worldwide not-for-profit organization that provides advocacy and support for gifted children. The website provides information on relevant publications and resources as well as details of the annual world conference.

Taking It into Your Classroom . . .

Including Students Who Are Gifted

When a student who is gifted is first placed in my classroom, I will

- review what I know about giftedness and locate resource materials,
- read the student's file,
- consult with the student's previous teachers,
- consult with the student's parents, and
- meet with the school-based team to discuss the student's current school year.
- Other: _____

When I suspect a student in my classroom is gifted, I will

- review what I know about giftedness and locate resource materials,
- collect information about the student through classroom interventions,
- consult with other school personnel who are familiar with the student,
- consult with the student's parents, and
- meet with the school-based team to present the information I have collected.
- Other: _____

Key points to remember in my daily interactions with a student who is gifted:

- The student may be easily bored with routine tasks.
- The student may be persistent about completing tasks of interest.
- The student may be emotionally sensitive.
- The student may be a perfectionist.
- The student may have a keen sense of right and wrong.
- Other: _____

Key points regarding curriculum differentiation for a student who is gifted:

- The student should be exposed to differentiation of the core curriculum.
- The curriculum should emphasize depth and not just the learning of facts.
- The student should be encouraged to develop higher-level thinking skills.
- The curriculum should emphasize interdisciplinary ideas.
- The student should have the opportunity to work independently.
- Other: _____

Key points regarding evaluation of the progress made by a student who is gifted:

- The student should have input into the development of an evaluation plan.
- Evaluation should be based on what the student is expected to know and understand.
- There should be recognition that the student may not be equally advanced in all areas.
- Evaluation should include assessment of products and performance.
- Evaluation should include assessment of effective outcomes.
- Evaluation should identify strengths and weaknesses.
- Evaluation should lead to new instructional goals.
- Other: _____

CHAPTER 8

Students with Intellectual Disabilities

LEARNING OBJECTIVES

After learning the material in this chapter, you should be able to:

- Define the term *Down syndrome*, including some of the clinical signs of the condition.

- Define the term *intellectual disability* and explain how this disability is diagnosed.

- Discuss the cognitive development of children with intellectual disabilities in terms of the delay or difference debate.

- Describe the relationship between intellectual disabilities and behaviour disorders.

- Provide several general strategies for teaching students with intellectual disabilities.

- Explain how to conduct observational assessments when monitoring student progress.

- Define the terms *Williams syndrome* and *Fragile X syndrome*.

- Discuss the importance of considering both academic and life-skills instruction for students with intellectual disabilities.

Name: David Robertson

Current Age: 17

School: King Street High School

Grade: 11

David is a high school student who enjoys being active whether it is through participation in sports or playing a role in an in-class drama production.

As a result of being born with Down syndrome, which is readily obvious through his physical characteristics, David has always had difficulty with academic tasks. His reading, writing, and mathematics abilities are significantly below those of his peers. Therefore, the focus of his high school program is on life skills and adapting to a workplace environment. David's story illustrates how the curricula in secondary school can accommodate students who need assistance as they move toward independent living.

Psycho-Educational Assessment

Age at Time of Assessment: 11 years, 1 month

Reason for Referral

David is currently placed in a Grade 5 classroom and his program is significantly modified to meet his needs. He has Down syndrome and receives support from the resource program, an EA (four periods a day), and a volunteer who is placed in the classroom to assist all students. He is also receiving treatment from the school board's speech-language pathologist. He is able to count to 20 and can add and subtract with the use of manipulatives. He enjoys matching and sorting activities and is very athletic. A psycho-educational assessment was requested to determine David's strengths and weaknesses and to assist school personnel in designing his program.

Assessment Techniques

- review of student file
- consultations with classroom teacher, resource teacher, and parents
- Bender Visual-Motor Gestalt Test
- Wechsler Intelligence Scale for Children-III (Canadian norms)

Assessment Results

Behavioural Observations

David was accompanied to the testing session by an EA. She was able to interpret most of David's gestures and vocalizations. David was not pleased to attend the session and complained to the EA after every request and often indicated that he wanted to leave.

Cognitive Potential

David was unable to complete many of the testing items. On those subtests where he was able to give a response, he was below the 6-year-old level. In a discussion with David's mother, she indicated that she believes that David is capable of more than these tests can measure. It was decided to put off assigning an IQ score at this time in the hopes that with maturity, David will be able to reliably complete more subtests in a future testing session.

Language Abilities

David's verbal comprehension skills are extremely limited. He appears to understand very little of what is said to him. His vocabulary, his general knowledge, and understanding of societal norms all fall below the 6-year-old level. David also has speech difficulties and can be quite difficult to understand. Not surprisingly, he has considerable difficulty expressing his thoughts, reasoning abstractly, and forming verbal concepts.

David Robertson

Tests of Achievement

Age at Time of Assessment: 15 years, 6 months

Test Administered: Woodcock–Johnson III Tests of Achievement

Test Results:

Cluster Test	Age Equivalent	Percentile Rank
Basic Reading Skills	6–9	<0.1
Academic Skills	6–8	<0.1
Academic Knowledge	4–2	<0.1

Additional Tests	Age Equivalent	Percentile Rank
Letter-Word Identification	6–8	<0.1
Calculation	7–1	<0.1
Spelling	6–2	<0.1
Word Attack	6–9	<0.1
Picture Vocabulary	3–8	<0.1

Test Observations

David's conversational proficiency seemed very limited for his age level. He was co-operative, appeared at ease, and was attentive to tasks. David responded promptly, but carefully, to test questions. He gave up easily when attempting difficult tasks.

Test Summary

When compared to others at his age level, David's academic knowledge and skills are both within the very low range. This includes his basic reading skills.

Teachers' Reports

Grade 9 (Semester 2)

David has done some good work in Dramatic Arts this semester. He is a pleasure to teach and always open to new ideas and creative critique. Well done!

In literacy, David has improved in the areas of word matching (beginning, middle, and end) and visual word matching at Level 1. The Academy of Reading has assisted David's development in these areas. His oral communication and social skills have been strengthened through journal presentations and role-playing.

In numeracy, David has developed his knowledge of one-number addition and subtraction as well as improving in the areas of money identification and graphing. His biggest area of improvement has been his positive attitude in learning these concepts.

In terms of physical education, David participated on a regular basis and showed a positive attitude. His teamwork has improved as he is more aware of passing to his fellow team mates in scrimmage situations. I encourage him to remain active over the summer.

Grade 10 (Semester 2)

David participated in meaningful activities during religion class this semester. The curriculum was modified to meet his learning needs and to maximize his skills. His prayer service was well prepared, and he showed understanding of the idea of prayer.

In drama, David continued his good work. He is willing to take risks and invests all of his dramatic endeavours with energy and commitment.

In numeracy, David has enhanced his knowledge of addition and subtraction facts to 100, money identification, and graphing. His work habits have improved significantly. The ability to complete tasks independently has improved his self-esteem.

David is a pleasure to have in physical education class. He demonstrates a positive attitude and excellent effort. He almost always participates to the best of his ability.

Grade 11 (Semester 1)

David demonstrated a moderate understanding of employer expectations during his work co-op placement. He has a limited understanding of job readiness skills and needs to improve his communication skills and appropriate work habits.

In social skills class, David has shown enthusiasm. He participated well in all activities. He is a pleasure to have in class.

David continues to be a positive influence in drama classes. I would like to see him take more initiative in developing ideas and incorporating instructions.

David regularly participates actively in physical activities. He often encourages his classmates. He is reminded to continue working toward attaining his fitness goals.

David Robertson

Excerpts from David's IEP

Grade:	11
Placement:	**Regular Classroom with Withdrawal Assistance** (David is working toward a Certificate of Accomplishment.)

Areas of Strengths

- expressive skills (with EA support uses gestures, sign language, and computer software to express ideas)
- gross motor skills (enjoys sports and drama)
- peer interaction
- visual cues result in more appropriate responses
- good sense of humour

Areas of Need

- communication skills (expressive and receptive language skills)
- fine motor skills
- functional academic skills
- life skills focusing on self-advocacy
- functional work-related skills

Instructional Accommodations

- Support verbal communication with natural gestures and facial expressions and non-verbal cues (e.g., pictures).
- Make use of augmentative communication devices (e.g., communication boards, pictogram programs, electronic picture communication books, and pointing and typing aids).
- Teach and model strategies that David can use to effectively communicate his strengths and needs.
- Focus on specific expectations that promote independence.
- Engage David's attention visually, verbally, and physically.
- Make use of alternative methods of sharing information (e.g., video, audiotapes).
- Provide a computer.

Assessment Accommodations

David is a kinesthetic learner. Assessments need to include diversity. Assessing participation, collaborative group work, and completion of tasks will provide alternate but meaningful assessments that reflect David's true abilities.

Accommodations may include

- adapting the assessment format (e.g., oral test, practical demonstration),
- allowing David to use assistive devices and technology resources (e.g., Kurzweil),
- providing prompts to return David's attention to the task, and
- reducing the number of tasks used to assess a concept or skill.

Subject:	Food and Nutrition
Current Level of Achievement:	David is not working toward an academic credit. The course has been modified to meet David's social and academic strengths.
Program Goal:	To enhance knowledge of the factors that affect attitudes and decisions about food.

Learning Expectations	Teaching Strategies	Methods for Assessment
• Demonstrate basic cooking and baking skills.	• Provide modelling and repetition of basic cooking and basic skills.	• Observation • Review self- and peer assessments
• Identify and demonstrate safe food-handling practices, including kitchen safety, sanitary methods, and proper food storage.	• Use signs/pictures/symbols necessary in daily routines to determine appropriate response or course of action.	• Review daily work • Observation
• Identify, select, and effectively use appropriate kitchen tools to plan and prepare interesting and appealing meals in co-operation with others.	• Provide opportunities for non-restrictive and creative endeavours.	• Review collaborative group work • Review daily work
• Plan meals that address factors such as nutritional needs, likes and dislikes, special diets, and considerations related to time, money, and effort.	• Allow for demonstration of this talent.	• Observation

David Robertson

Subject:	Numeracy and Numbers
Current Level of Achievement:	David is not working toward an academic credit. Expectations are from the Grade 3 math curriculum.
Program Goal:	To measure and compare the length, weight, mass, capacity, and temperature of objects, and demonstrate awareness of passage of time.

Learning Expectations	Teaching Strategies	Methods for Assessment
• Count by 1s, 2s, 5s, and 10s to 100 using multiples of 1, 2, and 5 as starting points.	• Use visual aids (e.g., printable number line, computer programs).	• Review daily work • Observation
• Demonstrate an understanding of some standard units of measure for length and distance (centimetre, metre) and time (second, minute, hour, day).	• Provide opportunities for system-based enriching activities (e.g., being punctual for school functions).	• Observation • Review individual and group presentations
• Name and state the value of all coins and demonstrate an understanding of their value.	• Use concrete materials to teach money identification, values, and counting.	• Observation
• Discuss the use of number and arrangement in the community (e.g., cans on a grocery store shelf, cost of a movie rental).	• Use real-life activities (e.g., counting money, grocery shopping).	• Review oral responses • Observation
• Read digital and analogue clocks, and tell and write time to the quarter-hour.	• Use computer games, clocks, worksheets, schedules, etc.	• Review class discussion • Observation

Subject:	Communication
Current Level of Achievement:	David is working at primary level in terms of reasoning skills and the ability to express his thoughts. His speech is affected by severe articulation difficulties.
Program Goal:	To increase David's oral and expressive language skills for the purpose of requests and social interaction (using signs and gestures to clarify).

Learning Expectations	Teaching Strategies	Methods for Assessment
• Enhance positive communication skills needed for future independence.	• Use drama, singing games, rhyming activities, etc., to enhance confidence and fluency.	• Observation
• Increase frequency/confidence in socialization/pragmatic skills.	• Teach and rehearse responses to social situations.	• Review individual and group presentations
• Improve articulation and individual sound production.	• Involve in small group expressive-language sessions.	• Review class discussion
• Use five- to six-word phrases.	• Use signs/pictures/symbols necessary in daily routines to determine appropriate response or course of action.	• Review daily work • Review self- and/or peer assessments

David Robertson

Subject:	Social Skills
Current Level of Achievement:	With adult intervention and support, David interacts in an age-appropriate manner with peers and adults.
Program Goal:	To improve social skills by maintaining appropriate behaviour in the classroom and improving peer interactions at school.

Learning Expectations	Teaching Strategies	Methods for Assessment
• Follow class rules, routines, and behaviour expectations.	• Model appropriate behaviour through role-playing and collaborative group work.	• Observation
• Participate in age-appropriate conversations with peers/staff.	• Provide opportunities for inclusionary activities to enhance David's verbal communication skills.	• Observation • Review self- and/or peer assessments
• Respect personal space of self and others.	• Empathetic prompting and cueing of appropriate personal space with peers and staff.	• Review daily work • Review class discussion
• Learn social cues.	• Model appropriate behaviour through role-playing and collaborative group work in classroom.	• Observation

Subject:	Healthy Active Living Education
Current Level of Achievement:	David is not working toward an academic credit. The course has been modified to meet David's social and academic strengths.
Program Goal:	To encourage David to use his knowledge of guidelines and strategies to enhance his participation in recreational and sports activities.

Learning Expectations	Teaching Strategies	Methods for Assessment
• Encourage David to develop greater independence and leadership skills whenever possible.	• Use inclusive language and facilitate group achievement.	• Consistently communicate with EA to assess David's effort and independent behaviour.
• Increase David's understanding of what constitutes healthy active living (i.e., exercise and healthy eating).	• Provide visual examples (e.g., overheads, pictures) to enhance comprehension.	• Alternate forms of evaluation that address David's strength as a kinesthetic learner.
• Maintain or improve fitness levels by participating in vigorous activities for sustained periods of time.	• Provide consistent reinforcement to motivate David to complete activities.	• Use charts and graphs to track David's success.
• Experience the benefits of participation in different physical activities (e.g., social interaction, enjoyment, relaxation, self-esteem).	• Recognize and praise efforts and improvements as well as task completion. Use verbal and non-verbal feedback.	• Use diverse assessment options, such as oral responses and role-playing.

David Robertson

Subject:	Computer and Information Science
Current Level of Achievement:	David is not working toward an academic credit. The course has been modified to meet David's social and academic strengths.
Program Goal:	To enable David to correctly create, name, copy, move, delete, and organize computer files. To increase David's understanding of how computers are used at home and at work.

Learning Expectations	Teaching Strategies	Methods for Assessment
• Use file management techniques correctly to create, name, copy, move, delete, and organize files.	• Teach and reinforce the use of key words, phrases, and terminology.	• Review daily work
• Identify and explore computer programs pertaining to Microsoft Word, Corel presentations, and All the Right Type.	• Permit and encourage use of support tools (e.g., dictionary, word lists, and spell check).	• Use Corel presentations • Observe oral response
• Describe how computers change the ways in which people live, work, and communicate, and apply these theories to own life.	• Provide real-life examples. • Encourage David to use the computer for a variety of tasks relevant to his life.	• Observe oral response • Use role-playing • Review daily work

Why Is David Considered to Have an Intellectual Disability?

Down Syndrome

David was born with Down syndrome. His diagnosis was made shortly after birth. However, even before the medical staff confirmed Down syndrome through a blood test that detects chromosomal abnormalities, David's parents knew immediately what they were facing. They both quickly recognized the implications of their baby's physical features: slanting eyes, flat nose, and small head. He was most definitely going to have intellectual challenges that affected not only his education but also his ability to live a fully independent life. David's mother described this moment in their lives as one of great joy and great sadness. They had a new baby, a sibling for their 2-year-old daughter, but their son was going to face many difficulties and perhaps never experience some of the dreams they had envisioned for him. In addition, they knew that Down syndrome is often accompanied by serious health concerns such as heart defects, gastrointestinal tract problems, low muscle tone, or difficulties with vision, hearing, or speech. David's parents were well aware that the road ahead was going to be challenging for the whole family.

What We Know . . .

Down Syndrome

Down syndrome is the most common and readily identifiable chromosomal condition associated with intellectual disability. It is caused by a chromosomal abnormality: For some unexplained reason, an accident in cell development results in 47 instead of the usual 46 chromosomes. This extra chromosome changes the orderly development of the body and brain. In most cases, the diagnosis of Down syndrome is made according to results from a chromosome test administered shortly after birth.

There are over 50 clinical signs of Down syndrome, but it is rare to find all or even most of them in one person. Some common characteristics include the following:

- Poor muscle tone
- Slanting eyes with folds of skin at the inner corners (called epicanthal folds)
- Hyperflexibility (excessive ability to extend the joints)
- Short, broad hands with a single crease across the palm on one or both hands
- Broad feet with short toes
- Flat bridge of the nose
- Short, low-set ears
- Short neck
- Small head

Continued

- Small oral cavity
- Short, high-pitched cries in infancy

Besides having a distinct physical appearance, children with Down syndrome frequently have specific health-related problems.

Source: Center for Parent Information and Resources, 2017.

Students with Down syndrome have a distinct physical appearance that will be easily recognizable by staff and other students.

Definition of Intellectual Disability

Sixteen years ago, David's diagnosis of Down syndrome meant that he was labelled as mentally retarded—the appropriate term at the time. While the term "mentally retarded," or "mental retardation," has been used for almost 50 years and is still being used today, it is slowly being replaced by other terms such as the one used in this text: *intellectual disability*. The problem with the term "mental retardation" is not that it was initially intended to be derogatory but rather, over the years, it has become associated with a negative stereotype and many feel it is disrespectful to label a person with a term that demeans him or her in any way. It is important to note that respected organizations, such as the American Association on Mental Retardation (AAMR), continued to use the language that was established in the 1950s until January 2007, when the AAMR officially became the American Association on Intellectual and Developmental Disabilities (AAIDD). Members of AAIDD decided it was time to move away from the term "mental retardation" so, like other similar organizations, they have officially replaced it with the term "intellectual disability."

What We Know . . .

Definition of Intellectual Disability

An intellectual disability is a disability characterized by significant limitations both in intellectual functioning and in adaptive behaviour, which covers many everyday social and practical skills. This disability originates before the age of 18.

Intellectual functioning—also called intelligence—refers to general mental capacity, such as learning, reasoning, problem solving, and so on. One criterion to measure intellectual functioning is an IQ test. Generally, an IQ test score of around 70, or as high as 75, indicates a limitation in intellectual functioning.

Standardized tests can also determine limitations in *adaptive behaviour*, which comprises three skill types:

- Conceptual skills—language and literacy; money, time, and number concepts; and self-direction
- Social skills—interpersonal skills, social responsibility, self-esteem, gullibility, naïveté (i.e., wariness), social problem solving, and the ability to follow rules/obey laws and to avoid being victimized
- Practical skills—activities of daily living (personal care), occupational skills, healthcare, travel/transportation, schedules/routines, safety, use of money, use of the telephone

On the basis of such many-sided evaluations, professionals can determine whether an individual has an intellectual disability and can tailor a support plan for each individual.

In defining and assessing intellectual disability, however, the AAIDD stresses that professionals must take additional factors into account, such as the community environment typical of the individual's peers and culture. Professionals should also consider linguistic diversity and cultural differences in the way people communicate, move, and behave.

Finally, assessments must also assume that limitations in individuals often coexist with strengths, and that a person's level of life functioning will improve if appropriate, personalized supports are provided over a sustained period.

Source: Republished with permission of the American Association on Intellectual and Developmental Disabilities (2013). Permission conveyed through Copyright Clearance Center, Inc.

Something to Think About

You will find that intellectual disabilities are classified in different ways by different groups. For example, sometimes intellectual disabilities are classified as mild, moderate, severe, or profound as defined in the *Diagnostic and Statistical Manual of Mental Disorders* (5th edition). You may also find that they are classified according to the amount of support an individual needs: intermittent, limited, extensive, or pervasive. How are intellectual disabilities classified in your home province or territory? Is there a difference in the classification systems used by different groups (e.g., the educational system versus advocacy groups)?

Diagnosing an Intellectual Disability

While David's intellectual disability was recognized from the time of his birth because of the physical characteristics of Down syndrome, the extent of his disability was not known until he was school age. At age 11, a psycho-educational assessment was conducted (see p. 221), and David performed below the 6-year-old level on all subtests to which he gave responses.

From the Psychologist's Notebook

David was first presented to me as an 11-year-old boy with Down syndrome who had difficulty adjusting to new situations and especially new people. At the time, he had been a student at the same school since kindergarten, moving with his peers from grade to grade. When I met him, he was in a Grade 5/6 classroom where his classmates assisted him with daily tasks. Class routines and timetables were consistent and structured. He responded well to routines and motivations, such as free time. All forms of classroom assessment were completed by the classroom teacher or the EA. Therefore, these two individuals had a good understanding of David's abilities. Consequently, I considered my psycho-educational assessment of David to be a small part of his overall profile. His in-class work, which was assessed regularly, provided a more accurate reflection of his abilities, especially given David's reaction to my testing sessions.

What Factors Contributed to David's Intellectual Disability?

Because David's mother was young and healthy, and her pregnancy progressed as it should, there was no early warning that her baby would have an intellectual disability. In terms of Down syndrome, the exact cause of the chromosomal rearrangement is unknown.

For example, David has Trisomy 21, which means there was abnormal cell division during the development of the sperm cell or the egg cell. Mistakes in cell division such as this are not an inherited condition. There is usually no history of Down syndrome in the family. There is also no known environmental cause of the syndrome. There is an increased risk of having an affected baby when the mother is older at the time of pregnancy, but this was not the case with David. However, if David's mother had been over the age of 35 at the time of pregnancy, she may have agreed to a screening test or a more definitive diagnostic test to determine the health of her baby. These tests are offered to parents as an option, not a requirement, since parents must carefully think through the implications of knowing whether or not their baby has a condition such as Down syndrome. Screening tests are not invasive—they simply require a sample of the mother's blood to assess the likelihood that the fetus has the condition. On the other hand, diagnostic tests like chorionic villus sampling and amniocentesis can predict with almost 100 per cent certainty whether or not Down syndrome is present. These tests are more invasive and do carry the risk of miscarriage.

chorionic villus sampling
A prenatal procedure in which samples of the placenta are used to determine genetic abnormalities in the fetus; usually done for women over 35.

amniocentesis
A prenatal procedure in which a small amount of amniotic fluid is extracted from the amnion surrounding the fetus to check for genetic abnormalities.

From the Psychologist's Notebook

While no one knows for sure why Down syndrome occurs, there are factors that are definitively known to cause other forms of intellectual disability. These factors are varied and can affect the child during the prenatal period (e.g., infections, drug or alcohol abuse), during the birthing process (e.g., a lack of oxygen to the brain), or after birth (e.g., meningitis, physical abuse, neglect, accidental injury). Generally, the younger the child is when any of these insults occurs, the more seriously he or she is affected. Children with severe intellectual disabilities are usually recognized early simply because of their obvious delays in development. However, in many cases of mild to moderate impairment, the disability is not detected until the child enters school. Unfortunately, by this point, valuable time has been lost and the benefits of early intervention are not realized.

How Has David's Intellectual Disability Affected His Development?

Cognitive Development

Just like all individuals with Down syndrome, David has an intellectual disability. Because David's parents knew that intellectual disability was a characteristic of the syndrome, they were quite aware that their son would probably not meet early developmental milestones at the expected age. What they did not know was David's *degree* of intellectual disability. According to his mother, "it was good to know in advance that David would need help with his early development, but it was difficult not to wonder just how severe his intellectual disability would be and how we might handle the different possible scenarios."

As an infant, David was a passive baby. He demanded little attention and his parents had to make purposeful attempts to pique his interest in his environment. His mother said that her nephew was born around the same time as David and she noticed that he was cooing, reaching for objects, and putting things in his mouth while David was content to sit quietly in his infant chair.

David did not begin talking during toddlerhood. He voiced few distinct sounds at the age when most young children are beginning to use several recognizable words. While he began to communicate his feelings through his body language and some vocalizations, he remained non-talkative until the age of four when he began to use words that were understandable to family members only.

He attended a preschool program for two years before entering kindergarten. He took part in all activities with the support of an EA. He showed little interest in colouring or using a pencil, and staying still long enough for a story to be read to him was challenging, to say the least, but he seemed to enjoy all activities that included large muscle movement. He especially liked to climb on the playground equipment and would cry when he had to come inside.

David entered school with few of the readiness skills identified as necessary for success in the kindergarten classroom. He also needed support with basic self-help skills (e.g., toileting and dressing himself). He was immediately assigned an EA who accompanied him throughout the school day. During the early elementary years, his IEP focused on math and reading readiness skills as well as self-help skills. By observing him in the classroom, more about his level of cognitive functioning was determined. His progress was slow but there were gains, especially in the areas of socialization. His mother commented on those gains:

> We tried to give David all the support and services he needed leading up to the time he started kindergarten, but even then he was well behind the other kids. I think he really started to make some gains during those first few years at school. He finally started to talk more and he became more interested in what was happening around him. He seemed to enjoy playing with the other kids rather than just being on the outskirts of the group, and he began to complete some academic tasks with the help of his educational assistant. While he still had trouble with new situations and being around strangers, he was fine around people he knew. I think most of this was due to him being a part of the regular classroom. It was the best decision we ever made.

What We Know . . .

The Cognitive Functioning of Students with Intellectual Disabilities

Mild Impairments

Exhibits mild functional problems occasionally and intermittently.

- Some difficulties acquiring new information, making connections, and generalizing
- Some difficulties understanding and following instructions
- Some difficulties with multi-step and complex tasks

- Skills and abilities unevenly developed across assessed areas
- Needs concrete task presentation
- Some difficulties with complex problem solving
- Can learn information, but may not generalize or easily apply concepts learned
- Some difficulties understanding social/interpersonal nuances

Moderate Impairments

Exhibits moderate functional problems not necessarily in every setting or at all times.

- Significant difficulties acquiring new information, making connections, and generalizing
- Significant difficulties understanding and following instructions
- Significant difficulties with multi-step and complex tasks
- Skills and abilities are significantly delayed
- Limited to concrete tasks
- Very limited problem-solving abilities
- Learns and uses skills exactly as taught (no generalization)
- Consistent difficulties understanding social/interpersonal nuances
- Significant difficulties with transitions or changes in routine

Complex Impairments

Exhibits significant functional problems across multiple settings.

- Profound difficulties with any learning
- No/very little ability to understand and follow instructions
- Unable to perform multi-step tasks
- Very serious delays in all areas of cognitive functioning
- Requires intensive, individualized support for all tasks
- Little to no problem-solving skills
- Learning tasks only when entirely individualized to personal level
- Unable to understand social/interpersonal nuances
- Unable to transition or change routine without significant support

Source: British Columbia Ministry of Education (2015).

Social and Emotional Development

As David's mother indicated, his social development progressed well once he entered school and he was able to participate in activities with his same-age peers. However, there was one significant challenge to his social and emotional development. That first became evident when he was around 3 years old; David often became physically aggressive with others when his frustration rose to high levels. This aggressiveness was obviously a concern because he was a robust little boy and he could quite easily hurt another child. These problematic behaviours have fortunately diminished significantly during his school years. The professionals working with David identified the antecedents of his aggressive behaviour (e.g., extended seatwork involving pencil-and-paper tasks, an inability to communicate his wants and needs, and being in new situations where he did not know the routines) and changed his education program to address his frustrations. They also implemented behaviour management techniques that helped with both his aggressive behaviour and his learning behaviours.

Emotionally, David was very much affected by the death of his father, which occurred unexpectedly when David was in Grade 5. He received a great deal of support during this time, especially from his mother and grandparents, but he still had much difficulty adjusting to life without his Dad. For a time, his aggressive behaviours returned and he became quite resistant to almost all activities at school. Eventually, however, he readjusted to the routine of school and his negative behaviours dissipated.

What We Know . . .

The Relationship between Intellectual Disabilities and Behaviour Disorders

According to Taylor, Richards, and Brady (2005), individuals with intellectual disabilities exhibit more behavioural problems than those without disabilities. Aggression is one of the most common of these behavioural problems. It is not known why this problematic behaviour occurs, but it has been hypothesized that it may be due to difficulties in processing and retrieving information, frustration, or lack of opportunities for recreation and leisure. Silka and Hauser (1997) emphasized that aggression is not necessarily an indicator of psychiatric illness. They stated that "when verbal expression is impaired, distress resulting from many possible causes may be expressed through maladaptive behaviour such as aggression . . . Such behaviour may be seen as a final common pathway for various medical, psychiatric, interpersonal, and environmental circumstances."

Motor Development

David has always exhibited a love for large muscle activities. His mother said that for as long as she can remember, David has expressed great delight in running, climbing, and playing different sports. He engages in these athletic-type movements with a sort of abandon, never faltering when he falls or hurts himself. While his gross motor movements have often lacked smoothness and fluency, there is no doubt that David is a willing and able participant in athletically based activities. On the other hand, David has always had difficulty with fine motor skills and has never shown much interest in paper-and-pencil activities.

When David entered school, the Movement Assessment Battery for Children, a performance test that provides screening, assessment, and management for children with motor skill disabilities, was administered to assess his fine and gross motor skills. Not surprisingly, David's strengths were in the areas of ball skills (i.e., rolling a ball at a target) and dynamic balance skills (i.e., jumping over an object). However, he struggled with activities involving manual dexterity, such as threading beads or using a pencil to trace a trail. These results have not really changed over his school years despite much exposure to these types of skills and considerable maturation. His gross motor skills remain his greatest strength, and he continues to struggle with fine motor skills.

What We Know . . .

Motor Development of Children with Intellectual Disabilities

Children with intellectual disabilities do not necessarily have difficulties with motor development. However, as reported by Harum (2006), it is not uncommon to find problems with fine motor control in this population. As well, Harum suggested that there may be subtle delays in gross motor acquisition recognized primarily as clumsiness.

In the case of children who have Down syndrome, the rate of gross motor development is affected by physical characteristics that commonly occur along with the intellectual disability. These children often have hypotonia (low muscle tone), ligamentous laxity (loose ligaments), decreased strength, and short arms and legs. As noted by Winders (2003), children with Down syndrome attempt to make up for these physical challenges by developing compensatory movement patterns that can develop into orthopedic and functional problems.

What Is School Like for David?

David loves to go to school. In fact, even when he is obviously not feeling well, he insists that he cannot stay at home. It has become a comfortable routine for him. His day begins with the task of getting his backpack ready and then setting out with a fellow student from his neighbourhood for the walk to school. He is greeted by many friends, both along the way and when he arrives at school, since most students in his small high school have known him since elementary school. He has always been a member of the regular classroom, so he is quite familiar to his peers and they are well aware of his communication and learning challenges.

David's school day is filled with activities he likes. He currently takes a gym class, a cooking class, and he gets to participate in drama and role-playing activities in communication and social skills classes. He is less enthusiastic about the time he spends doing more academically oriented activities. When he is required to do paper-and-pencil tasks or computer-related activities, his attention span is often quite short and he frequently begins displaying signs of frustration. When the frustration reaches a certain point, he will loudly voice his displeasure to his EA and often try to leave the room. According to his EA, "this is usually a sign that we have asked David to do too much and we need to re-look at whether or not we have moved along too quickly or he wasn't taught an important step that he needs to know in order to do the task at hand . . . David is getting much better, though, and seems to be able to stick with these types of activities much longer than he used to."

What We Know . . .

The Delivery of Special Services for Canadian Students with Intellectual Disabilities

There is ample evidence that students with intellectual disabilities benefit academically from receiving their education in an inclusive setting, both at the elementary and secondary levels. As Dore, Dion, Wagner, and Brunet (2004) revealed, when secondary students with intellectual disabilities moved from a self-contained classroom to a regular classroom (and when specific strategies to enhance such an integration were used) the students engaged more frequently in classroom activities and they increased their social interactions with regular-class peers.

However, not all Canadian students with intellectual disabilities are being educated in an inclusive setting. Bennett and Gallagher's (2012) report prepared for Community Living Ontario provides a snapshot of the situation in that province:

- While there has been a focused effort to provide instruction for diverse groups of students within the regular classroom, the degree of segregation for students who have an intellectual disability has seen frighteningly little movement.
- In 2010, at the elementary level, students with an identification of intellectual disability spent 68.7 per cent of their day in fully or partially self-contained settings. At the secondary level, students with an identification of intellectual disability spent 80 per cent of their day in fully or partially self-contained settings.
- In short, prioritizing for the needs of students who have an intellectual disability has not received due attention. Why? A sense of guardianship among education professionals is common as there is a pervasive notion that educational experiences that offer low student-to-teacher ratios, practise life skills, and provide specialized experiences and transportation all seem to demonstrate a high level of care and support.
- To reach the goal of full inclusive practice and to allow for all our students to engage in a truly diverse community we must make some seemingly radical but long overdue decisions to stop, once and for all, the systematic discrimination that blatantly exists within Ontario schools for students who have an intellectual disability.

Ontario is not the only province that could improve on its inclusion practices. In Alberta, the Alberta Teachers' Association (2015) investigated the state of inclusion in Alberta and reported the following:

Hundreds of teachers participated in the study of the Blue Ribbon Panel on Inclusive Education in Alberta Schools, contributing narrative responses that spoke to the importance of meeting student needs. Their voices were strong and the study results are clear—the ideals of inclusion are not in question, but the conditions required to support all students in the system are inconsistent and inadequate.

> *Creating an equitable, inclusive society in Alberta begins with the success-ful implementation of an inclusive education system. To facilitate this, compre-hensive short-, medium- and long-term plans to improve inclusive education must be put into place. As well, stakeholders must consider a systematic way of collecting data to evaluate the inclusive education model. We can only discern whether inclusion has been successful if stakeholders recognize a common aim and work together to reach it.* (p. 33)

David interacts well with his peers, both inside and outside of the regular classroom. He has a good sense of humour and enjoys being in the company of students who are being active and having a lot of fun. This is especially true when the students are engaged in sports activities. David is always willing to participate, and his peers include him fully in whatever they are doing.

One of the most positive aspects of David's school day is the time he spends with Andrew, his classmate and assigned buddy. Andrew volunteered to help David with the tasks he is re-quired to complete when he is in the regular classroom. While David has the support of an EA, it is Andrew who makes the attempt to fully involve him in the activities in which the rest of his classmates are participating. Andrew described his role as a buddy as follows:

> *I really like being David's buddy. It is my responsibility to help him in the class-room, and usually that means making sure he is taking part in all of the stuff we do. Sometimes I do help him to learn new things, but mostly that is his EA's job. I am more of a friend for David. I make sure that he is in my group if we do small-group work, and when we are given time to work on projects or free time to do whatever we want, I always check on David to see if he wants to be part of what I am doing. We have really become good friends. While it was hard at first to understand him when he spoke, I have gotten used to his speech. I pretty well know what he is trying to say most of the time. Once in a while he will get angry about something and I am not sure what is bothering him, but I am usually able to calm him down. The neat thing about being his buddy is the way he reacts when he sees me outside of class. He is always happy to see me and he loves to sit in the cafeteria with me at lunchtime. David is a real sports nut, so we sometimes go to the gym together. Even if I am not in any of David's classes next year, I am sure we will still get together and do things like that.*

What We Know . . .

Peer Buddy Programs

Service learning has become a common focus of high school curricula. In other words, students are encouraged to take part in activities that address actual societal needs, thus preparing them for an active and meaningful life in adult society. One type of ser-vice learning is participation in a buddy program. Students are given the opportunity to

Continued

spend time with peers who have special education needs. According to a group of high school students who worked with peers who have severe disabilities (Hughes et al., 2001), their participation in a buddy program resulted in growth in their interpersonal skills, new friendships, an increased knowledge and awareness of people with disabilities, new strategies for interacting with students with disabilities, and an increased comfort level during these interactions. These same students suggested that their peer buddy experiences could have been even better if they had been provided with detailed information about their peer's disabilities, strategies for handling different situations that arose when spending time with their peers, and ongoing support through scheduled conferences with their classroom teachers.

Clare Coe/Alamy Stock Photo

Best Buddies Canada is one organization that matches student volunteers with a peer who has an intellectual disability with the aim of providing meaningful friendships for all involved.

Something to Think About

It is estimated that nearly twice as many students with significant disabilities are included in regular elementary classrooms as compared to the number included in regular high school classrooms. Why do you think inclusive classrooms are less evident at the higher grade levels? How might this situation change as more inclusively educated students enter their high school years? To what extent would you support such a change?

What Educational Approach Is Best for David?

High School Curricula

David spent his early school years in an inclusive classroom, and when he entered high school the goal was for him to stay with his peers as much as possible. However, given that David's secondary school program was going to focus a great deal on both independent and community living skills, it was decided that he would need to be in a resource room for part of his school day. His mother agreed with this decision since she was eager to have David learn these skills and she knew it would require explicit instruction that would be difficult to deliver in the regular classroom. As well, she felt reassured that David would be just like other high school students, moving about the school attending different classes.

The decision to change the focus of David's program from the learning of academic skills to the learning of independent and community living skills was not a difficult one for the members of his school-based team. His mother gave her consent for this modification with the stipulation that his reading, writing, and math skills not be ignored, especially those that would help him in the real world. The team agreed that David could continue to work on the attainment of basic academic skills while acquiring new skills that would prepare him for adult living. Rather than David's program being devoid of academic instruction, it meant his schooling would consist of functional academics tailored to foster independence.

What We Know . . .

Academic Instruction for Students with Intellectual Disabilities

There is ample evidence that students with intellectual disabilities can learn academic skills (Browder, Wakeman, Spooner, Ahlgrim-Delzell, & Algozzine, 2006). However, the learning of these skills can be quite challenging for many of these students and, therefore, instruction must be well thought out, carefully delivered, and evaluated to determine if it is of value to the student.

When examining reading instruction for students with significant cognitive difficulties, Browder et al. (2006) concluded that this type of academic instruction should be a part of the students' school programming. They found evidence that students with moderate and severe mental intellectual disabilities "can learn to identify and comprehend sight words using **systematic prompting** methods with **concrete referents**." They noted that further research is required to determine the best possible instruction methods for teaching literacy skills to this special population. It is critical, then, that educators of students with intellectual disabilities not dismiss the importance of academic skill instruction for these children.

Continued

systematic prompting

An organized and predetermined series of prompts used to increase desired behaviours.

concrete referent

Something existing in reality or in real experience that is used to reinforce an abstract idea.

Downing and MacFarland (2010) summarized this issue well:

The question is not whether students can learn, but how much they can learn, and with what types of instruction and support. While early intervention is a recommended practice, learning can occur at any age. Those supporting the student need to know how to provide appropriate and effective instruction as well as how to challenge the student to attain higher goals. Changes regarding the education of students with severe disabilities involve maintaining high expectations for learning, inclusive education, and assuming more active roles in their communities upon leaving the educational system.

David settled into the routine of high school with relative ease. He still benefits from the support of an EA as he did in elementary school. His EA has been the same individual for the past three years, and that has facilitated smooth transitions from grade to grade. When David is in the regular classroom, his EA guides him through the activities set out by his teacher. His IEP (see pp. 224–230) serves as the guide for curricular direction, and it clearly outlines the learning expectations for each subject area. While David's program is modified significantly from that of his peers, it is still based on the general education curricular expectations whenever possible. For example, in his Food and Nutrition class, David participates just as other students do in planning and cooking meals. However, David is not expected to design elaborate menus or prepare written reports on issues such as safe food-handling practices. Instead, with the help of his teacher and his EA, he is expected to verbally or pictorially describe a menu for a simple meal, and he is taught such things as food-handling techniques through a completely hands-on approach. While there are occasions when David experiences a far different curriculum than his peers (e.g., during academically oriented classes like math), every effort is made to have him follow the same class routines as his peers (e.g., similar amount of seatwork and free time).

The teaching approach used in David's case is one that is highly recommended for students with intellectual disabilities. It includes direct step-by-step instruction, lessons that are linked to the real world, increased opportunities for hands-on learning, the use of numerous examples, and the provision of considerable positive reinforcement. As one of David's teachers stated, "we work on learning things in very small steps, making sure that David does the task successfully not only during that class but also the next day and even a week later . . . we make the task as relevant as we can to David's life, and of course we celebrate every time he learns something new; especially when he uses his new skill without our prompting."

What We Know . . .

Teaching Students with Intellectual Disabilities

General Strategies

- Provide instruction that is more explicit and is delivered at a slower pace than would normally be offered for students of that age.

- Consider that students with intellectual disabilities learn less well through abstract teaching, but learn more successfully from a multi-sensory approach, in which they participate in the activity with hands-on learning.
- Put skills in context so there is a reason for learning tasks.
- Be as concrete as possible. Demonstrate what you mean instead of just giving verbal directions. Rather than just relating new information verbally, show a picture. And then, rather than just showing a picture, provide the student with hands-on materials and experiences and the opportunity to try things out.
- Use strategies such as backward shaping, and role modelling as helpful teaching approaches.
- Break longer, new tasks into small steps. Demonstrate the steps. Have the student do the steps, one at a time. Provide assistance as necessary.
- Consider the use of technology-based tools as some students may be highly motivated by the visual aspects of computer applications as well as the instant rewards.
- Give the student immediate feedback.
- Ask students for their input about how they feel they learn best, and help them to be as in control of their learning as possible.

Source: Adapted from Hannell (2006), the National Dissemination Center for Children with Disabilities (2011), and Vise (2012).

backward shaping

Learning how to complete the last part of a task first so that a student can experience the sense of achievement.

Incorporating Assistive Technology

Assistive technology (AT) can be used to support individuals with intellectual disabilities in a variety of school activities. The technology may help them complete tasks independently or with less help. Consider the following:

- Audio books and etext supports for reading and listening comprehension
- SMART Boards in combination with computer-assisted software (e.g., digital flash cards to improve sight words)
- Personal digital assistants
- Graphic organizers
- Screen magnifiers

Examples of apps that support this domain include Money Equivalence (teaches about money equivalents and combinations of coins and bills) and Autism/DTT Shapes (teaches basic shapes using a discrete trial training technique).

Source: Evmenova, Ault, Bausch, and Warger (2013).

David's high school education has also included the opportunity to take part in a work placement. This is considered an important part of his schooling, especially by his mother who is worried about his transition from high school into the community. In Grade 10, David was assigned a "job coach" at his school who helped him prepare for this new experience and accompanied him during his time on the job. His coach commented about how the work placement was organized and implemented:

David's work placement last term was at a local grocery store. In past years, students from our school have completed placements at the same store, so the manager and the staff were quite familiar with how our placements work. I went to the store ahead of time and talked with them about David, giving them an idea of what he is like and how he may respond to his new job in the community. Together we decided that collecting and breaking down boxes might be the best job for him since he likes to do physical tasks and he can sometimes become upset when placed in situations where his speech is not understood (e.g., communicating with customers or other workers).

I helped David get ready for the placement by teaching him how to do the exact same job at school. We began collecting boxes from the office and the photocopy room and breaking them down so they could be placed in the recycling bin. David caught on fairly quickly and actually let me know whenever he saw an empty box anywhere in the building. The next thing we did was to visit the store. We made a couple of visits so David could get used to the environment. He had a chance to see all the parts of the building, and he met some of the staff. It was funny because he noticed all of the empty boxes before I even pointed them out to him.

When David first started working at the store, I was with him all the time. He didn't need much help with his job but he did need me there to keep him on task and to help him communicate with staff members and any customers who talked to him. Gradually, I stepped away a little and let him handle things on his own. I was always close by but David really could complete his work responsibilities fairly independently. He has made a few gains in his social interactions, too, but that is definitely an area that needs to be worked on. He has trouble responding to people he doesn't know. These types of things need to be addressed at school and then again in his next work placement.

From the Psychologist's Notebook

The coaching and support that David receives during his work placements are absolutely crucial to the quality of life he will lead once he gets out of school. The more independent he can become, the more fulfilling his day-to-day activities will be. Unfortunately, many teachers and parents are reluctant to change a student's curricular path away from academic subjects, stating that this "seals their fate" and puts a glass ceiling on the student's learning. This reluctance is even stronger if a student's academic abilities are better than David's. However, the reality is that even if a student can continue to progress academically, it is unlikely that his or her life after school will revolve around the ability to perform academic-type skills. Rather, the lives of students with intellectual disabilities are probably going to revolve around their proficiency with skills that allow them to work and participate in society. Given that these students learn slowly and need lots of help when learning new things, the earlier their schooling focuses on life skills, work skills, social skills, and functional academics the better. In my experiences with the **Canadian Association for Community Living** (CACL), students whose programs began addressing these types of living skills in Grades 5 or 6 have had many more successful work experiences as adults than students whose programs changed later (such as Grade 9 or 10).

Canadian Association for Community Living (CACL)
A Canada-wide association of family members and others who work for the benefit of individuals of all ages who have an intellectual disability.

Something to Think About

You have a student with a moderate intellectual disability who is going to complete a work placement as part of his or her secondary education. A business owner has contacted you to discuss the possibility of having the student work at her florist shop. She is concerned that the student will cause her problems, such as slowing down the pace of work at her establishment and annoying customers. How would you respond to these concerns? How might you help the business owner prepare for this work placement?

Evaluation of Progress

David's IEP recommends that his progress be evaluated primarily through oral testing and practical demonstration (see pp. 224–230). It is quite obvious that asking David to complete paper-and-pencil tasks to assess his learning is inappropriate. In fact, even relying solely on oral responses in David's case is inappropriate given his difficulty with communication. If David's teachers want to accurately evaluate his learning progress, they must depend mostly on their observation skills. And it is apparent that this is currently the method of evaluation that is used most often by his teachers. For example, his drama teacher watches his class performances and looks for signs that his expressive skills are improving (e.g., whether or not he can understand and emote the feelings of his character), and in his social skills class, the teacher observes his interactions with his peers to see if he is communicating more often and more effectively. However, none of David's teachers describe using a systematic approach to conduct observational assessments. They appear to rely on their own judgment as to whether or not they are observing any gains in David's skill or knowledge. When asked how he determines and reports David's progress in communication class, his teacher replied, "I just know when he has learned something because I can see that he is doing it better in class and that's what I write about in my report." Further conversations with David's teachers indicated that many of them were unaware of other effective ways to evaluate David's progress.

A concern regarding the evaluation method currently being used for David is that it does not clearly identify if learning is occurring, if it is occurring efficiently, and if the provided instruction is impacting on David's learning. As Taylor, Richards, and Brady (2005) indicated, "inference or indirect measures of progress are not sensitive enough to measure learning in many students with mental retardation" (p. 311). They emphasized that observational assessment must be carried out in a much more systematic fashion if it is going to be the basis for instructional decision making. This does not imply that teachers' general observations of student performance are of no value, but it does mean that these observations need to occur far more methodically to accurately identify what a student has learned and what instruction is necessary for the student to acquire the next step in his or her knowledge or skill development.

What We Know . . .

Conducting Observational Assessments

Taylor, Richards, and Brady (2005) recommended a four-step model of observation when monitoring the progress of student learning: (a) carefully and specifically identify the target behaviour/skill, (b) precisely measure the target behaviour/skill (e.g., compare the number of times the behaviour occurs in a specific time period with baseline data), (c) systematically introduce an intervention or teaching program, and (d) frequently evaluate the intervention/program effectiveness (p. 237).

Taylor et al. (2005) also presented three types of assessment (pp. 312–314) that can be made through observations to measure instructional effectiveness:

1. *Assess the percentage of accuracy or completeness:* Measure the total number of opportunities that the skill could have been given (e.g., peers provided 10 social initiations) and the number of times the target skill was actually given (e.g., the student responded to 8 of these social initiations). Calculate the percentage of accuracy (e.g., 8 out of 10 times indicates that the student responds to 80 per cent of peers' social initiations).

2. *Assess the rate of progress:* Measure the number of times a skill occurs during a fixed period of time (e.g., number of correct keystrokes in one minute). Calculate the number of student responses (e.g., 68 correct keystrokes), divide by the time taken to perform all the behaviours (e.g., four minutes), and convert to number of responses per minute as this is the standard convention for teachers who use rate measures (e.g., 17 correct keystrokes per minute).

3. *Assess progress in time intervals:* Determine the presence of a skill during a predetermined interval of time (e.g., the display of positive social comments during recess). The total number of intervals of observation is the denominator (e.g., 20 intervals during recess) and the number of intervals in which the student displayed the skill is the numerator (e.g., positive social comments were made by the student during five of the intervals). Calculate the overall finding (e.g., the student's measure of positive social comments is 25 per cent).

Source: Taylor, Richards, & Brody (2005). © 2005. Reprinted by permission of Pearson Education, Inc., Upper Saddle River, NJ.

How Is David Different from Other Students Who Have Intellectual Disabilities?

David is similar to other students who have intellectual disabilities in that he learns more slowly than students his age, he has limitations in his thinking skills, difficulties with attention and organizing information, and trouble seeing how things relate to each other. Given these challenges, David, like other students with intellectual disabilities, needs help with learning as well as assistance with attaining independent-living skills.

Again, however, as we have mentioned in previous chapters, children with special needs that fall in the same category of exceptionality can never be considered to be identical. David is unique within the population of students who have intellectual disabilities, and he is also unique within the population of students who have Down syndrome. He is undoubtedly most similar to those students with Down syndrome, but there are still many factors that set him apart and make it imperative that his education program be tailored to meet his specific needs (e.g., the severity of his intellectual disability, his specific difficulties with communication, his behaviour in social situations, and his desire to engage in large muscle activities).

To gain insight into the range of abilities and needs evident in students who have intellectual disabilities, consider the following two students. They have conditions other than Down syndrome, so their differences from David are readily apparent.

- *Williams syndrome*: Maarika is a popular 15-year-old high school student who loves to play piano and sing. If it was up to her, she would spend her entire school day in the music room. Her peers recognize her talents and often encourage her to perform for them. Maarika responds willingly, as she loves to immerse herself in music and she is always keen to please her classmates. She has a great memory for melodies and lyrics and can play and sing almost any song they request. Unfortunately, Maarika is not as happy and relaxed in the classroom. She has significant difficulties with academics and even though she is now in a special program in high school, she still struggles with any tasks that involve math or spatial abilities. Surprisingly, she does not experience the same level of difficulty with reading, and her vocabulary is quite impressive. Maarika has Williams syndrome, a genetic disorder that is marked by missing genetic material on chromosome seven. This syndrome is the reason for her physical appearance (small in stature, upturned nose, wide mouth, small chin, and puffiness around the eyes) and her cognitive difficulties (mild intellectual disabilities). Williams syndrome is distinguished from Down syndrome, and most other forms of intellectual disability, by the presence of both strong and weak cognitive abilities, as is evident in Maarika's case. It is expected that Maarika will master most self-help skills, complete her special program in high school, and live independently with some support.
- *Fragile X syndrome.* Sasha, who has been diagnosed with Fragile X syndrome, is an 11-year-old who looks and acts differently than his classmates. He has a large head, long face, prominent forehead, and large ears. His behaviour is described as "odd" by his peers. While he seems to want to be an active member of his peer group, he often stands at the periphery of the group and avoids eye contact. Sometimes he can be heard mumbling the same words over and over to himself, frequently mimicking the words of others. When he gets anxious, which is quite often, he begins biting his hands and "tuning out" even more than usual. This anxiety can be provoked by more than just social situations. It was apparent from the time he was a young child that he is hypersensitive to sounds, light, and touch. For example, Sasha becomes uncomfortable in environments that have bright lighting, and he does not like to participate in school activities, like physical education, where he may be touched by others. Sasha also has problems with academics. His IQ of 65 indicates mild intellectual disability, and this is most evident in his difficulty with higher-level thinking and reasoning skills. His strengths are his memory and his relatively extensive vocabulary. When

asked about his favourite TV show, *The Simpsons*, he is able to talk in detail about the characters and what happened in specific episodes, but he cannot describe the plots of the shows other than in simple terms. Sasha's parents report that he is quite calm and relaxed at home since they know the kind of environment that he requires. He is an active member of their household, performing regular chores just like his siblings. He is also able to perform self-care tasks with relative ease. Sasha's parents feel his greatest challenge is socializing with others. He has no friends despite wanting to be part of his peer group. He spends most of his out-of-school time alone.

What We Know . . .

Williams Syndrome

Williams syndrome is a rare neurobehavioural congenital disorder that impacts several areas of development including cognition, behaviour, and motor abilities. Due to the absence of the gene that produces the protein elastin, individuals with Williams syndrome have an elfin-like facial appearance: small upturned nose, curly hair, full lips, full cheeks, small teeth, a broad magnetic smile, and often especially bright eyes. Other common characteristics include an outgoing social nature, a sense of the dramatic, overfriendliness, an affinity to music, low muscle tone and joint laxity, a short attention span, difficulty modulating emotions, anxiousness, and learning difficulties. In terms of intellectual ability, individuals with Williams syndrome often demonstrate strengths (e.g., speech, long-term memory, and social skills) and weaknesses (e.g., fine motor and spatial relations).

Source: Williams Syndrome Association, www.williams-syndrome.org

What We Know . . .

Fragile X Syndrome

Fragile X syndrome is the most common form of inherited mental impairment. It involves changes in the X chromosome that affect the FMR1 gene. Because males have only one X chromosome, the syndrome usually affects them more severely than it does females. While the syndrome can affect individuals in a variety of ways, the most common characteristics include intellectual disability, hyperactivity, short attention span, tactile defensiveness, hand flapping, hand biting, poor eye contact, speech and language disorders, long face, large or prominent ears, large testicles, Simian crease or Sydney line, connective tissue problems, and a family history of intellectual disability.

Individuals with Fragile X syndrome often display autistic-like behaviours. While the syndrome is a cause of autism (15–33 per cent of individuals with Fragile X have autism), many individuals with the syndrome do not have autism despite the manifestation of these behaviours. Because they are interested in social interactions, they do not meet the diagnostic criteria for autism.

Source: National Fragile X Foundation (2017).

Closing David's File

David's schooling to date has addressed all of the skill areas that need to be taught to students with intellectual disabilities (i.e., academic skills, communication skills, independent-living skills, and community living skills). While he has not excelled in any of these areas, he has definitely benefited from the instruction provided by his many teachers. His early behaviour problems have diminished significantly, he has learned to communicate more effectively, and he has acquired skills that help him with independent living. It is noteworthy that his school placements have been predominantly in inclusive classrooms. He has undoubtedly enjoyed the company of his peers, and, in return, he has been considered a valuable member of the regular classroom. A glance at the teacher's comments on any of his report cards tells you what a "pleasure he is to have in the classroom."

David's education cannot be considered over as he gets ready to enter adulthood. Hopefully, he will benefit from further independent-living instruction and additional community work placements in his final years of high school. To give their children the maximal opportunity to learn and develop, many parents of students like David opt to have their child stay in school until they are 21 years of age. This is the child's legal right. Once David graduates, he will require considerable assistance in the transition from school to the community. It is important to remember that adults with Down syndrome can, and do, continue to learn throughout their lives.

As a single parent, David's mother has great concern regarding what will happen to him once he finishes high school. She has many questions about what the future holds for her son. What kind of supports are there in the community to help him with employment? Are there social and recreational activities in which he can participate? How will his mother manage to juggle her work responsibilities with the time she will need to spend looking after David? Who will care for him should anything happen to her?

It is these very questions that need to guide the curricular programming of students with intellectual disabilities. Every effort must be made to ensure they have the opportunity to learn the skills necessary for a productive, fulfilling life.

Updating David's Story

David has now finished school and settled into adult life in his community. He attended high school until he was 20 years of age. The last years of his formal education placed a great deal of emphasis on life skills and work placements. In fact, David's mother expressed concern that in the latter school years David's education did not include enough emphasis on academics. Therefore, his reading ability was very low. She has persisted with reading instruction at home with considerable success. David now reads at the Grade 2 level and continues to make progress.

The life-skill instruction prepared David for his first job, which was made possible due to the efforts of his local Association for Community Living. David currently works at a hardware store where he assists with stocking shelves and removing cardboard. David's mother reported that he is adjusting to his new job with enthusiasm:

> *His difficulty with speech has created some obstacles, but things are getting better and better. He is getting lots of support. I know from his demeanour that he really likes going to work. The support from the Association for Community Living has been exceptional,*

both for David and me. We are now planning to get David involved in the Special Olympics organization. You know I never really thought that David could have such a good life after high school. It is such a relief for me to see him find a place in society.

What We Know . . .

Employment for Canadian Individuals with Developmental Disabilities

Many people with developmental disabilities want to have a job, earn a wage, and be included and valued in their work. Despite this desire, the rate of people with developmental disabilities who are employed remains very low. Some believe that people with developmental disabilities should not or cannot work, and this leads to limited choices and opportunities to become employed. Current research shows that, contrary to this myth, people with developmental disabilities make valuable contributions to their communities, families, and to their workplaces when they have the proper supports and services available to them.

At Inclusion BC we believe that people with developmental disabilities can and should have as many opportunities to be employed as their non-disabled peers. With awareness and resources, employers in BC are willing to make reasonable accommodations to their employees. In turn, everyone in the workplace benefits from the value of diversity. The employee with a developmental disability gains confidence, independence, and enjoys an increased income as a result. What's more, community workplaces begin to truly reflect the makeup of the people that live in that community.

Relevant policies and regulations, training and education, job supports, and job-matching services can be designed to enable people to get and keep real jobs.

Source: Self Advocate Net (2017)

Summary

Students with intellectual disabilities exhibit significant limitations both in intellectual functioning and adaptive behaviour. These limitations, along with a student's strengths, are typically determined using standardized tests—usually an IQ test and tests that measure the individual's conceptual skills, social skills, and practical skills. While David's story highlights a chromosomal condition referred to as Down syndrome, intellectual disabilities are evident in a variety of conditions. The commonality among those with intellectual disabilities is a need for help with learning as well as assistance in attaining independent-living skills. Along with cognitive delays, there can be behaviour problems and motor difficulties. The best educational approach is the inclusion of behavioural management techniques along with direct step-by-step instruction, lessons that are linked to the real world, increased opportunities for hands-on learning, the use of numerous examples, and the provision of considerable positive reinforcement. In many cases, the focus is on learning self-supporting and community living skills while still addressing the attainment of basic academic skills.

Learning More about Students with Intellectual Disabilities

Academic Journals

American Journal on Intellectual and Developmental Disabilities
Journal of Applied Research in Intellectual Disabilities
Journal of Intellectual Disabilities
Journal of Intellectual Disability Research
Journal on Developmental Disabilities
Intellectual and Developmental Disabilities
Research in Developmental Disabilities

Books

Burack, J. A. (Ed.). (2011). *The Oxford handbook of intellectual disability and development* (2nd ed.). New York, NY: Oxford University Press.

Datta, P. (2014). *Intellectual disabilities: Insights, implications and recommendations.* New York, NY: Springer.

Richards, S. B., Brady, M. P., & Taylor, R. L. (2014). *Cognitive and intellectual disabilities: Historical perspectives, current practices, and future directions* (2nd ed.). New York, NY: Routledge.

Roberts, J. E., Chapman, R. S., & Warren, S. F. (Eds.). (2008). *Speech and language development & interaction in Down syndrome & Fragile X syndrome.* Baltimore, MD: Paul H. Brookes Pub.

Schalock, R. L., Borthwick-Duffy, S. A., Bradley, V. J., Buntinx, W., Coulter, D. L. et al. (2010). *Intellectual disability: Definition, classification, and systems of support* (11th ed.). Washington, DC: American Association on Intellectual and Developmental Disabilities.

Smith, P. (Ed.). (2010). *Whatever happened to inclusion? The place of students with intellectual disabilities in education.* New York, NY: Peter Lang.

Web Links

American Association on Intellectual and Developmental Disabilities

www.aaidd.org
AAIDD promotes progressive policies, sound research, effective practices, and universal human rights for people with intellectual and developmental disabilities.

Canadian Association for Community Living

www.cacl.ca
CACL is a family-based association that strives to lead the way in advancing the inclusion of people with intellectual disabilities in all aspects of community life.

Canadian Association for Williams Syndrome

http://caws.sasktelwebhosting.com
The CAWS was formed by a group of parents with the intent of raising awareness of Williams syndrome. The website reflects their goal of supporting research that examines the educational, behavioural, social, and medical aspects of this syndrome.

Canadian Down Syndrome Society

www.cdss.ca
The CDSS site is a resource linking parents and professionals through advocacy and education. The "Resources" link provides access to a library of past CDSS newsletters (*Canadian Down Syndrome Quarterly*).

Fragile X Research Foundation of Canada

www.fragilexcanada.ca
This not-for-profit organization, founded by parents and health professionals, funds research aimed at treatment and promotes awareness through a newsletter and information materials.

JP Das Centre on Developmental and Learning Disabilities

http://dascentre.educ.ualberta.ca
The mission of the Das Centre at the University of Alberta is to provide research, training, and some clinical services to people with developmental, perceptual, and learning disabilities.

Learning about Intellectual Disabilities and Health

www.intellectualdisability.info
The main aim of this site is to provide up-to-date information about the health needs of people with intellectual disabilities. Articles address prevention, diagnosis, social care issues, and family issues.

National Fragile X Foundation

http://fragilex.org
This site provides comprehensive information regarding Fragile X syndrome, including the discussion of educational issues and the presentation of current research findings.

Williams Syndrome Association—Information for Teachers

https://williams-syndrome.org/teacher/information-for-teachers
Recognizing that educators face unique challenges when teaching children with Williams syndrome, the WSA presents information specifically designed to assist teachers who have a child with Williams syndrome in their classroom.

Taking It into Your Classroom . . .

Including Students Who Have Intellectual Disabilities

When a student who has an intellectual disability is first placed in my classroom, I will

- review what I know about intellectual disabilities and locate resource materials,
- read the student's file,
- consult with the student's previous teachers,
- consult with the student's parents, and
- meet with the school-based team to discuss the student's current school year.
- Other:_____

When I suspect a student in my classroom has an intellectual disability, I will

- review what I know about intellectual disabilities and locate resource materials,
- collect information about the student through classroom interventions,
- consult with other school personnel who are familiar with the student,
- consult with the student's parents, and
- meet with the school-based team to present the information I have collected.
- Other: _____

Key points to remember in my daily interactions with a student who has an intellectual disability:

- The student may have a short attention span.
- The student may have both short-term and long-term memory problems.
- The student may have a limited ability to express and understand language.
- The student may need information delivered to him or her in short, simple chunks.
- The student may have a decreased ability to generalize information across settings.
- The student may exhibit behaviour problems, including aggression.
- Other: _____

Key points regarding programming for a student who has an intellectual disability:

- The classroom environment should be structured and consistent.
- Pay particular attention to the student's learning style and what motivates him or her.
- Present information/tasks in a progressive step-by-step fashion.
- Give immediate feedback.
- Take advantage of teachable moments and recognize when the student needs a break.
- Include life skills in the curricula.
- Promote independence rather than dependence on adult support.
- Other: _____

Key points regarding evaluation of the progress made by a student who has an intellectual disability:

- Evaluation should focus on teacher observation of student learning.
- Evaluation should include oral response and practical demonstration.
- Evaluation should occur on a frequent basis (e.g., daily in some cases).
- Evaluation should consider the measurement of target behaviours.
- Evaluation should provide data to assess instructional effectiveness (i.e., percentage of accuracy or completeness, rate of progress, and progress in time intervals).
- Other: _____

CHAPTER 9
Students with Autism

LEARNING OBJECTIVES

After learning the material in this chapter, you should be able to:

- Describe how autism spectrum disorder is diagnosed.

- Outline the levels of severity associated with autism spectrum disorder.

- Discuss the possible causes of autism.

- Describe the effects that autism can have on a child's development.

- Discuss how dysfunctional sensory systems can affect individuals with autism.

- Outline strategies for teaching students with autism.

- Differentiate between the three identified levels of autism.

- Discuss strategies that educators can use to reduce stress in educational settings.

Name: Zachary Wong

Current Age: 6

School: Sandhill Elementary School

Grade: Kindergarten

Zachary is a cognitively capable young boy who has had difficulty interacting with his environment since around the time of his first birthday.

Unfortunately, his sensitivity to sound and touch made his early years very painful and frustrating for both himself and his family members. It was because of his parents' desperation to help him that he received a relatively early diagnosis of autism and subsequent treatments that addressed his autistic behaviours. Zachary's story highlights the importance of early intervention and the ongoing need for considerable support in the school environment for students with autism.

Zachary Wong

Assessment Results

Age at Time of Assessment: 3 years, 4 months

Developmental Pediatric Assessment

Pregnancy was normal with no significant maternal illness nor substance exposure known to potentially damage a developing fetus. Mother's pre-pregnancy health and blood tests were normal. Maternal emotional health, during and after the pregnancy, was normal. Birth occurred at full term. Was breastfed until the age of two years. No significant illnesses or surgeries since birth. Developmental milestones achieved at expected rate except for language after 14 months and regression in social skills between 14 and 18 months. No dysfunctional family features recognized that might contribute to these problems. No significant relevant health problems in family history.

A limited physical examination (due to problems with co-operation) with an emphasis on the neurological system revealed no abnormality. No physical features to suggest a medical disease, syndrome, or substance exposure during pregnancy. Pattern of rocking and banging head was observed—appears to be a self-stimulating activity. Zach exhibited short concentration on chosen activities. Extensive jargon was evident with some understandable words. No immediate echolalia. Play activities were immature for age.

Conners' Rating Scales: scored in the very abnormal range for questions relating to anxious/shy behaviour, perfectionism, and emotional ability (mood swings). *Stony Brook Inventory:* scored "often or very often" on questions associated with 7 of 12 autistic behaviours. *Childhood Autism Rating Scale* (completed by parents alone, physician alone, parents and physician together, and the psychologist): all indicated behaviours in the autistic range. When considering the *DSM-IV-TR Criteria,* Zach showed a profile consistent with the diagnosis of autism (autistic disorder).

Psychological Assessment

Bayley Scales of Infant Development, Second Edition

2 years, 5 months developmental age-equivalent level

Vineland Adaptive Behavior Scales, Interview Edition

Communication skills domain   9th percentile

Daily living skills domain   1st percentile

Socialization skills domain   3rd percentile

Motor skills domain   19th percentile

Developmental Test of Visual-Motor Integration

2 years, 9 months age-equivalent level

Assessment Summary

Zachary has an autistic spectrum disorder. There is no evidence of an associated medical disease or psychosocial cause for his challenges. He meets the DSM-IV criteria for the diagnosis of mild autism (autistic disorder). He appears to qualify for provincial government funding for a child less than six years with this diagnosis.

The cause of autistic spectrum disorders is unknown. They probably represent a number of different causes with similar clinical presentations. All children with autism are different. We are learning more and more as extensive research in this area continues. Zachary is a unique individual who will certainly progress in learning, social skill development, and communication. His progress will be best followed by a coordinated team who work together with his parents to optimize learning strategies.

Zachary exhibits many non-autistic behaviours, which suggests that he will likely show positive progress in an intensive multi-disciplinary therapy environment with a strong emphasis on communication and social skills. It is recommended that he attend a highly structured preschool/daycare program several days per week where he can receive some one-on-one support in order to fully participate and benefit from the program. He will benefit from ongoing intensive speech-language therapy. Communication strategies should be shared with his preschool or daycare programs. Further, some support to reduce self-stimulatory behaviour and to encourage fine motor skills is recommended.

The prognosis for Zachary in school and later years is impossible to assess at this time. He will require intensive multi-disciplinary assistance in the school system. The present problems with program funding in the school system require strong, continuing parental advocacy to attain appropriate school programming. Often, supplementary privately paid therapists are needed for optimal management. Financial planning now may be wise.

Recommendations

Zachary will benefit from a review by professionals including a psychologist, developmental pediatrician, speech-language pathologist, occupational therapist, and educator prior to kindergarten entry. This will assist in preparation for school entry, appropriate designation, school program planning, the preparation of an individualized education program, and monitoring of progress to date.

Zachary will benefit from a visual assessment, and hearing should be assessed annually. He should have a single blood test to screen for Fragile X, blood lead level, and iron studies. Brain imaging studies such as CT and MRI scans are not recommended as they will not assist in management and rarely show significant findings. An EEG (electroencephalogram) is not recommended in the absence of symptoms that suggest seizures. Seizures are common in children with autism.

Zachary will benefit most if his mother and father seek to become highly knowledgeable about autistic spectrum disorders. We can assist with references if desired. Reassessment is advised if regression rather than improvement occurs or if significant management problems develop.

Note: Zachary was assessed based on criteria outlined in the DSM-IV. Diagnosis criteria and the terms used to refer to autism have recently been revised with the publication of the DSM-V. Other than actual documents obtained from Zachary's file, the information in this chapter adheres to the new criteria and the new terminology.

Zachary Wong

Mother's Comments Regarding Zachary's Diagnosis

Zachary was our second born, and for the first year of his life all seemed normal. In fact, he was a quiet and mellow baby compared to our first boy. He was born within a normal gestation period and he reached his developmental milestones of crawling, walking, and the beginnings of speech on time, albeit a bit later than our older child.

We started to notice subtle changes in Zach's behaviour after his first birthday and these changes became very apparent by 18 months. He had a vocabulary of around six words after his first birthday: "mama," "dada," "puppy," "bye," "car," and "hi." He stopped using these words altogether, and began to ignore us when we called his name. He went from being a happy and content baby to a toddler who appeared frustrated and inattentive. His constant smile seemed to evaporate, and he would only seek affection from me. His brother and father were now on the sidelines. Zach began to constantly bang his head on his high chair, and gradually destroyed it. I knew a bit about autism but the term seemed too frightening and overwhelming to consider.

At first, we believed his behavioural changes were due to a hearing loss, since he stopped responding to his name. In addition, my husband's family had a history of hearing loss, so it seemed logical to start from there. We had no idea how exhausting the process would be. My first visit was to the local family doctor who could not even examine Zach due to his high-pitched screams. The doctor actually asked if I needed anything! He referred Zach to a pediatrician who did not seem too concerned at first. He suggested that since Zach's older brother was slower to pick up words, this was probably the case for Zach as well. We were insistent that it was more than that. Zach had stopped speaking altogether. After a number of visits, the pediatrician put Zach on the waiting list for an autism assessment at the Children's Hospital in our region. We also began once-a-week visits with a private speech therapist.

I became consumed with reading everything I could find on autism. I spent hours researching the topic on the Internet. I also found some parents of autistic children and began to exchange emails with them. These resources helped me detect other signs of Zach's autism. He did not point at things, he developed terrible sleep patterns, and he did not play with his toys in an age-appropriate manner. As well, he did not take any interest in visitors to the household and was left out when kids came over to play. Noise and touch became overwhelming for him. Music could not be played at all. Washing, cutting, and brushing his hair were all out of the question. Despite sessions with the speech therapist, he was still not talking. The therapist said, "I would be very worried about this as a parent." It was a heartbreaking situation. Life was so difficult for our little guy.

One thing really nagged at me while I was doing my research on autism; I had read so much about the importance of therapy by the age of three years. We had been seeing doctors and speech therapists for close to a year, and the age of three was fast approaching. It would be another eight months before we would move up the waiting list and get our appointment at the Children's Hospital. We made the decision to see a developmental pediatrician who was in private practice. He had worked at the Children's Hospital and had diagnosed a number of children on the autism spectrum. The parents I spoke with considered him to be an expert in this field of medicine. At this point, we needed to know for sure if Zach was autistic. After four visits, the doctor confirmed that Zach was a high-functioning autistic child.

Excerpt from Zachary's IEP

Communication Goals for Kindergarten

Communication Needs

Zachary's expressive and receptive language skills are below age level. He is limited in his ability to respond to a communication partner, comment on what others are doing, maintain a conversation, and request information. He requires support to expand his play skills and engage in play activities with other children.

Communication Goals

- Broaden conversations with adults.
- Initiate conversations with peers.
- Make comments on what others are doing.
- Give and take instructions.
- Increase understanding of language concepts (all/except, either/or, match, when, before, then, farthest, top/bottom, unless, first/second/third/last).
- Use appropriate questions in communication (how, why, who, where, when).
- Improve use of gender-specific pronouns.
- Use adjectives and adverbs.
- Use language to describe pictures and stories.
- Use an outline of his day.
- Use social stories for social interactions.

Staff Responsibilities

- Speech-language pathologist will provide consultation and training for school personnel to work with Zachary in the classroom and one-on-one.
- Education assistant will support Zachary in the classroom and use modelling techniques and reminders to improve language skills.
- Classroom teacher will use modelling techniques and reinforcement for language skills.
- Parents will provide information and support for language goals. They will use a back-and-forth book to communicate with school. This book will be kept at the front of Zachary's binder.

Measurement of Progress

- Track communication skills in everyday interactions.
- Have formal and informal assessments by speech-language pathologist.
- Have parents keep record at home.

Zachary Wong

Zachary's Kindergarten Assessment: Term 1

Literacy

Your child's score was 90 out of a possible 100.

The range of scores for kindergarten children in this school was 5 to 100.

Lower Case Letters

Your child's lower case letter recognition score was 26 out of a possible 26.

The range of scores for kindergarten children in this school was 0 to 26.

Upper Case Letters

Your child's upper case letter recognition score was 26 out of a possible 26.

The range of scores for kindergarten children in this school was 0 to 26.

Letter Sounds

Your child's letter sound recognition score was 24 out of a possible 26.

The range of scores for kindergarten children in this school was 0 to 26.

Math

Your child's score was 98 out of a possible 100.

The range of scores for kindergarten children in this school was 24 to 100.

Counting Aloud

Your child was able to count aloud to 79.

The range for kindergarten children in this school was 4 to 109.

Counting Objects One-to-One Correspondence (up to 20)

Your child's score was 20 out of a possible 20.

The range of scores for kindergarten children in this school was 2 to 20.

Numeral Recognition 1-20

Your child's score was 20 out of a possible 20.

The range of scores for kindergarten children in this school was 0 to 20.

Teacher's Comments:

Academically, Zachary scored very high on this assessment. He is in the Grade 1 range for math and literacy. He reads at a Grade 2 level.

Why Is Zachary Considered to Be Autistic?

Diagnosis of Autism

While there has been much research, and many conjectures, regarding the causes of autism, diagnosis continues to be dependent on the observation of an individual's behaviour. Physicians and psychologists use the criteria contained in the most recent edition of the *Diagnostic and Statistical Manual of Mental Disorders* (DSM-5) to determine whether a young child like Zachary exhibits (a) persistent deficits in social communication and social interaction across multiple contexts and (b) restricted, repetitive patterns of behaviour, interests, or activities. According to the DSM-5 (American Psychiatric Association, 2013), *autism spectrum disorder* (ASD) is classified as a neurodevelopmental disorder that incorporates several previously separate diagnoses, including *autistic disorder, childhood disintegrative disorder, Asperger's disorder,* and *pervasive developmental disorder not otherwise specified* (PDD/NOS). ASD is now defined by a common set of behaviours and represented by a single diagnostic category that addresses three levels of severity—requiring support, requiring substantial support, and requiring very substantial support.

© natasa778/iStock

Children with autism will often engage in solitary activities.

What We Know . . .

Diagnosing Autism Spectrum Disorder

According to the DSM-5, the following criteria (A, B, C, D, and E) must be met for a diagnosis of ASD:

A. Persistent deficits in social communication and social interaction across multiple contexts, as manifested by the following, currently or by history:

1. Deficits in social-emotional reciprocity, ranging, for example, from abnormal social approach and failure of normal back-and-forth conversation; to reduced sharing of interests, emotions, or affect; to failure to initiate or respond to social interactions.
2. Deficits in nonverbal communicative behaviors used for social interaction, ranging, for example, from poorly integrated verbal and nonverbal communication; to abnormalities in eye contact and body language or deficits in understanding and use of gestures; to a total lack of facial expressions and nonverbal communication.
3. Deficits in developing, maintaining, and understanding relationships, ranging, for example, from difficulties adjusting behavior to suit various social contexts; to difficulties in sharing imaginative play or in making friends; to absence of interest in peers.

B. Restricted, repetitive patterns of behavior, interests, or activities as manifested by at least two of the following, currently or by history:

1. Stereotyped or repetitive motor movements, use of objects, or speech.
2. Insistence on sameness, inflexible adherence to routines, or ritualized patterns of verbal or nonverbal behavior.
3. Highly restricted, fixated interests that are abnormal in intensity or focus.
4. Hyper- or hypo-reactivity to sensory input or unusual interest in sensory aspects of environment.

C. Symptoms must be present in the early developmental period (but may not become fully manifest until social demands exceed limited capacities, or may be masked by learned strategies in later life).
D. Symptoms cause clinically significant impairment in social, occupational, or other important areas of current functioning.
E. These disturbances are not better explained by intellectual disability or global developmental delay.

Source: Reprinted with permission from the *Diagnostic and Statistical Manual of Mental Disorders*, Fifth Edition. (Copyright 2013). American Psychiatric Association. All Rights Reserved.

Table 9.1 Levels of Severity in Autism Spectrum Disorder

Severity Level for ASD	Social Communication	Restricted, Repetitive Behaviors
Level 3 *Requiring Very Substantial Support*	Severe deficits in verbal and nonverbal social communication skills cause severe impairments in functioning; very limited initiation of social interactions and minimal response to social overtures from others.	Inflexibility of behavior, extreme difficulty coping with change, or other restricted/repetitive behaviors markedly interfere with functioning in all spheres. Great distress/difficulty changing focus or action.
Level 2 *Requiring Substantial Support*	Marked deficits in verbal and nonverbal social communication skills; social impairments apparent even with supports in place; limited initiation of social interactions and reduced or abnormal response to social overtures from others.	Inflexibility of behavior, difficulty coping with change, or other restricted/repetitive behaviors appear frequently enough to be obvious to the casual observer and interfere with functioning in a variety of contexts. Distress and/or difficulty changing focus or action.
Level 1 *Requiring Support*	Without supports in place, deficits in social communication cause noticeable impairments. Difficulty initiating social interactions, and clear examples of atypical or unsuccessful responses to social overtures of others. May appear to have decreased interest in social interactions.	Inflexibility of behavior causes significant interference with functioning in one or more contexts. Difficulty switching between activities. Problems of organization and planning hamper independence.

Source: Reprinted with permission from the *Diagnostic and Statistical Manual of Mental Disorders*, Fifth Edition. (Copyright 2013). American Psychiatric Association. All Rights Reserved.

Assessing Autism Spectrum Disorder

It is not uncommon for a child's parents to be the first ones to suspect that their child is not developing normally. Since Zachary was their second child, Zachary's parents were even more aware of the behaviours that would be typical of a toddler his age. As his mother noted (see *Mother's Comments* on p. 260), by the time Zachary reached 18 months of age, she and her husband had real concerns about the regression of his language skills, his withdrawal from social interactions, his sensitivity to noise and touch, and his repetitive head banging. Through their own research they knew that early intervention was critical if they were indeed dealing with autism spectrum disorder; therefore, they decided to have Zachary assessed by highly qualified professionals who were in private practice rather than wait for an appointment at the regional hospital.

What We Know . . .

Early Identification of Autism

The importance of the early identification of autism cannot be overstated as it can only lead to both a better understanding of the disorder and the development of more effective interventions. Zwaigenbaum et al. (2015) noted that despite parents voicing concerns about their children within the first two years of life, the mean age of diagnosis remains between four and five years. The researchers suggested that a single behavioural marker of ASD is unlikely to be found given the heterogeneity of ASD expression. However, in an earlier Canadian longitudinal research study also headed by Zwaigenbaum (Zwaigenbaum et al., 2005) it was reported that by 12 months of age, siblings who were later diagnosed with autism were distinguishable from other siblings and low-risk controls on the basis of (a) several specific behavioural markers, including atypicalities in eye contact, visual tracking, disengagement of visual attention, orienting to name, imitation, social smiling, reactivity, social interest and affect, and sensory-oriented behaviours; (b) prolonged latency to disengage visual attention; (c) a characteristic pattern of early temperament, with marked passivity and decreased activity level at six months, followed by extreme distress reactions, a tendency to fixate on particular objects in the environment, and decreased expression of positive affect by 12 months; and (d) delayed expressive and receptive language (p. 149). Given these findings, Zwaigenbaum et al. (2015) emphasize the importance of considering combinations of symptomatic abnormalities in an effort to establish a risk-profiling approach (behavioural and biological markers) that could be used to identify ASD in very young children.

Zachary was subsequently assessed at age three years and four months by both a developmental pediatrician and a psychologist. The purpose of their assessments was to answer the following four questions:

1.   Does Zachary have autism?
2.   Is there evidence of any other medical disorder or abnormality?
3.   Can delays be explained by social or environmental causes?
4.   What recommendations can be made regarding further investigation and management?

As is evident from the resulting assessment report (see *Assessment Results* on p. 258), Zachary was diagnosed with autism spectrum disorder based on the DSM-IV autism criteria. The developmental pediatrician and the psychologist were able to determine through observation, standardized testing, and interviews with the parents that Zachary had significant difficulties with social interactions, verbal and non-verbal communication, age-appropriate play, and changes in routine. He also demonstrated repetitive patterns of behaviour. Neither the pediatrician nor the psychologist found any evidence of any other medical disorder or abnormality. Zachary's delays could not be explained by social or environmental causes. Therefore, the diagnosis of ASD was made with certainty, and recommendations for early intervention and preparation for entry into school were presented.

What Factors Contributed to Zachary's Autism?

The cause of autism is not yet known. However, research is focusing on several areas of study, including genetics, neuropathology, prenatal factors, and exposure to toxins. In Zachary's case, there were no obvious prenatal factors that may have altered his development. His mother's pregnancy was normal, and there were no birth complications. As well, there was no obvious exposure to any type of toxin; however, some may question the fact that Zachary received his childhood vaccinations. There is much conjecture that vaccinations may be a factor in autism; however, according to the Centers for Disease Control and Prevention (2015), there is no link between the two.

neuropathology
The study of diseases of nervous-system tissue, most often using tissue from small surgical biopsies or examination of whole brains.

Given Zachary's non-eventful prenatal and early childhood history, one must consider other factors that may have caused his autism. According to Locwin and Entine (2016), researchers are learning that random environmental factors appear to play far less of a role in autism than once thought, and it is genetics that is the current focal point. Tick, Bolton, Happe, Rutter, and Rijsdjik (2016) conducted a systematic review and meta-analysis of all the ASD twin studies published to date. They reported that the meta-analysis correlations for monozygotic twins with ASD were almost perfect at .98, and the dizygotic twin correlation was lower at .53. The genetic heritability of ASD was deemed substantial at 64–91 per cent. In other words, when considering the causes of ASD, strong genetic effects cannot be denied. However, from the genetic research to date, it appears that there is not an easily identifiable genetic marker for autism, but rather a number of genes interacting with each other and with non-genetic factors as well (Locwin & Entine, 2016).

monozygotic twins
Identical twins developed from the same fertilized ovum.

dizygotic twins
Two eggs are fertilized by two separate sperm resulting in fraternal or non-identical twins.

In Zachary's case, there is no history of autism in his immediate or extended family. Both his parents have college diplomas; his father is an accountant and his mother was trained as a dental assistant, but now stays home to care for her two sons. While Zachary's older brother was slow to speak, he is now a healthy 8-year-old boy who shows no signs of autism. However, having said that there is no evidence of autism in Zachary's family, Siegel (2003) noted that an inherited gene mutation may be passed through a family but it may not necessarily be expressed as autism, or it may cause a very mild case of autism that produces no notable problems.

genetic marker
A gene or DNA sequence that has a known location on a chromosome and is associated with a particular physical trait.

While we do not know if Zachary has any abnormalities in his brain structure, we do know that neuropathology is another factor identified by researchers as a possible cause of autism. There is believed to be a link between deficits in the cerebellum and individuals with ASD. Becker and Stoodley (2013) reported that "cerebellar findings in autism suggest developmental differences at multiple levels of neural structure and function, indicating that the cerebellum is an important player in the complex neural underpinnings of autism spectrum disorder, with behavioral implications beyond the motor domain" (p. 1).

cerebellum
A brain structure known to support motor learning and more recently thought to support cognitive functions as well as affective regulation.

How Has Zachary's Autism Affected His Development?

Cognitive Development

Zachary's parents were not concerned with his cognitive development during the first year of his life. In fact, he began to speak around the time of his first birthday, vocally identifying his "mama" and "dada" and a few familiar objects. However, not long after that, Zachary seemed to retreat from the outside world. He no longer spoke any words and seemed entirely uncomfortable with his environment. Much of his day was spent in distress as he struggled to cope with an extreme sensitivity to noise and touch, and a lack of sleep. Given these stressors, it was not surprising that he lacked an interest in exploration and demonstrated an inability to play with toys in an age-appropriate manner, two activities that are critical to a child's early cognitive development. His parents were concerned that he would fail to develop intellectually.

What We Know . . .

Autism Spectrum Disorders and Intellectual Abilities

While it was once thought that a large proportion of individuals with ASD had significant intellectual disabilities (Matson, 1994), recent research has shed new light on this topic. According to Sarris (2015), a significant study conducted in the United States found that almost half of the children with ASD had average or above-average intelligence, 23 per cent had IQ scores in the borderline range, and less than a third of the children with autism had an intellectual disability. Why the change? Sarris concluded that there may be several reasons, including the diagnosis of more individuals with milder forms of autism as well as the successes gained by early intervention.

Perhaps even more interesting, Clarke et al. (2016) conducted research that included over 10,000 participants who were tested for general cognitive ability and also had their DNA analyzed. Clarke and his colleagues were able to link genetic factors associated with autism to better cognitive ability in people who do not have the condition. In other words, genes linked with a greater risk of developing autism may also be associated with higher intelligence. As Olson (2015) stated, "Genetic research has unpacked fundamental questions surrounding how nature rules the abilities and disabilities humans are confronted with in life, autism being one of them."

During his psychological assessment at age three years and four months, Zachary's performance on the Bayley Scales of Infant Development, Second Edition, indicated a significant delay. The behaviours and skills he demonstrated during testing placed him at approximately the two years and five months developmental age-equivalent level, which is below the first percentile when compared to his same-aged peers. It should be noted, however, that most standardized ability measures were designed for use with neurotypical children, and results must be interpreted with caution when used with children with sensory, language, or motor difficulties. It is likely that Zachary's performance on the Bayley Scales of Infant Development was affected by his autism-related behaviours.

Once Zachary was diagnosed with autism and began a series of different therapies, it became apparent that he was making advancements in a number of areas of development, including his intellectual development. As he progressed through preschool, his teachers noted that one of Zachary's strengths was his mental ability. He learned to successfully complete tasks involving numbers, classification, seriation, and memory. These strengths were further confirmed when he entered kindergarten in 2006. His first Kindergarten Assessment (see p. 262), conducted in the fall term, revealed a student who was doing very well academically. This progress has continued throughout the school year; Zachary is performing at grade level in math and he is a proficient reader whose literacy skills exceed those expected for a child his age. His academic success is further confirmation that standardized test results must be interpreted with caution when a child's behaviour affects the completion of tasks during the testing session.

Social and Emotional Development

It is not at all surprising that Zachary is significantly delayed in his socio-emotional development given that ASD is characterized by impaired social interaction, problems with verbal and non-verbal communication, and unusual, repetitive, or severely limited activities and interests. Typical socio-emotional development during the first years of life includes the development of trust, security, and self-regulation, the development of play skills, and an increasing ability to understand and respond to the emotions of others. Zachary's behaviours during his preschool years obviously did not lend themselves to typical development in this area. He was a toddler who had great difficulty simply handling the environmental stimulation he faced on a daily basis. Playing with other children and relating to the emotions of others was given little attention as he and his family struggled to cope. While at age six Zachary is beginning to respond more to those around him, he is still very withdrawn and lacks the social skills necessary to independently take part in most play situations with his peers. It is likely he will have lifelong difficulties with social and emotional issues.

classification
The ability to recognize and construct relationships among objects, imagined objects, and classification systems themselves.

seriation
The ability to organize objects in a progressive sequence according to some measurable dimension (height, width, length, size, shape, etc.).

What We Know . . .

Autism and Social Development

From the start, typically developing infants are social beings. Early in life, they gaze at people, turn toward voices, grasp a finger, and even smile.

In contrast, most children with ASD seem to have tremendous difficulty learning to engage in the give and take of everyday human interaction. Even in the first few months of life, many do not interact and they avoid eye contact. They seem indifferent to other people, and often seem to prefer being alone. They may resist attention or passively accept hugs and cuddling. Later, they seldom seek comfort or respond to parents' displays of anger or affection in a typical way. Research has suggested that although children with ASD are attached to their parents, their expression of this attachment is unusual and difficult to "read." To parents, it may seem as if their child is not attached at all. Parents who looked forward to the joys of cuddling, teaching, and playing with their child may feel crushed by this lack of typical attachment behaviour.

Children with ASD are also slower in learning to interpret what others are thinking and feeling. Subtle social cues—whether a smile, a wink, or a grimace—may have little meaning. To a child who misses these cues, "Come here" always means the same thing, whether the speaker is smiling and extending her arms for a hug or frowning and planting her fists on her hips. Without the ability to interpret gestures and facial expressions, the social world may seem bewildering. To compound the problem, people with ASD have difficulty seeing things from another person's perspective. Most 5-year-olds understand that other people have different information, feelings, and goals than they have. A person with ASD may lack such understanding. This inability leaves them unable to predict or understand other people's actions.

Although not universal, it is common for people with ASD also to have difficulty regulating their emotions. This can take the form of "immature" behaviour such as crying in class or verbal outbursts that seem inappropriate to those around them. The individual with ASD might also be disruptive and physically aggressive at times, making social relationships still more difficult. They have a tendency to "lose control," particularly when they are in a strange or overwhelming environment, or when angry and frustrated. They may at times break things, attack others, or hurt themselves. In their frustration, some bang their heads, pull their hair, or bite their arms.

Sources: Strock (2004) and National Institute of Mental Health (2011).

Motor and Sensory Development

If you were to see Zachary's kindergarten class on the playground, at first glance any differences between Zachary and his peers might not immediately stand out. However, if you were to observe the children as they played, you would soon see a young boy who looks awkward when he runs and has difficulty balancing. Observation in the classroom would reveal further physical challenges. Zachary experiences problems with fine motor skills as well as gross motor skills. For example, he is not able to manipulate scissors like his peers and has some difficulties with printing using a pencil.

Zachary's low motor skills were noted when he was first diagnosed with autism. On standardized development tests, such as the Vineland Adaptive Behavior Scales, Interview Edition, he scored at the 19th percentile on the motor skill domain. His mother also reported at this time that he was exhibiting odd physical behaviours, such as head banging and an overwhelming response to noise and touch (see *Mother's Comments* on p. 260). This young boy was obviously not reaching his motor milestones as one would expect, and he was also responding differently than other children his age to basic sensations and perceptions.

What We Know . . .

Autism and Sensory Motor Difficulties

According to the US National Research Council (2001), a review of the literature revealed that most children with autism exhibit sensory and motor difficulties at some time in their development. Some children exhibit these difficulties as early as the first year of life, while others begin to manifest sensory difficulties during the toddler period and motor delays and clumsiness when more complex skills are required in preschool or elementary school.

Ayres (1972) proposed that children with autism exhibit sensory and motor difficulties because of dysfunctional sensory systems involving the following three basic senses: tactile, vestibular, and proprioceptive. Hatch-Rasmussen (2016) summarized how difficulties with these senses can affect children with autism:

The tactile system includes nerves under the skin's surface that send information to the brain. This information includes light, touch, pain, temperature, and pressure. These play an important role in perceiving the environment as well as protective reactions for survival. Dysfunction in the tactile system can be seen in withdrawing when being touched, refusing to eat certain textured foods and/ or to wear certain types of clothing, complaining about having his or her hair or face washed, avoiding getting his or her hands dirty (i.e., glue, sand, mud, fingerpaint), and using his or her finger tips rather than whole hands to manipulate objects. A dysfunctional tactile system may lead to a misperception of touch and/ or pain (hyper- or hypo-sensitive) and may lead to self-imposed isolation, general irritability, distractibility, and hyperactivity.

The vestibular system refers to structures within the inner ear (the semicircular canals) that detect movement and changes in the position of the head. For example, the vestibular system tells you when your head is upright or tilted (even with your eyes closed). Dysfunction within this system may manifest itself in two different ways. Some children may be hyper-sensitive to vestibular stimulation and have fearful reactions to ordinary movement activities (e.g., swings,

Continued

slides, ramps, inclines). They may also have trouble learning to climb or descend stairs or hills, and they may be apprehensive while walking or crawling on uneven or unstable surfaces. As a result, they seem fearful in space. In general, these children appear clumsy. On the other extreme, the child may actively seek very intense sensory experiences such as excessive body whirling, jumping, and/ or spinning. This type of child demonstrates signs of a hypo-reactive vestibular system; that is, they are trying continuously to stimulate their vestibular systems.

The proprioceptive system refers to components of muscles, joints, and tendons that provide a person with a subconscious awareness of body position. When proprioception is functioning efficiently, an individual's body position is automatically adjusted in different situations; for example, the proprioceptive system is responsible for providing the body with the necessary signals to allow us to sit properly in a chair and to step off a curb smoothly. It also allows us to manipulate objects using fine motor movements, such as writing with a pencil, using a spoon to drink soup, and buttoning his or her shirt. Some common signs of proprioceptive dysfunction are clumsiness, a tendency to fall, a lack of awareness of body position in space, odd body posturing, minimal crawling when young, difficulty manipulating small objects (buttons, snaps), eating in a sloppy manner, and resistance to new motor movement activities.

What Therapies Did Zachary Experience before Entering School?

Once Zachary was diagnosed at age three, his parents had to decide what therapies or programs would be best for him. They knew that early intervention was critical, so they arranged for continuing speech therapy (private) and added occupational therapy to deal with Zachary's sensory difficulties (funded through community services). They also established a home-based applied behavioural analysis (ABA) program. According to Zachary's mother, they chose this type of program for a number of reasons. First, they live in a small community where no centre-based programs are available. Second, they felt it was important to have Zachary learning from therapists who had experience working with autistic children, and the ABA therapists met this criterion. Third, they wanted their child in a program that was reputable and had a history of success with children like Zachary. From their research, they concluded that ABA has the longest and best-documented track record of any therapeutic intervention for children with autism. The ABA program requires therapists to use logically sequenced lessons to teach expressive, receptive, cognitive, fine motor, and gross motor skills, and the results of these lessons are carefully recorded. This meant that the data collected by Zachary's therapists would clearly indicate where he was excelling and where he needed extra help. Zachary's parents did consider other programs for him, such as auditory integration training and art therapy; however, these programs were not readily available in their region, so implementation would be difficult. ABA seemed the perfect fit for their family and their situation.

What We Know . . .

Interventions for Children with Autism

There are a number of specialized interventions, or teaching methods, that are used to assist children with autism with their learning. One of the most widely used of these teaching methods is applied behaviour analysis, or ABA. There have been reports (e.g., Reed, Osborne, & Corness, 2007) that children with ASD who receive ABA as an early teaching intervention make greater intellectual and educational gains than similar children in other types of teaching interventions. According to Autism Speaks Canada (2016a) and the Canadian Psychological Association (2015), early intensive intervention based on the scientifically derived principles of learning (ABA) has been proven to help children with ASD when used within a high-quality treatment program. Significant improvements are realized in learning, reasoning, communication, and adaptability. Key areas for intervention usually include communication and social skills, daily living skills, self-regulation or coping skills, and family support.

The Cambridge Center for Behavioral Studies (2012) describes some of the key features of ABA as follows:

1. The person's behavior is assessed through observations that focus on exactly what the person does, when the person does it, at what rate, and what happens before (antecedents) and what happens after behavior (consequences). Strengths and weaknesses are specified in this way.
2. Skills that the person does not demonstrate are broken down into small steps.
3. To teach each step: (a) give a clear instruction, provide assistance in following the instruction (for example, "prompt" by demonstration or physical guidance) and use materials that are at the person's level, (b) get a correct response, and (c) give a positive reinforcer (a consequence that will lead the person to do the behavior again in the future).
4. Many opportunities or trials are given repeatedly in structured teaching situations and in the course of everyday activities.
5. Instruction emphasizes teaching a person how to learn: to listen, to watch, to imitate.
6. As the person progresses, guidance is systematically reduced so that the person is responding independently; prompts are faded out.
7. As steps are acquired, the person is taught to combine them in more complex ways and to practice them in more situations.
8. Problem behavior is not reinforced. The person is not allowed to escape from learning and is redirected to engage in appropriate behavior.
9. The person's responses during every lesson are recorded. These data are used to determine if he or she is progressing at an acceptable rate. If not, that part of the program needs changing.

Source: Cambridge Center for Behavioral Studies (2012).

Initially, Zachary's ABA program included intensive therapy six days a week. Eventually, this was reduced to three to four times a week. Zachary still receives ABA therapy, even though he has entered school. A therapist visits his home twice a week after school hours.

From the Psychologist's Notebook

I first took the training necessary to become an ABA therapist from the consultant that the parents had chosen. I started working with Zachary when he was 3 years old and not talking. He only said a few words and was still in diapers. I worked three-hour shifts three days a week in the afternoons, and another therapist worked the same amount of hours on three other days. We have been doing this for three years now and he has certainly come a long way. We teach Zachary the drills that the consultant writes up. We try to do this in as many different settings as possible and with many different types of materials. We keep doing the drill until he has mastered it five times with at least two or three different therapists.

Zachary has changed a lot since I first started working with him. He is much more social with his peers and people in general. He doesn't seem to have a problem talking to people he doesn't know very well. His memory for things has improved. He remembers the words to songs he has only heard once, can tell you about certain movies that he likes, and has become a fairly good reader. He is reading at a Grade 2 level already. He loves to talk about, play with, or even read about airplanes, fire trucks, or big equipment. Zachary is doing great with his printing and has no problems spelling sight words out loud. He can do simple math questions, identify money, but has a hard time doing directive drawing. He loves the computer and has no difficulty playing games on it both at home or at school.

Zachary likes to go on outings with me to the beach, the park, McDonald's, and shopping. He never would go with anyone but his parents before. He is going to private swimming lessons and finally doesn't mind getting his hair wet. He also attends the "Friends" club once a week with other kids who have autism. Zachary is very eager to learn new things but at times needs some encouragement to keep going. We sometimes forget that he is a kid and needs to spend time doing things other than his ABA drills. He acts just like other kids do when it comes to interacting with his sibling. Sometimes they even get into trouble or have little arguments. Zachary is getting much better at not getting so mad when he doesn't get his own way.

If you were to meet Zachary, you would have no idea he has autism. He looks and acts just like any ordinary child, and that is the greatest compliment he could give us for all the hard work that we have put him through over the past three years.

Zachary's mother indicated that their only disappointment with the ABA program was that its intensive one-on-one approach did not help Zachary with his social development. They were aware of this quite early in Zachary's therapy program, so they arranged for a specially trained childcare worker to assist Zachary at daycare. Zachary attended daycare for two years prior to starting school.

What We Know . . .

Other Specialized Interventions for Autism

ABA (e.g., discrete trial training and the Lovaas Method) is only one of several specialized interventions used to help children with autism. Others that are commonly used include the Greenspan Method (Floortime), TEACCH (Treatment and Education of Autistic and Communication Handicapped Children), Picture Exchange Communication System (PECS), and Social Stories. Table 9.2, compiled by Ryan, Hughes, Katsiyannis, McDaniel, and Sprinkle (2011), addresses the demonstrated efficacy of each of these evidence-based interventions.

Table 9.2 Evidence-Based Interventions for Students with Autism Spectrum Disorders

Intervention	Program Description	Demonstrated Efficacy (as found in Ryan et al. [2011])
Developmental, Individual-Difference, Relationship-Based Model (DIR; Floortime; Wieder & Greenspan, 2003)	• Through challenging yet child-friendly play experiences, clinicians, parents, and educators learn about the strengths and limitations of the child, therefore gaining the ability to tailor interventions as necessary while strengthening the bond between the parent and child and fostering the social and emotional development of the child • Time requirement: 14–35 hours per week	• Shows increased levels of social functioning, emotional functioning, and information gathering • For ages: Approximately 2–5 years
Discrete Trial Training (DTT; Lovaas, 1987)	• Provides an intervention that focuses on managing a child's learning opportunities by teaching specific, manageable tasks, until mastery, in a continued effort to build upon the mastered skills • Time requirement: 20–30 hours per week	• Shows increased levels of cognitive skills, language skills, adaptive skills, and compliance skills • For ages: Approximately 2–6 years
Lovaas Method (Lovaas, 1987)	• Provides an intervention that focuses on managing a child's learning opportunities by teaching specific, manageable tasks, until mastery, in a continued effort to build upon the mastered skills • Time requirement: 20–40 hours per week	• Shows increased levels of adaptive skills, cognitive skills, compliance skills, language skills, IQ, and social functioning skills • For ages: Approximately 2–12 years

Continued

Table 9.2 continued

Intervention	Program Description	Demonstrated Efficacy (as found in Ryan et al. [2011])
Picture Exchange Communication System (PECS; Bondy & Frost, 1994)	• Provides a communication system developed to assist students in building fundamental language skills, eventually leading to spontaneous communication • The tiered intervention supports the learner in learning to identify, discriminate between, and then exchange different symbols with a partner as a means to communicate a want • Time requirement: As long as the child is engaged, typically 20–30 minutes per session	• Shows increased levels of speech and language development and social-communicative behaviours. • For ages: Approximately 2 years to adult
Social Stories (Gray & Garand, 1993)	• Provides personalized stories that systematically describe a situation, skill, or concept in terms of relevant social cues, perspectives, and common responses, and modelling and providing a socially accepted behaviour option • Time requirement: Varies per story; approximately 5–10 minutes prior to a difficult situation	• Shows increased levels of pro-social behaviours • For ages: Approximately 2–12 years
Treatment and Education of Autistic and Communication Related Handicapped Children (TEACCH; Schopler & Reichler, 1971)	• Provides an intervention that supports task completion by providing explicit instruction and visual supports in a purposefully structured environment, planned to meet the unique task needs of the student • Time requirement: Up to 25 hours per week (during the school day)	• Shows increased levels of imitation, perception, gross motor skills, hand-eye coordination, and cognitive performance • For ages: Approximately 6 years to adult

Source: Republished with permission of Sage publishing. "Research-based educational practices for students with autism spectrum disorders." Ryan, J.B., Hughes, E.M., Katsiyannis, A., McDaniel, M., & Sprinkle, C. *Teaching Exceptional Children*, 43 (3), 2011. Permission conveyed through Copyright Clearance Center, Inc.

What Was the Transition to School Like for Zachary?

School Readiness

Before Zachary entered kindergarten, he was assessed for *school readiness* by both daycare and school personnel. The daycare report reads as follows:

> *Zachary is a pleasant, happy boy who has been diagnosed with autism. He has attended daycare for two years and has acquired many skills during this time.*

Zachary appears to be comfortable in his daycare routine; he knows the daily routine and is usually able to make transitions smoothly as long as he is prepared ahead of time. Zachary is beginning to stand up for himself, for example he will say, "I sad" or "I frustrated."

Zachary can often be found playing with Lego and prefers to play alone or parallel to others. He enjoys spending long periods of time in the sandbox using the diggers. He is beginning to ask children to join his play. He is also taking part in more group games. Zachary will usually watch the children playing and then physically move into the play. If there is a conflict, he does not appear to understand how to resolve it.

Zachary's fine and gross motor skills have improved. He has been showing more interest in using scissors. He appears awkward at times in his running and hopping on one foot and tends to avoid balancing games.

One of Zachary's strengths is his cognitive development, particularly in classification, seriation, numbers, and memory. He exhibits some difficulties with time, such as knowing what happened yesterday.

Zachary's spoken language is usually clear and he has no difficulty expressing what he does or does not want. He uses echolalia frequently, either repeating something he has just heard or something he has heard in the past. Often these statements or sounds are ones he has heard on television.

Areas of development that appear to be in need of strengthening are prewriting and reading skills, art skills, and imaginary play. Zachary enjoys printing his name and will print some letters. He will draw basic shapes and has started to draw faces with eyes and mouths (no noses). Imaginary play is especially difficult for Zachary. He requires particular props to engage in pretend play and needs a lot of modelling before he will join in.

An area we have been focusing on with Zachary is respecting the personal space of others. He tends to get too close to his peers who in turn become upset. We have used booklets such as "A Tad Too Close" as well as role modelling to help Zachary with this. His teachers and his peers have also learned to say "Too close Zachary" in response to his behaviour.

We have seen Zachary grow in many areas of development over the past two years and have enjoyed being a part of his journey. We wish Zachary and his parents all the best!

Zachary was also assessed for school readiness by an early intervention specialist who works for the school district in which Zachary resides. Using the Brigance Preschool Screen, she had difficulty testing Zachary because he would not focus on task demands and required a great deal of prompting from both herself and his mother. Consequently, she stated that "the validity of the test results is questionable and must be viewed with caution." Zachary obtained a score of 41 per cent. A score of less than 92 per cent for a child Zachary's age indicates developmental delay. The early intervention specialist noted the following:

With prompting and one-on-one assistance where needed, Zachary was able to say his name and age, identify many body parts, build a tower with 10 blocks, identify colours, and name pictures of objects. Zachary was unable to give acceptable descriptions for the use of common objects, print his name, draw a picture of himself, or demonstrate one-to-one correspondence.

It is recommended that Zachary have an individualized education program (IEP) to define the goals he will work toward in kindergarten. Zachary will require support to function within the school setting. The nature and extent of this support will be outlined in his IEP. Strong communication is recommended to provide coordinated support and to facilitate Zachary's transition into the kindergarten program.

Transition to School

Zachary's transition into school was carefully planned. A "transition meeting" was held in the spring before his fall entry into kindergarten. The teacher and school support personnel met with Zachary's parents as well as all of the individuals who had provided therapy services during his preschool years (i.e., ABA therapists, occupational therapist, and speech therapist). The meeting provided the opportunity for all of these individuals to share information about Zachary and to take part in the decision making regarding his upcoming entry into school. As a result of this collaboration, the following decisions and recommendations were made:

- The support services teacher will develop an IEP for Zachary.
- Zachary's IEP will be adjusted regularly.
- Zachary will have a full-time educational assistant with him at school.
- The school will provide all of Zachary's current therapists with an outline of the school routine so that they can help Zachary become familiar with the routine before he enters school.
- Zachary will experience some mock trials of fire drills before entering kindergarten.
- Zachary will visit the current kindergarten classroom during the next month.

As a consequence of this attention given to Zachary's transition to school, his entry into the classroom went as smoothly as could be expected. He had moments when he was overwhelmed by his new surroundings, but he soon settled relatively well into the routine of school life. His teacher and his EA quickly learned how Zachary would respond to the different classroom activities and, as a team, adjusted their behaviours accordingly. In particular, they became especially sensitive to Zachary's need for time away from the classroom in order to "de-stress."

What We Know . . .

The Roles of the Teacher and Educational Assistant (EA)—Team Responsibilities

Teachers bear formal responsibility for the educational program for all students. It is their job to design the curriculum and instructional approach, to plan for assessment, to evaluate student progress, and to report to parents. EAs can play a variety of roles in support of this responsibility but at no time and in no dimension of this responsibility should they replace the teacher, either because they are willing to do so or because the teacher has asked them to do so. However, EAs have an important contribution to make as participants in the collaborative exercise of developing and enacting programs to meet student needs in collaboration with parents and other teachers. Although it is not uncommon for EAs to have more experience or training relative to a specific aspect of a student's personal circumstances, the teacher with responsibility for the student's overall program retains responsibility for using this expertise effectively and for overall design and delivery of the educational program.

EAs can play a wide role in support of student learning; they should be used in the most effective and meaningful way for students. This would typically mean that they do not spend large amounts of assigned time in tasks that might be considered purely clerical. However, there is nothing at all which prevents a teacher from requesting an EA to perform tasks such as preparing materials if that is appropriate in the larger context of the EA's role and if there are no higher-priority tasks to be performed within the school at that time. While an EA cannot take on the instructional role of the teacher, there may well be situations in which the EA could free up the teacher to work with a student rather than having the EA perform that task. Since the teacher is responsible for the educational program and would normally be more highly trained in this area than the EA, he or she should take on the task of instruction whenever possible and particularly in the most challenging situations.

Teachers and EAs have complementary roles. They may also have complementary expertise. Although teachers bear responsibility for all aspects of the educational program, it should not be assumed that a teacher can or needs to know everything that an EA knows. Thus, the collegial mentoring relationship between teachers and EAs may well be mutual.

Source: School District 38, Richmond, BC (2005).

What Is School Like for Zachary?

The educational assistant who currently works full time with Zachary in his kindergarten class keeps a journal of his school experiences. The following two journal entries are indicative of what a day at school is like for Zachary:

Journal Entry #1
First day after the holiday—Zachary's mother said he was reluctant to come to school. He was 10 minutes late, so we didn't have as much time as we usually do before recess. He was sad that we didn't do any ABA drills. We read two social stories and he was upset his name wasn't in the bus story while Jared's and Monica's were. He enjoyed playing "Memory." He was given a warm welcome by lots of his classmates at recess time. We went to the gym with about 10 kids. Zachary had lots of fun, but it was too noisy and he covered his ears a couple of times. He waited by the door at the end because of the noise. I will limit the group size to four or five from now on. We had a short music class because of an assembly. Zachary didn't want to go but when I said it would be just a short class, he agreed. He participated well but covered his ears again and bent over. I took him back to class and he played happily by himself until his classmates returned.

Journal Entry #2

Excellent day! Zachary was happily on task when I arrived. He had no problems with seatwork except that Sasha had a disagreement with him over a crayon. Zachary got up in frustration and said he wasn't working anymore and he was a very bad boy. I told him that wasn't true. I tried to engage him in his work at a different table, but he refused. He stood by himself for a few minutes and then returned to his chair and resumed his work. We had extra outside time in the morning. Zachary played on the swings. He and Cameron and Yannick had fun together pushing me on the swing. They thought this was hilarious. When we were eating lunch, Zachary suddenly announced that he didn't like everybody. I told him that sometimes we may feel that way for a while, but we shouldn't say it because it hurts people's feelings. Sasha agreed, saying that his feelings were hurt. Zachary was fine after that and he and Sasha interacted well. At lunch playtime we played tag with Moira, Andrea, and Craig. Zachary played happily for at least 10–15 minutes but was tired then and lay down on the ground. As I was about to get him up, Moira lay down next to him and they began to play "naptime," so I let them be. Another child came and joined them. In gym class, Zachary started out playing "freeze tag" but some kids were screaming and he became distressed and asked to leave. I said we'd leave for a few minutes and then try the gym class again. He led me to the library and chose a Pokémon book which he went through, telling me who all the characters were. He was very into this! Then he asked me to read him another Pokémon book. After this, we went back to the gym and had a great time playing "The Tide Is Coming In." Later, at centre time, Zachary was co-operative and there were no significant problems.

From the Psychologist's Notebook

The EA's journal entries reveal how Zachary is typical of students with ASD. He perceives returning to school and the music class as slightly threatening new experiences (even though he knows what they are), so he is reluctant to go. His sadness over not doing his ABA drills speaks to the predictability, comfort, and personal reinforcement he gets from the daily routine of the ABA therapy. Conversely, the "memory" game was enjoyed for the very same reasons. He wants his name to be in the story because of his strong egocentrism; a trait that makes the class's warm welcome that much more enjoyable, but also makes sharing the crayon that much more difficult. His emotional temperament makes recovering from the crayon exchange a longer-than-normal affair. His sudden announcement that he doesn't like everybody was probably caused by a sense of social discomfort with Sasha (and maybe others) that had slowly built up. He needed a way of releasing or diminishing it. Finally, the separation time and the book in the library were his solace from the noisy gym (and perhaps social stimulation overload).

When reading these journal entries, we react to what Zachary does with understanding because we "know" that this is what he is all about. We are more tolerant of the patience that is regularly required to work with him and we realize that not all activities or learning experiences will have positive outcomes. The success that the EA has with Zachary is directly attributable to these specific understandings.

What Educational Approach Is Best for Zachary?

An Emphasis on Communication and Socialization

While Zachary is currently a full participant in his kindergarten class, he does have a unique educational program that is clearly outlined in his comprehensive IEP. The learning expectations for his first school year were designed to specifically address his particular strengths and needs and do not necessarily match the learning expectations designed for his peers. One of Zachary's major areas of need is improved communication skills (see his *Communication Goals for Kindergarten* on p. 261). Other areas of need include improved social skills (sharing, waiting his turn, identification of emotions, and playing games with peers), gross motor skills (jumping, hopping, balancing, and ball skills), fine motor skills (printing using a pencil), and behaviour (ability to deal with transitions and frustrations).

The following adjustments to teaching methods and the learning environment were also identified for Zachary's kindergarten year and implemented by his teacher and the support staff:

- Demonstrate and/or model communication.
- Demonstrate and/or model tasks.
- Teach at a slow pace.
- Teach key concepts and vocabulary.
- Reduce oral language expectations.
- Emphasize visual and/or tactile clues and support.
- Assign a class "buddy" for Zachary.
- Use a student planner and/or home-school book.

Zachary is fortunate to live in a province that has a provincial outreach program dedicated to children with autism and related disorders. This program provides support to schools by offering workshops and training on autism. In addition, program professionals visit schools and consult with school-based teams regarding educational and behavioural programming. In other words, the school personnel involved in Zachary's education have access to resources, training, and expert consultation that enhance the services he already receives from the school-based team. Already, early in his kindergarten year, consultants from this outreach program have visited Zachary's school and observed him in the classroom. Based on their observations, and input from school personnel and Zachary's parents, they identified concerns and problems and proposed recommended strategies and interventions. For example, in terms of behaviour supports, the consultants' report stated the following:

Zachary is currently displaying some work avoidance behaviours. Zachary's educational assistant has implemented excellent supports. Consider implementing a visual timer (egg timer) to let Zachary know how long an activity or break lasts. Follow more difficult activities (journal, directed art) with a choice time. This would be a motivational strategy for Zachary ("first you do . . . and then you can . . . "). Define one to three specific rules for Zachary to work on between now and June. Create a portable visual reminder of the rules to show Zachary the expectations. Implement a token economy and reinforce Zachary with stickers/check marks each time he displays the desired rule. Once Zachary has gained five stars, he can earn a highly desired reward. Coupled with this behaviour technique, try reading social stories to him (ones that target the specific skills you are working on). When social stories are read regularly, they provide an internal script for Zachary to follow so that he can meet social expectations.

The consultants also observed that Zachary appeared to be an anxious child, which is common in children with autism spectrum disorder. The consultants suggested the following:

When Zachary shows signs of anxiety, offer him a break. This break can be outside and timed. Give Zachary a tangible item (Koosh ball) to use during these break times. Once Zachary becomes familiar with this item, it will signal him to "calm down." It can then be used to keep Zachary calm when he is in class (e.g., squeezing Koosh ball during circle time). Read a social story on calming. Because there is a pattern to Zachary's avoidance behaviours, pre-empt these avoidance episodes by offering breaks and decreasing the amount of work to complete (e.g., spend less time at circle, offer a break from circle, implement a choice time).

It is apparent, then, that the current educational approach implemented for Zachary is one that clearly recognizes his special needs. Academics are emphasized, but a great deal of attention is paid to helping Zachary with the communicative and social aspects of school. While his teacher is responsible for the delivery of curricula in the classroom, other professionals provide the additional support that is necessary to allow Zachary to function successfully in the school setting.

What We Know . . .

Teaching Students with Autism

Given the increasing use of inclusion as an educational strategy, this does not imply that the onus is solely on the regular classroom teacher to take full responsibility for the success or failure of the learning experiences of students with autism. As Autism Speaks (2012) noted, a team approach is necessary:

Each member of the team brings a unique perspective and set of observations and skills, all of which are helpful in assisting a student with complex and variable needs. It is also important to employ the knowledge and perspective of the family, since they offer another valuable and longitudinal view . . . Parents can contribute information and a history of successful (and unsuccessful) strategies, and may also benefit from information on strategies and successes at school that can help to extend learning into the home setting.

Strategies for Teaching Students with Autism

Use Task Variation

Vary tasks to prevent boredom, and alternate activities to reduce anxiety and inappropriate behaviours. For example, alternate familiar, successful experiences with less-preferred activities. It may be helpful to alternate large-group activities with calming activities completed in quiet environments. In addition, incorporating physical activity and exercise during scheduled activities can have positive benefits. All planned activities should be charted in visual forms and posted at or near the students' desks. Students can learn to use schedules independently and staff can direct students to the schedules when it is time to change activities.

Use Task Analysis

Task analysis involves breaking large tasks into small, teachable units. Teachers often need to break complex tasks down into subskills to ensure students are successful. Each subskill should be taught and reinforced in sequence.

Use Forward and Backward Chaining

Skill sequences that have been broken down through task analysis may be taught through forward and backward chaining. In forward chaining, the emphasis of instruction is placed on teaching the first behaviour or skill in the chain that the student has not mastered. Backward chaining has the advantage of allowing the student to experience the completion of the task immediately after instruction. For instance, if backward chaining were used to teach a student to put on his or her coat, the last step of the task would likely be pulling up his or her zipper. Following task completion, the student would probably be given an opportunity to go outside. As a result an activity that is reinforcing (going outside) immediately follows the task (pulling up his or her zipper). However, the decision to use backward or forward chaining often depends on the nature of the task.

Use Shaping Techniques

Teaching a new acceptable behaviour may involve shaping it by reinforcing approximations of that behaviour. Each reinforcement is provided for a closer approximation. For example, the teacher may accept the student's one-word request for a desired object until that skill is firmly established, then "up the ante" by requiring a two-word request.

Provide Precise, Positive Praise

Give students precise information about what they do right or well. Generalized praise may result in unintended learning that is hard to reverse. Accidental or unanticipated learning may occur if students mistakenly connect something else they are doing with praise.

Use Meaningful Reinforcements

Reinforcers can be anything from praise to tangible objects that increase the behaviour a student is trying to learn. It is only a reinforcer if it results in an increase in a specific behaviour. It is important to be aware that students with ASD may not be motivated by reinforcers that work with other students. For example, they might prefer time to spend alone, play with a desired object, or sit by the window. It is important to know what works as reinforcement for individual students.

Plan Tasks at an Appropriate Level of Difficulty

Students with ASD may become anxious and frustrated if they cannot perform assigned tasks. Teachers should support students through instructional adaptations. Teachers must select the most appropriate level of adaptation for a given activity for specific students. In general, students should be included in regular instruction to the greatest

Continued

extent possible. Adaptations should be carefully selected to ensure that students are successful and that their learning is extended.

Use Age-Appropriate Materials

It is important to treat students who have ASD with respect by ensuring instructional materials are appropriate. Even if instruction must be modified significantly, the learning materials should be appropriate to the age of the student.

Provide Opportunities for Choice

Because students with ASD are frequently frustrated by their inability to make themselves understood, they need instruction in communicating choices. Many parts of their lives are necessarily highly structured and controlled by adults. Sometimes, students continue to choose one activity or object because they do not know how to choose another. It may be helpful to develop a choice menu to help students select activities and tasks.

Break Down Oral Instructions

Avoid long verbal explanations when providing instruction for students with ASD. Supporting oral instruction with visual cues and representations helps students understand.

Prepare Students for Upcoming Lessons

Whenever possible, expose students with ASD to concepts and materials prior to presenting the information to the entire class. Students with ASD may require more time and repetition to learn a new skill or concept and incorporate it into their existing repertoire.

Pay Attention to Processing and Pacing

Students with ASD often need more time to respond than other students and may need to process each discrete piece of a message or request separately.

Use Concrete Examples and Hands-On Activities

Teach abstract ideas and conceptual thinking using concrete examples, and vary the examples so that a concept can be applied in a variety of ways.

Introduce Unfamiliar Tasks in a Familiar Environment

When possible, introduce unfamiliar tasks in a familiar environment. When that is not possible, prepare students for new tasks and environments using pictures, videotapes, or social stories.

Direct and Broaden Fixations into Useful Activities

If students are fixated on objects or topics, such as colours or shapes, use them to teach concepts.

Maintain a List of Individual Strengths and Interests

Family members can provide valuable information about what students know and do at home or in the community. Build on these interests and skills for instruction and to reinforce successful learning and behaviour.

Develop Talents and Interest Areas

If students demonstrate particular interests and strengths in specific areas, provide opportunities to develop further expertise in those areas.

Source: Adapted from Alberta Learning (2003).

Evaluation of Progress

Because of the complexity of Zachary's case, his progress in kindergarten is tracked by a number of people. First of all, his teacher evaluates how he is doing academically and how he is adjusting to the demands of school both inside and outside the classroom. Her guide for these evaluations is Zachary's IEP. The learning goals developed by the school-based team serve as the learning expectations designed specifically for him. Each goal is clearly stated and is followed by a description of how progress toward this goal should be measured. For example, one goal is for Zachary to improve his social skills by "sharing with others." His teacher is monitoring how well he is doing in this area by "observing and tracking appropriate behaviours on a monthly basis." In other words, she collects data each month (play time on Fridays), records how he is doing (the number of times he shares with others), and then compares the results across months. By following the recommendations in Zachary's IEP, such as how to monitor his progress, his teacher is able to provide valuable information to all members of the school-based team, including Zachary's parents.

Zachary is also evaluated regularly by his therapists (i.e., ABA therapists, speech therapist, and occupational therapist) and, as mentioned previously, the specialists from the provincial outreach program for autism. The advantage of having so many professionals involved in his education is that a comprehensive report of his progress is available to all those involved. The teacher is certainly not left to manage Zachary's education on her own. As she stated, "I really feel like part of a team that has the best interests of Zachary as its goal. I am learning so much from the other professionals and I can depend on their feedback to guide me in determining Zachary's progress."

What We Know . . .

Evaluating the Progress of Students with Autism

Scott, Clark, and Brady (2000) addressed the issue of how teachers can tell whether or not their teaching is effective and the student with autism is learning efficiently. They emphasized that these students have learning difficulties that are serious, and teachers cannot rely on guesswork to determine if learning is occurring as it should. Therefore, these researchers presented the following four principles for teachers to follow when evaluating their students:

1. Directly evaluate the skill being taught.
2. Measure the skill frequently.
3. Display the student's progress graphically.
4. Make instructional changes that reflect your findings.

How Is Zachary Different from Other Students with Autism?

The fact that autism is referred to as a "spectrum" disorder correctly implies that individuals who are autistic can display varying abilities and disabilities. Knowing that a child has been diagnosed with ASD provides some insight into the areas of development that may be affected;

however, it certainly does not provide a clear or precise picture of a child's level of functioning in each of these areas. As with other exceptionalities, each child who is autistic has a unique combination of strengths and needs.

Zachary has been diagnosed with Level 1 autism because he has less severe symptoms than many other children who are autistic. Zachary is very cognitively capable, which means he is a high functioning autistic child and most likely to benefit from being in an inclusive classroom with his same-age peers (Siegel, 2003). Zachary's cognitive abilities are what set him apart from many other children who have ASD.

The following examples highlight the varying abilities and needs of children with autism in terms of their cognitive functioning:

- *The low functioning (Level 3) child:* Daria is a 6-year-old child who was diagnosed with ASD when she was a toddler. It was not long after Daria's birth that her parents suspected something was wrong. She just never seemed to be like other babies her age. She slept a lot and seemed unresponsive to their attempts at playing with her. It did not seem to matter what environment she was in, nothing seemed to capture her attention. Instead, Daria responded to most new environments by crying, and despite their efforts to comfort her, her parents usually had to take her home to calm her down. Daria's troubling behaviours only increased as she entered the toddler period. She avoided cuddling and did not respond to any of her parents' attempts to connect with her. Most of the time, she simply stared into space and rocked back and forth. She showed no signs of beginning to use language other than using a high-pitched scream when agitated. She was diagnosed with ASD and an intellectual disability at age three. Despite great efforts by her parents and therapists, she has made few gains. As a 6-year-old, she attends her neighbourhood school and has the full-time support of an educational assistant. She joins her same-age peers for some of their daily activities, such as music, gym, and outdoor activities; however, she works one-on-one with her EA outside the classroom for much of the school day as she becomes too distraught in the classroom setting.

What We Know . . .

Students with Autism—Level 3

According to Manitoba Education (2016a), a student with autism (Level 3) meets the following criteria:

- A diagnosis of an ASD that is expressed in severe and pervasive difficulties in social interaction, verbal and non-verbal communication, and a narrow range of interests, activities, and behaviours
- A significant cognitive disability with corresponding delays in adaptive skill development
- May also experience severe difficulty with managing change in daily routines and activities, severe reactions to sensory stimuli, and a persistent pattern of behaviours that are dangerous to him- or herself or others

- Requires student-specific programming (e.g., adaptation or modification or individualized programming) and intensive support throughout the school day.

Schooling for these children involves a focus on four critical skills: (a) mobility, (b) self-care, (c) communication, and (d) social interaction (Scott et al., 2000). Their intellectual disabilities limit the rate at which they learn and, in the most severe cases, typical interventions for autism are not successful (Siegel, 2003).

- *The medium functioning (Level 2) child:* Nathaniel is a 6-year-old child who was diagnosed with ASD at age four. Like Zachary, he seemed to be developing normally for the first year of his life. While he was a "fussy" baby, he seemed to be reaching the milestones that are expected of a child his age. Then, it was as if his development stopped abruptly: no more babbling, no more playing with his toys, and no more interest in the activities going on around him. His fussiness increased and he could not be consoled with cuddling and attention. His parents were very concerned but somewhat reassured when told by a medical professional that their child was fine. As Nathaniel grew and his behaviour seemed to differ more and more from other children his age, his parents became convinced that their child was developmentally delayed. They had little knowledge of autism and it was not until a routine check-up that a doctor recommended an assessment by a specialist. Nathaniel was 4 years old when he was finally diagnosed with ASD and an intellectual disability. He had received no therapy to that point, and because his parents were not financially able to pay for private therapists Nathaniel's only treatment before entering school was speech therapy and attendance at a local preschool. He entered kindergarten with limited skills in the areas of language and social interaction. Nathaniel requires the full support of an EA and has been making the most gains in the areas of mobility and self-care.

What We Know . . .

Students with Autism—Level 2

According to Manitoba Education (2016b), a student with autism (Level 2) meets the following criteria:

- Has a diagnosis of an ASD that is expressed in significant difficulties with social interaction, verbal and non-verbal communication, and a narrow preoccupation with a fixed range of interests and activities
- May have a significant cognitive disability or delays in adaptive skill development resulting in the need for assistance with activities of daily living during the school day
- Demonstrates persistent patterns of behaviour that interfere with his or her ability to learn
- Requires student-specific programming, such as adaptation or modification beyond the usual education programming provided for students with moderate special needs for a major portion of the school day

- *The high functioning (Level 1) child:* Pierre is a 6-year-old kindergarten student who, like Zachary, is a high functioning child who has an autism spectrum disorder. Pierre has an above-average IQ and excellent expressive language skills. In fact, before he entered preschool at age four, his parents thought their only child was exceptionally clever and without any learning difficulties. Pierre had an insatiable appetite for knowledge about electricity, which his parents supported. Upon entry to preschool, concerns about Pierre rose immediately. He was having many problems interacting with his classmates, including an inability to take part in conversations and listen to others, an inability to understand non-verbal cues, and an inability to deal with others being in close proximity to what he perceived as his space. Preschool was extremely stressful for Pierre, and the tension was causing him to have outbursts of hand flapping and crying. At first, his parents attributed his difficulties to the fact that he had spent his early years as an only child with little exposure to other children. After all, he seemed like a little adult in the way he talked. However, when Pierre failed to "settle in" to preschool, he was assessed by a clinical psychologist who determined that he has ASD. Supports were immediately put in place to address Pierre's emotional, behavioural, and social skills.

What We Know . . .

Students with Autism—Level 1

According to Myles (2005), students who are diagnosed as high functioning within the autism spectrum are often misunderstood. They may have average to above-average intelligence as well as advanced verbal skills and good rote memory abilities; however, despite the fact that they appear to be like their peers, they do have difficulties that affect their success in school. Myles describes the characteristics of these students as follows:

- Unable to interact with others despite their desire for these interactions to occur (e.g., cannot share conversational topics, appear unwilling to listen to others, and engage in one-sided conversations)
- Inability to understand non-verbal cues
- Demonstrate concrete and literal thinking skills (e.g., difficulty comprehending abstract topics)
- Become easily stressed and show this stress in unconventional ways (e.g., unusual behaviours)
- Exhibit atypical sensory responses (e.g., exposure to loud noises may cause anxiety)
- Often have poor motor skills along with coordination and balance problems

Something to Think About

In 2016, the World Health Organization reported that 1 in 160 children has an autism spectrum disorder. According to Autism Speaks Canada (2016b), autism is now the fastest growing and most commonly diagnosed neurological disorder in Canada.

Because Canadian schools have adopted the inclusive approach to educating children with exceptionalities, more and more children with autism are being placed in the regular classroom. In your opinion, is the regular classroom the appropriate educational setting for all children who have autism?

A group of people gather at the World Autism Awareness Month (WAAM) event in Mumbai. Every April WAAM helps to raise awareness of a disorder that affects tens of millions of people around the world. Both the hand print and the puzzle piece have historically been symbols for autism.

Closing Zachary's File

The despair that Zachary's parents felt when their toddler began to retreat from the world is obvious from his mother's comments (see p. 260). Fortunately, that despair has turned to pride as his parents look back on the past three years. While it has not been an easy journey, Zachary is a much happier child who is able to attend kindergarten with his same-age peers. He has made great strides in his ability to communicate and in his ability to take part in daily activities, both at home and in the classroom. These gains have been due, in large part, to the involvement of Zachary's parents in his therapy. According to Siegel (2003), "research consistently points to parent involvement in a child's treatments as a critical factor in quality" (p. 444). Therapists and teachers can spend many hours working with a child who has autism, but it is the parents who have the most opportune moments for teaching, reinforcing, and encouraging the child.

Zachary's parents have been exemplary in their efforts to help their son. They searched unwaveringly for answers when Zachary first showed signs of not developing normally. They researched autism and intervention options when they received Zachary's diagnosis. They made sure he had the best therapists they could find. They took advantage of all the supports available to their family in the area in which they lived. They ensured that Zachary was prepared to enter kindergarten, and now that he is in school they continue to advocate for his special needs while supporting those who work with him. Zachary's parents believe strongly that the inclusive setting is where their son belongs.

Despite these efforts and successes, neither Zachary's parents nor his therapists or teachers are naive about the challenging road ahead. In terms of school, the early elementary years may be the easiest for Zachary. Once the emphasis in the classroom turns to independent learning primarily acquired through seatwork, Zachary may have difficulty coping with the learning environment. He probably will have difficulty learning non-rote material that requires him to understand the perspective of others, and many aspects of the curricula require this ability. Socializing with his peers will certainly be another challenge. In terms of life outside of school, he will need to further his communication and socialization skills in order to "fit in" and live an independent life. He will probably always be viewed as "different," but given his high intellectual functioning and the early interventions he has experienced Zachary's future holds great promise.

From the Psychologist's Notebook

When I first met Zachary's kindergarten teacher, she expressed concern about having a child with autism in her class. She was doubtful that she had the necessary skills to help Zachary learn. Her professional training had not included any course work in special education. We talked at length about Zachary, how he would be similar to other children in the class and how he might differ. We discussed his IEP and the role his educational assistant would play in helping him cope with the school environment. The more we talked, the more relaxed she became. I could see that it was her "not knowing" that was causing her anxiety. By the end of our conversation, she was the one making suggestions regarding teaching and classroom management strategies.

When Zachary's new teacher asked for one last word of advice, I told her to carefully foster the parent-teacher relationship because this is where she would get her greatest support. Once parents realize that a teacher truly cares and is trying his or her very best to help their child, a relationship of trust develops. The parents trust the teacher to be open about what is happening in the classroom, and the teacher trusts the parent to support his or her efforts. This means that when things do not go as well as expected, the teacher and the parents can work together to make things better. On the other hand, when things do go well and the child experiences learning successes, the teacher and the parents can share in the joy of watching the child grow.

Updating Zachary's Story

We revisited Zachary when he was in Grade 4. He was doing well academically, but he was still having difficulty coping in the busy environment of a regular classroom. His father described Zachary's situation as follows:

> This year Zach was transitioned into a regular class gradually from the social development class that he had at the end of his Grade 2 year and entire Grade 3 year. He was very successful in that environment, where the class size was small (seven students) and there were two teaching assistants along with the regular classroom teacher. He is having difficulties in the regular Grade 4 class, which is much larger and very noisy. There are some boys in the class who have not been diagnosed per se but definitely have behavioural issues. Zach is still very hearing sensitive and finds the environment very overwhelming. He has left the classroom on occasion as it has been unbearable in terms of the sensory overload. The staff and resource teacher have developed a plan where he receives positive breaks in the late morning. He is able to handle the mornings well, but is usually overloaded by the afternoon. He goes swimming and skating once a week in the late mornings and that has helped. We are now looking into having him go into the next level of a social development class on some afternoons. It would allow him be in a smaller class of eight students where the environment is quieter and calmer. He could use this time to finish up his core reading, math, and writing assignments. Unfortunately, the traditional class setting has not worked well for Zach. He is happiest and feels most in control in smaller settings with more teacher assistant support. The key is to keep Zach from feeling overwhelmed. When he feels in control, he is happy and, as a result, learning comes easier to him. He continues to spend time with friends outside of school as he is a social guy. In addition, he loves to swim, skate, and is an awesome downhill skier!

It is apparent that Zachary's sensitivity to the stresses of a busy classroom was having a negative impact on his learning experiences. Fortunately, he was doing well academically and had made many strides in his social skills, particularly when interacting with his friends outside of school. So what is it about school that continues to trigger Zachary's feelings of anxiety and sensory overload? Well, the classroom environment is an external stressor that can never be fully predictable. Think of all that can happen with absolutely no notice—a chair gets tipped over, a group of students begin to talk loudly, the fire alarm rings, someone knocks on the door, the teacher reprimands a student who is misbehaving—the list of possibilities is endless.

It is likely that Zachary will always experience stress within the school environment, as the potential stressors he will encounter will only become greater in his later school years. Consequently, it is critical that Zachary's parents and teachers remain acutely aware of his response to stress and help him regulate his stress levels to the greatest extent possible. The ultimate goal is to allow Zachary to reach his academic potential while continuing to develop emotionally and socially. This may be possible in the regular classroom if the appropriate supports are in place.

What We Know . . .

Stress and the Student with ASD

Hamlin (2016) has worked with families affected by autism for over 30 years. She noted that every time she meets a new family, the parents talk about how their child with ASD is anxious and stressed. One of their primary goals is to help their child feel calmer, both at home and at school. According to Lytle and Todd (2009), children with ASD have a heightened stress response and take longer to recover from stress. Their review of the literature revealed that research involving brain imaging, measurement of endorphins, and levels of cortisol have demonstrated that "stress and ASD are inseparable" (p. 38). In fact, the behaviour of children with ASD closely matches the behaviour of individuals with excessive stress and anxiety (e.g., repetitive movement, compulsive behaviour, hypervigilance, changes in cognitive function, and atypical attention). Therefore, Lytle and Todd recommended that teachers employ the following strategies to reduce stress throughout the instructional day and to help students with ASD learn to regulate their own stress levels.

Strategies to Reduce Stress in an Educational Setting

Environment

- Close doors or cover shelves to hide material that is not in use.
- Turn off or cover fluorescent lights, or replace with incandescent lighting.
- Minimize noise by speaking in a softer voice, turning down public address systems, and closing the door to the hallway.
- Avoid using loud noises, such as clapping or whistling, to get students' attention.

Familiarization

- Allow time for a student to become familiar with a new environment.
- Introduce a new environment just a few minutes at a time.
- Follow a visit to a new setting by a return to a comfortable setting.

Relaxation Corners

- Provide an area for relaxation or preferred sensory input.
- Encourage students to indicate when they might benefit from spending time in the relaxation corner.
- Make the student's preferred calming sensory activities available in the relaxation corner.

Routines

- Provide routines that are constant, visible, and followed.
- Provide schedules that show when activities will occur, their order, and how long they will last.
- Avoid surprises in the school-day routine.

Choice

- Provide choices and a variety of activities and materials.
- Build free time into the schedule and provide several activities the student may choose from.

Communication

- Present instructions at the student's level of understanding through preferred methods of communication.
- Be sure that instructions are clear and unambiguous.
- Clearly present expectations for success.

Exercise

- Provide physical activity breaks for the student.
- Take a brisk walk as often as every 90 minutes, which helps students to stay calm and focused.

Source: Republished with permission of Sage publishing, from Lytle, R., & Todd, T., "Stress and the student with autism spectrum disorders: Strategies for stress reduction and enhanced learning." *Teaching Exceptional Children*, 41(4), 2009. Permission conveyed through Copyright Clearance Center, Inc. .

Summary

Autism spectrum disorder is usually diagnosed at a young age based on the behavioural criteria contained in the *Diagnostic and Statistical Manual of Mental Disorders*. For example, Zachary was diagnosed with autism because he met the following specific behavioural criteria: (a) persistent deficits in social communication and social interaction across contexts, and (b) restricted, repetitive patterns of behaviour, interests, or activities. Students with autism spectrum disorder exhibit varying abilities and disabilities, but often have sensory and motor difficulties as well as some level of intellectual disability. Their education requires specialized interventions—ideally these interventions begin at a very early age and are delivered by specially trained professionals who continue to provide support upon the students' entry to school. Strategies for teaching these students include the use of task analysis, shaping techniques, visual cues, and task variation. Educators must also employ strategies to reduce the student's stress throughout the instructional day.

Learning More about Students with Autism

Academic Journals

Autism
Autism Research
Developmental Psychology
Journal of Applied Behavior Analysis
Journal of Autism and Developmental Disorders
Journal of Communication Disorders
Research in Autism Spectrum Disorders
Teaching Exceptional Children

Books

Bauman, M. L., & Kemper, T. L. (Eds.). (2006). *The neurobiology of autism* (2nd ed.). Baltimore, MD: The John Hopkins University Press.

Boutot, E. A. (2016). *Autism spectrum disorders: Foundations, characteristics, and effective strategies* (2nd ed.). Boston, MA: Pearson.

Canavan, C. (2016). *Supporting pupils on the autism spectrum in primary schools: A practical guide for teaching assistants.* Abingdon, UK: David Fulton Publishers.

Goldstein, S., Naglieri, J. A., & Ozonoff, S. (Eds.). (2009). *Assessment of autism spectrum disorders.* New York, NY: The Guildford Press.

Grant, R. J. (2016). *Play-based interventions for autism spectrum disorder and other developmental disabilities.* New York, NY: Routledge.

Herbert, M., & Weintraub, K. (2012). *The autism revolution: Whole-body strategies for making life all it can be.* New York, NY: Ballantine Books.

Lyons, T., & Siri, K. (2012). *Cutting-edge therapies for autism.* New York, NY: Skyhorse Publishing.

Webber, J., & Sheuermann, B. (2008). *Educating children with autism.* Austin, TX: PRO-ED, Inc.

Web Links

Autism Canada

http://autismcanada.org
Autism Canada is committed to adhering to the principles that guided both of its founding organizations, Autism Society Canada and Autism Canada Foundation. Autism Canada acts

as a united national voice focusing on the issues that affect individuals living on the spectrum and their families.

Autism Ontario

www.autismontario.com
Autism Ontario is dedicated to increasing awareness regarding the day-to-day issues faced by individuals with autism, their families, and the professionals with whom they interact.

Autism Society of America

www.autism-society.org
The ASA site provides comprehensive information about autism, including characteristics and causes, diagnosis, treatment, and educational issues.

Autism Spectrum Disorder

www.nimh.nih.gov/health/topics/autism-spectrum-disorders-asd/index.shtml?utm_source=rss_readersutm_medium=rssutm_campaign=rss_full
The US National Institute of Mental Health provides an overview of autism spectrum disorder, including signs and symptoms, treatments, and featured publications.

Autism Spectrum Disorders Canadian–American Research Consortium

www.autismresearch.ca
The ASD-CARC website includes interactive online questionnaires designed to uncover different information regarding individuals with autism spectrum disorders and their family members. It also provides links to important online resources and useful agencies.

Kilee Patchell-Evans Autism Research Group

http://kpearg.com
This research group, located at Western University, is focused on finding the basic processes involved in the symptomology of autism. They are particularly interested in how metabolic products of the gut microbiome control brain function and behaviour in autism.

Research Autism

www.researchautism.net
Research Autism strives to make a significant contribution to the understanding of autism by presenting information on autism issues, autism interventions, and the findings of evidence-based research.

Taking It into Your Classroom . . .

Including Students with Autism

When a student who has autism is first placed in my classroom, I will

- review what I know about autism and locate resource materials,
- read the student's file,
- consult with the student's previous teachers,
- consult with the student's parents, and
- meet with the school-based team to discuss the student's current school year.
- Other: _____

When I suspect a student in my classroom has autism, I will

- review what I know about autism and locate resource materials,
- observe the student's behaviour in different classroom or school situations,
- consult with other school personnel who are familiar with the student,
- consult with the student's parents, and
- meet with the school-based team to present the information I have collected.
- Other: _____

Key points to remember in my daily interactions with a student who has autism:

- The student may be unable to understand the social intentions of others.
- The student may lack the ability to engage in appropriate social interactions.
- The student may lack the ability to communicate through language.
- The student may use echolalia.
- The student may engage in repetitive activities.
- Other: _____

Key points regarding programming for a student who has autism:

- The classroom environment should be structured.
- Classroom activities should be predictable and routine with attention to transitions.
- Curricula should address weaknesses (e.g., attending and language skills).
- Curricula should address appropriate play and social interactions.
- A functional approach to behaviour should be implemented.
- Other: _____

Key points regarding evaluation of the progress made by a student who has autism:

- Evaluation should be based on what the student is expected to know and understand.
- Evaluation should include careful observations of the student's behaviour.
- Evaluation should identify any reduction in the behaviours that interfere with learning.
- Evaluation should include assessment of products as well as affective outcomes.
- Evaluation should identify strengths and weaknesses.
- Other: _____

CHAPTER 10
Students with Sensory Impairments

LEARNING OBJECTIVES

After learning the material in this chapter, you should be able to:

- Define the terms *sensory impairment* and *hearing impairment*.

- Describe how a hearing loss is categorized by degree of loss, type, and configuration.

- Provide examples of the type of tests used to assess the hearing of young children.

- Outline the types of communication used by individuals with hearing loss.

- Define the term *cochlear implant*.

- Outline the possible causes of both congenital and acquired hearing loss in children.

- Describe the developmental difficulties (e.g., speech and language, social and emotional) that children with hearing loss often experience.

- Provide examples of the specialized equipment used by students with hearing impairments.

- List several teaching strategies that teachers of students with hearing loss can use to ensure optimum opportunities for learning.

- Summarize the similarities and differences (e.g., definition and diagnosis, developmental issues, specialized equipment, education issues) between a student with a visual impairment and a student with a hearing impairment.

Name: Tyler Collins

Current Age: 14

School: Hillcrest Secondary School

Grade: 9

Tyler is a bright, friendly high school student who enjoys a variety of extracurricular activities.

At age two, it was determined that Tyler has a profound, sensorineural hearing loss. Until recently, he wore two hearing aids that allowed him to acquire well-developed language and communication skills. He is currently adjusting to receiving sound through his newly implanted cochlear devices. Even with a significant hearing impairment, Tyler has experienced much academic success over the years largely due to his advanced cognitive abilities and his parents' excellent working relationship with his school support team. However, he also experiences a significant level of difficulty with attention, concentration, and impulsivity and has been diagnosed with attention-deficit/hyperactivity disorder. Despite the challenges of his hearing loss, having ADHD, and being on the receiving end of some bullying at school, Tyler is a well-adjusted adolescent who exhibits excellent interpersonal relationship skills as well as good coping skills.

Summary of Children's Resource Services Psychological Assessment

Age at Time of Assessment: 5 years, 7 months

Tyler is a charming 5-year-old boy with a profound hearing loss in both ears. He wears hearing aids that correct his hearing to 25dB. He receives regular tutoring from an auditory verbal therapist and benefits from educational assistant support in his classroom. His teacher wears an FM system to maximize his ability to hear instructions.

For the most part, Tyler was co-operative during testing, although he was easily distracted when doing tasks that required listening and responding verbally. He tended to respond quickly and sometimes impulsively, not always waiting for all instructions to be given. Despite this impulsivity, Tyler often self-corrected his answers. He excelled at tasks that involved pointing at pictures and using blocks or other objects to answer questions.

According to the information gathered for this assessment, Tyler's cognitive skills are unevenly developed. His Nonverbal Cluster score on the Differential Abilities Scale fell at the 87th percentile, in the above-average range, indicating excellent development of his non-verbal abilities. Tyler's non-verbal reasoning skills are advanced, as are his visual-spatial analysis skills. His fine motor dexterity is age appropriate, and he is able to copy shapes using pencil and paper. His academic readiness skills are nicely developed.

In contrast to these good skills, Tyler's language skills remain weak for his age. His score on the Preschool Language Scale, 4, placed his receptive and expressive skills below the average range, although his receptive skills appeared to be better developed than his expressive skills. His performance on a test of spoken grammar was also weak—Tyler does not yet use certain grammatical structures when speaking. His working memory is also limited for his age. Tyler's weaker language skills need to be monitored carefully by his classroom teacher. His weaker language skills in combination with his weak working memory may make it difficult for him to comprehend verbal instructions and follow through appropriately. Tyler may also have some difficulty expressing his ideas coherently.

Tyler's phonological-awareness skills are developing, but are not strong. He has some trouble manipulating sounds within words and blending sounds together. These weaknesses could hamper his ability to learn to sound out words.

Tyler's visual-motor integration skills are adequately developed for his age, but his ability to print letters is lagging behind age expectations. He would benefit from direct instruction and practice in printing to prepare him for Grade 1. Tyler's gross motor skills are lagging behind age expectations.

Questionnaire results suggest that Tyler is somewhat impulsive and overactive. His attention is also poor, but only when he is engaged in tasks that are predominantly verbal. Tyler would benefit from a structured program to help curb his impulsivity. His teacher will need to be aware of his high activity level. Breaks should be provided at appropriate intervals to help Tyler cope with his need to move, thus allowing him to concentrate when required.

Tyler Collins

Speech and Language Assessment

Age: 6 years, 5 months

Test of Language Development, Primary (TOLD, P:3)

Subtest	Percentile Rank	Age Equivalent	Outcome
Picture Vocabulary	25	5.3 years	low average
Relational Vocabulary	75	7.6 years	high average
Oral Vocabulary	37	5.3 years	average
Grammatic Understanding	63	6.9 years	high average
Sentence Imitation	5	3.9 years	below average
Grammatic Completion	25	5.3 years	low average
Word Discrimination	91	9.6 years	above average

The Token Test for Children

Tyler's performance revealed that he experienced the most difficulty following instructions that exceeded one directive and those that contained linguistic concepts. He also experienced difficulty following instructions that involved reasoning. He was observed to occasionally use the effective strategy of re-auditorization, that is, repeating all or part of the instruction that had been presented to him.

Goldman Fristoe 2 Test of Articulation

An assessment of sound production skills revealed Tyler's use of several sound substitutions. There was also evidence of sound sequencing difficulties. Tyler's speech intelligibility was not impacted as a result of the above-mentioned sound substitutions.

Summary

Tyler's overall language abilities were found to be at the 30th percentile in comparison to his age-mates, revealing skills within the low-average range. It is recommended that Tyler receive 10 sessions with the school-based communicative disorder assistant under the direction of the speech and language pathologist. The focus should be on grammatical skills and strategies to assist with following verbal instructions.

Excerpt from Tyler's Current IEP

Accommodations

Instructional	Environmental	Assessment
• Use communication book.	• Minimize distractions.	• Provide more frequent breaks.
• Provide extra time for processing.	• Provide a small-group setting.	• Offer visual aids and concrete materials.
• Offer assistive technology, such as subtitles on videos.	• Offer preferential seating away from noise sources.	• Use scribing as applicable.
• Provide scribing, reduced written expectations, and computer options as applicable.		• Use alternative settings as applicable.
• Offer pre-teaching of new vocabulary and concepts.		• Offer computer options.
• Use visuals as a frame of reference.		

Annual Program Goals

Tyler will further develop higher-level writing skills at a rate of 90 per cent of the time. He will develop good self-advocacy skills related to his hearing needs at a rate of 90 per cent of the time. Tyler will develop executive functioning skills at a rate of 80 per cent of the time.

Learning Expectations	Teaching Strategies	Assessment Methods
• Learn new figurative language and apply it to his daily writing 70 per cent of the time.	• Pre-teach new vocabulary. • Use visual aids.	• Use oral and written activities.
• Proofread and revise his writing, and increase the complexity of his sentence structure 75 per cent of the time.	• Provide a checklist that describes the steps in a given process.	
• Take responsibility for appropriate FM system usage at a rate of 80 per cent of the time.	• Offer prompts. • Provide positive reinforcement. • Encourage self-checking.	• Demonstration • Data collection
• Develop his organizational, independent learning, and test-taking skills, meeting goals 70 per cent of the time (appropriate preparation for class, meets homework expectations).	• Encourage repeated practice. • Provide positive reinforcement.	• Demonstration • Data collection

Neurodevelopmental Assessment

Date of Assessment: January 26, 2012

Tyler is a 13-year-old boy with sensorineural hearing loss bilaterally caused by the Phelps malformation of the cochlear. He was referred for a pre-operative neurodevelopmental assessment in January 2012 as part of the Cochlear Implant Program.

Tyler's mother was 33 when he was born. The pregnancy was normal with the exception of a urinary tract infection at five months gestational age for which she took antibiotics. There were no other known infections or fevers during pregnancy, and she did not take any medications or use alcohol, drugs, or smoke at that time. She did not have gestational diabetes. Tyler was born at term weighing 7 lbs., 8 ozs. There was no need for resuscitation and his Apgars were approximately 9 and 10 at 1 and 5 minutes, respectively. He did have some jaundice in the first month and a half of his life.

His parents reported that at 2 years old Tyler was not developing speech. An audiologist's assessment revealed a moderate to severe hearing loss. A CT scan revealed the Phelps malformation of the cochlea. He has had hearing aids since that time and has participated in auditory verbal therapy for seven years.

At 10 years of age, a psycho-educational assessment indicated that Tyler has superior non-verbal skills and high-average verbal skills. He was also diagnosed with ADHD due to his attention difficulties, impulsivity, and hyperactivity; therefore, he takes slow-release Ritalin 40 mg daily and Melatonin 4 mg nightly. His parents report that Tyler enjoys socializing with peers but has some difficulties with subtle social cues and personal-space boundaries. He has a history of being bullied.

Developmental History

Tyler was slow to sit (7 months) and walk (19 months). As a toddler he walked with a wide-based gait, using his hand on the floor to provide balance. He has always had balance problems, which have caused him to be clumsy at times. He is able to ride a bike, catch a ball, skip and hop, and navigate stairs with no difficulties. He participates in basketball, wrestling, skiing, and baseball.

His language was delayed due to his hearing impairment. He said his first words at about 3 years of age. He currently speaks in complete sentences, can explain experiences in detail, and is able to give complex directions to others. As his hearing loss has progressed, he has demonstrated some articulation deficits and as a result his speech-recognition computer programs do not always correctly distinguish what he is saying. He demonstrates no unusual expressive language, no echolalia, and has had no language regression. He uses appropriate non-verbal gestures and facial expressions that are properly directed. Tyler can type, use word-processing software, and understand written material at the Grade 9 level or higher.

Tyler's social skills are very good, and he interacts well with a variety of peers, both in person and on Skype. He has many reciprocal friendships, he shares enjoyment with others, and often starts conversations with others on a topic of their interests. He plays computer games, can role-play, and has no history of non-functional play such as lining up toys or spinning or repetitive behaviours with toys. He is able to follow the rules in complex sports.

Tyler has attention difficulties as well as some impulsivity and hyperactiveness. He does not have any highly circumscribed interests or preoccupations. He is not rigid regarding routines, but does find transitions without warning (at least 10 minutes) difficult.

In terms of sensory interests, Tyler's parents reported that he does like sleeping on rough textures like a towel. He likes the smell of shampoo and the sensation of flannel. He also responds positively to the deep pressure of being cocooned and squeezed. There is no history of sensory aversions. He does not flap his hands or body tense or spin his body.

In terms of activities of daily living, Tyler is fully independent. There are no difficulties with feeding, toileting, or dressing.

There is no family history of learning disability or developmental disability, blindness, deafness, genetic or metabolic, or neurological or psychiatric conditions. Tyler has had seven ear infections (otitis media). His nutrition has been adequate, his immunizations are up to date, and he has an allergy to dust mites. Tyler's growth has been normal. There is no history of hospitalizations.

Psycho-Educational Assessment

The Vineland Adaptive Behavior Scales (2nd Edition) was administered. This is an interview-based developmental adaptive assessment that looks at skills in the areas of communication, daily living skills, and socialization.

Communication

Tyler's expressive language is very well developed (age equivalent of 22 years plus). His receptive language skills were at a moderately low adaptive level but were likely influenced by his inattentiveness and his inability to sit and talk for more than 10–15 minutes at a time. He likely did not fully grasp the testing instructions provided five minutes before the test. Nonetheless, he does have some difficulty understanding abstract language receptively. In terms of his written language skills, he achieved an adequate adaptive level.

Daily Living Skills

Tyler's daily living skills were adequate to moderately high.

- His personal adaptive level was adequate with an age equivalent of 14 years.
- His domestic skills were adequate with an age equivalent of 15 years.
- His community skills were at a moderately high level with an age equivalent of 16 years, 9 months.

Socialization

In terms of socialization skills, Tyler again achieved adequate to moderately high scores.
- His interpersonal relationship skills were adequate with an age equivalent of 14 years, 9 months.
- His play and leisure skills were at a moderately high level with an age equivalent of 22+ years.
- His coping skills were adequate with an age equivalent of 12 years.

Tyler Collins

Because of slight indications of previous autistic-like behaviours, the Autism Diagnostic Observation Schedule (Module III) (ADOS) was administered. The ADOS is a semi-structured play-based assessment that evaluates features on the autism spectrum. Tyler did not meet the criteria for autism spectrum disorder.

Language

Tyler's overall language was well developed. He uses complex sentences appropriately and correctly, and except for a few idiosyncratic uses of words and phrases, he demonstrated no speech abnormalities. He was able to have a conversation with the assessor that flowed and built on the assessor's dialogue. Tyler demonstrated a wide variety of descriptive, conventional, instrumental, and informational gestures.

Social Interaction

Tyler's reciprocal social interactions were very good during the assessment session. He provided good-quality social responses on most occasions. He demonstrated a number of appropriate facial gestures, exhibited his understanding of emotions and empathy for others, and had good insights into the nature of social relationships and his role in them.

Imagination and Creativity

Tyler demonstrated a well-developed imagination and creativity in play and creative story tasks.

Behaviour and Sensory

No sensory interests were observed. Tyler did not talk about an excessive interest or make reference to unusual or highly specific topics or have any repetitive behaviours. It was noted that he did display overactivity during the assessment and frequently stood up when expected to be sitting and frequently touched things around the room.

The Social Responsiveness Scale (evaluates social awareness, social cognition, social communication, social motivation, and autistic mannerisms) and the Sensory Processing Measure were both administered by Tyler's parents and his teacher. They all scored him in the typical range for social responsiveness, just below the cut-off for mild social behaviour deficiencies. In terms of sensory processing, his parents described, not surprisingly, some problems in hearing processing as well as balance. His teacher identified difficulties with social participation due to problems with sensory processing difficulties—hearing, body awareness, balance, and motion. Overall, Tyler does exhibit some problems that may be consistent with a sensory processing disorder.

Summary

Tyler is a 13-year-old boy with a history of progressive sensorineural hearing loss associated with the Phelps malformation of the cochlea. He has known balance difficulties. He also has a known diagnosis of ADHD. He has well-developed language and communication skills. His previous psychology assessment indicates high-average verbal skills and superior non-verbal cognitive skills. He has advanced personal, domestic, and community daily living skills. He also has well-developed social skills. He does have some sensory processing difficulties that could represent a sensory processing disorder. Tyler is scheduled to undergo surgery for a unilateral cochlear implant on February 6, 2012.

Tyler Collins

Why Is Tyler Considered to Be Sensory Impaired?

Definitions

An individual is deemed to be sensory impaired when one or more of his or her senses (i.e., hearing, vision, smell, touch, taste, or spatial awareness) is no longer functioning at a typical or normal level. Tyler's difficulties involve his sense of hearing, so he is more specifically described as having a hearing impairment. The term *hearing impairment*, which is typically used in Canadian schools, refers to the full range of possible degrees of hearing loss. Several other terms are used to describe the general categories of loss. For example, the Council for Exceptional Children (CEC; 2013) defines *deafness* as a hearing loss that has a negative effect on educational performance and is so severe that the individual has great difficulty processing linguistic information through hearing, with or without the use of hearing aids. The CEC also uses the term *hard of hearing* to describe children with a hearing impairment; these individuals are not deaf but have a hearing loss that adversely affects their educational performance and communication skills. Tyler fits into this category.

According to the Canadian Academy of Audiology (2016b), the more specific degrees of hearing loss are determined by measuring, in decibels (DB), how loud a sound must be to be just barely heard. The following categories are then used to describe an individual's hearing loss: minimal (16–25 DB), mild (26–40 DB), moderate (41–55 DB), moderate to severe (56–70 DB), severe (71–90 DB), or profound (90+ DB). In Tyler's case, he was diagnosed with a "profound" hearing loss in both ears (bilateral) at age 22 months. In other words, sounds must be above 90 decibels for Tyler to hear them without the use of an amplification aid.

What We Know . . .

Categories of Hearing Loss and the Effect on Students in Classrooms

According to the BC Ministry of Education, teachers may benefit from considering the general effects each category of hearing loss has on students:

Minimal loss	Students may have difficulty hearing faint or distant speech. Peer conversation and teacher instructions presented too rapidly, particularly in noisy classrooms, are likely to result in missed information.
Mild	Students may miss up to 50 per cent of class discussions, especially if voices are soft or the environment is noisy. Students will require the use of a hearing aid or personal FM system.

Moderate	Classroom conversation from three to five feet away can be understood if the structure and vocabulary is controlled. Hearing aids or personal FM systems are essential. Specific attention will need to be directed to language development, reading, and written language.
Moderate to severe	Without amplification students with this degree of loss can miss up to 100 per cent of speech information. Full-time use of amplification is essential. They will probably require additional help in all language-based academic subjects.
Severe	Students can only hear loud noises at close distances. They require individual hearing aids, intensive auditory training, and specialized instructional techniques in reading, language, and speech development.
Profound	For all practical purposes these students rely on vision rather than hearing for processing information. If you have a student in this category, he or she is usually a candidate for signing systems and specialized instructional techniques in reading, speech, and language development.

Hearing loss is not only categorized by the degree of loss, it is also classified by type and configuration. Type refers to the part of the auditory system that is damaged, the three basic types being conductive hearing loss, sensorineural hearing loss, and mixed hearing loss. Tyler has a sensorineural hearing loss. The configuration refers to the degree and pattern of hearing loss across frequencies—a loss can affect the ability to hear low tones, high tones, or both.

conductive hearing loss
Sound is not conducted efficiently through the ear canal, ear drum, or middle ear.

sensorineural hearing loss
Damage to the inner ear (cochlea) or hearing nerve in the brain.

mixed hearing loss
Having a combination of a conductive hearing loss and a sensorineural hearing loss.

What We Know . . .

How the Deaf Community Feels about Definitions of Hearing Impairment

According to the Canadian Cultural Society of the Deaf (2012), members of the Deaf community do not view themselves as having a disability:

Deaf is just a hearing loss, no matter how great or little the degree of loss . . . We do not view ourselves as deficient . . . The pathological terms "impaired" or "disabled" clearly do not reflect who we are. We are a cultural and linguistic minority group. We share a common language (American Sign Language and Langue des Signes Québécoise) . . . We prefer to call ourselves "Deaf" and proudly so. "Deaf" is a cultural, sociological term accurately reflecting our identity and our right to have and use our rich language, culture, and community.

Assessing a Hearing Impairment

Tyler's hearing impairment was not obvious at birth nor was it recognized during his first two years of life. While his parents, Peter and Lynda, were concerned about some of his early behaviours, Tyler's first hearing assessment did not occur until after his second birthday. Peter explained:

> *Tyler was born on November 11, Remembrance Day, and certainly for my wife, Lynda, and I it is a day we will never forget. His birth was uneventful albeit the fact that he was born in the middle of the night and the attending obstetrician's comment was that he "should have had a catcher's mitt" because Tyler entered this world in such a hurry, and he's never slowed down since. He was born weighing seven pounds eight ounces—a fussing, flushed infant.*
>
> *Not content from birth, Tyler always seemed fussy. He didn't sleep well, or for long, and was hard to quiet when he often cried at night. Tyler has an older sister, Mia, and she was easily contented with rocking and singing when she was upset, unlike Tyler. I feel like I'm characterizing Tyler as such an unhappy child, but really he was the happiest little boy I've ever seen during the daytime. He was quiet and busy, and always smiling and anyone who picked him up was greeted with the strongest and longest of hugs. At this point we knew nothing about the syndrome that Tyler would later be diagnosed with. One of our most amusing memories is how we could stop Tyler in his tracks at night literally with a light switch. The first time it happened Lynda, Mia, Tyler and I were full swing into the bedtime routine, and reading to Mia in her room. Tyler was still crawling at this point and was headed straight for a light socket (where he would most certainly stick his finger in if allowed) and Lynda yelled for me to grab him. I smiled and turned off the lights in the room. Lynda screamed at me "Peter! Get him." When I turned on the light, Tyler was lying asleep on the floor. However, with the light now back on, Tyler got up on all fours and immediately commenced his path to the light switch as if nothing had just happened, at which point I turned off the light again. Yes, when the light came on there was Tyler again lying asleep on the floor. It was a game we could play all evening.*
>
> *In retrospect, we should have realized something was amiss at this point. Years later, we were watching a family video of Tyler playing in the playroom, and I'm calling him, "Tyler, Tyler, Tyler . . ." to which I state into the camera "Lynda, I think we gave him the wrong name."*
>
> *At 18 months of age, Tyler had no language. My wife, concerned about his hearing, saw our pediatrician, who put these concerns down to "an overanxious mother." It wasn't until six months later that Lynda, now convinced that something was not right, using that strong intuition that mothers possess, booked an appointment with a local* audiologist. *I took Tyler to the appointment, and after an hour of beeps and tones, the audiologist ensured I was sitting down and then informed me that my son was deaf.*

audiologist
Healthcare professional who assesses and treats hearing and balance problems.

Unfortunately, it is not unusual that a child with a hearing impairment fails to be diagnosed during the first few years of life. After all, language development, which is certainly affected by hearing loss, is expected to flourish during toddlerhood. When language milestones are not met, parents often begin to worry and seek out help from health professionals. It should be noted that there are newborn screening tests for hearing that involve observing how an infant responds to sound. However, in Canada, these tests are not administered for all births.

Something to Think About

There are regions of Canada that have implemented newborn screening programs for hearing loss. However, there are other areas of Canada where such programs do not currently exist. As an educator, what concerns do you have about the lack of a universal screening program? How do you think an early diagnosis may facilitate a child's later success in school?

According to the Canadian Academy of Audiology (2016b), there are several tests that can be used to assess the hearing of young children. For very young children who are too young to respond, these include otoacoustic emissions (OAE), auditory brainstem response (ABR), and behavioural observation audiometry (BOA). For young children who are able to respond, tests that may be used include visual reinforcement audiometry (VRA) and play audiometry. Once children are four to five years of age, they can usually be assessed in the same manner that adults are tested (using a range of tests that require individuals to indicate whether or not they have heard a particular sound).

Hearing test results are typically presented on a graph that is referred to as an audiogram. This graph provides a picture of an individual's hearing ability. The vertical lines on the graph represent pitch or frequency, while the horizontal lines represent loudness or intensity. An example of Tyler's audiogram (at age 11) is presented in Figure 10.1.

Once assessment results demonstrate a hearing loss, especially in the case of young children whose cognitive and language development is at risk, the audiologist and other relevant professionals move quickly to determine what can be done to fully or partially correct the loss and what education and therapy is needed. Tyler's father, Peter, described how he and Lynda reacted during this emotional period:

My wife and I were devastated. There's really no other word for it. I felt that my son's future had been suddenly and irrevocably crushed. Period. Until you have a child diagnosed with a disability, there's really no way to understand the horrible mixture of feelings that comes with this knowledge. We were very fortunate to be quickly directed to a family who also had a deaf son. They had chosen an auditory route. He was a teenager who could not only talk to his family, friends, and neighbours, but was also on the honour roll at his local high school. Lynda and I sat in their living room still in a state of shock, but at least now we felt we had options. We had Tyler seen by an ear, nose, and throat (ENT) specialist, had him fitted with hearing aids by the local audiologist, and enrolled him in auditory verbal therapy (AVT) all within two weeks.

It is clear that while Tyler's diagnosis occurred later than desired, his parents moved quickly to give him the best support they could find. These efforts would prove beneficial in terms of Tyler's language development and school readiness skills.

otoacoustic emissions (OAE)
A microphone placed in the inner ear detects any response to sound that is introduced through a probe in the outer ear.

auditory brainstem response (ABR)
Electrodes placed on the scalp and each earlobe monitor the brain's response to clicking noises sent through earphones.

behavioural observation audiometry (BOA)
Child is presented with sounds while an audiologist watches for changes in behaviour to indicate that the sound has been heard.

visual reinforcement audiometry (VRA)
Child is presented with sounds. The expected response is localization to the sound source. Each expected response is reinforced with a visual distracter.

play audiometry
When a child hears a sound, he or she must pair the sound with an activity in a game.

ear, nose, and throat (ENT) specialist
A physician trained in the medical and surgical treatment of the ears, nose, throat, and related structures of the head and neck.

auditory verbal therapy (AVT)
A parent-centred approach that encourages the use of spoken language to help children learn to listen and to speak.

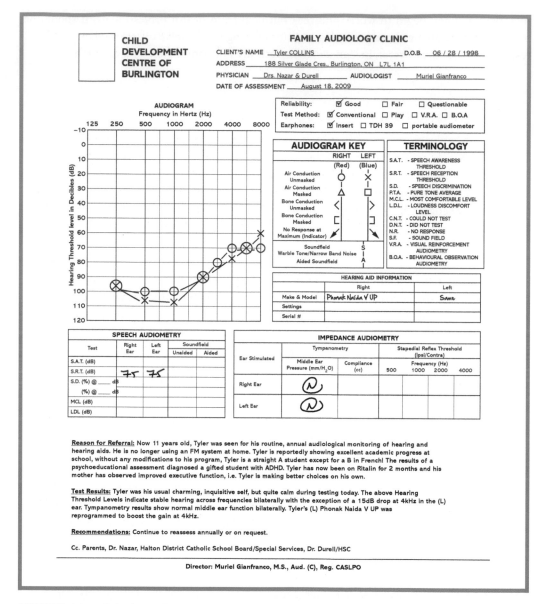

FIGURE 10.1 Tyler's audiogram.

What We Know . . .

Types of Communication Used by Individuals with Hearing Loss

- American Sign Language (ASL) is "a natural language used by members of the North American Deaf Community. It is a language that has developed naturally over time among a community of users. ASL exhibits all of the features of any language, in that it is rule-governed, its symbols are organized and used systematically, it is productive, the number of sentences that can be made is infinite, and new messages on any topic can be produced at any time. In ASL, hand shape, movement and other grammatical features combine to form signs and sentences." (Gallaudet University)

- The auditory oral approach is based on the principle that many "deaf and hard-of-hearing children can be taught to listen and speak with early intervention and consistent training to develop their hearing potential. The focus of this educational approach is to use the auditory channel (or hearing) to acquire speech and oral language." (Alexander Graham Bell Association for the Deaf and Hard of Hearing)

- The auditory verbal approach is "similar to the auditory oral approach in that there is a strong emphasis on maximizing a child's residual hearing and his ability to use it" (Alexander Graham Bell Association for the Deaf and Hard of Hearing). "It focuses on the use of sound (audition) as the primary channel for learning and gaining meaning from the environment. Parents are at the centre of this approach and take a full and active part in every session with the Auditory-Verbal therapist." (Auditory Verbal UK)

- Cued speech is "a visual communication system that uses eight hand shapes in four different placements near the face in combination with the mouth movements of speech to make the sounds of spoken language look different from each other." (National Cued Speech Association)

- Langue des Signes Québécoise is the Quebec sign language used by deaf people in Quebec and other centres in Canada. It is closely related to American Sign Language and French Sign Language.

- Manually Coded English systems refer to a number of sign language systems that use grammar and sentence structures of English (e.g., Contact Sign, Signed English).

- Speech reading is the ability to gain understanding of speech by watching lips, facial expressions, gestures, contextual cues, body language, as well as lip reading.

Source: Alberta Education (2007), p.9.

What Factors Contributed to Tyler's Sensory Impairment?

Not unlike most parents of children with exceptionalities, Peter and Lynda wanted to know the cause of their child's condition. As with other sensory impairments, like vision loss, it is extremely important to know whether or not the condition will worsen over time and if so what can be done to prevent or slow this progression.

The summer before Tyler entered school he experienced a change in his hearing. Peter and Lynda took him to be assessed for a cochlear implant. Part of that assessment included determining the cause of Tyler's hearing loss:

cochlear implant
A surgically implanted electronic device that helps to improve hearing in individuals with severe to profound impairments.

Up to this point in time, no one had been able to tell us the root cause of Tyler's hearing problems. When he had a sudden drop in his residual hearing, we were advised to go further in seeking out the reason for his deafness. What most people don't understand is that deaf people have a certain amount of "residual" hearing. It is this residual hearing that is exploited with high-powered hearing aids and intense therapy to allow deaf children to learn to listen and speak. Lynda and I began the process of having Tyler assessed for a cochlear implant at Sick Kids Hospital in Toronto. It was the first of what I would characterize as "a long string of bad news" from Sick Kids. After his first work-up, Tyler was assessed with a genetic condition called Phelps dysplasia—characterized by a highly malformed cochlea—and attention-deficit/hyperactivity disorder (ADHD) among other things. Then more bad news: Tyler was considered a high-risk candidate for a cochlear implant, and considering his current progress would not be implanted any time in the near future.

In her report, the geneticist who considered Tyler's case provided the following information on genetics and hearing loss, and she also explained how Tyler may have acquired a non-working gene:

Congenital hearing loss (hearing loss present at or around the time of birth) occurs in about 1 in 1,000 births. About half of the time, hearing loss of this nature is due to genetic causes. Many different genes have found to be associated with hearing loss. Genes are tiny packages of information that contain all of the instructions that determine how the body grows and develops. There are 30,000 to 40,000 genes in each cell in our bodies. Changes (mutations) can occur in genes, causing them not to work properly. Genes are found on structures called chromosomes. There are a total of 46 chromosomes in each of our cells, and they come in pairs. Twenty-two pairs of chromosomes are the same in males and females. The 23rd pair contains the sex chromosomes. They determine the sex of an individual: females have two X chromosomes and males have one X and one Y chromosome.

Tyler's CT scan of the inner ear showed bilateral Phelps dysplasia. This is consistent with a diagnosis of "conductive deafness with stapes fixation," also known as DFN3 or Gusher deafness. DFN3 is caused by a non-working copy of a particular gene called POU3F4 located on the X chromosome. It is inherited in an X-linked recessive manner. This means that females who carry a non-working copy of the gene are not clinically affected, since they have another working copy of the gene on their other X chromosome. However, since males only have one X chromosome, if they have a non-working copy of the gene, they will be affected.

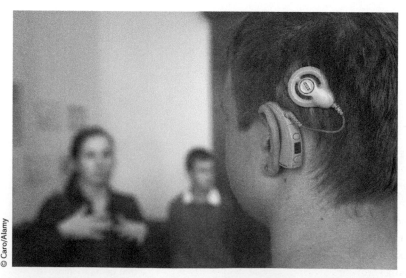

© Caro/Alamy

A great deal of controversy surrounds cochlear implants, particularly when the procedure is performed on children. Some members of the Deaf community don't believe there is anything to be fixed and consider its use to be an affront to their culture.

There are two ways Tyler could have a non-working POU3F4 gene. He could have inherited this change from his mother, or it could be a new change in him. If it was inherited from his mother, then his sister would have a 50 per cent chance of being a carrier. Unfortunately, there is currently no testing to determine which scenario occurred in Tyler's case.

What We Know . . .

The Causes of Hearing Loss in Children

According to the Canadian Academy of Audiology (2016a), hearing loss present at birth (congenital) can be caused by

- illness or infection the mother had during pregnancy,
- medicines taken by the mother during pregnancy,
- other medical problems (syndromes),
- physical abnormality of any part of the ear, or
- hereditary factors.

Hearing loss that develops later (acquired) can be caused by

- difficulty during birth,
- jaundice,
- meningitis, scarlet fever, mumps, or other illnesses associated with high fever,
- neurodegenerative disorders,
- medications that are toxic to the inner ear,
- head injury or trauma to the ear, or
- repeated or constant ear infections.

How Has Tyler's Sensory Impairment Affected His Development?

Cognitive Development

From an early age, it was clear that Tyler had strong cognitive abilities. When he was 5 years old, his general cognitive abilities were assessed using the Differential Ability Scale (DAS). Not surprisingly, given his delayed speech and language development, his non-verbal skills were the most advanced (see *Summary of Children's Resource Services Psychological Assessment* on p. 299). In fact, Tyler performed in the "above-average" range according to his non-verbal cluster score. During the same assessment, his school readiness skills were determined to be very good. He demonstrated that he had an excellent grasp of most of the concepts that are prerequisites for early academic success.

Tyler's cognitive abilities were also assessed at age 10 using the Wechsler Intelligence Scale for Children, Fourth Edition (WISC-IV). Again, his non-verbal cognitive ability proved to be advanced, as he scored in the "superior" range. His reasoning abilities on verbal tasks fell in the "average" range, as did his general working memory abilities and general processing speed abilities. According to the psychologist who administered the test, these results are noteworthy:

> *Tyler's achievement of an average verbal intelligence score, which must be considered a minimal estimate of his potential in this area, is quite remarkable given his profound hearing loss and the ensuing pervasive barriers to spoken language and communication. Tyler's intellectual capacity is clearly advanced.*

What We Know . . .

Characteristics of Students Who Are Both Gifted and Hearing Impaired

- Development of speech-reading skills without instruction
- Early reading ability
- Excellent memory
- Ability to function in the regular school setting
- Rapid grasp of ideas
- High reasoning ability
- Superior performance in school
- Wide range of interests
- Non-traditional ways of getting information
- Use of problem-solving skills in everyday situations
- Possibly on grade level
- Delays in concept attainment
- Self-starters
- Good sense of humour
- Enjoyment of manipulating the environment
- Intuition
- Ingenuity in solving problems
- Symbolic language abilities (different symbol system)

Source: Willard-Holt (1999).

Speech and Language Development

Tyler's speech and language development was significantly delayed as a very young child because of his hearing loss. This delay was in fact the impetus for his first visit with an audiologist. Once he was fitted with hearing aids and began receiving intensive AVT, his speech and language began to improve. By the time he entered Grade 1, a speech and language assessment revealed that many of his language skills were well within the average range. However, he still demonstrated delays in the area of expressive grammar (e.g., omitting final markers to indicate plurals and possessive nouns) and he had some problems with the intelligibility of his speech.

Overall, his language abilities were found to be at the 30th percentile (low-average range) in comparison to his age-mates (see *Speech and Language Assessment* on p. 300).

By Grade 5, Tyler's language abilities ranged from average to very superior, which is quite impressive given his profound hearing loss and his early delays in language development. During a psycho-educational assessment, his performance on the Wechsler Individual Achievement Test, Second Edition, revealed that his listening comprehension skills were in the "very superior range," his oral expression skills were in the "high average range," and his written language skills were in the "average range."

Currently, Tyler's teachers report that he is doing very well in all areas of language arts. In fact, he is obtaining grades of As and Bs in his English studies. He is performing at the same level in French. To put this in context, a psychologist who assessed Tyler stated:

Although Tyler clearly does very well with his hearing aids at school, and he communicates in spoken English, hearing aids do not provide users with normal hearing and barrier-free access to language and communication. Tyler, like other deaf students, has to work exceedingly hard at accessing spoken language. His success is a testament to his general level of intelligence, hard work, and perseverance.

What We Know . . .

The Language Development of Children with Hearing Loss

Vocabulary

- Vocabulary develops more slowly in children who have hearing loss.
- Children with hearing loss learn concrete words like *cat, jump, five,* and *red* more easily than abstract words like *before, after, equal to,* and *jealous.* They also have difficulty with function words like *the, an, are,* and *a.*
- The gap between the vocabulary of children with normal hearing and those with hearing loss widens with age. Children with hearing loss do not catch up without intervention.
- Children with hearing loss have difficulty understanding words with multiple meanings. For example, the word *bank* can mean the edge of a stream or a place where we put money.

Sentence Structure

- Children with hearing loss comprehend and produce shorter and simpler sentences than children with normal hearing.
- Children with hearing loss often have difficulty understanding and writing complex sentences, such as those with relative clauses ("The teacher whom I have for math was sick today.") or passive voice ("The ball was thrown by Mary.")

Continued

- Children with hearing loss often cannot hear word endings such as *"s"* or *"ed."* This leads to misunderstandings and misuse of verb tense, pluralization, non-agreement of subject and verb, and possessives.

Speaking

- Children with hearing loss often cannot hear quiet speech sounds such as *"s," "sh," "f," "t,"* and *"k"* and therefore do not include them in their speech. Thus, speech may be difficult to understand.
- Children with hearing loss may not hear their own voices when they speak. They may speak too loudly or not loud enough. They may have a speaking pitch that is too high. They may sound like they are mumbling because of poor stress, poor inflection, or poor rate of speaking.

Source: American Speech-Language-Hearing Association (2013).

Social and Emotional Development

According to his parents and his teachers, Tyler has always been a happy child who has been well-liked by his peers. His senior kindergarten teacher described him as an average student in terms of co-operation and self-control. She did say he was a little more assertive than most kindergarten students and he displayed some attention problems. However, she considered these behaviours fairly typical of children Tyler's age. At the time, Tyler's parents were a little more concerned than the teacher. They identified that Tyler had difficulties maintaining focus and attention and he exhibited hyperactivity. More specifically, they noticed that their son often acted without thinking, interrupted others when they were speaking, and could not sit still at mealtimes. It would be several years before a diagnosis of ADHD was confirmed and the appropriate medications were prescribed. In the meantime, Tyler coped well.

When Tyler was 10 years of age and in Grade 5, his teacher described him as "outgoing, pleasant, and energetic." However, she expressed concerns about his restlessness and difficulties with attention in terms of how these behaviours were impeding his learning and isolating him socially. It was at this time that another psycho-educational assessment was conducted. The psychologist who administered the testing interviewed both Tyler and his parents. He described these interviews as follows:

> *Tyler was very easy to interview. Information that he shared with me suggests that he feels very loved and supported by his parents. He was easily able to list some of his many strengths and positive qualities, particularly his sense of humour and interest in others. Tyler stated that he has some good friends at school and outside of school as well. He spoke to me freely about his deafness and the supports in place for him. He appears entirely at ease with his hearing loss and takes it very much in stride. He knows many other deaf children, one who attends his school. Tyler is very much aware that the adults around him would like him to listen more and follow directions more often and more quickly but, despite his efforts to do so, he finds this very difficult.*
>
> *Tyler's parents had an abundance of very positive comments to make about their son, including that he is friendly and outgoing, bright, kind, capable, and unique in*

many ways. Both parents, however, reported Tyler to have elevated levels of inattention and very high levels of physical activity/hyperactivity. They also expressed their concerns regarding Tyler's level of social skills and have enrolled him in a social skills learning program outside of school.

Now that Tyler is a teenager attending high school he faces new academic and social challenges. But as Tyler has displayed in the past, he is adaptable and not overly concerned about the challenges he faces. His Grade 9 teacher reported that he is very interested in socializing with his classmates and loves to chat with them. His parents also indicated that Tyler acts very much like a regular teenager—he talks on the phone, has friends over, plays sports, goes on group dates, attends birthday parties, and so on. Tyler certainly seems to enjoy the company of his peers, and this feeling appears mutual. While there have been difficulties along the way, the support Tyler has received from his parents, teachers, and other professionals, along with his obvious resiliency, have resulted in high levels of self-confidence and well-developed social skills.

What We Know . . .

Promoting the Social and Emotional Well-Being of Students with Hearing Impairments

According to Alberta Education, educators should do the following:

- Be aware of student–peer relationships and provide support and guidance, when necessary. Some students with hearing loss may be unaware or misunderstand incidental information and social nuances.
- Promote social interaction and reduce isolation for students who use sign language.
- Provide communication support during extracurricular activities, field trips, and assemblies.
- Foster students' understanding of their interests, strengths, and areas of need, and promote self-advocacy skills so students can ask for what they need.

Source: Alberta Education (2013).

From the Psychologist's Notebook

When considering a child's social or emotional development, it is often revealing to speak with siblings as well as parents. In Tyler's case, his sister wrote me a very honest letter about her life with her brother. It raises a number of issues about how all members of a family are affected by the high needs of a particular child. Tyler's sister wrote:

Ever since I was little, my brother has jumped at every opportunity to drive me insane. Growing up with him has definitely not

Continued

been easy, but I know someday I'll be able to look back and laugh at all his crazy antics. Although he has great characteristics, his multiple needs and disabilities cause him to be the biggest pain in the butt that you could ever imagine.

At first, living with Tyler was easy. This was when he wasn't talking, but after being diagnosed as deaf my entire family pretty much fell into chaos. Even though I was really little I can still remember the multiple trips to Sick Kids Hospital, and speech therapy, that my parents made weekly. In my eyes, I grew up attention deprived, and less important. This wasn't true. It just seemed that way, and even though I couldn't see it, life was much harder for my brother. The main focus of my family quickly became teaching my brother to speak and act like an ordinary individual. However, Tyler was and still is anything but ordinary.

From the day he got his hearing aids and onward, Tyler was difficult. It started out as tantrums in the supermarket and always wandering off and getting lost. Slowly, his shenanigans progressed and he realized that irritating me was one of the most entertaining things he'd ever experienced. Long car rides with him were absolute hell. At home he'd always be in my personal space. Wrestling and fighting became normal to us, as well as multiple time-outs and groundings. My parents did everything in their power to help us get along but that soon proved to be out of the question. I have learned to just ignore him, but occasionally he'll make me flip out.

Our problems soon became only his problems. Tyler didn't sleep at night when he was younger, and during the extra awake hours he managed to get himself into multiple problems. During the day he was also up to a lot of stuff. Tyler is also one of the clumsiest people I have ever seen and this is coming from me, a girl who walks into glass doors, and trips walking up stairs. My parents say that because of his syndrome his balance is off. This causes him to trip, "fly," and crash. A lot. There are so many stories of him in the emergency room that I wouldn't even know where to start, or end. Coincidentally, almost all of the times we've had to make a trip to the hospital because of him, it has ended up ruining a vacation, or a perfectly fine day. Along with his clumsiness, Tyler has managed to destroy many of my personal belongings. I can recall a time when I was 12 where he dropped my laptop, causing it to break into two pieces. At the time this felt like the end of the world.

Slowly our relationship began to disintegrate, but as I look back on the past I don't feel anger anymore. These events that have caused me to feel so much hatred toward a boy who didn't intentionally mean to cause me pain have turned into stories that can make an entire room laugh. For the longest time I grew up believing my brother was a reflection of me, and that he was an embarrassment. This is very far from true. I love him. I accept him for all his differences, and I hope that others can do the same.

What Is School Like for Tyler?

Tyler's mother, Lynda, who later became an educational assistant, spent many hours in Tyler's early grade classrooms as a volunteer. She describes Tyler's school experiences as follows:

When Tyler first started school (senior kindergarten), it was circle time that was the most stressful for him. He didn't like to sit, and what we really didn't understand was that he had a difficult time hearing the teacher. We became educated when we were called into the school to discuss a situation where Tyler, all of 5 years old, stood up during circle time and told two other children to "Shut up! Shut up! Shut up!" It was never the curriculum that challenged him—it was always the behavioural expectations. He was impulsive, busy, restless, and had no sense of personal space. I lived at the school in those days. I volunteered as much as possible, and kept in constant contact with Tyler's teachers, the support professionals, and the principal.

During the next few years, Peter and I focused on Tyler's language and school. Tyler continued to receive weekly auditory verbal therapy, and we put our efforts into building him a large support team. Together, his AV therapist, his audiologist, the Sick Kids cochlear team, the itinerant teacher*, his educational assistant, his occupational therapist, and the child and youth worker all ensured that Tyler never slipped through the cracks at school. We kept in constant contact with the school through team meetings and regular progress meetings as well as maintaining a constant dialogue with his teachers and professionals through his communication journal.*

Scholastically, Tyler was progressing well. There were obvious delays with his expressive language, but he was excelling. Throughout those years, the constant theme was Tyler's behavioural issues rather than how he was doing in his school work. Unfortunately, when Grade 5 rolled around, he began to be bullied. It was what every parent of a disabled child fears most in school, but it was still no less of a shock when it did happen. We immediately enrolled Tyler in a social skills group to try and provide him with strategies to deal with and avoid the bullies that could pervade his life. It seemed that no one had the answers we were seeking for our son. He was deaf, but we were running into a lot of different issues than the parents at our parent support group were encountering. I heard about a doctor who specialized in the assessment of deaf and hard-of-hearing children, so we immediately sought out her services.

Tyler received a very in-depth assessment. The doctor's synopsis was like a splash of cold water in the face. Tyler had "mastered deafness." It was ADHD that was his major obstacle in life at this moment. Peter and I had never fully accepted a diagnosis of ADHD prior to this assessment, feeling that Tyler's issues were more linked to our failings as parents than any real and additional diagnoses. Faced with the facts of this assessment we sought out a medical intervention for Tyler. We found a pediatrician who specializes in children with ADHD. Tyler was put on Ritalin, and, within a few days, his teachers, who recently labelled him as "unteachable," were amazed at the difference.

Our life stabilized. For the first time we began to focus on our other child. We could almost run Tyler on auto-pilot. Sure there were the constant audiologist and doctor appointments, tutors, and tantrums. But Tyler had graduated from AVT in Grade 5, and because of the Ritalin and melatonin, our lives, for the first time since Tyler's birth, felt normal.

itinerant teacher

A fully qualified teacher who usually specializes in an area of education (e.g., the education of students with hearing or visual impairments) and provides assistance to teachers and students in a number of schools.

During Tyler's Grade 8 year, we were at what was now a routine visit at Sick Kids when the audiologist noticed a significant drop in Tyler's perceptive language. Concerned, we reopened the discussion of a cochlear implant. Another child with Phelps had recently been successfully implanted by our surgeon, Dr. Leask, and suddenly what seemed as too high risk was now conceivable. In February 2012, Tyler received a cochlear implant. On March 28 his implant was activated. Unlike the other Phelps child, Tyler's implant was giving him a lot of facial nerve stimulation. The outcome was that after one month of being activated, Tyler had only seven electrodes (of a possible 22) activated. He was re-enrolled in auditory verbal therapy with his original therapist. Again, we would begin the process of teaching our child to learn to listen, this time with a cochlear implant. Now, eight months later, Tyler has regained six electrodes and now has 13 activated. However, progress is slow.

Tyler is currently in Grade 9. He has really matured over the past year, and he loves high school. He's really risen to the level of responsibility and independence that high school requires. He's happy and confident. His story hasn't been completely written yet. Peter and I can only imagine where this will all end up. Wherever it is, we're ready because we are confident that Tyler will be happy.

Tyler recently wrote in his journal about the importance of his cochlear implant. It is quite apparent that his positive outlook has been affected by his ability to hear. He stated:

The choice to have surgery on my ear to hear well had a huge impact on my life and my Mom and Dad's life. It has created a new journey of hearing and it has helped me with my hearing and, to this day, I am still hearing new sounds and I am extremely happy of the choice I made. The three greatest joys in my life are hearing, speaking and understanding. Hearing is given from my hearing aids and my cochlear implant. Speaking was given from my Mom's confidence and seven years of non-stop therapy. Understanding is knowing and getting information from what is being heard. Those will stay as my greatest joys.

From the Psychologist's Notebook

Over the years I have come to know Tyler, I am struck by how outgoing and lively he is and by how his so-called impairment is the absolute least of his worries. Unless you were to observe him in certain situations, you would never know he is a student with special needs. He is carefree and precocious and exhibits a great deal of compassion toward others. However, he can be forgetful and impulsive at times.

Even though Tyler presents with co-occurring conditions, he is just like many students with exceptionalities. He has definite strengths and needs, each of which must be considered in his educational programming. He is very bright and very capable in some domains, yet he struggles with others.

Given his educational struggles, his recent surgeries and recoveries, and having to adapt to a new level of hearing, he is to be commended for his superb attitude. His new-found hearing, due to the cochlear implants, seems almost magical to him, opening up a whole new world that he seemed only on the fringe of previously. He definitely takes every day as it comes with total vim and vigour. Much of his educational success appears due to his temperament and outlook and, of course, the immense support and care provided by his parents. Over the years, I have become more and more convinced that the educational and personal success of students with exceptionalities is more a function of the student's attitude, his or her parental support, and the compassion of his or her teachers than it is a function of precise programming. That is not to say that proper programming can be ignored; it means that proper programming alone is not enough.

Something to Think About

What do you think are the characteristics of a compassionate teacher? In the case of a child like Tyler, how might a teacher balance being compassionate with making sure that Tyler learns the appropriate skills to be successful inside and outside of the school environment?

What Educational Approach Is Best for Tyler?

While Tyler is a very bright young man who does well with the regular curricula, there are two important factors—specialized equipment and classroom supports—that facilitate his success at school.

Specialized Equipment

Tyler's ability to do well academically can be largely attributed to the specialized equipment he has had access to since the start of school. First, and foremost, up until this year when he received his cochlear implant, Tyler benefited from wearing hearing aids, which were regularly adjusted by his audiologist to provide the amplification necessary for optimal hearing. Second, Tyler's teachers have always used an FM system to maximize Tyler's ability to hear what is being said within the classroom. According to the Canadian Academy of Audiology (2016a), an FM system, or assistive listening device, improves the signal-to-noise ratio for the listener and reduces the effects of poor acoustics. It has two parts; in Tyler's case, the teacher wears a transmitter when speaking to the class so that his or her voice is heard clearly through a receiver worn by Tyler. This device makes listening much easier and it also allows teachers to speak at a normal volume.

FM system

A frequency modulation system. It consists of a transmitter microphone used by the speaker (e.g., teacher) and a receiver used by the listener. The receiver transmits the sound to the listener's ears or directly to the hearing aid.

Changes within the Learning Environment

In order for Tyler to receive and process the information communicated by his teachers and keep pace with his peers, there are some necessary accommodations that have been established by the school-based team who monitors his progress (see *Excerpt from Tyler's Current IEP* on p. 301). The following adjustments to the classroom environment and to teaching methods were also suggested as a result of one of Tyler's psycho-educational assessments:

- Provide seating at the front of the classroom, near to and facing the instructor, to ensure that visual cues are optimally received.
- Face the student when using the board and visual aids, even when wearing a microphone for a student's FM system. Turning your back does not allow for lip-reading cues. Speak clearly at a normal rate. Speak in a natural tone of voice.
- Ensure that the lighting is adequate and that speakers are alerted to potential distractions such as gum chewing and hand placement that may interfere with lip reading.
- Visual aids should be used whenever possible. Use the board, maps, charts, illustrations, and captioned videos.
- When showing slides or videos, provide the student with an outline or summary of the materials to be covered in advance. Be careful not to speak over sound portions even if the student is using an assistive listening device.
- Repeat questions from others in the classroom before answering.
- Do not exaggerate pronunciation as this will deter understanding.
- Keep environmental noise to a minimum.
- Do not give out procedural information while handing out exams, papers, and so on. Make sure that instructions or information are clearly understood by the student after handouts are viewed.
- Emphasize important information such as assignments or schedule changes by providing written details to students (on the board or in handouts).
- Make sure the student understands the information presented to him or her. Do not accept a nod or smile as an indication of understanding. Ask the student content questions rather than yes or no questions.
- Include the student in all class experiences (e.g., student conversations and small-group activities).
- Keep in close communication with qualified specialists on the student's team, especially the itinerant teacher for the deaf or hard of hearing. The student may not yet have developed skills to advocate for him or herself in a general education setting.
- Help the student understand his or her own hearing loss and provide an opportunity for the student to share information with the class about hearing loss and how his or her hearing aids and FM system work.

These teaching strategies can ease the stresses experienced by all students with hearing loss, regardless of the degree of loss. It is most important that this information be communicated to teachers who, for the first time, find themselves responsible for the education of such students.

From the Psychologist's Notebook

With strong disclaimers about the dependability and accuracy of available data, the Canadian Association of the Deaf states that approximately 350,000 Canadians are profoundly deaf and approximately 3.2 million Canadians are hard of hearing (Canadian Association of the Deaf, 2012). Currently, because of newborn screening programs in some regions and early intervention services in most regions, the vast majority of Canadian children who are deaf or hard of hearing are diagnosed before they go to school, and many will have prescribed educational intervention programs before they enter a teacher's classroom. This means that barring any other co-occurring disorders (e.g., ADHD in Tyler's case), the student will likely master in the early years whatever adjustments he or she has to make to learn properly and to express that learning in appropriate ways. In this regard, students who are deaf or hard of hearing are noticeably different than many other students with exceptionalities. Most of those students are not diagnosed before they enter school, and many have to continually alter their modes of learning and their expressions of learning as they progress through the grades. For students who are deaf or hard of hearing, the primary focus is on the adjustments that teachers have to make.

Evaluation of Progress

Just like any student who has an individual education plan, Tyler's IEP (see *Excerpt from Tyler's Current IEP* on p. 301) outlines his current level of achievement, his annual learning goals, his short-term learning expectations, and the assessment methods to be used when determining whether or not goals have been met. Because Tyler is quite capable of completing the regular curricula, his progress is evaluated in a manner very much like that of his peers. However, there are some differences that are important in terms of allowing Tyler to fully demonstrate his knowledge. For example, the choice of evaluation methods (e.g., oral, written, or demonstration) must be carefully considered depending on the subject and task. Tyler's strengths (non-verbal reasoning abilities) and his relative weaknesses (sustaining attention and processing spoken language) must be acknowledged in an effort to allow him to express what he has learned. It is most important that students with hearing impairments, like Tyler, be consulted on a daily basis about their progress in terms of understanding instruction and assignments. Catching areas of confusion quickly prevents these students from lagging behind simply because they have not clearly understood the teacher. It is essential that educators recognize the added attention and energy resources that Tyler must expend to access communication. There are bound to be times when he is tired from listening and watching intently. Therefore, he is likely to miss important information, and his progress will be affected.

In the 2016 Census of Canada, 27,510 people reported that sign language (American Sign Language, Quebec Sign Language, or other) is the language used to communicate at home (Statistics Canada, 2016).

© Hemera/Thinkstock.com

How Is Tyler Different from Other Students Who Have Sensory Impairments?

There are two primary sensory impairments—hearing loss and vision loss. Tyler, with his profound hearing loss, shares many similarities with other students who also experience auditory difficulties. For example, he requires specialized equipment to enhance his ability to receive and process sound, and changes within the learning environment are also necessary for him to thrive in the classroom. Obviously, not all students with hearing impairments are just like Tyler. Their degree of loss as well as the type and configuration of their impairment may differ, and unlike Tyler, they may have acquired a hearing loss after birth. Furthermore, they may use a non-oral form of communication (e.g., a sign language system) and identify more closely with the Deaf community. They may even attend a school for the deaf.

Visual Impairments

retinopathy of prematurity
A disorder that affects the blood vessels in the eyes of premature babies.

There are also similarities and differences between Tyler's situation and that of students with visual impairments. This is best exemplified by considering the case of another high school student, Veena, who, like Tyler, was diagnosed with a sensory impairment at a very young age by medical specialists. In Veena's case, pediatric ophthalmologists determined that she had an eye disease called retinopathy of prematurity due to her early birth. While the retinopathy was treated with laser procedures and eventually healed, the long-term effects were significant myopia (nearsightedness) and a reduced field of vision. Veena's vision is partially corrected through the use of contact lenses, but she remains visually impaired—with correction she does not have normal sight.

What We Know . . .

Students with Visual Impairments

low vision
Diminished visual capability that cannot be improved to a sufficient level to enable an individual to perform common visual tasks adequately.

Visual impairment refers to a significant loss of vision in both eyes that cannot be corrected with glasses. The degree of loss may vary significantly, which means that each student with low vision or blindness needs individual adjustments to learn most effectively.

There are two main categories of visual impairment: low vision and blind. Most students with visual impairments have **low vision**, which means they are print users but require special equipment and materials. They should be encouraged to use their residual vision in their educational programs as much as possible. Students who are described as **legally blind** usually have some usable vision. The term *legally blind* is used to indicate entitlement to important government and private agency services.

legally blind
Worse than or equal to 20/200 acuity in the better eye or a visual field extent of less than 20 degrees in diameter horizontally.

Visual impairments are also classified as congenital (vision loss that is present at birth) or adventitious (vision loss later in life as a result of illness or accident). The age of onset and level of development before sight loss occurs are critical factors in the student's ability to acquire skills and concepts.

It is important for you to be aware that although two children with visual impairment may be assessed as having the same visual acuity, they may each learn and function in very different ways. Vision may actually fluctuate or may be temporarily influenced by such factors as fatigue, light glare, or inappropriate lighting. An understanding of the type of visual impairment is certainly important, but generalizations about the student's visual functioning cannot be made solely on the basis of the diagnosed eye condition.

Source: British Columbia Ministry of Education, 2017.

During her preschool years, Veena's vision capabilities were examined using a functional vision assessment (FVA). As in the case of Tyler, the goal was to ensure that Veena be given every opportunity to develop and learn at the same pace as her peers. The information gathered in this type of assessment is different from that gathered during a clinical vision evaluation or an eye test. While the goal of a clinical examination is to determine whether a child can see, and to what degree, the purpose of an FVA is to determine how and what a child sees and what can be done to best facilitate his or her learning. FVA information can make an immeasurable contribution to the design of a child's educational program.

An ideal FVA gathers information from the child's existing medical records, from the family, and from any other medical or educational professionals who may offer a unique perspective on the child's abilities. This variety of information from several sources is used to determine and confirm the quality and quantity of functional vision evident in the child's normal routines such as play, communication, self-help, and mobility. With this type of information, educators can design interventions to properly reinforce the transfer of available functional vision abilities to the child's real-life settings. Again, this is similar to how those involved in all aspects of Tyler's young life contributed to a plan for optimizing his strengths and minimizing his weaknesses.

Developmental Issues Related to Visual Impairments

Even though Veena met most of her developmental milestones as a young child, she did experience a delay in her speech and language development. Her parents were surprised to learn that this delay could be partially attributed to her visual impairment. Like Tyler, Veena benefited from speech and language therapy. Her parents had expected some delays in her cognitive and motor development, due to her inability to see well, but Veena actually excelled in both of these areas. She has, however, had some ongoing social and emotional issues, mostly related to feeling different. She says she is often left out in terms of the activities engaged in by her peers.

```
From the Psychologist's Notebook

There are some developmental issues that are not uncommon in children with
visual impairments.

Speech and Language

A common misconception about children who are visually impaired or blind is
that they are equally or more capable in terms of language skills than their
                                                                    Continued
```

normally sighted peers. In actuality, severe and early vision impairments often negatively affect language development because of a limited access to the environment and because these children lack the visual references that accompany the integration of other forms of information from the individuals around them.

Social and Emotional

Children with visual impairments often struggle to adapt socially because they miss the social cues of body language and they are usually not aware of the reactions of others to their own body language. Hence, they may transmit body language that erroneously suggests feelings they are not experiencing. These children also appear to demonstrate higher incidences of psychiatric disorders, but there is considerable concern about such findings among educators because the criteria used to determine the diagnoses are based on the sighted population. Therefore, it is difficult to determine whether the manifestations are the actual symptoms of a psychiatric disorder or whether they are a representation of the child's visual impairment. As in the case of many exceptionalities, it is therefore crucial that assessments for such disorders be conducted by professionals familiar with visual impairment. For example, many totally blind children engage in autistic-type stereotypic movements such as hand or finger flicking, rocking, body swaying, and tapping. But their behaviours are more likely an expression of under- or overstimulation. As a result, these children resort to repetitive behaviours as a means of coping with an environment that has become too visually complex to manage. When the environmental stimuli become more visually acceptable, the excessive behaviours are usually reduced.

The Education of Students with Visual Impairments

Veena's educational experiences parallel Tyler's quite closely. She depends on specialized equipment and technology to receive and communicate information, and her IEP outlines several adjustments within the learning environment that are necessary if she is to keep pace with her classmates. Her itinerant teacher for the visually impaired has been a great support in ensuring that her school experiences are positive and conducive to efficient and effective learning.

What We Know . . .

Facilitating Learning for Students with Visual Impairments

A student with visual impairments typically requires a variety of adjustments within the classroom environment to facilitate learning as he or she progresses through school. These are usually determined by an itinerant teacher or consultant who conducts the functional visual evaluation, acquires the specialized materials needed by teachers and the student, and collaborates with educators to make sure that all components of the educational plan are coordinated and understood by everyone. Depending on the student's needs, the itinerant teacher or consultant may serve the student directly in the classroom, or simply provide consultation to the educational team.

A variety of adaptations and accommodations may be used by students who have varying degrees of visual impairment. For students with low vision, these may include increased contrast and colour highlighting, lighting adaptations, optical devices, and auditory materials. For students who are blind, these will likely include the use of Braille, tactile adaptations such as raised maps, the use of real objects and materials, and auditory descriptions in place of notes. Students with visual impairments may also benefit from instruction in orientation and mobility skills that are not part of the standard curriculum. Curricular areas that are important for many students who are visually impaired include instruction in daily living skills, career development, communication literacy, use of assistive technology, use of functional vision, and social skills.

A learning media assessment is often used to identify the primary and secondary media necessary for reading and other learning activities. Students who are visually impaired may need one or more of the following to enable them to read:

- Reading stands or reading positions that allow reduced viewing distances
- Decreased viewing distance or the use of a handheld or stand magnifier or other optical devices to read standard print
- Enlarged print
- Braille
- Monoculars and telescopes for distance viewing
- Technological accommodations such as closed circuit televisions (CCTVs) or screen enlargement programs for computers
- Auditory learning in combination with the above

Many students who do not use vision will rely heavily on tactile and auditory materials. Braille is the most efficient tactile code used for reading. It is produced in standard paper and book form and can be written and read using portable note-takers with Braille displays or computer output. Most students with visual impairments rely on auditory information for part of their learning. Books on tape or CD, spoken output from the computer, and use of tape recorders for memos provide a quick means of access.

Source: Adapted from Liyange (2002).

Something to Think About

Having read about Tyler and Veena's sensory impairments, in your opinion, which type of impairment—hearing or vision—presents the most barriers to learning? As an educator, would you be most comfortable teaching a student with a hearing impairment or a student with a visual impairment? Why?

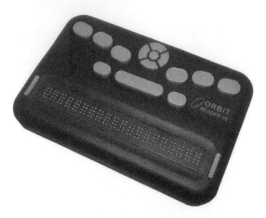

Increasingly sophisticated technology is revolutionizing how Braille readers obtain written information and communicate. Portable, refreshable Braille readers can receive information from free smartphone applications such as BrailleBack, through a wireless Bluetooth connection.

Photo: © dennizn/Shutterstock.com

Closing Tyler's File

Tyler, like many other students with special needs, faced many challenges in his preschool and elementary school years. His current success with the transition to high school has much to do with how these early challenges were addressed. His teachers, his therapists, his audiologist, all members of his school-based team, and especially his parents continually monitored his progress and immediately acted on any identified concerns. When his language development was delayed, he was assessed, fitted with hearing aids, and immersed in auditory verbal therapy. When he had trouble with his first year at school, his mother became a classroom volunteer. When his behaviour was not appropriate, he was assessed and treated for ADHD. When he was bullied, he was enrolled in a social skills group. Tyler never fell through the cracks. Instead, he thrived. He has been given every opportunity to develop his strengths and lessen the effects of his weaknesses. Because of this, just as a psychologist told his parents, "Tyler has mastered deafness." In fact, it appears that this effort to help Tyler has resulted in the attainment of many skills that would serve any student well in high school and life in general. Tyler's story is one that educators can learn much from. Perhaps, most importantly, it shows how educators should refrain from focusing on what may appear to be the student's "biggest problem." Rather, educators should concentrate on what they do best—helping students learn—by taking advantage of all the expertise, recommendations, and assistance provided by other key individuals, including the student's parents. When the student does face problems in the classroom, whether they are academic, behavioural, or social, it is the educator who will likely first notice these problems and bring them to the attention of the student's team of support personnel. Together, solutions can be decided upon and then put in place and monitored by the educator, all the while keeping all aspects of a student's development in mind.

Summary

Students with sensory impairments, like Tyler and Veena, have one or more senses (e.g., hearing, vision) that no longer function at a typical or normal level. These impairments are most often diagnosed before entry to school and, as a result, maximum benefit is gained from early intervention services. In general, the more severe the impairment, the more difficult it is for the student to learn in a classroom setting without specialized equipment. Adjustments or changes to teaching methods, as well as the learning environment, are also usually necessary to ensure that the student has every opportunity to receive information, process it, and communicate what he or she has learned. Students with sensory impairments receive much support from a school-based team. Their strengths and needs are clearly identified in their individualized education plans.

Learning More about Students Who Have Sensory Impairments

Academic Journals

American Annals of the Deaf
British Journal of Visual Impairment
The Hearing Journal
Hearing Review
Journal of Deaf Studies and Deaf Education
Journal of Speech, Language, and Hearing Research
Journal of Visual Impairment and Blindness

Books

Barclay, L. A. (2012). *Learning to listen/listening to learn: Teaching listening skills to students with visual impairments*. New York, NY: AFB Press.

Bishop, V. E. (2004). *Teaching visually impaired children* (3rd ed.). Springfield, IL: Charles C Thomas.

Marschark, M., & Hauser, P. (2011). *How deaf children learn: What parents and teachers need to know*. New York, NY: Oxford University Press.

Marschark, M., & Spencer, P. E. (2010). *Oxford handbook of deaf studies, language, and education* (Vol. 2). New York, NY: Oxford University Press.

Moores, D. F., & Martin, D. S. (Eds.) (2006). *Deaf learners: Developments in curriculum and instruction*. Washington, DC: Gallaudet University Press.

Nanci, A. S. (2012). *Deaf education in the 21st century: Topics and trends*. Boston, MA: Pearson.

Salisbury, R. (Ed.). (2008). *Teaching pupils with visual impairment: A guide to making the school curriculum accessible*. New York, NY: Routledge.

Spencer, P. E., & Marschark, M. (2010). *Evidence-based practice in educating deaf and hard-of-hearing students*. New York, NY: Oxford University Press.

Web Links

American Foundation for the Blind

www.afb.org
The AFB presents information about living with visual impairments. Professional development opportunities for educators are offered.

Blind and Low Vision

www.teachspeced.ca/blind-and-low-vision
The Ontario Teachers' Federation provides teaching strategies and resources for those working with students who have visual impairments.

Bright Hub Education

www.brighthubeducation.com/special-ed-hearing-impairments/67528-tips-and-strategies-for-teaching-hearing-impaired-students
This site outlines strategies for teaching students with hearing impairments, including classroom adaptations, communication considerations, visual strategies, curriculum accommodations, and evaluation.

Hard of Hearing and Deaf Students: A Resource Guide to Support Classroom Teachers

www.bced.gov.bc.ca/specialed/hearimpair/toc.htm
The British Columbia Ministry of Education provides a resource guide for classroom teachers to assist them in educating students with hearing impairments.

Hearing Health and Technology Matters

http://hearinghealthmatters.org/hearingviews/2012/eleven-misconceptions-that-teachers-should-know-about-children-with-hearing-loss/
The Hearing Views forum discusses misconceptions teachers should know about children with hearing loss.

Medical/Disability Information for Classroom Teachers

www.learnalberta.ca/content/inmdict/html/index.html
This site provided by the Alberta Government offers teachers medical and disability information on a number of conditions including hearing loss and vision impairment. The critical information is not necessarily what the medical conditions or disabilities are, but rather how they impact a student's learning, social or emotional behaviour, and the classroom environment.

Professional Resource Centre for the Visually Impaired

www.prcvi.org/professional-resources.aspx
The Provincial Resource Centre for the Visually Impaired (PRCVI) is a British Columbia Ministry of Education Provincial Resource Program established to assist school districts in educating students whose access to learning is restricted because of a visual impairment or blindness.

Students with Visual Impairments

www2.gov.bc.ca/assets/gov/education/kindergarten-to-grade-12/teach/teaching-tools/inclusive/students-with-visual-impairments.pdf
The British Columbia Ministry of Education provides teachers with a comprehensive resource guide for teaching students with visual impairments.

VOICE for Hearing Impaired Children

www.voicefordeafkids.com
The VOICE network develops and implements programs and services in four principal areas—parent support, public education, advocacy, and auditory verbal therapy.

Taking It into Your Classroom . . .

Including Students Who Are Hearing Impaired

When a student who is hearing impaired is first placed in my classroom, I will

- review what I know about hearing impairments and locate resource materials,
- read the student's file,
- consult with the student's previous teachers,
- consult with the student's parents, and
- meet with the school-based team to discuss the student's current school year.
- Other: _____

When I suspect a student in my classroom is hearing impaired, I will

- review what I know about hearing impairments and locate resource materials,
- collect information about the student through observation,
- consult with other school personnel who are familiar with the student,
- consult with the student's parents, and
- meet with the school-based team to present the information I have collected.
- Other: _____

Key points to remember in my daily interactions with a student who is hearing impaired:

- The student may benefit from additional visual cues when receiving information.
- The student may rely on lip-reading cues when communicating with others.
- The student may need to receive some information in written form.
- The student may be working very hard to understand spoken language.
- The student may feel embarrassed about asking for verbal information to be repeated.
- Other: _____

Key points regarding programming for a student who is hearing impaired:

- The student should be exposed to the regular curricula unless otherwise indicated.
- The student may need additional time to process and complete language-related tasks.
- The student may require additional help in all language-based academic subjects.
- The student may benefit from specialized instructional techniques.
- The student may benefit from the pre-teaching of new vocabulary and new concepts.
- The student may require assistive technology, such as FM systems and subtitles.
- The student may need access to scribing and special computer programs.
- Other: _____

Key points regarding evaluation of the progress made by a student who is hearing impaired:

- The evaluation methods for the student should be clearly outlined in an IEP.
- Evaluation methods should be varied (e.g., oral, written, and demonstration).
- There should be recognition that the student may not be equally advanced in all areas.
- The student should be asked to provide daily feedback on his or her understanding of class lessons and assignments.
- Evaluation should identify strengths and weaknesses.
- Evaluation should lead to new instructional goals.
- Other: _____

CHAPTER 11
Students with Multiple Disabilities

LEARNING OBJECTIVES

After learning the material in this chapter, you should be able to:

- Explain what is meant by the term *multiple disabilities* and describe the impact that multiple disabilities can have on a child.

- Discuss how teachers can proactively build positive relationships with parents of children with exceptionalities.

- Describe how teachers can increase the likelihood that non-communicative students will show an interest in their environment and make attempts to communicate.

- Describe intervention strategies that teachers can implement to facilitate peer relationships in the inclusive classroom.

- Describe the collaborative approach to providing educational services to students with multiple disabilities.

- Discuss the use of transition portfolios and describe types of items they may contain.

- Discuss the importance of addressing the social needs of students with multiple disabilities throughout their school years.

Name: Monique Levesque

Current Age: 14

School: Munroe Junior High School

Grade: 8

Monique is a good-humoured teenager who loves to hum the melodies of her favourite songs.

She also enjoys attending local sporting events and being around animals, especially horses and dogs. Due to her physical disabilities, Monique is dependent on a wheelchair for mobility. She also has severe communication problems that make conversing with others a significant challenge. It is apparent from Monique's story that it takes a great deal of support from a variety of professionals in order for some students to be accommodated in the regular classroom. However, it can be done if these professionals work together to provide an appropriate learning environment for the student. Regular classroom teachers certainly play a role in educating students with multiple disabilities, but they must never be in a situation where they feel solely responsible for meeting the needs of these very special students.

Monique Levesque

Monique's Transition into Kindergarten Summary of Skills and Abilities

Age at Time of Transition: 4 years, 11 months

Monique is an engaging child who was born with multiple physical needs. She has decreased range and ease of movement in her joints. She may not have typical muscle groups and the muscles she has are weak. Monique has had surgery on her feet but has otherwise been healthy. Both hips are dislocated, but stable. Her right knee is unstable and causes some discomfort when bent, so she cannot tolerate kneeling. Monique tends to tip her head back to look at things; however, vision is reported as normal.

Summary of Child's Current Functional Abilities

Mobility/Positioning

Monique can use a manual wheelchair to propel herself 10 to 15 feet on smooth, flat terrain. She requires assistance to negotiate corners and to travel longer distances. Monique can roll from her back to her side and can assist in sitting up. She lies down from sitting independently and tolerates lying on her stomach for five minutes. She sits independently in long-leg sitting but needs a pillow behind her as her balance reactions are slow. She can sit on a low bench with one person nearby, but needs full assistance to get on and off of it. Monique uses a standing frame for up to 40 minutes but needs full assistance to get in and out of it. She wears ankle-foot-orthoses daily.

Self-Care

Monique can finger- and spoon-feed herself independently. She needs a raised edge on the plate/bowl to help her scoop. Monique is slow in organizing and chewing food, may have decreased oral sensation, and tends to get distracted. In the past, Monique has had some coughing/choking episodes and therefore needs supervision while eating, especially for crunchy and chewy foods. She drinks from a regular cup. Monique needs maximal assistance for dressing, but she should be encouraged to assist as much as she is able. She is not toilet trained. In school, she will require a change table and a supportive toilet seat with side/trunk support and a footrest.

Hand Skills

Monique needs to be well supported during fine motor activities. She can be seated in her wheelchair or in an adapted wooden chair but the table height must be no higher than her bellybutton in order for Monique to use her arms successfully. Monique has limited range of movement in her shoulders and arms and has difficulty reaching above shoulder height, turning her hands palm-side up, and bending her knuckles. She does best with movements when her hands are close to her body and in midline. Monique can participate in crafts and activities with larger objects; however, she has difficulty manipulating smaller objects. She uses loop scissors mounted on a wooden block for cutting. Activities using two hands together are challenging and she does better if she can stabilize objects against her body.

Communication/Symbols

Monique has a few words that she is able to say: "mom," "dad," and "yeah." Her vocalization typically consists of vowel sounds and "g" or "k" sounds. She tends to vocalize to indicate pleasure and has recently begun to vocalize the melody of songs. Monique has a small vocabulary of "signs" that have been modified in consideration of her limited hand and arm mobility. She tends to use her signs when prompted but not often spontaneously. At home, Monique typically communicates through signs, looking, pointing, and gesturing.

Monique uses a laptop computer that is programmed for voice output. The computer is mounted on Monique's wheelchair by a metal post with a plastic key guard covering the keyboard. Monique can turn the computer on and off independently. She has six "pages" of pictures and she can move between the pages independently. The computer is set up with a touch-screen such that when Monique touches a picture on the screen her message is spoken aloud. Monique has been taking the computer to playschool since February 1997.

Monique attends playschool two afternoons a week. She uses the computer in the kitchen centre to interact with the other children and at circle time when taking turns.

Monique needs encouragement to use the computer to interact verbally with the other children. She wants to be close to the other children but tends to watch them or play parallel to them. Communication delays make co-operative play difficult. Monique uses paper picture boards at other centres in the classroom (i.e., playdough, craft, snack). The paper boards are taped to the table and the vocabulary is activity specific. Monique uses these boards if prompted.

Learning

Monique was seen by a psychometrist in June 1996 for an assessment of her developmental abilities to aid in decision making regarding therapy and learning goals. Monique demonstrated delayed performance in all areas with receptive comprehension of language and various terms and concepts being a relative strength for her.

Child's Support Needs

Monique requires assistance to move around on the floor and to get in and out of her wheelchair. She needs assistance with dressing/undressing and toileting and should be supervised when eating. Monique needs prompting to use her computer, signs, picture boards, and words to interact with the other children and she needs support in helping the other children learn her ways of communicating.

Monique Levesque

Pediatric Review

Age at Time of Review: 6 years, 10 months

Monique is an only child. Monique's mother was 33-years-old at the time of her pregnancy. Monique's father is a business owner who is in good health. There is a paternal cousin with mild cerebral palsy and developmental delay. He is ambulatory.

The pregnancy was complicated by pneumonia during the first month of gestation. The mother was treated with the drug erythromycin. An ultrasound done at 16 weeks gestation was normal. Movements were not very active throughout the pregnancy. Monique was born by spontaneous vaginal delivery at 39 weeks. Birth weight was 5 pounds, 11 ounces. Resuscitation was required after birth. Monique was removed from the delivery room for a few minutes but then brought back to her parents. There was meconium stained amniotic fluid (may be aspirated during labour and delivery causing neonatal respiratory distress). Monique was noted to have multiple deformities of her limbs.

Monique is currently a 6-year, 10-month-old girl with the following problems:

Arthrogryposis Multiplex Congenital

Monique has bilaterally dislocated hips, a subluxed right knee, and kyphosis. She has had extensive investigations including an MRI, muscle and skin biopsy, and EMG, but no underlying diagnosis has been found. There is no current need for surgery.

Duane Syndrome

Monique recently had eye surgery. On examination, Monique now has much less extension of her neck when fixating on items in front of her. Her posture is very functional and much improved over one year ago. There continues to be limited abduction and adduction of the eyes.

Expressive Language Disorder

Monique is using some PIC symbols and has these on her table. Monique has a small vocabulary of signs and seems eager to learn more. She uses some single words; however, she does not use them consistently. She has made excellent progress in early reading skills and recognizes letters of the alphabet. She attends well to conversation directed at her and has comprehension skills that are well beyond her expressive skills.

Developmental Delay

Psychological testing done one year ago revealed a developmental delay. On the Leiter International Performance Scale, Monique's non-verbal abilities fell within the mild developmental handicap range. Completion of the Peabody Picture Vocabulary Test indicated a receptive vocabulary at approximately the three-year level when her chronological age was five years, four months. On the Boehm Test of Basic Concepts, Monique's performance again indicated a mild developmental delay. Social adaptive functioning was at a similar level.

Speech and Language Progress Report

Age at Time of Review: 13 years, 9 months

Monique was seen for regular speech and language therapy throughout the school year. The following report assesses how she progressed toward the stated goals

Answering Questions

Monique enjoyed having stories read to her. During the reading of these stories, the therapist would ask simple comprehension questions related to characters, time/place, feelings, and events. Generally, it was observed that Monique would not typically want to respond using her Dynamite (a communication device with picture communication symbols); instead, she preferred to point to pictures or vocalize a response. When encouraged to use her Dynamite, Monique preferred responding with single words. Most often her responses were correct but limited in scope.

Monique participated fully in answering questions using her Dynamite when asked questions of a personal nature. She revealed many of her interest areas and activities both inside and outside of school.

Asking Questions

Throughout the year, a question page on her Dynamite was being referred to more and more within her academic program. Monique was shown where her page was but appeared to have difficulty finding it efficiently. Examples of asking questions related to her basic needs were demonstrated, and attempts were made to encourage Monique to practise. However, Monique had not demonstrated the implementation of a single question word located on the Dynamite with the therapist. It was possible that since her routines have been established at school, perhaps the need for asking questions is limited to specific locations or people.

Building on Early Phonemic Awareness Training or Early Reading Skills

Monique was asked to match an orally presented rhyming word with a key word located on a familiar page of her Dynamite. While several examples and practice opportunities were provided, Monique only showed a 50 per cent success rate. It appeared that this activity did not hold her interest for very long, and at times she would stop participating.

Monique was also encouraged to use her alphabet board to demonstrate initial letter and initial letter sound identification. The therapist would attempt to give either an isolated sound or an initial sound in a word and ask her to identify it on her key pad. Monique demonstrated some success; however, this task also had limited interest for Monique and typically she would stop participating after several turns.

Overall, Monique has a high interest in books and relaying personal information. These were areas in which she participated fully. As far as developing more functional and academic skills, she appeared less inclined to participate and thus actual progress was difficult to determine at this time. This may have been related to how the skill was presented, her ability to attend during the sessions, and her interest level.

Monique Levesque

Excerpt from Monique's IEP

Strengths

- receptive language skills (comprehension)
- social skills
- interpersonal relations
- receptive language skills (listening)
- positive outlook
- rote memory skills
- visual awareness skills
- visual information skills

Needs

- expressive language skills (speaking)
- expressive language skills (writing)
- fine motor skills
- gross motor abilities
- problem-solving skills
- receptive language skills (decoding)
- motor coordination skills
- perceptual reasoning skills
- phonological awareness skills
- visual tracking skills

Health Support Services

- chokes very readily
- requires occupational therapy, physiotherapy, and speech and language pathology

Individualized Equipment

- computer, monitor, and printer
- alternative keyboard-producing software
- symbol-writing software
- talking word processor software
- augmentative communication device
- wheelchair
- change table and commode
- lift

General Accommodations

Instructional

- Assign one task at a time.
- Encourage use of assistive technology (symbol-writing software, text-to-speech software, and word-processing software).
- Encourage use of augmentative communication system.

- Provide concrete/hands-on materials.
- Minimize distractions.
- Prioritize tasks for completion.
- Read all written instructions.
- Reduce new skills to small steps.
- Provide work samples on desk.
- Provide a scribe.
- Use a homework/communication book.
- Provide visual aids.

Environmental
- Provide alternative work space.
- Provide shelves for material storage.
- Provide a slant board, special chair, and special desk.

Assessment
- Allow use of assistive technology (talking word-processor software and word-processing software).
- Extend time limits.
- Provide extra time for processing.
- Allow frequent breaks.
- Read questions on tests.
- Reduce the number of tasks used to assess a skill.
- Provide visual materials.
- Provide updated subject-specific vocabulary as required.
- Allow use of augmentative communication system.
- Provide a scribe.
- Allow use of adaptive technology (touch-screen).

Example of Teacher-Parent Daily Communication Sheet

Date:	September 20, 2006
Arrival:	Happy—She told me she had a good time horseback riding yesterday.
Language:	Grammar (appositives): We did this together with Monique using Dynamite.
Mathematics:	Patterning with beads: Monique used Dynamite to identify patterns. I will get large beads to make manipulation easier for Monique.
Science:	Quiz: Monique did well!
Geography:	Quiz: 12/12 well done!
French:	Reviewed phrases on Dynamite.
Phys. Ed:	Practised softball throws.
Special Events:	Monique went to Skipping Class at recess and loved it. Physiotherapist worked with Monique in the afternoon.
Comments:	Monique wheeled down and got her own tickets today. We are really trying to encourage independence.
Reminders:	Monique should wear red and white or Canada shirt tomorrow.
Homework:	Geography: Practised locating continents in an atlas. French: Find pictures on computer for highlighted vocabulary words.

What Are Monique's Multiple Disabilities?

As is apparent from the terminology, a student with multiple disabilities has more than one significant disability. According to NICHCY (2013), these disabilities often include difficulties with speech and communication skills as well as mobility issues. Frequently, there is a need for assistance in performing everyday activities. This is true in Monique's case, as she has physical, expressive language, visual, and developmental disabilities. It is important to note that each of her disabilities must be addressed individually, but educators must also address the combined impact of the challenges she faces.

Physical Disability

Monique has been diagnosed with *arthrogryposis multiplex congenital* (AMC), a condition in which there are multiple joint contractures at birth. A contracture is a limitation in the range of motion of a joint. Unfortunately, Monique has a severe form of AMC, resulting in contractures that affect many of her joints, including her hands, wrists, elbows, hips, feet, and jaw. She also has muscle weakness, which further limits her movement. As a consequence, Monique is non-ambulatory and uses a wheelchair for mobility. She is dependent on caregivers for transfers in and out of her wheelchair, and for self-care activities such as dressing, bathing, and toileting. Her physical challenges are evident in most everything she does since she has difficulty with arm and hand movements and lacks the ability to speak clearly. She also has difficulty swallowing.

What We Know . . .

Physical Disabilities

Students with a physical disability may not be able to
- control spontaneous limb movement,
- control speed of movement,
- move quickly or have coordination,
- perform manual tasks such as gripping and turning a handle, holding a pen, and typing,
- move arms or legs fully (e.g., negotiate stairs),
- move around independently (e.g., walking any distance, standing for extended periods of time),
- reach, pull, push, or manipulate, or
- perform tasks that require endurance and strength.

Source: University of Guelph (2008).

Continued

According to Heller, Forney, Alberto, Schwartzman, and Goeckel (2000), physical disabilities that result in an inability to move well "can result in problems with most major systems of the body, including the musculoskeletal, integumentary (skin), sensory, respiratory, immune, and gastrointestinal systems, in addition to other body systems (e.g., renal, cardiovascular, and immune systems)" (p. 5). In other words, when an individual has a condition such as AMC, the lack of normal muscle tone and movement can significantly impact his or her physical health. Therefore, a number of professionals (e.g., physiotherapists and occupational therapists) are usually involved in the individual's care. To maximize the health of the musculoskeletal system, attention is paid to muscle strength, range of joint motion, and bone strength and density.

Expressive Language Disability

Monique's physical disabilities have affected her ability to speak. Early in her development it was apparent that while she could comprehend language, she was unable to express language. This is not surprising given that speech relies on a complex system of sounds made by precise movements of the lips, tongue, and palate (Parker, 1997). Just as Monique has difficulty swallowing, her AMC has affected her ability to complete the movements necessary to produce language. According to Parker (1997), it is much more likely that it will be speech rather than language that will be affected by the structural problems encountered in AMC.

In order to allow her optimal opportunities to communicate, Monique was introduced to sign language and encouraged to use a picture board. By age two and a half, she was using some signs and had about 50 symbols on her board. By age four and a half, she was still using some signs but they were modified due to her limited hand and arm mobility. By this time, her picture board was now on a computer and programmed for voice output (simply touching a picture on the screen results in a spoken message). At age six, there was still concern regarding Monique's limited ability to express herself. She tried to vocalize single words, but these words were rarely understood. While she knew about 20 signs at this point, she usually pointed or used eye gaze to indicate what she wanted. She only used her picture symbols when encouraged to do so.

As a teenager, Monique still relies on vocalizations, facial expressions, and gestures to indicate her needs. She supplements these communication skills by using her computer. While the computer is not usually her first choice of communication, she uses it more frequently and independently than she did in the past. According to Monique's speech-language pathologist, vocabulary pages on Monique's computer are customized. Programming, typically completed by Monique's parents or her educational assistant, allows vocabulary to be added as necessary (e.g., vocabulary highlighted in curricula). There are currently a large number of pages available to Monique, and she is reported to be able to navigate through these pages to find required words and messages. She is noted to understand pop-up pages and can combine up to five words into a sentence, although the words are not always in correct sentence order. See *Speech and Language Progress Report* on p. 337 for more details on how Monique's limited communication skills affect her academic development.

What We Know . . .

Augmentative and Alternative Communication

Augmentative and alternative communication (AAC) includes all forms of communication (other than oral speech) that are used to express thoughts, needs, wants, and ideas. We all use AAC when we make facial expressions or gestures, use symbols or pictures, or write.

People with severe speech or language problems rely on AAC to supplement existing speech or replace speech that is not functional. Special augmentative aids, such as picture and symbol communication boards and electronic devices, are available to help people express themselves. This may increase social interaction, school performance, and feelings of self-worth.

Unaided communication systems rely on the user's body to convey messages. Examples include gestures, body language, or sign language. Aided communication systems require the use of tools or equipment in addition to the user's body. Methods can range from paper and pencil to communication books or boards to devices that produce voice output (speech-generating devices) or written output. Electronic communication aids allow the user to use picture symbols, letters, or words and phrases to create messages. Some devices can be programmed to produce different spoken languages.

Source: American Speech-Language-Hearing Association (2017).

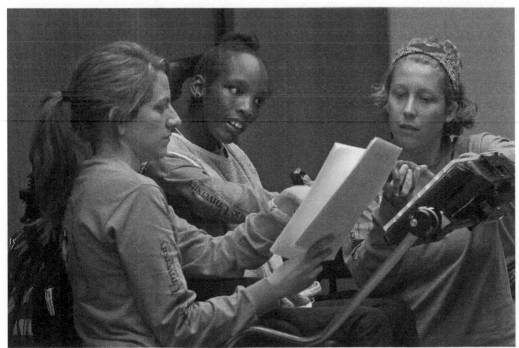

At the Augmentative and Alternative Communication Theater Camp in St. Louis, participants such as Terriona Ingram (centre) use AAC language programs on their computers to recite their lines in a stage production.

Sensory Impairment

Monique was also born with an eye movement disorder called Duane syndrome (DS). While she has good vision in terms of the ability to see, she has difficulty moving her eyes inward toward her nose (adduction) and outward toward her ears (abduction). Since Monique was trying to maintain ocular alignment by using poor head posture (chin up), it was decided that eye muscle surgery may be of benefit. When Monique was 7 years old, she underwent a procedure designed to align her eyes and thereby reduce her abnormal head posture. Since the procedure, Monique's posture has significantly improved, but she continues to have limited adduction and abduction. Because of her visual disability, Monique requires a larger-than-normal computer screen that is carefully positioned to allow optimal accessibility.

What We Know . . .

Visual Disabilities

The term *visual disabilities* refers to a broad spectrum of impairments. Individuals may be legally blind, have low vision, or have visual impairments that require special learning supports. According to Erin (2003), about one in 1,000 school-aged children has a visual impairment that significantly affects his or her ability to learn. Professionals with expertise in visual disabilities are required to help these students and their teachers with the necessary supports and services needed to facilitate learning. These may include special lighting, optical devices for reading, enlarged print, materials written in Braille, auditory materials, or assistive technology.

Developmental Disability

When she was a preschooler, Monique was diagnosed as being "developmentally delayed." A developmental delay indicates a significant difference between a young child's current level of functioning (i.e., cognitive, motor, communicative, social, and adaptive) and his or her chronological age. In Monique's case, it was obvious that her motor development and her communicative abilities were delayed. However, Monique's cognitive abilities were unknown, especially given her inability to communicate effectively. Testing by a psychometrist at age four resulted in a report stating that Monique was "delayed in all areas" with a relative strength being her receptive language. On the Leiter International Performance Scale, a totally non-verbal test of intelligence and cognitive abilities, she scored in the mild developmental handicap range. Similar results were revealed when the Boehm Test of Basic Concepts, a test of basic positional concepts (e.g., size, direction in space, and quantity), was administered. Completion of the Peabody Picture Vocabulary Test, a measure of receptive vocabulary and a screening test of verbal ability, indicated a two-year developmental delay. Despite these indicators of cognitive delay, there was, and still is, considerable concern on the part of both Monique's parents and the professionals testing her that these results may not be accurate. As stated by Monique's pediatrician, "It continues to be difficult to make an accurate assessment of Monique's under-lying intellectual abilities based on standardized psychological tests due to Monique's physical limitations and her expressive language disorder."

What We Know . . .

Developmental Disabilities

People with developmental disabilities learn, understand, or remember things at a slower pace than others. This can affect their language and social skills. It may also mean they need help with daily life as well as other assistance to be as independent and success-ful as possible. A developmental disability that is present at birth or develops before 18 years of age limits a person's ability to learn, is permanent, and can be mild or severe.

Source: Developmental Services Ontario (2013).

Something to Think About

It is clear that Monique requires considerable specialized attention from a wide variety of professionals, and she needs very particular programming to derive benefit from her school experiences. Despite the current move toward more inclusive classrooms and schools, is it possible that Monique's educational needs exceed what can be reasonably expected from regular classroom teachers? What are the advantages and disadvan-tages of having Monique in an inclusive classroom versus a segregated classroom?

What Factors Contributed to Monique's Disabilities?

Monique's most significant challenge is her physical disability. According to medical profes-sionals at Avenues (www.avenuesforamc.com/index.htm), a support group for people with arthrogryposis multiplex congenital, a genetic cause is found in only 30 per cent of individu-als diagnosed with AMC. Monique's case is similar to those of the majority of AMC cases; no genetic link can be found.

Furthermore, no definitive cause of Monique's AMC has been determined in terms of en-vironmental causes either. However, there were some complications during pregnancy that must be considered as possible factors that lead to Monique's physical disabilities. Monique's mother developed pneumonia during the first month of gestation and was treated with an antibiotic drug. While an ultrasound done at 16 weeks gestation was normal, movements were not very active throughout the pregnancy.

What We Know . . .

The Causes of Arthrogryposis Multiplex Congenital

Research on animals has shown that anything that prevents normal joint movement before birth can result in joint contractures. The joint itself may be normal. However, when a joint is not moved for a period of time, extra connective tissue tends to grow around it, fixing it in position. Lack of joint movement also means that tendons connected to the joint are not stretched to their normal length; short tendons, in turn, make normal joint movement difficult.

In general, there are four causes for limitation of joint movement before birth:

1. Muscles do not develop properly (atrophy). In most cases, the specific cause for muscular atrophy cannot be identified. Suspected causes include muscle diseases (e.g., congenital muscular dystrophies), maternal fever during pregnancy, and viruses, which may damage cells that transmit nerve impulses to the muscles.
2. There is not sufficient room in the uterus for normal movement. For example, the mother may lack the normal amount of amniotic fluid or have an abnormally shaped uterus.
3. Central nervous system and spinal cord are malformed. In these cases, arthrogryposis is usually accompanied by a wide range of other conditions.
4. Tendons, bones, joints, or joint linings may develop abnormally. For example, tendons may not be connected to the proper place in a joint.

Source: Avenues for AMC (2017).

Monique's physical disability has further affected her ability to speak as well as her ability to swallow. Therefore, AMC is a direct cause of her expressive language disorder. The causes of developmental expressive language disorder in children who are not limited by a physical disability are still not known.

In terms of Monique's visual problems, Duane syndrome is a rare, congenital disorder that is more common in females. Unlike Monique, most individuals who have DS have no other disorders. The cause of DS is unknown; however, according to the National Human Genome Research Institute (2010), many researchers believe that DS results from a disturbance (either by genetic or environmental factors) during embryonic development. Since the cranial nerves and ocular muscles are developing between the third and eighth week of pregnancy, this is most likely when the disturbance happens. It is interesting to note that this is the same period when Monique's mother was being treated for pneumonia.

The causes of intellectual disabilities are also varied. Again, genetic causes (e.g., Down syndrome) or environmental factors (e.g., complications during pregnancy) must be considered. Given that AMC does not usually affect intelligence, Monique's intellectual disability may be due to environmental factors. Resuscitation was required after birth, so it is possible that Monique's brain was deprived of oxygen during that time.

How Have Monique's Disabilities Affected Her Development?

Monique's difficulties with movement and communication from the time of birth have undoubtedly affected her development. Her physical development has obviously been significantly delayed because of her severe case of AMC. Movement of both her upper and lower body is problematic, limiting her ability to care for herself and to interact fully with her environment. The fact that communication is also a problem for Monique impacts greatly on her cognitive development. Babies and young children use their mobility (e.g., reaching, crawling, and walking) and their development of language (e.g., babbling, talking, and questioning) to learn about the world around them. Theories of child development indicate that children are active learners who are influenced by adults and other children (Piaget, 1952; Vygotsky, 1978). In other words, mobility and communication facilitate intellectual development. According to Forney and Heller (2004) and Hamilton (2016), when infants and young children are unable to experience sensory and motor experiences at critical periods in their development, many areas of development can be affected. This is also true of language disorders, since they have the potential to isolate the child from his or her environment, thus reducing learning opportunities. Monique has been fortunate in that her parents have attempted to provide her with rich learning experiences that emphasize what she can feel, see, and hear. Despite their efforts, however, she has been challenged intellectually by her inability to actively seek out knowledge and extend what she knows by communicating with peers and adults.

```
From the Psychologist's Notebook

When considering Monique's development, it is sometimes easy to get caught
up in what she cannot do. However, there is lots of positive behaviour that
we can talk about too. In terms of emotional development, Monique has always
displayed a great deal of emotionality. She may not be able to communicate
her feelings with words, but her body language and vocalizations exude a
great deal of personal expression. Her smile can light up a room, as it does
so quite often. Monique is a very happy child; she experiences great de-
light in attending hockey games, playing with her two dogs, and being around
horses. She has a great sense of humour and shares it with all those who
she comes in contact with. She also loves music, and while she has trouble
speaking she has no trouble humming along to her favourite melodies. Monique
also uses her body language to express sadness, frustration, and pain. She
is a wonderful child who has a great ability to make those around her see
the joy in life.
```

What Is School Like for Monique?

Monique's parents have always been very involved in her education. They believe strongly that she belongs in the regular classroom, and not just as a "token member of the class." They continue to advocate for her full participation in classroom activities, and they provide support to school personnel to make sure this happens. As they expressed, "We don't want Monique sitting at the back of the English class doing an unrelated activity and having that considered inclusion." They are in constant contact with Monique's teacher, her EA, and all of the professionals involved in providing services to their child. They realize that "the school system isn't perfect," so they have taken it upon themselves to ensure that all of these people work together in a unified effort. This means constantly monitoring and participating in their daughter's education. One way they do this is by attending school-based team meetings where they share information and make suggestions regarding Monique's current needs. This has not always been a positive experience for them. There have been school personnel who have not appreciated their high level of participation. As Monique's father stated, "It hasn't been easy when you see so many areas that could be improved in terms of how Monique is educated . . . as parents we have learned that we have to pick our battles and take some satisfaction in seeing small changes."

Due to the efforts of her parents and the dedicated professionals involved in her care, Monique is currently active and involved in all Grade 8 subject areas. Her EA describes a typical school day as follows:

Monique arrives by bus in the morning. While I am there to meet her, we always arrange for a peer to help her off the bus and into the schoolyard. Once the bell goes, Monique enters the school and I take off her coat and unpack her backpack. I have a look at her Home Communication Book (see example on p. 340) to see if her parents have written anything that is important for me to know. Her parents are really involved in her education, so that makes my job easier. Around this time in the school day, I also initiate communication with Monique by asking her things like what she did the previous night. Monique rarely initiates this type of communication, but she does respond when I ask her questions. It is easy to tell if Monique isn't feeling well because she is usually smiling and very pleasant to work with.

Monique's school day starts with science. She is part of a small group, so I usually stand back and let her fully participate with the other students. Her classmates are really good at helping her. For instance, when they have to look at things through the microscope, one of the students in her group will carry the microscope over to Monique so she can look through it. With prompting, Monique uses her Dynamite computer program to take part in discussions.

After science, it is recess time. Monique accompanies her peers to the playground. I don't go with her since an adult is always supervising the schoolyard. After recess, it is snack time. I open Monique's snack and then stay with her while she eats. We have to be careful, because she sometimes has trouble with swallowing.

Then it is time for French class. Sometimes we miss this and/or other classes as Monique receives in-school speech, physio, and occupational therapy on a regular basis. After French class, toileting is scheduled. Monique wheels herself to the specially equipped washroom. I get help from another EA to lift her into the sling and onto the commode. The whole process takes us about 20 minutes.

Next, the class has either history or art. I help Monique with art activities. She needs hand-over-hand support to do things like colouring. Then it is time for lunch.

I set up her food and monitor her as she eats. Lunch is followed by math class and then geography class. Monique again takes part in the regular class activities. Her teachers modify the activities for her. I also take note of any new vocabulary that needs to be added to Monique's Dynamite computer program. I usually send the list home to her parents and they enter it into the computer.

Physical education is the last class of the day. Monique really loves this class. A recreation therapist has provided Monique's gym teacher with ideas that allow Monique to fully participate in the class. For example:

- *Volleyball: Monique holds hands with a partner. A beach ball is placed on her hands/forearms. She moves her arms (guided by her partner) in a small up and down motion to bounce the ball without dropping it. She counts the number of successful bounces while trying to beat her personal best.*
- *Basketball: Monique throws a lightweight all-purpose ball to a target on the floor. She also practises passing the ball to a partner.*
- *Bowling: Bowling pins are set up approximately two feet from the gym wall. Using a ramp that rests on her lap, Monique rolls a medium-sized ball down the ramp and knocks down as many pins as possible.*
- *Baseball: Using a baseball bat and a T-ball stand that Monique owns, she attempts to make contact with a ball placed on the T-ball stand.*

Monique's school day ends at 3:20. I dress her in her outdoor clothing, get her backpack ready, and strap her up for the bus ride home. Then I accompany her out to the bus.

What We Know . . .

Family Involvement

Given the complicated learning needs of children with severe and multiple disabilities, it is critical that educators and families work together to provide the best educational experiences possible for these children. As Chen and Miles (2004) stated, teachers too often view parents who are very involved in their child's education as nuisances since they take up valuable time in the teacher's work day. They suggest that teachers need to consider the following process of building effective family–professional relationships (p. 32):

1. Analyze how the structure of educational programs affects family involvement.
2. Acknowledge that each family is a complex and unique system.
3. Understand the significant impact that a child with disabilities has on the family.
4. Implement family-friendly strategies that invite family participation and value family contributions.

Continued

Chen and Miles (2004) also presented the following tips that teachers can use when speaking with parents (pp. 41–42):

1. Pay attention to the parent's non-verbal expressions and listen carefully to what is said.
2. Monitor your own non-verbal behaviours and facial expressions.
3. Allow the parent sufficient time to express and describe his or her feelings.
4. Acknowledge and validate the parent's feelings and demonstrate that you understand him or her by reflecting the feelings the parent has shared.
5. Respond to the parent's expression of difficult situations and emotional issues in a sensitive and caring way.
6. Do not ignore a parent's emotional statement about the child's disability by making superficial comments that ignore the parent's feelings and concerns.
7. Paraphrase what the parent says by restating the message. Paraphrasing helps to clarify the intended message.
8. Summarize what the parent has said to communicate that you understand and to check your perception.
9. Weigh what is being said, and do not make quick judgments. Resist the temptation to give advice or make recommendations too quickly.

Source: Republished with permission of Paul H. Brookes Publishing Company. "Working with families," in *Educating children with multiple disabilities: A collaborative approach*. Chen, D., & Miles, C., 2004. Permission conveyed through Copyright Clearance Center, Inc.

What We Know . . .

Encouraging Communication

Sometimes school personnel are too quick to meet the needs of the non-communicative student and, in doing so, they eliminate the student's need to communicate at all. Kaiser and Grim (2006, p. 464) suggest that those working with non-communicative students make use of the following strategies to increase the likelihood that these students will show an interest in their environment and, subsequently, make communicative attempts:

1. *Interesting materials:* Students are likely to communicate when things or activities interest them.
2. *Out of reach:* Students are likely to communicate when they want to gain access to something they cannot reach.
3. *Limited portions:* Students are likely to communicate when they do not have the necessary materials to carry out an instruction.
4. *Choice-making:* Students are likely to communicate when they are asked which of several options they prefer.
5. *Assistance:* Students are likely to communicate when they need assistance in operating or manipulating materials.
6. *Unexpected situations*: Students are likely to communicate when something happens they do not expect.

Janine Wiedel Photolibrary/Alamy Stock Photo

Stimulating objects and activities will encourage students to actively communicate.

What We Know . . .

Peer Relationships

Sometimes the physical and learning needs of a student with multiple disabilities are so great that their social needs are given much less attention. However, when discussing students with severe disabilities, Schwartz, Staub, Peck, and Gallucci (2006) note that "the level of importance and value that teachers place on supporting and facilitating their students' relationships will influence greatly their successful development" (p. 400). They offer the following intervention strategies that were designed to facilitate peer relationships in the inclusive classroom (pp. 384–386):

Small-Group Membership (Teacher Developed)

Be sure there are opportunities for all students to make a substantial contribution to the group. This may mean making accommodations for students with disabilities. Encourage students within the small groups to suggest accommodations for their peers who are disabled.

Small-Group Membership (Peer Developed)

Create unstructured situations for play and exploration. Plan ahead for peer support by conducting ability awareness training, setting up buddy systems, and having class discussions about ways in which peers with disabilities can be included in peer-directed activities.

Continued

Class Membership

Develop a strong sense of community in your classroom. Have regular class meetings that create opportunities for students to have a voice in decisions about how the class is conducted and the expectations for behaviour in the classroom community.

School Membership

Include students with disabilities in active roles at school (e.g., bringing the daily attendance sheet to the principal's office or taking tickets at a basketball game). Ensure the necessary supports are in place so that students with disabilities are included in school-wide rituals and celebrations (e.g., wearing a school sweatshirt, carrying a school bag, hanging out in a certain area during lunchtime, and attending graduation).

Susan Leggett/Alamy Stock Photo

Creating opportunities for students to fully participate in group activities like physical education will influence their successful development.

From the Psychologist's Notebook

It is obvious that Monique's educational assistant plays a greater minute-by-minute role in her educational life than any of her teachers. EAs typically help students like Monique with everything they do at school. Because they get to know the student so well, EAs often provide help with program development and implementation, the adaptation of teaching materials, and the fostering of student independence. EAs are usually assigned on a one-to-one basis for students like Monique, but they can also be employed to help several different students in the run of a school day. It is also not uncommon that EAs are the main caregivers for students who may need assistance with feeding, toileting, taking medication, or participating in various therapeutic programs, such as speech and language training or physical therapy. EAs also often help students participate in extracurricular activities such as sports, plays, and school clubs, and in some jurisdictions, they even assist with bus transportation.

Given all that goes on in a student's life, day after day, there is an obvious need for close connections between students with exceptionalities and their EAs. In many cases, students have such great needs that they are wholly dependent on their EA. It stands to reason, therefore, that teachers can also become dependent on a child's EA because of the EA's intimate knowledge. Nonetheless, it is important that teachers and EAs understand and respect their respective educational boundaries when it comes to helping the student in the classroom. Sometimes teachers allow EAs to take on more direct teaching responsibilities than they should. Therefore, it is worth noting that the role of an EA is to deliver specific services and programming to students with exceptionalities under the direction of the classroom teacher.

What Educational Approach Is Best for Monique?

The Collaborative Model

Thus far, Monique's education can be best described as having been based on inclusive principles using a transdisciplinary model. In other words, her placement in the regular classroom has been planned and monitored by educators (i.e., teachers, special education specialists, and educational assistants), her parents, and professionals who provide her with specific therapies. While the therapists have developed their own therapy-related goals for Monique and provided direct services in the school setting, it has been primarily the teacher and the educational assistant who have been responsible for the delivery of Monique's education. They have received assistance from other members of the team, especially in terms of special education practices, physical positioning, and the use of assistive technology.

As is evident from Monique's current IEP (see excerpts on pp. 338–339), the transdisciplinary team has gathered general information about Monique, including her strengths and needs. They have also summarized the special equipment she requires and the health services that are necessary. A large portion of her IEP is dedicated to the supports and services (i.e., instructional, environmental, and assessment) that are needed in the classroom for Monique to meet her learning goals.

Is this the best educational approach for Monique? Monique's parents feel it is "a good start, but there is room for improvement." They would like the transdisciplinary approach to be replaced by more of a collaborative approach. In other words, they would like the team members to work even more as a unit rather than as individuals who provide domain-specific services. "We would like the entire team to work together, learn from each other, and share the responsibility of the delivery of services."

What We Know . . .

Collaborative Educational Services

The most effective service delivery model for the education of students with multiple disabilities is the collaborative approach (Cloninger, 2004; Horn & Kang, 2012). It involves forming a team of individuals (parents, educators, therapists, etc.) who are willing to share their knowledge and collaborate on all aspects of the student's school program, including assessment, development of instructional goals, intervention, and evaluation. As Horn & Kang (2012) explain:

> Through the process of working together, team members acquire a shared understanding and knowledge of each other's expertise. New ideas are then generated and incorporated into collaborative evaluation, planning, implementation, and on-going progress monitoring of child and family outcomes. (p. 242)

Cloninger (2004, p. 20) identified the following essential components of the collaborative approach:

- Appropriate team membership
- A shared framework of assumptions, beliefs, and values
- Distribution and parity of functions and resources
- Processes for working together
- A set of shared goals agreed to by the team

Monique's parents also have concerns about the IEPs that have been developed for their daughter since she has been in school. While they are supportive of the IEP process, they are concerned that "the IEP doesn't really have enough information, especially when it is for a child with multiple disabilities." For instance, they point out that the current IEP fails to detail how teachers make programming decisions within each subject area: "There seem to be general recommendations, but the IEP doesn't really give specifics about how Monique should be taught in a specific area—like what level she is at now, what the goals are for her in that subject, and how these goals can be met by teaching her skills in a proper sequence." These concerns appear to be legitimate. When one of Monique's current teachers was asked how he decides the content of Monique's program, he was unable to explain how curricular decisions are made. Instead, he described how Monique just does what the other children do but in a simplified form.

Something to Think About

One of Monique's past teachers, who received limited support from resource personnel in the school, was vague when asked to describe how she modified the curricula to meet Monique's needs. She indicated that while she did modify activities for Monique, her teaching was mostly guided by Monique's emotional expressions. She said her goal was to keep Monique happy so that school was an enjoyable experience for her. How do you feel about this teacher's goal? How would you react as a teacher if you received limited support in modifying curricula for a high-needs child?

What We Know . . .

Developing Curriculum and Instruction

It is apparent that having an IEP for a student does not guarantee that the best educational practices are in place. IEPs can look very different depending on who has developed them and how they are intended to be used. In the case of students with multiple disabilities, the development of the IEP may require significant effort, yet the results ensure that everyone involved knows the student's program and how it will be implemented. Developing curriculum and instruction must be given considerable attention so that the student is not simply kept busy during the school day, but rather skills are learned in a sequence that leads to the attainment of stated learning goals.

Gee (2004, p. 97) points out that there should also be support plans for each curricular period of the student's day. These plans can be developed by answering the following questions:

1. What are the typical class activities and routines within this curricular unit?
2. What typical teaching strategies will be used?
3. What are the expectations for all students?
4. What are the expectations for the focus student?
5. How will the focus student receive information?
6. How will the focus student provide information?
7. What additional types of support are needed for the focus student?

Source: Gee (2004). Reprinted with permission of the Paul H. Brookes Publishing Company.

The Use of Assistive Technology

Given Monique's multiple disabilities, it seems logical that she would use assistive technology (AT) in the classroom. While she does use both low- and high-tech communication aids, there may be AT products and devices that would further enhance her functional capabilities. However, it is apparent that her teachers are not fully involved in the AT she currently uses (e.g., her parents are responsible for updating the vocabulary in the Dynamite program). In fact, her teachers have expressed their lack of confidence when it comes to choosing and using AT. This is not uncommon, as research has identified the need for increased teacher preparation in the use of AT in the classroom (Allen, 2015). After all, there are thousands of AT products and devices to choose from, and each requires knowledge about how to use it to support and facilitate student learning. This may explain why many students (as many as 80 per cent) stop using AT devices because they are a poor match for their actual needs (Petschauer, 2016). The solution to these poor results may be a concerted effort by school-based teams to consult with AT specialists when considering a particular child's requirements. Ideally, these specialists should then work closely with teachers, educational assistants, and parents to ensure that best practices are applied as long as the technology is used.

Evaluation of Progress

Just as Monique takes part in the same learning opportunities as her classmates, she is also evaluated on the same schedule as her peers. According to her teachers, they simply modify the test they are giving to the class (i.e., usually fewer questions) and they allow Monique to communicate her knowledge through the use of her computer. For example, the vocabulary that is used in a particular subject is programmed into her computer so that when she is asked a question, she can indicate the answer by touching the correct symbol on her screen.

When Monique's teachers were asked about how they decide the content of her test, they were again rather vague about their decision-making process. The IEP was not mentioned, nor were any specific learning objectives.

What We Know . . .

Evaluating the Progress of Students with Multiple Disabilities

According to Kleinert and Kearns (2004), evaluating the learning outcomes of students with severe and multiple disabilities should be an integral component of a continuous process that revolves around the IEP. This process involves program planning (establishing appropriate learning objectives), instruction (providing opportunities for the student to meet the learning objectives), and outcomes assessment (monitoring and measuring student progress to facilitate ongoing program planning). Kleinert and Kearns emphasize that the IEP is not a static document, but rather an ever-evolving student plan based on the standards set for all students. In other words, the IEP is developed with the general curricula in mind. Just like their peers, students with severe and multiple disabilities work toward meeting the curricula demands. There should be no guesswork involved in what the student with disabilities should be doing in class, and the evaluation of their progress is critical to ensuring that continuous learning occurs.

There are many evaluation or assessment formats that may be appropriate for students with severe and multiple disabilities (Kleinert & Kearns, 2004; Ysseldyke & Olsen, 1999):

- Structured interviews (reports of performance from parents and school personnel)
- Checklists (using a list of targeted skills to assess performance)
- Performance records (instructional data, graphs, anecdotal records)
- Performance tests (observations of the student performing predetermined tasks)
- Student portfolios (documents that provide a complete picture of overall performance)

It is important to use as many of these formats as is necessary to determine the student's progress. The continuous development of new learning objectives is only effective if the student has mastered the prerequisite skills that are required to move on to the next level of skill.

Something to Think About

Monique's father was busy one weekend programming her Dynamite computer program to include the symbols necessary for Monique to express her knowledge in a science test on Monday. The test was to be on the parts of a microscope and safety in the lab, topics that had been covered in class the previous week. On Friday, the teacher sent home the information that Monique's father needed to program her computer. Once the information was entered, he helped Monique prepare for the test. Do you think Monique was given the best opportunity to learn and to be evaluated? How could her communication technology be used more effectively?

How Is Monique Different from Other Students Who Have Multiple Disabilities?

When multiple disabilities are involved, each child's situation is obviously unique. There are many possible combinations of cognitive, sensory, and physical disabilities, and each disability can vary greatly in both its severity and how it impacts other existing disabilities. However, despite the uniqueness of each child's case, there are general similarities that can also be identified across individuals with multiple disabilities. Like Monique, many children with multiple disabilities look different than other children. They are perhaps the group most readily identified as having special needs. They often have significant medical needs, difficulty communicating, difficulty with physical mobility that requires special equipment, and an inability to care for themselves. In other words, they require significant, ongoing support. In fact, many of these children are only seen in the company of an adult, since they must have constant supervision for a variety of reasons. The children in the following examples typify the similarities that are often seen in people with multiple disabilities, but their individual circumstances also illustrate the uniqueness that one can expect to see in this special population:

- *Cognitive delay, visual impairment, and cerebral palsy:* Caleb is a 16-year-old teenager who charms everyone he comes in contact with. He attends a high school where he spends one period per day in a special resource class and the rest of the day in the regular classroom. Due to his cognitive delay, he is working slightly below grade level in math and reading. His most significant disabilities, however, are a visual impairment and cerebral palsy. He was born prematurely and, as a result, he has retrolental fibroplasias, a condition where the development of retinal blood vessels is disrupted. Consequently, he has low vision that requires him to wear glasses and make use of low vision aids, such as large print. In terms of his mobility, he is limited in both his poor vision and his cerebral palsy. Cerebral palsy is a group of neurological disorders that affect body movement and muscle coordination. Caleb has spastic cerebral palsy that is apparent in one leg. It causes stiffness, and he has difficulty moving. Because Caleb basically drags the affected leg, he uses a rolling walker to get around the school. This is not always easy, as his visual impairment sometimes prevents him from predicting what is in his path. Caleb takes it all in stride, however, and tries his best to keep up with his peers. He is very well-liked by his classmates and is included in all school activities both inside and outside of the classroom.

- *Hearing impairment, microcephaly, and intellectual disability:* Tara is a 15-year-old high school student who lives with foster parents due to her parents' inability to deal with her disabilities. She has facial distortions and a small head. She is also short in stature. Her mother contracted rubella (German measles) during the first trimester of her pregnancy, which impacted Tara's development across a number of areas. Tara is hearing impaired and, even with the use of hearing aids, she is unable to hear normally. As a result, her speech is not easily understood. Tara also has an intellectual disability and performs well below the cognitive level of her same-age peers; she has microcephaly, a medical condition in which the circumference of the head is smaller than normal because the brain has not developed properly. Tara experienced inclusive education during elementary school but now that she is in secondary school, she spends limited time in the regular classroom. The emphasis of her high school curriculum is on the acquisition of life skills. She takes part in a special program designed to give students the opportunity to develop independent living abilities. Her progress has been slow, but Tara continues to exhibit an eagerness to learn. She especially enjoys repetitive tasks that allow her to experience the satisfaction of working independently and following a task through to completion. Unfortunately, Tara has few friends but she does enjoy the company of her dog, Buddy. Her foster parents have encouraged her to be Buddy's primary caretaker, and she takes this job very seriously.

Something to Think About

Imagine that Caleb and Tara are students in your high school classroom. How would you build on their strengths while addressing their areas of need?

Closing Monique's File

As a result of concerted efforts by her parents and dedicated professionals within the education system, Monique will soon complete her middle school years and move on to secondary school. This transition evokes both pride and apprehension on the part of her parents. There is pride in the fact that Monique will complete middle school with her same-age peers, and in the fact that she has been a valued student of the regular classroom. As her father stated, "We worked very, very hard to make sure that Monique participated in all the same activities the other children were doing . . . each year we had to work with new school personnel to make sure everyone was aware of Monique's needs, and it wasn't always easy but we were driven by the belief that Monique belonged with other kids her age." Now Monique's parents are expressing some apprehension about the new challenges that Monique will face in secondary school. While they still want Monique to be a member of the regular classroom, they realize it will require significant adjustments on the part of all those involved. Their current focus is on the transition process itself; they are actively preparing a transition portfolio that will help them consolidate all of the information that will be of interest to the staff at Monique's new school. Their hope is that this portfolio will prevent them from having to "start all over again." Their comment was that "we and others have learned so much about Monique and how she learns that we just want to pass it along to help others who work with her . . . we know how daunting it can be to be responsible for the education of a child with multiple disabilities, and this portfolio will only help reduce that anxiety."

What We Know . . .

Transition Portfolios

According to Demchak and Greenfield (2003, p. 2), a transition portfolio is a strategy that documents critical information about a student. It may be prepared by a teacher, support personnel, or parents. Demchak and Greenfield point out that transitions are likely to be more successful if relevant, student-specific information is provided in a non-technical manner. They recommend transition portfolios contain the following components:

- Personal information (history, strengths, and interests)
- Medical information (medical issues and needs)
- Education programming suggestions (educational focus and unique learning characteristics)
- Ideas for adaptations and supports (modifications to environment/instruction and the use of technology)
- Recommendations for physical impairments (adaptive positioning equipment and therapeutic handling techniques)
- Expressive and receptive communication strategies (current methods of communication and instructional suggestions)
- Reinforcement strategies and positive behavioural support plans (effective reinforcers and summary of behaviour assessment and behaviour plan)
- Problem-solving techniques and team notes (past challenges and how they were resolved)

The idea is to present a whole picture of the child—one that allows teachers and support personnel to understand the strengths and needs of their new student without having to repeatedly sift through the many reports that may exist in the student's school file. The transition portfolio presents succinct yet comprehensive information written in an easy-to-read format.

From the Psychologist's Notebook

From a schooling perspective, the greatest hurdle that Monique faces, and will continue to face, is her inability to easily and accurately convey to educators what she knows. It is clear from what her parents and teachers have reported that Monique often knows and understands much more than she is able to tell them. Therefore, it is important that teachers assess the full scope of Monique's learning with a variety of tests and assignments that provide her with the best opportunity to convey her knowledge. This type of careful assessment and evaluation allows for a more precise determination of Monique's progress and also allows for the development of a more definitive set of future educational objectives. By encouraging Monique to demonstrate her learning more often, she may use her computer as her first choice of communication rather than her last.

Updating Monique's Story

We have learned that Monique attended her local high school along with the classmates she had in elementary school. While her parents continued to advocate for her full inclusion in the regular classroom, she did spend approximately one third of her day in a special resource room. Throughout the school day, she was always accompanied by an educational assistant. Some of the same difficulties the family faced in the lower grades were still evident (e.g., a lack of collaboration in the delivery of support services as well as a lack of adherence to Monique's education plan). In addition, new challenges arose. In the high school environment, educators paid less attention to Monique's social needs. Peer relations were not emphasized as they had been in the elementary school classroom. As a result, Monique was more isolated and had fewer interactions with her classmates. According to Snowdon (2012), this is not uncommon. Parents of Canadian children with disabilities identified late-elementary school to early-secondary school as a particularly difficult time for their children in terms of friendships and social interactions. These parents indicated that their children often felt isolated and lonely in the secondary school setting. Furthermore, Snowden's work revealed that many children and youth with disabilities lacked close, interactive friendships. Over half of the children or youth in the study had either no friends or had only one close relationship with a friend, and the amount of time spent by the children or youth interacting with their peer networks was very minimal.

What We Know . . .

Fostering Social Relationships in Secondary School

According to Carter, Sewdeen, and Kurkowski (2008), the limited general education curriculum experiences schools provide to students with significant disabilities, the restrictive classroom contexts in which these students spend their days, the narrow range of approaches teachers use to deliver instruction, the extensive reliance on individually assigned paraprofessionals to provide direct support, and the limited extent to which extracurricular activities and other after-school events are considered by planning teams, all contribute to limited opportunities for youth with significant disabilities to develop relationships with their classmates. They identified the following five important actions that schools should take when fostering friendships:

1. Reflect on existing opportunities and current practices.
2. Design frequent shared activities.
3. Promote valued roles for all students.
4. Equip youth with relevant information, ideas, and strategies on how to support each other.
5. Offer "just enough" support.

Walton (2012) also addressed the issues of inclusion and exclusion among students in secondary schools. She described how the fostering of "sympathetic imagination" through literacy activities can increase inclusivity:

> Literature offers much to education in general, and it provides the pedagogic space to address issues of inclusion and exclusion, particularly of people with disabilities. Selecting literary texts that feature people with disabilities for high school students can be challenging, but once chosen, such texts can be used to promote inclusivity by developing sympathetic understanding, by addressing sensitive issues using the characters and context of the text, and by engaging in critical literacy that exposes power and positioning in texts. These strategies can be applied in classrooms through various written and verbal activities and can be used with a range of texts. (p. 224)

Summary

A student with multiple disabilities has more than one significant disability. These coexisting impairments may include movement difficulties, sensory loss, or intellectual disabilities. As is evidenced by Monique's story, students with severe multiple disabilities often experience delays in their development and require significant supports, especially in the school setting. These supports are usually provided by education assistants and a number of professionals, such as physiotherapists, occupational therapists, and speech and language therapists. All of these individuals address the student's physical and learning needs. While social needs are not always the priority, peer relationships should not be forgotten or undervalued. It is also important for students with multiple disabilities to have comprehensive IEPs that include appropriate learning objectives and details on measuring student progress. Along with this ever-evolving education plan, transition portfolios are an important tool for introducing students to their new teachers.

Learning More about Students with Multiple Disabilities

Academic Journals

Augmentative and Alternative Communication
Journal of the American Academy of Audiology
Journal of Developmental and Physical Disabilities
Journal of Special Education Technology
Journal of Speech, Language, and Hearing Research
Journal of Visual Impairment and Blindness
Physical Disabilities: Education and Related Service
Research and Practice for Persons with Severe Disabilities

Books

Dell, A. G., Newton, D. A., & Petroff, J. G. (2012). *Assistive technology in the classroom: Enhancing the school experiences of students with disabilities* (2nd ed.). Boston, MA: Pearson.

Demchak, M., & Greenfield, R. (2003). *Transition portfolios for students with disabilities.* Thousand Oaks, CA: Corwin Press, Inc.

Downing, J. E. (2008). *Including students with severe and multiple disabilities in typical classrooms: Practical strategies for teachers.* Baltimore, MD: Paul H. Brookes.

Heller, K., Forney, P., Alberto, P., Schwartzman, M., & Goeckel, T. (2000). *Meeting physical and health needs of children with disabilities: Teaching student participation and management.* Toronto, ON: Nelson Thomson Learning.

Orelove, F., Sobsey, D., & Gilles, D. (2016). *Educating children with severe and multiple disabilities: A collaborative approach* (5th ed.). Baltimore, MD: Brookes Publishing Company, Inc.

Schwartz, H. D. (2012). *A primer on communication and communicative disorders.* Boston, MA: Pearson.

Sileo, N. M., & Prater, M. A. (2012). *Working with families of children with special needs: Family and professional partnerships and roles.* Boston, MA: Pearson.

Snell, M., & Brown, F. (2010). *Instruction of students with severe disabilities* (7th ed.). Upper Saddle River, NJ: Pearson Education, Inc.

Web Links

AMC Support

www.amcsupport.org
This support organization provides educational material and information to those who wish to learn more about AMC and how it affects children.

Council for Exceptional Children

www.cec.sped.org
The CEC is the largest international professional organization dedicated to improving educational outcomes for individuals with exceptionalities, students with disabilities, and the gifted.

Education for Students with Multiple Disabilities

www.perkinselearning.org/scout/multiple-disabilities-educational-resources
This information clearinghouse provides educators with an introduction to the educational needs of students with multiple disabilities. It also addresses policy and best practices.

Speech and Language Disorders

http://speechandlanguagedisabilities.weebly.com/teaching-resources--strategies.html
This site offers basic information on speech and language disorders as well as classroom implications and teaching strategies.

TASH

www.tash.org
TASH is a civil rights organization that advocates for human rights and inclusion for people with significant disabilities and support needs. The site includes information, links to resources, and targeted advocacy.

Taking It into Your Classroom . . .

Including Students with Multiple Disabilities

When a student with multiple disabilities is first placed in my classroom, I will

- review what I know about the different disabilities and locate resource materials,
- consider how the disabilities may impact upon each other,
- read the student's file,
- consult with the student's previous teachers,
- consult with the student's parents, and
- meet with the school-based team to discuss the student's current school year.
- Other:_____

Key points to remember in my daily interactions with a student who has multiple disabilities:

- The student may struggle to communicate both verbally and non-verbally.
- The student's attempts to communicate may often go undetected.
- The student may comprehend more than he or she is able to express.
- The student may benefit from the use of multiple means of communication.
- The student may need encouragement to use aided communication (i.e., technology).
- Other:_____

Key points regarding programming for a student with multiple disabilities:

- A collaborative approach to service delivery is considered ideal.
- A carefully developed IEP should clearly outline the student's program.
- The student should be actively involved in all relevant school activities.
- Skills should be taught in a logical sequence.
- The student's school day should be carefully planned with supports in place.
- Other:_____

Key points regarding evaluation of the progress made by a student with multiple disabilities:

- Evaluation should measure the student's proximity to the standards set for all students.
- Evaluation should be based on the learning objectives stated in the IEP.
- Evaluation should include the most appropriate assessment formats for that student.
- Evaluation should include as many formats as is necessary to determine learning.
- Evaluation should provide the feedback necessary to develop new objectives.
- Evaluation should be ongoing.
- Other:_____

CHAPTER 12

Students Who Are At-Risk

LEARNING OBJECTIVES

After learning the material in this chapter, you should be able to:

- Define the term *at-risk* and describe the dimensions of the at-risk concept.

- Present the environmental factors that can put students at-risk.

- Discuss why a holistic approach to assessment is important when dealing with students who are at-risk.

- Define the term *trauma* and describe how trauma can affect students who are at-risk, including the effects that trauma can have on a child's development.

- List several strategies that educators can use when dealing with traumatized students.

- Discuss the primary understandings that have come from the resiliency research and outline the aspects of resilience evident across different cultures.

- List several strategies that teachers and schools can implement to enhance resiliency in students.

Name: Owen Bachman

Current Age: 16

School: H.G. Cook High School

Grade: 11

Owen is a high school student who has had a tumultuous life from birth.

His parents failed to provide the necessities of life, so by the time Owen was 6-years-old he was under the care of the Children's Aid Society. Unfortunately, he lived in several group settings and foster homes before being placed in his current foster home with the Kelly family. Over his school years, he has been identified as having ADHD, a communication learning disorder, and emotional/behavioural problems. He has received limited special education services for each of these challenges. Owen's life both inside and outside of school has improved significantly since moving to his current foster home three years ago. With the support of Marianne and Bill Kelly, he has begun to thrive. He is doing very well in school, and while he still has an IEP, his school supports have been reduced significantly. His goal is to become an electrician when he graduates. Owen is an example of a child who has demonstrated considerable resiliency; he has benefited most from a stable, loving family life that includes consistent and appropriate behavioural demands.

Elementary School Referral for Assessment

Date: September 2006

Owen Bachman is being referred for a psycho-educational assessment due to concerns regarding his social and emotional well-being, as well as his behaviour and academic difficulties.

He is a student who demonstrates well-developed athletic ability and he can be very polite and charming. He also gets along well with his peers. However, concerns exist regarding Owen's ability to stay focused at school. He is easily distracted, and he requires encouragement to stay on task. Owen also has difficulty with organization. He has had a previous diagnosis of ADHD. His academic skills are felt to be weak at this time. Reading, written communication skills, and math appear to be below grade level.

Of far greater concern is Owen's emotional well-being. He is easily upset and often hides in the school or runs from the school building. He frequently becomes agitated and uncommunicative and has talked about harming himself or others. He has been hospitalized for actions related to these thoughts. Owen often appears sad and sullen at school. His behaviour is also of great concern as he can be very defiant and disrespectful. Owen has also demonstrated aggressive, non-compliant behaviour. He is currently in foster care.

Owen Bachman

Excerpts from Owen's Psycho-Educational Assessment

Date: September 2006

Intellectual Functioning

Owen's intellectual abilities were assessed using the WISC-III. The results suggest that Owen's intellectual functioning falls within the average to low-average range (Full Scale = 80–92; 17th percentile), although this is somewhat misleading because of a discrepancy between his verbal and non-verbal abilities. Owen performed significantly better on non-verbal tasks than he did on tasks requiring auditory verbal functioning. He is a visual learner with a strong preference for processing visual-spatial information. A significant relative weakness in processing verbal information is evident. These scores suggest a general delay in verbal processing abilities.

Owen's verbal skills on this assessment fell within the low-average to below-average range (Verbal IQ = 74–89; 9th percentile). There was little variability among subtests. Owen generally experienced mild difficulty on tasks requiring the processing and interpreting of verbal information and verbal reasoning skills. Comprehending what he hears and reads will likely continue to be somewhat difficult for Owen at school. It is likely that this weakness will impact on all academic subject areas.

Owen's non-verbal abilities, at the time of testing, fell within the average range (Performance IQ = 78–104; 37th percentile). There was no significant variability among subtest scores. His ability to process non-verbal information appears to be a relative strength. Owen is able to perform adequately on tasks requiring hands-on, visual-spatial skills.

Owen performed within the average to high-average range on tasks measuring processing speed (Processing Speed Index = 95–114; 61st percentile). Owen is able to demonstrate well-developed motor skills and speed.

Attention

Owen performed within the low-average to below-average range on subtests measuring auditory attention and working memory (Freedom from Distractibility Index = 72–92; 8th percentile). Some difficulty with auditory attention is evident. Owen may have difficulty recalling and comprehending what he hears, particularly if the information is lengthy and complex. This is consistent with his previous diagnosis of ADHD.

The Conners' Scales are designed as brief screening tools to assess difficulties in the following categories: Hyperactivity, Hyperactivity-Impulsivity, Inattention, and Learning Problems. No significant problems for Owen (> 95th percentile) were identified in any of these areas at the time of assessment. Owen may have been on prescribed medication at this time.

Academic Functioning

Owen's academic development was assessed with the WIAT-II. He performed below the average range on a subtest measuring spelling skills (9th percentile) and within the average to low-average range on a subtest measuring computational arithmetic skills (34th percentile).

Social/Emotional Functioning

Owen's responses on the Reynolds Depression Scale did not suggest significantly elevated scores corresponding to symptoms of depression at the time of administration. It is my understanding that concerns in this area exist at the present time.

Problems including Anxiety, Perfectionism, Social, Emotional, and Oppositional Behaviour were also assessed using the Conners' Scales. Owen's classroom teacher did not express concerns at the time in any of these areas. It must be noted that Owen's behaviour has deteriorated since this time.

The Achenbach Scales were also used to assess possible problems in the following areas: Anxiety, Depressive Symptoms, Social Problems, Attention Problems, Rule-Breaking Behaviour, and Aggressive Behaviour. Owen's classroom teacher supplied the relevant information. No significant problems were identified at the time these scales were completed.

Conclusions

This assessment was undertaken to observe the pattern of Owen's learning strengths and needs. Owen demonstrated weaknesses in his ability to process verbal information. He will require more time and more assistance to acquire the basic skills being taught. His auditory verbal weakness will affect all subject areas at school and will make it more difficult for him to cope unless a great deal of academic assistance is provided. His behaviour may in part be a result of academic frustration. Owen is considered at-risk for increased behaviour problems if his academic needs are not addressed.

Weaknesses in reading and spelling are evident. Owen's skills in these areas appear to be well below average for his age and grade placement. His academic difficulties will continue to make it challenging for him to cope with the regular curriculum.

While no significant social, emotional, or behaviour problems were in evidence at the time of the assessment, significant concerns exist at this time. Owen has been under psychiatric care. Appropriate referrals have been made.

Owen Bachman

Overview of Formal Assessment Results

Date	Type	Age	Results
September 2006	Psycho-Educational Assessment	10 years, 2 months	Behaviour problems may be a result of academic needs. Results indicate a profile consistent with an identification of Communication Learning Disability.
April 2008	Speech and Language Assessment	11 years, 10 months	Owen presented with age-appropriate language comprehension and expression. Auditory memory skills were moderately delayed. He had slow processing speed for language information and required extra support to understand directions. He requires support to improve decoding skills and written language organization.
March 2009	Social Services Assessment	12 years, 9 months	Owen requires a strong support system and needs to know how to access it.
May 2009	Canadian Achievement Test	12 years, 11 months	Reading: Grade equivalent 3.9 Language: Grade equivalent 3.6 Math: Grade equivalent 4.3

Children's Aid Society Report

Date: March 2010

Re: Owen Bachman (14 years of age)

The above-named child is currently a child in care of the Children's Aid Society under a Crown Wardship with access order. He currently resides with Marianne and Bill Kelly. Prior to this placement, several treatment foster homes were unsuccessful and he resided for a short time at a Home for Boys. Unfortunately, Owen has experienced many moves and a difficult upbringing. When he was first taken into care, he had visits with his mother and stepfather but they stopped making contact in late 2007. His father continues to make sporadic contact.

Owen is currently on medication for ADHD, ODD, and CD. This medication (Zyprexa and Adderall) is administered in the foster home.

Owen makes friends easily and is a very likeable child. However, he has experienced difficulty expressing any upsetting emotions he may be having. When he is emotionally stressed, he sometimes shuts down by refusing to talk, or he becomes unco-operative, or his defiant behaviours escalate. If Owen is able to get a negative reaction from those around him, his problematic behaviours continue to intensify. His current foster parents deal with this exceptionally well by ensuring that he is aware that if he chooses to continue with these behaviours, his choices will only impact himself. They always encourage Owen to make good choices. Currently, the school has a plan in place to address Owen's emotional needs during class time. If he is unable to regulate his emotions, he can use a special signal to let the teacher know that he needs to leave the room. He is given this special privilege so that he has time to calm down before continuing with his academic activities. There is no punishment associated with this type of situation as it is viewed as a coping strategy. If Owen is still unable to manage his emotions after this time away, he is allowed to contact his foster parents and ask to be picked up. Owen is encouraged to use this plan when required.

In terms of Owen's transition into secondary school, we hope that more supports such as the one above are put into place. There was a recent incident at Owen's current school where the police were called about Owen having marijuana in his possession. We are concerned about him making positive peer choices. If there is a mentoring program at the school, this may be one way that Owen could be connected with positive role models. Currently, he is taking diving lessons and doing very well given his athletic abilities. The Kellys are also educating Owen about the dangers of drug and alcohol use. It is hoped that his involvement in these pro-social activities will motivate him to make positive choices for himself in the future.

Owen Bachman

Excerpt from Owen's IEP

Student	Owen Bachman
Current Grade	11
Reason for IEP	Student identified as exceptional
Exceptionality	Behaviour/communication learning disorder
Placement	Regular classroom with resource assistance

Accommodations

INSTRUCTIONAL

- Provide access to computer for written work.
- Provide extra review/drill.
- Increase task completion time.
- Reduce the learning of new skills into smaller steps.

ENVIRONMENTAL

- Minimize background noise.
- Minimize distractions.

ASSESSMENT

- Allow notes/open book for tests.
- Allow extra time to respond.
- Provide prompts.
- Repeat/reword instructions.
- Allow use of computer for written work.

Actions

- Access resource room assistance for help with major assignments and exams.
- Develop self-advocacy skills.
- Become comfortable communicating with teachers about strengths, needs, and accommodations.
- Complete a co-op placement to gain practical work experience and information for postsecondary planning.

Long-Term Goals

- Attain Secondary School Diploma.
- Complete 40 hours of community service.
- Consider postsecondary options.

Owen's Report Card—Grade 11

Course	Percentage Grade	Comments
Regional Geography	75%	Demonstrates considerable knowledge of course content. Improved use of critical thinking processes.
Foundations of Mathematics	93%	Has demonstrated very high achievement in meeting expectations in this course. An excellent effort has been made.
Healthy Living Co-Op	86%	Excellent demonstration of initiative and self-motivation. Improved making appropriate choices for future goals. Practised the employability skills required for success in the workplace.

Owen Bachman

Why Is Owen Considered to Be At-Risk?

Definition of At-Risk

Students who are "at-risk" for school failure are found in all walks of life; all racial, ethnic, linguistic, and socio-economic backgrounds are affected. While there is no universal definition of the term *at-risk*, most educators and researchers concur that those individuals who have an increased probability of having problems in school can be identified as having biological (e.g., factors related to pregnancy and child health) or environmental risk factors (e.g., extreme poverty and abuse) present in their lives (Kopp, 1983). These students are at considerable risk for failing school, enduring ongoing social and behavioural difficulties in school, dropping out, and experiencing significant difficulties throughout their lives.

What We Know . . .

Dimensions of the "At-Risk" Concept

Schonert-Reichl (2000) recognized the ambiguities in the use of the term *at-risk* and subsequently explored the origins of the risk concept as well as the current state of knowledge regarding the conceptualization of risk in children and youth. In her review of the literature, she found the following salient dimensions of the "at-risk" concept:

- Risk status should be viewed as steps along a continuum, ranging from low risk to high risk.
- Risk factors are multi-dimensional and interactive.
- Risk factors include factors from the individual level reaching far out to the societal level (e.g., individual factors, family factors, peer factors, school factors, social or community factors, and social-cultural factors).
- The "at risk" label assumes prediction (e.g., antecedent conditions or predisposing factors).
- Risk is multiplicative (exposure to multiple risks increases the likelihood of having one or more problem outcomes).
- The nature and timing of risk factors may differentially affect outcomes.
- Risk propensity is heightened during periods of transition.

In summary, Schonert-Reichl (2000) stated that "the 'at-risk' label is relative and not absolute, it is the result of environmental as well as individual factors, it is not a fixed quantity, and it is dependent on context. Moreover, risk is not a monolithic construct that, once achieved, will always be present. It cannot be seen as a fixed attribute of the student, because the circumstances in which it may occur are dynamic" (p. 11).

Source: Schonert-Reichl (2000).

As in Owen's case, there are environmental factors that can certainly affect a child's success in school. Table 12.1 outlines some of these factors and presents the behavioural and physical indicators of child abuse and neglect.

TABLE 12.1 Physical and Behavioural Indicators of Child Abuse and Neglect

Type of Abuse/Neglect	Physical Indicators	Behavioural Indicators
Physical abuse: Any act which, regardless of intent, results in a non-accidental physical injury to a child	Questionable injuries, such as: • bruises, welts, or other injuries; • burns; • fractures; or • lacerations or abrasions	• Being uncomfortable with physical contact • Being wary of adult contacts • Showing behavioural extremes, either aggression or withdrawal • Not wanting to go home • Reporting an injury by a parent • Complaining of soreness or moving uncomfortably • Wearing excessive clothing to cover the body • Chronically running away from home (adolescents) • Reluctance to change clothes for gym activities (attempt to hide physical injuries)
Neglect: A caregiver's failure to provide something that a child needs	• Undernourished appearance • Lethargic • Signs of inadequate food or sleep • Untreated injuries • Evidence of unattended illness	• Begging for or stealing food because of persistent hunger • Poor hygiene • Inappropriate dress for the weather • Accidents and injuries • Risky adolescent behaviour • Promiscuity, drugs, and delinquency • Being shunned by peers • Clinging behaviour
Sexual abuse: The misuse of adult authority by involving children in sexual activities	• Most physical indicators would be found during a physical exam by a medical practitioner	• Expressions of age-inappropriate knowledge of sex and sexually "pseudomature" behaviours • Sexually explicit drawings • Highly sexualized play • Statements of unexplained fear of a person or place • Stated desire to avoid a familiar adult • Expressions of excessive concern about gender identity (boys) • Nightmares • Sleep interruptions • Withdrawal • A child's statement of sexual abuse

Source: Republished with permission of Sage publishing. "Teacher Perceptions of Mainstreaming/Inclusion, 1958–1995." T.E. Scruggs and M.A. Mastropieri. *Teaching Exceptional Children*, 63 (1), 1996. Permission conveyed through Copyright Clearance Center, Inc.

Owen suffered both abuse and neglect in his early years. Unfortunately, things did not get much better for him when he began school and entered foster care. He was placed in multiple foster homes each year, and he attended at least two different schools (sometimes more) in any given school year. He ran away from home countless times, often refused to go to school, and never did any homework. Owen was considered a "problem child" by both his foster parents and teachers because he exhibited numerous and persistent problematic behaviours. Upon reflection, he and his current foster parents feel that these behaviours were primarily caused by his pervasive feeling that he was not loved or cared for by his parents, his foster parents, or any of his teachers; his frustrations with non-success in school; and because he felt he was stupid. Owen remembers one of his Grade 4 resource teachers telling him he was too dumb to even be in school.

Assessing the Student Who Is At-Risk

Owen displayed problematic behaviours and difficulties with learning from the time of his entry into school. In Grade 2, he was diagnosed as having ADHD (inattentive type) and was put on Ritalin. In addition to his inattentive ADHD behaviours, he also exhibited many other behaviours that aggravated his caregivers and educators. He was known as a "bad kid" and, unfortunately, this became his pervasive persona. For the most part, Owen was well known for simply not wanting to do anything that any adult asked or told him to do. He was defiant and belligerent and non-compliant all the time.

In the early elementary grades, Owen received help from resource room teachers. However, because he moved from school to school so often during this period, he was not referred for a psycho-educational assessment until the age of 10. The referral for this assessment was put forth by Owen's teacher. Her biggest concern was Owen's emotional well-being despite the fact that he was working below grade level in most subjects.

The psycho-educational assessment included a battery of standardized tests (see *Excerpts from Owen's Psycho-Educational Assessment* on p. 368). Owen's intellectual functioning was assessed using the WISC-III. Overall, he was determined to be in the average to low-average range with his non-verbal abilities being his strength; in other words, he is a visual learner. He did exhibit "mild difficulties" on tasks requiring the processing and interpreting of verbal information. Consistent with his previous diagnosis of ADHD, Owen also had difficulty with auditory attention. Owen's academic functioning was assessed using the Wechsler Individual Achievement Test, Second Edition (WIAT-II). He demonstrated weaknesses in both reading and spelling skills. According to the psychologist, "if these academic needs are not addressed, Owen is considered at risk for increased behaviour problems." The psychologist acknowledged that while he did not note any significant social, emotional, or behaviour problems at the time of the assessment, he had been told that there were some psycho-social concerns about Owen and that the appropriate referrals were being made.

From the Psychologist's Notebook

It is not at all surprising that Owen's psycho-educational assessment made little reference to the environmental factors (e.g., family situation and foster care) that surely affected his early school life. It is common for such an assessment to primarily focus on intellectual and academic functioning since these are considered most relevant to a student's success with learning. However, while Owen's emotional and behavioural difficulties were apparently being addressed through other referrals and other assessments, it may have been beneficial to consider an at-risk student from a more holistic perspective. A growing body of literature is providing consistent evidence that psychological trauma or traumatic stressors create barriers to student learning, classroom functioning, and overall well-being. Therefore, to ignore this aspect of Owen's life when determining his educational programming seems to have resulted in a less than optimal plan for his schooling. This is especially true because Owen's risk factors occurred in clusters (e.g., neglected by parents, moved from foster home to foster home, and moved from school to school) and probably negatively contributed to each other. It is known that the higher the number of stressors, the more likely the child will suffer poor educational outcomes (Bernardini & Jenkins, 2002; Jensen, 2009).

What We Know . . .

Trauma and the At-Risk Student

Trauma and stressor related disorders are defined by the DSM-5 as follows:

> *These disorders are caused by exposure to a stressful or traumatic event. They have a close relationship and are often diagnosed with other disorders such as anxiety disorders, obsessive-compulsive and related disorders, and dissociative disorders. The most common characteristics of these disorders are the absence or ability to experience pleasure, an emotional state of anxiety, depression, or unease, outbursts of anger or aggression, or removal from association.* (American Psychiatric Association, 2013)

The vast majority of youth with emotional and behavioural symptoms have experienced one or more traumatic events (Copeland, Keeler, Angold & Costello, 2007) with some specific at-risk populations experiencing much higher rates of trauma (Arroyo, 2001). As the American Psychological Association (2008) stated, traumatic stress responses evoke intense fear, horror, terror, and helplessness and cause a debilitating form of distress that compromises the ability to function effectively. The identifying factors in children and youth, such as sleep disturbance, sadness, irritability, the development of new fears, reduced concentration, anger, loss of interest in normal activities, and a decline in school work are not indicative of pathology. These factors are

Continued

natural products of our instinctive human desire to cope and survive whereby we automatically activate our fight-or-flight-or-freeze response to a perceived threat. While this natural response is usually a healthy and protective feature of the psyche, constantly retriggering this threat-response cycle can alter a person's psychological security and his or her ability to make sense of the world. For some students, trauma-related stress is evident in their externalized behaviours, but others provide no signs whatsoever that they are struggling to cope. Unfortunately, there is also evidence that educators are mostly unaware of the occurrence or effects of trauma on students and the challenges they bring to school. Without externalized evidence or disclosure, it is unlikely that educators will consider trauma the cause of a student's demonstrated emotions and behaviours. Sadly, without an awareness of the trauma, educators falsely attribute a student's resulting poor grades, lack of compliance, decline in attendance, and other problematic actions that negatively affect schooling to the student's making deliberate (defiant and manipulative) choices. These misunderstandings and the usually negative consequences that follow (e.g., detentions, suspensions, expulsions) further exacerbate the student's fragile psychological situation and often lead to school failure and poor overall well-being.

Much research has demonstrated that trauma negatively affects students' behaviour, attention, memory, personality, grades, peer relationships, compliance, and attendance (Cook, et al., 2005; Dorado & Zakrzewski, 2013; Slade & Wissow, 2007; Yasik, Saigh, Oberfield, & Halamandaris, 2007). Students in special education are not immune from these effects (Ferguson et al., 2005; Meichenbaum, 2006). Additionally, many students with exceptionalities, including those at-risk, have histories of behaviours indicating a need for mental health supports (Kline & Silver, 2004). Those at-risk typically suffer from a lack of school connectedness—they do not believe that adults in the school care about their learning and about them as individuals (Blum, 2005). This is a grave concern for educators because school connectedness is viewed by many researchers as the number-one protective factor for students who have suffered trauma (Saewyc, Wang, Chittenden, Murphy, & The McCreary Centre Society, 2006).

How Has Owen's Development Been Affected by the Trauma He Has Experienced?

While Owen's physical development has flourished and resulted in great athletic success, the same cannot be said about his social and emotional development or his cognitive development. He has clearly been viewed as an emotionally troubled student who has difficulty with the behavioural and learning expectations of school. According to Owen:

> Not that long ago, I didn't care about anyone or anything—especially not school. I
> was constantly getting into trouble, having fights, swearing, and being suspended for

one thing or another. My foster parents and my teachers didn't like me, and thought I couldn't do anything in school. Even the other kids didn't like me because of the way I acted. Whenever I felt stressed out or threatened or felt that there was some sort of conflict, I used to just zone out. I'd curl up and shut out the world and sleep or I'd run away. I'd walk the streets, sometimes for hours at a time just to stay away from the trouble. Or, I'd get mad at something and just leave class. One time I climbed up on the roof of the school just to see if I could do it and because I wanted to see what it looked like from up there.

Then I got to come and live here with Marianne and Bill, who are my parents now. My brother was living here with them so I got placed here too. It has taken a while to get it, but now I am a much happier person. This is the first time I have ever felt loved by anyone. My Mom and Dad love and care for me unconditionally. I don't even mind that they make me responsible for my actions.

Owen was obviously greatly affected by his early life experiences. It is not surprising that a child who dealt with such significant ongoing trauma was unable to develop normally under such adversity. This disruption in his development has had long-lasting effects. His current foster parent, Bill Kelly, describes these effects as follows:

When Owen first came to live with us, he exhibited tics and monumental mood swings—he was either in a very calm state or he was very, very agitated and angry.

School environments are often loud and unpredictable. Children who have experienced trauma may find these environments stressful or triggering for their hyperarousal and hypervigilance, which can impact their ability to listen, pay attention, and learn.

He was virtually inconsolable during these periods and could not be reasoned with at all. In addition to his anger, he exhibited lots of high-risk-taking tendencies like climbing on top of the school and trying drugs. He was diagnosed with bipolar disorder and has been on medication for it ever since. He still takes a maintenance dose of Zyprexa for the bipolar disorder and a 12-hour dose of Adderall for his ADHD. It took several attempts at drug combinations to get his dosages right. While Owen has come a long, long way, he still has some problems. He struggles through many tough days, ones that are filled with angry outbursts, meltdowns, and lots of emotional and behavioural setbacks. As his parents, it can be really hard. We are always thankful that at least one of us is not willing to give up on him on any of those troublesome days.

What We Know . . .

The Effects of Trauma on a Child's Development

Trauma affects children differently at different ages, depending on their temperament and existing resilience factors. Chronic childhood trauma interferes with the capacity to integrate sensory, emotional, and cognitive information into a cohesive whole; it sets the stage for unfocused and irrelevant responses to subsequent stress. The solutions to life's problems used by traumatized children seem unconnected and unhelpful. Yet these are all they have. Children who have suffered chronic abuse or neglect often experience developmental delays across a broad spectrum, including cognitive, language, motor, and socialization skills. One of the key messages to emerge in recent times is that trauma affects the whole person: their mind, brain, body, spirit, and relationships with others.

Impacts on Academic Performance

- Reduced cognitive capacity
- Sleep disturbance (causing poor concentration)
- Difficulties with memory (making learning harder)
- Language delays (reducing capacity for listening, understanding, and expressing)

Impacts on Social Relationships

- Need for control (causing conflict with teachers and other students)
- Attachment difficulties (making attachment to school problematic)
- Poor peer relationships (making school an unpleasant experience)
- Unstable living situation (reducing learning and capacity to engage with a new school)

The impact of abuse and neglect on children's academic performance and social functioning are closely associated with affect dysregulation. There are two forms in which affect dysregulation can be manifested: hyperarousal and dissociation. Hyperarousal often goes hand in hand with hypervigilance. Hypervigilant children will often perceive neutral stimuli as threatening. Although physiologically prepared for danger, they are in practice very poor at assessing real danger and often put themselves in situations of risk. Attention and concentration are both severely reduced by hypervigilance, as the child is constantly on the alert for danger and not relaxed enough to listen and learn. Dissociative children often do not know how they feel; seem distant, vague, and unreachable; and they may become oppositional as a response to a demand for attention, contact, and closeness. They are often just not thinking, and they do not want to think.

Source: Excerpted from *Calmer classrooms: A guide to working with traumatized children*, Child Safety Commissioner of Victoria, Australia (2007).

What Has School Been Like for Owen?

Owen's education up to Grade 8 consisted of special education services provided by many different teachers in many different schools. These services were delivered mostly through pull-out programming with some dedicated time in a special class during his Grade 1 year. Owen's academic performance was poor, and his report cards showed no signs of progress in any of the fundamental curricular areas of the elementary program. As Owen's current foster mother (who is a teacher) stated:

> There were no indications that he could succeed in school, but this appears mostly due to the fact that he purposefully did as little as possible and, because he demonstrated so many outrageous and offensive behavioural problems, his teachers were content to let his academic growth slide as long as he was not causing trouble. And, because he was constantly being moved from foster placement to foster placement, none of his guardians paid much attention to how he did in school. Therefore, due to a litany of interrelated circumstances, the education system was not held accountable for Owen's demise.

During the later elementary years, Owen was a frequent-but-mild drug user (e.g., marijuana) and sometimes abused alcohol as a way of running away from or avoiding his tumultuous world. He did not care about the consequences that were levied against him—he would simply get up and leave the situation (in his home or school) and sometimes disappear for days at a time. As a result, he was "running the streets" from an early age.

At 16 years of age, Owen is now a personable young man who is quite able to clearly describe his school experiences. Owen shared what school is like for him now:

> I am doing much better in school since I started living here. I am taking applied courses and my average is in the 80s, and that's without doing a stitch of homework. All the comments on my report cards say that my school work and my attitude are "excellent." I am taking applied math, construction, applied English, and gym. Even though I am only in Grade 11, I only have one mandatory course left to do before I can get my high school diploma. When I finish school, I want to do an electrical apprenticeship. That means I have to do Grade 11 physics and Grade 12 math. I am

looking forward to those courses. My teachers like me and they treat me nice and I like school . . . I like going to school more than I ever did before. Now I know what goal setting is and how important it is to work for something. I just got a part-time job so that I can save up enough money to pay for my Driver's Ed course . . . then I can get my licence.

Before I moved in here, it was easier to not do stuff. I now know what it is like to have to do something even though I don't want to. I know that I can trust people more and that things will turn out okay. Before, I knew that things would always turn out bad, and they did. Kids like me just need someone to teach them how to deal with things that are stressful, like taking a walk, playing the guitar, reading a book, or going off to their room for some alone time.

As Owen indicated, his life changed dramatically when he moved in with the Kellys. It marked the beginning of a complete transformation of both his personal life and his school life. Marianne and Bill were well aware of Owen's history when he arrived on their doorstep. At the very beginning, they made it very clear that attending the local high school was mandatory and not up for negotiation and that the use of drugs was not going to be tolerated. They also clearly established that they wanted him to be part of their family—that they cared for him. This is not to say that things went smoothly from the start. Marianne describes Owen's move to their home as follows:

We told Owen he had to participate in a series of trade-offs if he was to get what he wanted. This meant that if he wanted something, he had to do something. This mostly involved doing chores or just being good in order to earn what he wanted. He was so socially inept that we had to teach him even the simplest social skills and then give him opportunities to practise and use them. He really resisted taking any risks, even though many situations were actually no risk or very low risk. Owen had been hurt or betrayed or uncared for so many times that he was very risk adverse. Instead of taking part in new or unfamiliar situations where he felt anxious or had little-to-no control, he would run from them or avoid committing himself.

As for school, Owen was first put on the Essentials Program, which places very few academic demands on students and is mainly designed to keep them in school. This was ideal for Owen because he needed time to adjust and to feel like he was having some success in school. Now he is doing great and feels ready to tackle some academic high school courses. We are very proud of him.

We also told Owen when he came to live with us that he had to participate in some sort of out-of-school activity. It just happened that a Learn-to-Dive program was available on Tuesdays . . . the best possible day in our family's schedule. We thought this would be a good fit because Owen had indicated that he loved diving/ jumping off a local bridge. Thankfully, the diving program was very structured and demanded high levels of commitment, dedication, and self-regulation; all the things that we required of Owen at home. One of the major trade-offs that Owen had to negotiate between home, school, and diving was that he had to get good grades to be allowed to spend more time on training and travelling to diving meets with the team.

Diving has become very important in his life because both coaches welcomed him with open arms and did not pre-judge him like many of his teachers had done in the past.

From the Psychologist's Notebook

Undoubtedly, Owen was a problem student for most of his school years. His well-documented, persistent, and highly irritating actions were enough to put any teacher off. It is not surprising that nearly all of his more than 20 teachers (up until Grade 9) did little except discipline him or refer him to the principal. The question that usually gets asked is "How can a teacher be expected to put up with what Owen was doing when they have a professional obligation to the rest of the students in the class?" In simple and realistic terms, no teacher has to put up with what Owen did. In more complex terms, Owen's teachers obviously had no understanding of at-risk students and their symptomatic behaviours. Without a proper and logical explanation of why Owen did what he did, he was, in his teachers' eyes, simply a bad kid who was making deliberate choices to misbehave and cause people misery. This was probably even more the case as Owen got older and was expected to exercise more emotional and behavioural restraint.

   This perspective is not uncommon for educators facing students who constantly exhibit highly problematic behaviours. However, there is no intention here to infer that Owen's teachers deliberately cast him in a bad light so they could wash their hands of their responsibilities to help him. In fairness, his teachers simply did not know that his actions were those of a traumatized child because his actions looked exactly like someone who was making conscious choices to wreak havoc whenever he was in school. His teachers were probably well intentioned but they were not well informed.

What Educational Approach Is Best for Owen?

Now that Owen's home life is stable and many of his emotional and behavioural issues are being addressed, learning has become a more positive experience for him. In fact, he is excelling in the high school courses he is taking and looking forward to the challenges of even more difficult academic courses. While he still has an IEP to address some of his developmental delays (i.e., language disabilities and behavioural issues), his teachers have indicated that his IEP is not really as relevant as it once was: "Owen is usually quite capable of doing his work without the accommodations listed in his IEP . . . sometimes we forget just how much he has been through and just how negative school was for him at one time." It is unfortunate, however, that it took so long for Owen to find a home where he is loved and supported and an environment where education is now a priority. School could have been more of a haven for him in his early school years if educators had been more knowledgeable about his needs.

What We Know . . .

Strategies for Dealing with Traumatized Children

Understand the Child

Understanding trauma and attachment difficulties brings compassion and empathy; understanding that the child may be developmentally younger than his or her chronological age will guide teaching practices.

Manage Your Own Reactions

Working with traumatized children can bring strong emotions; staying calm will help the child to calm him- or herself.

Acknowledge That Children May Need Help

Help children to comply with requests. Because they don't necessarily want to please adults, helping them comply will avoid power battles.

Structure and Consistency

Traumatized children often have little internal structure and need firm boundaries, rules, expectations, and consequences—applied with sensitivity and calm.

Time-In, Not Time-Out

Traumatized children experience time-out as yet more rejection, increasing their feelings of shame and worthlessness; time-in keeps them engaged in a relationship.

Connect

Dissociative children, who are often quiet and compliant, need gentle and consistent attempts to connect with them.

Consequences, Not Punishment

Use natural consequences that relate to the problem behaviour and are designed to repair damaged property or damaged relationships.

Structure Choices to Remain in Control

Offer choices with humour and creativity to avoid power battles; keep the child responding to you rather than allowing them to control the interaction.

Acknowledge Good Decisions and Choices

Traumatized children often don't respond well to praise, but still need positive reinforcement for doing something well. Comment on the job well done rather than intrinsic characteristics.

Support Parents and Caregivers

Get to know the parents or caregivers; keep up good communication and don't communicate through the child. Try to be understanding and compassionate. Living with a child who has trauma and attachment difficulties can be very stressful.

Maintain Your Role

Don't be tempted to move too far out of your role (e.g., taking on a caregiver role). These children need caring and competent teachers.

Plan for Challenging Incidents

Many traumatized children will have outbursts of extreme anger and aggression. Be prepared for these situations as soon as they occur—establish safety, stay calm, calm the child, assist the child to understand what happened, assign well-thought-out consequences, help the child take responsibility, and debrief the child's classmates.

Source: Excerpted from Child Safety Commissioner of Victoria, Australia (2007).

Owen's early-year experiences were certainly dire and he faced many obstacles. His behaviour during this time is not surprising; in fact, it is a reflection of how a child with few supports and little nurturing tries to cope. By acting out in extreme ways he was able to control his environment, to some degree, even though it produced unpleasant ramifications. So, how did Owen make it? It appears that he is a very strong individual. This is especially evident in his rapid progression from novice diver to National B Champion in his age group. Diving at that level is not for the timid. This raises the importance of the concept of resiliency, especially in terms of how educators can help their students become more resilient.

resiliency
A dynamic process whereby an individual exhibits positive behavioural adaptations when encountering significant adversity; a two-dimensional construct involving exposure to adversity and the positive adjustments that result.

What We Know . . .

Resiliency

Modern contemporary views of resiliency clearly indicate that it is not a magical personality trait evident in some children yet absent in others. Rather, resilience is best described as a psycho-socio-cultural construct wherein external factors are also deemed salient (Leadbeater, Dodgen, & Solarz, 2005). This means the child's environment as well as his or her development of coping and managing skills are equally important. This also means that with proper instruction and support, all children can learn to be resilient. Benard (2006) provides us with four primary understandings that have come out of resilience research over the last 35 years:

1. Resilience is a capacity all youth have for healthy development and successful learning.

Continued

2. Certain personal strengths are associated with healthy development and successful learning.

3. Certain characteristics of families, schools, and communities are associated with the development of personal strengths and, in turn, healthy development and successful learning.

4. Changing the life trajectories of children and youth from risk to resilience starts with changing the beliefs of the adults in their families, schools, and communities. (p. 4)

Similarly, Ungar and colleagues (2007) identified seven aspects of resilience evident across several different cultures. It is noteworthy that each of the aspects below depends in some way on the others. These aspects of resilience include the following:

1. Access to material resources (availability of financial, educational, medical, and employment assistance or opportunities, as well as access to food, clothing, and shelter)

2. Access to supportive relationships (relationships with significant others, peers, and adults within one's family and community)

3. Development of a desirable personal identity (desirable sense of one's self as having a personal and collective sense of purpose, ability for self-appraisal of strengths and weaknesses, aspirations, beliefs and values, including spiritual and religious identification)

4. Experiences of power and control (experiences of caring for one's self and others, the ability to effect change in one's social and physical environment to access health resources)

5. Adherence to cultural traditions (adherence to, or knowledge of, one's local or global cultural practices, values, and beliefs)

6. Experiences of social justice (experiences related to finding a meaningful role in one's community that brings with it acceptance and social equality)

7. Experiences of a sense of cohesion with others (balancing one's personal interests with a sense of responsibility to the greater good; feeling a part of something larger than one's self socially and spiritually) (p. 302)

Learning to Be Resilient

Schools that provide refuge from high-stress situations are crucial in the development of resilience. Three essential protective factors are required—caring relationships, high expectations, and opportunities to make meaningful contributions. According to Hurlington (2010) at Trent University:

[C]aring relationships must acknowledge strengths within children and build from there. High expectations for students' performance and behaviour are essential because they help students understand that they have the capacity to be successful. Boundaries are clearly delineated and rich resources (those that allow a child to reach beyond their independent abilities) are made available. Finally, it is critical for young people to have opportunities for meaningful

participation. These are authentic tasks wherein students can demonstrate their abilities in real-world settings and experience the rewards that come from benevolence. (pp. 2–3)

Hurlington also explained how educators can help to enhance resilience in students by implementing seven key strategies:

1. Affirm relationships by getting to know your students and their non-school environments. Teachers need to be more aware of the environments where students spend time outside of school. These environments can be enriching or problematic. Getting to know your students and their life contexts allows for early intervention when risky issues arise . . . Research suggests that the short-term intervention of even a single caring adult can make a profound difference.

2. Affirm relationships by seeking to understand individual strengths . . . accepting that each student comes to school with unique understandings, knowledge, and awarenesses encourages us to appreciate their strengths. With students who are most at-risk, this can be a challenge. Resilience, however, develops out of existing strengths, so this step is essential. Keeping a log of the actions of your students that impress you can help when there are conflicts.

3. Affirm relationships by encouraging students to know each other. Equally important is the need to encourage students to develop positive social relationships with each other. Providing time for students to be celebrated for who they are and to be appreciated for their complexity (ethno-cultural, social, gender, and otherwise) in a sensitive context is key to these relationships. Bulletin boards featuring interesting facts about or abilities of students can help to achieve this community connection and foster a sense of belonging.

4. Set high expectations: Cooperatively build the parameters of the learning environment. A focus on resilience means using the existing strengths of students to deal with the areas of weakness. Teachers need to acknowledge the challenges that students face, but must still hold them to high expectations. In collaboration with students, teachers can set high expectations demarcated by clear boundaries. Consider developing boundaries in collaboration with students as one of the first tasks of the new school year; this will ensure that students have an operational understanding of rules and policies . . .

5. Set high expectations: Cooperatively build realistic goals with individual students. Setting meaningful goals means that students will have something to celebrate throughout the year. These goals must be student-focused, student driven, personalized, and documented. Teachers need to be involved in the acknowledgement of milestones. This celebration becomes a systematic element of learning communities where personal growth is lauded within one's social environment. Teachers can encourage deeper learning through opportunities for reflection with their students, using strategies such as student-led interviews.

Continued

6. Ensure opportunities for meaningful participation. A resilience-rich environment will allow for the development of skills and attitudes that should have come from other learning environments. Teachers help to develop critical life skills like conflict resolution, problem solving, and stress management. Opportunities for meaningful participation mean that youth are encouraged to take sensible risks, to make the world a laboratory for exploring the ramifications of their positive actions. Service learning is an excellent way for students to try out their newly-developed life skills . . .

7. Live resilience development as a process . . . When we understand the complexities of the lives of young people, it may seem that nothing can be done to address the significant challenges they face in their lives. The systematic application of resilience principles in the classroom and school may provide a young person with the only/best environment to develop good coping mechanisms. It is a process that is worth it! (pp. 3–4)

How Is Owen Different from Other Students Who Are At-Risk?

There are many students within the Canadian education system who are considered at-risk despite the fact they are not all formally identified as such. Their family backgrounds and life situations may be somewhat similar to Owen's (e.g., abuse, neglect, lack of stable home) or they may be very different (e.g., war-affected refugees, immigrants, minority students, Indigenous students). Despite any differences, the trauma experienced by all students who are at-risk is likely to have a negative impact on their academic performance and on their social relationships. And, like Owen, they can all benefit from resiliency, which can be enhanced in classrooms and schools. The goal is to increase student engagement and inclusivity rather than leaving these students on the periphery. Further, educators play a key role in recognizing how students from all backgrounds are coping with the at-risk factors in their lives. It is critical that students who are having difficulties are referred for the mental health supports they require. Immediate intervention is obviously most desirable when students who are at-risk are struggling.

Something to Think About

Consider a 12-year-old student who just arrived in Canada as a war-affected refugee. What might this student be facing in her life, both inside and outside of school? How might you as a teacher help this child with the obstacles she is facing? Read "Students from Refugee Backgrounds: A Guide for Teachers and Schools" published by the British Columbia Ministry of Education (2015).

Language barriers as well as different school systems and customs can potentially cause students from refugee backgrounds to feel isolated at school. Teachers and school staff have the opportunity to avoid this by providing specialized and additional services.

Closing Owen's File

Owen's life has been difficult to say the least. Whether or not it was intentional, many people failed him over the course of his childhood. Yet, despite significant trauma and feelings of being unloved and unable to learn, he has survived to become a well-liked young man who is learning to cope with the demands of school and everyday life. The key to his recovery lies with the Kellys. After all, recovery from trauma is not possible if the traumatized individual does not feel safe. Marianne and Bill are the trusted, caring adults that Owen needed to begin healing from his experiences of abuse and neglect. They know that traumatized children often require time to change and, therefore, they continue to never give up on Owen. As a result, he now has a more positive view of himself, especially in terms of what he is capable of achieving. There will undoubtedly be difficult times ahead. Owen will likely have long-term effects from his negative childhood experiences, but he is learning how to be responsible and how to cope. It is now possible that he will "overcome the odds" and become a confident and accomplished adult. He certainly has begun to show signs of resiliency in that he is more socially competent, he is developing a healthy sense of identity, and he has goals and a sense of purpose in terms of his future. He now has the protective factors within his family and his school to successfully continue his recovery.

From the Psychologist's Notebook

Owen's externalized behaviours (defiance, overreactions, severe dissociation, verbal abuse, etc.) were a combination of flight-fight-freeze responses that certainly got him into trouble. Unfortunately, none of his educators in the years up to and including Grade 8 made any connections between his horrendous home life and his outrageous actions. They probably did not have any understanding of the traumas he may have suffered as a result of his compounding at-risk factors. Since connections to caring adults as well as stable home environments are known protective factors for at-risk youths, Owen's educators may have assumed that his foster parents were meeting these needs. However, Owen's ever-changing sets of foster parents were the very instability that caused a great deal of his trauma. His substance abuse and risk-taking and defiant behaviours were attempts to cope.

Owen's trauma ended in the time between Grade 8 and 9 when he moved to his current foster placement. As a result of the overall structure imposed by the Kellys as well as the supports they provided, Owen was able to feel less like he was constantly under duress and, consequently, he developed much better coping skills. These have made the biggest impact on his schooling and overall well-being. The key message here for educators is that when the stressors in a child's life are removed or mitigated, the child is able to access underlying strengths and capabilities.

Summary

Students deemed to be at-risk have an increased probability of having problems in school and can be identified as having biological or environmental risk factors. These students are in jeopardy of failing school, enduring ongoing social and behavioural difficulties, dropping out, and experiencing significant difficulties throughout their lives. Most of the factors that have made the difference in Owen's school life, and in his life in general, are related to the concept of resilience. Given that Owen's turnaround did not occur because of significant educational interventions, it behooves every teacher to consider how their personal contact with individual students can be purposefully targeted to build students' resilience against the potential life traumas they may face. Many of the resilience elements described in this chapter are also found in the fundamental features of good classroom management found in Chapter 4.

Learning More about Students Who Are At-Risk

Academic Journals

American Psychologist
Canadian Journal of School Psychology
Child Development
Journal of Education for Students Placed at Risk

Books

Craig, S. E. (2008). *Reaching and teaching children who hurt: Strategies for your classroom.* Baltimore, MD: Paul H. Brookes Pub.

Geldard, K. (Ed.). (2009). *Practical interventions for young people at risk.* Los Angeles, CA: Sage.

Goldstein, S., & Brooks, R. (Eds.). (2013). *Handbook of resilience in children* (2nd ed.). New York, NY: Springer Science+Business Media.

McGrane, G. (2010). *Building authentic relationships with youth at risk.* Clemson, SC: National Dropout Prevention Network.

Oehlberg, B. (2006). *Reaching and teaching stressed and anxious learners in grades 4–8: Strategies for relieving distress and trauma in schools and classrooms.* Thousand Oaks, CA: Corwin Press.

Snow, D. R. (2005). *Classroom strategies for helping at-risk students.* Aurora, CO: Mid-Continent Research for Education and Learning.

Stormont, M., Reinke, W. M., Herman, K. C., & Lembke, E. S. (2012). *Academic and behaviour supports for at-risk students: Tier 2 interventions.* New York, NY: Guilford Press.

Vaughn, S., Bos, C. S., & Schumm, J. S. (2011). *Teaching students who are exceptional, diverse, and at risk in the general education classroom* (5th ed.). Upper Saddle River, NJ: Pearson Education.

Web Links

Bolstering Resilience in Students: Teachers as Protective Factors

www.edu.gov.on.ca/eng/literacynumeracy/inspire/research/WW_bolstering_students.pdf
This document is a research-into-practice series produced by a partnership between The Literacy and Numeracy Secretariat and the Ontario Association of Deans of Education.

Centre for Research on Youth At Risk

http://w3.stu.ca/stu/sites/cryar/index.aspx
This centre at St. Thomas University in Fredericton, New Brunswick, engages in applied research on at-risk youth. The purpose of the website is to disseminate knowledge both across Canada and from the research community to the broader public.

Developmental Issues for Young Children in Foster Care—American Academy of Pediatrics

http://pediatrics.aappublications.org/content/106/5/1145.full
This article reviews the following developmental issues relevant to young children in foster care: (a) the implications and consequences of abuse, neglect, and placement in foster care on early brain development; (b) the importance and challenges of establishing a child's attachment to caregivers; (c) the importance of considering a child's changing sense of time in all aspects of the foster care experience; and (d) the child's response to stress.

Imagining a Future: Reaching At-Risk Students by Teaching the Whole Child

http://etfovoice.ca/node/229/page/0/4
The author of this article encourages teachers of Indigenous students to learn more about First Nations cultures and histories by taking on a learner role. The First Nation students themselves are identified as critical pedagogical resources.

National Dropout Prevention Center/Network

www.dropoutprevention.org
The National Dropout Prevention Center/Network (NDPC/N) is an established resource for sharing solutions for student success and does so through its clearinghouse function, active research projects, publications, and through a variety of professional development activities.

School Connectedness: Strategies for Increasing Protective Factors among Youth

www.cdc.gov/healthyyouth/protective/pdf/connectedness.pdf
This document provides a comprehensive consideration of school connectedness—the belief by students that adults in the school care about their learning as well as about them as individuals.

Using Technology to Support At-Risk Students' Learning

https://edpolicy.stanford.edu/sites/default/files/scope-pub-using-technology-report.pdf
This brief describes approaches to technology use as they apply to high school students who have been at risk of failing courses and exit examinations or dropping out due to a range of personal factors (such as pregnancy, necessary employment, mobility, and homelessness) and academic factors (special education needs, credit deficiencies, and lack of supports for learning English).

Taking It into Your Classroom . . .

Including Students Who Are At-Risk

When a student who has been traumatized is first placed in my classroom, I will

- review what I know about trauma, attachment difficulties, and resulting developmental delays,
- read the student's file,
- consult with the student's previous teachers,
- consult with the student's parents or caregivers, and
- meet with the school-based team to discuss the student's current school year.
- Other: _____

When I suspect a student in my classroom is at-risk, I will

- review what I know about students who are at-risk,
- consult with other school personnel who are familiar with the student,
- consult with the student's parents or caregivers,
- observe the student's behaviour across several school settings, and
- meet with the school-based team to present my findings and discuss how to proceed.
- Other: _____

Key points to remember in my daily interactions with a student who has experienced trauma:

- The student may have trouble controlling anger and impulses.
- The student may be quiet and compliant and need gentle persuasion to connect with others.
- The student may need firm boundaries, rules, expectations, and consequences.
- The student may tend to engage in power battles.
- The student may not respond well to praise but still needs positive reinforcement.
- The student may view time-out as yet more rejection.
- Other: _____

Key points regarding the education of a student who is at-risk:

- The student may have delays in all areas of development.
- The student may have poor concentration.
- The student may have difficulties with memory.
- The student may have a reduced capacity for listening, understanding, and expressing.
- The student may benefit from strategies that enhance student resiliency.
- Other: _____

CHAPTER 13

Creating Your Own Special Stories

LEARNING OBJECTIVES

After learning the material in this chapter, you should be able to:

- Define the term *mentoring* and explain how it relates to the teaching profession.

- Explain how having a mentor can benefit a beginning teacher.

- Describe the behaviours of effective teacher mentors.

- Describe the type of mentor you feel would be best for you and why.

- Define the term *professional development* (PD) and explain how it relates to the teaching profession.

- Discuss how you will develop your own professional development plan.

- Provide examples of how you plan to take the information learned in this course into the classroom.

Learning More

In this text, we have introduced you to several different categories of exceptionalities. As we stated in Chapter 1, it was not our intent to provide comprehensive information that would qualify you as an expert once you had read and discussed the material. However, we do hope that you have learned a great deal from each of the chapters, and you will now take the time to learn more about aspects of exceptionalities that are of particular interest to you.

Something to Think About

There is a plethora of information available on the Internet about education, including information about students with exceptionalities. Sometimes this information is not complete or entirely accurate. How can you best use the Internet as a resource for your teaching needs? Are there any sites that you would recommend to your fellow students? What makes these sites better than others you have accessed?

Mentoring

Perhaps one of the most undercrused resources available to beginning and less-experienced teachers is mentoring. While much can be learned from print material, there is often nothing more effective than learning from an expert in the area, someone who has a great deal of experience in carrying out the same tasks you will be expected to perform and in the same setting with similar students. Appropriate mentors include experienced teachers, educational specialists, and school administrators who are willing to share their experiences and advice and answer questions on a regular basis. Many of these individuals already perform a nearly identical task when mentoring prospective teachers during practicum placements. Therefore, they are quite comfortable with the mentoring process including having less-experienced teachers observe them while working in classroom situations.

mentoring
Providing ongoing guidance and support to an individual who is less experienced in a particular field.

If your school does not have an established mentoring program, you may want to discuss with your principal the possibility of acquiring a mentor or starting a school-wide mentoring program. Or, you may choose to approach a staff member, or a teacher you know in another school, with whom you seem to relate well and ask if he or she would be willing to serve as your mentor on an informal basis. Either way, you will certainly benefit from having someone to talk with regarding your concerns and ideas.

What We Know . . .

The Mentoring of Beginning Teachers

According to the Mentoring and Leadership Resource Network (www.mentors.net), an international initiative designed to help educators with best practices, mentoring has a significant impact on beginning teachers. Evaluations of mentoring programs have

Continued

revealed that when experienced teachers engage in meaningful conversations with new teachers, and provide them with ongoing support, the mentored teachers are better able to confront the challenges in their classrooms. Feedback from teachers who have been part of mentoring programs indicates that having a mentor in their first year impacted their decision to stay in teaching. The participants emphasized that the emotional support the mentor provided, the non-judgmental feedback, and the opportunity to grow professionally were all critical to their positive feelings about their chosen career.

What Can You Expect from a Mentor?

According to the self-reflections of Petersen (2007), a mentor often observes interactions in a teacher's classroom, especially when there are challenging student behaviours, and then offers advice on how to better manage the situation. Mentors also recommend appropriate resources and provide general teaching tips and strategies.

More specifically, the American Institutes for Research (2015) identified the behaviours of effective mentors. These individuals

- know they will learn from the beginning teachers and the mentoring experience and express this to the beginning teachers;
- demonstrate that they are reflecting on their own practice while working with beginning teachers;
- are open to feedback and willing to adapt as needed;
- establish goals with the beginning teachers for their partnership;
- continue to build their own content knowledge and familiarity with emerging research and practices in the field;
- can articulate the art of teaching;
- do not feel the need to prove competence by having all the answers or pre-empting the beginning teachers' discoveries;
- know when to share knowledge and when to help beginning teachers discover things on their own;
- use learner-centred approaches with beginning teachers;
- encourage beginning teachers to assess their own conclusions and decisions;
- set high expectations for beginning teachers and recognize and build on teachers' strengths;
- are able to articulate clearly what they know and have experienced;
- ask open-ended questions to elicit thinking; and,
- probe for specificity, clarity, elaboration, and precision so that teachers learn to reflect on their practice and learn to better articulate their thinking and reasoning.

How Do Mentors Benefit from the Mentoring Experience?

The mentoring experience has also proven to be positive for the mentors themselves. Huling (2001) summarized the benefits experienced by teacher mentors: (a) an increase in their own professional development, (b) a focus on their own reflective practice, (c) a strengthening of their commitment to the teaching profession, (d) an enhancement of their self-esteem, (e) the development of strong collegial collaborations, and (f) an improvement in their leadership skills.

What Does Mentoring Look Like in the Delivery of Special Education?

In a comprehensive analysis of 10 studies of mentoring related to special education, Griffin, Winn, Otis-Wilborn, and Kilgore (2003) outlined the elements of mentoring that were associated with successful teaching experiences: (a) a culture of shared responsibility and support, (b) interactions between new and experienced teachers, (c) a continuum of professional development, (d) de-emphasized evaluation, (e) clear goals and purposes, and (f) diversified content.

Something to Think About

What are the characteristics that you would look for in a mentor? What kind of mentoring style would best suit your personality and your teaching needs? How might you approach a staff member about becoming your mentor?

Ongoing Professional Development in Special Education

As teachers, you are probably aware that you are expected to engage in professional development (PD) throughout your teaching career as another way to learn more about educational issues and best practices. This expectation is common, if not mandatory, for most teachers around the world and, if it is not, it should be. We encourage you to make this type of ongoing professional growth a personal mission rather than merely treating it as a professional obligation.

Based on our years of experience in developing and delivering PD sessions for educators, we know that special education is always one of the most requested topics. As you begin to experience the joys and challenges of teaching students with exceptionalities, you will quickly recognize areas of knowledge and training that you may want to augment. Professional development sessions addressing some of these areas may be provided by your school, school board, or teachers' union, but it is highly probable that your specific learning needs will not be addressed at the time you require the new information or skills. In these instances, we recommend you seek out professional development that provides you with exactly what you need. Think of this as your own form of special education. The British Columbia Teachers' Federation (www.bctf.ca) offers helpful tools for developing self-directed professional development plans.

> **professional development (PD)**
> An ongoing commitment to ensure that one's skills and abilities to do one's job are always relevant and up to date.

Something to Think About

If you are a beginning teacher, consider the coursework you will complete in your teacher education program. What professional development are you likely to need in your early years as a classroom teacher?

Continued

If you are a more experienced teacher, consider both the coursework you have completed and the professional development experiences you have had to date. What professional development are you likely to need over the next five years?

One of the best sources for special education PD is the Council for Exceptional Children (CEC), the largest international professional organization dedicated to improving the educational success of individuals with disabilities or gifts and talents. The CEC offers different types of PD, including webinars, podcasts, hot topic workshops, and conferences. If you feel you need some specific information about a certain topic, the CEC also provides professional development–related documents that can be downloaded. Within the CEC, a Canadian/ US committee advises the board of directors on communication, networking, liaising, professional knowledge and skills, and advocacy. In Canada, there are provincial CEC units in Alberta, British Columbia, Manitoba, Ontario, and Saskatchewan. Each of their websites lists the types of professional development they will offer throughout the current year.

Some examples of past sessions provided by the CEC (Canada) include "Positive Behaviour Support and Functional Behaviour Assessment" (Saskatchewan CEC, 2016), "Paradigm Shifts and Unusual Techniques for Managing Resistance" (Manitoba CEC, 2016), "Level B Testing— What Now? From Interpretation to Implementation" (Alberta CEC, 2015), and "Universal Design for Learning" (British Columbia CEC, 2016). Some examples of past instructional sessions that were provided by the CEC (US) include webinars entitled "Determining What Works Best for Students: From Philosophy to Practice: Enacting Authentic School Inclusion" and "Teaching Emotional Regulation: Essential Skills for Students with Disabilities." The current PD listings offered by the CEC can be found at www.cec.sped.org.

Finally, make a note to yourself to check out the annual CEC Convention and Exposition. This event is one of the most attended conferences on special education in North America, especially by teachers. Each year teachers, academics, researchers, and parents (and often students) gather to learn more about advances and changes in special education. There are a wide variety of sessions to suit whatever your requirements or interests may be. It is also a great forum for networking with others who work with students with exceptionalities. This often leads to the informal sharing of excellent teaching ideas and the establishment of professional friends whom you can call on for resources and moral support.

What We Know . . .

Reflective Practice

reflective practice
An ongoing process that involves both a consideration of one's current practice and contemplation of how that practice may be improved based on various credible sources of information.

While a lot of the research on teacher practice has centred on pedagogy, curriculum knowledge, and theories of motivation and learning, more attention is now being paid to the significance of teachers' awareness and understandings of their own practice; this trend is known as **reflective practice**. Teachers need a clear vision of what teaching expertise is, or what they want it to be, so they can observe their own work with an eye toward growth and progress and envision themselves making changes as required;

"without a clear vision of one's ultimate goals and responsibilities as a professional, the metacognitive reflection needed for assessing progress is difficult if not impossible to achieve" (Bransford, Derry, Berliner, Hammerness & Beckett, 2005, p. 76). Therefore, it is imperative to develop the inquiry skills needed to look critically at one's own practice and to adapt as one sees fit.

The pervasive mindset of teachers, therefore, should be to embody an explicit plan to reflect on, appraise, and learn from their teaching in a continual and organized fashion. This plan has to include a variety of sources of information about good teaching that ranges from evidence contained in the literature, to the practices of colleagues and mentors, to one's local knowledge about specific students and classrooms. These intertwined perspectives provide an informed expert base that is indispensable when exercising one's professional judgment. This is not to say that teachers without this specific type of plan are not good teachers; but it does say that teachers with this type of plan will be much better teachers and will continue to get better throughout their careers.

Step 1: Identify and analyze the elements of your teaching you think need attention.

Step 2: Gather new information about these elements (or these types of elements).

Step 3: Decide whether or not the new knowledge has implications for your identified elements.

Step 4: Design and implement your desired changes.

Step 5: Choose a time when you plan to go through this process again.

Taking It into Your Classroom

We know from experience that knowledge gained through participation in a college or university course does not always transfer readily into the classroom. In other words, it is sometimes difficult to remember and use information you have been exposed to as a student. You may find yourself a little panicked as you stand in front of your class trying to recall exactly what you are supposed to do in a certain situation. While this is normal for a beginning or less-experienced teacher, it is somewhat disconcerting and can sometimes be avoided with proper preparation. This was our intention when providing you with the *Taking It into Your Classroom* summary at the end of each chapter. These summaries were designed to be used well after you have completed your coursework. Ideally, you will have copies of these summaries, with your own notes attached, in a binder or stored on a computer so that you can easily access them while working as a teacher. Then, when you are faced with a particular situation, you can quickly review your notes to see if you have the information that will help in your decision making or in your choice of teaching strategies. Acting without thinking or being improperly informed is obviously not recommended in the classroom, especially in the case of students with exceptionalities where many assumed norms do not apply.

As an example, suppose you have a student in your class who has an identified learning disability. During the first few weeks of school, the student is disruptive during reading and math classes and does not respond well to your stern looks or your prompts for him or her to focus and attend to his or her work. You wonder if you should implement more severe consequences for the disruptive behaviours. A quick scan of your notes on learning disabilities reminds you of the "Key points to remember in your daily interactions with a student who has a learning disability":

- The student may have low self-esteem and low self-concept.
- The student may exhibit a discrepancy between ability and performance.
- The student may be impulsive and speak without thinking.
- The student may not be able to interpret body language and tone of voice.
- The student may have difficulty understanding spoken language.
- The student may not react well to change.

In light of this information, you reflect on what your student is experiencing: a new classroom (i.e., a change in his or her routine and environment), a new teacher (i.e., may be difficult to understand the meaning of the teacher's body language and tone of voice), and exposure to the subjects he or she finds most difficult (i.e., reading and math). To complicate matters, the student is impulsive and blurts out comments without intending to disrupt the class. You now realize that implementing more severe consequences for the unwanted behaviours is not the ideal response. In fact, it would probably have a negative impact on his or her self-esteem and self-concept and result in an increase in the very behaviours you are trying to eliminate. Instead, you decide to help the student settle into the routine of the classroom and speak with him or her about the unacceptable behaviours and how the two of you can work together to reduce these behaviours over time. You also decide to review his or her reading and math abilities with the special education expert in your school. This more thoughtful and informed response to your student was simply prompted by a quick review of your own notebook. We hope that this simple suggestion does not feel patronizing in any way. We present it here as a reminder, because in the reality of a busy classroom the specific details of working with students who have exceptionalities often get overlooked.

It is important to have resources such as your notes available to you, even if they only contain brief summaries of information. You will be extremely busy as a teacher with little time to research relevant issues by thumbing through a book or sifting through sites on the Internet. On many occasions, as in the example above, reviewing your notes will be enough to help you with a particular situation or at least get you started looking in the right direction. Other times, you will have to access more comprehensive resources and your existing notes will serve as an excellent guide in your search for the necessary information.

Because we believe in the importance of collecting informational summaries, we encourage you to add to your notebook whenever you come upon new information that may be useful at a later date. For instance, there may be a time when you have to research a new issue that relates to a student in your class (e.g., the first time you find yourself teaching a student who has a profound hearing impairment). Making notes to summarize this newly researched information will help you with your teaching throughout the school year and in any subsequent years when you have a student with a similar disability.

We are convinced that *Taking It into Your Classroom* will not be an onerous task, and as you build upon your teaching experiences you will not have to access your notes quite as often as you do during your first years in the classroom. Perhaps, when you have many years of teaching behind you, and you have the opportunity to mentor beginning and less-experienced teachers, you can share your notes with them and encourage them to include the same practice in their school life.

Your Own Special Stories

If you already have experience as a teacher, you are certainly cognizant of the heterogeneity of students. If you are a beginning teacher, you will quickly become aware of the uniqueness of each and every one of the students who enters your classroom. Their varied strengths and needs may seem daunting to you at first, but you will soon come to appreciate what each student has to offer to the classroom as a whole.

Undoubtedly, some of your future students will have needs that are significant enough to require the input of a team of professionals. As a member of this team, you will benefit from the support of team members who have expertise in delivering various special services. In other words, you should take advantage of the input offered by others and not be afraid to ask for advice and help in meeting the needs of a particular student. As we have mentioned previously, no regular classroom teacher is expected to be a specialist in the area of exceptionalities. However, you will most likely spend more time with the student than most other team members, so you should also feel confident about sharing your observations regarding the student's experiences in the classroom. What may seem insignificant to you may be quite valuable to your colleagues who view the student from an entirely different perspective.

Being observant is an important characteristic of being an exemplary teacher. While this will not only assist you in your teaching of all students in the inclusive classroom (i.e., recognizing whether or not a particular student's needs are being met), it will also help you spot those students who may have unidentified disabilities. We recommend that you keep a notebook on your desk so that you can easily record any observations that you make during the school day. This notebook should have a designated section for each student in your class. Simply arrange the sections in alphabetical order (by last name) according to your class or attendance list. It will allow you to quickly make note of what you have observed. These observations may be random at first, but you will probably notice a trend when a student is consistently having a particular difficulty. Once a trend is apparent, you can then make more specific observations, perhaps while trying some minor interventions that you feel may be of immediate help. If the student continues to have problems, you will have readily available documentation to bring to the appropriate special services personnel and the school-based team.

Over the school year, as you learn more about your students who have been identified as exceptional, you will begin to develop your own collection of special stories. You will undoubtedly build upon the information you first received in a particular student's file and, by the end of the school year, you will have a more detailed story to tell the teachers who will have that student in their classes the following year. So often this information is lost as teachers fail to communicate with one another in this way across grade levels. However, you can certainly make a difference and set an example in your school. By being open to learning more about special education and actively playing a role on all your students' special services teams, you will be able to use what you have learned and what you have observed to enrich the stories that unfold in your classroom. By putting these stories into words, either verbally or in writing, you will allow future teachers of your students to have the insight you have had when reading the eight stories in this text.

Something to Think About

Imagine that at the beginning of the school year one of the students presented in this text is assigned to your classroom. What effect would knowing the student's story have on your feelings about teaching a student with this particular exceptionality? How would the information you have learned about the student aid in your preparation for the school year? How would the student benefit from your extensive knowledge about his or her situation?

Closing Our File

Just as we have closed the file on the stories of each of the eight students presented in this text, we now must close our file on the third edition of *Special Education in Canada*. Being an educator means always being open to learning, and we have certainly learned a great deal in the writing of all three editions of this book. We sincerely hope that you too have increased your understanding of special education; your future students will certainly benefit from this knowledge.

Something to Think About

Now that you are familiar with the stories of the students presented in this text, how do you feel about teaching in an inclusive environment? Did any particular story from this text have a significant impact on how you think and feel about special education? How will you use the information you have learned to better prepare for the inclusion of children with exceptionalities in your classroom?

Glossary

amniocentesis A prenatal procedure in which a small amount of amniotic fluid is extracted from the amnion surrounding the fetus to check for genetic abnormalities.

anecdote A brief narrative account of a student's behaviour that is of interest to the observer.

antecedents Behaviours that occur immediately before an identified problematic behaviour; often the cause of the behaviour.

assistive technology Application or device used to maintain or improve physical ability or academic performance.

audiologist Healthcare professional who assesses and treats hearing and balance problems.

auditory brainstem response (ABR) Electrodes placed on the scalp and each earlobe monitor the brain's response to clicking noises sent through earphones.

auditory verbal therapy (AVT) A parent-centred approach that encourages the use of spoken language to help children learn to listen and to speak.

autonomous learners Students who can learn, solve problems, and develop new ideas with minimal external guidance.

backward shaping Learning how to complete the last part of a task first so that a student can experience the sense of achievement.

behavioural observation audiometry (BOA) Child is presented with sounds while an audiologist watches for changes in behaviour to indicate that the sound has been heard.

Canadian Association for Community Living (CACL) A Canada-wide association of family members and others who work for the benefit of individuals of all ages who have an intellectual disability.

cerebellum A brain structure known to support motor learning and more recently thought to support cognitive functions as well as affective regulation.

chorionic villus sampling A prenatal procedure in which samples of the placenta are used to determine genetic abnormalities in the fetus; usually done for women over 35.

classification The ability to recognize and construct relationships among objects, imagined objects, and classification systems themselves.

cloze format A fill-in-the-blank activity in which students use the context of other written or spoken words to comprehend the concept being conveyed.

cochlear implant A surgically implanted electronic device that helps to improve hearing in individuals with severe to profound impairments.

cognitive-behavioural therapy An action-oriented form of therapy used to alter distorted attitudes and resulting problem behaviours by identifying and replacing negative or inaccurate thoughts with more positive ones.

co-morbid condition A condition evident in an individual at the same time he or she has another distinguishable condition.

conceptual information Mental representations of the knowledge one has about concrete (dog) or abstract (love) objects.

concrete referent Something existing in reality or in real experience that is used to reinforce an abstract idea.

conductive hearing loss Sound is not conducted efficiently through the ear canal, ear drum, or middle ear.

differentiated curriculum A program of study that is altered in content or instructional method to suit the specific needs of a student who has an exceptionality.

dizygotic twins Two eggs are fertilized by two separate sperm resulting in fraternal or non-identical twins.

dysfunctional environment Surroundings that contain or perpetuate a persistent series of high-stress incidents that threaten one's sense of psychological security.

ear, nose, and throat (ENT) specialist A physician trained in the medical and surgical treatment of the ears, nose, throat, and related structures of the head and neck.

enriched curriculum A program of study that is expanded beyond its typical depth and scope, usually involving independent study.

formal assessment Testing that has standardized administration procedures, is usually scored on norm-referenced criteria, and uses a formal interpretive procedure to provide reliable and valid assessment data.

formative assessment Determination of a student's level of understanding on an ongoing basis during the instructional period.

FM system A frequency modulation system. It consists of a transmitter microphone used by the speaker (e.g., teacher) and a receiver used by the listener. The receiver transmits the sound to the listener's ears or directly to the hearing aid.

frequency sampling Counting how many times a particular behaviour occurs during a designated period of time.

functional behavioural analysis (FBA) A process of determining why a student engages in problematic behaviour and how that behaviour relates to his or her environment.

genetic marker A gene or DNA sequence that has a known location on a chromosome and is associated with a particular physical trait.

grade acceleration Skipping a grade to participate in appropriate levels of curricula.

individualized education program (IEP) A document that describes a student's specialized learning expectations and the educational services that will be implemented to help the student meet these expectations.

informal assessment A variety of data-gathering processes that allow variation in administration procedures and more subjective interpretations of results.

integration The process of reintegrating students with exceptionalities back into the regular classroom, if possible.

itinerant teacher A fully qualified teacher who usually specializes in an area of education (e.g., the education of students with hearing or visual impairments) and provides assistance to teachers and students in a number of schools.

Kurzweil Software designed for those who struggle with reading. It provides a text-to-speech reader.

legally blind Worse than or equal to 20/200 acuity in the better eye or a visual field extent of less than 20 degrees in diameter horizontally.

low vision Diminished visual capability that cannot be improved to a sufficient level to enable an individual to perform common visual tasks adequately.

mainstreaming The selective placement of students with exceptionalities in regular classrooms on a part-time basis where possible (dependent on ability).

mentoring Providing ongoing guidance and support to an individual who is less experienced in a particular field.

meta-analysis A quantitative and systematic analysis of the results of two or more studies that have examined the same issue in the same way.

meta-cognitive ability The ability to understand and monitor one's own cognitive systems and their functioning.

mixed hearing loss Having a combination of a conductive hearing loss and a sensorineural hearing loss.

mnemonics Simple mental aids such as abbreviations, rhymes, or images that help people remember more complex material.

monozygotic twins Identical twins developed from the same fertilized ovum.

neuropathology The study of diseases of nervous-system tissue, most often using tissue from small surgical biopsies or examination of whole brains.

norm-referenced tests Tests that indicate a student's performance based on how the student's score compares with the scores of other similar students.

occupational therapist A certified specialist who evaluates and treats muscle and joint disorders to determine their impact on daily living activities.

otoacoustic emissions (OAE) A microphone placed in the inner ear detects any response to sound that is introduced through a probe in the outer ear.

phonological awareness The awareness that language is composed of sounds and these sounds (syllables) are related to letters.

phonological memory The coding of information according to its sounds for temporary storage in working or short-term memory.

physical therapist A certified specialist who evaluates and treats physical ailments using physical therapy programs.

play audiometry When a child hears a sound, he or she must pair the sound with an activity in a game.

positive reinforcement When desired student behaviour is increased through the use of rewards.

postmodernist approach An approach that negates the concept of scientific truth and supports the fragmentation of all academic subjects into a variety of perspectives—with no "answers."

professional development An ongoing commitment to ensure that one's skills and abilities to do one's job are always relevant and up to date.

psychiatrist A medical specialist who deals with the diagnosis, treatment, and prevention of mental and emotional disorders.

psychometrist A certified specialist who administers educational, psychological, and psychometric tests under the supervision of a psychologist.

reflective practice An ongoing process that involves both a consideration of one's current practice and contemplation of how that practice may be improved based on various credible sources of information.

resiliency A dynamic process whereby an individual exhibits positive behavioural adaptations when encountering significant adversity; a two-dimensional construct involving exposure to adversity and the positive adjustments that result.

response cost Removal of a student's previously received reward as a consequence of misbehaviour.

retinopathy of prematurity A disorder that affects the blood vessels in the eyes of premature babies.

scaffolding A teaching method that enables a student to complete a task through a gradual reduction of teacher support.

self-efficacy Beliefs about one's capability to produce certain levels of performance in order to influence events that affect one's life.

self-esteem Our subconscious beliefs about how worthy, lovable, valuable, and capable we are.

sensorineural hearing loss Damage to the inner ear (cochlea) or hearing nerve in the brain.

seriation The ability to organize objects in a progressive sequence according to some measurable dimension (height, width, length, size, shape, etc.).

simultaneous processing difficulties A deficit in the ability to efficiently process multiple pieces of information at the same time.

social worker A certified specialist trained in psychotherapy who helps individuals deal with mental health and daily living problems in an effort to improve overall functioning.

speech-language pathologist A certified specialist who evaluates and treats communication disorders.

standardized tests Tests prepared by experts, administered under exactly the same conditions, and used primarily to compare students' performances with other students' performances.

systematic prompting An organized and pre-determined series of prompts used to increase desired behaviours.

teratogens Agents classed as radiation, maternal infections, chemicals, or drugs that disturb the development of an embryo or fetus.

test reliability Refers to the consistency of a measure; degree to which test items give the same results.

test validity Degree to which a test measures what it purports to measure.

time-out Removal of a student from a learning activity or learning situation as a consequence of misbehaviour.

time sampling Observations of student behaviour that are recorded at fixed, regular intervals.

visual perception The ability to see and to interpret what is seen.

visual reinforcement audiometry (VRA) Child is presented with sounds. The expected response is localization to the sound source. Each expected response is reinforced with a visual distracter.

visual-spatial abilities The ability to efficiently visualize and manipulate objects in space.

WordQ Software designed for those who struggle with writing. It integrates word prediction and text to speech.

References

Chapter 1

Bedgell, J., & Molloy, A. (1995). Eleven-year-old Emily Eaton wins landmark Charter victory. *Forum/Abilities, 23*, 52–54.

Eaton v. Brant County Board of Education. [1997] 1 S.C.R. 241.

Jay, J. K. (2004). Variations on the use of cases in social work and teacher education. *Journal of Curriculum Studies, 36*(1), 35–39.

Learning Disabilities Association of Canada. (2005). *Eaton v. Brant County Board of Education* [1997] 1 S.C.R. 241; (1996) 31 O.R. (3d) 574 (1996) 142 D.L.R. (4th) 385; 1997, Supreme Court of Canada. *LD and the law: Case summaries.* Retrieved from www.ldac-taac.ca/LDandtheLaw/casesBrant_Law-e.asp

Kantar, L. D. (2013). Demystifying instructional innovation: The case of teaching with case studies. *Journal of the Scholarship of Teaching and Learning, 13*(2), 101–115.

Kuntz, S., & Hessler, A. (1998). *Bridging the gap between theory and practice: Fostering active learning through the case study method* (Report No. SPO37985). Washington, DC: Association of American Colleges and Universities. (ERIC Document Reproduction Services No. ED420626).

King, A. (2000). Situated cognition. In A. Kazdin (Ed.), *Encyclopedia of psychology* (pp. 289–291). Washington, DC, and New York, NY: American Psychological Association and Oxford University Press.

Nath, J. (2005). The roles of case studies in the educational field. *International Journal of Case Method Research & Application, 17*(3), 396–400.

York University's Daily News. (2013). York students get a personal lesson on inclusive education. Retrieved from http://yfile.news.yorku.ca/2013/08/07/york-students-get-a-personal-lesson-on-inclusive-education/

Chapter 2

Bennett, S. (2009). *Including students with exceptionalities. What works? Research into practice.* Research Monograph #16. Government of Ontario. Retrieved from www.edu.gov.on.ca/eng/literacynumeracy/inspire/research/Bennett.pdf

British Columbia Ministry of Education. (1985). *Special Programs: A manual of policies, procedures and guidelines.* Vancouver, BC: Author.

British Columbia Ministry of Education. (2016). Student statistics 2015–2016: Province—public and independent schools combined. Retrieved from www.bced.gov.bc.ca/reports/pdfs/student_stats/prov.pdf

CBC News. (2016, March 9). Classroom inclusion review is unnecessary, say supporters. Retrieved from www.cbc.ca/news/canada/new-brunswick/inclusion-classrooms-policy-review-1.3482926

Council for Exceptional Children. (2006). *New flexibility in testing students with disabilities: A positive step.* CEC position document. Arlington, VA.

Council for Exceptional Children. (2013). *CEC's 2012–2014 strategic plan.* Retrieved from www.cec.sped.org/About-Us/Mission-and-Vision/Strategic-Direction

Council for Exceptional Children. (2016). *CEC's summary of selected provisions in Every Student Succeeds Act (ESSA).* Retrieved from http://cecblog.typepad.com/files/cecs-summary-of-selected-issues-in-every-student-succeeds-act-essa-1.pdf

Crawford, C. (2005). *Inclusive education in Canada: Key issues and directions for the future.* Toronto, ON: L'Institut Roeher Institute.

Edmunds, A. L. (2003). The inclusive classroom—Can teachers keep up? A comparison of Nova Scotia and Newfoundland & Labrador perspectives. *Exceptionality Education Canada, 13*(1), 29–48.

Edmunds, A. L., Halsall, A., Macmillan, R. B., & Edmunds, G. A. (2000). *The impact of government funding cuts on education: Report from a teacher survey.* Halifax, NS: Nova Scotia Teachers' Union.

Ellis, J. (2014). *Special education.* Retrieved from http://eugenicsarchive.ca/discover/encyclopedia/535eee5c7095aa000000025d

Enculescu, S. (2015). Inclusive education benefits all students, with or without disabilities. Retrieved from http://e-include.eu/news/279-inclusive-education-benefits-all-students-with-or-without-disabilities

Exceptionality Education Canada. (2003). *Preparing Canadian teachers for inclusion, 13(1).*

FSU Center for Prevention & Early Intervention Policy. (2002). *What is inclusion? Including school-age students with developmental disabilities in the regular education setting.* Tallahassee, FL: Florida State University. Retrieved from www.cpeip.fsu.edu/resourceFiles/resourceFile_18.pdf

Goguen, L. (1993). Right to education for the gifted in Canada. In K. A. Keller, F. J. Monks, & A. H. Passow (Eds.), *International handbook of research and development of giftedness and talents* (pp. 771–777). New York, NY: Pergamon Press.

Human Rights Watch. (2016, September 21). We are still fighting for a school for my child. Retrieved from www.hrw.org/news/2016/09/21/we-are-still-fighting-school-my-child

Hutchinson, N.L. (2010). *Inclusion of exceptional learners in Canadian schools: A practical handbook for teachers.* Toronto: Pearson Canada Inc.

King, W., & Edmunds, A. L. (2001). Teachers' perceived needs to become more effective inclusion practitioners: A single school study. *Exceptionality Education Canada, 10*(3), 23–37.

Kohama, A. (2012). Inclusive education in India: A country in transition. Retrieved from http://intldept.uoregon.edu/wp-content/uploads/2012/12/INTL-UG-Thesis-Kohama.pdf

Korte, G. (2015, December 11). Every Student Succeeds Act vs. No Child Left Behind: What's changed? *USA Today*. Retrieved from www.usatoday.com/story/news/politics/2015/12/10/every-student-succeeds-act-vs-no-child-left-behind-whats-changed/77088780/

Lieberman, L. M. (1992). Preserving special education for those who need it. In W. Stainbeck & S. Stainbeck (Eds.), *Controversial issues confronting special education: Divergent perspectives*. Boston, MA: Allyn and Bacon.

Lupart, J. (2000). Students with exceptional learning needs: At-risk, utmost. Paper presented at the Pan-Canadian Education Research Agenda Symposium, Ottawa, April 6–7.

Lupart, J., & Odishaw, J. (2003). Canadian children and youth at-risk. *Exceptionality Education Canada, 13*(2&3), 9–28.

MacKay, W. A. (1987). The *Elwood* case: Vindicating the educational rights of the disabled. *Canadian Journal of Special Education, 3*(2), 103–116.

McKenzie, J. (2003). Gambling with children. *No Child Left, 1*(1). Retrieved from http://nochildleft.com/2003/jancov03.html#index

Meijer, J. W. (2010). Special needs education in Europe: Inclusive policies and practices. *Zeitschrift für Inklusion, 2*. Retrieved from www.inklusiononline.net/index.php/inklusion/article/viewArticle/56/60

Mertler, C. (2011). Teachers' perceptions of the influence of No Child Left Behind on classroom practices. *Current Issues in Education, 13*(3). Retrieved from http://cie.asu.edu/

National Association of School Psychologists. (2002). *Rights without labels*. Position statement adopted by NASP Delegate Assembly, 2002, July 14. Retrieved from www.nasponline.org/information/pospaper_rwl.html

People for Education. (2014). *Special education*. Retrieved from www.peopleforeducation.ca/wp-content/uploads/2014/04/special-education-2014-WEB.pdf

Pudlas, K. A. (2003). Inclusive educational practice: Perceptions of students and teachers. *Exceptionality Education Canada, 13*(1), 49–64.

SEAC Learning. (2007). *Unit 1: An historical overview of special education in Ontario*. Retrieved from www.seac-learning.ca/unit1.htm

Siegel, L. (2000). *A review of special education in British Columbia*. Victoria, BC: British Columbia Ministry of Education.

Smith, S. (2010). Applying a response to intervention framework for noncategorical special education identification. Retrieved from www.readperiodicals.com/201006/2061410611.html

Sokal, L., & Sharma, U. (2014) Canadian in-service teachers' concerns, efficacy, and attitudes about inclusive teaching. *Exceptionality Education International, 23*, 59–71.

Taylor, G. R., & Harrington, F. (2001). Incidence of exceptionality. In G. R. Taylor (Ed.), *Educational interventions and services for children with exceptionalities* (2nd ed.) (pp. 3–13). Springfield, IL: Charles C. Thomas Publisher.

US Department of Education. (2002). *Twenty-third annual report to Congress on the implementation of the Individuals with Disabilities Act* (p. AA3). Washington, DC: Author.

Woloshyn, V., Bennett, S., & Berrill, D. (2003). Working with students who have learning disabilities—Teacher candidates speak out: Issues and concerns in preservice education and professional development. *Exceptionality Education Canada, 13*(1), 7–28.

Chapter 3

Alberta Education. (2013). *Inclusive education*. Retrieved from http://education.alberta.ca/department/ipr/inclusion/faq.aspx

Beery, K. E., Buktenica, N. A., & Beery, N. A. (2010). *Beery Buktenica Developmental Test of Visual-Motor Integration* (6th ed.). San Antonio, TX: Pearson.

Bloom, B. S. (1964). *Stability and change in human characteristics*. New York, NY: Wiley.

Canadian Test Centre. (2008). *Canadian Achievement Test* (4th ed.). Markham, ON: Author.

Center for Applied Special Technology. (2013). *UDL guidelines—Version 2.0: Research evidence*. Retrieved from www.udlcenter.org/research/researchevidence

Council for Exceptional Children. (2005). *Universal Design for Learning: A guide for teachers and educational professionals*. Arlington, VA: Pearson Merrill Prentice Hall.

Council for Exceptional Children. (2013). *Individualized education plans*. Retrieved from www.cec.sped.org/Special-Ed-Topics/Hot-Topics/Individualized-Education-Plans?sc_lang=en

Edgar, E., & Pair, A. (2005). Special education teacher attrition: It all depends on where you are standing. *Teacher Education & Special Education, 28*(3/4), 163–170.

Edmunds, A. L., Edmunds, G. A., & Hogarth, L. (2012, February). The behaviour management network: KNAER knowledge mobilization. Paper presented at the 2012 Ontario Education Research Symposium, Toronto, Ontario.

Flanagan, D., Mascola, J., & Hardy-Braz, S. (2009). *Standardized testing*. Retrieved from www.education.com/reference/article/standardized-testing/

Fuchs, L., & Fuchs, D. (1996). Linking assessment to instructional interventions: An overview. *School Psychology Review, 15*(3), 318–324.

Gregory, R. J. (2000). *Psychological testing: History, principles, and applications* (3rd ed.). Toronto, ON: Allyn and Bacon.

Hale, L. (2015). *Behind the shortage of special ed teachers: Long hours, crushing paperwork*. Retrieved from www.npr.org/sections/ed/2015/11/09/436588372/behind-the-shortage-of-special-ed-teachers-long-hours-crushing-paperwork

King-Sears, M. E., Burgess, M., & Lawson, T. L. (1999). Applying curriculum-based assessment in inclusive settings. *Teaching Exceptional Children, 32*(1), 30–38.

Manitoba Education. (2010). *Student-specific planning: A handbook for developing and implementing individual education plans (IEPs)*. Winnipeg, MB: Manitoba Education.

McLoughlin, J. A. & Lewis, R. B. (2005). *Assessing students with special needs* (6th ed.). Columbus, OH: Pearson/Allyn Bacon.

Newfoundland and Labrador Department of Education. (2007). *Focusing on students: The ISSP and pathways commission report*. St. John's, NL: Government of Newfoundland and Labrador.

Nova Scotia Department of Education. (2009). *The program planning process: A guide for parents*. Halifax, NS: Government of Nova Scotia.

Ontario Ministry of Education. (2004). *The individualized education plan (IEP): A resource guide*. Toronto, ON: Queen's Printer for Ontario.

Overton, T. (1996). *Assessment in special education: An applied process* (2nd ed.). Columbus, OH: Merrill.

Reynolds, C. R., & Kamphouse, R. W. (2015). *Behavior assessment system for children* (3rd ed.). Circle Pines, MN: American Guidance Service.

Roid, G. (2003). *Stanford–Binet Intelligence Scale* (5th ed.). Chicago, IL: Riverside Publishing.

Salvia, J., & Ysseldyke, J. E., with Bolt, S. (2007). *Assessment: In special and inclusive education* (10th ed.). Belmont, CA: Cengage Learning.

Salvia, J., Ysseldyke, J., & Bolt, S. (2010). *Assessment in special and inclusive education* (11th ed.). Belmont, CA: Wadsworth Cengage Learning.

Salvia, J., Ysseldyke, J., & Witmer, S. (2016). *Assessment in special and inclusive education* (13th ed.). Belmont, CA: Wadsworth Cengage Learning.

Saskatchewan Education. (2009). *Personal programs (PPP) guidelines*. Regina, SK: Saskatchewan Ministry of Education.

Sternberg, R. J., & Salter, W. (1982). Conceptions of intelligence. In R. J. Sternberg (Ed.), *Handbook of human intelligence* (pp. 3–28). Cambridge, UK: Cambridge University Press.

UDL-Universe. (2016). *A comprehensive universal design for learning faculty development guide*. Retrieved from www.udluniverse.com

US Department of Education. (2000). *A guide to the individualized education program*. Washington, DC: Office of Special Education and Rehabilitative Services.

Vygotsky, L. S. (1978). *Mind in society: The development of higher psychological processes*. (M. Cole, V. John-Steiner, S. Scribner & E. Souberman, Eds.). Cambridge, MA: Harvard University Press.

Wechsler, D. (1974). *Manual for the Wechsler Intelligence Scale for Children-Revised*. Cleveland, OH: Psychological Corporation.

Chapter 4

Bandura, A. (1977). *Social learning theory*. Englewood Cliffs, NJ: Prentice-Hall.

Bandura, A. (1986). *Social foundations of thought and action*. Englewood Cliffs, NJ: Prentice-Hall.

Berk, L. E. (1996). *Infants and children: Prenatal through middle childhood*. Boston, MA: Allyn & Bacon.

Brophy, J. (2006). History of research on classroom management. In C. M. Evertson & C. S. Weinstein (Eds.), *Handbook of classroom management: Research, practice and contemporary issues* (pp. 17–46). Mahwah, NJ: Lawrence Erlbaum.

Canter, L., & Canter, M. (1993). *Succeeding with difficult students: New strategies for reaching your most challenging students*. Santa Monica, CA: Lee Canter & Associates.

Doyle, W. (2006). Ecological approaches to classroom management. In C. M. Evertson & C. S. Weinstein (Eds.), *Handbook of classroom management: Research, practice and contemporary issues* (pp. 97–126). Mahwah, NJ: Lawrence Erlbaum.

Dreikurs, R., & Cassel, P. (1992). *Discipline without tears* (2nd ed.). New York, NY: Plume.

Edmunds, A. L. (2010, April). The effectiveness of a school-wide approach to classroom management. Paper presented at American Educational Research Association, Denver, Colorado.

Edmunds, A. L., & Edmunds, G. A. (2015). *Educational psychology: Applications in Canadian classrooms* (2nd ed.). Toronto, ON: Oxford University Press.

Edmunds, A. L., Edmunds, G. A., & Hogarth, L. (2012, February). *The behaviour management network: KNAER knowledge mobilization*. Paper presented at the 2012 Ontario Education Research Symposium, Toronto, Ontario.

Evertson, C. M., & Weinstein, C. S. (2006). Classroom management as a field of inquiry. In C. M. Evertson & C. S. Weinstein (Eds.), *Handbook of classroom management: Research, practice and contemporary issues* (pp. 4–42). Mahwah, NJ: Lawrence Erlbaum.

Farrell, M. (2012). *New perspectives in special education: Contemporary philosophical debates*. New York, NY: Routledge.

Friedman, I. A. (2006). Classroom management and teacher stress and burnout. In C. M. Evertson & C. S. Weinstein (Eds.), *Handbook of classroom management: Research, practice and contemporary issues* (pp. 925–944). Mahwah, NJ: Lawrence Erlbaum.

George, H. V. (1991). Organization of one's classroom. *Guidelines, 13*, 95–99.

Greenberg, J., Putnam, H., & Walsh, K. (2014). Training our future teachers: Classroom management. Retrieved from www.nctq.org/dmsView/Future_Teachers_Classroom_Management_NCTQ_Report

Johnson, F. L., & Edmunds, A. L. (2006). *From chaos to control: Understanding and responding to the behaviours of students with exceptionalities*. London, ON: The Althouse Press.

Jones, V. (2006). How do teachers learn to be effective classroom managers? In C. M. Evertson & C. S. Weinstein (Eds.), *Handbook of classroom management: Research, practice and contemporary issues* (pp. 887–908). Mahwah, NJ: Lawrence Erlbaum.

Kauffman, J. M., & Sasso, G. M. (2006a). Toward ending cultural and cognitive relativism in special education. *Exceptionality, 14*(2), 65–90.

Kauffman, J. M., & Sasso, G. M. (2006b). Certainty, doubt, and the reduction of uncertainty. *Exceptionality, 14*(2), 109–120.

Klopfer, K. (2014). Pre-service teacher education and classroom management: An evaluation of EDU5572. Retrieved from https://tspace.library.utoronto.ca/bitstream/1807/43994/1/Klopfer_Kristina_M_201403_MA_thesis.pdf%20.pdf

Landrum, T. J., & Kauffman, J. M. (2006). Behavioral approaches to classroom management and effective teaching. In C. M. Evertson & C. S. Weinstein (Eds.), *Handbook of classroom management: Research, practice and contemporary issues* (pp. 47–72). Mahwah, NJ: Lawrence Erlbaum.

Lane, K., Falk, K., & Wehby, J. (2006). Classroom management in special education classrooms and resource rooms. In C. M. Evertson & C. S. Weinstein (Eds.), *Handbook of classroom management: Research, practice and contemporary issues*, (pp. 439–460). Mahwah, NJ: Lawrence Erlbaum.

Levin, J., & Nolan, J. F. (2000). *Principles of classroom management: A professional decision-making model* (3rd ed.). Boston, MA: Allyn & Bacon.

Lewis, T. J., Newcomer, L. L., Trussell, R., & Richter, M. (2006). Schoolwide positive behavior support: Building systems to develop and maintain appropriate social behavior. In C. M. Evertson & C. S. Weinstein (Eds.), *Handbook of classroom management: Research, practice and contemporary issues* (pp. 833–854). Mahwah, NJ: Lawrence Erlbaum.

Lickona, T. (1987). Character development in the elementary school classroom. In K. Ryan & G. F. McLean (Eds.), *Character development in the schools and beyond*. New York, NY: Praeger. Retrieved from www.crvp.org/book/Series06/VI-3/chapter_vii.htm

Maag, J. W. (2004). *Behavior management: From theoretical implications to practical applications* (2nd ed.). Belmont, CA: Thompson Wadsworth.

Marzano, R. J., & Marzano, J. S. (2003). The key to classroom management. *Educational Leadership, 61*(1), 6–13.

McCaslin, M., Rabidue-Bozack, A., Napoleon, L., Thomas, A., Vasquez, V., Wayman, V., & Zhang, J. (2006). Self-regulated learning and classroom management: Theory, research, and considerations for classroom practice. In C. M. Evertson & C. S. Weinstein (Eds.), *Handbook of classroom management: Research, practice and contemporary issues* (pp. 223–252). Mahwah, NJ: Lawrence Erlbaum.

Mostert, M. P., Kauffman, J. M., & Kavale, K. R. (2003). Truth and consequences. *Behavioral Disorders, 28*, 333–347.

Paintal, S. (1999). Banning corporal punishment of children. *Childhood Education, 76*, 36–40.

Scott, T. M., Gagnon, J. C., & Nelson, C. M. (2008). School-wide systems of positive behavior support: A framework for reducing school crime and violence. *Journal of Behavior Analysis of Offender and Victim: Treatment and Prevention, 1*(3), 259–272.

Sugai, G., & Horner, R. (1999). Discipline and behavioral support: Preferred processes and practices. *Effective School Practices, 17*, 10–22.

Sugai, G., Horner, R. H., Dunlap, G., Hieneman, M., Lewis, T. J., Nelson, C. M., . . . Wilcox, B. (2000). *Applying positive behavioral support and functional behavioral assessment in schools*. Washington, DC: OSEP Center of Positive Behavioral Interventions and Support.

Thomas, A., & Chess, S. (1977). *Temperament and development.* New York, NY: Bruner/Mazel.

Turecki, S. (2000). *The difficult child.* New York, NY: Bantam Books.

Weinstein, C. S. (1997). *Secondary classroom management.* New York, NY: McGraw-Hill.

Whelan, R. (1995). Emotional disturbance. In E. L. Meyen & T. Skirtic (Eds.), *Special education and student disability: An introduction* (pp. 271–336). Denver, CO: Love.

Woolfolk-Hoy, A., & Weinstein, C. S. (2006). Student and teacher perspectives on classroom management. In C. M. Evertson & C. S. Weinstein (Eds.), *Handbook of classroom management: Research, practice and contemporary issues* (pp. 181–222). Mahwah, NJ: Lawrence Erlbaum.

Chapter 5

Alberta Education. 2010. *Making a difference: Meeting diverse learning needs with differentiated instruction.* Edmonton, p. 173.

American Psychiatric Association. (2013). *Diagnostic and statistical manual of mental disorders.* (5th ed.). Washington, DC: Author.

Brigham, N., Morocco, C. C., Clay, K., & Zigmond, N. (2006). What makes a high school a good high school for students with disabilities? *Learning Disabilities Research & Practice, 21*(3), 184–190.

Campbell, W., & Missiuna, C. (2016). Bullying risk in children with disabilities: A review of the literature. Retrieved from www.canchild.ca/en/resources/32-bullying-risk-in-children-with-disabilities-a-review-of-the-literature

Conte, R. (1998). Attention disorders. In B. Wong (Ed.), *Learning about learning disabilities* (2nd ed.) (pp. 67–105). San Diego, CA: Academic Press.

Council for Exceptional Children. (2013). *Disability terms and definitions.* Retrieved from www.cec.sped.org/Special-Ed-Topics/Exceptional-Learners?sc_lang=en

Edmunds, A. L., & Blair, K. (1999). Nova Scotia teachers' use of the Cognitive Credit Card. ATEC *Journal, 5*(1), 7–13.

Fiedler, C. R., Simpson, R. L., & Clark, D. M. (2007). *Parents and families of children with disabilities: Effective school-based support services.* Upper Saddle River, NJ: Pearson Education, Inc.

Fuchs, D., Fuchs, L. S., & Compton, D. L. (2012). Smart RTI: A next-generation approach to multilevel prevention. *Exceptional Children, 78*(3), 263–279.

Goldberg, R. J., Higgins, E. L., Rasking, M. H., & Herman, K. L. (2003). Predictors of success in individuals with learning disabilities: A qualitative analysis of a 20-year longitudinal study. *Learning Disabilities Research & Practice, 18*(4), 222–236.

International Dyslexia Association. (2013). *What is dyslexia?* Retrieved from www.interdys.org/FAQWhatIs.htm

LD@School. (2016). What are nonverbal learning disabilities? Retrieved from www.ldatschool.ca/learn-about-lds/nonverbal-lds/

Learning Disabilities Association of Canada. (2016). *Official definition of learning disabilities.* Retrieved from http://www.ldac-acta.ca/learn-more/ld-defined

Learning Disabilities Association of Ontario. (2015). Some common signs of LDs. Retrieved from www.ldao.ca/introduction-to-ldsadhd/what-are-lds/some-common-signs-of-lds/

Lerner, J. W., & Kline, F. (2006). *Learning disabilities and related disorders.* Boston, MA: Houghton Mifflin Company.

Mayes, S. D. (2000). Learning disabilities and ADHD: Overlapping spectrum disorders. *Journal of Learning Disabilities, 33*(5), 417–424.

McIntosh, K., MacKay, L. D., Andreou, T., Brown, J. A., Matthews, S., Gietz, C., & Bennett, J. L. (2011). Response to intervention: Definitions, the evidence base, and future directions. *Canadian Journal of School Psychology, 26*(1), 18–43.

National Center on Response to Intervention. (2010). *Essential components of RTI—A closer look at response to intervention.* Washington, DC: US Department of Education, Office of Special Education Programs, National Center on Response to Intervention.

National Joint Committee on Learning Disabilities. (2005). *Responsiveness to intervention and learning disabilities.* Austin, TX: Author.

Nowicki, E. A. (2006). A cross-sectional multivariate analysis of children's attitudes towards disabilities. *Journal of Intellectual Disability Research, 50*, 335–348.

Ogle, D. (1986). K-W-L: A teaching model that develops active reading of expository text. *The Reading Teacher, 38*, 564–570.

Pavri, S., & Monda-Amaya, L. (2000). Loneliness and students with learning disabilities in inclusive classrooms: Self-perceptions, coping strategies, and preferred interventions. *Learning Disabilities Research & Practice, 15*(1), 22–33.

Reiff, H. B. (2004). Reframing the learning disabilities experience redux. *Learning Disabilities Research & Practice, 19*(3), 185–198.

US National Institute of Health. (2014). What causes learning disabilities? Retrieved from www.nichd.nih.gov/health/topics/learning/conditioninfo/Pages/causes.aspx

Wilson, A. M., Armstrong, C. D., Furrie, A., & Walcot, E. (2009). The mental health of Canadians with self-reported learning disabilities. *Journal of Learning Disabilities, 42*(1), 24–40.

Young, G., & MacCormack, J. (2014). Assistive technology for students with learning disabilities. Retrieved from www.ldatschool.ca/technology/assistive-technology/

Chapter 6

American Psychiatric Association. (2013). *Diagnostic and statistical manual of mental disorders.* (5th ed.). Washington, DC: Author.

Banerjee, T. D., Middleton, F., & Faraone, S. V. (2007). Environmental risk factors for attention-deficit hyperactivity disorder. *Acta Paediatrica, 9*, 1269–1274.

Barkley, R. A. (1998). *Attention-deficit hyperactivity disorder: A handbook for diagnosis and treatment.* New York, NY: Guildford Press.

Bertin, M. (2011). ADHD *and high school planning: What it takes to thrive.* Retrieved from www.psychologytoday.com/blog/the-family-adhd-solution/201106/adhd-and-high-school-planning-what-it-takes-thrive

Bloom, B., Cohen, R. A., & Freeman, G. (2010). *Summary health statistics for US children: National Health Interview Survey, 2009.* National Center for Health Statistics. *Vital Health Stat 10, 247.*

British Columbia Ministry of Education. (2006). *Awareness of students with diverse learning needs: What the teacher needs to know, Volume 1.* Retrieved from http://www.bced.gov.bc.ca/specialed/awareness/24.htm

Cantwell, D. P. (1999). *Comorbidity in ADHD and associated outcomes.* Retrieved from http://gradda.home.isp-direct.com/sp99como.html

Doyle, A. E., Faraone, S. V., DuPre, E. P., & Biederman, J. (2001). Separating attention deficit hyperactivity disorder and learning disabilities in girls: A familial risk analysis. *American Journal of Psychiatry, 158*, 1666–1672.

DuPaul, G. J., Gormley, M. J., & Laracy, S. D. (2013). Comorbidity of LD and ADHD: Implications of DSM-5 for assessment and treatment. *Journal of Learning Disabilities, 46*(1), 43–51.

Environmental Health News. (2012, September 21). Kids exposed to mercury or lead more likely to have ADHD symptoms, Canadian study finds. Retrieved from www.environmentalhealthnews.org/ehs/news/2012/adhd-lead-and-mercury

Faraone, S. V., & Biederman, J. (1998). Neurobiology of attention-deficit hyperactivity disorder. *Biological Psychiatry, 44*, 951–958.

Faraone, S. V., Sergeant, J., Gillberg, C., & Biederman, J. (2003). The worldwide prevalence of ADHD: Is it an American condition? *World Psychiatry, 2*, 104–113.

Hannell, G. (2006). *Identifying children with special needs: Checklists and action plans for teachers.* Thousand Oaks, CA: Corwin Press.

Hinshaw, S. P., Owens, E. B., Sami, N., & Fargeon, S. (2006). Prospective follow-up of girls with attention-deficit/hyperactivity disorder into adolescence: Evidence for continuing cross-domain impairment. *Journal of Consulting and Clinical Psychology, 74*(3), 489–499.

Jensen, P. M. (2001). AD/HD: What's up? What's next? *CHADD: Attention, 7*(6), 24–27.

LD Online. (2006). *What causes ADHD?* Retrieved from www.ldonline.org/adhdbasics/causes

Massachusetts General Hospital. (2011, May 6). Combination of ADHD and poor emotional control runs in families, study suggests. *Science Daily.* Retrieved from www.sciencedaily.com/releases/2011/05/110505103341.htm

Mueller, K. L., & Tomblin, J. B. (2012). Examining the comorbidity of language disorders and ADHD. *Topics in Language Disorders, 32*(30), 228–246.

National Human Genome Research Institute. (2012). The ADHD Genetic Research Study at the National Institutes of Health and the National Genome Research Institute. Retrieved from www.genome.gov/10004300/

National Institute of Mental Health. (2008). *Attention deficit hyperactivity disorder.* NIH Publication No. 08-3572. Retrieved from www.nimh.nih.gov/publicat/adhd.cfm

Rief, S. F. (2005). *How to reach and teach children with ADD/ADHD: Practical techniques, strategies, and interventions* (2nd ed.). San Francisco, CA: Jossey-Bass.

Rief, S. F. (2015). *The ADHD book of lists: A practical guide for helping children and teens* (2nd ed.). San Francisco, CA: Jossey-Bass.

Schnoes, C., Reid, R., Wagner, M., & Marder, C. (2006). ADHD among students receiving special education services: A national survey. *Exceptional Children, 72*(4), 483–496.

Toppelberg, C. O., & Shapiro, T. (2000). Language disorders: A 10-year research update review. *Journal of the American Academy of Child & Adolescent Psychiatry, 39*(2), 143–152.

Chapter 7

Alberta Education. (2010). Making a difference: Meeting diverse learning needs with differentiated instruction. Retrieved from https://education.alberta.ca/media/384968/makingadifference_2010.pdf

Baldwin, A. Y., & Vialle, W. (1999). *The many faces of giftedness: Lifting the masks.* Belmont, CA: Wadsworth Publishing Company.

Bender, S. J. (2006). Struggles of gifted children in school: Possible negative outcomes. *Gifted Education Press Quarterly, 20*(2), 10–13.

British Columbia Ministry of Education. (2016). *Special education services: A manual of policies, procedures and guidelines.* Retrieved from http://www2.gov.bc.ca/assets/gov/education/administration/kindergarten-to-grade-12/inclusive/special_ed_policy_manual.pdf

Colangelo, N., & Assouline, S. G. (2000). Counseling gifted students. In K. A. Heller, F. J. Monks, R. J. Sternberg, & R. F. Subotnik (Eds.), *International handbook of giftedness and talent* (2nd ed.) (pp. 595–608). Oxford, UK: Elsevier Science Ltd.

Coleman, L. J., & Cross, T. L. (2001). *Being gifted in school: An introduction to development, guidance, and teaching.* Austin, TX: Prufrock Press Inc.

Dabrowski, K. (1972). *Psychoneurosis is not an illness.* London, UK: Gryf Publications.

Dabrowski, K., & Piechowski, M. M. (1977). *Theory of levels of emotional development.* Oceanside, NY: Dabor Science.

Edmunds, A. L, & Edmunds, G. A. (2005). Sensitivity: A double-edged sword for the pre-adolescent and adolescent gifted child. *Roeper Review, 27*(2), 69–77.

Edmunds, A. L., & Noel, K. (2003). Literary precocity: An exceptional case among exceptional cases. *Roeper Review, 25*(4), 185–194.

Fowler, W. (1981). Case studies of cognitive precocity: The role of exogenous and endogenous stimulation in early mental development. *Journal of Applied Psychology, 2*, 319–367.

Frasier, M. M., García, J. H., & Passow, A. H. (1995). *A review of assessment issues in gifted education and their implications for identifying gifted minority students* (RM95204). Storrs, CT: The National Research Center on the Gifted and Talented.

Gardner, H. (2000). The giftedness matrix: A developmental perspective. In R. C. Friedman & B. M. Shore (Eds.), *Talents unfolding: Cognition & development* (pp. 77–88). Washington, DC: American Psychological Association.

Goldsmith, L. T. (2000). Tracking trajectories of talent: Child prodigies growing up. In R. C. Friedman & B. M. Shore (Eds.), *Talents unfolding: Cognition and development* (pp. 89–117). Washington, DC: American Psychological Association.

Horowitz, F. (2009). Introduction: A developmental understanding of giftedness and talent. In F. Horowitz, R. F. Subotnik, & D. J. Matthews (Eds.), *The development of giftedness and talent across the life span* (pp. 3–20). Washington, DC: American Psychological Association.

Johnson, L. J., Karnes, M. B., & Carr, V. W. (1997). Providing services to children with gifts and disabilities: A critical need. In N. Colangelo & G. A. Davis (Eds.), *Handbook of gifted education* (pp. 516–527). Boston, MA: Allyn and Bacon.

Lerner, J. W., & Kline, F. (2006*). Learning disabilities and related disorders.* Boston, MA: Houghton Mifflin Company.

Lindsey, M. (1980). *Training teachers of the gifted and talented.* New York, NY: Teachers College Press.

Marland, S. P., Jr. (1972). *Education of the gifted and talented: Report to the Congress of the United States by the U.S. Commissioner of Education and background papers submitted to the U.S. Office of Education*, 2 vols. Washington, DC: US Government Printing Office. (Government Documents Y4.L 11/2:G36).

Matthews, D. (2013). Canadian Aboriginal students: What they can teach us all about gifted education. Retrieved from https://donamatthews.wordpress.com/2013/11/06/canadian-aboriginal-students-what-they-can-teach-us-all-about-gifted-education/

Mendaglio, S. (1995). Sensitivity among gifted persons: A multi-faceted perspective. *Roeper Review, 17*(3), 169–172.

Merriam-Webster's Collegiate Dictionary (11th ed.). (2003). Springfield, MA: Merriam-Webster, Inc.

Michael-Chadwell, S. (2011). Examining the underrepresentation of underserved students in gifted programs from a transformational leadership vantage point. *Journal for the Education of the Gifted, 34*(1), 99–130.

Mrazik, M., & Dombrowsk, S.C. (2010). The neurobiological foundations of giftedness. *Roeper Review, 32*(4), 224–234.

Newfoundland and Labrador Department of Education. (2013). *Teaching students who are gifted and talented: A handbook for teachers.* Retrieved from http://www.ed.gov.nl.ca/edu/k12/studentsupportservices/publications/TeachingStudentsGiftedTalented.pdf

Newman, S. D., & Just, M. A. (2005). The neural bases of intelligence: A perspective based on functional neuroimaging. In R. J. Sternberg & J. E. Pretz (Eds.), *Cognition and intelligence: Identifying the mechanisms of the mind* (pp. 88–103). Cambridge, UK: Cambridge University Press.

Nielsen, M. E. (2002). Gifted students with learning difficulties: Recommendations for identification and programming. *Exceptionality, 10*, 93–111.

Nielsen, M. E., & Higgins, L. D. (2005). The eye of the storm: Services and programs for twice-exceptional learners. *Teaching Exceptional Children, 38*(1), 8–15.

Noel, K., & Edmunds, A. L. (2007). An analysis of highly precocious writing. *Roeper Review, 29*(2), 125–131.

Nova Scotia Department of Education. (2010). *Gifted education and talent development.* Retrieved from https://studentservices

.ednet.ns.ca/sites/default/files/Gifted%20Education%20and%20Talent%20Development.pdf

Olszewski-Kubilius, P., Lee, S., Ngoi, M., & Ngoi, D. (2004). Addressing the achievement gap between minority and nonminority children by increasing access to gifted programs. *Journal for the Education of the Gifted, 28*(2), 127–158.

Plomin, R. (1997). Genetics and intelligence. In N. Colangelo & G. A. Davis (Eds.), *Handbook of gifted education* (pp. 67–74). Boston, MA: Allyn and Bacon.

Porath, M. (2000). Social giftedness in childhood: A developmental perspective. In R. C. Friedman & B. M. Shore (Eds.), *Talents unfolding* (pp. 195–215). Washington, DC: American Psychological Association.

Renzulli, J. S., Hartman, R. H., & Callahan, C. M. (1971). Teacher identification of superior students. *Exceptional Children, 38*, 211–214, 243–248.

Renzulli, J. S., & Reis, S. M. (1997). *The Schoolwide Enrichment Model: A how-to guide for talent development.* Waco, TX: Prufrock Press Inc.

Renzulli, J. S., & Reis, S. M. (2014). *The Schoolwide Enrichment Model: A how-to guide for talent development* (3rd ed.). Waco, TX: Prufrock Press Inc.

Robinson, N. M. (2000). Giftedness in very young children: How seriously should it be taken? In R. C. Friedman & B. M. Shore (Eds.), *Talents unfolding: Cognition & development* (pp. 7–26). Washington, DC: American Psychological Association.

Roeper, A. (1995). Participatory vs. hierarchical models for administration: The Roeper School experience. In A. Roeper, *Annemarie Roeper: Selected writings and speeches* (pp. 109–123). Minneapolis, MN: Free Spirit.

Shavinina, L. V. (1999). The psychological essence of the child prodigy phenomenon: Sensitive periods and cognitive experience. *Gifted Child Quarterly, 43*(1), 25–38.

Siegle, D., & McCoach, D. B. (2005). Making a difference: Motivating gifted students who are not achieving. *Teaching Exceptional Children, 38*(1), 22–27.

Silverman, L. K. (Ed.). (1993). *Counseling the gifted and talented.* Denver, CO: Love.

Simonton, D. K. (2005). Giftedness and genetics: The emergenic-epigenetic model and its implications. *Journal for the Education of the Gifted, 28*(3/4), 270–286.

Snow, R. E. (1994). Aptitude development and talent achievement. In N. Colangelo, S. G. Assouline, & D. L. Ambroson (Eds.), *Talent development: Volume II* (pp. 101–122). Dayton, OH: Ohio Psychology Press.

Stephens, K. R., & Karnes, F. A. (2001). Product development for gifted students. In F. A. Karnes & S. M. Bean (Eds.), *Methods and materials for teaching the gifted and talented* (pp. 181–211). Austin, TX: Prufrock Press Inc.

Sternberg, R. J., & Grigorenko, E. L. (2003). Teaching for successful intelligence: Principles, procedures, and practices. *Journal for the Education of the Gifted, 27*(2/3), 207–226.

Tucker-Drob, E. M., Briley, D. A., & Harden, K. P. (2013). Genetic and environmental influences on cognition across development

and context. *Current Directions in Psychological Science, 22*(5), 349–355.

VanTassel-Baska, J. (1997). What matters in curriculum for gifted learners: Reflections on theory, research, and practice. In N. Colangelo & G. A. Davis (Eds.), *Handbook of gifted education* (pp. 126–135). Boston, MA: Allyn and Bacon.

VanTassel-Baska, J. (2003). *Curriculum planning and instructional design for gifted learners.* Denver, CO: Love.

VanTassel-Baska, J., & Brown, E. F. (2001). An analysis of gifted education curriculum models. In F. A. Karnes & S. M. Bean (Eds.), *Methods and materials for teaching the gifted and talented* (pp. 93–132). Austin, TX: Prufrock Press Inc.

Vygotsky, L. S. (1978). *Mind in society: The development of higher psychological processes.* (M. Cole, V. John-Steiner, S. Scribner & E. Souberman, Eds.). Cambridge, MA: Harvard University Press.

Wenke, D., Frensch, P. A., & Funke, J. (2005). Complex problem solving and intelligence: Empirical relation and causal direction. In R. J. Sternberg & J. E. Pretz (Eds.), *Cognition and intelligence: Identifying the mechanisms of the mind* (pp. 160–187). Cambridge, UK: Cambridge University Press.

Chapter 8

Alberta Teachers' Association. (2015). The state of inclusion in Alberta schools. Retrieved from www.teachers.ab.ca/SiteCollectionDocuments/ATA/Publications/Research/COOR-101-5%20The%20State%20of%20Inclusion%20in%20Alberta%20Schools.pdf

American Association on Intellectual and Developmental Disabilities. (2013). Definition of intellectual disability. Retrieved from http://aaidd.org/intellectual-disability/definition#.V-lPXJMrLBI

Bennett, S., & Gallagher, T. (2012). The delivery of education services for students who have an intellectual disability in the province of Ontario. Community Living Ontario. Retrieved from www.inclusiveeducation.ca/documents/CLO%20Delivery%20of%20Education%20Services.pdf

British Columbia Ministry of Education. (2015). Intellectual disabilities: Instructional support planning process. Retrieved from http://www.bced.gov.bc.ca/specialed/docs/id_instructional_support_tool.pdf

Browder, D. M., Wakeman, S. Y., Spooner, F., Ahlgrim-Delzell, L., & Algozzine, B. (2006). Research on reading instruction for individuals with significant cognitive disabilities. *Exceptional Children, 72*(4), 392–408.

Center for Parent Information and Resources. (2017). *Down syndrome.* Retrieved from www.parentcenterhub.org/repository/downsyndrome/#def

Dore, R., Dion, E., Wagner, S., & Brunet, J. (2004). High school inclusion of adolescents with mental retardation: A multiple case study. *Education and Training in Mental Retardation and Developmental Disabilities, 37*(3), 253–261.

Downing, J. E., & MacFarland, S. (2010). Severe disabilities: Education and individuals with severe disabilities—Promising practices. In J. H. Stone & M. Blouin (Eds.), *International*

Encyclopedia of Rehabilitation. Retrieved from http://cirrie .buffalo.edu/encyclopedia/en/article/114/

Evmenova, A., Ault, M., Bausch, M., & Warger, C. (2013). Assistive technology provides supports for individuals with intellectual and developmental disabilities. Retrieved from www.tamcec .org/wp-content/uploads/2013/05/AT-Supports-IDD.pdf

Hannell, G. (2006). *Identifying children with special needs: Checklists and action plans for teachers.* Thousand Oaks, CA: Corwin Press.

Harum, K. H. (2006). *Mental retardation.* eMedicine. Retrieved from www.emedicine.com/neuro/topic605.htm

Hughes, C., Copeland, C., Guth, C., Rung, L., Hwang, B., Kleeb, G., & Strong, M. (2001). General education students' perspectives on their involvement in a high school peer buddy program. *Education and Training in Mental Retardation and Developmental Disabilities, 36*(4), 343–356.

National Dissemination Center for Children with Disabilities. (2011). *Intellectual disability.* Retrieved from http://nichcy.org/ disability/specific/intellectual#teachers

National Fragile X Foundation. (2017). Fragile X syndrome. Retrieved from https://fragilex.org/learn

Self Advocate Net. (2017). Real jobs for real pay. Retrieved from http://selfadvocatenet.com/real-jobs-for-real-pay/

Silka, V. R., & Hauser, M. J. (1997). Psychiatric assessment of the person with mental retardation. *Psychiatric Annals, 27*(3). Retrieved from www.psychiatry.com/mr/assessment.html

Taylor, R. L., Richards, S. B., & Brady, M. P. (2005). *Mental retardation: Historical perspectives, current practices, and future directions.* Boston, MA: Pearson Education, Inc.

Vise, A. (2012). *Intellectual disabilities in the classroom.* Retrieved from www.brighthubeducation.com/special-ed-inclusion-strategies/9893-teaching-students-with-intellectual-disabilities

Winders, P. C. (2003). The goal and opportunity of physical therapy for children with Down syndrome. *Down Syndrome Quarterly.* Granville, OH: Denison University. Retrieved from www .denison.edu/collaborations/dsq/windersphysicaltherapy.html

Chapter 9

Alberta Learning. (2003). Teaching students with autism spectrum disorders. Retrieved from http://education.alberta.ca/ media/511995/autism.pdf

American Psychiatric Association. (2013). *Diagnostic and statistical manual of mental disorders.* (5th ed.). Washington, DC: Author.

Autism Speaks. (2012). Educating students with autism. Retrieved from www.autismspeaks.org/sites/default/files/sctk_educating_ students_with_autism.pdf

Autism Speaks Canada. (2016a). Applied behaviour analysis. Retrieved from www.autismspeaks.ca/about-autism/treatment/ applied-behaviour-analysis/

Autism Speaks Canada. (2016b). Facts and FAQs. Retrieved from www.autismspeaks.ca/about-autism/facts-and-faqs

Ayres, J. (1972). Improving academic scores through sensory integration. *Journal of Learning Disabilities, 5,* 338–343.

Becker, E. B., & Stoodley, C. J. (2013). Autism spectrum disorder and the cerebellum. *International Review or Neurobiology, 113,* 1–34.

Bondy, A., & Frost, L. (1994). The picture exchange communication system. *Focus on Autistic Behavior, 9,* 1–19.

Cambridge Center for Behavioral Studies. (2012). Frequently asked questions about applied behavior analysis (ABA) and autism. Retrieved from www.behavior.org/resource.php?id=551

Canadian Psychological Association. (2015). Autism spectrum disorder. *Psychology Works Fact Sheet.* Retrieved from www.cpa.ca/docs/File/Publications/FactSheets/Psychology WorksFactSheet_Autism.pdf

Centers for Disease Control and Prevention. (2015). *Vaccines do not cause autism.* Retrieved from www.cdc.gov/vaccinesafety/ concerns/autism.html

Clarke, T. K., McIntosh, A. M., Lupton, M. K., Pujals-Fernandez, A. M., Starr, J., Davies, G., et al. (2016). Common polygenic risk for autism spectrum disorder (ASD) is associated with cognitive ability in the general population. *Molecular Psychiatry, 21,* 419–425.

Gray C., & Garand J. D. (1993). Social stories: Improving responses of students with autism with accurate social information. *Focus on Autistic Behavior, 8*(1), 1–10.

Hamlin, T. (2016). *Autism and the stress effect.* London, UK: Jessica Kingsley Publishers.

Hatch-Rasmussen, C. (2016). *Sensory integration.* San Diego, CA: Autism Research Institute. Retrieved from www.autism.com/ symptoms_sensory_overview

Locwin, B., & Entine, J. (2016). *Autism in our DNA? Slew of studies points to genetics as main driver, but there is no "autism" gene.* Retrieved from www.geneticliteracyproject.org/2016/07/21/ autism-in-our-dna-slew-of-studies-points-to-genetics-as-main-driver-but-there-is-no-autism-gene

Lovaas, O. I. (1987). Behavioral treatment and normal educational and intellectual functioning in young autistic children. *Journal of Consulting and Clinical Psychology, 55,* 3–9.

Lytle, R., & Todd, T. (2009). Stress and the student with autism spectrum disorders: Strategies for stress reduction and enhanced learning. *Teaching Exceptional Children, 41*(4), 36–42.

Manitoba Education. (2016a). *Annotated descriptor for severe to profound autism spectrum disorder Level 3.* Winnipeg, MB: Author. Retrieved from www.edu.gov.mb.ca/k12/specedu/ funding/asd_III.html

Manitoba Education. (2016b). *Special needs categorical funding criteria for Level 2 and Level 3.* Winnipeg, MB: Author. Retrieved from www.edu.gov.mb.ca/k12/specedu/funding/level2-3.html

Matson, J. L. (1994). *Autism in children and adults: Etiology, assessment, and intervention.* Pacific Grove, CA: Brooks/Cole Publishing Company.

Myles, B. (2005). *Children and youth with Asperger syndrome.* Thousand Oaks, CA: Corwin Press.

National Institute of Mental Health. (2011). *A parent's guide to autism spectrum disorder.* NIH Publication No. 11-551. Retrieved from www.nimh.nih.gov/health/publications/a-parents-guide-to-autism-spectrum-disorder/complete-index.shtml

Olson, S. (2015). Autism genes linked to higher intelligence: Treading a fine line between intellectual disability and superiority. Retrieved from www.medicaldaily.com/autism-genes-linked-higher-intelligence-treading-fine-line-between-intellectual-325798

Reed, P., Osborne, L. A., & Corness, M. (2007). Brief report: Relative effectiveness of different home-based behavioral approaches to early teaching intervention. *Journal of Autism and Developmental Disorders, 37*(9), 1815–1821.

Ryan, J. B., Hughes, E. M., Katsiyannis, A., McDaniel, M., & Sprinkle, C. (2011). Research-based educational practices for students with autism spectrum disorders. *Teaching Exceptional Children, 43*(3), 56–64.

Sarris, M. (2015). Measuring intelligence in autism. Interactive Autism Network. Retrieved from https://iancommunity.org/print/13820

School District 38, Richmond, BC. (2005). A discussion paper on the role of educational assistants. Retrieved from www2.sd38.bc.ca/SD%2038%20Policy/Related%20Resources/RoleEAs%20Disc%20Paper%20Mar05.pdf

Schopler, E., & Reichler, R. J. (1971). Parents as co-therapists in the treatment of psychotic children. *Journal of Autism and Child Schizophrenia, 1*, 87–102.

Scott, J., Clark, C., & Brady, M. (2000). *Students with autism.* San Diego, CA: Singular Publishing Group.

Siegel, B. (2003). *Helping children with autism learn: Treatment approaches for parents and professionals.* New York, NY: Oxford University Press.

Strock, M. (2004). *Autism spectrum disorders (pervasive developmental disorders).* NIH Publication No. 04-5511, National Institute of Mental Health, National Institutes of Health, U.S. Department of Health and Human Services. Retrieved from www.nimh.nih.gov/publicat/autism.cfm

Tick, B., Bolton, P., Happe, F., Rutter, M., & Rijsdijk, F. (2016). Heritability of autism spectrum disorders: A meta-analysis of twin studies. *Journal of Child Psychology Psychiatry, 57*(5), 585–595.

US National Research Council. (2001). *Educating children with autism.* Committee on Educational Interventions for Children with Autism. Division of Behavioral and Social Sciences and Education. Washington, DC: National Academy Press.

Wieder, S., & Greenspan, S. I. (2003). Climbing the symbolic ladder in the DIR model through floor time/interactive play. *Autism, 7*(4), 425–435.

World Health Organization. (2016). Autism spectrum disorders. Retrieved from www.who.int/mediacentre/factsheets/autism-spectrum-disorders/en/

Zwaigenbaum, L., Bryson, S., Rogers, T., Roberts, W., Brian, J., & Szatmari, P. (2005). Behavioral manifestations of autism in the first year of life. *International Journal of Developmental Neuroscience, 23*, 143–152.

Zwaigenbaum, L., Bauman, M. L., Stone, W. L., Yirmiya, N., Estes, A., et al. (2015). Early identification of autism spectrum disorder: Recommendations for practice and research. *Pediatrics, 136*, S10–S40.

Chapter 10

Alberta Education. (2007). Essential components of educational programming: Students who are deaf or hard of hearing. Retrieved from https://education.alberta.ca/media/1477210/ecep_deaf_or_hard_of_hearing.pdf

Alberta Education. (2013). Hearing loss. Retrieved from www.learnalberta.ca/content/inmdict/html/hearing_loss.html

American Speech-Language-Hearing Association. (2013). Effects of hearing loss on development. Retrieved from www.asha.org/public/hearing/disorders/effects.htm

British Columbia Ministry of Education. (2017a). Special education: Hard of hearing and deaf students: A resource guide to support classroom teachers. Retrieved from http://www.bced.gov.bc.ca/specialed/hearimpair/range.htm

British Columbia Ministry of Education. (2017). Students with visual impairments: The nature and degree of visual impairment. Retrieved from http://www.bced.gov.bc.ca/specialed/visimpair/nature.htm

Canadian Academy of Audiology. (2016a). Causes of hearing loss. Retrieved from https://canadianaudiology.ca/for-the-public/causes-of-hearing-loss

Canadian Academy of Audiology. (2016b). Hearing loss in adults and children. Retrieved from https://canadianaudiology.ca/for-the-public/hearing-loss-in-adults-and-children

Canadian Association of the Deaf. (2012). Statistics on deaf Canadians. Retrieved from www.cad.ca/statistics_on_deaf_canadians.php

Canadian Cultural Society of the Deaf. (2012). *Hearing impaired? Hearing handicapped? Hard of hearing? Deaf? What's in a label? Everything!* Retrieved from http://deafculturecentre.ca/Public/Default.aspx?I=295&n=Hearing+Impaired%3F

Council for Exceptional Children. (2013). Disability terms and definitions. Retrieved from www.cec.sped.org/Special-Ed-Topics/Exceptional-Learners?sc_lang=en

Liyange, A. G. (2002). Visual impairment: Its effect on cognitive development and behaviour. *Understanding Intellectual Disability and Health.* Retrieved from www.intellectualdisability.info/physical-health/visual-impairment-its-effect-on-cognitive-development-and-behaviour

Statistics Canada. (2016). Census in brief: Linguistic diversity and multilingualism in Canadian homes. Statistics Canada. Retrieved from http://www12.statcan.gc.ca/census-recensement/2016/as-sa/98-200-x/2016010/98-200-x2016010-eng.cfm.

Willard-Holt, C. (1999). Dual exceptionalities. ERIC EC Digest #E574, Office of Educational Research and Improvement, U.S. Department of Education. Retrieved from www.gifted.uconn.edu/siegle/tag/Digests/e574.html

Chapter 11

Allen, E. (2015). Assistive technology for students with multiple disabilities. Retrieved from http://fisherpub.sjfc.edu/cgi/viewcontent.cgi?article=1300&context=education_ETD_masters

American Speech-Language-Hearing Association. (2017). Augmentative and alternative communication (AAC). Retrieved from: www.asha.org/public/speech/disorders/AAC

Avenues for AMC. (2017). Avenues: A National Support Group for Arthrogryposis Multiple Congenita. Retrieved from: http://www.avenuesforamc.com/publications/pamphlet.htm

Carter, E.W., Sewdeen, B., & Kurkowski, C. (2008). Friendship matters: Fostering social relationships in secondary schools. TASH Connections. Retrieved from http://tash.org

Chen, D., & Miles, C. (2004). Working with families. In F. Orelove, D. Sobsey, & R. Silberman (Eds.), *Educating children with multiple disabilities: A collaborative approach* (pp. 31–65). Baltimore, MD: Paul H. Brookes Publishing Company.

Cloninger, C. J. (2004). Designing collaborative educational services. In F. Orelove, D. Sobsey, & R. Silberman (Eds.), *Educating children with multiple disabilities: A collaborative approach* (pp. 1–30). Baltimore, MD: Paul H. Brookes Publishing Company.

Demchak, M., & Greenfield, R. (2003). *Transition portfolios for students with disabilities: How to help students, teachers, and families handle new settings.* Thousand Oaks, CA: Corwin Press, Inc.

Developmental Services Ontario. (2013). *What is a developmental disability?* Retrieved from www.dsontario.ca/whats-a-developmental-disability

Erin, J. (2003). *Educating students with visual impairments.* Retrieved from http://ericec.org/digests/e653.html

Forney, P. E., & Heller, K. (2004). Sensorimotor development: Implications for the educational team. In F. Orelove, D. Sobsey, & R. Silberman (Eds.), *Educating children with multiple disabilities: A collaborative approach* (pp. 193–247). Baltimore, MD: Paul H. Brookes Publishing Company.

Gee, K. (2004). Developing curriculum and instruction. In F. Orelove, D. Sobsey, & R. Silberman (Eds.), *Educating children with multiple disabilities: A collaborative approach* (pp. 67–114). Baltimore, MD: Paul H. Brookes Publishing Company.

Hamilton, J. (2016). How to best support early learning for children with physical disabilities. Retrieved from www.brighthubeducation.com/special-ed-physical-disabilities/129310-early-learning-for-children-with-physical-disabilities/

Heller, K. W., Forney, P. E., Alberto, P. A., Schwartzman, M. N., & Goeckel, T. M. (2000). *Meeting physical and health needs of children with disabilities: Teaching student participation and management.* Toronto, ON: Nelson Thomson-Learning.

Horn, E. M. & Kang, J. (2012). Supporting young children with multiple disabilities: What do we know and what do we still need to learn? *Topics in Early Childhood Special Education, 31*(4), 241–248.

Kaiser, A. P., & Grim, J. C. (2006). Teaching functional communication skills. In M. Snell & F. Brown (Eds.), *Instruction of students with severe disabilities* (pp. 447–488). Upper Saddle River, NJ: Pearson Education, Inc.

Kleinert, H., & Kearns, J. (2004). Alternate assessments. In F. Orelove, D. Sobsey, & R. Silberman (Eds.), *Educating children with multiple disabilities: A collaborative approach* (pp. 115–149). Baltimore, MD: Paul H. Brookes Publishing Company.

National Human Genome Research Institute. (2010). *Learning about Duane syndrome.* Retrieved from www.genome.gov/11508984

NICHCY. (2013). *Multiple disabilities.* Retrieved from www.parentcenterhub.org/repository/multiple

Parker, C. (1997). *Feeding and speech problems in AMC.* Paper presented at the Arthrogryposis Group Conference. Retrieved from www.tagonline.org.uk/articles/feeding_speech.txt

Petschauer, D. (2016). What is an assistive technology assessment? Retrieved from http://assistivetechnology.about.com/od/ATCAT3/f/What-Is-An-Assistive-Technology-Assessment.htm

Piaget, J. P. (1952). *The origins of intelligence in children.* New York, NY: International Universities Press.

Schwartz, I. S., Staub, D., Peck, C. A., & Gallucci, C. (2006). Peer relationships. In M. Snell & F. Brown (Eds.), *Instruction of students with severe disabilities* (pp. 375–404). Upper Saddle River, NJ: Pearson Education, Inc.

Snowdon, A. (2012). *Strengthening communities for Canadian children with disabilities.* Toronto, ON: The Kids Health Foundation. Retrieved from http://sandboxproject.ca/wpcontent/uploads/2012/01/SandboxProjectDiscussionDocument.pdf

University of Guelph. (2008). *Teaching students with a physical disability.* Teaching Support Centre. Retrieved from www.uoguelph.ca/tss/resources/pdfs/Mobility2.pdf

Vygotsky, L. S. (1978). *Mind in society: The development of higher psychological processes.* (M. Cole, V. John-Steiner, S. Scribner, & E. Souberman, Eds.). Cambridge, MA: Harvard University Press.

Walton, E. (2012). Using literature as a strategy to promote inclusivity in high school classrooms. *Intervention in School and Clinic, 47*(4), 224–233.

Ysseldyke, J., & Olsen, K. (1999). Putting alternate assessments into practice: What to measure and possible sources of data. *Exceptional Children, 65*(2), 175–186.

Chapter 12

American Psychiatric Association. (2013). *Diagnostic and statistical manual of mental disorders.* (5th ed.). Washington, DC: Author.

American Psychological Association. (2008). Children and trauma: Update for mental health professionals. Retrieved from www.apa.org/pi/families/resources/children-trauma-update.aspx

Arroyo, W. (2001). PTSD in children and adolescents in the juvenile justice system. In S. Eth (Ed) *Review of psychiatry: Vol. 20. PTSD in children and adolescents* (pp. 59–86).

Benard, B. (2006). *Resiliency: What we have learned.* San Francisco, CA: WestEd.

Bernardini, S. C., & Jenkins, J. M. (2002). *An overview of risks and protectors for children of separation and divorce.* Ottawa: Department of Justice Canada; Family, Children and Youth Section (2002-FCY-2E).

Blum, R. (2005). A case for school connectedness. *Educational Leadership, 62*(7), 16–20.

British Columbia Ministry of Education. (2015). Students from refugee backgrounds: A guide for teachers and schools. Retrieved from www2.gov.bc.ca/assets/gov/education/administration/kindergarten-to-grade-12/diverse-student-needs/students-from-refugee-backgrounds-guide.pdf

Child Safety Commissioner. (2007). Calmer classrooms: A guide to working with traumatized children. Melbourne, AU. Retrieved from www.ocsc.vic.gov.au/downloads/calmer_classrooms.pdf

Cook, A., Spinazzola, P., Ford, J., Lanktree, C., Blaustein, M., Cloitre, M., et al. (2005). Complex trauma in children and adolescents. *Psychiatric Annals, 35*(5), 390–398.

Copeland, W. E., Keeler, G., Angold, A., & Costello, E. J. (2007). Traumatic events and posttraumatic stress in childhood. *Archives of General Psychiatry, 64*(5), 577–584.

Dorado, J., & Zakrzewski, V. (2013). How to help a traumatized child in the classroom. Retrieved from http://greatergood.berkeley.edu/article/item/the_silent_epidemic_in_our_classrooms

Ferguson, B., Tilleczek, K., Boydell, K., Rummens, J. A., Cote, D., & Roth-Edney, D. (2005). *Early school leavers: Understanding the lived reality of student disengagement from secondary school.* Final report submitted to the Ontario Ministry of Education, May 31, 2005.

Hurlington, K. (2010). *Bolstering resilience in students: Teachers as protective factors.* What Works? Research into Practice, Monograph #25. Ontario Literacy and Numeracy Secretariat. Retrieved from www.edu.gov.on.ca/eng/literacynumeracy/inspire/research/WW_bolstering_students.pdf

Jensen, E. (2009). *Teaching with poverty in mind: What being poor does to kids' brains and what schools can do about it.* Alexandria, VA: ASCD.

Kline, F., & Silver, L. (Eds.). (2004). *The educator's guide to mental health issues in the classroom.* Baltimore, MD: Paul H. Brookes Publishing Co.

Kopp, C. B. (1983). Risk factors in development. In M. Haith & J. Campos (Eds.), *Infancy and the biology of development* (Vol. II of *Mussen's Manual of Child Psychology*). New York, NY: Wiley Publishing.

Leadbeater, B., Dodgen, D., & Solarz, A. (2005). The resilience revolution: A paradigm shift for research and policy. In R. D. Peters, B. Leadbeater, & R. J. McMahon (Eds.), *Resilience in children, families, and communities: Linking context to practice and policy,* (pp. 47–63). New York, NY: Kluwer.

Meichenbaum, D. (2006). How educators can nurture resilience in high-risk children and their families. Retrieved from www.teachsafeschools.org/Resilience.pdf

Saewyc, E., Wang, N., Chittenden, M., Murphy, A., & The McCreary Centre Society. (2006). *Building resilience in vulnerable youth.* Vancouver, BC: The McCreary Centre Society.

Schonert-Reichl, K. (2000, April). *Children and youth at risk: Some conceptual considerations.* Paper presented at the Pan-Canadian Education Research Symposium, Ottawa. Retrieved from http://educ.ubc.ca/research/ksr/docs/schonert-reichl_childrenatrisk2000.pdf

Scruggs, T. E., & Mastropieri, M. A. (1996). Teacher perceptions of mainstreaming/inclusion, 1958–1995: A research synthesis. *Exceptional Children, 63*(1), 59–74.

Slade, E. P., & Wissow, L. S. (2007). The influence of childhood maltreatment on adolescents' academic performance. *Economics of Educational Review, 26*(5), 604–614.

Ungar, M., Brown, M., Liebenberg, L., Othman, R., Kwong, W. M., Armstrong, M., & Gilgun, J. (2007). Unique pathways to resilience across cultures. *Adolescence, 42*(166), 287–310.

Yasik, A. E., Saigh, P. A., Oberfield, R. A., & Halamandaris, P. V. (2007). Posttraumatic stress disorder: Memory and learning performance in children and adolescents. *Biological Psychiatry, 61*(3), 382–388.

Chapter 13

American Institutes for Research. (2015). Promoting teacher effectiveness: Teacher induction and mentoring brief. Retrieved from http://lincs.ed.gov/publications/te/mentoring.pdf

Bransford, J., Derry, S., Berliner, D., Hammerness, K., & Beckett, K. (2005). Theories of learning and their roles in teaching. In L. Darling-Hammond & J. Bransford (Eds.), *Preparing teachers for a changing world: What teachers should learn and be able to do* (pp. 40–87). San Francisco, CA: Jossey-Bass.

Griffin, C. C., Winn, J. A., Otis-Wilborn, A., & Kilgore, K. L. (2003). *New teacher induction in special education.* (COPSSE Document number RS-5). Gainesville, FL: University of Florida.

Huling, L. (2001). Teacher mentoring as professional development. ERIC Digest: ED460125. Retrieved from www.ericdigests.org/2002-3/mentoring.htm

Petersen, L. K. (2007). Mentoring as a support mechanism for teaching practice by teachers in higher education. Retrieved from www.aare.edu.au/07pap/pet07120.pdf

Index

ABA. *See* applied behavioural analysis (ABA) program

accommodation. *See* educational intervention

Achenbach Scales, 369

activity level, 80

adaptability, 80

adaptation. *See* educational intervention

adaptive behaviour, 233

Adderall, 380

ADHD. *See* attention-deficit/hyperactivity disorder (ADHD)

adolescence: ADHD and, 175–8; giftedness and, 214

affect disregulation, 380–1

aggression: conduct disorder and, 173; intellectual disabilities and, 237–8

Alberta: inclusion in, 28; special education in, 12, 34

Alberta Education, 317; "Conduct Disorder: Strategies That Make a Difference," 180; *Inclusive Education Planning Tool* in, 41

Alberta Teachers' Association, 240–1

AMC. *See* arthrogryposis multiplex congenital (AMC)

AMC Support, 362

American Academy of Pediatrics: "Developmental Issues for Young Children in Foster Care," 392

American Association on Intellectual and Developmental Disabilities (AAIDD), 233, 253

American Association on Mental Retardation (AAMR), 233

American Foundation for the Blind, 329

American Institutes for Research, 396

American Psychiatric Association, 110; *see also Diagnostic and Statistical Manual of Mental Disorders*

American Psychological Association, 377; "Classroom Management," 100

American Sign Language (ASL), 310–11, 323

amniocentesis, 235, 403

anecdotes, 44, 403

antecedents, 41, 403

anxiety, 90, 159, 163, 282, 292

Anxiety and Depression Society of America, Childhood Anxiety Disorders, 180

anxiety disorder, 139, 155, 172–3, 174, 377

applied behavioural analysis (ABA) program, 272–5

approach/withdrawal, 80

arthrogryposis multiplex congenital (AMC), 336, 341, 345–6, 347

Asperger's disorder, 263; *see also* autism spectrum disorder

assessment: accuracy or completeness, 248; at-risk students and, 376–7; autism spectrum disorder and, 262, 265–7; curriculum-based, 66; definition, 39–40; developmental pediatric, 258, 260, 266; ESSA and, 16–17; evaluation of student progress, 66–8; formal, 48, 404; formative, 67, 404; fundamental principles of, 41; giftedness and, 191–2; hearing impairments, 308–9; and IEP process, 42–68; identification, 42–5; importance of, 40–1, 57–8; informal, 48, 404; NCLB Act and, 15; observational, 247–8; overview of process, 42, 43; progress in time intervals, 248; rate of progress, 248; psycho-educational, 48, 49–50; screening, 44

assistive technology (AT), 403; intellectual disabilities and, 245; learning disabilities and, 127; multiple disabilities and, 335, 355; visual impairments and, 344

Association for Bright Children of Ontario, 217

association reactions, 81

at-risk students, 4, 96, 366–90; assessing, 376–7; definition, 374–6; development and, 378–81; educational approach and, 383–8; dimensions for concept, 374; environmental factors and, 376; IEP for, 372; others who are at-risk and, 388–9; resiliency and, 385–8; resources, 391–2; school experience and, 381–3; tips for teachers in classroom, 392–3; trauma and, 377–8, 378–81

attention, disorders of, 120

attention-deficit/hyperactivity disorder (ADHD), 79, 119, 132; adolescence and, 175–8; at-risk students and, 376; behaviour plan and, 148–9, 170; behaviours of, 153; classroom strategies and, 165–6, 170–1; definition, 152–7; diagnosing, 153, 154–5, 302; environmental causes of, 157; exposure to mercury and, 158; factors contributing to, 157–8; friendships and, 161–2; genetics and, 157; hearing impairments and, 319; high-school and, 177–8; homework and, 166–8; learning disabilities and, 132, 159; medication, 156; placement options, 164–71; presentations of, 153–4; prevalence of, 155–6; resources, 179–80; speech-language difficulties and, 161; temperament vs., 80; tips for teachers in classrooms, 180–1

attention span and persistence, 80

audiogram, sample, 310

audiologist, 308, 403

auditory association problems, 81

auditory awareness problems, 82

auditory brainstem response (ABR), 309, 403

auditory discrimination problems, 82

auditory-figure-ground problems, 82

auditory oral approach, 311

auditory sequencing problems, 82

auditory verbal approach, 311

auditory verbal therapy (AVT), 309, 319, 320, 403

augmentative and alternative communication (AAC), 343

Australia: inclusion and, 23

autism. *See* autism spectrum disorder (ASD)

Autism Canada, 294

Autism Diagnostic Observation Schedule, Module III (ADOS), 304

autistic disorder 263; *see also* autism spectrum disorder

Autism Ontario, 294

Autism Society of America, 295

Autism Speaks Canada, 273, 282, 288

autism spectrum disorder (ASD), 257–93; ABA and, 272–5; assessing, 262, 265–7; behaviours and, 265; causes of, 259; cognitive development and, 268–9; communication and socialization, 281–4; criteria, 258, 259, 263, 264, 286–7, 293; development and, 268–72; diagnosing, 293–5; diet and, 268; in DSM, 263, 264, 266; early identification of, 266; educational approaches and, 281–5; emotional development, 269–70; environmental causes of, 267; evaluation of progress, 285; factors contributing to, 267–8; Fragile X syndrome and, 250; genetics and, 267; high functioning (level 1), 288; IEP for, 261; intellectual abilities and, 268–9; interventions for, 273, 275–6; levels of severity in, 265; low functioning (level 3), 286–7; medium functioning (level 2), 287; motor and sensory development and, 270–2; neuropathology and, 267; onset of, 260; other students with, 285–9;

parents and, 265, 267, 270, 282, 289, 290; parent-teacher relationship and, 278–9, 290; prevalence of, 25; provincial outreach program for, 281–2; resources, 294–5; school experience and, 279–80, 291–3; school readiness and, 276–8; social communication and, 265; social development, 269–70; stress and, 291, 292–3; teaching students with, 282–4; tips for teachers in classroom, 295–6; transition to school, 276–9

Autism Spectrum Disorders Canadian—American Research Consortium, 295

autonomous learners, 44, 403

Ayres, J., 271

Bachman, Owen (case study), 366–90. *See also* at-risk students

backward shaping, 245, 403

Bandura, A., 83

Banerjee, T.D., F. Middleton, and S.V. Faraone, 157

Barkley, R.A., 159

BASC-3. *See* Behaviour Assessment System for Children (BASC-3)

Bayley Scales of Infant Development, Second Edition, 269

Becker, E.B. and C.J. Stoodley, 267

Beery–Buktenica Developmental Test of Visual-Motor Integration (VMI), 112

behavioural differences, 40–1; *see also* antecedents

behavioural disorders: anxiety disorders, 172–3, 174; cognitive development and, 158–9; conduct disorder, 172, 173–4; definition, 152; development and, 158–62; educational approaches, 164–71; emotional development, 161–2; evaluation of progress, 171; factors contributing to, 157–8; intellectual disabilities and, 238; other behavioural disorders, 172–4; placement options, 164–71; resources, 179–80; school experience and, 163–4; social development, 161–2; speech and language development, 159–61; tips for teachers in classroom, 180–1; *see also* attention-deficit/hyperactivity disorder (ADHD)

behavioural intervention plan (BIP), 96, 97; IEP and, 98–9

behavioural observation audiometry (BOA), 309, 403

behavioural problems, 48; back-up plan for, 92–3; behavioural analysis, 96–8; environmental causes of, 83–4; learning difficulties and, 81–3; psychological causes of, 78–81; responding to, 96–7; solving, 92

Behaviour Assessment System for Children (BASC-3), 56–7

Behaviour Management Network, The, 100

Behaviour Rating Inventory of Executive Functioning (BRIEF), 120

Benard, B., 385–6

Bennett, S., 30

Bennett, S. and T. Gallagher, 240

Bertin, M., 177–8

Best Buddies Canada, *242*

"Big Five, The," 88–9

bipolar disorder, 380

Bloom, B.S., 44

Boehm Test of Basic Concepts, 344

"Bolstering Resilience in Students: Teachers as Protective Factors," 391

boys: ADHD and, 155, 156; exceptionalities and, 4; sensitivity and, 200

Braille, 327, 328

brain injury: acquired, 116; ADHD and, 158; traumatic, 116

Brant County School Board, 6

Brigance Preschool Screen, 277

Bright Hub Education, 330

British Columbia: Human Rights Code, 19; prevalence of students with exceptionalities, 24, 25; Schools Act in, 22; special education in, 12, 34; students with special needs in, *26*

British Columbia (Education), Moore v., 19–20

British Columbia Ministry of Education: categories of hearing loss, 306–7; definition of giftedness, 190; "Gifted Education: A Resource for Teachers," 217; "Hard of Hearing and Deaf Students: A Resource Guide to Support Classroom Teachers," 330; "Special Education Manual," 70

British Columbia Teachers' Federation, 397

Brophy, J., 72, 85

Browder, D.M. et al., 243

buddy programs, 168, 241–2

bullying, 123, 319

Cambridge Center for Behavioral Studies, 273

Canada: approaches to special education in, 28–35; autism in, 288–9; concept of inclusion across, 28–9; IEPs across, 41; prevalence of students with exceptionalities, 24; RTI model in, 114; similarities with US, 18–19; special education practices compared to those of outside North America, 23–4

Canadian Academy of Audiology, 306, 313, 321

Canadian Achievement Test (CAT-4), 55

Canadian ADHD Resource Alliance, 156

Canadian Association for Community Living (CACL), 246, 253, 403

Canadian Association for the Deaf, 323

Canadian Association for Williams Syndrome, 254

Canadian Attention Deficit Hyperactivity Disorder Resource Alliance, 180

Canadian Cultural Society of the Deaf, 307

Canadian Down Syndrome Society, 254

Canadian Journal of Education: "Accelerating Gifted Students in Canada," 216

Canadian Psychological Association, 273; "Professional Practice Guidelines for School Psychologists in Canada," 70

Canadian Test of Basic Skills: Spelling subtest, 55

Cantwell, D.P., 161

Carter, E.W., B. Sewdeen, and C. Kurkowski, 360–1

case studies, 2–3

catastrophic response, 82

categorical approach, 31; non-categorical approach vs., 31–2

Center for Applied Special Technology, 63

Centers for Disease Control and Prevention, 267

Centre for Research on Youth At Risk, 391

cerebellum, 267, 403

cerebral palsy, 65, 208, 357–8; *see also* Eaton, Emily

chaining, forward and backward, 283

Charter of Rights and Freedoms, 6, 18–19; *Elwood* case and, 19

Chen, D. and C. Miles, 349

child abuse, physical and behavioural indicators of, 375

childhood disintegrative disorder, 263; *see also* autism spectrum disorder

Children and Adults with Attention-Deficit/Hyperactivity Disorder (CHADD), 180

Children's Aid Society, 366, 371

Children's Mental Health Ontario: "Behaviour Problems in Children and Adolescents," 180

choice: students with autism and, 284, 293

chorionic villus sampling, 235, 403

Clarke, T.K., et al., 268–9

classification, 269, 403

class membership, 352

classroom, taking it into, 399–400

classroom management, 72; ADHD and, 165–6; behavioural view of, 75; causes of problematic behaviours and, 77–84; classroom behaviour and, 73–6; class rules, 86, 87–9, 90–1; consequences, 89–90; current views of, 74–6; definition, 72; effects of problematic behaviour, 73–4; environment and, 83–4, 93–4; perceptions of, 73, 74; postmodernist approach and, 75; psychologically secure classroom and, 84–99; rewards, 89–90; teachers' skills, 76; tenets of, 77; *see also* dynamic classroom management (DCM)

Clonidine, 146, 156

Cloninger, C.J., 354

cloze format, 46, 62, 403

Cochlear Implant Program, 302

cochlear implants, 298, 311–12, 320, 403

cognitive-behavioural therapy, 173, 403

Cognitive Credit Card (CCC), 128–9

cognitive delay, 357–8

cognitive development: autism spectrum disorder and, 268–9; behavioural disorders and, 158–9; giftedness and, 195–8; intellectual disabilities and, 235–7; learning disabilities and, 116–18; multiple disabilities and, 347; sensory impairment and, 313–14

cognitive discrimination problems, 82

cognitive sequencing problems, 82

cognitive strategies, poor, 121

collaborative model, 353–4

Collins, Tyler (case study), 298–328; *see also* sensory impairments, students with

communication: autism and, 293; expressive language disability and, 342; hearing loss and, 310–11; multiple disabilities and, 335, 347, 350; options for, 66

co-morbid condition, 132, 403

comprehension, 51, 64

Comprehensive Test of Phonological Processing (CTOPP), 112

computers, 127, 128; expressive language disability and, 342; learning disabilities and, 122

conceptual information, 193, 403

conceptual skills: adaptive behaviour and, 233

Concerta, 146, 156

concrete referents, 243, 403

conduct disorder, 79, 172, 173–4

conductive hearing loss, 307, 312

Conners' Rating Scales, 146, 147, 153, 368, 369

constructivism, 3

Conte, R., 132

contractures, 341, 346

Council for Children with Behavioural Disorders, 180

Council for Exceptional Children, 12, 16, 41, 63, 110, 306, 362; Gifted Education, 216–17; professional development and, 398; publications of, 70

Council of Ministers of Education, Canada (CMEC), 37

creative, 191

critical education juncture, 44

crossing the midline, 82

cued speech, 311

curriculum: developing, 355; differentiated, 203–4, 204–5, 403; educational interventions and, 62; enriched, 203, 404; high school, 243; IEPs and, 58; gifted and talented, students who are and, 202–6; multiple disabilities, students with and, 354; visual impairments, students with and, 327; structure applied to, 95

curriculum-based assessment (CBA), 66–7, 68

Dabrowski, K., 200

Dabrowski, K. and M.M. Piechowski, 200

DCM. *See* dynamic classroom management (DCM)

Deaf community: on categories of hearing impairment, 307

deafness, 306; prevalence of, 323; *see also* hearing impairment; hearing loss

Demchak, M. and R. Greenfield, 359

demonstration schools, 164–5, 168

depth perception problems, 82

detail recognition, 51

Developmental, Individual-Difference, Relationship-Based Model, 275

developmental delay, 336, 344

developmental disabilities, 345; employment and, 252

Developmental Test of Visual-Motor Integration, 55–6

development of class meetings, 166, 352

Diagnostic and Statistical Manual of Disorders, Fifth Edition (DSM-V), 153, 173, 234; autism diagnosis and, 263, 264; trauma and stressor related disorders, 377; diagnostic criteria for specific learning disorder, 113

Diagnostic and Statistical Manual of Disorders, Fourth Edition (DSM-IV); autism diagnosis and, 266

Diagnostic Centre (BC), 20, 22

diagnostic instruction, 45–7

differences, interpersonal and intrapersonal, 61

Differential Ability Scale (DAS), 313

differentiated curriculum, 203–4, 204–5, 403

directional problems, 82

disabilities: ESSA and, 17–18; terminology, 14; *see also specific disabilities*

disciplinary interventions, 72

Discipline Without Tears (Dreikurs and Cassel), 78

Discrete Trial Training (DTT), 275

discrimination, 18, 51

disinhibition, 82

dissociation, 380, 381, 384

distractibility, 80

dizygotic twins, 267, 404

Dore, R., E. Dion, S. Wagner, and J. Brunet, 240

Downing, J.E. and S. MacFarland, 244

Down syndrome, 220, 231–2, 249; diagnosing, 234; factors contributing to, 234–5; motor development and, 238, 239; *see also* intellectual disability

Dreikurs, R. and P. Cassel, 78

Dr. Mac's Amazing Behaviour Management Advice Site, 100

DSM-V. *See Diagnostic and Statistical Manual of Disorders*, Fifth Edition (DSM-V)

Duane syndrome, 336, 344, 346

DuPaul, G.J., M.J. Gormley, and S.D. Laracy, 159

dynamic classroom management (DCM), 85–96; behavioural problem-solving, 92–3; "The Big Five," 88–9; class rules and, 87–9; consequences and rewards, 89–90; diagram of, 87; effectiveness of, 94–5; effects on classroom environment, 93–5; effects on students with exceptionalities, 95–6; implementation of, 86; overview of, 85–6; planning for re-entry, 93; structure applied to curricula, 95

Dynamite, 337, 355, 357

dyscalculia, 82

dysfunctional environment, 172, 404

dysgraphia, 82

dyslexia, 82, 134

dystaxia, 82

dystonia, 82

ear, nose, and throat (ENT) specialist, 309, 404

Eaton, Emily, 2, 5, 6, 7, 7–9

Eaton v. Brant, 2, 6

echolalia, 258, 277, 302

Edmunds, A.L., 94

Edmunds, A.L., G.A. Edmunds, and L. Hogarth, 95

educated for life vs. education for success, 214

educational assessment, 39–40

educational assistant (EA): autism, students with and, 278–9, 279–80; intellectual disabilities, students with and, 236, 239, 244; multiple disabilities, students with and, 348–9, 352–3, 360

educational intervention: categories of, 61–2; defining, 61; learning environment and, 62; phase of assessment and IEP process, 61–3; therapeutic, 62; Universal Design for Learning, 62–6

Education for Students with Multiple Disabilities (website), 363

effort, 177

Ellis, J., 13

Elwood, Luke, 19

Elwood v. The Halifax County-Bedford District School Board, 18, 19

emotional control, poor, 157

emotional development: multiple disabilities and, 347; autism spectrum disorder and, 269–70; behavioural disorders and, 161–2; giftedness and, 198–200; hearing loss and, 316–17; intellectual disability and, 237; learning disabilities and, 119–20; visual impairments and, 326

emotional disturbance, 152, 178

emotionally sensitive, 199

employment: students with intellectual disabilities and, 252

Enculescu, S., 23

engagement, principle of, 64–5

enriched curriculum, 203, 404

enrichment: curricula and, 203, 404; School-Wide Enrichment Model (SEM), 206

environment: ADHD and, 157; autism spectrum disorder and, 267, 292; classroom management and, 83–4, 93–4; giftedness and, 193–4; learning disabilities and, 115–16

Erin, J., 344

Europe: special education in, 23

evaluation of student progress: autism spectrum disorder and, 285; behavioural disorders and, 171; giftedness and, 207; hearing impairments and, 323; intellectual disabilities and, 247–8; learning disabilities and, 130–1; multiple disabilities and, 356; phase of assessment and IEP process, 66–8, 131; sensory impairments and, 323

Evertson, C.M. and C.S. Weinstein, 93

Every Student Succeeds Act (ESSA) (US), 16–18, 41

exceptionalities: high-incidence, 4, 21, 22, 49, 58, 67; low-incidence, 4, 22; see also students with exceptionalities

Exceptionality Education Canada, 29

executive function: ADHD and, 177; options for, 66

exercise: autism and, 293; multiple disabilities and, 349

expert, 191

expression: options for, 66; principle of, 65–6

expressive language disorder/disability, 336, 346

extremely compassionate, 199

familiarization, 292

family involvement: students with multiple disabilities and, 349–50; see also parents; siblings

Farrell, M., 75

feedback, 91, 130, 168, 202, 207, 245

flight-fight-freeze responses, 378, 390

fluency, 125

fluid reasoning, cognitive index of WISC-V, 52

FM system (assistive listening device), 299, 306, 307, 321, 404

Forney, P.E. and K. Heller, 347

foster care, 376, 381, 382–3, 389

Fragile X Research Foundation of Canada, 254

Fragile X syndrome, 249, 250

Frasier, M.M., J.H. García, and A.H. Passow, 213

frequency sampling, 44, 404

From Chaos to Control (Johnson and Edmunds), 77

full scale IQ, 112, 159, 192

functional behavioural analysis (FBA), 48, 404

functional behaviour assessment, 96, 97–8, 98–9

functional MRI scans, 195

functional vision assessment (FVA), 325

funding, for special education: NCLB Act and, 15, 16

GATE–Gifted and Talented Education Parent Association, 217

Gee, K., 355

generalization, 51

genetic marker, 267, 404

genetics: ADHD and, 157; autism and, 267, 269; giftedness and, 193, 194, 215; hearing loss and, 312–13; intellectual disabilities, 249, 346; learning disabilities and, 115; multiple disabilities and, 345

genius, 191

Gifted Education: A Resource for Teachers (BC Ministry of Education), 217

gifted minority, 208–9

gifted students/giftedness, 183–215; assessing, 191–2, 207; biological influences on, 195; characteristics of, 197–8; cognitive development and, 195–8; curriculum and, 202–6; definitions, 189–91; development and, 195–200; different types of, 207–13; educational approaches and, 202–6; emotional development, 198–200; environment and, 193–4; evaluation of progress, 207; factors contributing to, 193–5; genetics and, 194, 215; and hearing impaired, 314; heredity and, 193, 194; identification issues, 213; learning disability and, 208, 210–11; minority students and, 208–9, 212–13; other types of, 207–13; physical disability and, 208, 212; resources, 216–17; school experience and, 200–1, 215; sensitivity and, 186, 198, 199–200; social development, 198–200; teachers of, 201–2; terms related to, 15, 190–1; testosterone and, 195; tips for teachers in classroom, 218; underachieving students and, 208, 209–10; in US, 24

gifted underachievers, 208, 209–10

girls: ADHD and, 155, 156, 175; exceptionalities and, 4

goal-directed adaptive behaviours, 51, 194

Goldberg, R.J., E.L. Higgins, M.H. Rasking, and K.L. Herman, 137

grade acceleration, 203, 404

Greenspan Method (Floortime), 275

Griffin, C.C., J.A. Winn, A. Otis-Wilborn, and K.L. Kilgore, 397

Halifax County-Bedford District School Board, Elwood v., 19

Hall–Dennis Report (*Living and Learning: The Report of the Provincial Committee on Aims and Objectives of Education in the Schools of Ontario*), 13–14

Hamilton, J., 347

Hamlin, T., 292

Handbook of Classroom Management (Evertson and Weinstein), 93

Hanlon, Jamie, 195

Hannell, G., 174

hard of hearing, 306; prevalence of, 323; see also hearing impairments

Harum, K.H., 239

Hatch-Rasmussen, C., 271

Health Canada: brain stimulants and, 156–7

health impairments, 4, 25, 26

hearing aids, 298, 299, 321

Hearing Health and Technology Matters, 330

hearing impairments, 4, 358; ADHD and, 319; assessing, 308–11; categories of, 306–7; changes within learning environment and, 322; Deaf community on definitions of, 307; definitions, 306–7; emotional development and, 317; evaluation of progress, 323; family life and, 317–18; genetics and, 312–13; giftedness and, 314; language development and, 315–16; school experience and, 319–21; social development and, 317; tips for teachers in classrooms, 331; see also sensory impairments

hearing loss: acquired, 313; categories of, 306–7; causes of, 313; conductive, 307, 403; diagnosing, 302; genetics and, 312–13; communication and, 310–11; congenital (at birth), 312–13; mixed, 307, 404; newborn screening programs, 309, 323; sensorineural, 307, 405

Heller, K.W., et. al, 342

heredity: autism spectrum disorder and, 267; giftedness and, 193, 194; learning disabilities and, 115

Hildebrandt, Karl (case study), 102–39; see also learning disabilities

Hinshaw, S.P., E.B. Owens, N. Sami, and S. Fargeon, 175

homework: ADHD and, 166–8; journal, 166

Horn, E.M. and J. Kang, 354

Huling, L., 396

human rights, 13–14

Human Rights Watch, 23–4

Hurlington, K., 386–7

hyperactivity, 56, 79, 368; ADHD and, 155, 316

hyperarousal, 380–1

hypervigilance, 381

hypotonia, 239

IDEA. See Individuals with Disabilities Education Act (IDEA)

identification: of children with exceptional needs, 14; assessment and IEP process and, 42–5

Identification, Placement, and Review Committee (IPRC), 6, 25, 112

IEP. See individualized education program (IEP)

"Imagining a Future: Reaching At-Risk Students by Teaching the Whole Child," 392

immature tactile abilities, 82

impulsivity, 79, 86, 119, 132, 155, 161

inattention, 119, 132, 154, 161

inattentiveness, 79

inclusion, 22, 23, 27, 36; ADHD, students with and, 165, 170–1; approaches to, 33; in Canadian jurisdictions, 28–9; intellectual disabilities, students with and, 240–1; practices, 27–8; teachers' views of, 29–30; teacher training and, 30; as term, 27, 29

Inclusion BC, 252

Inclusive Education Planning Tool, 41; see also individualized education program (IEP)

inclusive classroom; peer relationships in, 351–2; teaching strategies for, 31, 124–6, 401

individualized education program (IEP), 14, 41, 57–61, 404; at-risk students and, 372,

383; autism spectrum disorder and, 261; behaviour plan and, 98–9; benchmarks, 57; components of, 57, 59; condensed version of, 58–61; developing curricula and instruction, 355; evaluation of, 58; intellectual disabilities and, 224–30, 244; learning disabilities and, 123–4; multiple disabilities and, 338–9, 353–4; problems with, 58; regular curriculum and, 58; sensory impairments and, 301, 323; teachers' views of, 29–30; various terms for, 41

Individualized Education Plan (IEP), The: A Resource Guide (Ontario Ministry of Education, 59

individualized education program (IEP) process, 42, 69; assessment/IEP phase, 49–61; diagnostic instruction, 45–7; educational intervention, 61–3; evaluation of student progress, 66–8; fundamental principles of, 41; identification, 42–5; overview, 42, *43*; referral, 47–9

individual program plan (IPP), 41; *see also* individualized education program (IEP)

individual services support plan (ISSP), 41; *see also* individualized education program (IEP)

Individuals with Disabilities Education Act (IDEA), 14–15, *25, 26*, 41, 114

induction, 51

infants, with special needs: legislation for, 14

information-processing skills, 64

instruction: developing, 355; differentiated, 203–4; direct and strategy, 130

integration, 27, 404; *see also* inclusion

intellectual abilities, 51; autism spectrum disorder and, 268–9

intellectual disabilities, 220–52, 358; academic instruction for, 243–4; adulthood and, 251; autism spectrum disorder and, 268–9; behaviour disorders and, 238; causes of, 346; classification of, 234; cognitive development and, 235–7; cognitive functioning and, 236–7; definition of, 232–4; delivery of special services, 240–1; development and, 235–9; diagnosing, 234; educational approaches and, 243–8; emotional development, 237; employment and, 252; evaluation of progress, 247–8; factors contributing to, 234–5; high school and, 243–6, 251; inclusion and, 240–1; motor development and, 238–9; observational assessments, 247; peer buddy programs, 241–2; other types of, 247–50; resources, 253–4; prevalence of, 25; school experience and, 239–42; social development, 237; strategies for teaching, 244–5; terminology and, 13, 232–3; tips for teachers in classroom, 254–5; work placement and, 245–6; *see also* Down syndrome

intellectual functioning, 233; *see also* intelligence

intelligence, 233; genetics and, 194; tests of, 50–4, 189, 192, 233

intensity of reaction, 80

International Association of Special Education, 37

intersensory problems, 82

interventions: behavioural problems and, 96–8; referral phase and, 49; RTI model and, 114–15; students with autism and, 273, 275–6; *see also* educational interventions

Inuit, 158

IPP. See individual program plan (IPP)

IQ-Achievement discrepancy model, 114

isolation, 123

ISSP. See individual services support plan (ISSP)

Jacob Javits Gifted and Talented Students Education Act (US), 14, 17

Jay, J.K., 3

Jensen, P.M., 157

Johnson, F.L. and A.L Edmunds, 81; *From Chaos to Control*, 77

JP Das Centre on Developmental and Learning Disabilities, 254

Kaiser, A.P. and J.C. Grim, 350

Kauffman, J.M. and G.M. Sasso, 74–5

Kilee Patchell Evans Autism Research Group, 295

King-Sears, M.E., M. Burgess, and T.L. Lawson, 67

Klopfer, K., 76

knowledge, 51; postmodernist approach to, 74; SB5 and, 54

Kohama, A., 23

Kuntz, S. and A. Hessler, 3

Kurzweil, 122, 126, 404

K-W-L (Know-Want-Learn) strategy, 129–30

Landrum, T.J. and J.M. Kauffman, 75

Lane, K., K. Falk, and J. Wehby, 76

language: giftedness and, 196; options for, 64

language development: behavioural disorders and, 159–61; hearing loss and, 315–16; visual impairments and, 325–6

Langue des Signes Québécoise, 311

LD@School, 140

LD Online, 140

"LD students," as term, 15; *see also* learning disabilities

lead exposure, 158

Learn Alberta: Medical/Disability Information for Classroom Teachers, 330

learners, autonomous, 44

Learning about Intellectual Disabilities and Health, 254

learning differences, 40

learning difficulties: behavioural problems and, 81–3

learning disabilities, 22, 23; ADHD and, 132, 159; assessment of, 111–15; assistive technology and, 127; cognitive development and, 116–18; common characteristics of children with, 118, 120–1; definition, 110–11; development and, 116–21; educational approaches, 123–31; emotional development, 119–20; environment and, 115–16; evaluation of progress, 130–1; factors contributing to, 115–16; giftedness and, 208, 210–11; heredity and, 115; high school and, 137–9; identification process in US, 114; learning environment and, 126–8; learning strategies and, 128–30; mental health and, 139; motor development and, 120–1; note-taking and, 46; other learning disabilities, 131–5; organizational difficulties, 124; resources, 140–1; prevalence of, 25; school experience and, 121–3; social development and, 119–20; successful attributes and, 137; teaching strategies for, 124–6; as term, 15; tips for teachers in classroom, 399–400; *see also* dyslexia

Learning Disabilities Association of Canada (LDAC), 110, 115

Learning Disabilities Association of Ontario, 140

learning disorders: assessing specific, 111–13; in DSM-V, 113; non-verbal, 133–4

learning environments: educational interventions and, 62; effects of DCM on, 93–5; exemplary, 72, 77; hearing impairments, students with and, 322; learning disabilities, students with and, 126–8; visual impairments, students with and, 326–7

learning media assessment, 327

learning problems, 56, 78, 1114, 132

learning strategies: direct and strategy, 130; learning disabilities and, 128–30

least restrictive environment, 14

legally blind, 324, 404; *see also* visual impairments

legislation: special education and, 14–18

Leiter International Performance Scale, 344

Levesque, Monique (case study), 333–61; *see also* multiple disabilities

Lewis, T.J. et al., 85

Lieberman, L.M., 22

life-skill instruction, 246, 251

ligamentous laxity, 239

Living and Learning (Hall–Dennis Report), 13–14

Locwin, B. and J. Entine, 267

"logicalization of thought," 196

loneliness, 123

Lovaas Method, 275

low vision, 324, 404; *see also* visual impairments

Lytle, R. and T. Todd, 292

McCaslin, M. et al., 91
MacInnis, Geoffrey (case study), 183–215; *see also* gifted students/giftedness
McIntosh, K. et al., 114
MacMurchy, Helen, 13
mainstreaming, 27, 404
Manitoba: IEPs in, 41; inclusion in, 28
Manitoba Education, 286, 287; *A Handbook for Developing and Implementing* IEPs, 70
Manually Coded English, 311
Marland, Sidney, 189
Massachusetts General Hospital, 157
mathematics, 64, 121, 124–5
medication: ADHD and, 156–7, 163, 380; for bipolar disorder, 380
Meijer, J.W., 23
memory, 51, 168–9
Mendaglio, S., 200
mental health, 139
mentally retarded/mental retardation. *See* intellectual disabilities
mental operations: intelligence testing and, 51
mentoring, 395–7, 404
Mentoring and Leadership Resource Network, 395–6
mercury, 158
Mertler, C., 16
meta-analysis, 74, 404
meta-cognitive ability, 128, 404
Michael-Chadwell, S., 213
microcephaly, 358
minority students: giftedness and, 208–9, 212–13
mixed hearing loss, 307
mnemonics, 124, 404
modelling, 72, 91, 130, 166
modification. *See* educational intervention
monozygotic twins, 267, 404
mood: quality of, 80; swings, 152
Moore, Jeffrey, 19–20, 20–3
Moore v. British Columbia (Education), 18, 19–20, 20–3
morally sensitive, 199
motivation, 177, 178; giftedness and, 197
motor abilities, poor, 120
motor development: autism spectrum disorder and, 270–2; Down syndrome and, 238, 239; intellectual disabilities and, 238–9; learning disabilities and, 120–1
Movement Assessment Battery for Children, 238
Mrazik, M. and S.C. Dombrowsk, 195
Muckle, Gina, 158
multiple disabilities, 333–61; development and, 347; educational approaches and, 353–7; encouraging communication, 350; evaluation of progress, 356; factors contributing to, 345–6; family involvement and, 349–50; IEPs for, 338–9; other multiple disabilities, 357–8; peer relationships and, 351–2; resources, 362–3; school experience

and, 347–53, 358–9; secondary school and, 358–9, 360–1; tips for teachers in classroom, 363–4
Myles, B., 288

National Association for Gifted Children, 217
National Association of Special Education Teachers: "Classroom Management Series," 100
National Center for Learning Disabilities, 141
National Center on Response to Intervention, 114
National Fragile X Foundation, 254
National Human Genome Research Institute, 157, 346
National Institute of Mental Health, 157, 159; "Attention-Deficit/Hyperactivity Disorder," 179
National Resource Center on ADHD (NRC), 180
neglect: physical and behavioural indicators of, 375
neuropathology, 267, 405
New Brunswick: inclusion in, 28
New Brunswick Teachers' Association, 30
Newfoundland and Labrador: inclusion in, 28; giftedness, 190 in; special education in, 34
Newfoundland and Labrador Department of Education: Individual Support Services Plan, 41, 70
New Zealand: inclusion and, 23
NICHCY, 341
No Child Left Behind Act (NCLB), 15–16
Noel, K. and A.L. Edmunds, 196
non-categorical approach, 31–2; categorical approach vs., 32–5
non-verbal learning disorders (NVLD), 133–4
norepinephrine reuptake inhibitor, 156
Northwest Territories: inclusion in, 28
note-taking, 46, 62
Nova Scotia: giftedness in, 190; inclusion in, 29; IPPs in, 41; special education in, 34
Nowicki, E.A., 123
numeracy, 169
Nunavut: inclusion in, 29

Obama, Barack, 16, *17*
Obamsawin, Alanis, 213
observation, 401; direct, 56; strategies, 44
observational assessments, 247–8
occupational therapists, 50, 405
Olson, S., 269
Ontario: Education Act in, 6, 112; IEPs in, 41, 59, 70; prevalence of students with exceptionalities, 24–5; special education in, 35
Ontario Court of Appeal, 6
Ontario Ministry of Education: *The Individual Education Plan*, 70; *The Individualized Education Plan (IEP): A Resource Guide*, 59
Ontario Special Education Tribunal, 6, 8

Ontario Teachers' Federation: "Blind and Low Vision," 329
oppositional defiance, 79
oral language difficulties, 121
organizational difficulties, 110, 124
otoacoustic emissions (OAE), 309, 405

parent rating scale, 57
parents: as advocates, 136; giftedness and, 193–4; referral phase of assessment and IEP process and, 47–8; at-risk students and, 385; autism, students with and, 289–90
parent-teacher communications: ADHD, students with and, 167, 177; autism, students with and, 290; giftedness and, 214; multiple disabilities, students with and, 340, 347–8, 349–50
Parker, C., 342
participatory decision making, 87–8
part-to-whole relationships, 55
pattern completion, 51
Pavri, S. and L. Monda-Amaya, 123
PBIS. *See* positive behavioural interventions and supports (PBIS)
PBIS-SCP Canada, 100
PD. See professional development (PD)
Peabody Picture Vocabulary Test, 344
peer buddy programs, 241–2
peer relationships: intellectual disabilities, students with and, 241; multiple disabilities, students with and, 351–2, 360
"people-first approach," 14, 15
perception: options for, 63; tests of, 55–6
perceptual-motor skills: problems, 82; tests of, 55–6
performance deficits, 76
personal program plan (PPP), 41; *see also* individualized education program (IEP)
pervasive developmental disorder not otherwise specified (PDD/NOS), 263; *see also* autism spectrum disorder
Petersen, L.K., 396
Phelps dysplasia, 305, 312
phonological awareness, 112, 405; lack of, 121
phonological memory, 112, 405
physical action: options for, 66
physical disabilities, 341–2, 346; giftedness and, 208, 212
physical therapists, 50, 405
Picture Exchange Communication System (PECS), 275, 276
placement options: behavioural disorders and, 164–71
play audiometry, 309, 405
Porath, M., 199–200
positive behavioural interventions and supports (PBIS), 85
positive reinforcement, 171, 405
postmodernist approach, 74–6, 405
power, 74
PPP. *See* personal program plan (PPP)

practicum placements, 29, 76, 84, 395
praise, 283
precocious, 191; assessing, 192
pregnancy/prenatal period: autism spectrum
    disorder and, 267; Down syndrome and,
    235; intellectual disabilities and, 235;
    rubella during, 358; multiple disabilities
    and, 336
prevalence: of ADHD, 155–6; autism spectrum
    disorder and, 25; hearing impairments
    and, 323; intellectual disabilities and, 25;
    of learning disabilities, 25; of students with
    exceptionalities, 24–6
Primer for Teaching Students with ADHD, A, 179
Prince Edward Island: special education in, 35
problematic behaviours: causes of, 77–84;
    in classroom, 77; learning difficulties
    and, 81–3; temperament and, 80; see also
    classroom management
processing speed, cognitive index of WISC-V, 52
prodigy, 190, 191
professional development (PD), 397–8, 405;
    inclusion and, 30, 31
Professional Resource Centre for the Visually
    Impaired, 330
proprioceptive senses, 272
provinces and territories: inclusion across,
    28–9; jurisdiction over education, 37;
    special education in, 34–5
psychiatrists, 153, 405
psycho-educational assessment, 40, 49–50
psychological processing deficits, 121
psychologists, 49, 50
psychometrists, 40, 405
Public Law 94-142, the Education for All
    Handicapped Children Act (US), 14
punishment, 85, 86, 166, 168, 384

Quebec Sign Language, 307, 311, 323

Raven's Progressive Matrices (RPM), 192
reaction, intensity of, 80
reading difficulties, 33, 121
reading skills: ADHD and, 169; giftedness and,
    195; teaching strategies for, 125
reasoning: abstract, 51; analogical, 51; fluid, 52,
    54; perceptual, 112, 133; quantitative, 54
reciprocal determinism, 83–4
referral, 47–9
reflective practice, 398–9, 405
refugee students, 388
Reiff, H.B., 136
reinforcements, 283
relaxation corners: students with autism
    and, 292
relaxation techniques, 120, 174, 292
Renzulli, J.S. and S.M. Reis, 203, 206
Renzulli Center for Creativity, Gifted
    Education, and Talent Development, 217
representation, principle of, 63–4
Research Autism, 295

resiliency, 385–8, 405
resource room, 121, 243
response costs, 171, 405
responsiveness, threshold of, 80
responsiveness-to-intervention (RTI), 114–15
retinopathy of prematurity, 324, 405
retrolental fibroplasias, 357
rhythmicity, 80
Rief, S.F., 167
Ritalin (methylphenidate), 146, 156, 163, 302
Robertson, David (case study), 220–52; see also
    intellectual disabilities
Roeper, A., 214
Roeper Review, 195
routines: students with autism and, 293
rules class: "The Big Five," 88–9; designing,
    87–9; enforcing, 90–1; serious violation of,
    173; see also classroom management
Ryan, J.B., E.M. Hughes, A. Katsiyannis, M.
    McDaniel, and C. Sprinkle, 275

Sarris, M., 268
Saskatchewan: PPPs in, 41; special education
    in, 35
Saskatchewan Ministry of Education: Inclusion
    and Intervention Plan, 70
SB5. See Stanford-Binet Intelligence Scale (SB5)
scaffolding, 66, 405
Schnoes, C. R. Reid, M. Wagner, and C.
    Marder, 159
Schonert-Reichl, K., 374
school-based teams, 47–8, 49
"School Connectedness: Strategies for
    Increasing Protective Factors among
    Youth," 392
school experience: at-risk students and, 381–3;
    autism, students with and, 279–80, 291–3;
    behavioural disorders, students with and,
    163–4; giftedness and, 200–1; hearing
    impairments, students with and, 319–21;
    intellectual disabilities, students with and,
    239–42; learning disabilities, students with
    and, 121–3; multiple disabilities, students
    with and, 347–53, 358–9
school membership, 352
school readiness, 44, 236, 276–8
School-Wide Enrichment Model (SEM), 206
Schwartz, I.S., D. Staub, C.A. Peck, and C.
    Gallucci, 351
Scott, J., C. Clark, and M. Brady, 285
screening assessments, 44
SEAC Learning, 14
seatwork, 237, 290
secondary school: at-risk students and, 371;
    intellectual disabilities, students with and,
    243–6, 251; learning disabilities, students
    with and, 137–9; multiple disabilities,
    students with and, 358–9, 360–1; special
    education in, 24
segregation, 6, 23, 35, 240
self-analysis, 3

self-contained classrooms, 165, 240
self-efficacy, 49, 405
self-esteem, 49, 405
self-regulation, 64–5, 91
self-report of personality, 57
sensitivity, 186, 198, 199–200
sensory development: autism spectrum
    disorder and, 270–2
sensory impairments, 298–328; cognitive
    development and, 313–14; definitions,
    306–7; development and, 313–18;
    educational approaches and, 321–3;
    emotional development and, 316–17;
    evaluation of progress, 323; factors
    contributing to, 311–13; other sensory
    impairments and, 324–7; resources, 329–
    30; social development and, 316–17; speech
    and language development and, 314–16;
    tips for teachers in classroom, 331; See also
    hearing impairments; visual impairments
Sensory Processing Measure, 304
sentence structure: hearing loss and, 315–16
sequencing, 51
sequential processing problems, 82
seriation, 269
service learning, 241–2
sexual abuse: physical and behavioural
    indicators of, 375
shaping techniques, 283
Shavinina, L.V., 199
short-term memory problems, 82
Siegel, B., 267, 289
sign language, 307, 310–11, 317, 323, 324, 342,
    343
Silka, V.R. and M.J. Hauser, 238
Silverman, L.K., 200
Simonton, D.K., 193
simultaneous processing difficulties, 46,
    83, 405
situational measures or groups, 56
small-group membership, 351
Snow, R.E., 196
Snowdon, A., 360
social development: autism spectrum disorder
    and, 269–70; behavioural disorders and,
    161–2; giftedness and, 198–200; intellectual
    disabilities and, 237; learning disabilities
    and, 119–20; sensory impairment and,
    316–17; visual impairments and, 326
social cognitive theory, 83, 91
social constructivist approach, 2–3
socialization, 72; autism spectrum disorder
    and, 281–2; trauma and, 380
social relationships, 360–1; see also peer
    relationships
Social Responsiveness Scale, 304
social skills, 121; adaptive behaviour and, 233
Social Stories, 275, 276
social workers, 50, 405
Sokal, L. and U. Sharma, 30
South Africa: inclusive education and, 23–4

speaking: giftedness and, 195–6; hearing loss and, 316

special education, 35–6, 39; in Canada, 13, 31–35; in Canada and outside of North America, 23–24; Canadian and American compared, 18–19; categorical approach to, 31; defining, 12; effects of postmodernism on, 74–6; as implementation of exemplary teaching practices, 39; inclusionary practices, 27–8; legislation and, 14–15; modern history of, 12–14; non-categorical approach to, 31–2; professional development in, 397–9; use of term, 27

Special Education Appeal Board, 6

speech: ADHD and, 161; autism spectrum disorder and, 260, 268; behavioural disorders and, 159–61; intellectual disabilities and, 236; sensory impairment and, 314–16; visual impairments and, 325–6

Speech and Language Disorders (website), 363

speech-language pathologists, 50

speech-language therapy, 159–60

speech reading, 311

spelling: teaching strategies for, 126

Stanford–Binet Intelligence Scale (SB5), 54

Statistics Canada: "Education, Training, and Learning," 37

Stephens, K.R. and F.A. Karnes, 207

sterilization, 13

Sternberg, R.J. and W. Salter, 51

Sticky Keys, 128

stimulants, 156, 156–7

stories, of children with exceptionalities, 3–4, 401; choosing, 4; value of, 4–5

Strattera, 146, 156

stress: autism spectrum disorder and, 291, 292–3; trauma-related, 377–8

structured development history, 57

student observation system, 57

students with exceptionalities, 12, 13; behavioural intervention plans and, 12, 48, 50; categories in US legislation, 14; DCM and, 95–6; definition, 12; identification of, 112; inclusion and, 27–8, 31, 33; loneliness and, 123; prevalence of, 24–6; terminology and, 13, 14; see also specific exceptionalities

Students with Visual Impairments, 330

Supreme Court of Canada: Eaton v. Brant, 2, 6; Moore v. British Columbia, 18, 19–20, 20–3; interpretation of Charter and, 18–19

Surman, Craig, 157

symbols, options for, 64

systematic prompting, 243, 406

tactile defensiveness, 83

tactile discrimination problems, 83

tactile pressure problems, 83

tactile senses, autism spectrum disorder and, 271

TASH, 363

task analysis, 283

task variation, 282–3

Taylor, R.L., S.B. Richards, and M.P. Brady, 238, 247, 248

TEACCH (Treatment and Education of Autistic and Communication Handicapped Children), 275, 276

teacher rating scale, 57

teachers, 12; at-risk students and, 383, 384–5; autism spectrum disorder, students with and, 278–9, 290; behavioural problems and, 84, 92–3; categorical approach and, 31, 32; CBA and, 67, 68; classroom application of learning, 399–400; class rules and, 90; developing special stories, 401; diagnostic instruction and, 45–7; as facilitators of social relationships, 123; gifted and physically disabled, children who are and, 212; gifted, students who are, 185, 200, 201–2, 218; gifted underachievers and, 210; hearing impairments, students with and, 322; identification process and, 45; intellectual disabilities, students with and, 247; itinerant, 319, 326–7, 404; mentoring and, 395–7; NCLB Act and, 15; need for classroom management skills and, 76; non-categorical approach and, 32; parents and, 167, 177, 214, 290, 340, 347–8, 349–50; professional development and, 397–8; reflective practice and, 398–9; resiliency and, 387–8; resources for, 395, 400; role of; screening assessments and, 44; views of inclusion, 29–30; see also classroom management

"Teacher's Guide, The: Classroom Management" (website), 100

Teacher Vision: "Behaviour Management Resources" (website), 100

technology. See assistive technology

temperament: behavioural problems and, 80

teratogens, 115, 406

terminology, 14, 15; intellectual disabilities and, 232–3

testosterone, giftedness and prenatal exposure to, 195

test reliability, 54, 406

tests: academic achievement, 54–5; audiology, 309; intelligence, 50–4; multi-skill achievement, 55; norm-referenced, 49, 405; of perception and perceptual-motor skills, 55–6; screening achievement, 55; of social and emotional behaviour, 56–7; standardized, 49, 66, 67, 405; standardized scores, 111

test validity, 54, 406

theft, 173

therapeutic interventions, 62

Tick, B., et al., 267

time-outs, 171, 406

time sampling, 44, 406

toxins: autism spectrum disorder and, 267

transition portfolios, 359

trauma: diversity of experiences, 388; at-risk students, 377–8, 378–81; strategies for dealing with, 384–5

traumatic brain injury, 116

Trisomy 21, 235

twice-exceptional learners, 211

underachieving students: giftedness and, 208, 209–10

Ungar, M. et al., 386

United States: ADHD in, 155; Department of Education, 14, 15, 24; Every Student Succeeds Act (ESSA), 16–18; "A Guide to the Individualized Education Program," 70; identification of learning disabilities and, 114; legislation affecting special education in, 14–18; No Child Left Behind Act (NCLB), 15–16; Office of Special Education and Rehabilitative Services, 37; prevalence of students with exceptionalities, 24; similarities with Canada, 18–19

Universal Design for Learning (UDL), 62–3; principles of, 63–6

"Using Technology to Support At-Risk Students' Learning" (website), 392

US National Centre for Education Statistics, 24

US National Institute of Mental Health: "Autism Spectrum Disorder" (website), 295

US National Research Council, 271

VanTassel-Baska, J., 202

verbal comprehension, cognitive index of WISC-V, 52

vestibular senses: autism spectrum disorder and, 271–2

Vineland Adaptive Behavior Scales, 271, 303

vision loss, 311

visual disabilities, 344, 346; see also visual impairments

visual discrimination problems, 83

visual figure-ground problems, 83

visual impairments, 4, 324–5, 357–8; adventitious, 324; congenital, 324; developmental issues related to, 325–6; education and, 326–7

visual orientation problems, 83

visual perception, 112, 406

visual reinforcement audiometry (VRA), 309, 406

visual sequencing problems, 83

visual spatial: abilities, 406; cognitive index of WISC-V, 52, 54

vocabulary, 51, 125, 315

VOICE for Hearing Impaired Children, 330

Vygotsky, L.S., 63, 196

Walton, E., 361

Wechsler, D., 51

Wechsler Individual Achievement Test, Second Edition (WIAT-II), 369, 376
Wechsler Intelligence Scale for Children (WISC), 52; cognitive indexes of WISC-V, 52; Third Edition (WISC-III), 192, 368, 376; Fourth Edition (WISC-IV), 112, 159, 313–14
Whelan, R., 96
Wide Range Assessment of Memory and Learning (WRAML), 112
Williams syndrome, 249, 250
Williams Syndrome Association: Information for Teachers, 254
Wilson, A.M., C.D. Armstrong, A. Furrie, and E. Walcot, 138–9
Winders, P.C., 239
WISC. See Wechsler Intelligence Scale for Children (WISC)

Wong, Zachary (case study), 257–93; *see also* autism spectrum disorder
Woodcock–Johnson III Tests of Achievement (WJ-III), 112
Woodcock–Johnson Tests of Cognitive Ability (WJIV), 52–3; Tests of Achievement, 52, 53; Tests of Cognitive Abilities, 52, 53; Tests of Oral Language, 52, 53
Woods, Lindsey (case study), 144–78; *see also* attention-deficit/hyperactivity disorder (ADHD); behavioural disorders
WordQ, 122, 126, 406
working memory, 54; cognitive index of WISC-V, 52
work placement: students with intellectual disabilities and, 245–6
World Autism Awareness Month (WAAM), 289

World Council for Gifted and Talented Children, 217
World Health Organization, 288
writing: difficulties, 121; giftedness and, 196; teaching strategies for learning disabilities, 126
written expression, 126
written language, 110, 131, 139

Young, G. and J. MacCormack, 127
Youth 2 Youth, 141
Yukon: special education in, 35

zero tolerance rule, 88, 90
Zwaigenbaum, L., et al., 266
Zyprexa, 380